MARCRAFT INTERNATIONAL CORPORATION

Train with the Pros!™

NETWORK+ CERTIFICATION TRAINING GUIDE

COPYRIGHT 1999 MARCRAFT International Corporation

Trademark Acknowledgements

Written by Randy L. Ratliff.
Edited by Whitney G. Freeman
Original graphics created by Michael R. Hall and Cathy J. Boulay

ISBN: 1-58122-012-X

P/N DC-400T
Printed in the United States of America
1-9/00

ACKNOWLEDGEMENTS

The author wishes to make the following acknowledgements in appreciation for the help obtained in the writing, and preparing, of this book.

No one can write a book of this scope and magnitude without a lot of help. I'm grateful to the following for their expertise, encouragement, criticisms, suggestions, and general good will: Whitney Freeman for studious and demanding editorial comments. Cathy Boulay for finding each and every item that was missing. Michael Hall for incredible graphics created from indecipherable sketches of mine. Wanda Dawson and Paul Havens for their help with NetWare. Gary Gregg for showing me what's around the corner. John Mohl at Computer Learning Centers for an exhaustive review. Todd Kaczor from Computer Learning Centers for redefining the-straight-and-narrow for me. Ray Stroud for identifying the missing links. Grant Socal and Shawn Ratliff at Cisco for bearing with me, while still answering my questions as if they made sense. Chuck Brooks, who was with me a long time ago—when this was just an idea.

Numerous companies for access to their resources: Cisco systems, Cabletron Systems, 3Com, Bay Networks and Nortel, Rockwell, Intel, Lucent Technologies, Zoltrix, Hayes, Marcraft Iternational, Red Hat, Computer Learning Centers and all the folks at the April 99 Net+ seminar in Virginia, CompTIA and Doug Bastianelli, Microsoft, Novell, and the Branike Corp for their excellent work with cable modems.

My wife, Jan. My daughter, Phoebe. My son, Nick.

To Jan,
for venturing with me
into the
wide open spaces...

FEDERAL COMMUNICATION COMMISSION NOTICE

This equipment generates and uses radio-frequency energy, which may cause interference to radio and TV reception if it is not installed and used according to the manufacturer's instructions. This equipment has been tested and found to comply with the limits for a Class B computing device, in accordance with FCC specifications in Subpart J, Part 15. These specifications are designed to provide reasonable protection against radio-frequency interference in a residential installation.

However, there is no guarantee that interference will not occur in a particular installation. If this equipment does cause interference to radio or television reception, which can be determined by turning the equipment off and on, the user is encouraged to try and correct the interference by one or more of the following measures:

Reorient the receiving antenna.

Relocate the computer/modem with respect to the receiver.

Move the computer/modem away from the receiver.

Ensure that the expansion slot covers are in place when no option board is installed.

Use properly shielded cables and connectors.

Plug the computer/modem into a different outlet so that the computer and the receiver are on different branch circuits.

If necessary, the user should consult the dealer, or an experienced radio/television technician, for additional suggestions. The user may find the following booklet prepared by the Federal Communications Commission helpful: "How to Identify and Resolve Radio-TV Interference Problems."

This booklet is available from the U.S. Government Printing Office, Washington, D.C., 20402. Refer to Stock No. 004-000-00345-4 when ordering this booklet.

Table of Contents

CHAPTER 1—DATACOMM FUNDAMENTALS

CHAPTER 2—DATA TRANSMISSION

CHAPTER 3—THE TELEPHONE SYSTEM ..3-1

CHAPTER 4—MODEMS

CHAPTER 5—PROTOCOLS

CHAPTER 6—LOCAL AREA NETWORKS

CHAPTER 7—NETWORK OPERATIONS

CHAPTER 8—WIDE AREA NETWORKS

CHAPTER 9—NETWORK MANAGEMENT

CHAPTER 10—ERROR CONTROL AND DATA SECURITY

CHAPTER 11—SATELLITE COMMUNICATION

APPENDIX A - GLOSSARY

INDEX

CHAPTER

1

DATACOMM FUNDAMENTALS

LEARNING
OBJECTIVES

LEARNING OBJECTIVES

Upon completion of this chapter and its related lab procedures, you should be able to perform the following tasks:

1. State three fundamental components of a communications systems.

2. State several applications of networking.

3. Prepare a brief definition of protocols.

4. Prepare a brief definition of the Open Systems Interconnect (OSI) model.

5. Prepare a brief definition of network topology.

6. Identify the basic attributes, purpose and function of baseband and broadband.

7. Prepare a brief definition of access methodology.

8. Prepare a brief definition of DTE and DCE.

9. Identify the basic attributes, purpose and function of server-based and peer-to-peer networking.

10. Study technology options, such as Network Interface Cards.

11. Explain the difference between RISC and CISC microprocessors.

12. Recognize visually or by description common peripheral ports, external SCSI ports (especially DB-25 connectors), and common network components.

13. List the limitations of the ATE standard for IDE hard drive units.

14. Explain the reason why a UPS may be essential.

15. Implement a disaster recovery plan, using a UPS.

16. Identify the use of repeaters, hubs, switching hubs and their differences.

17. List the primary purpose of a bridge in a network.

18. State the primary function of a router.

19. Prepare a brief definition of multiplexing and demultiplexing.

20. Prepare a brief definition or baud and bit rate.

21. Prepare a brief definition of bandwidth.

22. State three common modulation methods used in networking.

23. Briefly describe characteristics of the Baudot, ACSII, and EBCDIC codes.

24. Prepare a brief definition of synchronous and asynchronous communication.

25. Identify the basic attribute, purpose and function of simplex, half-duplex and full-duplex transmission systems.

26. Provide a general description of EIA/TIA-232, -449 and -484 interfaces.

27. Realize that relevant SOPs must be obtained prior to network implementation.

28. Develop network documentation by stating six characteristics common to all procedures.

29. Provide input for documentation to corporate users by determining who is responsible for following standard operating procedures (SOPs) and who is responsible for changing them.

30. Develop network documentation by determining when an SOP is needed, as well as when it isn't.

31. Provide input for documentation to corporate users by making a list of titles typical to a networking environment.

CHAPTER 1

Datacomm Fundamentals

INTRODUCTION

There's "all of that information out there, and no way to get it." Truly, we are living in the information age. Hordes of salesmen want information describing our age, sex, income, preference for toothpaste, preference for shoes, socks and soap. Engineers, scientists and technicians search through manufacturer's product literature for the newest devices. Law enforcement officers would like to know if the driver they are pulling over for speeding has a history of shooting policemen. And perhaps we would like to have access to a million volume library of electronics books, preferably accessed from our home or office. Or maybe you are planning a flower garden and would like to know the plants that do well in direct sunlight, those that prefer shady areas, and those that like a little of both. Possibly you're planning to mix a few chemicals together in the hope of curing the common cold. But you're not sure if the mixture will result in the comfort of millions of people, or the destruction of all life on the planet.

All of that information is indeed out there, but getting to it is a bit of a problem. Information access has improved significantly in the past decade. Advances in communications products, greater standardization, and the proliferation of personal computers have thrust the data communications industry to the forefront of information processing. The widespread use and acceptance of the Internet is transforming the way we live and work. Although the reliability of network systems has improved tremendously, many snags and glitches prevail in the industry making the transfer of data somewhat of a gamble.

However, we've made considerable strides from the first telegraph line from Baltimore to Washington, D.C. in 1884. Today, billions of dollars are transferred electronically all around the world. The composition of planets millions of miles away can be determined. A telephone conversation spanning the globe takes mere seconds to connect. By accessing corporate intranets, more of us are working at home.

Accomplishments in electronic communications over the past century have been phenomenal. The fundamental nature of the problem has not changed-that is, to get information from one point to another-but the methods and techniques of moving information have radically changed. The emphasis of data transfer these days is on efficiency, accuracy, quantity and transparency. The basic function of a communications system is to transfer data. If, in order to transfer the data, a large amount of extra baggage must be carried, then efficiency suffers. Certainly, the receiver expects to receive an exact replica of the data that was transmitted. Our tolerance for errors is extremely low. The search continues for transmission techniques that minimize, detect, or correct errors occurring on the way to the receiver.

A large portion of data is transmitted through long distance telephone facilities.

These are the same facilities we use when making a long distance call. The long distance carriers bill data communications users in a similar way telephone companies bill their customers: by the amount of time their facilities are used in processing the call. If we could somehow quadruple our rate of speech, our phone bills would be cut by a fourth. Data communications users do just that. The idea is that the larger amount of data transmitted in a unit of time, the cheaper will be the charge for using the facilities of long distance carriers.

The designers of networking systems have one rather strange aspect inherent in the job: they develop incredibly complex techniques for achieving the system characteristics described above, and then mask all of their work so that it appears to the every day user as if it doesn't exist. Their goal is to make data transfers transparent to users. In turn, the user can concentrate on initiating the transfer at one end, and receiving data at the other end. All the things occurring in between appear invisible, or nonexistent, to them.

In this chapter, we'll begin to penetrate the transparency so carefully cloaking data communications. Basic concepts are introduced, common terms are defined and equipment fundamental to the industry is described. Some of the more common standards and protocols are introduced along with characteristics common to the many areas comprising data communications.

SYSTEM COMPONENTS

A communications system consists of three fundamental components: a sender, message and receiver.

Figure 1-1 illustrates a familiar communication system, a telephone call. The caller is the sender, voices contain the message, and the individual answering the call is the receiver. All communication-written, oral, microwave, television, printed, or by telephone-consists of these components. We usually think of data communications as involving the exchange of data between computers. It would be valid to substitute computers for the telephones in Figure 1-1.

When data is exchanged between computers the sender is generally referred to as the **transmitter** and the computer accepting data is called the **receiver**.

As in the case of a telephone call, the assignment of transmitter and receiver to a specific computer is relative; it depends on which computer is sending and which is receiving at any given time. As in telephone calls, the roles of computers reverse frequently from transmitter to receiver and vice versa. In the interest of simplification and coherency, the transmitting device in this book should be considered the transmitter, and the device on the other end considered the receiver.

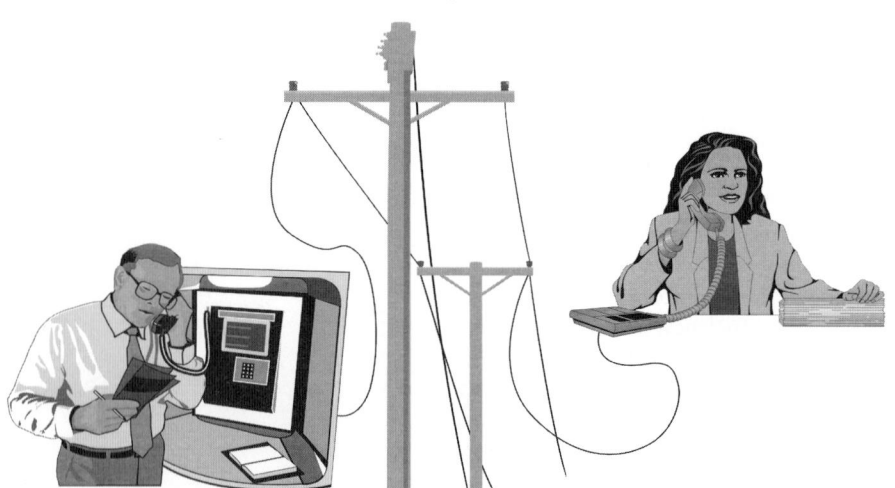

Figure 1-1 Components of a Basic Communications System

DATA COMMUNICATIONS APPLICATIONS

Nearly every business has found a need for data communications in one form or another. For the most part, the **communication medium** (all hardware and software between transmitter and receiver) used by businesses is the local and long distance telephone network.

> The phone system is a convenient pathway for carrying the exchange of data between computers.

The reason the phone system has taken on a dominate role in data communications is because telephone wires are in nearly every home and office. The existing wire is a logical choice to use in linking computers together since it's already installed. The major drawback to using the telephone system is that it is intended to carry voice communication and not data. As will be seen in the chapters ahead, this has presented unique challenges to designers of data communications and has resulted in unique responses to the challenges.

A communication system proves its value most readily for a company with offices or stores scattered about the country. Consider a large, general merchandise retailer with 100 stores in twenty states. Each store may maintain 10,000 different items for sale. In order for the store to continue making money, it must restock the items it has sold. A network could be implemented using point-of-sale terminals.

These are the check-out registers with a bar code scanner or a stock number the cashier enters into the register at the time of check-out. Most point of sale terminals track the inventory of a store. The registers are linked to a computer—either at the store or at a centralized remote site—and when an item is sold, an inventory adjustment is made to the data maintained in the computer memory. Perhaps a report is automatically generated listing all items whose quantity in the store is below a specific level. The store manager then knows it's time to re-order that item.

Data communications readily lends itself to industrial plants. The communication system may monitor a hazardous or toxic process and send information about the process to employees who are at a safe distance. The system could also be used when portions of the process have been split, or distributed, among different areas of the plant. The system would monitor the progress of the processing and provide operators with status reports.

The financial community has made extensive use of data communications. Stock, bond, or currency traders need to know exactly what is happening in market exchanges around the world. If they receive dated or inaccurate information, their clients may lose thousands of dollars. The banking industry evaluates loan applications from reports maintained by credit bureaus. High volume banks usually maintain an on-sight terminal linked to credit bureau computers. The bank requests a report from the credit bureau. The bureau pulls the report from a large database, and sends it to the bank where it is printed on a local printer. The data travels back and forth on telephone lines.

More and more, computer users are discovering that access to a **database** provides them with a key "to all that information out there."

> A database is generally contained in the memory of a large computer, and typically specializes in a specific subject.

For example, there are databases specializing in stock trading on the New York Stock Exchange, databases for lawyers providing the results of court decisions, databases for the chemical industry describing sources for raw materials or new break-throughs.

A company that maintains a database is called an **information service**.

The company sells access to its database. Generally, all that's needed to gain access is a computer, a modem, and a password. You buy the password from the information service and are usually billed for the time you use their database.

Another application of data communications revolves around networks. A data communications network consists of a number of computers tied together in such a way that data can be exchanged among them. Generally, networks are **wide area networks** (WANs) or **local area networks** (LANs). The distinction between the two is not obvious.

For the purposes of this text, a LAN consists of computers linked together in a room, a building or in a metropolitan area, while a WAN consists of computers connected together over a large geographical area; that is, areas falling outside a specific metropolitan area.

As a point of interest, networks which cover a city are sometimes referred to as metropolitan area networks (MAN). However, this text will describe networks in general as either a WAN and a LAN.

Networks are such an important part of data communications that the next section explains the various methods used to classify and describe them.

As a general rule, a data communication system is applied in those situations in which it makes a positive financial impact on an organization. This means the system will assist the organization in earning more money, or improve the efficiency of the way business is conducted. At a minimum, an organization with timely information has the means to make better informed decisions affecting its markets, products and employees.

CNST OBJECTIVE
I-A

PROTOCOLS

Protocols are the rules used with data communications.

The data frames discussed for asynchronous and synchronous communications have specific protocols describing frame formats. The telephone industry has detailed protocols and standards describing how data is to be packaged, multiplexed, and switched on its way to a destination. An understanding of protocols is essential to an understanding of data communications, because much of the industry has been built around protocols.

The intention of protocols is to bring a sense of standardization to data communications.

The tendency of many data processing vendors has been to carefully safeguard the technical details of their products. They do this so their products are not duplicated by their competitors. But the computer industry has grown to the point of touching the lives of nearly everyone. Access to data files may mean life or death to an accident victim who is unable to tell a doctor about the medicines he is currently taking, or is allergic to. Timely access to information is a concern to the national defense. These situations, and many more like them, cross the boundaries of corporate competitiveness and the desire to protect trade secrets.

Several highly respected standards organizations as well as several large data processing vendors recognize the implications of computer products on our daily lives, and have sought to bring a sense of order to the industry. Many of the standard protocols in use today were once proprietary products of large computer vendors. The process of standardizing data communications is an ongoing process. Standards change as technology changes. Many protocols have built-in flexibility that allows for changes without affecting other protocols.

There exists a basic blueprint that describes the function of protocols for data communications called the **Open System Interconnection** (OSI) Reference Model.

CNST OBJECTIVE
I-A

It was published in 1978 by the **International Standards Organization**, and is shown in Figure 1-2. The OSI model takes a layered approach to a communication system in a manner similar to the layers of an onion. As the heart of an onion lies at the innermost, or lowest layer, so the lowest layer of the OSI model concentrates on the most basic concepts of data transfer. The succeeding layers deal with progressively higher-order concepts until the final, or outermost layer, which involves the interaction of a user with the data communications system.

The ISO OSI model is one of many data communications models. Throughout this book, you'll have an opportunity to study other models. The OSI model is widely quoted in equipment specifications and is central to the Network + exam. See Chapter 5 for a detailed description of the layers.

Closely related to the model are protocols that delineate the layers. At the Physical layer are interface standards such as EIA/TIA-232, formerly known as RS-232C. A standard isn't a protocol; a standard explains how to implement a protocol, whereas the protocol describes outcomes. At the Data Link layer are protocols associated with Local Area Networks. IEEE 802.3 is usually referred to as Ethernet, while 802.5 is called Token Ring. Protocols at this level are very well documented and implemented within the networking community.

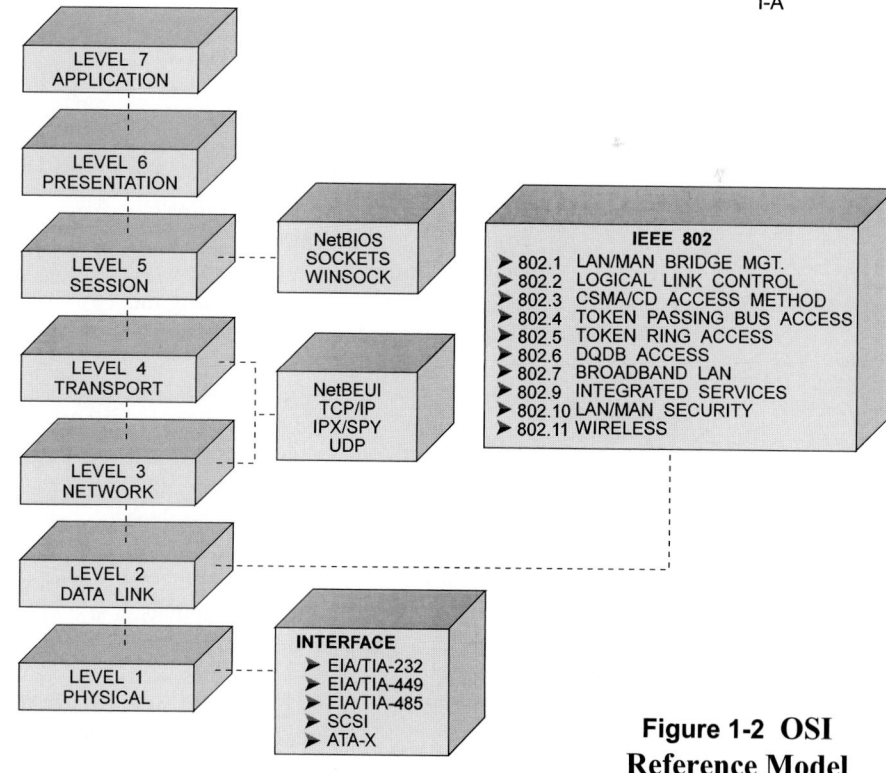

Figure 1-2 OSI Reference Model

Protocols used to connect networks, or to send data across large networks are defined at the Network and Transport layers, with the most common being TCP/IP.

Although later chapters of this book describe various protocols in significant detail, understand that the model describes protocols only; it does not specify how to implement them. That is for vendors to decide. Portions of the model are incomplete, particularly at the upper levels. The lower levels have, for the most part, been accepted by data communications designers and vendors, and a concerted effort has been made to be faithful to the standards. However, the protocol implementation is determined by the vendor, and the temptation to protect the product from duplication is never out of reach. This often results in little modifications made here and there, to the point that it would be wise to thoroughly examine any claims of compatibility and quotes of adherence to specific protocols.

NETWORKS

A network consists of hardware and software designed to direct and control data traffic.

Why bother with a network? The single most important reason is that it simplifies data transfer. Figure 1-3 shows five computers connected to one another without the benefit of a network. In order for the computers to exchange data, each must have a wire connected to the other. In the worst case, as shown in the illustration, each computer has output wires connected to each of the other computers as well as input wires from the other computers. The total number of wires linking the five computers together is twenty.

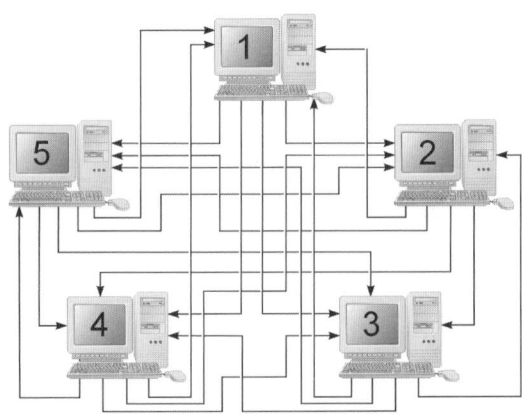

Figure 1-3 Connection Problems Linking Computers

In Figure 1-4, the same five computers have been linked in a network. Now, data transfer can take place with the use of only five wires. From a troubleshooting standpoint, it would be much easier to track down a wiring problem in Figure 1-4 than in Figure 1-3. If the system itself is simplified, then it is reasonable to assume that it will be more reliable.

Five computers connected together is a small network. A local area network in an office building may tie together hundreds or thousands of computers. If Figure 1-3 looks like a wiring nightmare, you can imagine the difficulty of maintaining connections for a thousand computers.

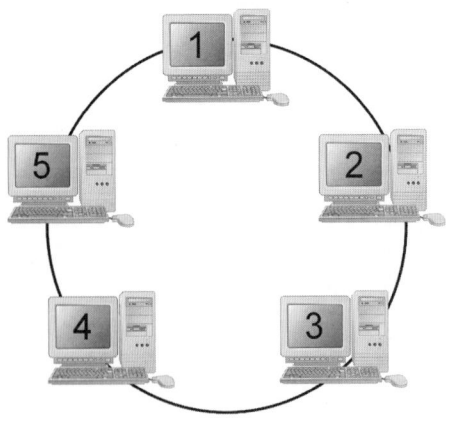

Figure 1-4 Connecting With a Network

A network has many characteristics. The tendency to describe or classify a network is often rooted in the characteristics having the greatest importance to the user. For example, the most important aspect may be the physical arrangement, or topology, of the network. To another network user, the primary concern may be the type of transmission medium selected—existing telephone wiring, coaxial cable or fiber optic cable. The different characteristics affect the performance of a network. In and of themselves, none is any better or worse than the other. But when considered collectively, the overall characteristics define the level at which the network will operate.

The operational level of the network is dictated by the application.

To achieve the desired application the network must possess characteristics that, when used in conjunction with each other, will produce the desired result.

The following is a general discussion of methods used to describe LANs and WANs.

CNST OBJECTIVE
I-A, IV-B & VII-A

Topology

Topology refers to the architecture, or physical arrangement, of a network.

The most commonly used topologies are illustrated in Figure 1-5. The title of the topology is a good description of the arrangement of computers and connections between them. The **point-to-point** topology of Figure 1-5(a) is the simplest type. A personal computer and printer communicate in a point-to-point fashion. Strictly speaking, it is stretching it a bit to call it a network. It is included here because it illustrates the parts of many networks. If you have a personal computer connected to the Internet, you probably configured the connection as point-to-point.

The protocol used for a PC-to-Internet connection is called **Point-to-Point Protocol**, or PPP. In this case, the protocol specifies how data will flow back and forth on a simple topology.

The **ring** network in Figure 1-5(b) has computers connected in a daisy-chain fashion. Data flows from computer, or terminal, to computer in a circular manner, as indicated by the arrows. Each computer takes turns loading data onto the network. The disadvantage to ring networks is that if the ring is broken, the entire network is disabled. Token Ring protocols are run on a ring topology.

A **star** configuration is illustrated in Figure 1-5(c). The computers are connected to a central processor, called a **hub**. The hub is basically a high-speed data switch that routes data through the network. From the view of the computers, they communicate with the hub in a point to point arrangement. Star networks, if properly designed and installed, are noted for their high speed. The drawback to the topology is the hub itself. If it malfunctions, the entire network is affected.

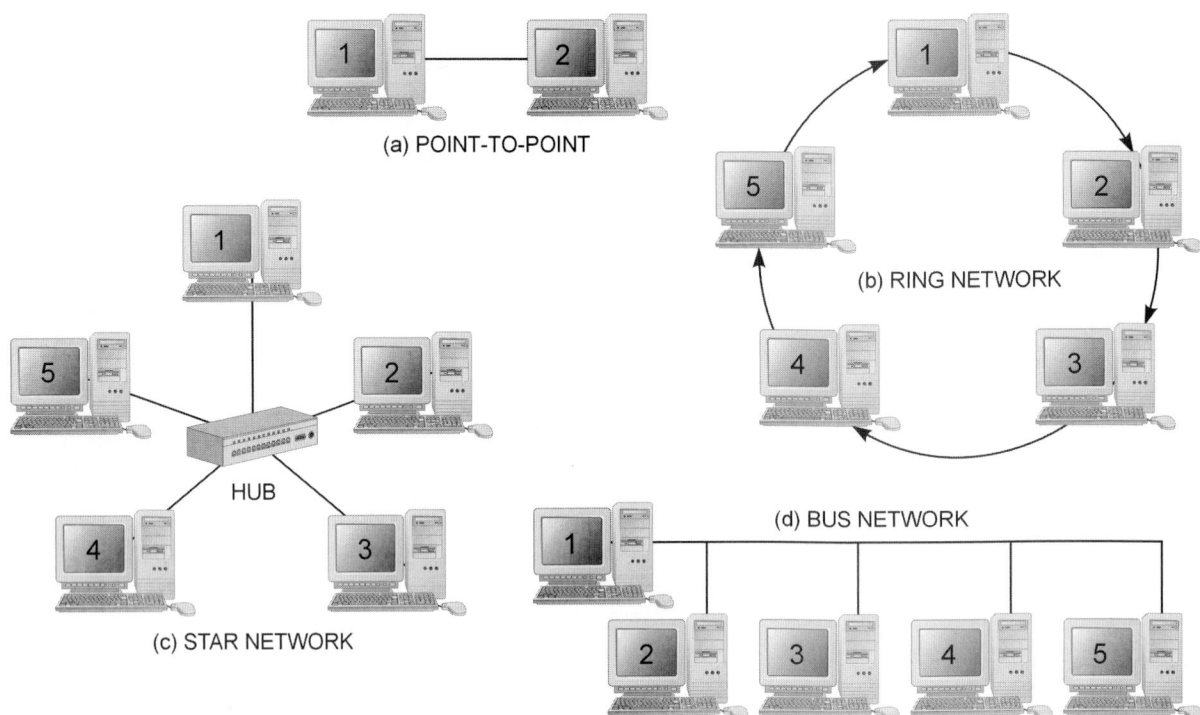

Figure 1-5 Network Topologies

Hub-based topologies are very common in a local area network, and in situations where a hub is used to link networks.

Hub-based topologies are very common in a local area network, and in situations where a hub is used to link networks. Hubs may be as simple as hard-wired connections or they may be extremely sophisticated. Many protocols are run on star topologies with Ethernet being the most common for LANs. Note that a huge advantage of a star topology using a hub is that if a connection brakes to any one of the end-nodes, only that portion of the network is affected.

The **bus** topology shown in Figure 1-5(d) is a commonly used architecture. Each end of the bus includes a terminator that's used to stop the network signal. On a bus network using Ethernet, devices on this network communicate with one another by competing for access to the bus. The device winning the competition has control of the network for a period of time. Using a different protocol, devices may gain access to the bus by receiving a token which permits them a specified time to send data. As you can see, bus networks are attractive to users because of the flexibility of the topology. A user can be added or deleted without affecting the operation of any other part of the network. Of course, the attached computers could be seriously damaged if there was an electrical problem (a short) in the bus.

Generally speaking, the topology of a network is independent of the protocol running the network.

For example, the majority of installed networks are Ethernet (IEEE 802.3) or Token Ring (IEEE 802.5). Ethernet may be installed on a bus-style LAN or on a star topology, with the star topology being the most common implementation. Token Ring, on the other hand, must be installed on a ring topology, but Token Passing can be installed on either a bus or ring network.

The specific techniques computers use to gain access to the network, and the flow of data in the network, is the subject of succeeding chapters.

Figure 1-6, in addition to being a wide area network, can also be classified as using a **mesh** topology. In a mesh topology, all nodes are either logically or physically connected together. The public telephone system is an example of a mesh network. The Internet is composed of a mesh network.

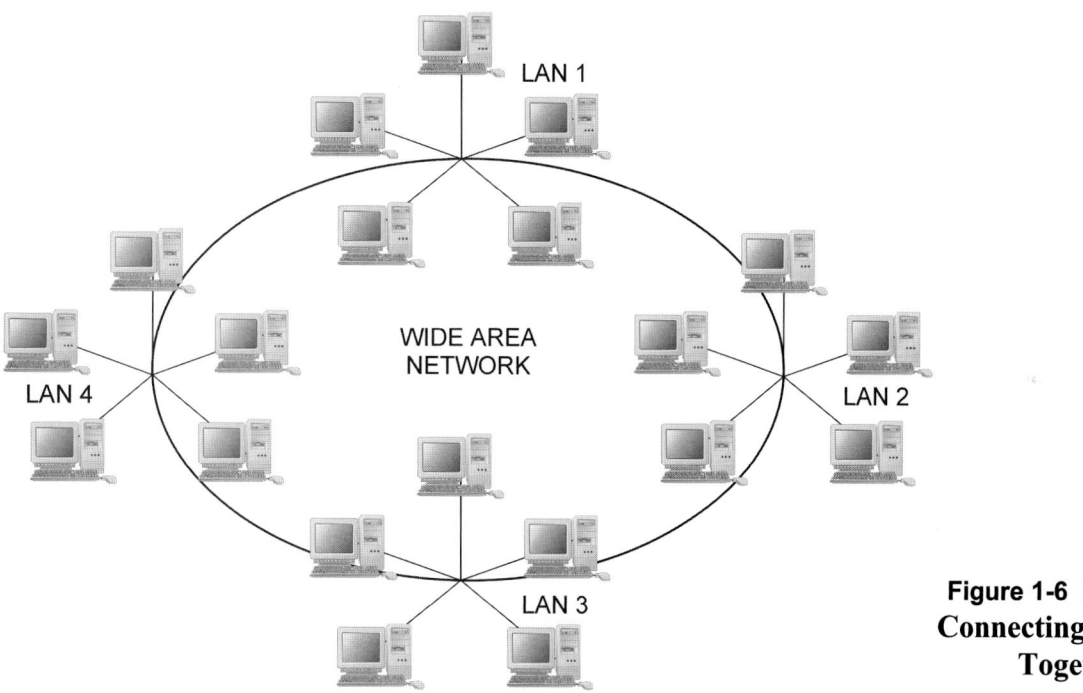

Figure 1-6 Networks Connecting Networks Together

Increasingly, topologies are mixed in a practical environment. Fiber optic rings operating at data rate speeds of 100MBS are often used as a backbone for interconnecting LANs. The LANs may be of any topology, and have any protocol running them. The ring may be connected to another ring via a long distance carrier to form a large intranet. There's no practical limit to the size, topology, or protocols running networks. The network may be large, complex, and expensive; but global information systems are a reality, and an expected way of conducting business.

Method of Transmission

NET+ OBJECTIVE
I.1.7

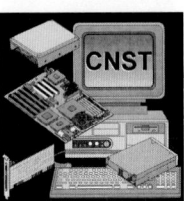

CNST OBJECTIVE
I-A

Networks are sometimes described by the method used to transmit data. Generally, two alternatives are available: **baseband** and **broadband**. Originally, a baseband network transmitted data directly onto a network. The receiving network station simply removed and processed the data. Baseband networks covered a small area—a room or building. Because of the short distances involved, the data could, be transmitted without the need for a carrier frequency. The lack of a carrier distinguished a baseband network.

Broadband networks had a wider area to cover. Cable runs that were long—from building to building or from one part of a city to another—covered a sufficient distance that the data had to modulate a carrier frequency. The increased energy inherent in the higher-frequency carrier transported the data.

With improvements in network design, these definitions for baseband and broadband are not necessarily valid. A baseband network may very well be found using an assigned carrier.

> A baseband network is now thought of as a network—using any topology—in which data is transmitted at rates up to 10MHz.

Broadband systems have been installed in increasing numbers, primarily as a result of growth in the cable television industry. They find high usage when large volumes of data are to be transmitted. High data rates require a considerable amount of bandwidth, and the bandwidth of broadband systems is much larger than that of baseband.

> Broadband networks carry data at rates over 10MHz, up to around 100MHz.

Physical Connection Medium

> The medium refers to the physical path taken by data.

A network can use a wide variety of connection media. The medium refers to the physical path taken by data. Typical media include copper wire, fiber optic cable, microwaves, infrared and radio waves.

> Copper wire includes twisted wire pairs, and **twisted pairs** refers to voice and data network cabling.

It is composed of 22- or 24-gauge copper wire twisted together like a braid. The wire is twisted together to eliminate common noise voltages that may be induced into the wire. Another copper wire medium in common use is **coaxial cable**. Coax cable has a single insulated copper wire enclosed with a copper braid. Enclosing the braid is the outer insulation. Historically, coaxial cable has been used in wide-bandwidth applications, particularly in the cable television industry as well as in many earlier computer networks.

In recent years, twister pair cabling has advanced to where it competes equally with coax in a network environment. In fact, there's little justification in using coax for an Ethernet LAN with the availability of wide bandwidth (Category 5) twisted pair cabling which has a bandwidth of 100MBS. Whenever possible, use CAT5 twisted pair for the local network cabling infrastructure.

A **fiber-optic cable** consists of a thin strand of glass or plastic cable surrounded by a jacket.

Fiber optic cable is rapidly becoming the choice medium for ground base communication systems. The data to be transmitted is converted from electrical energy to light energy and transmitted through the cable.

Fiber optic cable has significantly lower losses than copper wire, and is immune from external electrical interference (lightening, motors, generators, microwaves) that creates much of the distortion found in copper-based systems.

Microwaves offer another alternative for transmission media.

Satellites use microwaves for relaying data from transmitter to receiver.

Microwaves offer another alternative for transmission media. Satellites use microwaves for relaying data from transmitter to receiver. In recent years, satellite systems have experienced a surge of growth due to improvements in ground-based antennas and a decrease in the relative costs of utilizing satellites. Long distance telephone companies frequently employ microwave systems in their trunk lines, along with traditional land-based microwave.

A **trunk line** is a major artery capable of carrying thousands of calls.

The telephone companies modulate the many calls onto the carrier using sophisticated multiplexing techniques.

Wireless networks offer another approach using microwave-based media.

A wireless network—either local or in a wide area—offer the greatest flexibility of all media types.

More and more, the need have a network mobile is becoming increasingly important. Often, a copper or fiber connection isn't available where the need is; so companies are turning to wireless technology, particularly as a temporary solution.

Access Control

A network user has to decide how the computers connected to the network will gain access to it. In a point to point arrangement, one of the devices is given authority over the other. This is the case in communication between a personal computer and printer. The printer is subordinate to the PC.

In many cases computers (or intelligent terminals which are often referred to simply as a station) are connected in a similar point to point topology. Most of the time, one of the computers is designated the primary station and the other designated the secondary station. Essentially, the secondary receives data when told to do so by the primary, and if it has data to transmit, waits until permission is given by the primary. In a similar situation, such as a peer network, all stations are at once primaries and may access the network using one of many technologies.

The star topology sometimes makes use of a similar access method. In a star network, the stations take direction from the hub.

Since the hub is managing network traffic, it makes decisions concerning which should transmit or which should receive data. Of course, in other hub-based topologies, the hub has no management authority; all controls originate in a server, the client nodes, or both.

Ring and bus networks use different access methods.

> Access may be granted to a bus network through contention. In a **contention-based network**, the stations vie for access.

Eventually, a winner emerges and the winner has a limited time to transmit data. The process is a bit like "first come, first served". Once the transmission time has expired, the stations contend once again for control of the network.

> In a ring network, a token is passed from station to station. This type of access method is called a **token-based system**.

The station in possession of the token has control of the network, and is free to transmit for a limited time. The later sections of this book have been written around the characteristics of networks. Much of the transparency that users find so pleasing is a result of the nuts and bolts details associated with networks.

DTE AND DCE

There is some confusion in regards of how to describe a terminal connected to a network, or a personal computer, modem, multiplexer or, for that matter, another network. In order to alleviate the confusion in terminology, the data communications industry has settled on two terms that describe devices attached to a communication system. The terms are **data terminal equipment** (DTE) and **data communication equipment** (DCE).

DTE refers to any device in which the primary purpose of the device is the manipulation or processing of data.

Examples of DTEs are computers and terminals. The two are used interchangeably as generic terms for DTE, even though the terminal may be used only as a data input device. Printers and all passive peripherals are classified as DTEs. Data communication literature may also refer to a DTE as a station, primary or secondary, transmitter or receiver (although it is technically incorrect), and as a node. The same convention is followed in this text.

DCE refers to any device directly involved in transmitting and receiving data.

Generally, if a device alters data in some way, it is a DCE. Examples of DCE are modems, multiplexers, routers and switches. Figure 1-7 is an example of DTE and DCE. The personal computer sends data to be transmitted to the modem.

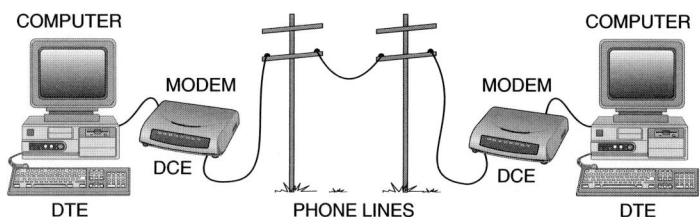

Figure 1-7 Use of DTE vs. DCE Terminology

A **modem** is used to modulate a carrier with the data for transmission over a long distance.

Once the signal arrives at its destination, another modem demodulates, or detects, the data from the carrier. The receiving modem then sends the data to the receiving computer. It is the function of the computers to process the data, so the PCs have been labeled as DTE.

In modulating a carrier with data, the modem has not only altered the data, it has eliminated it entirely.

The carrier retains only an effect of the data. Note that a similar phenomenon occurs with broadcast radio. The audio modulating a carrier at a radio station is filtered-out before the carrier is transmitted. However, the carrier is distorted in some manner (by amplitude, frequency or phase, for example) which corresponds to the original audio. A modem performs similarly. The receiving modem analyzes the effect of data on the carrier and generates a replica of the data. Since the modem has been used to alter the data, it's labeled DCE.

Networks Propagate Themselves

In an earlier section of this chapter, several simple networks were described to illustrate topologies. In reality, a "simple network" is an oxymoron—that is, there's no such critter! There are two fundamental reasons for this.

The first is the commercialization of the Internet in the early nineties. Seemingly overnight, the world has shrunk to the distance between our eyes and our terminal screen. As a technological leap, the Internet will, one day, be ranked next to the invention of the telephone. It is having a profound effect on the way we do business, manage our personal lives, communicate, and learn.

The second reason is a technological shift in data management. You have to go back a decade or two to appreciate that we take for granted the millions of personal computers sitting around homes and offices. Just twenty years ago, it wasn't uncommon for a company to have a data processing department, which included a room (off limits to nearly everyone) with a main-, or mini-computer that had a group of terminals connected to it. Programmers managed all of the electronic data quite jealously, and—as it turned out—fruitlessly.

As personal computers proliferated (thanks in large part to Apple), it became difficult to justify the sterile computer rooms. Gradually, the power of IBM 370's and System 36's represented overkill to many companies, when stand-alone computers could do many of the same tasks. The programmers were reluctant to let go, though. They compromised with an interesting tool called a **server**.

A server was a powerful computer that had full control of any other computers connected to it, and usually contained all of the resident software. The terminology is Machiavellian, since the device controlled everything and served no one.

But the user connected to the server wasn't powerless. With a little hard work, that user discovered a few instances here and there in which the server wasn't even needed. The user now had computing power and a bit of control over tasks that traditionally required a work order, and a two-week wait. The user, of course, wanted more.

Computer manufacturers responded with more powerful computers; a response that shows no signs of slowing. As the personal computers evolved toward independence, the task of managing them grew in complexity.

Sub-industries were born that existed solely to make some software sense of the rules governing the server, and connected clients. Novell certainly had a significant impact on smaller networks, and soon dominated the LAN market. Novell software managing a network worked. Once it was installed (which in the early days was about as easy as flying to the moon), the network could be expected to perform in a manner that was transparent to the user.

With powerful computers connected to the server, many mundane server tasks were off-loaded to the client computers. In other words, the network functions became somewhat distributed among all computers connected to the network. This freed the server, so that it could spend more time responding to requests from the client PCs. What an interesting idea! The server would now respond to the client needs. Finally, it would fulfill its namesake.

The concept of viewing servers as tools for users has dramatically changed the data processing landscape. Today, we work with servers. We utilize the services of a server. We change their functionality if they no longer meet our needs. In some cases, we scrap them entirely because they aren't needed. Many smaller offices opt for peer-to-peer networks, which don't have a file server.

It's interesting to note that **combination networks** are used frequently. A combination network shares characteristics of both server-based networks and peer-to-peer networks. A good example would be a local area network consisting of a server running Windows NT and ten client computers all running Windows 98. The clients may share one another's files in a peer-to-peer arrangement, while also utilizing the server resources.

The important point is that network servers are an integral part of networks, but a part that enhances, rather than stifles, productivity, efficiency, and harmony.

In the sections to follow, we'll look at a server-based LAN, and grow it until it's meshed into a conglomerate, wide area network. Along they way, you'll have an opportunity to see how many of the common network devices are used. It's a bird's-eye tour, lacking in detail, but rich in breadth.

Server-Based LANs

Figure 1-8 shows five personal computers connected to a server through a hub. A printer is also attached to the network, and all are functioning under the Windows NT operating system. The personal computers are referred to as clients, or nodes. These are stand-alone computers that may or may not have Windows NT installed in them.

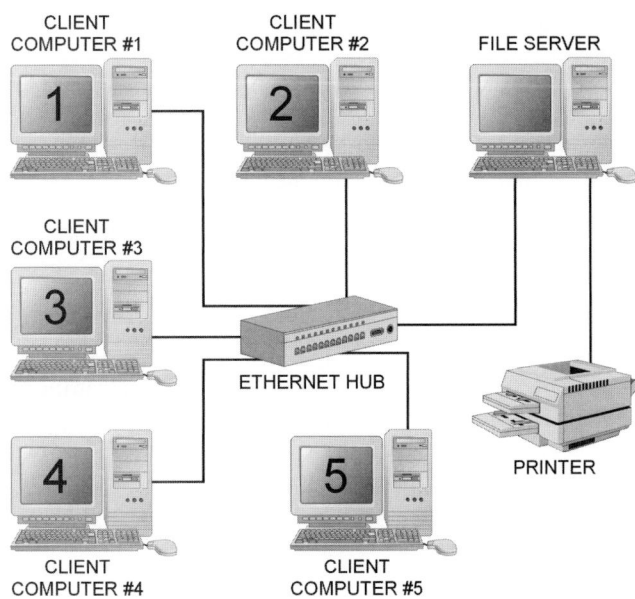

Figure 1-8   Server-Based LAN

There are many specifications which affect the performance of a network. This section is intended to provide you with an overview of common devices used in the networking industry, how the devices work together, as well as the definitions of the devices. Details are available in later chapters of this book.

Let's take a closer look at the LAN.

The hub may come in many varieties, but essentially it's a point-to-point connection for all nodes (which includes the server and printer). As shown in the illustration, the ports of the hub are dedicated to a port of the nodes. The hardware configuration inside the hub could take many forms, but for the moment, think of it as a switch which allows communication between any of the nodes.

The node ports connect via a **Network Interface Card** (NIC), also called a network interface controller card, or data network interface card.

The NIC is an inexpensive card that slips into an expansion slot of the PCs. The NIC is media and protocol dependent; that is, it will be equipped for unshielded twisted pair or fiber cable but not, typically, both. It's protocol dependent because it contains hardware and software designed to format data according to specific and standardized protocols. Ethernet and Token Ring NIC cards, for example, can't be interchanged. However, it's not uncommon to find NIC cards equipped for UTP and coaxial cable on the same card.

NET+ OBJECTIVE
I.1.7

> The NIC is an important consideration when building a LAN, because it contains addressing information that identifies a node on a network.

The address is unique, and without it, the node is lost to any other nodes attempting to communicate with it. When scouting NIC cards, buy from a reputable manufacturer. Buy cards that will operate in the types of computers on your LAN (usually stated by the bus size of client/server microprocessors such as 16 or 32 bits), and according to the LAN protocol, and type of media, used to access the network (twisted pairs, fiber cable, coaxial, etc.).

The clients are personal computers. An NT operating system installed on the server works quite well with Windows 95 installed on the PCs. NT also has a client component (called Windows NT Workstation), which was intended to work in tandem with NT Server. However, we'll assume Win 95 is running on the clients.

> The hardware configuration of the clients may span the gamut of personal computer microprocessors, RAM size and fixed-disk size. It doesn't matter to the server.

The client may be a slow Intel 386, or a fast MMX—perhaps faster than the server processor. Other than the NIC card and operating system, the clients are whatever you imagine them to be. Although the server doesn't care about the particulars of its clients, these same particulars affect the performance of the network. The type and speed of the MPU, bus architecture, amount of cache, seek rates of hard drives, size and type of RAM, buffer size of the NICs—all contribute to network performance.

The server, on the other hand, is another matter. This is because it's our friend; it manages the flow of data on the network, and it does so transparently. Rather, it should be transparent to us. If not, we need to reexamine its usefulness. What, exactly, begs examination? Specific server considerations are similar to those of the client:

- Microprocessor speed.

- Peripheral Interface.

- RAM memory.

- Cache.

- Size and specifications of the hard drive.

- Operating system.

- Fault tolerance.

GHz microprocessors, while not readily available, were announced in 1998. These are fast microprocessors, and a server can't be fast enough. Why? As MPUs become faster, users will demand they be installed in their machines to handle complex software routines. These same routines may be installed on the server, and made available to multi-users simultaneously. Not only is the software complex, but each of the multi-users expects to use it as if no one else was. That's network transparency!

Servers may contain several MPUs to handle requests quickly and transparently.

You can setup a standard PC as a file server, and in a lightly loaded network containing a small number of clients, it will work fine. But if the network grows, the server can only respond to requests as fast as its MPU can process them. Buy a server, rather than a PC with server software installed in it, that includes provisions for multiple processors.

There are two basic types of microprocessors:

- **Complex Instruction Set Computing** (CISC) microprocessors.

- **Reduced Instruction Set Computing** (RISC) microprocessors.

Of the two, CISC designs are the most widely used, since all Intel processors use this type of architecture. RISC is quicker and more efficient because less hardware is utilized to execute commands.

Which is better? There's far more software support for CISC than for RISC; so, even though RISC will perform better, this advantage is offset by the lack of software compatibility available for it. Until the full benefits of RISC can be exploited, use a CISC-based processor.

Note that motherboards containing the microprocessor will ship with ZIF sockets which allow easy extraction and insertion of microprocessor integrated circuits. This is important because it allows the IC to be replace with a newer microprocessor while still retaining the motherboard.

CNST OBJECTIVE
X-A

RAM memory is where most of the "application" part of application software is temporarily stored. Buy 72 pin SIMM boards (or 30 pin for older PCs) or 132 pin DIMMs, and install as much on the server as it will hold. As a general rule, fill the SIMM slots in increments of two.

The system cache is a **buffer**, which stores data going to and from the microprocessor.

The MPU is running at a rate that may be ten-fold higher than the network, or the internal bus of the computer the MPU is installed in. The buffer holds data temporarily when the processor is finished with it, and until the bus becomes available to send it to its destinations. It's a misconception to think that a 233MHz computer is swapping files at that rate; the MPU is running at a high data rate, but data exchanges between the MPU and memory or I/O devices is limited to the speed of the system bus.

The server will interface to numerous peripherals besides the clients and hub. Web-access modems, tape backups, CD-ROM, a printer, or other devices linking a LAN to other networks may all be connected to the server. It's important than these peripherals don't interfere with the primary job of the server of handling file transfers and managing the network.

The preferred interface is the **Small Computer Systems Interface** (SCSI—pronounced "scuzzy").

With a SCSI interface card installed in a server, all devices can operate independently since the interface circuitry will queue requests, then service them when it's most efficient for the device to deliver the service.

Not all system board-connected devices transfer data at the same rate. Some are faster than others.

NET+ OBJECTIVE
II.1.3

An Ultra-SCSI interface allows for speeds up to 200MBS.

The connected devices can interface with the MPU at a speed that's closer to their native capabilities, rather than a system-dictated speed.

Another reason for using SCSI is that a device needn't shutdown when the processor is communicating with another device.

CNST OBJECTIVE
X-A

A single SCSI card in a PCI slot allows simultaneous operation of up to 60 devices (using Ultra-SCSI with 15 devices on each of the four, wide ports).

When purchasing server hardware, include a SCSI interface card, and then buy peripherals that are SCSI compatible. The cabling is more complex with SCSI (Devices external to the server are connected in a daisy chain manner using a cable than may have up to 60 pins), but other than making the connections, the rest is configurable from the card software or hardware configurable via jumpers or switches. Figure 1-9 depicts two 50-pin SCSI connector pinouts, while Figure 1-10 shows the 50-pin Mini-Micro SCSI-2 connector pinout, and the 68-pin, Wide SCSI-3 primary connector pinout. In addition, a common, though unstandard connector, is a DB-25 SCSI that's used frequently.

A hard drive is where user files, and in many cases, all application software will be stored. There are two important considerations, then, for a server hard drive. It should be big, and fast! It's impossible to separate a discussion of hard drives and **interface** technology, since the two are intrinsically linked. Most hard drives are the IDE type, which stands for **Integrated Device Electronics**. An IDE hard drive is the same as an **Advanced Technology Attachment** (ATA) hard drive, although ATA is actually a reference to the type of bus attachments used in a computer. This text will use the terms IDE and ATA synonymously.

CNST OBJECTIVE
X-B

An improvement to IDE is EIDE. EIDE competes head-on with SCSI as a means of transferring data, with EIDE specifically referring to fixed disks (hard drives, tape drives and CD-ROM) while SCSI includes all attached devices. Currently, EIDE hard drives transfer data to and from the drive (or drives, since the IDE/ATA standard supports more than two hard drives) at a maximum burst rate of 33MBS for ATA3 compliant hard drives. Compare this to the maximum data rate of a SCSI interface burst rate of 200MBS.

Currently, IDE hard drives transfer data to and from the drive at a maximum of 33MBS, for ATA3 compliant hard drives.

DD-50P SCSI RIBBON CABLE

Pin	Description	Pin	Description
1	Ground	2	Data 0
3	Ground	4	Data 1
5	Ground	6	Data 2
7	Ground	8	Data 3
9	Ground	10	Data 4
11	Ground	12	Data 5
13	Ground	14	Data 6
15	Ground	16	Data 7
17	Ground	18	Data Parity (Odd)
19	Ground	20	Ground
21	Ground	22	Ground
23	Ground	24	Ground
25	No Connection	26	No Connection
27	Ground	28	Ground
29	Ground	30	Ground
31	Ground	32	Attention
33	Ground	34	Ground
35	Ground	36	Busy
37	Ground	38	ACK
39	Ground	40	Reset
41	Ground	42	Message
43	Ground	44	Select
45	Ground	46	C/D
47	Ground	48	Request
49	Ground	50	I/O

MALE

DD-50SA (OLD STYLE SUN SCSI)

Pin	Description	Pin	Description	Pin	Description
1	GND	18	GND	34	-DB (0)
2	-DB (0)	19	-DB (2)	35	GND
3	GND	20	GND	36	-DB (3)
4	-DB (4)	21	-DB (5)	37	GND
5	GND	22	GND	38	-DB (6)
6	-DB (7)	23	-DB (P)	39	GND
7	GND	24	GND	40	GND
8	GND	25	RST	41	RST
9	OPEN	26	RST	41	RST
10	RST	27	GND	42	TERMPWR
11	GND	28	GND	43	GND
12	GND	29	BSY	44	-ATN
13	GND	30	GND	45	GND
14	-RST	31	-MSG	46	-ACK
15	GND	32	GND	47	GND
16	-C/D	33	-REQ	48	-SEL
17	GND			49	GND
				50	-I/O

MALE

"CENTRONICS" 50 PIN

Pin	Description	Pin	Description
26	-DB (0)	1	GND
27	-DB (1)	2	GND
28	-DB (2)	3	GND
29	-DB (3)	4	GND
30	-DB (4)	5	GND
31	-DB (5)	6	GND
32	-DB (6)	7	GND
33	-DB (7)	8	GND
34	-DB (8)	9	GND
35	GND	10	GND
36	GND	11	GND
37	RST	12	RST
38	TERMPWR	13	OPEN
39	RST	14	RST
40	GND	15	GND
41	-ATN	16	GND
42	GND	17	GND
43	BSY	18	GND
44	-ACK	19	GND
45	-RST	20	GND
46	-MSG	21	GND
47	-SEL	22	GND
48	-C/D	23	GND
49	-REQ	24	GND
50	-I/O	25	GND

MALE

Figure 1-9 SCSI-2 50-Pin Connector Pinouts

MINI-MICRO (SCSI-2)

Pin	Description	Pin	Description
26	-DB (0)	1	GND
27	-DB (1)	2	GND
28	-DB (2)	3	GND
29	-DB (3)	4	GND
30	-DB (4)	5	GND
31	-DB (5)	6	GND
32	-DB (6)	7	GND
33	-DB (7)	8	GND
34	-DB (8)	9	GND
35	GND	10	GND
36	GND	11	GND
37	RST	12	RST
38	TERMPWR	13	OPEN
39	RST	14	RST
40	GND	15	GND
41	-ATN	16	GND
42	GND	17	GND
43	BSY	18	GND
44	-ACK	19	GND
45	-RST	20	GND
46	-MSG	21	GND
47	-SEL	22	GND
48	-C/D	23	GND
49	-REQ	24	GND
50	-I/O	25	GND

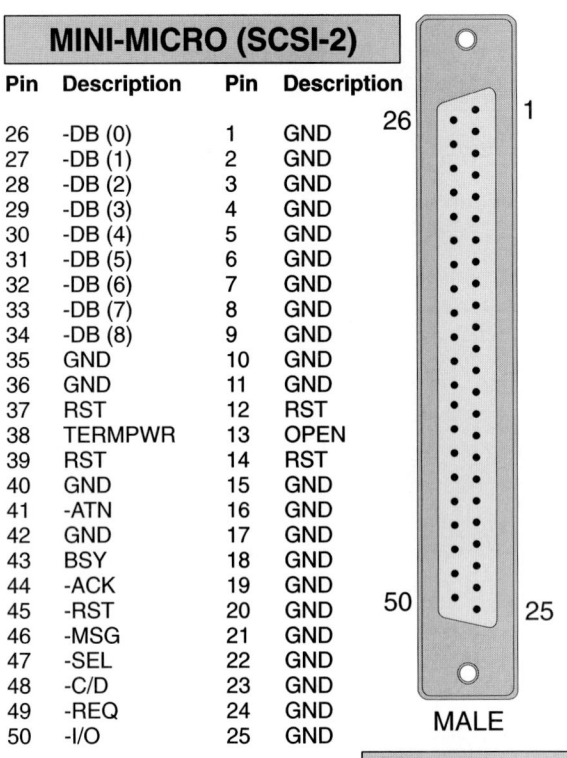

MALE

Figure 1-10 SCSI-2, 50-Pin Mini-Micro Pinout, and SCSI-3, 68-Pin Primary Connector Pinout

16 BIT (WIDE SCSI-3 P)

Pin	Description	Pin	Description
35	-DB (12)	1	GND
36	-DB (13)	2	GND
37	-DB (14)	3	GND
38	-DB (15)	4	GND
39	-DB (P1)	5	GND
40	-DB (0)	6	GND
41	-DB (1)	7	GND
42	-DB (2)	8	GND
43	-DB (3)	9	GND
44	-DB (4)	10	GND
45	-DB (5)	11	RST
46	-DB (6)	12	OPEN
47	-DB (7)	13	RST
48	-DB (P)	14	GND
49	GND	15	GND
50	GND	16	GND
51	TERMPWR	17	TERMPWR
52	TERMPWR	18	TERMPWR
53	RSRVD	19	RSRVD
54	GND	20	GND
55	-ATN	21	GND
56	GND	22	GND
57	BSY	23	GND
58	-ACK	24	GND
59	-RST	25	GND
60	-MSG	26	GND
61	-SEL	27	GND
62	-C/D	28	GND
63	-REQ	29	GND
64	-I/O	30	GND
65	-DB (8)	31	GND
66	-DB (9)	32	GND
67	-DB (10)	33	GND
68	-DB (11)	34	GND

MALE

Compare this to the maximum data rate of a SCSI interface of 200MBS. The interface used with fixed disks—there may be more than one in a server—is critical to getting data to and from the disk.

A SCSI interface competes with the MPU for speed, so data movement outside the drive isn't a problem. Getting it off the disk is the bottleneck.

The hard drive seeks the requested file, and the time it takes to do so slows the system down considerable. One way to offset the delay (known as latency in a hard drive) is to provide the disk with a large cache to store data, while the hard drive mechanics fetch and store files. Hard drives have built-in caches, but choose the drive with as much as you can get.

Hard drive sizes exceeding 10 Gigabytes are readily available. How much do you actually need? Enough to meet your current demands, as well as future needs. A quick way to determine size is to make a best-guess estimate of your current storage (add up the disk space used on all stand alones), and multiply that total by 1.5. The future is difficult to predict, but keep in mind that new software releases can be counted on to hog memory. That's the case for purchasing a server that has room to add-on hard drives. You may not need the space now, or want to budget money for additional hard drives, but when the time comes, you'll have room to do so.

An **operating system** controls and directs the operation of a computer system.

Windows NT has become a popular operating system because it combines operations of the computer hardware and network hardware—a combination that's hard to beat. But it's certainly not the only one available, even if it seems to be at times. Other operating systems are MS-DOS, OS/2, Windows 3.x, Windows 95, Windows 98, MacOS, and Unix.

Operating systems run beneath and, ideally, independent of networking software. It doesn't make a lot of sense to scrap all stand alones when designing a network because their OS is Unix, or Apple. Granted, some OS's are far more supported than others, but you must be sensitive to the needs of users, and determine if a new operating system is a good idea when they must also learn conventions associated with a networking environment.

Fault tolerance refers to the ability of a network to recover from problems.

Implied in fault tolerance is reliability and this, in turn, is a specification of the components comprising the system. Buy quality equipment for a network. Buy from manufacturers who can show you an ISO9000 Quality System certificate. Make sure all of the products you buy are built in a factory that has been certified by an outside agency as having a viable Quality System. Then, spend a little extra and add an **Uninterruptable Power Supply** (UPS) to the network.

A UPS is a battery-operated power supply that kicks in if you loose power to the network.

Depending on the type of OS used, a UPS is critical. For example, a Unix system may crash, and important data lost, if the power drops out long enough to cause the server to try and reboot. Data integrity is reason enough to add UPSs to a network.

CNST OBJECTIVE
IX-B

NET+ OBJECTIVE
II.5.8

> As a rule of thumb, add a UPS to each segment of a LAN. This keeps the server and the client PCs running.

Even if the power doesn't drop out occasionally, there are many other disasters waiting to destroy electronic files. The best recourse is preventive.

> **Backup** the data on a server, automatically, once each day, at a minimum.

The easiest auto-backups are SCSI tape drives. Configure the backup to occur at a time when no one is working; usually, the middle of the night.

Now that you have an idea of the hardware components of a LAN, let's assume we need to expand it. There are limits to the number of nodes, which can be connected to Ethernet or Token Ring LANs. If more nodes must be added, then the LAN will have to be extended.

> A **repeater** connects separate LANs, extends a single LAN's physical size.

Figure 1-11 shows two LANs connected by a repeater. The **repeater** is little more than a signal amplifier that also regenerates and conditions signals to remove noise and distortion. A repeater is a physical device that is only concerned with data streams, and is not capable of making decisions as to where data originates, or where it's going—it simply releases it on to the next node, a hub or a server.

NET+ OBJECTIVE
I.2.2

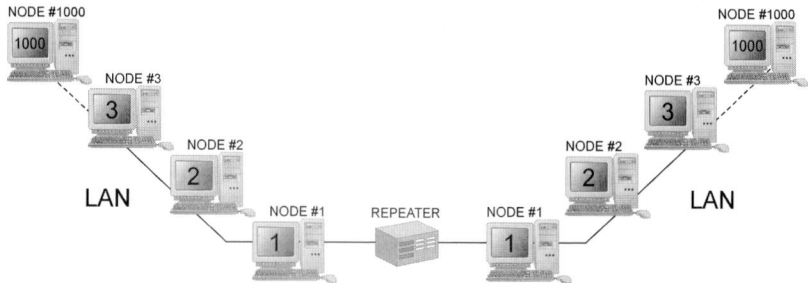

Figure 1-11   Repeater Regenerating Network Signals

It's dependent on the physical media (twisted pairs, fiber optic, etc.), but independent of the access protocol type, such as Ethernet, FDDI, and Token Ring. Since it works at the physical level, a repeater is unaware of any protocol formatting,

CNST OBJECTIVE
VI-A

Many repeaters serve a dual role as a hub, and are called active hubs. Therefore, a hub without any signal regenerating capabilities, such as a punchdown block or wiring panel, is known as a passive hub. A **hub** contains from 4 to 132 ports to which network nodes may be connected. Typically, the connected workstations share and communicate through the hub. A close relative of a hub is a **switching hub**, which operates at a higher level than a conventional hub, and is used to transfer packets of data that have been broken into small portions.

Separate LANs may need to be connected in order to exchange files between different groups. For example, the Payroll department may be on one LAN, while the Sales department may be on another. Since the size of paychecks for Sales reps are dependent on how much they sell, the Payroll department needs to know whenever a sale is made. So, each time a Rep makes a sale, the sale is forwarded to Payroll. However, it's not necessary for the Sales Rep to have access to the files in Payroll.

If a repeater is used to connect these two LANs, it won't be able to stop requests for files from Sales to Payroll.

A repeater doesn't have the capability to filter network traffic, but a **bridge** does.

The bridge looks at addressing information in each frame passing through it to determine if the frame should be sent on. If an address has access to the next LAN, the data bits are reconditioned as in a repeater, and the frame is forwarded. If the frame doesn't have access, the bridge will forbid the delivery of the frame. It has decision-making capabilities that repeaters don't possess.

Bridges, pictured in Figure 1-12, are dependent on the type of protocol. Two Ethernet LANs can be bridged, but an Ethernet and a Token Ring LAN can't. The media type used in the two LANs must be the same; a twisted pair Ethernet can't be bridged to a fiber cable Ethernet.

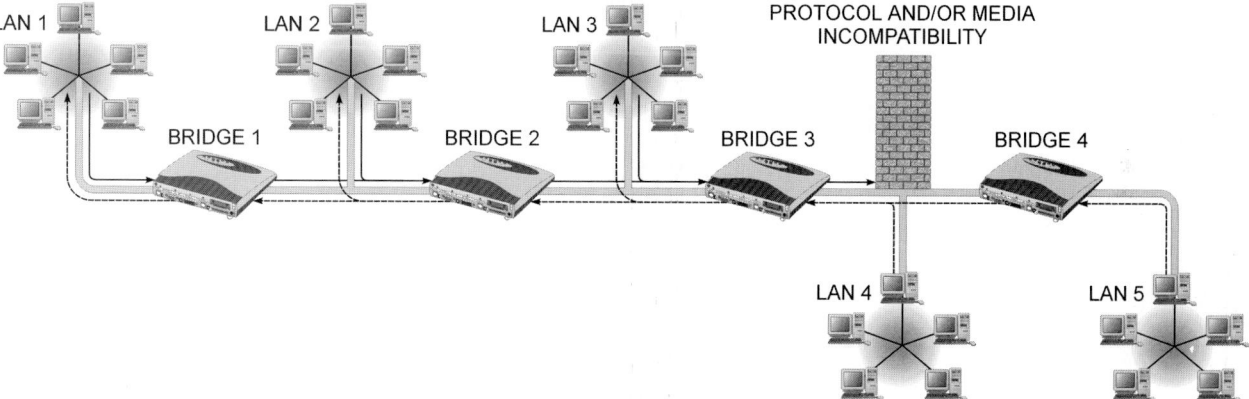

Figure 1-12   Bridges Filtering Network Traffic

Bridges offer filtering capabilities between LANs. The drawback to them is the lack of flexibility in connecting LAN protocols and different media types.

To overcome this shortcoming, routers, shown in Figure 1-13, may be used in place of bridges.

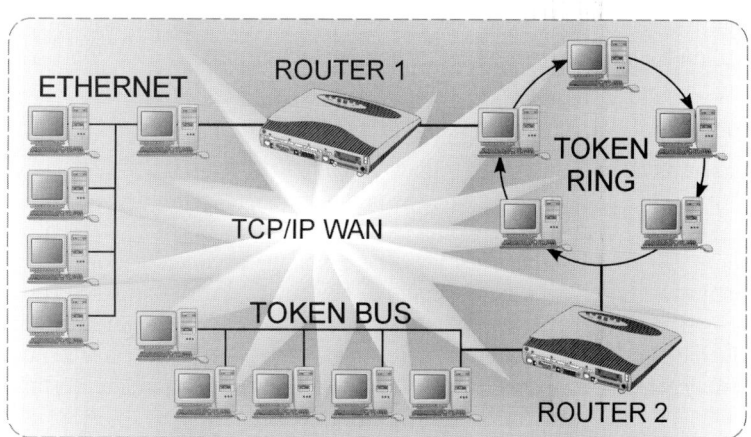

Figure 1-13   Router Filtering Traffic between LANs with Different Protocols

A **router** works independently of the LAN protocol.

This means that Ethernet, Token Ring or FDDI LANs can be connected with the router in a wide area network. The protocol used for the WAN, though, must be consistent for all interconnected LANs.

A **gateway** may be required when a network is using incompatible protocols such as IBM SNA, ISO OSI, or DEC DNA.

These protocols define the full outcomes of a data communication system, and in the implementation, use diverse designs in hardware and software.

Chapters 7 and 8 examine the details of bridges, routers, and higher-level protocols, along with details of clients and servers. Protocols for local area networks are examined in Chapters 5, 6 and 7.

MODEMS AND MULTIPLEXERS

As mentioned earlier, a modem converts data into a format suitable for transmission over a long distance. What is meant by "a long distance"?

A modem is required whenever data is transmitted over a distance greater than 50 feet.

Having stated that, we will risk some confusion by stating there are many exceptions to the statement. In particular, some networks cover far greater distances, but modems are not required. However, a modem is required in order to use the local and long distance telephone network to transmit data. In fact, modems find their greatest application serving as an interface between a computer, and the telephone system.

The majority of modems have been designed specifically to serve as an interface to the telephone company.

Unfortunately for data communication users, the most widely installed communication medium was never intended to transfer data. Telephone lines have a frequency response of 300Hz-3300Hz. This is adequate for voice communication, but painfully slow for high-speed computers. The job of a modem is to alter data in such a way that it can be sent through the phone system. Figure 1-14 illustrates how the exchange between stations occurs. Binary information from terminal 1 is sent to modem A. Note that the waveform out of the modem is an analog signal, with very little resemblance to the square wave input. In fact, the frequency output of the modem falls within the 3kHz response of the telephone channel. For example, the modem may generate a carrier frequency of 1200Hz, and the data modulates this carrier.

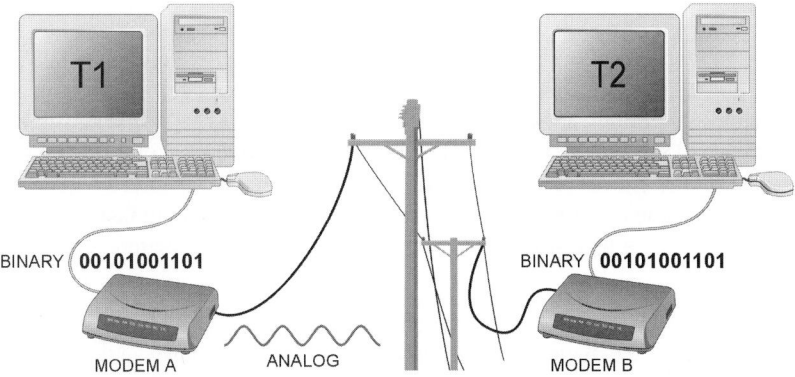

Figure 1-14   Transferring Data Over Phone Lines

Modem B receives the modulated carrier, detects the data out of it, and sends the data to terminal 2. If terminal 2 has a response for terminal 1, the process is reversed. Terminal 2 will transmit back at a different carrier frequency than terminal 1.

Frequently, several terminals in an office may need to transmit data. Each terminal could have a modem attached to it, and the local phone company could install a line to each terminal. A simpler, and certainly a more cost-effective approach is to connect the terminals to a **multiplexer**, as shown in Figure 1-15.

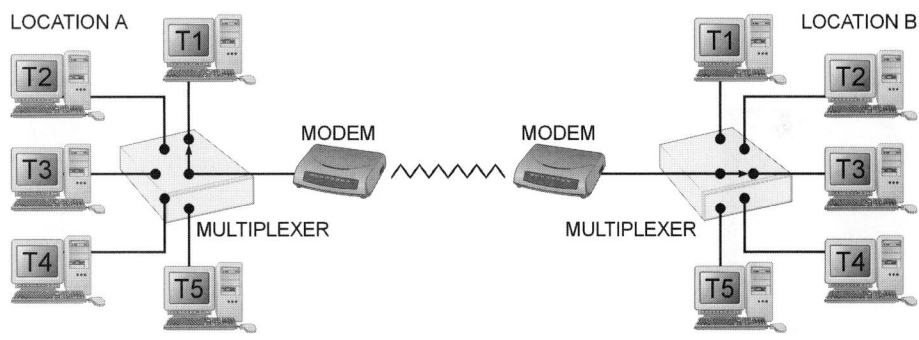

**Figure 1-15
Multiplexing Data**

A multiplexer is an electronic switch capable of selecting one of several input signals, and connecting it to a single output line.

The switch moves from terminal to terminal in a rotating manner. When the switch connects to a terminal, the terminal can transmit data if it has any to send. The multiplexer will remain connected to the terminal for a predetermined length of time, and then move to the next terminal. If the terminal does not have time to transmit all of its data in the allotted time, it must wait until its turn comes back around.

The data out of the multiplexer is applied to a modem. The modem transmits a carrier modulated with data. At the receive end, the modem extracts data from the carrier and applies the data to another multiplexer. The receive multiplexer is functioning as a demultiplexer. A demultiplexer applies the data from a single input line to several output lines. As shown in Figure 1-15, the data from terminal 1 will be transmitted from location A, through the telephone lines to location B, and then terminal 3.

The justification for multiplexers is one of economics; it is simply cheaper than running dedicated lines. Most long-distance telephone calls are extensively multiplexed. Multiplexing data channels is extensively done in satellite systems as well.

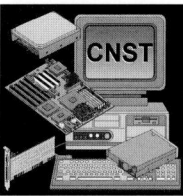

CNST OBJECTIVE
I-A

Closely related to multiplexers are switches. A network switch allows nodes to be connected as members of workgroups on a network. The node is physically connected to a port on a switch, but frequently, it is virtually connected to a workgroup. A virtual connection is a programmatic connection; that is, the node is represented with a logical port assignment that is under control of network management software. The software assigns ports based upon the destination of a message from the node, the level of traffic to the destination, the receiving speed of the destination, and so on. Switches are extremely fast because logical port assignments occur as fast as the microprocessors inside the switch.

> The speed of a switch, incidentally, is published according to how fast the switch can switch port assignments, and not by how fast data moves through it.

More will be said about network switches in a later chapter.

BAUD AND BIT RATE

CNST OBJECTIVE
VI-D

> The speed at which data is transmitted is quoted in much of the technical literature as either the **baud rate** or bit per second (BPS) rate. Baud rate describes the number of data symbols (The information that's modulated onto a carrier) transmitted per second.

> A **symbol** is a small group of bits into which data is organized at the time of modulation.

The use of symbols effectively increases the number of bits transmitted in the allotted bandwidth of a communication channel. A data communications symbol can contain 1, 2, 3, or 4 or more data bits. The specific number of bits contained in the symbol is determined by the method used to modulate the carrier.

Baud rate is calculated by:

$$Baud = BPS/N$$

where BPS is bits per second, and N is the number of bits per symbol.

For example, a Bell 201 modem has a specified data rate of 2400 BPS. The number of bits per symbol is 4. The baud rate is equal to:

$$Baud = 2400\ BPS/4 = 600$$

The **bit rate**, or bits per second, describes the number of discrete binary bits transmitted per second. It is a true measure of data rate. The bit rate is calculated by:

$$BPS = 1/T$$

where T is the bit time in seconds.

For example, if the time of a single bit is measured with an oscilloscope and found to be 10 milliseconds (ms), then:

$$BPS = 1/.01 = 100$$

Notice that baud is an indication of the amount of information transmitted, while BPS is the amount of total data transmitted.

Baud is a unitless quantity, and therefore can't be quantified. It has little meaning in evaluating the performance of a network, or the components comprising a network. Its value lies in the concept that many of the data bits which are sent over a network contain no user data. Therefore, in order to gain insight as to how much information is sent using a particular modulation scheme, we sometimes focus on baud rather than BPS.

Increasingly, data communications literature uses baud and BPS interchangeably. The usage is incorrect, and represents an attempt to subvert the English language. The two are only equal at lower data rates of less than about 1200 BPS.

All modems are classified by their BPS rate.

Multiplexing schemes are devised around the BPS rate of a channel, and the digital systems of long distance carriers are specified by BPS. All data rates in subsequent chapters will be given in BPS.

DATA TRANSMISSION

Information in a data communication system is transmitted in digital or analog formats. Analog data is common in many parts of the telephone system, although most regional and long distance carriers are aggressively replacing their analog systems with digital systems. The principle reason for the change to digital is that it is easier to generate, is compatible with the structure of data in computer systems, and noise and distortion is easier to remove from digital signals.

An analog signal has many discrete values representing a physical process (a voice, for example).

It's difficult, if not impossible, to remove some types of distortion in an analog signal without simultaneously degrading the signal. Analog to digital, and digital to analog integrated circuits have advanced to the point that an analog signal can be converted to digital, transmitted through a digital communication system, and converted back to analog at the receiver with nearly perfect clarity. Still, many segments of analog communications remains. The most notable is the **subscriber loop**, also called the local loop, of the local telephone exchange.

> The subscriber loop is the circuit from a residential or office telephone to the local central office. A central office is designated by the first three digits of a local telephone number.

A computer user wishing to connect to the Internet utilizes the same loop circuit through a modem. The problem is that these circuits were designed for analog signals, and in particular, voice signals.

Figure 1-16 depicts the subscriber loop voice channel. The frequency response of the channel is 300Hz-3300Hz for a bandwidth of 3kHz (3300-300=3000). All data transmitted through this channel must have a bandwidth no greater than 3kHz.

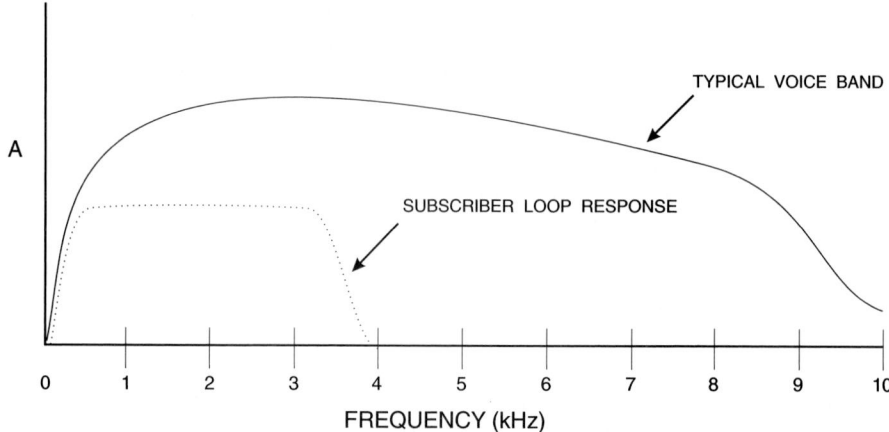

Figure 1-16 Frequency Response of Voice Channel

> **Bandwidth** (BW) is a particularly important aspect of data because it is a measure of the amount of actual data being transmitted.

And the amount of transmitted data is related to channel capacity.

> Channel capacity, measured in bits per second, is directly proportional to bandwidth.

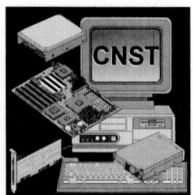

CNST OBJECTIVE
I-A

This means that a channel with large BW can carry large amounts of information; a channel with a narrow BW can carry small amounts of information. The local subscriber loop has a narrow BW. The problem is compounded if a digital square wave is applied to a subscriber loop. Square waves, as we will see in the next chapter, require far greater BW than does an analog signal. In order to achieve the benefits of digital data communications systems designers have resorted to considerable subterfuge in developing modulation and multiplexing techniques that allow an analog system to behave as a digital system.

Compromise is the key criteria in bandwidth considerations. The greater the bandwidth, the more data can be transmitted in a given time. The costs of transmitting the data will also be cheaper; however, equipment costs are greater for large bandwidth systems than for narrower bandwidth systems.

MODULATION METHODS

Data may be modulated onto a carrier for several reasons. The frequency of the data may not be the same frequency as the frequency of an assigned, or allotted, channel.

The FM radio-frequency range is from 88 MHz to 108 MHz.

Obviously, that is out of the audible range. In the telephone voice channel, the carrier must be between 300 Hz and 3,300 Hz.

It is usual to have MBPS data rates modulating a 1,200-Hz carrier because the data frequency falls far outside of the voice channel. In a microwave system, high carrier frequencies keep antennas down to manageable sizes. The use of a carrier is essential with some types of multiplexing techniques. A carrier with a broad bandwidth can be used to carry several thousand data signals by sharing the bandwidth.

Fundamentally, **modulation** is the process of superimposing data on a carrier.

Once the modulated carrier is transmitted, the data is detected at the receiving end. Detection, or demodulation, is the process of recovering data from the modulated carrier. There are three basic modulation methods: amplitude modulation (AM), frequency modulation (FM), and phase modulation (PM). In practice, it is very common to use various combinations of the three or to use a variation of one of the three basic methods. Furthermore, there is digital modulation and analog modulation. Nearly all variations of analog modulation can be traced back to AM, FM or PM. Some digital modulation methods—pulse width modulation, for example—resemble FM since a digital carrier is modulated by varying the width of square waves. Other digital modulation techniques involve varying the amplitude of square waves in a manner similar to AM.

Specific modulation methods are discussed in appropriate areas of the text. The following discussion describes the fundamentals of AM, FM and PM.

Amplitude Modulation

Amplitude modulation is produced by simultaneously applying a carrier and data to any non-linear device.

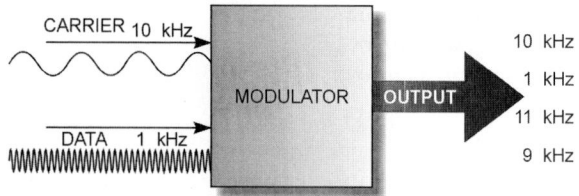

Figure 1-17 Producing Amplitude Modulation

As shown in Figure 1-17, this results in a 10kHz carrier, the original 1kHz data signal, the sum of the carrier and data (11 kHz), and the difference of the carrier and data (9 kHz). The sum frequency is called the upper sideband and the difference frequency is called the lower sideband.

In a conventional AM transmitter, the 1kHz original data signal is filtered out. The carrier, upper sideband and lower sideband are the transmitted frequencies. Each of these waveforms are depicted in Figure 1-18 in the time domain, as seen on an oscilloscope.

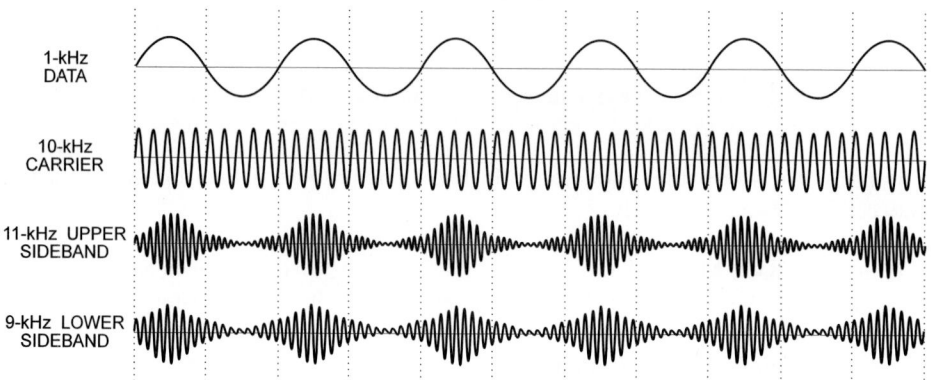

Figure 1-18 AM Modulation Envelope

There are several points to consider with the waveforms. First, notice the transmitted carrier contains no data; it is the same as when it was input to the modulator. In conventional AM, the carrier can contain up to 40% of the transmitted power. This is power containing no data. The carrier is used at the receiver to assist in recovering the original data. In some AM systems, the carrier is suppressed and not sent at all. This results in an improvement in the power efficiency.

Another interesting observation of the waveforms in Figure 1-18 involves the sidebands. The upper and lower sidebands are identical in all aspects except frequency. As mentioned earlier, it is the sidebands that contain the effects of the original data.

If one sideband were suppressed at the transmitter and the other transmitted, it would make little difference because they share the same characteristics.

Single-sideband (SSB) systems operate on the principle of suppressing one sideband and transmitting the other.

The peculiar shape of the sidebands is called the **modulation envelope**.

The effect of the 1kHz data signal can be seen by tracing the modulation envelope. The outline of the modulation envelope—either the positive or negative alternations of the sideband; they are identical—corresponds to the 1kHz data. The amplitude of the modulation envelope is directly proportional to the amplitude of the data. The rate of amplitude changes is directly proportional to the frequency of the data. Note that the sidebands contain only the effect of the data frequency and amplitude variations, but the data itself is lost.

AM is a simple and low-cost method of modulation. Conventional AM detectors are simple and easy to implement at the receiver. AM modulation requires a conservative amount of bandwidth. The bandwidth is equal to the difference of the upper and lower sideband.

A major drawback to AM is its poor power efficiency.

With the carrier requiring 40% of the transmitted power, the other 60% divides between the two sidebands. Since the sidebands are identical, the efficiency is calculated by 30/100=30%.

Another drawback is the difficulty in removing any noise picked up on the way to the receiver.

With analog AM it is sometimes impossible to eliminate noise. In a digital AM system in which square waves are transmitted, greater successes are achieved in reducing noise.

Frequency Modulation

Frequency modulation (FM) is produced by varying the frequency of the carrier.

FM is illustrated in Figure 1-19.

On the positive alternation of the 1kHz data, the frequency of the carrier increases. The amount of frequency increase is proportional to the amplitude of the data signal—the frequency of the carrier will be at its greatest at the peak value of the carrier. The negative alternation of the data causes the carrier frequency to decrease. As with the positive alternation, the greatest amount of frequency change occurs at the peak negative alternation.

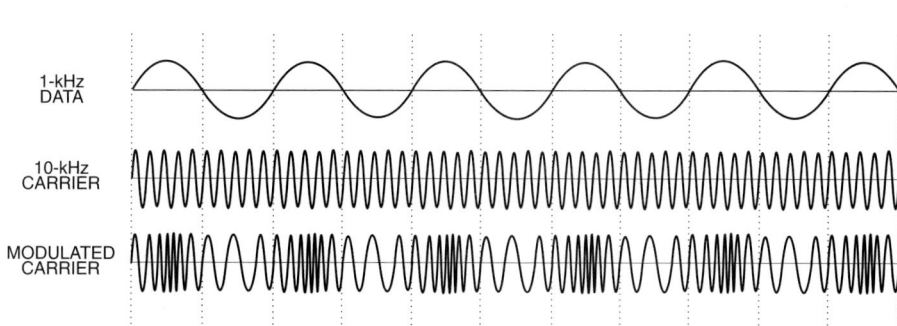

Figure 1-19 Frequency Modulation

The amount of frequency change, or deviation, is directly proportional to the amplitude of the data signal.

How quickly the carrier frequency changes is determined by the frequency of the data signal. In Figure 1-19, the carrier frequency is deviating at a 1kHz rate. If the data frequency increases to 2kHz, the rate of the carrier deviations will also increase to 2kHz.

The deviation of the carrier above and below the center frequency does not readily lend itself to the bandwidth of the FM signal. In calculating BW for an AM signal, the lower sideband was subtracted from the upper sideband. Bandwidth calculations for FM are not quite as straightforward because the carrier, as it deviates above and below the center frequency, generates an infinite number of sidebands. The intelligence contained in the modulating signal is contained in the sum of all the sidebands. As a practical matter, those sidebands containing less than 1% of the total voltage of the waveform are considered negligible and can be deleted from bandwidth considerations. As a general rule, the sidebands are repetitively duplicated at diminishing voltage levels for a distance above and below the carrier. The distance between those sidebands that contain more than 1% of the waveform voltage comprises the bandwidth. Just how much is that?

A method of calculating the bandwidth known as **Carson's rule** recognizes all sidebands containing 96% of the total radiated power.

Using this rule, bandwidth is calculated by:

$$BW = 2(\Delta F_c + F_m)$$

where Fc is the deviation produced by the modulating signal, and Fm is the frequency of the modulating signal.

Let's assume a 1kHz data signal produces a deviation of the FM carrier of 1kHz. This is consistent with the sideband placement of the earlier example used for AM, and will provide us a reference for comparing AM and FM. The bandwidth of the FM signal is:

$$BW = 2(\Delta F_c + F_m)$$
$$BW = 2(1 \text{ kHz} + 1 \text{ kHz})$$
$$BW = 2(2 \text{ kHz})$$
$$BW = 4 \text{ kHz}$$

This is twice the bandwidth of an equivalent AM signal. The FM bandwidth could be reduced by lowering the amplitude of the modulation, but the sideband energy would be reduced as well. Although larger bandwidths increase channel capacities, the bandwidths available are usually sharply defined, which makes bandwidth considerations a high priority.

Using our example of a 1kHz data signal, the BW from a conventional AM transmitter is 2kHz. A 100kHz communication channel can accommodate 50 AM transmissions (100kHz/2kHz=50). The same 100kHz channel can only contain 25 FM transmissions with a 4kHz bandwidth (100kHz/4kHz=25).

The wide bandwidth requirements of FM are somewhat offset by the superior noise-rejection qualities of FM. Since an FM signal contains no amplitude variations, noise can be eliminated by passing the signal through a **limiter**.

A limiter clips the positive and negative alternations of the signal, thereby eliminating most of the noise.

Another advantage of FM is the distribution of radiated power. Less than 10% of the radiated power is contained in the carrier. The rest of the power is contained in the sidebands, of which there are many in FM.

Phase Modulation

Phase modulation (PM) is a form of FM. Occasionally, it is referred to as indirect FM.

Phase modulation is produced by summing together a carrier frequency, generated by a crystal oscillator, with the data signal. The resulting signal is phase-distorted. The amount of distortion is proportional to the amplitude of the data signal, and the rate at which the phase shifts occur is proportional to the frequency of the data signal.

Phase-modulated systems are extremely stable, since the carrier is generated by a crystal. They find widespread use in data communications because of their stability and very narrow bandwidth. The bandwidth is comparable to AM.

A PM system shares the same noise-rejection qualities and power-efficiency advantages of FM.

Figure 1-20 illustrates PM using square waves, as would be found in a digital communications system.

At the positive alternation of the 1kHz data signal, the 2kHz carrier phase is shifted 90 degrees ahead of the unmodulated carrier. The negative alternation of the data signal shifts the carrier phase to lag the unmodulated carrier by 90 degrees. In practice, the actual phase shift (leading or lagging) is conducted in reference to the position of the previous phase shift. For example, when the square waves in Figure 1-20 have two positive alternations in succession, the modulated carrier shifts forward 90 degrees for each alternation.

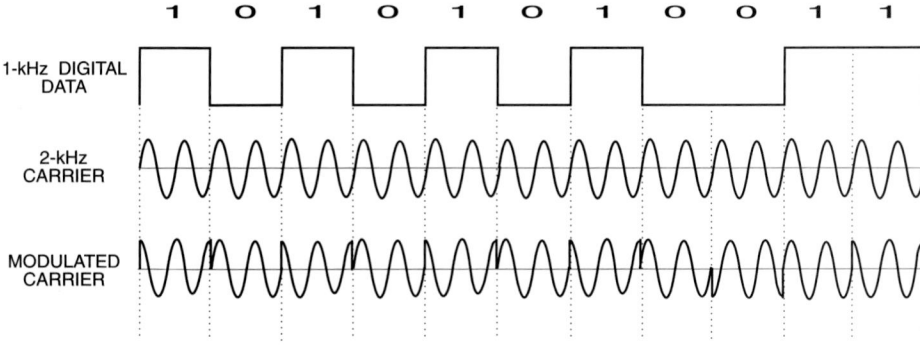

Figure 1-20 Phase Modulation

TERMINAL CODES

Terminal codes consist of binary numbers representing alphanumeric characters and special control functions.

The control functions include arithmetic symbols, spaces, grammar characters, as well as codes that are used to process or transfer data. A code is a method of expression that data processing equipment can understand. Terminal codes are expressed in the language of computers (binary 1's and 0's).

The most common terminal codes are **Baudot**, the **American Standard Code for Information Interchange** (ASCII), and the **Extended Binary Coded Decimal Interchange Code** (EBCDIC).

Baudot

The Baudot code is an older code that was developed to permit teletypewriters to operate at high speeds. Originally, it was intended to be used by Morse-code operators.

The idea was twofold: the operators needed a code that was standard in the length of the dots and dashes, and machines could assist in transferring the code if it were standardized. The Baudot code was never fully accepted by operators because they found it too difficult to standardize the length, or on/off characteristics, of the code.

There are many varieties of Baudot code, but the most common are 5-bit codes. The maximum number of characters represented by a 5-bit code is:

$$max\ characters = 2^B$$

where B is the length of the code.

$$max\ characters = 2^5$$
$$= 32$$

The Baudot code can represent 32 characters. If you consider 26 letters in the alphabet, 10 numbers (0-9), and codes for space, comma, period, etc., you can see the major disadvantage of Baudot. The code length restricts the flexibility of communications. It is a slow code that does not incorporate error-detection mechanisms. This makes it inappropriate for most modern communication equipment. The standardized Baudot code is shown in Figure 1-21.

Start	1 (LSB)	2	3	4	5 (MSB)	Stop	No Shift	Shift — U.S.A Teletype Commercial Keyboard
	●	●				●	A	—
	●			●	●	●	B	?
		●	●	●		●	C	:
	●			●		●	D	$
	●					●	E	3
	●		●	●		●	F	!
		●		●	●	●	G	&
			●		●	●	H	#
		●	●			●	I	8
	●	●		●		●	J	Bell
	●	●	●	●		●	K	(
		●			●	●	L	)
			●	●	●	●	M	.
			●	●		●	N	,
				●	●	●	O	9
		●	●		●	●	P	0
	●	●	●			●	Q	1
		●		●		●	R	4
	●		●			●	S	'
					●	●	T	5
	●	●	●			●	U	7
		●	●	●	●	●	V	;
	●	●			●	●	W	2
	●		●	●	●	●	X	/
	●		●		●	●	Y	6
	●				●	●	Z	"
						●	Blank	
	●	●	●	●	●	●	Letters shift	↓
	●	●		●	●	●	Figures shift	↑
			●			●	Space	■
				●		●	Carriage return	<
		●				●	Line feed	≡

Figure 1-21 Standardized Baudot Code

EBCDIC

In 1962, IBM developed EBCDIC to overcome the deficiencies of Baudot codes. It is a true binary-based code, widely used in IBM machines. EBCDIC assigns 8 bits for each alphanumeric character and each of the control functions. An 8-bit code can produce 256 unique characters. Unfortunately, nearly half of the characters are unassigned. This represents a lot of waste, while at the same time it permits quite a bit of flexibility. The EBCDIC code is shown in Figure 1-22.

		MSD															
		0 0000	1 0001	2 0010	3 0011	4 0100	5 0101	6 0110	7 0111	8 1000	9 1001	A 1010	B 1011	C 1100	D 1101	E 1110	F 1111
0	0000	NUL	DLE			SPACE	&	–									0
1	0001	SOH	DC1					/		a	j			A	J		1
2	0010	STX	DC2	SYN						b	k	s		B	K	S	2
3	0011	ETX	DC3							c	l	t		C	L	T	3
4	0100		RES	BYP						d	m	u		D	M	U	4
5	0101	HT	NL	LF	DC4					e	n	v		E	N	V	5
6	0110		BS	EOB						f	o	w		F	O	W	6
7	0111	DEL			EOT					g	p	x		G	P	X	7
8	1000		CAN							h	q	y		H	Q	Y	8
9	1001		EM							i	r	z		I	R	Z	9
A	1010					¢	!		:								
B	1011	VT				.	$	'	#	{	}						
C	1100	FF	FLS			<	*	%	@								
D	1101	CR	GS	ENQ	NAK	(	)	—	'			[		]			
E	1110	SO	RDS	ACK		+	;	>	=								
F	1111	SI	US	BEL	SUB	|	¬	?	"								

LSD

Figure 1-22 EBCDIC Code

ASCII

ASCII was first published in its present form in 1967. ASCII is a 7-bit code. It is capable of producing 128 unique characters. Certain versions of ASCII use 8-bit character lengths. ASCII is the most widely used information code in the world today, because it was designed specifically for data-processing equipment. There are no unassigned ASCII characters. The ASCII code is shown in Figure 1-23.

As an example, consider the letter "A". The code for this letter is 41_{16}. The most significant digit (MSD) is 4_{16}, while the least significant digit (LSD) is 1_{16}.

The codes presented in this section—**terminal codes**—are a category of a far larger group called **information codes**.

			MSD							
			0 000	1 001	2 010	3 011	4 100	5 101	6 110	7 111
LSD	0	0000	NUL	DLE	SPACE	0	@	P	`	p
	1	0001	SOH	DC1	!	1	A	Q	a	q
	2	0010	STX	DC2	"	2	B	R	b	r
	3	0011	ETX	DC3	#	3	C	S	c	s
	4	0100	EOT	DC4	$	4	D	T	d	t
	5	0101	ENQ	NAK	%	5	E	U	e	u
	6	0110	ACK	SYN	&	6	F	V	f	v
	7	0111	BEL	ETB	'	7	G	W	g	w
	8	1000	BS	CAN	(	8	H	X	h	x
	9	1001	HT	EM	)	9	I	Y	i	y
	A	1010	LF	SUB	*	:	J	Z	j	z
	B	1011	VT	ESC	+	;	K	[	k	{
	C	1100	FF	FS	,	<	L	\	l	|
	D	1101	CR	GS	-	=	M	]	m	}
	E	1110	SO	RS	.	>	N	^	n	~
	F	1111	SI	US	/	?	O	—	o	DEL

Figure 1-23 ASCII Code

Information codes have a variety of applications, but share the common intent of manipulating data without changing the original meaning of the data.

Some information codes, such as **Manchester** and **nonreturn-to-zero**, are used to change the structure of an ASCII-coded word so that it can be transmitted with a minimum of errors. Other information codes, such as the **Cyclic Redundancy Check** (CRC), are used for error-detection. Still others are used to correct errors, such as **Hamming codes**.

In all of the examples above, it is common to refer to the process of manipulating data bits as simply, **coding**. As in the example of coding an ASCII word, the coding process may occur many times over, for a variety of applications, and to address the many problems that are encountered when transmitting data streams.

One of the challenges in transmitting data is for the receiver to determine that a character is being received. The receiver also needs a method of determining the start of a character and the end of a character. The problem is addressed at the transmitter by framing data words.

Framing refers to methods of transmitting data that identify the start and stop of a character, or of long strings of characters. The two common methods of framing are called **asynchronous** and **synchronous**.

ASYNCHRONOUS AND SYNCHRONOUS DATA

Asynchronous

Asynchronous transmission is characterized by keeping the line in a steady-state condition until transmission occurs. One it begins, each character is separated by start and stop bits (or equivalent characters).

> The steady-state condition is referred to as a **mark**, and is represented by a logic 1.

> When the line makes the transition from the binary 1 to binary 0, this is referred to as a **space**, and the receiver will decipher the transition as the start of a data stream.

> The receiver will know the data stream is completed by detecting a **stop bit**.

Once the data has been sent, the line returns to the mark condition until more data are transmitted.

The format for asynchronous transmission is illustrated in Figure 1-24. The ASCII letter "T" is being transmitted. Prior to sending the letter, the line is in the mark state.

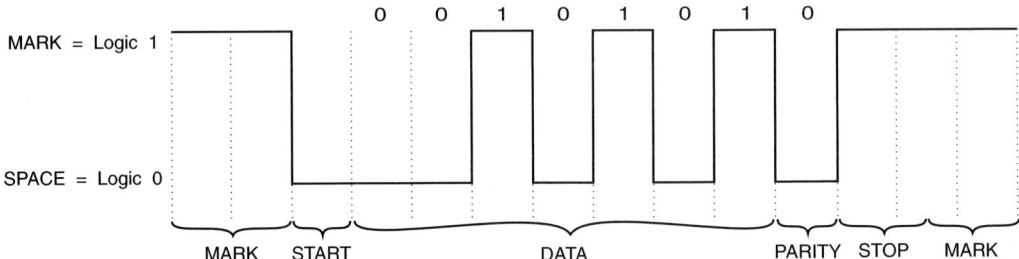

Figure 1-24 Asynchronous Data Format

> The line makes the transition from high to low, or space, with the **start bit**.

Immediately following the start bit is the data. The stop bit, which may be 1, 1.5, or 2 bits long, tells the receiver the transmission is ended. The line will remain in the mark condition until more data is transmitted.

> The **parity bit** is used for error detection.

Asynchronous transmission is fairly easy and inexpensive to implement. The major disadvantage is the time taken to transmit start and stop bits which contain no data. Many personal computers utilize asynchronous communications.

Synchronous

Synchronous literally means that the transmitter and receiver are synchronized. It improves upon asynchronous techniques by greatly reducing the bit space used for start and stop instructions.

> Synchronous transmission is characterized by one character immediately following another without the inclusion of start/stop bits.

In addition, each bit contains a synch pulse.

> The synch pulse tells the receiver the exact time a bit occurs.

CNST OBJECTIVE
I-A

To appreciate the value of synchronization, imagine a message transmitted 2,000 miles over long-distance telephone networks. By the time it arrives at the receiving end, it may be heavily distorted by propagation delays and noise. The receiver may begin extracting data too early or too late, thereby garbling the transmission. The problem is compounded at high data rates when bit times are short. When both the receiver and transmitter are synchronized, errors are less likely to occur. Each end will know if data is lost, because the synchronization pulse will also be lost.

The synchronous format is shown in Figure 1-25. The word "TWO" is being transmitted in ASCII. The line is held in the mark state until the start bit (or flag), occurs. The characters are sent and the transmission is terminated with a stop flag, at which time the line returns to the idle condition.

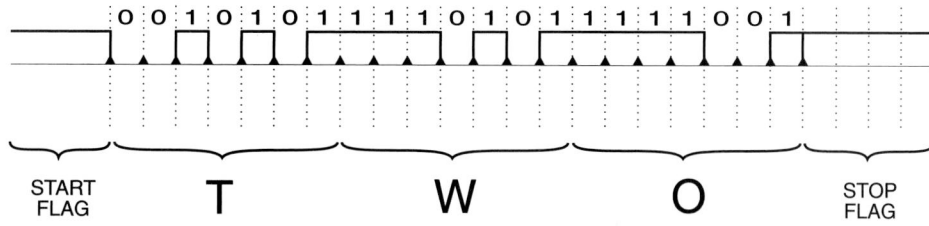

Figure 1-25 Synchronous Data Format

The carrier provides the synchronizing information. The synch pulse is depicted in Figure 1-25 by carrots at each data bit. A common method of synchronization is achieved by shifting the relative phase of each bit for mark and space conditions, with a mark being a 90-degree shift forward, and a space represented by a 90-degree lagging shift. The shift is relative to the preceding bit. For example, the first two bits of the ASCII T are 0's.

As the two logic 0's occur, the carrier shifts back by 90 degrees, once for each logic 0. The third bit is a logic 1, so the carrier is shifted forward 90 degrees. If a long stream of binary 1's is transmitted (a mark state), the carrier will shift forward 90 degrees for each logic 1.

The receiver detects each 90-degree phase shift as a data bit. In this way, the receiver and the transmitter are synchronized.

> Synchronous transmission is common at higher data rates, when long blocks of information are transmitted.

The advantage of synchronous over asynchronous is that communicating nodes can start and stop based on bit sequences, rather than driving the communication line high or low to represent the start or stop bits. When a receiver detects an agreed upon sequence (usually, 10101010), it begins decoding the remaining bits based upon their bit position following the sequence. Hundreds of bits may be decoded before the actual user data is decoded but the receiver will still pick it out because it's synchronized by each received bit.

DATA FLOW STRUCTURE

Earlier, it was stated that a communications system consists of the sender, the message, and the receiver. Implicit in the description is that there exists a medium in which the data will flow. The medium can consist of copper wire, fiber optics, or the atmosphere for microwaves. In a data communication system, the medium is structured in accordance with the direction of data flow. The flow of data can be structured in one of three different ways: **simplex**, **half duplex**, and **full duplex**.

NET+ OBJECTIVE
I.1.7

CNST OBJECTIVE
I-A

Simplex

> Simplex communication is one-way communication.

A simplex system is shown in Figure 1-26.

Data flows from the transmitter to the receiver, but not from the receiver to the transmitter. Examples of a simplex system are the terminals found in airports which list flight arrivals and departures.

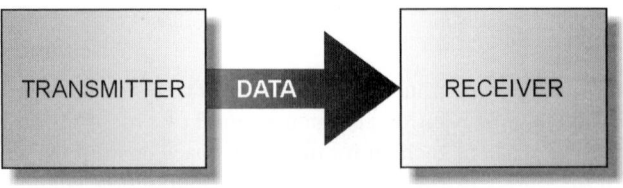

Figure 1-26 Simplex Communication

Half Duplex

A half-duplex system allows data to flow from the transmitter to the receiver, and from the receiver to the transmitter, but only in one direction at a time.

In the half-duplex system of Figure 1-27, a computer is transmitting a message to another computer. Once the message has been received, the second computer sends back an acknowledgment that the message was received. Note that the terms, transmitter and receiver, are relative to the direction the data is traveling.

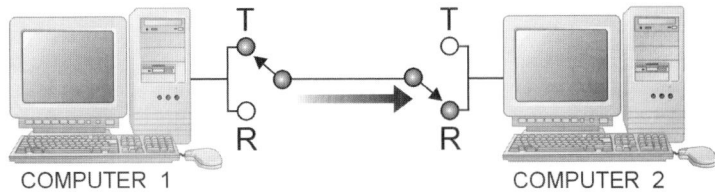

Figure 1-27 Half-Duplex Communication

The top of the figure shows the computer on the left serving as a transmitter, but when the computer on the right sends a reply, it serves as a receiver.

Full Duplex

Full-duplex systems permit data to flow in both directions simultaneously.

The most common full-duplex system is the telephone service. Conversations on the telephone can take place with both parties talking at the same time.

Full-duplex operation requires additional wiring and greater circuit complexity than simplex and half duplex. A full-duplex system is shown in Figure 1-28.

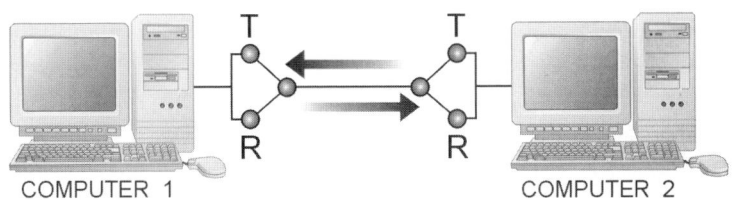

Figure 1-28 Full-Duplex Communication

NET+ OBJECTIVE
I.1.7

CNST OBJECTIVE
I-A

Once again, a computer is sending a message to another computer. In the half-duplex system, the first computer waited for an acknowledgment from the second computer. In full duplex, the first computer could continue to transmit rather than wait for the line to become free. As with half duplex, equipment on both ends of the communication link assumes the dual role of transmitter and receiver.

Full-duplex is typically associated with a need high speed communication between nodes. Half-duplex is used when speed is not a priority but costs are. Simplex is primarily used to supply a peripheral with information, or to collect information from a peripheral.

INTERFACES

An interface provides a connection between dissimilar devices. An interface is required between a personal computer and a printer because they are entirely different machines. An interface is a physical device, such as a connector or adapter. The specifications for an interface are usually described in the literature for protocols. Over a period of time, the physical device may become an industry standard, primarily through wide acceptance in the industry.

Some of the more popular interfaces are the **EIA/TIA-232**, the **EIA/TIA-449**, and the **EIA/TIA-485.** These interfaces are responsible for implementing protocols found in level 1, the **Physical layer**, of the OSI model.

Physical layer protocols are involved with the actual transfer of data through a communication system (at all other levels, physical data transfer does not occur).

The characteristics of a logic 0 and a logic 1 are defined, the activation and deactivation of a connection is described, and procedures for controlling and detecting errors are discussed. The result has been the implementation of interface standards.

EIA/TIA-232

The standard specifies a D-type, 25 pin connector. For many applications, less than ten of the pins are used. The other pins are available for specialized configurations.

The EIA/TIA-232 interface is commonly used with personal computers and peripherals.

The interface is generally well suited to single-user environments free of electromagnetic noise produced by motors and generators, such as may be found in an industrial setting. The maximum distance a DCE can be located from a DTE is 50 feet when using an EIA/TIA-232 interface. In actual practice, the maximum length varies with the data rate. The standard specifies a maximum data rate of 20 kBPS and a maximum cable length at this rate of 50 feet. For data rates less than 20 kBPS, the cable length can be increased without adversely affecting the data. The EIA/TIA-232 is not a good choice for multi-user settings, since it only supports two users.

The EIA/TIA-232 pinout is shown in Figure 1-29.

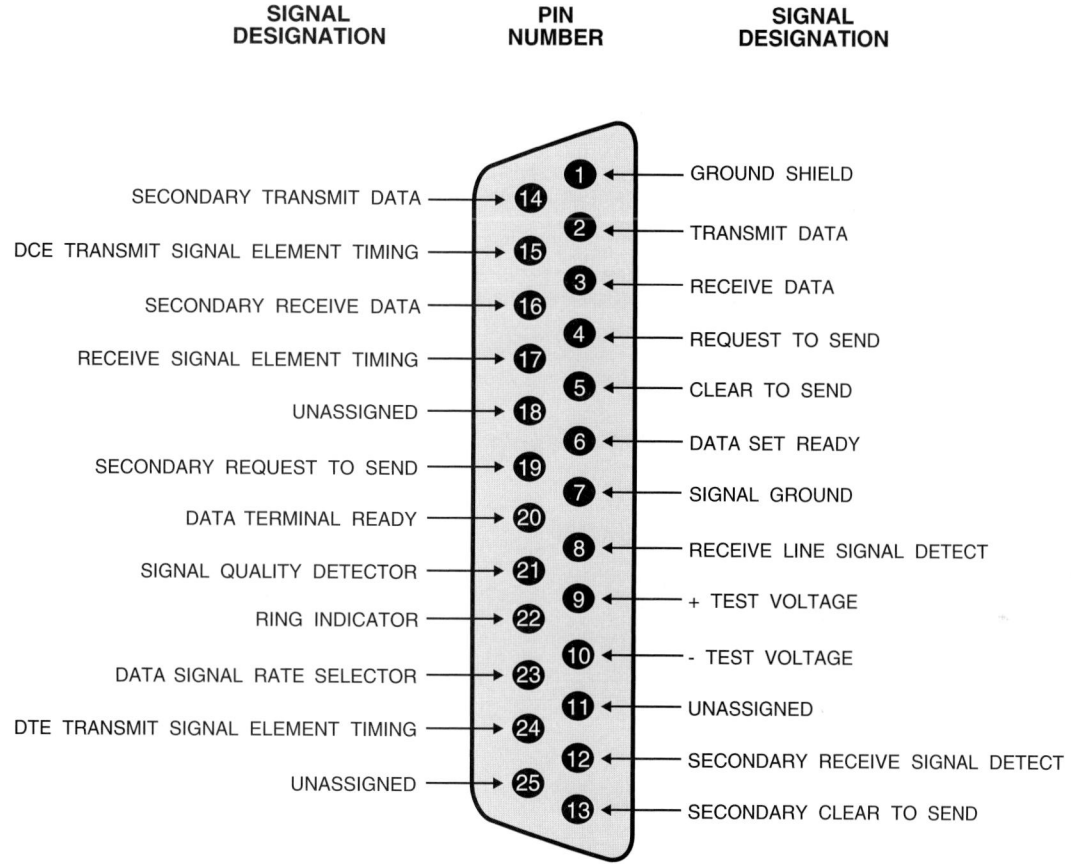

SIGNAL DESIGNATION   **PIN NUMBER**   **SIGNAL DESIGNATION**

SECONDARY TRANSMIT DATA — 14   1 — GROUND SHIELD
DCE TRANSMIT SIGNAL ELEMENT TIMING — 15   2 — TRANSMIT DATA
SECONDARY RECEIVE DATA — 16   3 — RECEIVE DATA
RECEIVE SIGNAL ELEMENT TIMING — 17   4 — REQUEST TO SEND
UNASSIGNED — 18   5 — CLEAR TO SEND
SECONDARY REQUEST TO SEND — 19   6 — DATA SET READY
DATA TERMINAL READY — 20   7 — SIGNAL GROUND
SIGNAL QUALITY DETECTOR — 21   8 — RECEIVE LINE SIGNAL DETECT
RING INDICATOR — 22   9 — + TEST VOLTAGE
DATA SIGNAL RATE SELECTOR — 23   10 — - TEST VOLTAGE
DTE TRANSMIT SIGNAL ELEMENT TIMING — 24   11 — UNASSIGNED
UNASSIGNED — 25   12 — SECONDARY RECEIVE SIGNAL DETECT
   13 — SECONDARY CLEAR TO SEND

Figure 1-29 EIA/TIA-232 Interface

When a long string of logic 1's or 0's are transmitted through a cable, the average line voltage tends to drift. For example, if a logic 0 is to be equal to 0 volts, and hundreds of 0's are transmitted, the line voltage will gradually creep to some positive voltage. The receiver may begin to interpret the positive voltage levels as logic 1's, rather than logic 0's. A DTE/DCE interface addresses the problem of dc drift by assigning opposite polarity voltages to a logic 1 and a logic 0. The specified EIA/TIA-232 voltage range describing a logic 1 is –3 to –25 Vdc, while a logic 0 is specified as +3 to +25 Vdc.

EIA/TIA-449

The EIA/TIA-449 is an interface that improves upon the noise, cable-length, and data-rate limitations of the EIA/TIA-232.

It performs in a much superior manner than the EIA/TIA-232. Unfortunately, the EIA/TIA-232 is the **de facto** interface standard in the United States, and equipment manufacturers, as well as users, have been quite reluctant to make a change.

The EIA/TIA-449 offers two modes of operation: the **balanced mode**, and the **unbalanced mode**.

The balanced mode transmits only **differential voltages**, and rejects all **common-mode voltages**.

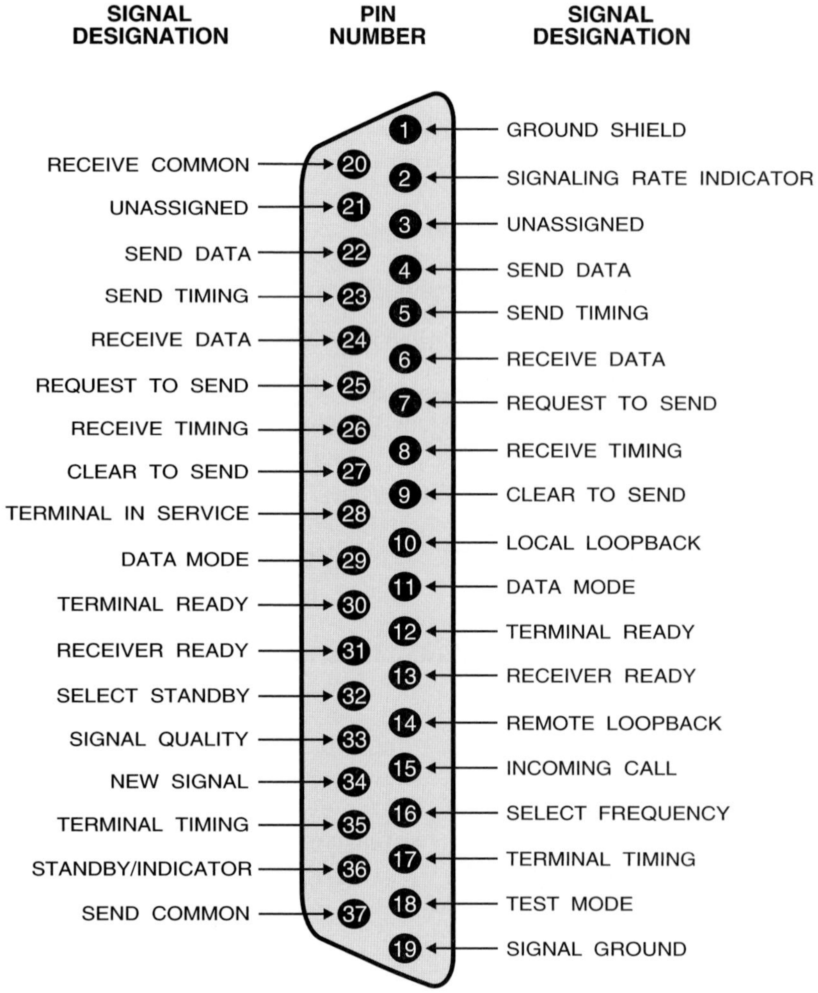

Common-mode voltage is usually noise induced into the cables.

SIGNAL DESIGNATION	PIN NUMBER	SIGNAL DESIGNATION
	1	GROUND SHIELD
RECEIVE COMMON	20, 2	SIGNALING RATE INDICATOR
UNASSIGNED	21, 3	UNASSIGNED
SEND DATA	22, 4	SEND DATA
SEND TIMING	23, 5	SEND TIMING
RECEIVE DATA	24, 6	RECEIVE DATA
REQUEST TO SEND	25, 7	REQUEST TO SEND
RECEIVE TIMING	26, 8	RECEIVE TIMING
CLEAR TO SEND	27, 9	CLEAR TO SEND
TERMINAL IN SERVICE	28, 10	LOCAL LOOPBACK
DATA MODE	29, 11	DATA MODE
TERMINAL READY	30, 12	TERMINAL READY
RECEIVER READY	31, 13	RECEIVER READY
SELECT STANDBY	32, 14	REMOTE LOOPBACK
SIGNAL QUALITY	33, 15	INCOMING CALL
NEW SIGNAL	34, 16	SELECT FREQUENCY
TERMINAL TIMING	35, 17	TERMINAL TIMING
STANDBY/INDICATOR	36, 18	TEST MODE
SEND COMMON	37, 19	SIGNAL GROUND

Figure 1-30 EIA/TIA-449 Interface

With differential inputs, common voltages subtract from one another. Since they are of equal amplitude, the result is 0 volts of common-mode voltage. The unbalanced mode does not contain common-mode rejection; consequently, it does not perform well at rejecting noise.

A complete EIA/TIA-449 interface contains a 9-pin connector, and a 37-pin connector. Both connectors are used when the interface is in the balanced mode. When in the unbalanced mode, only the 37-pin connector is used. The complete pinout is shown in Figure 1-30.

The EIA/TIA-449 standard is a description of the signaling elements of the interface—the name of signals, assignment of voltage levels, the function of signals, and so forth. The electrical characteristics of the unbalanced mode of operation of the physical interface are contained in **EIA/TIA-423**, while the electrical characteristics of the balanced mode are specified by **EIA/TIA-422**.

EIA/TIA-423 is the electrical equivalent of EIA/TIA-232. It does offer some improvements in cable lengths and data rates. Bit rates of up to 100 kBPS are permitted, and cable lengths of up to 4,000 feet are supported. The EIA/TIA-423 connector contains 37 pins. It is compatible with the 25-pin EIA/TIA-232.

To connect two devices, one with an EIA/TIA-232 interface and the other with an EIA/TIA-423 interface, a cable is used with the EIA/TIA-423 connector on one end and the EIA/TIA-232 connector on the other. The EIA/TIA-423 can support up to 10 receivers from one transmitter. Logic 1 is represented by –3.6 to –6 Vdc, and logic 0 by +3.6 to +6 Vdc.

The EIA/TIA-422 interface is the balanced mode of operation. It uses the 37-pin connector and, as an option, the 9-pin connector as a second channel. The interface can accept data rates up to 10 MBPS, and specifies maximum cable lengths of 4,000 feet. A logic 1 is represented by –2 to –6 Vdc, and a logic 0 by +2 to +6 Vdc.

EIA/TIA-485

The EIA/TIA-485 is a high-performance standard. It is the only interface designed for a multi-user environment.

It can support 32 transmitters and 32 receivers on a single cable. It is capable of transmitting small signal levels over the maximum 4,000-foot cable length. A logic 1 is represented by –1.5 to –6 Vdc, and a logic 0 by +1.5 to +6 Vdc. It handles data rates up to 10 MBPS, and shares the excellent noise rejection qualities of the EIA/TIA-422 since it also uses differential inputs. For a D-type 37-pin connector, the EIA/TIA-485 resembles the EIA/TIA-449 pinout of Figure 1-30, except that the drivers are wired for tri-state operation. In addition, the optional second channel is usually provided, wired to a D-type 9-pin connector. Its pinout is depicted in Figure 1-31.

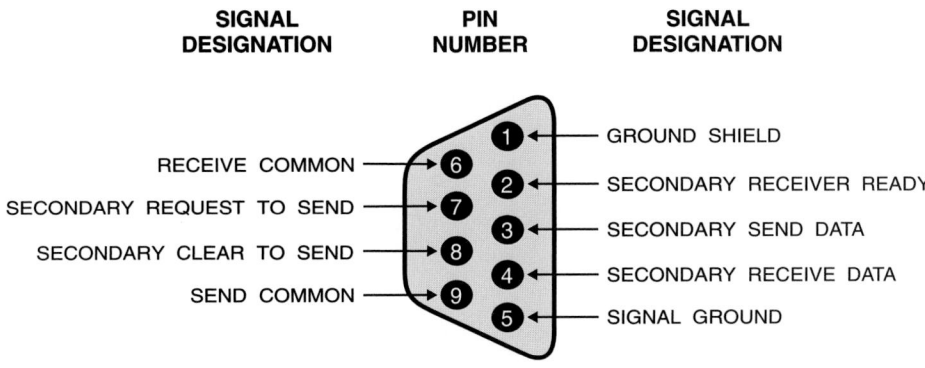

Figure 1-31 EIA/TIA-485 Interface

Table 1-1 lists the major characteristics of the EIA/TIA family of interfaces.

The EIA/TIA standards presented here are a sampling of commonly used interfaces, but there are many more. Certain local area networks specify special connections. For example, **Ethernet** is a widely used LAN that uses specific connectors.

Table 1-1 Operating Characteristics of Electrical Interfaces

INTERFACE	Sensitivity to Noise	Maximum Noise	Logic 1 Mark	Logic 0 Space	Maximum Data Rate	Maximum Receivers	Maximum Xmitters	Wiring
EIA/TIA-232	High	50 ft	−3V to −25V	+3V to +25V	20 KBPS	1	1	Unbalanced
EIA/TIA-423	High	4,000 ft	−3.6V to −6V	+3.6V to +6V	100 KBPS	10	1	Unbalanced
EIA/TIA-422	Low	4,000 ft	−3.6V to −6V	+3.6V to +6V	10 MBPS	10	1	(Balanced) Differential
EIA/TIA-485	Low	4,000 ft	−1.5V to −6V	+1.5V to +6V	10 MBPS	32	32	(Balanced) Differential

Another type of network is called **Packet Switching**. It specifies a particular interface as well, but because of the popularity of EIA/TIA-232, there are equivalent packet switching interfaces nearly indistinguishable from EIA/TIA-232. All of the interfaces discussed have described voltages to represent logic levels. An alternative method is to use current to represent data.

Current Loop

The use of current in data communication systems has resulted in an informal standard known as the current loop.

The **current loop** is based on a 20mA value, and the presence of the 20mA current flow represents a logic 1.

The absence of current represents a logic 0. A typical system using the current loop is shown in Figure 1-32.

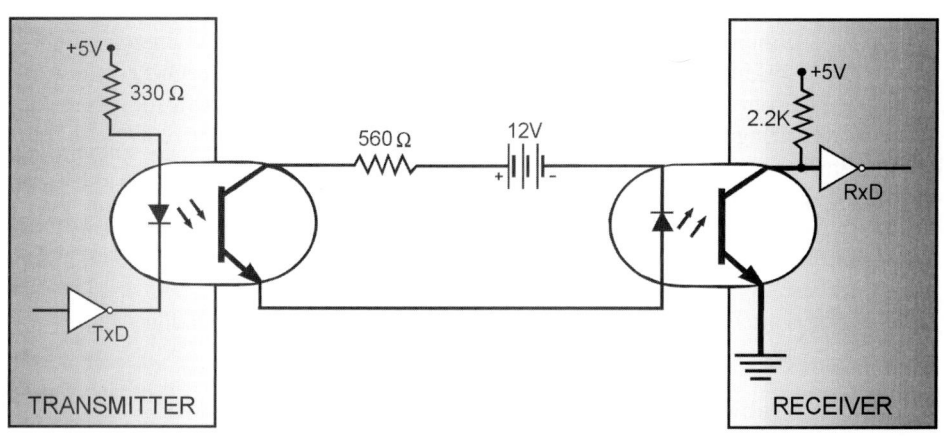

Figure 1-32
Communication System
Using Current Loop

The system illustrated in this figure is simple; there is data movement from a transmitter to receiver only. In order for the receiver to transmit, it would have to have a separate current loop with a current source.

Typically, current is generated in the loop through an **isolation transformer** or with a **photo-isolator**.

An LED may be focused on a photo transistor. When the LED turns on, the transistor is biased on, and collector current flows. The use of source and load isolation from the current loop gives it excellent noise rejection qualities. This is an asset particularly valuable in industrial environments, where the arcing of large motors can cause many noise problems. An induced voltage from a motor or generator would have to be quite large to generate 20mA of current in the loop.

There is no standard connector used with current loops.

Many times, EIA/TIA-232 connectors are installed, and a current source is located at some point between the transmitter and receiver. The location of the current source is not required to be at the transmitter. EIA/TIA-232 is usually a fairly good choice, since the standard specifies one transmitter and one receiver. This meets the current-loop requirement of one loop for each transmitter and receiver.

NET ENGINEERING AND DOCUMENTATION

Technology changes on a daily basis. This is a fact that's at once intimidating, and exciting, because it makes the job of those involved in network decisions extremely difficult, while at the same time, keeps the job interesting.

Technicians and Engineers who make those decisions are expected to do so systematically, and with the best interests of the company and users at the forefront of their thinking. They must do this because a bad decision could cost a company millions of dollars, or crash a critical component of the network. In other words, networks, whether new or existing, must operate under a strategic plan. There are many lines of thought on how to strategically plan a new network, but in this book, we'll reference those who do it for a living.

In 1997, the Computing Technology Industry Association (CompTIA) commissioned a survey of networking professionals to try and determine what they did each day when they went to work. From this information, CompTIA is developing a base certification (Net+) for employees entering the networking industry. While the survey, one of the first of its kind of network professionals, is extensive in the summarized results, we'll focus on duties that have been identified as particularly important. The survey delineates these duties into a series of tasks the employee routinely performs—or is expected to perform—in order to earn a paycheck.

The duty areas are listed in Table 1-2. We will begin with the documentation aspect.

Table 1-2 CompTIA Duty Area Survey Results

NETWORKING TASKS
Planning the Customer's Job
Designing the Network
Implementing the Installation of the Network
Managing the Support Efforts
Developing/Coordinating/Delivering the Training
Analyzing/Evaluating the Network Implementation
Developing Documentation (SOPs)
Setting Up Standard Operating Procedures (SOPs)
Operating the Network Management System
Maintaining the Network
Administering the Network
Administering the Change Control Systems
Implementing the Change Control Systems
Analyzing/Evaluating the Applicability of New Technology
Troubleshooting the Network

Developing Documentation

Why is it important to document a network? It may not be apparent until you try troubleshooting a network that hasn't been documented; it's a nightmare. The cables connecting computers and printers to hubs and servers may not be labeled, so you have no idea what's hooked to what. Software may been installed one time, and never upgraded for new releases; or it may have been upgraded with each new release. You don't know because no one bothered to keep a record of it.

NET+ OBJECTIVE
II.1.1

Equipment upgrades may be canceled because you have to know exactly what processors are running in the machines, but there is nothing written down reflecting the current state of the machine technology. Users are password-protected from one another, but you later discover that they all have access to the payroll files, and some are upset that the person in the next cubicle makes twice as much, and to their critical eye, does far less.

Do you get the idea? Someone needs to be properly managing the network, and an important part of the management is documenting any changes in the network, along with its current state (physical and logical). In this section, you'll look at methods and practices used to document the network, as well as how to write a **Standard Operating Procedure** (SOP).

Normally, industry documentation explains how to do something—add a new user to the network, complete a work order, backup data on the server, etc. There are a multitude of formats for creating documentation, and which format you select will depend on conventions currently used at your place of work, along with the audience that the procedure has been written for. In this book, the format follows a very effective presentation scheme that's widely used in industry.

Basically, the format is designed to convey knowledge, as opposed to data, to the reader. The material is presented so that the reader will actually use the document. A sample procedure is shown in Figure 1-33.

Before getting to the nuts and bolts of how to write a SOP, there a several characteristics, or information fields, that all procedures share. They are:

NET+ OBJECTIVE
II.1.1

- A unique title.

- Revision control.

- Approvals.

- Date.

- Revision (or change) history.

- Distribution list.

Large Corporation Quality System		
TITLE: Product Handling For ESD Protection		
REVISION: A		DATE: 10-1-98
APPROVALS: • Network Manager (Signature and date) • Quality Manager (Signature and date) • General Manager (Signature and date)		
REVISION HISTORY • 10-1-98 Initial release of procedure.		
DISTRIBUTION LIST • Network Engineering • Field Service • Technical Support • Quality Assurance		
Purpose of Procedure	The purpose of this standard operating proceure is to specify precautions personnel are to take when handling printed circuit boards to prevent electro-static damage (ESD).	
Effects of ESD	ESD may cause catastrophic failures of electronic devices (printed circuit boards and integrated circuit components) that may be immediately apparent, or become apparent weeks or months after the event.	
ESD Precautions	To prevent ESD damage, observe the following precautions: • Wear an anti-static wrist strap when handling printed circuit boards or electronic components. • Do so for all components, even if you suspect they aren't ESD sensitive. • Hold printed circuit boards by the edges. • When moving a printed circuit board, place it in an anti-static bag, or approved container. • In the presence of ESD flooring, wear an anti-static ankle strap on both shoes.	
Related Documents	• 3M Corp. Standard For ESD Protection • Anti-Static Strap Check • SOP For Wiring Work-Surfaces For ESD Protection	

Figure 1-33 Sample SOP

A unique title differentiates the procedure from any others. This is done so there's no confusion when referencing SOPs.

A Standard Operating Procedure is revision controlled.

This means that if it's changed, the revision, or version, of the documents will change as well. Why document revisions? Because procedures change. They aren't static, and must be updated when the network environment changes. In a large organization, the SOPs may be distributed to many locations, and those using the procedures need to know if the procedure they're using is accurate for the current environment. Revision controls helps them to know.

Typically, all SOPs are listed in a **Master Index** that includes the title and revision of the document.

The user needs only to reference the master list to determine if a procedure is current, or has been made obsolete by a change.

The approvals field documents who authorized the procedure, or approved a change to the procedure. Approvals give a SOP credibility. The individual(s) approving the document is/are not only authorizing its release, but is/are always indicating that the procedure is accurate for its intended purpose.

The date field lists the date that the procedure became effective. This date is important because it also indicates the date that previous versions of the document became obsolete. Note that the approval signature/date may not correspond to the release date of the document; but the release date should never occur before the date that a procedure is approved.

A revision history is a section of the SOP that details changes made to the procedure. An SOP may go through dozens of revisions, and without a history documenting the changes, it's possible (likely, actually) that the changes will become redundant.

Adequately controlled documents are assigned to the areas where they will be used. Not all documents will be assigned to the same areas. It's unlikely that a mechanic in the motor pool needs to know how to configure a server, and equally unlikely that an engineer needs to know how to use a caliper for measuring brake pad thickness.

Since the procedures may be distributed to multiple locations, it's imperative to maintain a **Master Distribution List** which shows where each document is located.

When a document is revised, it's a matter of referencing the distribution list to determine where the affected documents are located so that the old revisions can be destroyed, and the new ones distributed.

All so-called controlled documents share the characteristics that you see in the header of the sample procedure. The implementation may vary from company to company, but the structure as described above will be noticeable.

The content of a SOP is written for the individual using it.

That same individual should be held accountable for following the procedure (or for changing it by submitting a revision to those approving the document). As you can see from the sample, the first heading in the body of the document is labeled Purpose. This is followed by the Related Documents section, and then the actual procedure is detailed.

The Purpose heading should answer why the SOP has been written; or the objective that the reader should achieve by being familiar with the document.

The Related Documents is a list of SOPs that are cited in the procedure.

NET+ OBJECTIVE
II.1.1

The reason for listing them is that it's redundant to spell out the steps for conducting a task related to the subject at-hand, when those steps are already detailed in another procedure. Conventionally, the related tasks are cited in a procedure which the reader can then reference if necessary.

If you set up a documentation system, consider electronically linking all documents in the system so that it's relatively easy for the reader to bounce back and forth between SOPs. Both Microsoft Word and Corel Wordperfect support HTML links between documents on a computer, or distributed on file servers.

Optional headings used with SOPs include:

- Safety.

- Required Training.

- Associated Forms.

- Equipment Needed.

When writing SOPs, keep the following in mind:

- Be informal. Write to the level of the reader/ user. But also be specific. Avoid vague words like maybe, should, sometime, occasionally, etc.

- List "how-to" instructions as a series of steps, as shown in the sample procedure. But be brief whenever possible. Avoid long blocks of text. Whenever possible, replace text with graphics—photos, sketches, flowcharts, etc.

- Be consistent in format and heading information. A standard operating procedure is not the sort of writing that encourages imaginative accounts.

- Create a SOP for situations or tasks that, if done incorrectly, could have serious consequences for the organization or network. Before submitting these SOPs for approvals, have those who will be using them read and critique them. It's pointless to write a procedure that no one will use.

- Update procedures as needed. When a change occurs which affects the information in a procedure, change the document and have it approved and distributed before implementing the change. Again, it's pointless to create a documentation system if it won't be followed by all involved.

What are the consequences of not having a controlled documentation system? Chaos—certainly; pandemonium—probably; and for you, days that stretch on like an endless wasteland.

Create SOPs where they are needed. Don't create them if they aren't needed.

The following is a list of titles that are representative of the scope of network documentation systems:

- How to Configure Network Software.

- SOP for Disaster Recovery.

- Troubleshooting Flowcharts.

- Cable Labeling Conventions.

- How to Document System Changes.

- SOP for Internal and External Security.

- System Floorplan.

- How to Setup User Accounts.

NET+ OBJECTIVE
II.2.1

- Location and Pertinent Information About Service Contracts.

- How to Change User Accounts.

- Format for Controlled Documents.

- SOP for Problem Escalation Protocol.

- Distribution of Controlled Documents.

- How to Identify a Problem.

- Revision Control of Controlled Documents.

- SOP for Strategic Plan for Growth and Capacity.

- How to Backup Server Data.

- How to Setup Peripherals.

- How to Setup Servers.

- Establishing Testing Standards Benchmarks.

- How to Setup Clients.

KEY POINTS REVIEW

This chapter has presented an extensive exploration of the fundamentals of data communications.

- A large portion of data is transmitted through long distance telephone facilities.

- A communications system consists of three fundamental components: a sender, message and receiver.

- When data is exchanged between computers the sender is generally referred to as the transmitter and the computer accepting data is called the receiver.

- The phone system is a convenient pathway for carrying the exchange of data between computers.

- A database is generally contained in the memory of a large computer, and typically specializes in a specific subject.

- A company that maintains a database is called an information service.

- A LAN consists of computers linked together in a room, a building or in a metropolitan area, while a WAN consists of computers connected together over a large geographical area; that is, areas falling outside a specific metropolitan area.

- Protocols are the rules used with data communications.

- The intention of protocols is to bring a sense of standardization to data communications.

- There exists a basic blueprint that describes the function of protocols for data communications called the Open System Interconnection (OSI) Reference Model.

- Protocols used to connect networks, or to send data across large networks are defined at the Network and Transport Layers, with the most common being TCP/IP.

- A network consists of hardware and software designed to direct and control data traffic.

- The operational level of the network is dictated by the application.

- Topology refers to the architecture, or physical arrangement, of a network.

- The protocol used for a PC-to-Internet connection is called Point-to-Point Protocol, or PPP. In this case, the protocol specifies how data will flow back and forth on a simple topology.

- Hub-based topologies are very common in a local area network, and in situations where a hub is used to link networks.

- Generally speaking, the topology of a network is independent of the protocol running the network.

- A baseband network is now thought of as a network—using any topology—in which data is transmitted at rates up to 10 MHz.

- Broadband networks carry data at rates over 10 MHz, up to around 100 MHz.

- The medium refers to the physical path taken by data.

- Copper wire includes twisted wire pairs, and twisted pairs refer to telephone wiring.

- A fiber optic cable consists of a thin strand of glass or plastic cable surrounded by a jacket.

- Fiber optic cable has significantly lower losses than copper wire, and is immune from external electrical interference (lightening, motors, generators, microwaves) that creates much of the distortion found in copper-based systems.

- Satellites use microwaves for relaying data from transmitter to receiver.

- A trunk line is a major artery capable of carrying thousands of calls.

- A wireless network—either local or in a wide area—offer the greatest flexibility of all media types.

- In a star network, the stations take direction from the hub.

- Access is granted to a bus network through contention. In a contention-based network, the stations vie for access.

- In a ring network, a token is passed from station to station. This type of access method is called a token-based system.

- DTE refers to any device in which the primary purpose of the device is the manipulation or processing of data.

- DCE refers to any device directly involved in transmitting and receiving data.

- A modem is used to modulate a carrier with the data for transmission over a long distance.

- In modulating a carrier with data, the modem not only alters the data, it eliminates it entirely.

- Network servers are an integral part of networks, but a part that enhances, rather than stifles, productivity, efficiency, and harmony.

- The node ports connect via a Network Interface Controller (NIC) card.

- The NIC is an important consideration when building a LAN, because it contains addressing information that identifies a node on a network.

- The hardware configuration of the clients may span the gamut of personal computer microprocessors, RAM size and fixed-disk size. It doesn't matter to the server.

- Servers may contain several MPUs to handle requests quickly and transparently.

- CISC microprocessor designs are the most widely used, since all Intel processors use this type of architecture. RISC is quicker and more efficient because less hardware is utilized to execute commands.

- The system cache is a buffer, which stores data going to and from the microprocessor.

- The preferred interface is the Small Computer Systems Interface (SCSI—pronounced "scuzzy").

- An Ultra-SCSI interface allows for speeds up to 200 MBS.

- A single SCSI card in a PCI slot allows simultaneous operation of up to 60 devices (using Ultra-SCSI with 15 devices on each of the four, wide ports).

- Currently, IDE hard drives transfer data to and from the drive at a maximum of 33 MBS, for ATA3 compliant hard drives.

- A SCSI interface competes with the MPU for speed, so data movement outside the drive isn't a problem. Getting it off the disk is the bottleneck.

- An operating system controls and directs the operation of a computer system.

- Fault tolerance refers to the ability of a network to recover from problems.

- A UPS is a battery-operated power supply that kicks in if you loose power to the network.

- As a rule of thumb, add a UPS to each segment of a LAN. This keeps the server and the client PCs running.

- Backup the data on a server, automatically, once each day, at a minimum.

- A repeater is used to connect separate LANs, or to extend the physical size of a single LAN.

- A repeater doesn't have the capability to filter network traffic. But a bridge does.

- A router works independently of the LAN protocol.

- A gateway may be required when a network is using incompatible protocols such as IBM SNA, ISO OSI, or DEC DNA.

- A modem is required whenever data is transmitted over a distance greater than 50 feet.

- The majority of modems have been designed specifically to serve as an interface to the telephone company.

- A multiplexer is an electronic switch capable of selecting one of several input signals, and connecting it to a single output line.

- The speed of a switch, incidentally, is published according to how fast the switch can switch port assignments, and not by how fast data moves through it.

- The speed at which data is transmitted is quoted as the baud rate or bits per second (BPS). Baud rate describes the number of data symbols transmitted per second.

- A symbol is a small group of bits into which data is organized at the time of modulation.

- Baud is an indication of the amount of information transmitted, while BPS is the amount of total data transmitted.

- All modems are classified by their BPS rate.

- An analog signal has many discrete values representing a physical process (a voice, for example).

- The subscriber loop is the circuit from a residential or office telephone to the local central office, which is designated by the first three digits of a local telephone number.

- Bandwidth (BW) is a particularly important aspect of data because it is a measure of the amount of actual data being transmitted.

- Channel capacity, measured in bits per second, is directly proportional to bandwidth.

- The FM radio-frequency range is from 88 MHz to 108 MHz.

- Fundamentally, modulation is the process of superimposing data on a carrier.

- Amplitude modulation is produced by simultaneously applying a carrier and data to any non-linear device.

- Single-sideband (SSB) systems operate on the principle of suppressing one sideband and transmitting the other.

- The peculiar shape of the sidebands is called the modulation envelope.

- A major drawback to AM is its poor power efficiency.

- Another drawback to AM is the difficulty in removing any noise picked up on the way to the receiver.

- Frequency modulation (FM) is produced by varying the frequency of the carrier.

- The amount of frequency change, or deviation, is directly proportional to the amplitude of the data signal.

- A method of calculating the bandwidth known as Carson's rule recognizes all sidebands containing 96% of the total radiated power.

- A limiter clips the positive and negative alternations of the signal, thereby eliminating most of the noise.

- Phase modulation (PM) is a form of FM. Occasionally, it is referred to as indirect FM.

- A PM system shares the same noise-rejection qualities and power-efficiency advantages of FM.

- Terminal codes consist of binary numbers representing alphanumeric characters and special control functions.

- The Baudot code is an older code that was developed to permit teletypewriters to operate at high speeds. Originally, it was intended to be used by Morse-code operators.

- The codes presented in this section—terminal codes—are a category of a far larger group called information codes.

- Some information codes, such as Manchester and nonreturn-to-zero, are used to change the structure of an ASCII-coded word so that it can be transmitted with a minimum of errors. Other information codes, such as the Cyclic Redundancy Check (CRC), are used for error-detection. Still others are used to correct errors, such as Hamming codes.

- Framing refers to methods of transmitting data that identify the start and stop of a character, or of long strings of characters. The two common methods of framing are called asynchronous and synchronous.

- The steady-state condition is referred to as a mark, and is represented by a logic 1.

- When the line makes the transition from the binary 1 to binary 0, this is referred to as a space, and the receiver will decipher the transition as the start of a data stream.

- The receiver will know the data stream is completed by detecting a stop bit.

- The parity bit is used for error detection.

- Synchronous transmission is characterized by one character immediately following another without the inclusion of start/stop bits.

- The synch pulse tells the receiver the exact time a bit occurs.

- Synchronous transmission is common at higher data rates, when long blocks of information are transmitted.

- Simplex communication is one-way communication.

- A half-duplex system allows data to flow from the transmitter to the receiver, and from the receiver to the transmitter, but only in one direction at a time.

- Full-duplex systems permit data to flow in both directions simultaneously.

- Full duplex is high-speed communication. Half duplex is used when speed is not a priority, but costs are. Simplex is primarily used to supply a peripheral with information, or to collect information from a peripheral.

- Physical layer protocols are involved with the actual transfer of data through a communication system (at all other levels, physical data transfer does not occur).

- The EIA/TIA-232 interface is commonly used with PCs and peripherals.

- The EIA/TIA-449 is an interface that improves upon the noise, cable-length, and data-rate limitations of the EIA/TIA-232.

- The EIA/TIA-449 offers two modes of operation: balanced and unbalanced.

- Common-mode voltage is usually noise induced into the cables.

- The EIA/TIA-485 is a high-performance standard. It is the only interface designed for a multi-user environment.

- The EIA/TIA standards were devised by the Electronic Industry Association (EIA).

- The current loop is based on a 20mA value, and the presence of the 20mA current flow represents a logic 1.

- Typically, current is generated in the loop through an isolation transformer or with a photo-isolator.

- There is no standard connector used with current loops.

- A Standard Operating Procedure is revision controlled.

- Typically, all SOPs are listed in a Master Index that includes the title and revision of the document.

- Since the procedures may be distributed to multiple locations, it's imperative to maintain a Master Distribution List which shows where each document is located.

- The content of a SOP is written for the individual using it.

- The Purpose heading should answer why the SOP has been written; or the objective that the reader should achieve by being familiar with the document.

- The Related Documents is a list of SOPs that are cited in the procedure.

At this point, review the objectives listed at the beginning of the chapter to be certain that you understand and can perform them. Afterward, answer the review questions that follow to verify your knowledge of the information.

LAB MANUAL

Lab Exercises

The lab manual that accompanies this book contains hands-on lab procedures that reinforce and test your knowledge of the theory materials presented in this chapter. Now that you have completed your review of Chapter 1, refer to the lab manual and perform Procedure 1, "Creating Standard Operating Procedures."

REVIEW QUESTIONS

The following questions test your knowledge of the material presented in this chapter:

1. In terms of geography, describe the difference between a local and a wide area network.

2. Define DTE and DCE.

3. Calculate the bits per second rate for a bit time of .1mS.

4. Calculate baud for a modem transmitting at 14.4 KBPS in which the number of bits per symbol is 4.

5. Describe the relationship between bandwidth and the amount of information that a data communication channel can carry.

6. Write a brief definition of simplex, half-duplex and full-duplex.

7. What is the advantage to specifying a broad range for logic levels for an electrical interface?

8. Briefly describe the term "access method" as it relates to networking.

9. Describe the architecture of a client-server network.

10. What is meant by the "topology" of a network?

11. Describe the difference between server-based and peer-to-peer networking.

12. Why is it important to prepare SOPs for a network before it's installed?

13. Differentiate between, simplex, half-duplex and full-duplex transmission.

14. What are six characteristics common to all SOPs?

15. Why is it necessary to include revision controls with SOPs?

MULTIPLE CHOICE QUESTIONS

1. What is the main advantage of the SCSI interface?
    a. It's a fiber optic channel.
    b. It connects a single peripheral.
    c. It's a wireless interface.
    d. It connects multiple peripherals.

2. Which of the following is an example of a terminal code?
    a. ASCII
    b. SCSI
    c. FDDI
    d. IEEE

3. A communications system consists of sender, receiver and:
    a. Modem.
    b. Message.
    c. Transmitter.
    d. Protocol.

4. The type of network utilizing a central hub is called a:
    a. Ring.
    b. Star.
    c. Bus.
    d. Point-to-point.

5. A type of communications media that's immune to electrical interference is:
    a. Twisted Pairs.
    b. Coaxial.
    c. Fiber Optics.
    d. Microwaves.

6. Why is a modem necessary for sending data through the telephone network?
    a. The bandwidth of the telephone network is too wide.
    b. Only squarewaves can be sent through the telephone system.
    c. The telephone network bandwidth is too narrow for squarewaves.
    d. Only voice communication can go through the telephone network.

7. An asynchronous data frame is characterized by:
    a. A start bit and stop bits.
    b. A start bit and no stop bits.
    c. No start or stop bits.
    d. FM modulation.

8. Data bits in asynchronous network are synchronized by:
   a. Counting each bit.
   b. Measuring the bit times.
   c. Inverting the logic levels.
   d. Shifting the bit phase to represent 1's and 0's.

9. What is an interface?
   a. The physical connection between similar devices.
   b. The physical connection between dissimilar devices.
   c. The layers of the OSI model.
   d. The topology of a network.

10. The interface with the highest data rate is:
    a. Current Loop.
    b. EIA/TIA-232.
    c. EIA/TIA-449.
    d. EIA/TIA-422.

CD-ROM

Net+ Practice Test

Additional Net+ Certification testing is available on the CD that accompanies this text. The testing suite on the CD provides Study Card, Flash Card, and Run Practice type testing. The Study Card and Flash Card feature enables you to electronically link to the section of the book in which the question is covered. Choose questions from the test pool related to this chapter.

CHAPTER 2

DATA TRANSMISSION

**LEARNING
OBJECTIVES**

Upon completion of this chapter and its related lab procedures, you should be able to perform the following tasks:

1. Discuss the advantages and disadvantages of analog and digital waveforms when used in networking.

2. Define "media" as applied to networking.

3. State several factors that influence the choice of media.

4. Recognize and describe the advantages/disadvantages of coax, CAT3, CAT5, fiber optic, UTP and STP media and connectors, and the conditions under which their use is appropriate.

5. Explain how CAT5 UTP increases bandwidth capabilities of twisted-pair cable.

6. List differences between the various categories of UTP.

7. Given an application, select the best category of UTP.

8. Given an installation scenario, demonstrate an awareness that the compatibility of RJ-45 connector use depends on the cabling.

9. Identify the use of the (MAU) transceiver network component.

10. Discuss the differences between Thicknet and Thinnet coaxial cable.

11. Recognize and describe the visual appearance of RJ-45 and BNC media and connectors, and how they are crimped.

12. Provide a basic description of how light propagates through a fiber optic cable.

13. Describe the physical and optical characteristics of a fiber optic cable.

14. Describe the Data Link layer 802 specs, especially those covered in 802.3.

15. Provide a description of how to connect a connector to a fiber optic cable.

16. Describe the differences between the IEEE 803 fiber optic protocols for 10BASE-FP, 10BASE-FB, 10BASE-FL, and 100BASE-FX.

17. Define the following characteristics related to cable: distributed reactance, characteristic impedance, ISI, and equalization.

18. Explain the purpose of a terminator, and the problems encountered through improper use of a terminator.

19. Describe how equalization decreases ISI.

20. Draw a graphical illustrating the following types of encoding: NRZ, Manchester and AMI.

21. State the differences between bipolar and unipolar signaling.

22. Define atmospheric noise, impulse noise, frequency noise, and crosstalk.

23. Calculate signal-to-noise ratio of a communication channel.

24. Calculate noise factor of a communication channel.

25. Determine the value of a parity bit for a data word given even or odd parity.

26. Provide a description of analog-to-digital and digital-to-analog conversion.

27. Demonstrate awareness of the need to document the current status and configuration of the workstation (creating a baseline), prior to making changes.

28. Given a configuration scenario, select a course of action that would allow the return of a system to its original state.

Data Transmission

INTRODUCTION

Imagine planning a family vacation to a resort area located 2,000 miles away. On the date of departure you and the family are packed and ready to go, except...you don't have a map, money, car, or reservations of any sort. In short, you're totally unprepared for any problems that may arise; the first one being getting out of the driveway. It's a little far-fetched to imagine ourselves in that situation but it isn't too far off from what a data stream encounters upon leaving the transmitter. The data in a communication system faces many obstacles from the moment it's transmitted to the time it arrives at the destination.

Nearly all communication systems incorporate an error detection component. Error detection is based upon the data transmitted. Data frames may be as basic as the detection incorporated in a character sent from a PC to a printer, or the cyclic error detection used with a PC hard-disk unit that also provides for correcting errors. As you'll see throughout this book, data bits are exposed to a surprising amount of manipulation that renders them nearly indecipherable—until the manipulation is reversed and the original data restored. If the standard manipulations of data communication (coding, encoding, modulation, multiplexing, equalization, quantization) are combined with noise, distortion, and distributed reactances, then the fact that data moves in any organized manner at all is an accomplishment. In fact, data communications is a very reliable, fault-tolerant segment of the communications industry.

One of the reasons for high reliability is that many of the obstacles facing data transmission have been identified and techniques selected to address the problems. Often, the techniques chosen are implemented before the data is transmitted. For example, if a transmission channel is found to attenuate the higher-frequency components of a channel, those frequencies may be over-amplified before the data is transmitted. The amplified frequencies will be attenuated on the way to the receiver, but because they've been over-amplified, they will arrive at the receiver with the same amplitude as the lower frequencies. This is the basic concept of **line equalizers**.

In many cases the success rate of data arriving intact at the receiver is a function of media and environments. **Electromagnetic Interference** (EMI) is radio-frequency noise transmitted through the atmosphere. The source of EMI can be motors, generators, radio stations, lightening, or high-frequency electronic circuits. It causes problems when the EMI cuts through a metallic conductor and a voltage is induced into the wire. For example, the EMI caused by lightening has an average period of 1ms. If data is transmitted through a channel at 1MBPS, then the lightening will distort, or destroy, 1,000 bits of data, or about 125 bytes. In many cases, precautions can be taken to recover the data or to prevent the interference from distorting the information. Selecting the proper media for transmitting data goes a long way in preventing problems.

Fiber optics has been hailed as the transmission media totally immune from EMI interference—and it is. Fiber-optic cable can be run side-by-side with industrial grade motors and not be affected by radiated noise. However, fiber remains an expensive option when compared to alternative, copper-based media. The coaxial-cable-based systems of cable television companies will offer an intriguing communication system in the near future. More than half of U.S. households are cable subscribers. Coaxial cable has a bandwidth several times that of telephone twisted wires, which means the time is not so far off that the household subscriber or business office, may be able to rent space for transmitting data.

Where fiber-optic cable seemed destined to capture the majority of wiring closets, unshielded twisted pair (UTP) cabling that's been configured for networking is now the media of choice for network runs to the desktop. Although structurally identical to telephone wire pairs, UTP nearly eliminates much of the noise problems that gave fiber an advantage, while doing so at a lower cost.

The cost of a network can't be minimized. Somewhere, an accountant's teeth will gnash each time you spend money and the cabling infrastructure is a significant investment—about 30% or more of the total network cost. When tens of thousands of feet of cabling are installed in a medium-sized network, you can't afford to make too many cabling mistakes, and still expect to keep your job.

Increasingly, the look of data outside the local environment is becoming digital. The local and long distance telephone companies are converting analog systems to digital. Digital data has the advantage of being much more resistant to noise than analog data. It is also in the same format as the square waves found in computers and other types of data processing equipment. When information from computers is transmitted through an analog system, it must first be converted from digital to analog, and at the receiving end be converted back to digital. With a fully digital system, this conversion need never take place.

The types of problems encountered by data signals are analyzed in this chapter. In many cases, the problems are a natural symptom of the characteristics of the channel. Occasionally, system designers have utilized channel problems in such a way as to assist data transmission. For example, the principle of equalization, which is the process of overemphasizing the weak component of a signal, has been modified and used in data concentrators. With the use of concentrators the amount of data transmitted can be reduced 75% without any loss of the original information.

ANALOG AND DIGITAL WAVEFORMS

Digital data is preferred over analog data because noise and distortion is easier to remove, it's in the same format as computer data, and the sharp edges of square waves provide for more reliable bit recognition.

In its earliest form, electrical communication was digital. The telegraph of Samuel Morse operated by alternately opening and closing a switch. When the switch was closed, current flowed in the telegraph line. The **Morse code** characters were composed of dots and dashes which, in an open-and-close type circuit, described digital square waves. Oddly, it was the simplicity of telegraphy that ultimately resulted in its demise as a commercial method of communication. As communication systems became more sophisticated, the code associated with Morse code proved to be quite slow and cumbersome for the fast operations of machines.

The ASCII and EBCDIC codes described in Chapter 1 originated with Morse code as well as a variety of others. Most of the codes in use today are of a digital nature. These codes were originally in an analog format, usually in the form of speech. To get a clear understanding of why digital communications have had such a special place in data communications, it's necessary to analyze the structure of analog and digital signals.

Analog Signals

An analog signal is shown in Figure 2-1. It has a peak value of 1 V, a frequency of 1 kHz, and a **period** of 1 ms. As an ac waveform, it has positive and negative alternations, and it recurs in time in a predictable manner. It was stated that the period of the signal is 1 ms. This was found by taking the inverse of the frequency, or:

$$T = 1/F$$

measured at the 0–degree **crossover points**. But the conventional method of measuring the pulse width, or time of an alternation, is to measure from the 10% point at the leading edge of the signal and the 90% point at the trailing edge, as shown in Figure 2-1. The pulse width at these points is 0.4 ms. Because of the sine structure of the ac wave, it is extremely difficult to determine how much the voltage level is since the amplitude is different for each moment in time through the alternation. The same can be said of the period, pulse width, or time. If the point at which the pulse width is measured is taken in respect to voltage levels around the alternations, then the pulse width becomes as relative as the amplitude measurements. The extreme variety of change in an analog signal makes it a difficult waveform with which to establish a predictable pattern suitable for digital equipment.

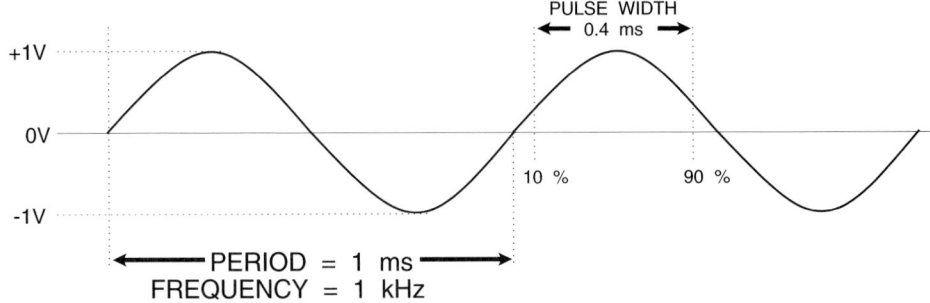

Figure 2-1 Analog Signals of Constant Variation

As a practical example of the problem of analog signals in data communications, consider an ac sine wave with a frequency of 1 kHz and a peak amplitude of 6 volts. If this signal were transmitted through an EIA/TIA-232 interface, it could create a considerable amount of confusion. The interface may not recognize amplitude levels of less than 3 volts, so the amplitude may be cut in half. Now, if a synchronizing pulse had been sent with the signal, it may be lost. The portion of the alternations not cut off will be transmitted as bits. Due to the sine of the alternations, the time between bits will not be equal to the time of a bit and the receiver may fail to correctly identify the proper bit times.

Ac waveforms of any type—analog or digital—are susceptible to **noise distortion** en route to the receiver. But analog data distorted by noise presents a particularly difficult problem because the noise is difficult to remove without causing further distortion of the signal.

In fact, in some types of channels, the noise may be of proper frequency that it actually passes through the line easier than the signal. The receiver may reject the signal and accept only noise–in which case, the receiver will futilely process noise. The constant change of analog signals and the problem with removing noise from these signals are their most serious drawbacks.

An analog signal is not without redeeming qualities. A 1kHz sine wave has a **bandwidth** of 1 kHz. As will be shown shortly, a 1kHz square wave used in digital systems has an 11kHz bandwidth. An analog system would be the best choice to use in channels with a scarce amount of bandwidth. A channel with a 10kHz bandwidth can accommodate ten analog signals but can barely contain one digital signal.

Digital Signals

Square waves are used in digital communications because they're representative of the base two, binary number system. **Binary numbers** consist of 1 and 0, and a square wave is either on or off, high or low. It's the equivalency to binary that makes square waves the reasonable choice of data communications. A square wave is relatively easy to generate as well as to code to represent alphanumeric systems. Of course, analog signals can be coded, too; but keep in mind that the first communication systems—telegraph and, later, the Teletype—were digital systems. Much of the development in data processing can be traced back to an effort to improve the transmission and reception of telegraph signals. Since the data being transmitted was digital, it follows that the machines developed to automate telegraphy would be digital systems.

Figure 2-2 illustrates a square wave of 1-volt peak amplitude, a frequency of 1 kHz, and a period of 1 ms. In terms of basic specifications it's no different than the sine wave discussed earlier. But those are about the only similarities shared by the two waveforms. The pulse width of a square wave—the time of a single bit—is measured in a manner similar to that of a sine wave except it doesn't matter if the measurement is taken on the leading or trailing edge. (Assuming, of course, that both edges are identical.) If the pulse width is measured between 10% and 90%, or 40% and 60%, the pulse width is the same. The vertical slope of leading and trailing edges provides transmitting and receiving equipment with a very predictable waveform. Compare pulse-width measurements of square waves to sine waves whose pulse widths are open to interpretation, dependent on where the measurement is taken.

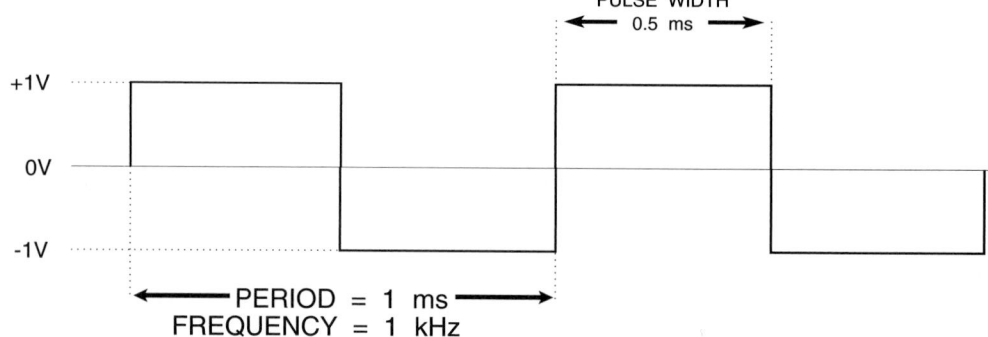

Figure 2-2 Predictable Square Waves

Having said that, consider data bits switched through wide area networking machines—routers, for example—that are clocked at GHz rates. At high data rates, bit edges are all that matters. The bits have been manipulated by coding and modulation beyond recognition so that the 10/90% measuring points are critical.

Undesired noise may be superimposed on a square wave as shown in Figure 2-3. The square wave has been heavily distorted. The regenerator, or repeater, is an in-line amplifier that boosts the signal level and restores the square wave to its original shape. Many network hubs on the market today incorporate repeaters as a matter of course. The regenerator can contain an **astable multivibrator** (Schmitt Trigger) designed with threshold voltages equal to the original amplitude of the signal. At the output of the regenerator, the square wave is clean of noise and distortion. If the distance from transmitter to receiver is long, there may be many **repeaters** along the way. Since the repeaters regenerate a new signal at each point, the overall performance of the system and the quality of the data is much higher than for analog systems.

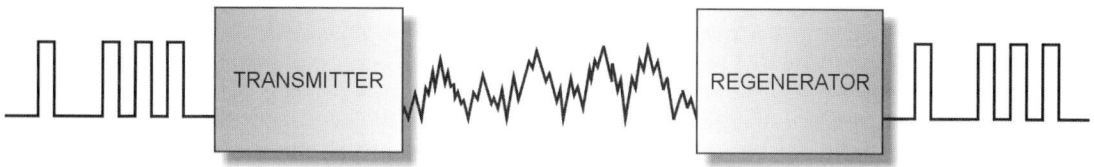

Figure 2-3 Digital Data is Less Sensitive to Noise than Analog Signals

Can repeaters be used with analog systems? They can, and frequently are. But the disadvantage to regenerating an analog signal is that the corrupting noise is amplified along with the signal. At best, analog repeaters serve to compensate for losses resulting from long cable lengths, but do very little to eliminate or decrease noise.

You may be tempted to wonder why the analog repeater can't simply restore the signal to its original shape, since this is essentially what a digital repeater does. To answer this, think about the definitions of analog and digital. A digital signal is composed of only two states, whereas an analog signal contains an infinite number of states. No matter how complex a digital waveform becomes, only one of two state changes (even if occurring multiple times within a bit) will ever be used to represent some part of the data. In the analog signal—take your pick as to how many of the infinite possibilities are actually incorporated. The only way to be sure is to know what was originally transmitted, and if at each repeater station you knew that , repeaters wouldn't be needed since the destination node would also know.

> Digital square waves have the disadvantage of requiring at least five times as much bandwidth as analog.

The disadvantage of a digital signal is the wide bandwidth required to transmit it. Figure 2-4 depicts the components that are combined to create a 1kHz square wave. Square waves are composed of an infinite number of odd harmonics of a fundamental frequency. In Figure 2-4, the fundamental frequency is 1 kHz, so the odd harmonics 3 kHz, 5 kHz, 7 kHz, and so forth, are summed together to create the square wave.

In practice, harmonics beyond the fifth order (11 kHz, in this example) have a negligible effect on the structure of the square wave and can be ignored. Each alternation of the square wave is composed of two vertical sides (the leading and trailing edges) and the horizontal peak. The sides are representative of a rapid change which is descriptive of the higher-order harmonics: the higher frequencies are primarily responsible for the vertical slope of the leading and trailing edges.

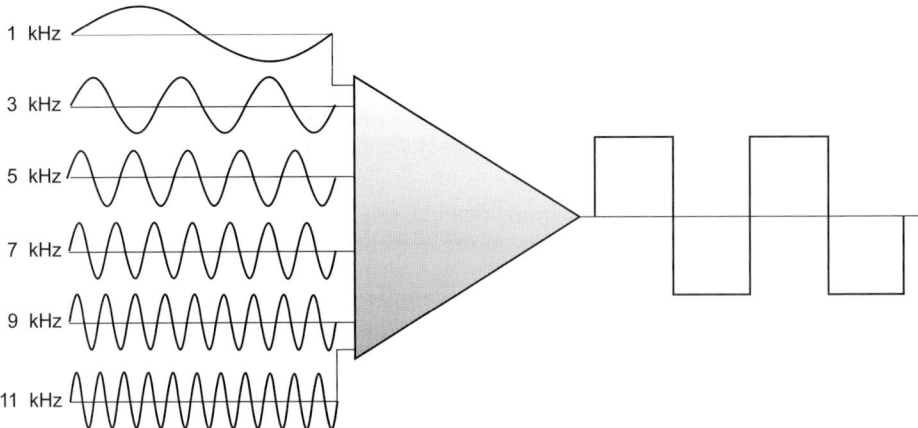

Figure 2-4 Square Wave Produced from a Fundamental Sine Wave and its Odd Harmonics

The flat top of the square wave is representative of the lower-order harmonics: the lower frequencies are responsible for the horizontal peak of a square wave.

In order to transmit the square wave through a channel, it must have a bandwidth at least equal to the fifth harmonic of the frequency of the square wave. If the bandwidth isn't wide enough, one or more of the higher-order harmonics will be attenuated and the square wave distorted. Harmonic distortion is illustrated in Figure 2-5.

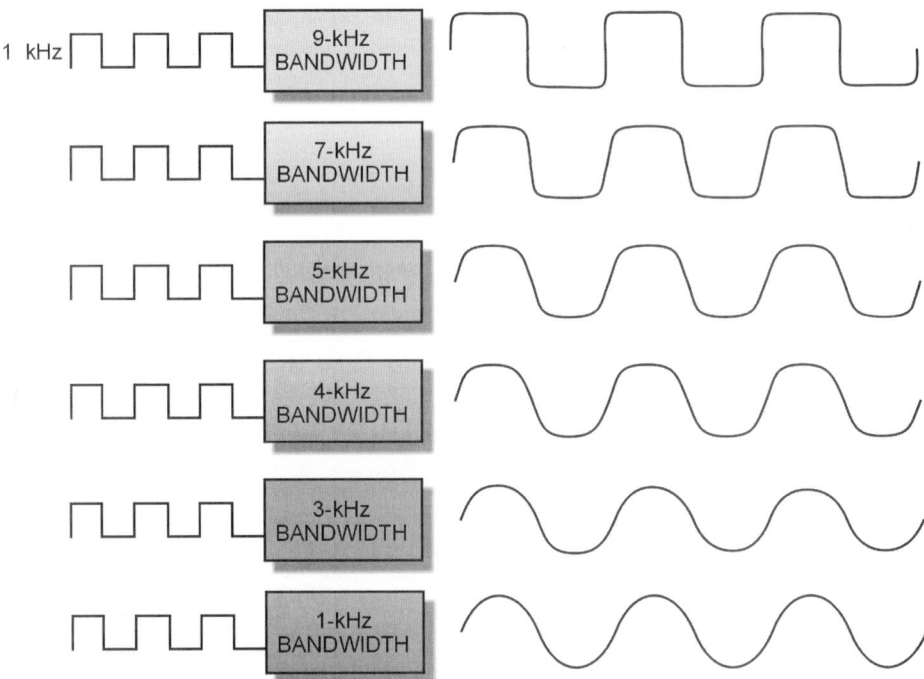

Figure 2-5 Inadequate Bandwidth Causes Harmonic Distortion

When the 1kHz square wave is passed through a circuit (**communication channel**) with a 9kHz bandwidth, the corners of the square wave are rounded slightly, but the square wave remains flat on top. The loss of the 11kHz fifth harmonic has caused the rounding of the corners, as well as increased the rise and fall time of the square wave. If the same 1kHz square wave is transmitted through a channel with a 7kHz bandwidth, the rounding of the corners is more severe and the rise and fall times increase. The square wave takes on the characteristics of the first-order harmonic when it's applied to a channel with a 1kHz bandwidth. At this point, what was once a digital signal with sharply defined edges is now an analog signal whose characteristic amplitude and pulse width are open to the interpretation of the receiver.

The wide bandwidth requirements of digital signals are a disadvantage to digital communications. However, the disadvantage can easily be turned into an opportunity to improve the performance of a data system. It was mentioned earlier that channel capacity (the volume of data) is proportional to bandwidth. This means that the greater the bandwidth, the greater is the volume of data that can be transmitted. Various multiplexing schemes have been devised to utilize as much of the available bandwidth as possible to transmit many channels of data through a single, wide-bandwidth, channel.

Increasingly, the terms, "data communication" and "digital communication", are used interchangeably. The digital structure of **machine language**, the superior quality and performance of digital systems, and simpler digital multiplexing methods have combined to make digital methods the choice data structure for networks. The telephone system still retains a small segment of analog networks, but these are being gradually replaced with digital networks.

TRANSMISSION MEDIA

Transmission media is the physical path data travels en route to its destination. There are four basic mediums: **twisted-pair wire**, **coaxial cable**, **fiber-optic cable**, and radio frequencies (**microwaves**). In the case for each medium, there are characteristics that make one type a better choice than another. It would be an oversimplification to say that one is better than another, because there are several factors to consider when selecting a transmission media.

> Transmission media refers to the channel data travels enroute to the receiving station and includes coaxial cable, twisted wire pairs, fiber optics and microwave.

CNST OBJECTIVE
VII-A

The **cost** of media is certainly a primary concern. Too often, the temptation to use the exotic or superior performer is given into, when a cheaper, although less glamorous, medium would have done an acceptable job. An example is to lease satellite time to send data across the country, when the long-distance carriers could probably transmit everything at a significantly lower cost.

Compatibility with existing media and machines demands a thoughtful analysis. If an extension to an existing network is under consideration, and the network is wired with coaxial cable, then it probably wouldn't be a good idea to wire the extension with twisted pairs. Existing media, also called the cabling infrastructure, accounts for about 30% of the cost of a network. Considerable thought must be given the initial infrastructure because future changes that include a different cable type will be expensive.

Signal losses, or **attenuation**, due to a wrong media selection require an expensive fix: the entire medium has to be replaced, or an extensive amount of repeaters, filters and shielding must be installed. The effects of noise that a signal may be exposed to can be minimized with the correct media choice.

Attenuation results in a gradual loss of signal strength from one end of a cable to another. The loss is measured in decibels (dB). There are two ways of looking at signal loss in a cable. The first is based on characteristics of the cable and is stated as dB/m, dB/km, or dB/ft. These specs are readily available from cable manufacturers, but they should correspond to certain accepted standards in the networking business.

The other way of viewing attenuation is to measure the loss of signal integrity across a cable run. For example, the losses from a node placed 100 feet from a hub will be greater than one placed 10 feet from the hub. When measured within a network, the losses are specific to the protocol and media type. A 10BaseT Ethernet LAN, for example, is not to have losses exceeding 11.5 dB. This means that whatever the power level is at the transmitting node, it's not to lose any more that 11.5 dB of it's signal strength once a signal arrives at the receiver.

The **impedance** of a cable directly affects losses. The higher the impedance, the higher the losses. Since impedance is influenced by resistive as well as reactive characteristics of the cable, it will vary for each cable type. The frequency (in BPS) will also effect losses.

The **bandwidth characteristics** of the medium are an important factor in making a selection because bandwidth in data communications is synonymous with channel capacity and data rates. Twisted pairs are the least expensive cable medium but, depending on their implementation (CAT 3 versus CAT 5 UTP, for example) may also have restricted bandwidth; fiber optics have the widest bandwidth but it's also the most expensive cable medium.

Cabling also affects the time that a signal arrives at the receiving node. This characteristic is called **propagation delay**, and is stated in microseconds. The delay, in either copper-based or optical cables, is appreciable and will ultimately limit the physical size of the network. The implication is that larger networks require cabling with shorter delays, or must come with in-line equipment that has signal regeneration capabilities.

Noise immunity of a cable may be important depending on the environment surrounding the infrastructure. An industrial environment is likely to generate considerably more electrical interference than an office environment. On the other hand, a building that's extensively wired for networking may have a problem with crosstalk. **Crosstalk** is the coupling of electrical energy between wires lying in a parallel plane.

The topology of a network may effect your decision on the type of media. Bus networks, for example, require that the ends of the bus be terminated with a proper resistance so that data signals aren't reflected back through the wire and create distortion of data signals.

Other factors to consider when evaluating the cable plant are ambient temperature, the type of data to be exchanged on the network (voice, data, video, etc.), future growth, and mobility of the users. It costs about three times as much to move a network connection as it does to relocate a telephone connection. The reason is that telephone connections are typically installed already, whereas network connections are typically installed when they're needed.

Twisted pairs, coaxial cable, fiber optics, and radio-frequency transmission media are analyzed in the following sections. The final criteria for selecting the medium is ultimately determined by the level of performance required of the communications system.

NET+ OBJECTIVE
I.1.6

CNST OBJECTIVE
VII-A

Twisted Pairs

Twisted-pair cables consist of copper wire twisted into a spiral shape as show in Figure 2-6. They're normally associated with telecommunications because it's the most common type of subscriber loop wiring. Twisted pairs have been used extensively in networking since they're a major component of the installed telephone network. Using the existing twisted-pair cables for data communications represents a significant cost savings, although, as you'll see shortly, this isn't a good idea.

Twisted pairs may be 22, 24 or 26 **American Wire Gauge** (AWG). The copper wire (solid or stranded) is insulated by a polyethylene or polyvinyl chloride jacket. The wires are twisted together to reduce noise and, in particular, **crosstalk**. Recall that crosstalk is the magnetic induction of a signal from wires lying in a parallel plane. The twisting of the wires causes a great deal of the unwanted crosstalk signals to cancel.

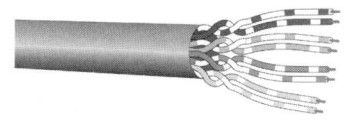

Figure 2-6 Twisted-Pair Wire

Twisted pairs, referred to in this book as unshielded twisted pairs (UTP), represent the largest installed base of cable media used in networks. Not only is there a lot of it out there, it's also capable of handling data rates from GBPS, all the way down to voice band frequencies.

> Twisted pair is the most widely installed media. Its size ranges from 16 to 24 AWG, and may be found in cables encasing from 1 to 6,000 pairs in a single sheath. Unshielded twisted pair (UTP) is the preferred cabling for LANs. UTP is classified by the EIA/TIA according to categories. Whenever possible, use CAT 5 UTP.

Twisted-pair wires outside of a residence are of a larger gauge. They may be stretched above ground between telephone poles or buried beneath the ground. Buried cable is cable that's buried in the earth without underground conduit. You may also see twisted-pair wires referred to as underground cable. This cable runs through ducts installed underground. The cables running outside, whether above ground or underground, are 16 to 19 AWG. They're designed to carry thousands of telephone channels and, in order to handle such a large volume, the twisted pairs are grouped in as many as 6,000 pairs encased in a plastic sheath.

As mentioned earlier, twisted pairs are the widest used transmission medium due to the sheer numbers installed in homes and businesses. But of all the media, twisted-pair wire is the easiest to work with as well. In order to make a connection or splice, it's necessary to just strip the insulation, connect the wire and solder.

When speaking of twisted pair wiring, it's important to distinguish between voice- and network-grade cabling. Structurally, the two are identical, and voice can be transmitted equally well over either type. The difference is the mechanical connection to DTEs and DCEs on each end of the cable. If you have a PC at home connected to the Internet, you're using voice-grade twisted pairs (actually, the wire pair may or may not be twisted).

If you have several PCs connected together in a network, you're using (or should be) network-grade twisted pairs. We'll take a look at both types of cabling.

There are several disadvantages to consider with voice-grade twisted pairs. The data rates that can be transmitted through the medium are around 1 MBPS for unconditioned cable installed in a residence or business. With **conditioning** and special care, the data rate can be increased to about 10 MBPS for voice-grade cabling, and in excess of 100 MBPS for data cabling.

> Conditioning refers to the deliberate loading of twisted pairs with inductance. The most common loading is 19H–88 loaded pair. This means 19 AWG cable is loaded with 88 mH (milliHenrys) of inductance every 6,000 feet.

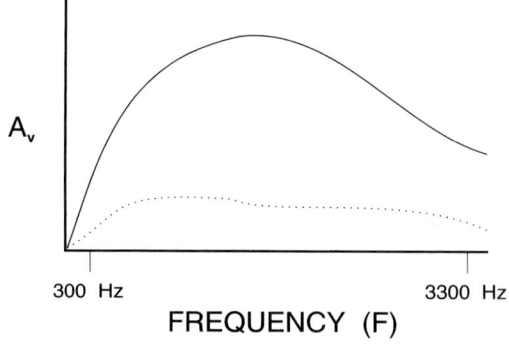

Figure 2-7 Effects Of 19H-88 Loading

The effects of 19H-88 loading are shown in Figure 2-7.

The solid line on the graph illustrates the **frequency response** of an unloaded line. Recall that the range of frequencies in a telephone voice channel are from 300 Hz to 3,300 Hz.

The unloaded line shows a sharp increase in signal attenuation over the channel. The dotted line indicates the response of the same channel that's been 19H-88 loaded. The insertion of the induction increases the attenuation over the frequency range of the voice channel, but it also results in a flat response. The graph in Figure 2-7 illustrates one of several of the methods of line conditioning. Other types will be discussed in the chapter on the telephone system.

Another consideration of voice-grade twisted pairs is the rather narrow bandwidth (about 100 kHz). The narrow bandwidth is a serious disadvantage since it ultimately restricts the volume of data that can be transmitted. There are a couple of reasons that voice-grade UTP is bandwidth restricted. The maximum distance from telephone to switching centers is often violated, usually by the telephone subscriber. Connections made within a house or business are often of poor quality resulting in signal losses. But the most important reason is that only two wires are used in a voice-grade connection. Some of the induced noise and crosstalk is eliminated by twisting the wires, which has the effect of canceling much of the noise, but it doesn't eliminate all or enough of it. The single most important reason, though, is that voice-grade UTP was designed for voice communication. As you'll see shortly, network-grade UTP, even though it's structurally identical to voice UTP, extends data rates by taking a preventive approach to eliminating problems.

Figure 2-8 shows a UTP cable used for networking. This is the type of cable used in a typical Ethernet LAN. It's also 22, 24 or 26 AWG unshielded copper (solid or stranded) wire. A connection between two nodes on a network will have four wires (two cable pairs) between them. Normally, four pairs are sheathed within a polyvinyl chloride jacket.

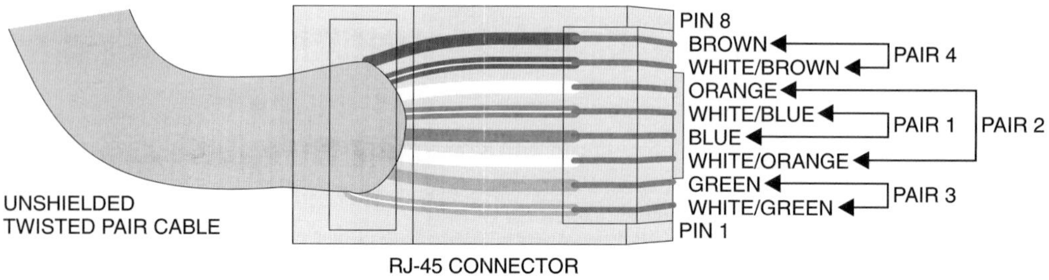

Figure 2-8 UTP Networking Cable

The wires are segregated into pairs which are then twisted and labeled as transmit and receive pairs. In each pair, one wire carries the transmission, while the other wire carries an inverted copy of the transmission. Hence, when a node sends data, the actual transmission is carried on Tx+ while an inverted copy of the transmission is carried on Tx–. In other words, all transmission on an Ethernet LAN includes an opposite mirror of the original transmission.

When a node transmits, both signals propagate on the cable at the same rate and are influenced by the same factors. This is because the wires are constructed identically and are twisted about one another. If external noise induces a noise signal into the wires, it will be induced into both in an identical manner.

Figure 2-9 shows the sequence of events as a signal is transmitted from a node. As you can see, the signal is first inverted and both signals are sent at the same time. En route to the receiver, a noise spike causes distortion of the data bits. Notice that the noise affects both Tx+ and Tx– in the same manner. When the signals arrive at the receiving node, the Tx-signal is inverted back to its original polarity and summed with the Tx+ signal. The induced noise on Tx– is inverted as well, then summed along with the Tx+ noise. The noise spikes are summed as reverse polarity signals that are identical in all aspects except for polarity. The summing action eliminates the noise spikes.

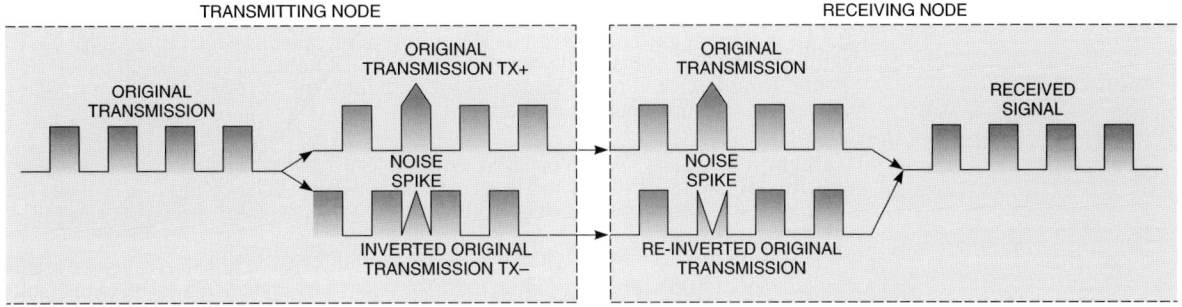

Figure 2-9 Summing Reverse Polarity Noise Spikes

Since UTP uses separate receive and transmit wire pairs, it's important not to connect the Tx+ of one station to the Tx+ of another station. If this happens, both stations will eventually try to transmit to one another on the same wire at the same time. Ethernet is designed so that, ultimately, the link between the two stations will crash. The IEEE 802.3 protocol, as part of the Data Link layer concept, is designed for straight-through wiring from network device (a hub) to network stations (a personal computer). Straight-through wiring means that you attach RJ-45 connectors to the ends of the UTP cable, and then plug the connectors into the station ports. No special precautions are needed on your part. The wire pair switch is built into the hub. A hub that's compliant with the standard will reverse the Tx wires at one end of the cable so that they connect to the Rx wires at the other end. Compliant hubs are marked with an X at each port.

If similar network devices are connected—two hubs, for example—a cross-over cable must be connected between them. The **crossover** is a connector that performs the switch between Tx and Rx. Note that a link requiring a crossover must have an odd number of cross-over cables, or the transmit and receive wire pair switch won't occur.

By using two wires for both the transmit and receive signals, network-grade UTP is able to virtually eliminate noise, including crosstalk.

NET+ OBJECTIVE
I.3.1

UTP Standards

UTP is differentiated according to specifications published by the Electronic Industry Association (EIA) and Telecommunications Industry Association (TIA). The standard used most often is EIA/TIA-568. The standard details the types of connectors used with UTP, how far the cable must be located from electrical sources, how to install the cable to prevent damage to personnel or equipment, and other aspects that may effect the system's quality.

An often repeated UTP specification is EIA/TIA Categories for UTP. These categories define the minimum quality level requirements for various applications of the cable. The cable is then specified by the category. The categories are as follows:

- **Category 1:** 22 or 24 AWG untwisted wire. This is common telephone cable and is the cable used to connect many telephones to phone drops as well as connect extensions within a building.

- **Category 2:** 22 or 24 solid wire, twisted pairs. CAT2 cable was the first networking UTP but is now considered obsolete. It supports data rates up to 1MBPS and is not tested for crosstalk distortion.

- **Category 3:** 24 solid wire, twisted pairs. Originally used in IBM Token Ring LANs, CAT3 is seldom used outside an IBM environment, and has been replaced by CAT5 cabling. CAT3 is occasionally used in 10MBPS Ethernet LANs as well as 4MBPS Token Ring LANs. It has been tested for data rates up to 16MPBS. The wire has a characteristic impedance of 100 ohms.

- **Category 4:** 22 or 24 AWG solid wire, twisted pairs. This category has been specified for up to 20MPBS and is specific to 16MBPS Token Ring LANs. The wire has a characteristic impedance of 100 ohms.

- **Category 5:** 22 or 24 AWG solid wire, twisted pairs. CAT5 cable has a characteristic impedance of 100 ohms and is specified for data rates up to 100 MBPS. This is the preferred cabling installation for Ethernet and Token Ring, and is recommended for all new installations, even if an existing LAN is running at 10 MBPS (Standard Ethernet speeds). If you choose to upgrade to the 100MPBS Fast-Ethernet, the cabling will already be installed and ready to go.

When you buy UTP, you need to know, in addition to the category, whether the cable is PVC or plenum rated, and whether the cabling scheme is compliant to EIA/TIA-568 A or B. "Plenum" rated UTP has a higher heat resistance rating so that it can be run in HVAC (Heating/Ventilation/Air Conditioning) plenum. PVC UTP without the plenum rating should be used when the cabling will be routed through walls, sub-flooring, or overhead—but not through heat plenum.

NET+ OBJECTIVE I.1.6

EIA/TIA-568A/B compliant refers to which of the four pairs in the UTP cable are designated as transmit, and which are designated as receive. Use the following as a guide:

- **EIA/TIA-568A:** 10BaseT (10MBPS) and 100BaseTX (100MBPS) devices transmit over pair 3, and receive over pair 2.

- **EIA/TIA-568B:** 10BaseT and 100BaseTX devices are configured to transmit over pair 2, and to receive over pair 3.

It's important to terminate all cables at a location according to the same standard, either A or B, but not both at the same facility. If you don't, you'll have a situation in which one device is trying to transmit along a wire connected to a transmit side of the receiving device; invariably, the two will try to transmit at the same time and the data will collide, eventually crashing the network.

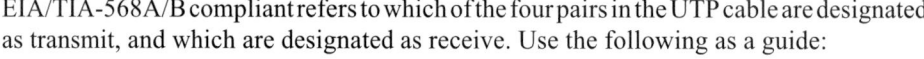

UTP 4-Pair and 25-Pair Cabling Schemes

Wire Color	EIA/ TIA Pair	Ethernet Signal Use	
		568A	**568B**
White/ Blue (W-BL)	Pair 1	Not Used	
Blue (BL)			
White/ Orange (W-OR)	Pair 2	RX+	TX+
Orange (OR)		RX-	TX-
White/ Green (W-GR)	Pair 3	TX+	RX+
Green (GR)		TX-	RX-
White/ Brown (W-BR)	Pair 4	Not Used	
Brown (BR)			

UTP in the LAN environment is installed using 4-pair, or 25-pair cable. The larger bundle is used to connect together wiring closes or hubs that service different parts of a network. The smaller four-pair cable is dedicated to network devices such as the connection between a hub and a personal computer. The jackets of either cable will vary in color, and may be orange, green, white or blue. Figure 2-10 illustrates a 4-pair color coding scheme.

Figure 2-10 Four Wire-Pair Color Codes

Four of the eight wires will be solid colors of brown, blue, orange and green. The other four wires will consist of a solid white base color and an accent color consisting of rings of the other four colors. When referring to the wires in a jacket, use the following convention:

- **Solid Color Wires:** Blue (bl), Brown (br), Green (gr), Orange (or).

- **White Base Color with Accent:** White/Color. For example, a white base with blue accent is written as white/blue (w/bl).

As mentioned above, 25-pair cabling is used where many connections are run between two points. Wiring closets in two different locations will be connected with 25-pair cable. The fifty wires in each cable are identical to their four-pair counterpart in all aspects other than the color coding of the insulation. In Figure 2-11, each wire is identified by two colors, and the convention for referring to the color is base color/accent color.

PORT NUMBER	+-Rx/Tx	COLOR CODE	RJ21 PIN NUMBER	PUNCHDOWN IN NUMBER	PUNCHDOWN OUT NUMBER
1	RX+	White/Blue	26	A1	B1
	RX-	Blue/White	1	A2	B2
	TX+	White/Orange	27	A3	B3
	TX-	Orange/White	2	A4	B4
2	RX+	White/Green	28	A5	B5
	RX-	Green/White	3	A6	B6
	TX+	White/Brown	29	A7	B7
	TX-	Brown/White	4	A8	B8
3	RX+	White/Gray	30	A9	B9
	RX-	Gray/White	5	A10	B10
	TX+	Red/Blue	31	A11	B11
	TX-	Blue/Red	6	A12	B12
4	RX+	Red/Orange	32	A13	B13
	RX-	Orange/Red	7	A14	B14
	TX+	Red/Green	33	A15	B15
	TX-	Green/Red	8	A16	B16
5	RX+	Red/Brown	34	A17	B17
	RX-	Brown/Red	9	A18	B18
	TX+	Red/Gray	35	A19	B19
	TX-	Gray/Red	10	A20	B20
6	RX+	Black/Blue	36	A21	B21
	RX-	Blue/Black	11	A22	B22
	TX+	Black/Orange	37	A23	B23
	TX-	Orange/Black	12	A24	B24
7	RX+	Black/Green	38	A25	B25
	RX-	Green/Black	13	A26	B26
	TX+	Black/Brown	39	A27	B27
	TX-	Brown/Black	14	A28	B28
8	RX+	Black/Gray	40	A29	B29

Figure 2-11 Color Codes for 25 Wire Pairs

	RX-	Gray/Black	15	A30	B30
	TX+	Yellow/Blue	41	A31	B31
	TX-	Blue/Yellow	16	A32	B32
9	RX+	Yellow/Orange	42	A33	B33
	RX-	Orange/Yellow	17	A34	B34
	TX+	Yellow/Green	43	A35	B35
	TX-	Green/Yellow	18	A36	B36
10	RX+	Yellow/Brown	44	A37	B37
	RX-	Brown/Yellow	19	A38	B38
	TX+	Yellow/Gray	45	A39	B39
	TX-	Gray/Yellow	20	A40	B40
11	RX+	Violet/Blue	46	A41	B41
	RX-	Blue/Violet	21	A42	B42
	TX+	Violet/Orange	47	A43	B43
	RX-	Orange/Violet	22	A44	B44
12	RX+	Violet/Green	48	A45	B45
	RX-	Green/Violet	23	A46	B46
	TX+	Violet/Brown	49	A47	B47
	TX-	Brown/Violet	24	A48	B48
UNUSED	N/A	-	25 50	N/A N/A	N/A N/A

Figure 2-11 Color Codes for 25 Wire Pairs (continued)

For example, a wire with a green base color that has white rings imprinted on it is written as white/green (w/gr).

With a 25-pair cable, 12 devices can be connected (one of the wire pairs is not used). Each device requires two pairs designated as Tx+, Tx–, Rx+ and Rx–. In addition, the pairs must be mated. An RJ21 connector is one way to mate cable pairs. In addition to the color scheme used with the cable, Figure 2-11 also shows how the cable transmit and receive pairs are mated to specific pins of the connector. Another method used for mating cable pairs is to use a **punchdown**.

> A punchdown is a device used to connect large cable runs, then to distribute wire pairs to network devices.

The wires are clamped to **bayonet pins** to hold them in place, and are distributed according to the scheme shown in Figure 2-12. All wires entering the punchdown do so on the "A" side and exit on the "B" side.

UTP four-pair cables use an RJ-45 connector, pictured in Figure 2-13. Physically, it resembles an oversized telephone jack (RJ-11). To make a cable, the insulation is stripped from the ends of each wire using a commercial wire stripping tool. The bare wires are then slipped into the connector and an end piece, or cover, is snapped over the connector to retain the wires. Alternatively, the connector may be installed using a crimping tool.

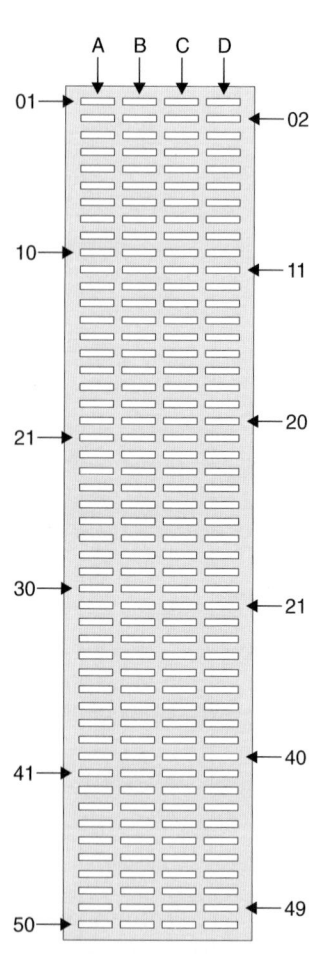

**Figure 2-12 Punchdown
for 25 Wire Pairs**

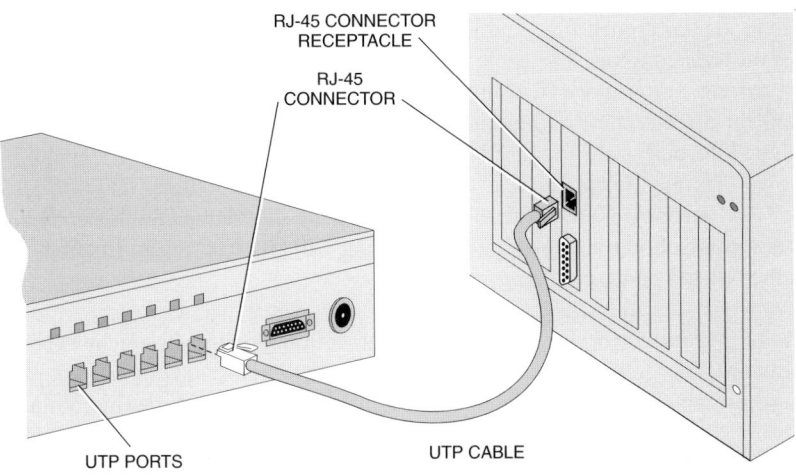

RJ-45 CONNECTOR
RECEPTACLE

RJ-45
CONNECTOR

UTP PORTS

UTP CABLE

Figure 2-13 UTP RJ-45 Connector

The bare wires are then slipped into the connector and an end piece, or cover, is snapped over the connector to retain the wires.

It should be noted that while CAT5 UTP is widely used as networking media, it doesn't necessarily follow that RJ-45 connectors are used only with CAT5 cable. RJ-45 is a generic, 8-pin connector that may be found in any of the other categories of UTP as well. The connector may be used for single wire pairs, or in cases when only two wire pairs are needed.

On a cost-per-foot basis, twisted pair is the cheapest medium. It offers an extensive amount of compatibility with the existing telephone network as well as with devices designed to work with the telephone network. However, it's not an acceptable practice to connect voice-devices such as telephones to unused CAT5 UTP. Interference from the network cable may distort voice signals. In addition, using excess pairs for voice prevents their use for network connections if the need arises in the future. A disadvantage of UTP is that it's the least secure of all media types. It's as easy to **tap** a telephone line as it is to make a connection. A **security breach** is also difficult to detect.

UTP and STP

STP is an abbreviation for **Shielded Twisted Pair**. It contains a metal shielding fully encircling the twisted pairs that's intended for reducing **ElectroMagnetic Interference** (EMI). EMI is produced by sources such as motors, generators, power lines, or high-wattage radio signals. The shielding—when grounded properly—causes a current to be induced in it from the interference. This same current will generate electromagnetic flux that induces an opposite polarity current into the twisted pairs. Since the two noise signals are of opposite polarities, they cancel, thereby eliminating the interfering noise.

The shielding may be either a metal foil (called Foil Twisted Pair, or FTP), or it may consist of a fine mesh of braided metal (called Screened Twisted Pair, or STP). STP using the foil shield is thinner, and somewhat easier to install, than the type that contains a braided shield. The braided shielding contributes to the bulk of the cable, which limits the bending radius in an installation. FTP is cheaper than ScTP, but the differences in installation savings can be negligible since both types must be carefully installed.

NET+ OBJECTIVE
I.1.6

CNST OBJECTIVE
VII-A

The reason that care must be taken is that STP works only as well as the shielding that encloses the twisted wires. The cable must be properly grounded to an earth ground that's neither too long, or too short. If, at any point along the length of the cable, the foil becomes disrupted, the effectiveness of the shield diminishes. A disrupted shield may occur due to a tear in the shield, or it could be caused by a manufacturing defect that may not manifest itself until the cable is installed in the field. Other factors contribute to the shield's effectiveness, as well. The frequency of the noise, the thickness of the shield, the ground connections, the cable's end connections, and the type of grounding will all affect the ability of the shield to protect the twisted pairs.

STP may be grounded at one or both ends of a connection. For high-frequency applications, both ends must be grounded in order to prevent the signal-carrying twisted pairs from inducing crosstalk into adjacent wires. The ground from end-to-end must be continuous.

If, during installation, the cable is pulled beyond the tinsel strength of the shield, or if it's bent to the point that the strength is stressed, EMI will be radiated from the wire pairs, or be induced into them from an outside source.

UTP doesn't have these drawbacks. The use of two transmit and receive wires virtually eliminates crosstalk, as well as outside magnetic field interference. It's also cheaper and easier to install. The problem associated with grounding doesn't occur.

It makes sense to install STP when it's already installed in a network, and you don't want to spend the money to rewire the media. This is particularly true if the current system is working adequately. However, for new installations, choose CAT5 UTP.

NET+ OBJECTIVE
I.1.6

CNST OBJECTIVE
VII-A

Coaxial Cable

> Networking coaxial cable has a maximum data rate of 100 MBPS, and fair noise immunity. In other applications, it has a maximum data rate of 4,000MBPS, bandwidths of up to 1,000 MHz and is more expensive to install than twisted wire

Originally, coaxial cable offered better noise immunity that UTP, and in some situations this remains the case. It consists of two conductors insulated from one another and enclosed in a **polyethylene** jacket. A cut-away view of coax cable is shown in Figure 2-14. The center conductor is surrounded by a flexible polyethylene insulator. Wrapped about the insulator is the second conductor consisting of braided wire, foil or both. The braid is connected to ground potential. Since it entirely encircles the center conductor, external noise such as crosstalk is effectively shorted to ground. The braided conductor is covered with an outer jacket of polyethylene insulation. Polyethylene is a very resistant to substances that damage the conductors, such as salt, water, or oil. It retains a high degree of flexibility over broad temperature ranges.

Coaxial cable is most effective at frequencies over 100 kHz. At lower frequencies, the skin effects are minimal, and external noise "leaks" through the braid to cause distortion of the signal carried on the center conductor. The upper frequency limit for data transmission rates using coaxial cable can exceed 400 MBPS. However, resistive losses increase rapidly with the frequency necessitating the use of repeaters for long-distance transmission.

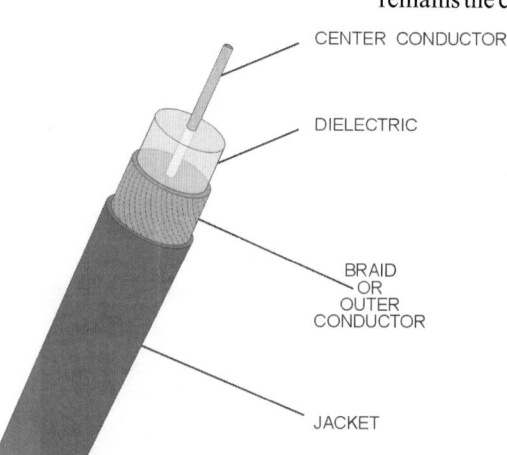

CENTER CONDUCTOR

DIELECTRIC

BRAID
OR
OUTER
CONDUCTOR

JACKET

Figure 2-14 Coaxial Cable

The cable television industry has used coaxial cable extensively. Many local area networks owe their high data rates to cable advancements brought about by the cable TV industry. Cable TV networks can utilize coaxial cable with a 400MHz bandwidth. At this size bandwidth, 52 TV channels can be carried on a single cable with the assistance of multiplexing. LANs typically transmit on coax from 1 MBPS up to about 100 MBPS.

The disadvantage to coaxial cable is the cost and lack of compatibility with twisted wires. The cost is only slightly more per foot than twisted wire, but this can grow to significant proportions when thousands of feet of cable are needed. Compatibility to UTP is a problem since most Ethernet networks now use UTP.

Thicknet

Originally, all Ethernet LANs used coax as the transmission medium. The cable was called **thicknet** due to its strength and resistance to bending. Because of its bulkiness (.4 inches thick), thicknet is used primarily as a backbone for interconnecting network devices. Thicknet, also referred to 10base5, supports 100 transceivers on each segment. Any unused ends must be terminated with a 50-ohm resistance to prevent signal reflections. The cable is yellow or orange with dark colored rings spaced every 2.5 meters. The rings represent the minimum spacing of in-line transceiver taps to the backbone. The number of connections are limited to prevent signal attenuation and interference. The transceivers, in turn, connect to the coax cable via a 15-pin connector and cable (no longer than 50 feet) through one of two methods—intrusive taps, or non-intrusive taps. Figure 2-15 shows a typical thicknet connection.

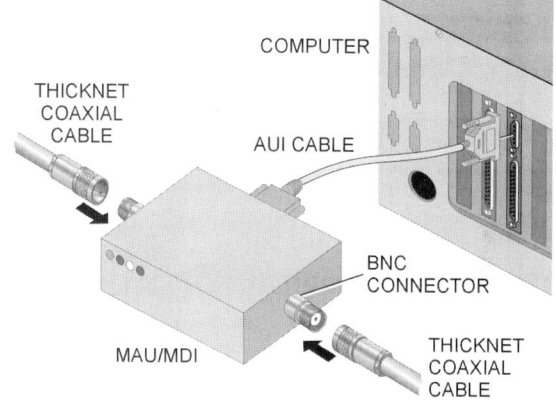

Figure 2-15 Thicknet Connections

Note the terminology used. MAU, or Medium Attachment Unit, contains the transceiver circuitry along with various digital devices used to format data bits into Ethernet frames. A transceiver, as used with coaxial cable, simply receives and transmits signals. It lacks the sophistication to manage or massage the signal in any way. It doesn't amplify it, or remove noise, and it can't be assigned to another physical device through software configurations. An AUI, or Attachment Unit Interface, is a DB15 connector (either male or female) which is used to connect a 15-wire AUI cable between a MAU and the computer interface. Figure 2-16 shows the AUI cable and its associated pinout. Notice the reversal of pin number designations between the male and female connectors.

NET+ OBJECTIVE I.2.2

The frames formatted in the MAU are up and downloaded to the thicknet coaxial cable via the MDI, which stands for Medium Dependent Interface. The MDI is nothing more than a mechanical connection, or interface from the MAU to the coax. There are two types of MDI, **intrusive taps** and **non-intrusive taps**.

PIN FUNCTION	PIN NUMBER
LOGIC REF	1
COLLISION +	2
TRANSMIT +	3
LOGIC REF	4
RECEIVE +	5
POWER RETURN	6
NOT USED	7
LOGIC REF	8
COLLISION –	9
TRANSMIT –	10
LOGIC REF	11
RECEIVE –	12
POWER (+12 Vdc)	13
LOGIC REF	14
NOT USED	15

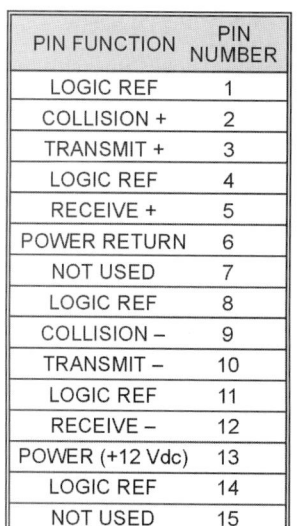

Figure 2-16 AUI Connector Point

NET+ OBJECTIVE
I.1.6

CNST OBJECTIVE
VII-B

An intrusive tap, shown in Figure 2-17, requires the coax to be cut and a barrel connector inserted, which allows the transceiver and cable to join the coax backbone. The barrel connector fits to an interface that also joins the transceiver's 15-pin cable from the node.

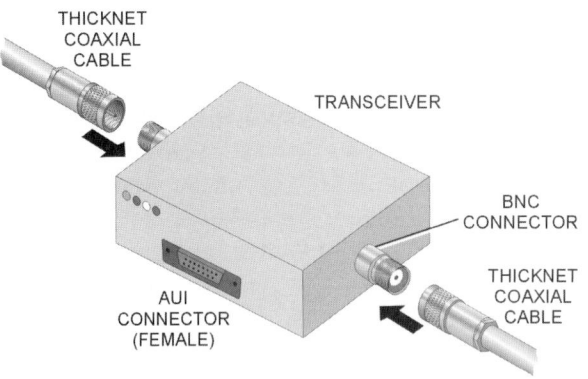

Figure 2-17 Thicknet Non-Intrusive Tap

A non-intrusive tap (also called a "vampire tap") doesn't require the cable to be broken and, therefore, the network doesn't have to be brought down each time another user is added. A hole is pierced through the coax and a bayonet spear inserted into the hole which contacts the center conductor of the cable. The non-intrusive method is the favored practice because the network continues to run while the procedure takes place. Figure 2-18 illustrates a non-intrusive tap.

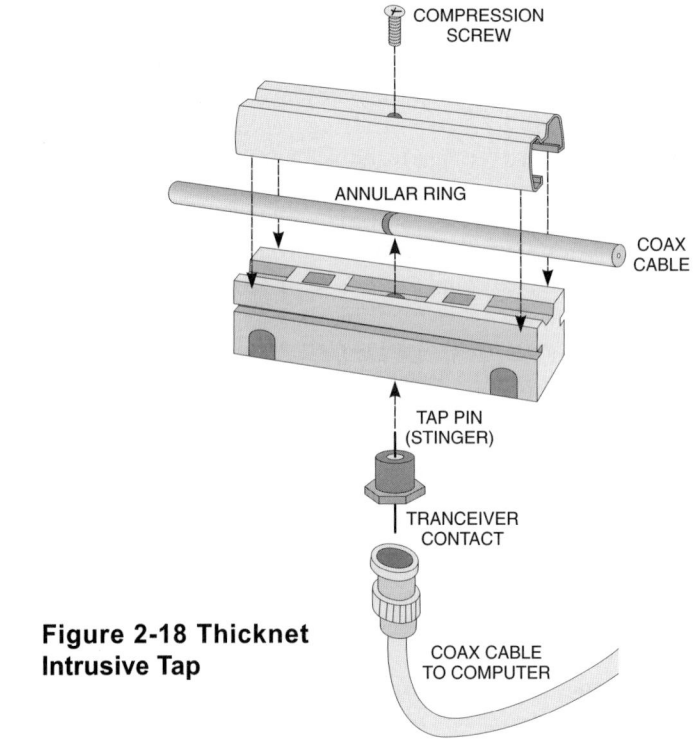

Figure 2-18 Thicknet Intrusive Tap

Thinnet

Thinnet, or 10Base2 (also called cheapernet, RG-58A/U, or thin coaxial) coaxial cable has less shielding than thicknet, and consequently, smaller permissible segment lengths in a LAN. The maximum length of thinnet is 185 meters (compared to 500 meters for thicknet) and each unused segment end must be equipped with a 50-ohm termination to prevent undesired signal reflections. It can support up to 30 transceivers on each segment, but the transceivers can be placed as close together as 0.5 meters.

To connect a transceiver, the cable is cut and the ends prepared for BNC connectors and a T-connector installed at the break. One of the leads from the T connects back to the NIC card of the computer (which contains the transceiver circuitry), while the other two leads form an Ethernet bus. Figure 2-19 shows a typical arrangement. Barrel connectors can be used to join two short RG-58 cables, if necessary.

Coaxial cable is seldom used at the LAN level of networking in modern networks. UTP and fiber optics have exceeded it in terms of bandwidth and channel capacity, although in a small peer-to-peer LAN, it may be easier to configure than UTP, and will work just as well.

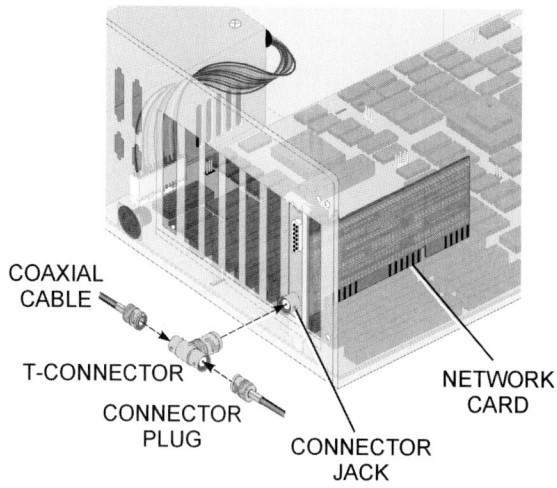

COAXIAL CABLE

T-CONNECTOR

CONNECTOR PLUG

CONNECTOR JACK

NETWORK CARD

Figure 2-19 Thinnet Connections

Fiber Optics

Fiber optics represents a very important stride in the development of data communications systems. A fiber-optic system offers much higher data rates, bandwidth, and noise immunity than do copper-based systems. At present, fiber systems are used in point-to-point configurations using conventional star, ring and, in some cases, bus topologies. Due to the large capacity capability of a fiber system, it's installed where it will be expected to carry large volumes of data. Telecommunications and cable television industries have used it for many years because of this.

Within the last ten years, fiber has bubbled down to the local network level due to a drop in prices—although it remains the most expensive media—and broader standardization. The actual cost of fiber cable isn't expensive. The connectors, special tools needed, hardware to convert signals from electrical to light and vice versa, all combine to drive up the cost of an optical system.

Even though it's an expensive choice, there are several reasons to install fiber in a network. Since no copper is used in the cable, data bits won't be corrupted by electromagnetic interference (EMI), crosstalk, or other external noise that may garble bits in a UTP or coaxial system. The optical cable isolates devices connected to either end of it which makes it a good choice where completely separate systems are linked together. An example is two LANs in different buildings. Connecting them can be tricky because of ground loops caused by common electrical planes. A fiber-optic connection avoids the problem and eliminates the danger to personnel and equipment.

Laboratory experiments with fiber optics have produced data rates as high as 200,000 MPBS. Telecommunication carrier frequencies hover in the 40MBPS to 8,000MBPS range. At the local level, data rates are standardized at 10MBPS and 100MBPS, using the IEEE 802 protocols and the FDDI (Fiber Distributed Data Interface) protocol. Losses are quite small compared to copper systems. At the long-distance carrier level, losses are not to exceed 2dB/km (over 1kilometer). Compare this to 11.5db/km over 100 meters using UTP. This means that a fiber cable will carry more data farther, and with fewer losses, than its copper-based cousin.

> Fiber-optic media relay data via light waves through a glass or plastic conductor. It offers the best in noise immunity but is the most expensive to install. Data rates may run as high as 200,000 MBPS and bandwidths as high as 1,000 GHz. The disadvantage of fiber optics is the expense, special splicing tools, and need for very careful alignment of splices and connections.

How does fiber optics achieve such high data rates and bandwidths? In the next section, the basic structure of light will be reviewed and slanted toward answering that question.

Light Structure

Light is electromagnetic radiation that has a wavelength falling within the infrared, visible, or ultraviolet ranges, broadly referred to as the **Optical Spectrum**. The ranges are illustrated in Figure 2-20.

Typical wavelengths used in fiber optic networks fall in the near infrared and into the visible light spectrum.

Wavelength is described as a portion of a meter and will be stated using one of the following units:

- Micron (μm): 10^{-6} meters
- Nanometer (nm): 10^{-9} meters
- Angstrom (A): 10^{-10} meters

Specifications could have described light using frequencies within the optical spectrum, but it would have been inconvenient due to the large numbers used at these high frequencies.

Light is recognized as having two primary properties as it moves, or propagates. It has a wave-like nature and a particle-like nature. When it passes through, or is deflected from, an object (such as a piece of glass), it resembles a wave much like ac current traveling through a wire. But when it is absorbed by an object (such as semiconductor material), it behaves as particles of energy that strike an object. As far as fiber cable is concerned, think of the light going through it as a single, two-dimensional (it has direction and amplitude) particle stream.

ULTRAVIOLET (390nm-10nm)	10nm
	Far Ultraviolet
	300nm
	Near Ultraviolet
VISIBLE (770nm-390nm)	390nm
	770nm
INFRARED (1000nm-3nm)	Near Infrared
	3um
	Middle Infrared
	30um
	Far Infrared
	1000um

Figure 2-20 Optical Spectrum

Light from any source will disperse, or separate with distance. But it's convenient to think that it doesn't when creating a model to describe how it travels in a fiber cable. Figure 2-21 shows a ray of light (the **incident ray**) striking a surface at an angle. Assume the surface has mirror-like qualities and the ray reflects (**reflected ray**) from it. The incident ray strikes the mirror at some angle called θi (**incident angle**), and is reflected at θr (**reflected angle**).

The relationship between the incident ray and the reflected ray is given by **Snells Law** which says that when light is reflected, θi = θr.

Snell's angle is measured from an imaginary line drawn perpendicular to the incident point. The incident point is the point where the ray of light strikes an object, a mirror in the figure. The imaginary line is called **line normal**, and it provides a reference for measuring both the **angle of incident** and the **angle of reflection**.

Not all surfaces reflect light. Some surfaces absorb all or part of the light that strikes it, while other surfaces refract light. **Refraction** is the bending of a light ray that occurs when light passes through materials of different densities. Snell has a law for this, too, and it is called **Snell's Law of Refraction**. The law says that the amount of refraction is determined by the difference in densities of two materials. The greater the relative difference, the greater the refractive angle.

When light passes from air to water, it changes direction (refracts) because the water is denser than the air. You've probably witnessed the effects of this phenomenon by looking at an object at the bottom of a swimming pool. The object looks much closer than it actually is because light entering the pool refracts and slows its rate of propagation in the denser water.

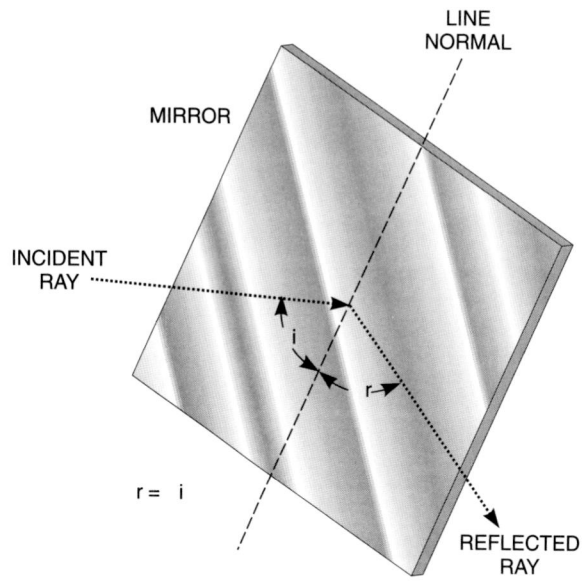

Figure 2-21 Reflection of Light Rays

Figure 2-22 shows a light ray passing from air to glass. The dotted line shows the course of the light ray if it didn't refract, while the solid line shows the actual course of the ray due to refraction. The refracted ray is traveling at a slower rate than the incident ray.

Figure 2-23 is the vector representation of light rays in the dense glass material. Line normal is illustrated as Time, while the incident surface is illustrated by describing the Amplitude of the light.

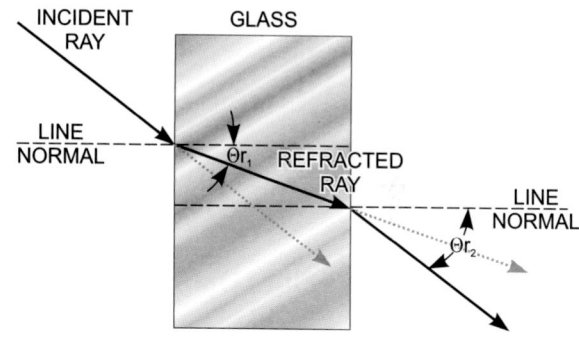

Figure 2-22 Refraction of Light Rays

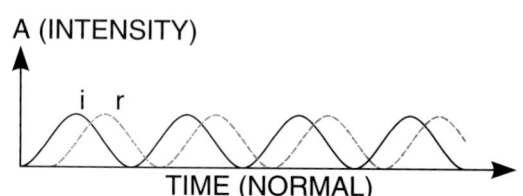

Figure 2-23 Vector Comparison of Incident and Refracted Light

The projected incident ray reaches some maximum amplitude at a time prior to the refracted ray reaching the same amplitude. The only explanation for this is that the refracted ray must be traveling slower than the projected incident ray.

If, after passing through the glass, light were to reenter air, it would speed up again. This is pictured in Figure 2-22. Notice that the refracted ray bent toward line normal when it entered the denser glass material, but bent away from normal once it reentered the air. This actually makes sense because the velocity of light in air is faster than through the glass. It will now reach its maximum amplitude (called intensity in the optical world) at the same rate as the original incident ray, but the event will occur at some later point in time.

A fiber cable makes good use of both reflection and refraction when propagating light. In either case, light must pass through one type of material and strike another type. That is, two types of material (or, two materials with differing densities) are needed to manipulate the direction of light. No matter if the ray is reflected or refracted, two materials will always be used in the construction of a fiber optic cable. These materials are called the **core** and the **cladding** and they are further described by their diameter in microns.

The conventional method for specifying fiber cable is to state the diameter of the core versus cladding. For example, a 62.5/125 cable has a 62.5-micron core and a 125-micron cladding.

Fiber Cable Propagation

A cut-away view of a fiber cable is shown in Figure 2-24. The core is composed of either a glass or plastic strand, and the cladding which encircles it is also composed of glass or plastic.

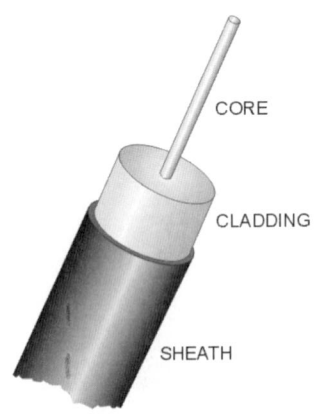

The only difference between core and cladding is the difference in density the two offer to light beams. Examining a fiber cable doesn't help to distinguish between core and cladding, as they are manufactured in the same strand. The density difference is a cable manufacturing specification called refractive index. Refractive index is the ratio of the velocity of light through a material, to the velocity of light through a vacuum (300,000,000m/s). In practice, the refractive index is also influenced by the angle of incidence.

In a fiber optic cable, the refractive index for the cladding will always be less than the index for the core. Or, in other words, the density of the cladding material will be less than the density of the core. Since the two differ in density, light striking the junction of core and cladding will either reflect or refract. Which phenomenon is used to propagate light is determined by the manner used to construct the cable. There are two basic methods used to construct fiber cable—**singlemode** and **multimode**.

Figure 2-24 Fiber Optic

Multimode Graded Index Fiber Optic Cable

Multimode cable is the most commonly used because it's cheaper and will transmit light over distances used in local area networks. Mode refers to the way light traverses a fiber cable, and this, in turn, is partly determined by the manner in which light enters the cable. A working definition of "mode" is the various paths that light takes along the cable.

A multimode cable means that light will travel in many paths from transmitter to receiver. This is shown graphically in Figure 2-25.

Light emanating from the source strikes the fiber at many angles. The angle at which light enters the cable is the incident angle. Light wave A1 strikes the fiber end at a very small incident angle. The wave passes through the core, through the cladding, and is absorbed in the sheath which is opaque. Light wave A2 reaches the core at a much wider angle of incident. As the wave leaves the core and enters the cladding, it's bent from its original path. The core of the cladding is much more dense than the cladding material. The lower cladding density refracts the wave in the direction shown but the angle of refraction is too wide for the wave to reenter the core and it's subsequently lost in the cladding and sheath.

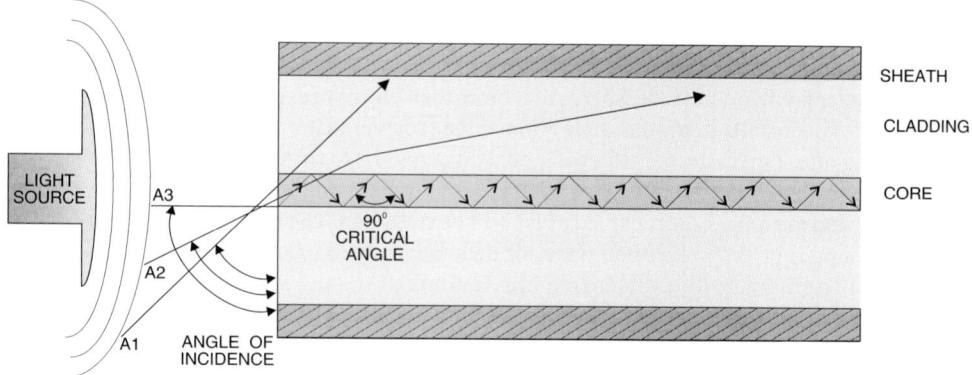

Figure 2-25 Various Light Paths in a Multimode Cable

The third light wave, A3, moves through the core and strikes the cladding interface at a specific angle that, when it strikes the junction of core and cladding, will cause it to refract back into the core. This angle is called the **critical angle**. All light waves that strike the interface will reflect away from the cladding according to Snell's Law of Reflection.

When the reflected ray once again encounters the core/cladding junction, its bent back (reflected back) again. This zig-zagging continues along the length of the cable. The A3 light wave, or all light waves which fall within the spread of the critical angle, is the beam that will carry data from transmitter to receiver. Information carried in A1 and A2 is lost which results in an attenuated signal at the receiver.

The critical angle that's necessary for internal reflection in a fiber covers a range of degrees. The specific range is a function of the composition and physical construction of the fiber, as well as the angle that light enters the fiber cable. Light waves leave the source in many directions, not all of which will cause the rays to reflect within the critical angle. The precise alignment of source to fiber is an important aspect of an optical system.

The manner of propagation in the figure is reflection. As long as light strikes the surface within the critical angel, it will reflect when it encounters the core/cladding interface, and will internally reflect along the length of the cable.

As light enters the core, it does so at many angles of incidence. Some of these will fall within the critical angle necessary for propagation. Consider only those rays that enter within the critical angle. Some will do so at a steeper angle than others and they will zig-zag through the cable more times than a ray entering at a slightly wider angle.

The steeper angle means the wave will take longer getting to the end of the cable than the wave that enters at a wide angel. At the receiving end of the cable, the rays arriving at different times causes a variance in phase of the light beams. This effect is called **modal dispersion** since the light rays strike the core at different angles causing them to propagate through the fiber in different modes, or manners.

The remedy for modal dispersion is to restrict the size (diameter) of the core. If the thickness of the cladding is at least three times the thickness of the core, modal dispersion can be eliminated. Multimode cables should consist of 50/125m, 62.5/125m or 100/140m. The cable should be tested at a wavelength of 850nm over 1km (in an Ethernet application) for losses not to exceed –13dB, –16dB and –19dB respectively for the core/cladding sizes.

Singlemode Fiber Optic Cable

The problem with multimode fiber is that more than one path exists for light to travel along the core. This results in **modal distortion** at the receiver that may cause a loss of data bits over long runs. (Visually, the effect of modal dispersion is to stretch a transmitted pulse. The greater the dispersion, the longer it will take for all components of a pulse to arrive at the receiver and the longer the received pulse will be stretched. The implication is that data bits will no longer be the prescribed width or data rate, causing a complete signal loss in the system.) To eliminate the problem requires limiting the modal paths. This is accomplished by using a very small core strand so that only one wavelength of light will radiate through the cable. Figure 2-26 shows a singlemode cable connected to a LASER light source.

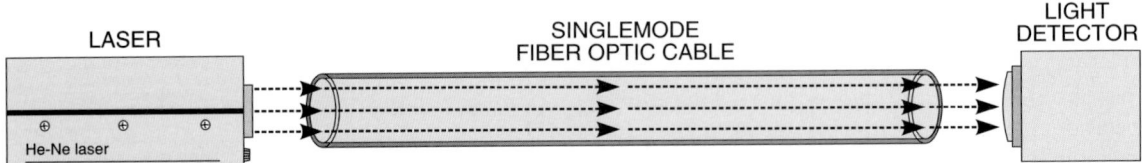

Figure 2-26 Singlemode Fiber Optic Light Propagation

Notice that light travels axially through the cable, and not in the zig-zag fashion that's typical of multimode. Since there's only one wavelength of light that's being transmitted, modal dispersion is entirely eliminated. The bits arriving at the receiver will have phase characteristics identical to the bits at the transmitting end of the cable.

A LASER is necessary to drive singlemode cable because it produces energy that's coherent (in phase), monochromatic (of the same wavelength), and collimated (traveling in the same direction, not radiating in many directions like light from a LED). At the receiving end, the detector is specialized to the wavelength of transmitted light.

The LASER, even if it's a semiconductor device, drives up the cost of a singlemode system. Singlemode cable is also the most expensive and difficult to work with because of its small size, and the precise alignment needed between cable and end connections. It is, however, the most efficient and less distorting of all fiber cable types.

Singlemode cable is limited by the FDDI protocol to a diameter of 8.7/125 microns. The length of the cable is determined by topology. When used in point-to-point configuration, the maximum length is 40km (24 miles), but in a ring topology the length can be extended to 100km (62 miles) for dual-rings, and 200km (124 miles) for single rings. It typically uses light with a wavelength of 1,305 nm with cable attenuation of .5dB/km.

Singlemode fiber cable is used in applications where data speed and distance (limited to 5km, maximum in an Ethernet network) are the concern. Multimode fiber isn't acceptable over long runs due to excessive modal dispersion.

Fiber Cable Losses

Although fiber cable has many advantages over copper wire, it's not without its drawbacks. As mentioned earlier, light disperses with distance causing a gradual loss in signal strength.

Varying angles of incidence will cause rays to arrive at the receiver out of phase causing modal dispersion. Losses due to dispersion and scattering are also dependent of the wavelength of the source light. At wavelengths of 1.3u and 1.5u, light travels at a relatively constant speed with low losses (about 2dB/Km). These wavelengths are called **zero-dispersion** wavelengths and are used in commercial long-distance fiber optic networks.

Connection losses contribute to signal degradation. Connection losses result from fiber splices, the interface of light source to fiber, and fiber to light detector. The actual amount of signal attenuation is measured with a photometer. Gallium-arsenide LEDs are common light sources but the light ends of these are rounded. Optical connectors are available that will focus the beam from the LED end so it's directed into the fiber core. This helps to reduce modal dispersion but it decreases the amount of available light by about one-third. The decrease in light is a connection loss. Note that copper systems don't have this problem.

Misaligned connections also limit the amount of available light. Even when the alignment is perfect, the light coupling won't be 100% because the rays will reflect and refract at a splice or connection junction. **Numerical Aperture** (NA) losses are a result of connection mismatches, as well. NA loss occurs when the critical angle of light emitted from a cable is different than the critical angle of the receiving cable. NA is a published specification of fiber cable and should be low (less than .5). The lower the NA, the tighter will be the critical angle and more light will likely couple within the critical angle of the receiving cable.

Spectral dispersion causes losses in a fiber cable because of the fact that some wavelengths travel faster along the cable length than others. By using LASER energy, spectral dispersion is eliminated since only one wavelength is transmitted. However, when LASERs aren't available (LEDs will likely be used), a broad spectrum of light will be sourced into the cable. At the receiving end, a data bit will appear to be stretched because not all wavelengths are arriving at the same time. This effect is similar to modal dispersion. Recall that a LASER generates collimated light. This means that the light is traveling in the same direction, and if you imagine the light as a series of single rays, they would travel in a nearly parallel manner.

When injected into a fiber cable, the rays travel as axial beams through the cable, neither reflecting or refracting in a perfectly straight cable. In a bent cable, the axial ray will strike the core/cladding interface and reflect along the remaining distance to the receiver. Some of the energy will refract into the cladding and be lost. A bind in a fiber optic cable will produce losses and signal attenuation. This is true of all optical cable types, so cable runs should be kept as straight as possible. Liberally, use wire ties to bundle cable groups, and then anchor the bundle to supports in ceilings or walls. This will help to reduce sagging in the cable.

Fiber Connections, Splices, and Standards

Fiber connections are considerably more difficult than the solder connections of copper wire. Usually, a light source (LED) and the fiber are coupled together with a plastic connector, as shown in Figure 2-27. The same is true of the fiber-to-light detector connection. The two most important considerations of connecting fibers is that the connection offer the proper alignment so as to avoid any more than the minimum amount of connector loss, and that the end of the fiber be unblemished.

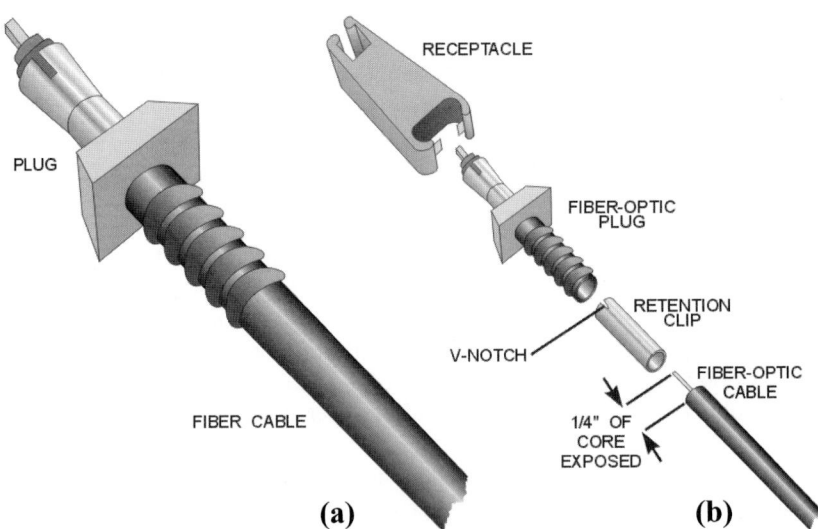

Figure 2-27 Fiber Connections

The proper alignment of the fiber is accomplished by correctly fitting the cable plug as shown in Figure 2-27(a). Shown is a standard cable plug that can be used to connect the cable to fiber-optic equipment. Figure 2-27(b) shows a breakdown of the plug and a typical fiber cable receptacle. The cable sheath should be stripped to expose approximately 1/4 inch of the fiber. The retention clip is then slid onto the cable with the notched "V" on the exposed end of the fiber. The cable and retention clip assembly are then pressed into the plug. The connector—plug and receptacle—will generally ensure a good alignment of the fibers.

The end of the fiber must be unblemished (not be scratched, nicked, or dirty). There are two methods for preparing the fiber ends. The first method involves polishing the fiber ends.

The other method involves using a **hot knife**. Ideally, the knife should have an adjustable temperature range since different sizes and types of fibers have optimum heat ranges for cutting. The fiber cable is slipped into a cutting fixture that has a flat circular surface on one end, as shown in Figure 2-28. The beveled edge of the hot knife is slid along the flat surface of the cutting tool to make a clean, smooth cut.

If the ends of the fiber are not prepared so they are smooth and clean, the connection loss can be significant. It is analogous to a cold solder joint with copper wires.

The preceding discussion serves to highlight some of the difficulties you encounter when working with fiber. Fortunately, many of the connection problems described for the connector have been eliminated through better designs. But before describing the new and improved models, let's take a paragraph or two to clear up some confusions concerning fiber optic standards.

The first fiber standard was published in the early 1980's and was called Fiber Optic Inter-Repeater Link (FOIRL). The original intent of the standard was to specify fiber backbones connecting repeaters, which were separated by up to 1,000 meters. However, as Ethernet LANs propagated and the cost of fiber cable decreased, the IEEE added fiber protocols in the 803 standards which permitted fiber Ethernet to be run directly to the desktop.

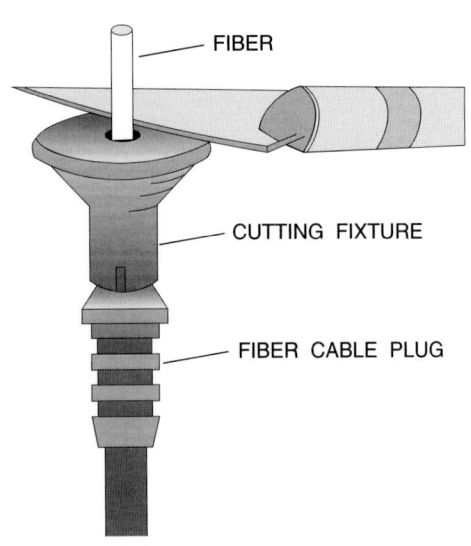

Figure 2-28 Cutting Fixture and Hot Knife

The IEEE 803 standards for fiber are collectively called the 10BaseF specifications, and have replaced the original FOIRL standard. The specification is broken up into the following categories:

- **10BaseFP, Passive Fiber Optic Star:** In a 10BaseFP network, nodes connect through a hub that doesn't alter the signal; it simply relays it form one port to another using mirrors.

- **10BaseFB, Active Fiber Optic Backbone:** This describes a high-speed backbone between repeaters.

- **10BaseFL, Active Fiber Optic Link:** The most common standard used when connecting two devices on a network such as node to hub, it is a full-duplex protocol which allows a cable length up to 2km (6558 feet). As the fiber standard to actually replace FOIRL, it remains backward compatible with it when the older FOIRL hubs are used, although the maximum segment length is reduced to 1km (3279 feet).

- **100BaseFX, Fiber Optic Fast-Ethernet:** This specification is similar to 10BaseFL, except date travels at 100MBPS rather than at 10MPBS for the categories described above.

Another fiber protocol is FDDI, **Fiber Distributed Data Interface**. The details of this specification are described in Chapter 6, Local Area Networks. FDDI requires a special connector, and it is described in Chapter 6 as well.

Now, let's take a look at current connectors used with fiber optic cables. The cable shown in Figure 2-27 is called a Sub-Miniature Assembly, or SMA. These are gradually being replaced with connectors that provide better alignment with fewer opportunities for problems. Figure 2-29 shows an ST, or Straight Tip, connector that is defined in the 10BaseF specifications.

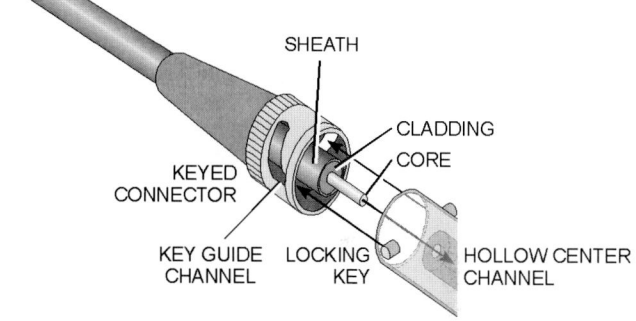

The ST has a keyed locking connector that automatically aligns the center strands of the fiber cable to the network device it's connected to. An integral spring helps to keep the fiber strands from being crushed together and damaging the cable ends. There are different ST connector types for singlemode cable and multimode cable, and the two can't be interchanged.

Figure 2-29 Straight Tip Fiber Optic Connector

100BaseFX cable requires the use of an SC connector pictured in Figure 2-30. While no standard has been defined for connectors in a 100BaseFX network at the time of this writing, the SC seems to predominate in the industry.

At the high data rates used with 100BaseFX, the fiber strands must be very accurately aligned so as to avoid signal loss. This is done in an SC cable by including floating ferrules which contact the fiber strands. The ports of devices connected to an SC connector also have floating ferrules. Since the ferrules are floating, they're held loosely in place and will move slightly when contacting the fiber strands. The small amount of movement addresses slight alignment differences found from connector to connector and from port to port.

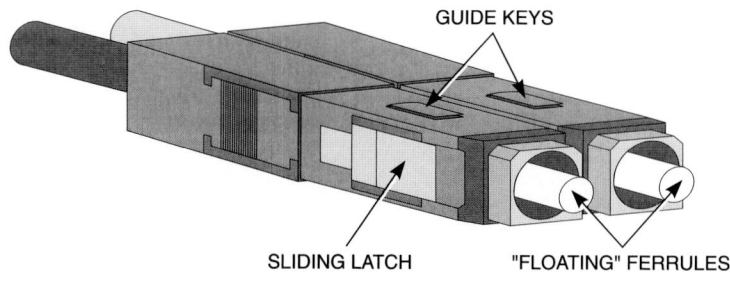

Figure 2-30 SC 100BaseFX Fiber Optic Connector

Microwaves

Microwaves are used with **satellites** and in the telecommunication's industry where cable isn't practical, such as across oceans. Microwaves are susceptible to solar disturbance and weather conditions. At the LAN level, microwaves and infrared are used in wireless networks.

Microwave communication systems consist of a transmitter, receiver, and the atmosphere is the transmission medium. The long-distance telephone carriers frequently use microwaves in **line of sight** (point-to-point) configurations with the assistance of repeaters spaced from one to thirty miles apart. The advantage of microwaves is that communication can be transferred across areas in which geography is an obstacle such as large lakes or the oceans.

Microwave communications also include satellites. Historically, satellites have been an expensive method to send information, but in recent years the costs have declined, primarily due to advances in Earth station antennas.

Microwave communications for the telephone system and satellites take place in the 3–6GHz frequency range. Table 2-1 shows common frequency bands.

Table 2-1 Common Frequencies Used With Satellites, the Telephone Industry, and Wireless Networks

SATELLITE FREQUENCY BANDS		
BAND	UPLINK (GHz)	DOWNLINK (GHz)
C	6	4
Ku	14	11/12
K	29/30	19/20

DIGITAL TELEPHONE CARRIER BANDWIDTH (MBPS)	
MEDIUM	BANDWIDTH
T1 CABLE	1.544
1A MICROWAVE	1.544
T1C CABLE	3.152
T2 CABLE	6.312
FT3 FIBER	44.736
T4M COAX	274.176
DR18 MICROWAVE	274.176

Microwave systems are quite insecure. Since the information is transmitted through the air, it's relatively easy to intercept. Microwaves are also at the mercy of the elements, particularly rainfall which can entirely obscure portions of a transmission in the Ghz frequencies.

Microwave communication within long-distance carrier facilities and data exchanges that are beamed up and down via satellite are specialized across wide areas. For the local arena, we have the IEEE 802.11 standard for Wireless Local Area Networks (WLAN). While wireless LANs have been around for many years, there hasn't been an agreed-upon standard as to how to implement them until 1997. After seven years of wrestling with compatibility issues among working vendors, the IEEE ratified the first widely accepted standard.

The WLAN standard is the wireless equivalent to the IEEE802.3 protocol for Ethernet. There are several differences, notably data rates for 802.11 are a maximum of 2MBPS. Recall that Ethernet is 10MBPs while fast-Ethernet is 100MBPs. Still, the realization that your workstation is no long restricted to UTP cabling routed through walls and ceilings is seductive, making wireless networking one of the fastest growing sub-industries in networking.

Wireless LANs are discussed in detail in Chapter 7, but the following information should give you a general idea of the variety available at the physical interface level of WLANs. The standard specifies three different types of physical interfaces. You select one of the three, then make sure your vendors are aware of your selection, since the three can't be mixed-and-matched easily.

The interfaces are:

- **Direct Sequence Spread Spectrum (DSSS):** Data rates at 1 and 2MBPS, and five overlapping 26MHz sub-bands centered around 2.4GHz.

- **Frequency Hop Spread Spectrum (FHSS):** Data rates at 1 and 2MBPS, operating in the 2.4GHz range and consisting of 79 sub-bands. Each of the sub-bands has a bandwidth of 1MHz and data packets are required to traverse a minimum of 22 hops among the 79 sub-bands. The idea is that data packets are likely to be loss or garbled but the number of minimum hops nearly guarantees that if this happens, the packet will be restored at another hop.

- **Infrared Red:** Data Rates are 1 and 2MBPS and the range between transmitter and receiver is ten meters. Unlike the radio frequencies used in DSSS and FHSS, infrared does not require a clear line-of-sight between communicating stations. In other words, it's said to be diffused. Infrared operates in the 850nm to 950nm range.

Microwave telephone and satellite systems are discussed in greater detail in later chapters.

ELECTRICAL PROPERTIES OF CABLE

Twisted-pair wire and coaxial cable are in more common use than fiber optic cable. The wide base of installed copper media virtually guarantees it will not be superseded by optical systems in the near future. Indeed, in some cases, fiber is a very awkward media choice. In a bus configuration, it's difficult to install a fiber system because of the station taps to the bus. Twisted pair is the preferred medium in architectures where multiple data paths exist.

But, whereas, fiber optic system performance is unaffected by frequency changes, copper wire is greatly affected. The effects of increasing frequency through copper produces the greatest disadvantages to the media. For either twisted pairs or coaxial cable, the performance drops with increases in frequency. The maximum frequency limit of voice-grade twisted-pair wiring is about 1 MHz, for UTP CAT 5 it's 100 MHz, and for thick or thinnet coaxial cable, it's 10 MHz. For the most part, copper media is limited at the upper frequency range because of the distributed capacitance and inductance of the wire runs. The reactive effects distort binary data to the point that a receiver will not be able to interpret the data. The following sections explore the nature of **distributed reactance**, the effects on data, and methods used to avoid some of the effects.

Distributed Reactance

Parallel conductors, separated by an insulator, represent a capacitor. Coaxial cables are wrapped in a sheath, but inside, the solid center wire is separated from the braided conductor by a **polyurethane** insulator. The wires act like capacitor plates across the entire cable length. Twisted pairs are separated from one another by the insulating jacket. Similar to coax, the wire pairs represent capacitor plates, and the insulation represents a capacitor **dielectric**.

As a current moves through coaxial and twisted pairs, magnetic lines of force radiate from the wires and a voltage is induced into the other wire. As the lines of force cut into the conductors, the existing current in the wires opposes the change and the wires exhibit inductive properties.

> Copper cables contain a **characteristic impedance** of series inductance and parallel capacitance, which gives the cable the properties of a **lowpass filter**.

An equivalent circuit of a two-conductor cable is shown in Figure 2-31.

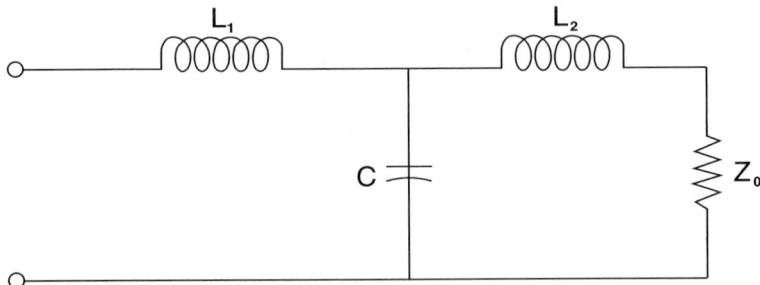

Figure 2-31 Equivalent Two-Conductor Cable Circuit

L1 an L2 represent the inductance of each wire, while C represents the capacitance exhibited by the cable. In actual practice, each wire length contains a series resistance and parallel conductance. The series resistance consists of the actual resistance of the wire and the parallel conductance is the leakage of energy through the insulating material. These two factors have a negligible effect on the data signal and for this reason have not been included in the illustration.

The circuit of Figure 2-31 also contains Zo which is the characteristic impedance of the cable. The characteristic impedance of a transmission line is a value of pure resistance which the line must be terminated with in order to transfer the maximum amount of energy to a load. An improperly terminated line results in reflected waves, or the amount of energy not coupled to the load, and they travel back through the line producing constructive as well as destructive effects on the line signal. Once a long transmission line is terminated properly, the energy propagating through the line is transferred to the load—the receiver—and reflected waves cease to degrade the data signal. To prevent undesired signal reflections and to ensure the maximum signal strength is transferred to the receiver, unused ends of copper-based cabling must be terminated with a resistance equaling the characteristic impedance of the cable.

Use Table 2-2 as a guide for selecting various terminating resistances.

Table 2-2 Terminating Resistance Guide

CABLE TERMINATIONS		
CABLE TYPE	**TERMINATION**	**CABLE TECHNOLOGY**
RG-58A/U Thinnet	$50\Omega \pm 10\%$	Ethernet, 10Base2
Thicknet Ethernet	$50\Omega \pm 10\%$	Ethernet, 10Base5
RG-59/U	$50\Omega \pm 10\%$	CATV, ARCNET
RG62/U	$93\Omega \pm 10\%$	ARCNET, IBM Networks
Unshielded Twisted Pair	$100–120\Omega$	Ethernet, 10BaseT, 100BaseTX
Shielded Twisted Pair	$150\Omega \pm 10\%$	Token Ring

Characteristic impedance is not dependent upon cable length; in fact, it depends only upon the effective capacitance and inductance of a particular cable. These values are found in manufacturers' data sheets. Characteristic impedance can be approximated by:

$$Z_o = \sqrt{L/C}$$

For example, a common coaxial cable is RG-58. It has a capacitance of 29.5 pF/Ft and an inductance of 73 nH/Ft. For any length of RG-58, the characteristic impedance is:

$$Z_o = \sqrt{\frac{73 \times 10^{-9}}{29.5 \times 10^{-12}}}$$

$$Z_o = 49.745 \text{ ohms}$$

This means that the RG-58 cable will behave as any circuit with a capacitor, and inductance, and a 50-ohm load. It will exhibit phase-shifts and time constants as in any RCL circuit.

Notice that Figure 2-31 is essentially a lowpass filter. As the applied frequency increases, the reactance of C decreases resulting in less voltage being developed across Zo. At some frequency, the impedance voltage drop will be 70% of the applied voltage. This represents the **half-power point**, or –3 dB loss, and defines the upper frequency limit of the cable. As has been mentioned, the upper frequency limit of coax is 10 MHz, for voice-grade twisted pairs, it's 1 MHz, and for CAT5 UTP, it's 100 MHz.

One other observation can be made of Figure 2-31. At higher frequencies, or data rates, the impedance will **integrate** the data signals. The extent of integration is determined by the **time constant** (TC) of the circuit; in particular, that of the capacitor and characteristic impedance. When the width of the signal—a square wave—is equal to the time constant, there is little integration. But, when the width of the data signal is much shorter, integration is severe and the data signal is heavily distorted.

Don't leave unused copper cables dangling in the air. Terminate them properly.

Intersymbol Interference

The reactive components of cables cause **Intersymbol Interference** (ISI).

The combined effects of distributed inductance and capacitance and the characteristic impedance causes the ISI type of distortion. ISI is produced by a long charge or discharge of reactive components. The effect on a data signal is illustrated in Figure 2-32.

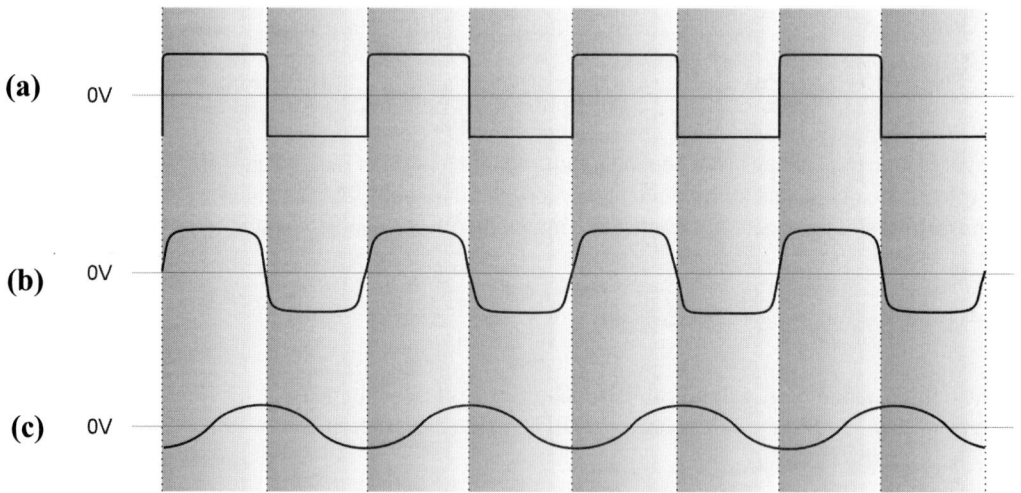

Figure 2-32 Effects Of Intersymbol Interference on Data Signals

In Figure 2-32(a), the corners of the square wave are slightly rounded. A binary signal propagating through a properly terminated line may arrive at the receiver with this mild amount of distortion. Circuitry at the receiver can return the signal to its original condition of sharp, clean edges. In Figure 2-32(b), the square wave has rounded corners and it's also been **phase shifted**.

Recall that a capacitor and inductor produce voltage and current phase shifts. In most transmission lines, the phase angle characteristics of the capacitor predominates, causing the line current to lead line voltage by some amount of time. The line-induced phase shifts can cause quite a few problems in a system in which the data is phase modulating a carrier.

In many cases, the receiver will have difficulty discerning where a data bit begins and ends. As components of the square wave shift, some harmonic frequencies will travel faster through the line than others but will arrive at the receiver with similar amplitudes. The delays cause the bits to run together. The worst case appears to the receiver, as shown in Figure 2-32(c). Here, the cumulative effects of ISI have severely degraded the data bits of Figure 2-32(a) so that a receiver will no doubt be unable to differentiate a logic 1 from a logic 0. Not only have the bits been shifted in time but the BPS rate is high compared to the reactive time constants, so that the inductor and capacitor do not have time to discharge before the next data bit occurs.

> ISI is the blurring together of data bits. It's most noticeable in narrow bandwidth channels, as in telephone networks, and increases with data rates.

In a digital system, it's not very important how much distortion an individual bit receives (since the wave shape is easily restored) as is the specific **segregation** of logic 1's and 0's. ISI blurs the segregation between bits. A square wave requires a considerable amount of bandwidth. If the bandwidth is limited to begin with, maintaining distinct logic levels is even more difficult. If, in Figure 2-32(c), the receiver interpreted a logic 0 as 0-volts dc, it would decipher this data stream as continuous logic 1's.

The amount of ISI can be determined by evaluating the **eye pattern** of data bits with an oscilloscope. The scope is set to trigger on the edge of each bit with the time base adjusted so that one bit is displayed on the scope screen. A normal eye pattern appears as in Figure 2-33(a). By having the scope trigger on each data bit, a series of bits are superimposed one on each other. If the internal scope trigger won't do this, use an external trigger taken from the data bits. The pattern shown in the figure shows four bits. Notice the corners of the bits are slightly rounded, and all of the bits are of similar amplitudes. In this transmission channel, the bandwidth is adequate for the data rate since the square-wave corners are not severely rounded, indicating that the higher frequency harmonics have not been attenuated.

The frequency components have also maintained their proper phase position, as indicated by the trigger. The scope triggers at the start of the data bit; if the bit components had been phase shifted, some portion of the bit would delay from other portions.

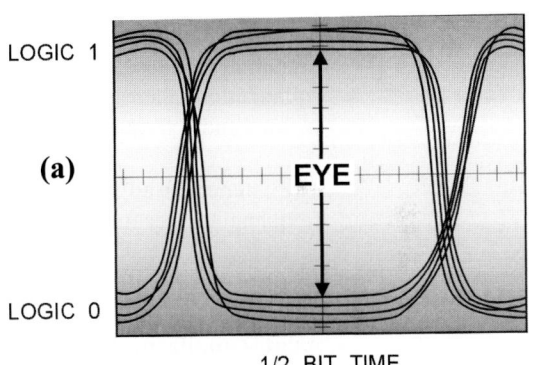

Figure 2-33 **Evaluating the Eye Pattern with an Oscilloscope for ISI Distortion**

Figure 2-33(b) shows a bit stream with ISI. The eye pattern has partially closed. This tells us that some frequencies have been attenuated. The rounded corners indicate that the bandwidth of the circuit is not adequate for the BPS of the bit stream. The narrowness of the eye tells the difference between a logic 1 and a logic 0. If the eye in this figure were to close much further, the receiver probably wouldn't be able to distinguish the binary 1 from a 0. Notice that in Figure 2-33(b), a phase shift is indicated since the bits are offset from the half-bit time. This time is simply one half of the pulse width of the bit. In the example, many components of the bit stream have been delayed due to phase distortion, or **jitter**.

A receiver also evaluates eye patterns by evaluating a sample data stream that is sent ahead of the data. The eye pattern tells the receiver how the cable, or channel, characteristics will affect data bits. The sampling of data bits is called a **training period**. Once the receiver determines how the bits will be affected, it can take measures to compensate for the ISI. The compensation on the part of the receiver is called **equalization**.

Equalization

ISI can be compensated for by equalizing the data stream. An **equalizer** separates signal frequencies through filtering and incorporates phase shifts to counter the effects of the channel.

Equalization of data signals can be related to equalizers used with audio equipment. The equalizer is placed at the receiver and has a series of slide switches that are associated with various audio frequencies.

The listener can adjust the switches so the higher frequencies are attenuated and the lower frequencies over-amplified. The result will be a more bass sound. An **audio equalizer** gives the listener a much greater degree of control to compensate for any weaknesses perceived in the audio.

A **data equalizer** follows a similar approach, except that the compensation is based upon an analysis of data after it has been transmitted through a communication channel. An equalizer is capable of examining each symbol, or bit group, for ISI.

If a receiver (repeater, hub, etc.) could anticipate the amount of each bit's degradation, it would know the bit sequence (knowing what was being transmitted before it was sent), in which case, there would be no point in transmitting the data.

An equalizer's greatest strength lies in its ability to correct phase jitters and frequency attenuation. A block diagram of an equalizer is shown in Figure 2-34. The equalizer consists of filters D1, D2, D3; amplifier A1, A2, A3; and a summing amplifier. Filter D1 is designed to shift a frequency forward by 10 ms; D2 incorporates no forward or delay shifts, and D3 produces a 10ms delay to frequencies falling within its narrow bandpass range.

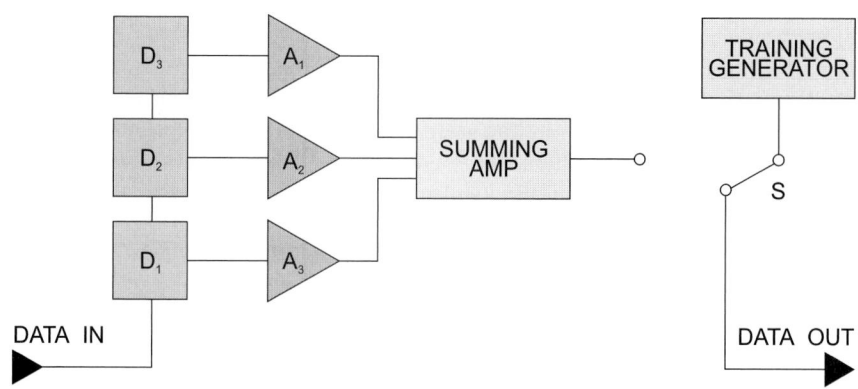

Figure 2-34 Equalizer Block Diagram

As an example of how the equalizer works, two frequency components from a data signal have been identified by the receiver as having been phase distorted by the channel. One frequency has been phase shifted forward by 10 ms and another is phase delayed, also by 10 ms. The equalizer samples the data and extracts a portion of it that has not been phase distorted and uses it as a reference. The reference is applied to filter D2. The frequency that was shifted forward is applied to D3. The D3 filter will delay this component 10 ms. The frequency that was delayed is applied to D1, and D1 shifts it forward 10 ms. The three signals are equally amplified and summed together in the **summing amplifier**. The output of the summing circuit should be a reasonable version of the original data.

The data equalizer described above is placed at the receiver and generally is a part of a modem circuitry as well as intelligent repeaters and hubs. Figure 2-34 contains a training generator. The training generator in a modem either transmits or receives (depending upon whether it is acting as transmitter or receiver) a data stream of alternating 1's and 0's. The receiver analyzes the bits during a training period (about 10ms for a 2,400BPS modem) to determine phase distortion and logic-level noise in a way similar to examining eye patterns with an oscilloscope.

Once the training period is ended, logic circuits in the equalizer activate the appropriate filtering action and any data received is equalized accordingly. Unfortunately, if line conditions change during the middle of a transmission, as is frequently the case, the equalizer will not respond to the change. It is left up to error-detection circuits in the receiver to identify problems resulting from spontaneous changes.

The foregoing described equalization at the receiver. If a system designer knows what distortion will occur in a channel, measures can be taken at the transmitter to compensate. The process of compensation at the transmitter is called **pre-equalization**. For example, if it was determined that a channel consistently delays a specific frequency range, these frequencies can be phase shifted forward at the transmitter. In this way, they will arrive at the receiver in phase with other frequencies. Pre-equalization at the transmitter and equalization at the receiver are common functions of high-speed modems.

A more sophisticated method of equalizing data is the use of an **adaptive equalizer**. An adaptive equalizer constantly samples and evaluates data for ISI. If a change occurs in the data transmission, the adaptive equalizer compensates for it. This overcomes the disadvantage of the equalizers discussed earlier, where, once the transmission begins, spontaneous problems are not compensated for.

Adaptive equalization adds expense and complexity to a data communication system. A signal that has been conditioned with an adaptive equalizer is also difficult to evaluate from a troubleshooting standpoint, because it may have very little resemblance to the square waves associated with digital logic. In satellite systems, signals have a tendency to ether fade or arrive at the receiver as an echo. The adaptive equalizer will identify fading or echoes as they happen and will generate the appropriate phase shifts.

ENCODING

Encoding is the process of physically manipulating data. ASCII and EBCDIC are common examples of encoding. An **alphanumeric character** is encoded in a format that can be processed by a machine—the format in this example is binary.

The ASCII character may be further encoded to allow for compensation of phase differences or the effects of reactive components in a channel. In the previous section, the problems caused by intersymbol interference were discussed with a particular emphasis placed upon data distortion caused by phase, or frequency delays. Once the delays and forward frequency shifts were accounted for, the data signal was equalized so that all components of the signal could be processed by the receiver.

ISI is also responsible for another type of distortion called **dc shift**, which is a gradually increasing line voltage caused by channel reactance. It happens because of the charge and discharge of the line capacitance and inductance, and is especially a problem when long strings of 0's or 1's are transmitted. If several thousand logic 0's are transmitted, the average line voltage will charge in accordance to the charging rate of the distributed line capacitance, and eventually settle at a steady-state, or dc, value.

A long series of 0's may be transmitted, but the receiver could interpret them as logic 1's due to the dc component. For this reason, the logic levels of EIA/TIA-232 should be spaced as far apart as possible.

Figure 2-35 shows the letter "A" being transmitted in ASCII. The dc shift has been greatly exaggerated to illustrate the confusion the distortion can cause at the receiver. Notice there is not an immediate transition from the logic 1 at bit 1 to the logic 0 at bit 2. The receiver may very well interpret bit 2 as a logic 1 rather than a logic 0. The reactance is nearly discharged at bit 5, but bit 6 is a logic 1. The data rate here is much faster than the channel is capable of responding to, and a logic 1 at bit 6 does not quite develop before the channel is driven to a low at bit 7. The receiver will likely garble the original message due to the distortion of dc shift.

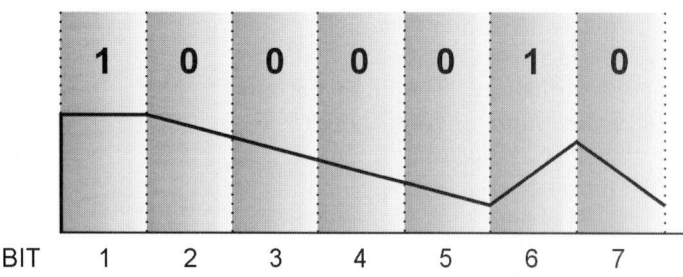

Figure 2-35 ASCII Character "A" Distorted by dc Level Shift

In many communication systems, the receiver and transmitter maintain proper clock timing through a clock **synchronization pulse**. Ordinarily, this synch pulse is the edge of the data bits. If the synch pulse is lost to the receiver, it can signal to the transmitter to send the data again. But if a portion of the transmitted message contains several thousand 0's, there will not be a bit edge for the receiver to lock on to for an extended period of time. The receiver will signal the transmitter that it has lost the data, the transmitter will send it again, and the receiver will once again lose the data on the long run of logic 0's. As you can see, this network would effectively crash.

Data bits are encoded to alleviate the ISI problems just described. Most encoding schemes are structured to continuously alternate the bits so that the channel will not charge to a dc value. In many data systems, dc voltages are prohibited by the type of equipment used. For example, a channel may be coupled to the receiver by a transformer that has been installed as an impedance matching device. The transformer will not pass a dc voltage, and any dc values contained in the transmission will be blocked from the receiver. In a system containing ac-only components-like a transformer—data encoding is a necessity.

> Codes that eliminate ISI and dc drift are **Nonreturn To Zero**, **Manchester** and **Alternate Mark Inversion**.

Nonreturn To Zero (NRZ), Manchester, and Alternate Mark Inversion (AMI) are common encoding methods, and each will be described in the following sections.

Nonreturn to Zero (NRZ)

NRZ encoding may be unipolar or bipolar, as shown in Figure 2-36.

CNST OBJECTIVE
I-A

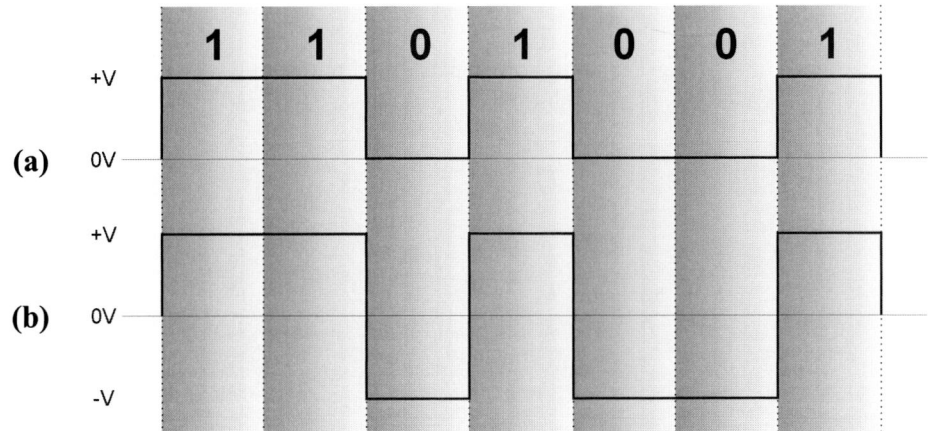

Figure 2-36 Unipolar and Bipolar NRZ Encoding

Unipolar NRZ, shown in Figure 2-36(a), is the type of encoding found in situations where transmission runs are short and there is little noise to interfere with the data bits. A good example would be inside of a computer when square waves are transmitted between integrated circuits or PC boards. Data encoded with unipolar NRZ assigns a positive dc voltage to logic 1's and 0 volts to logic 1's. Within a computer, the logic 1's are generally +5 V and the logic 0's are 0V. This type of encoding does very little in addressing ISI problems and dc shift. In fact, if unipolar NRZ is coupled through a transformer have data will, at a minimum, be heavily distorted.

If a long string of logic 0's or 1's are transmitted through a long transmission line, the line will gradually charge to the average value of the dc. Also, timing synchronization will be lost between long bit runs of logic 1's and 0's.

Bipolar NRZ, shown in Figure 2-36(b), offers a little better performance. Logic 1's are assigned a positive voltage while logic 0's are represented by a negative voltage. If a data transmission contained an equal number of logic 1's and 0's, the average line voltage would be 0 V, and there would not be any dc shift. But the probability of adjacent bits being the same (a logic 1 followed by another logic 1) is much greater than having the bits consistently alternating between 1 and 0. If a long string of 1's or 0's are transmitted, bipolar NRZ will generate a dc shift as well as lose clock timing between the transmitter and receiver. These problems are the same as was found with unipolar NRZ, but because of the use of opposite polarity voltages used with bipolar NRZ, it consumes 50% less power than unipolar NRZ.

NRZ gets its name from the fact that the line voltage does not go to 0V between adjacent bits. Notice that the two logic-1 bits at the left hold the line in the high state. This can cause trouble in asynchronous channels because the line is held in the **mark**, or positive voltage, state during the time between transmission. Since the line will charge to the average value of the voltage, it may not immediately respond to a logic 0 when it is transmitted.

Manchester II

Manchester II, or **biphase**, encoding is a popular encoding scheme since it eliminates the loss of clock signals as well as dc shift. Manchester II is shown in Figure 2-37.

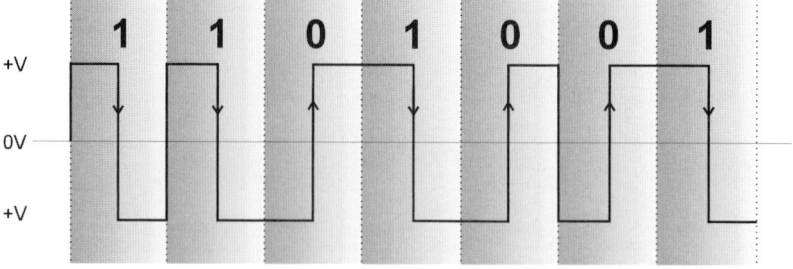

Figure 2-37 Manchester II Encoding

The logic bits are represented by the transition occurring in the middle of a bit; a logic 0 is represented by a low-to-high transition occurring in the middle of the bit. As you can see, there will never be a gradual increase in the line voltage because the voltage changes with each bit. In an asynchronous line, when the channel is held in the mark condition between transmissions, the channel voltage will continuously alternate as in an ac signal. The predictable alternations provide a ready-made clock signal for maintaining synchronization between the receiver and transmitter. Since the encoded data has the characteristics of an ac voltage, it will not be blocked or garbled by ac devices like transformers.

While Manchester II solves the problems of dc shift and loss of clock signals, it does so at the price of requiring twice as much bandwidth as does NRZ. The wider bandwidth is needed because each bit is represented by +V and –V, or two states, whereas an NRZ bit is either +V or –V, but not both. The mid-bit transitions of Manchester II encoding effectively doubles the signaling rate, which necessitates doubling the bandwidth.

Alternate Mark Inversion (AMI)

AMI is an encoding technique popular with long-distance digital telephone systems. It is illustrated in Figure 2-38. Logic 0's are represented by 0V while a logic 1 is represented by alternating the line voltage between +V and –V. AMI prevents dc shift due to the alternation from +V and –V for the 1 bits. Loss of timing between the receiver and the transmitter can occur for long 0-bit runs, but not for extended transmissions of logic 1's.

AMI is actually a variation of NRZ, except that the line voltage is permitted to return to 0V for logic 0's. It improves upon the clock-timing performance of NRZ as well as drastically reducing dc shift. Notice that the logic 1 pulses are only half as wide as the prescribed bit times. By reducing the transmitted 0, the **duty cycle** of AMI is 50%. This means the data is transmitted using

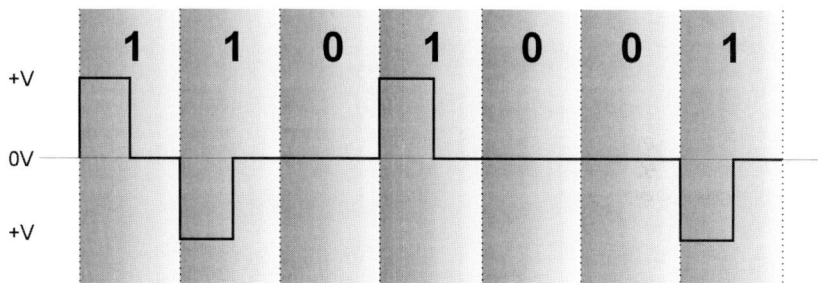

Figure 2-38 Alternate Mark Inversion Encoding

50% less energy which results in a significant power savings. The long-distance carriers find AMI attractive because all the power consumed in the telephone system is provided (or purchased) by the long-distance company. AMI saves money for these companies while simultaneously eliminating or reducing dc shift and timing problems.

NOISE AND DISTORTION

Noise can be defined as any interference that causes a signal to deviate from its normal structure. This deviation from normal is commonly called **distortion**. Intersymbol interference is distortion that can disable an entire network. The effects of noise (distortion) on individual data bits, data frames, as well as on the complete network, is of vital concern. At a minimum, an error is generated, and in the worst case the network may become inoperable.

In the sections to follow, various types of noise are discussed along with techniques for measuring noise and distortion. In many cases, distortion is measured with respect to reference levels of power, voltage, or current, and described as a decibel that is above or below the reference. For this reason, decibels will be reviewed before describing the various types of noise affecting data signals.

Decibels

A **decibel** (dB) describes the exponential way in which the ear responds to sound. Over the years, dBs have come to be used as a standard for evaluating the signal quality of electronic waveforms in general, and in particular, the gain or loss of signal strength.

You may recall that dBs (a dB is a tenth of a Bel, and is named after Alexander Bell, which is why the "B" is capitalized in "dB") are derived from converting an electronic relationship to a logarithmic relationship. Logarithms are intended to simplify the arithmetic involved with exponents. In fact, a common logarithm (log) is the exponent of any Base 10 number. The following illustrates examples of **common logs**:

$$10^4 = 10,000 = \text{a log of } 4$$
$$10^3 = 1,000 = \text{a log of } 3$$
$$10^2 = 100 = \text{a log of } 2$$
$$10^1 = 10 = \text{a log of } 1$$
$$10^0 = 1 = \text{a log of } 0$$
$$10^{-1} = .1 = \text{a log of } -1$$
$$10^{-2} = .01 = \text{a log of } -2$$
$$10^{-3} = .001 = \text{a log of } -3$$
$$10^{-4} = .0001 = \text{a log of } -4$$

Common logs have the number 10 as a base. A common log, then, represents the number of times that the number 10 has been multiplied by itself, along with any fractional amounts of 10. For example, the log of 144 = 2.15836. The log represents the number of times ten must be multiplied by itself to equal 144. Common logs are integrated with decibels in the following formula:

$$dB = 10 \log (Po/Pi)$$

where Po = Power out and Pi = Power in. The following examples show how dBs are used.

Example 1

An amplifier has an input power of 10 mW (milliWatts) and a power out of 20 mW. Calculate the **gain** in decibels.

$$dB = 10 \log (Po/Pi)$$
$$dB = 10 \log (20 \text{ mW}/10 \text{ mW})$$
$$dB = 10 \log (2)$$
$$dB = 10 (.3)$$
$$dB = 3$$

Example 2

The power received through a transmission line is .25 mW. Using decibels, evaluate the performance of the line if the power at the transmitter is 1 mW.

Notice in the first example, the power from input to output doubled for a gain of 3 dBs. With each doubling of the power, the dB gain will increase by a factor of 3. So, if Po = 40 mW in example 1, the dB gain will be 6.

$$dB = 10 \log (Po/Pi)$$
$$dB = 10 \log (.25 \text{ mW}/1 \text{ mW})$$
$$dB = 10 (-.6)$$
$$dB = -6$$

In the second example, the power at the receiver was less than the power transmitted. A **loss** of signal strength is indicated by a negative dB. It is sometimes difficult, as in example 2, to determine what is Po and what is Pi. If you are unsure, it is usually helpful to draw a rough sketch of the problem and label it according to what is given. As dBs increase by three for each doubling of the power, they also decrease by three each time the power is halved, as in example 2. The amount of received power is one fourth of the transmitted power; consequently, −6 dB represents the loss of signal strength. Signals for a particular frequency are often compared to a **reference level**. One milliwatt (mW) is a common audio and telephone industry reference. For example, a telephone transmission channel may exhibit a 6-dB loss. What is the value of the signal strength?

$$dB = 10 \log (Po/Pi)$$
$$-6 dB = 10 \log (x/1 \text{ mW})$$
$$-.6 dB = \log (x/1 \text{ mW})$$
$$.25 = x/1 \text{ mW}$$
$$.25 \text{ mW} = x = Po$$

When solving for one of the unknown power levels, begin with the basic decibel formula, fill in the given values, and solve for the unknown. The following examples should help to clarify the use of decibels.

Example 3

A **power amplifier** has 5-dB gain referenced to 6 mW. What is the output power?

$$dB = 10 \log (Po/Pi)$$
$$5 \ dB = 10 \log (Po/6 \ mW)$$
$$.5 \ dB = \log (Po/6 \ mW)$$
$$\text{Inverse log } .5 = Po/6 \ mW$$
$$3.16 = Po/6 \ mW$$
$$18.96 \ mW = Po$$

Example 4

A data signal is permitted no more than 1 dB of **attenuation**, or loss, from transmitter to receiver. You measure the transmitter power at 24.2 mW and the power received at 19.5 mW. Is this an acceptable amount of attenuation?

$$dB = 10 \log (Po/Pi)$$
$$dB = 10 \log (19.5 \ mW/24.2 \ mW)$$
$$dB = 10 \log (.806)$$
$$dB = 10 \ (-.0936)$$
$$dB = -.936$$

The signal loss in this example is acceptable.

Decibels are used to express the ratio of many values. But a dB is significant only when referenced to some agreed upon value. For example, it is meaningless to say a twisted-pair cable has 4 dBs of loss.

If it is understood the loss is referenced to 1 mW, then the -4 dB is of practical value, because an indication is given of the severity of the loss. If a reference hasn't been agreed upon, then -4 dB could represent a loss from 100 W or from 10 mW. A 10mW loss would cause very few problems in a twisted-pair line, but a 100W loss would mean the line isn't functioning.

In a local network, power loss is a symptom, not a root cause of problems. If the power level of a data stream has degraded, and all segment lengths are within specification (described in Chapter 6), the problem isn't likely to be the cable. Look for faulty transceivers in the network interface cards (NIC), hub malfunctions, or power supply problems in the PC nodes.

Atmospheric Noise

Atmospheric noise results from **lightning**, solar activity and stellar radiation.

The static that results from lightning during thunderstorms is classified as atmospheric noise. It distorts radio and television signals for a few milliseconds, and is a nuisance in these situations, but usually doesn't disrupt the entire communication system. In data communications, a few milliseconds can represent hundreds of data bits which could include several sentences of text.

Microwave communications forms the basis of satellite systems, and is used extensively in the telephone industry. A bolt of lightning releases vast amounts of energy into the surrounding atmosphere, and the energy radiates from the lightning source. As the radiated energy cuts any material capable of conducting electricity, a voltage is induced into the conductor, and the resulting current obliterates any signals that happen to be traveling through the conductor at the time.

In addition to lightning, **sunspot activity** creates atmospheric noise. On the sun, a sunspot is an explosion that releases a tremendous amount of energy which travels through the solar system, striking the Earth, and creating noise in a way similar to lightning strikes. Sunspots are cyclical, occurring about every 11 years, and can therefore be anticipated. Lightning is unpredictable, and the best solution for dealing with it is one of prevention: shielding of transmission lines is the usual remedy, and the extensive use of an **Uninterruptable Power Supply** (UPS) to support the system with battery power when the ac line voltage is down.

Fortunately, most solar noise is attenuated by the Earth's atmosphere and doesn't reach the surface. Since satellites don't have the benefit of the atmosphere to shield them, they're the most susceptible to sunspot noise, and to a barrage of noise emanating from the distant stars.

Impulse Noise

> Impulse noise is sporadic and of short duration, usually caused by periodic use of electro-mechanical equipment or from a **glitch** that occasionally appears.

Mechanical switches, motors, generators, and engine ignition systems all contribute to the distortion of data bits, and are collectively called "impulse noise". It's generally of short duration and in close proximity to the affected data system.

The most troublesome aspect of impulse noise is locating the source of it. The source could be a few feet away or it could be hundreds of feet. It may be a mobile source such as a portable generator or motor, or a device that's rarely activated, such as a flood pump. The simplest solution for impulse noise is to avoid installing networking equipment near devices that may radiate interfering noise. Impulse noise is of very short duration but capable of the highest intensity levels. It will jam data signals completely, but usually for less than a microsecond.

Frequency Noise

> Frequency noise originates from 60Hz wire, system clocks, or carrier frequencies.

Frequency noise is of a constant time but of variable amplitude. The most common type of frequency noise is the **60 Hz** radiated from fluorescent lights and the associated wiring.

Recall from earlier discussions on the electrical characteristics of cables that they act as lowpass filters. The cable's distributed capacitance offers a high capacitive reactance to lower frequencies, making those frequencies available at the load. Realizing the problems of 60 Hz and 120 Hz (from **full-wave rectification** in power supplies), data communication systems are designed to have a lower **cutoff frequency**, above 200 Hz. For example, audio frequencies below 300 Hz are blocked from telephone channels to avoid 60 Hz interference.

Within digital communication equipment, **system clock** frequencies can also distort data signals. The solution in this situation involves the careful placement of clock generators in the equipment, and avoiding paralleling the clock printed-circuit board runs with data signal runs. Another solution involves the frequency separation between the clock and data signal.

Crosstalk

Crosstalk is the electro-magnetic induction (transmitted noise) that results from **unshielded cables** laying in parallel.

Each cable acts as a transmitter and a receiver to/from the cable next to it. The earlier example of the clock signal interfering with data signals illustrates the problem of crosstalk. You may have been talking on the telephone and have heard another conversation. Crosstalk is a frequent problem in the telephone system because hundreds of cables may run in parallel. The energy from a cable radiates and cuts across adjacent cables inducing a signal into them. While crosstalk in a telephone conversation is annoying, it generally doesn't prevent you from continuing your own conversation. But crosstalk between data signals can blur the distinction between logic levels and introduce a considerable error component into data.

Shielding is the common solution to crosstalk. Each cable can be shielded, as is the case with coaxial cable, or a bundle of cable may be shielded. The unfortunate effect of shielding is that it raises costs and consumes space. Due to the costs involved in shielding, other alternatives have been examined. For example, category 5 UTP has all but eliminated crosstalk of parallel network cables. However, these same data lines may induce a signal into voice cables if run side by side with them. This is why it's not a good idea to connect unused network UTP to voice circuits such as telephone extensions. The next section describes an effective method for obscuring noise.

Noise Analysis

It's one thing to have noise present in a communication system, and another to determine the extent of the problem resulting from noise. In many situations, the noise induced into communication channels can be prevented through shielding, changing the physical positions of interacting signals, by conditioning a channel, or with the use of equalizers. Or, the noise can be ignored. Ignoring the noise, or taking no action, is a common technique and, certainly, the cheapest remedy. Ignoring noise is effective when the desired signal is much stronger than the offending noise. Two common methods are used to analyze the strength of the desired signal to the noise: **Signal-to-Noise Ratio** (SNR) and **Noise Factor** (NF). Both calculations provide an indication of the relative signal strength. If the signal is large compared to the noise, the noise is often ignored.

How large the difference can be varies with the application. Table 2-3 lists several acceptable SNRs. For any application, SNRs will decrease with bandwidth, source impedance, lack of shielding, increases in temperature, and increasing data rates.

Noise and distortion is expressed in **decibels**. The decibel results from the ratio of an actual value to a reference value. Reference values for data communications are 1mW and 6mW.

An analysis of noise can be found by calculating the signal to noise ratio.

Table 2-3 Typical SNRs of Communication Channels

CHANNEL	SNR
Digital Communication	40 dB
Voice Telephone Channel	35 dB
Video Channel	50 dB
Microwave Systems	10 dB

The signal-to-noise ratio is a measure of the desired signal power to the noise signal power at the same point in a circuit. It's expressed mathematically as:

$$SNR = Ps/Pn$$

where Ps = the power of the desired signal and Pn = the power of the noise. It's often expressed in decibels as:

$$SNR = 10 \log (Ps/Pn)$$

For example, if the SNR is to be determined at the output of a transmitter, and the signal level is determined to be 2 mW and the noise is 500 μW, the SNR is:

$$SNR = 2 \text{ mW}/.5 \text{ mW}$$
$$SNR = 4$$

or, as a decibel:

$$SNR = 10 \log (Ps/Pn)$$
$$SNR = 10 \log (2 \text{ mW}/.5 \text{ mW})$$
$$SNR = 10 \log (4)$$
$$SNR = 10 (.602) \text{ dB}$$
$$SNR = 6 \text{ dB}$$

The SNR defines the amount of noise found in a signal at a given point—as at the transmitter output in the example above—but it doesn't give an indication of how much noise is picked up from the transmitter to receiver; that is, the amount of noise acquired across a cable run.

> Noise factor (NF) is another method of analyzing noise, and is a more useful calculation for analyzing the noise characteristics of a system or device. It's the ratio of signal-to-noise at the system's input to the signal-to-noise at its output.

Noise factor is calculated as:

$$NF = 10 \log ((Si/Ni)/(So/No))$$

where Si/Ni is the signal-to-noise ratio at the input, and So/No is the signal-to-noise ratio at the output.

For example, the NF of a transmission line is to be calculated. The signal level at the transmitter is 22 mW and the noise level is 1 mW. At the receiver, the signal level has dropped to 18.5 mW and the noise increased to 2.25 mW.

$$NF = 10 \log ((Si/Ni)/(So/No))$$
$$NF = 10 \log ((22 \text{ mW}/1 \text{ mW})/(18.5 \text{ mW}/2.25 \text{ mW}))$$
$$NF = 10 \log (22/8.22)$$
$$NF = 10 \log (2.676)$$
$$NF = 10 (.427) \text{ dB}$$
$$NF = 4.27 \text{ dB}$$

The SNR and NF are important to data communications because each provides an indication of the performance of the **communications system**. Specifically, they provide general information about the number of errors likely to be generated by the noise. The greater the S/N or NF, the fewer errors will occur. Why? Figure 2-39(a) shows a data stream with no noise, and at 2-39(b), the same data that's been distorted with large-amplitude noise.

The amplitude of the noise may be of sufficient amplitude that the receiver will interpret it as a logic 1 rather than a logic 0. In Figure 2-39(c), the level of noise is drastically reduced. At this level, the receiver will appropriately ignore it and interpret it as a logic 0.

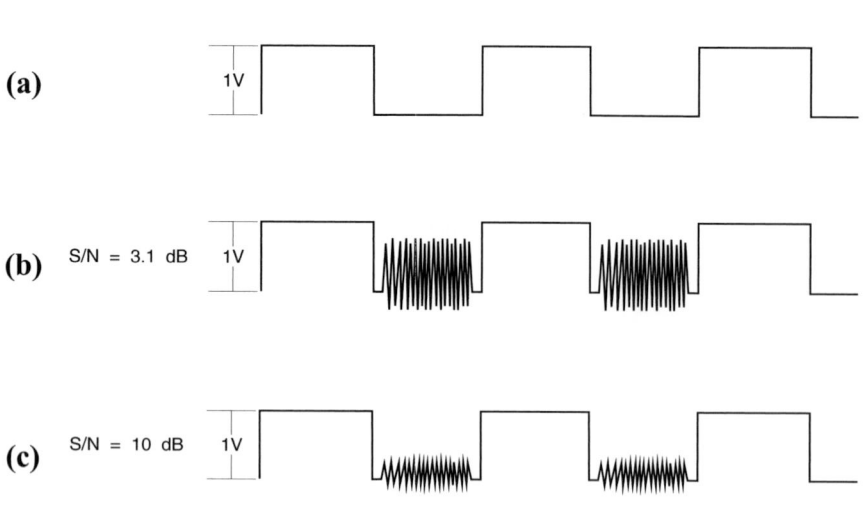

Figure 2-39 Noise and Distortion Contribute to Data Errors

Earlier, it was stated that noise is sometimes ignored. If the volume of noise is small compared to the signal strength, then ignoring it offers a realistic solution. A SNR of 40 dB in a digital data communication system will introduce about 5 errors for each one million bits. Most error detection schemes will detect errors occurring at that rate, so an attempt to decrease the noise further may be a questionable exercise for most applications.

ERROR CONTROL

Once data leaves a transmitter, it enters the rather nebulous region known as the **communication channel**. The channel is composed of the path between transmitter and receiver. Just about anything could happen to the data bits while traveling through the communication channel. The data could experience severe harmonic distortion, and arrive at the receiver as a jumbled group of bits and pieces of the original data. A thunderstorm could obscure critical pieces of the data message, or the logic levels could be so distorted that the receiver can't decipher the original message.

A bit here and there may become inverted resulting in data that looks right but doesn't make any sense. Finally, the data may not make it to the receiver at all. A relay somewhere along the path could trip and send the message to points unknown. How does the receiver even know if the received bits are accurate replicas of the bits that were transmitted?

Error control is the segment of data communications responsible for detecting errors, and in some cases, corrected them. The details of error control are analyzed in Chapter 8, but a basic understanding will be needed for the next section, as well as the following chapters.

The premise of detecting errors lies in the redundancy of binary bits. Digital logic is either high or low. This is convenient for developing a mechanism that counts bits, then adds bits to the count, counts them again, adds more bits, counts the bits, adds bits, etc. Since a bit stream is composed of only a 1's or 0's, there are only two numerical states to keep track of.

If a receiver constantly adds bits to a previous count of data bits, and then makes a comparison to what the expected count is versus the actual count, any missing—or extra—data bits will be discovered. Any error-detecting schemes that redundantly counts data bits in a never ending cycle is called a **Cyclic Redundancy Check** (CRC). A CRC is a complex technique, but it's quite effective at detecting errors. Since it has a high success rate, it's a very common technique used with the more advanced frame format protocols.

A simpler, but also very common, technique is **parity**. In a less sophisticated manner than CRC, parity makes use of redundancy to detect an error. The detection technique adds a parity bit to a data word, giving each word either an even or odd number of total bits.

Most all data communication systems utilize error control. It follows then, that there are two types of parity checks: **even parity** and **odd parity**.

Even Parity

Even parity is shown in Figure 2-40(a).

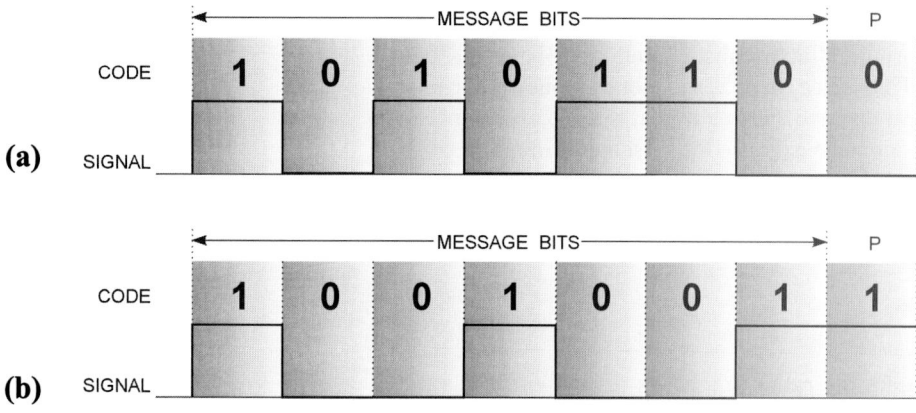

Figure 2-40 Even Parity

An asynchronous, 7-bit data word is shown, along with a parity bit. With even parity, the number of logic 1's in the data word are counted, and if the count is an even number, the parity bit is made a logic 0. If the number of bits in the data word is an odd number, the parity bit is made a logic 1. In other words, the parity bit is set to either a 1 or 0 so that when added to the word count, the total number of logic 1's is an even number.

The second example of even parity is shown in Figure 2-40(b). Count the number of logic 1's in the data word, and check for yourself to see that the parity bit has been set so that the total number of logic 1's is an even number.

Odd Parity

Odd parity is nearly identical to even parity, except the parity bit is selected so that when added to the number of logic 1's in the data word, the total amount of logic 1's will be an odd number. Notice in Figure 2-41(a), the data word has four logic 1's. The parity bit is made high to give a total logic 1 bit count of 5, for odd parity.

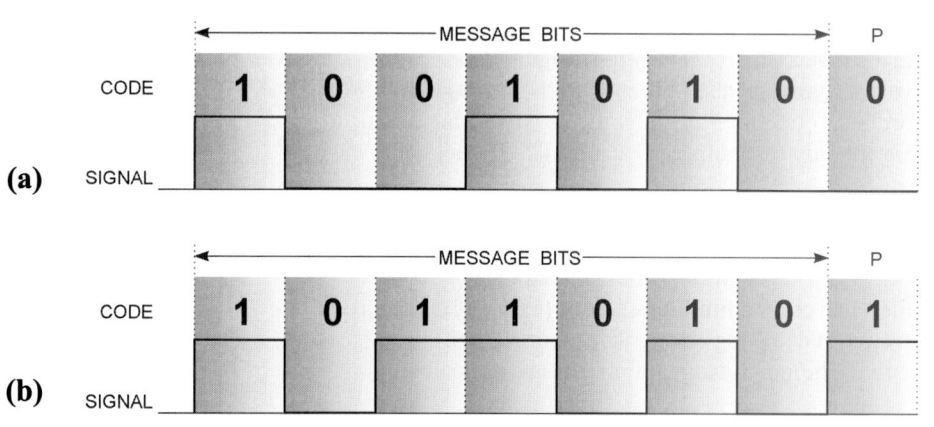

Figure 2-41 Odd Parity

A second example of odd parity is shown in Figure 2-41(b). As you did for even parity, count the logic 1's in the data word and check the parity to ensure that the total bit count is an odd number.

Parity doesn't correct errors, and it doesn't tell the receiver which bit is in error. Variations of parity have been designed to identify the corrupted bits, and to correct them. But for the purposes of providing a quick check for errors in situations where the tolerance for error is wide, parity is hard to beat because it's easy to implement. It's a common error-detection technique used in **asynchronous communications** between a personal computer and a printer.

If a **parity error** is detected, the receiver sends a command to the transmitting device to retransmit. If a printer detects a parity error, it will tell the computer it didn't get the last character and the computer will send it again. If the printer doesn't calculate a parity error, it will inform the computer that the character was received successfully. Even in the most sophisticated error-detection systems, the receiving device usually asks the transmitter to send the message again.

This is frequently done because it's often cheaper and less time consuming to retransmit, than to find the offending bit and correct an error. Once the error has been detected and corrected, there's still a margin of error. This is because the receiver can't know for sure if the problem was resolved, without comparing the corrected data to the original, errorless data. But, in order to do that, the receiver would need to "know" what the transmitter actually transmitted. If it knew that, there would be no need to detect and correct the error in the first place, much less transmit the data.

DATA CONVERSION

Data is frequently converted from analog to digital, and from digital to analog.

Not all data flowing through network cabling originates from computers. Voice communication, for example, originates as an analog waveform, and is ultimately converted to digital at some point in the huge telephone network. Modems routinely convert digital data into analog data in order to send it across telco lines. Hundreds of industrial applications begin as analog measurements which are converted to digital for ease-of-use through networks, and then converted back to analog for the end-application. Nearly all process control techniques require the conversion of analog and digital data.

This section describes basic analog-to-digital and digital-to-analog technologies. As networking professionals, we would be imposing tunnel vision on our ability to service the industry if we focused only on digital office settings.

It's often necessary to convert an analog signal into a digital format to be processed by a computer. Temperature or fluid monitoring, in process control, are examples of analog signals. Since most data processing equipment is digital, these signals must be converted to digital. The conversion may take place at the source of the signal, or it may be transmitted as analog data and converted to digital at the computer port. The digital signal may be converted back to an analog waveform at another point.

Figure 2-42 shows an example of an **Analog-to-Digital Converter** (ADC), data acquisition equipment, and a reconversion from digital to analog. The thermocouple is a transducer that converts a change in temperature to a corresponding voltage change. This analog voltage is then applied to the ADC where it's converted into a digital signal and sent to the data acquisition system. Data acquisition devices are generally small computers that process data by performing calculations, making comparisons, generating error-correction signals or provide a visual display of the process via a CRT screen.

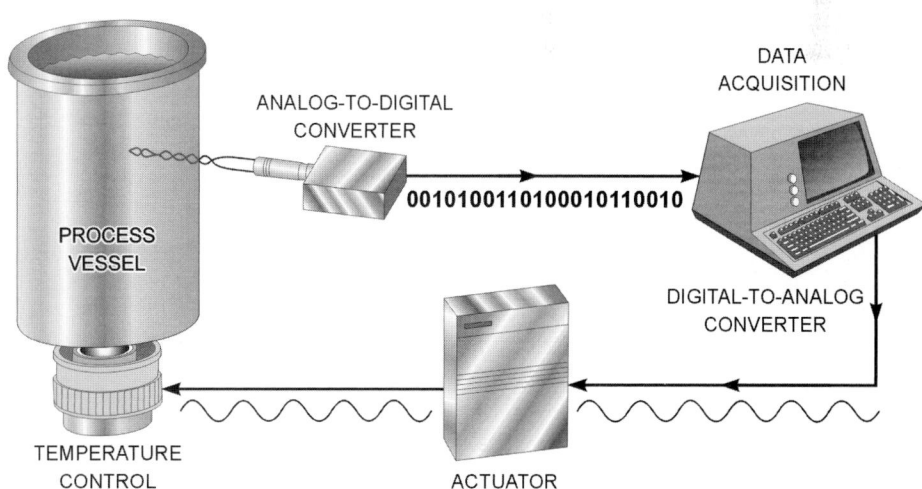

Figure 2-42 Analog Voltage Thermocoupler

In this example, an error signal is generated at the output of the data acquisition system, applied to a **Digital-to-Analog Converter** (DAC) and used to control an actuator. The actuator varies the temperature of the process being monitored. As the temperature at the thermocouple varies above and below a desired setting, the actuator will increase or decrease the temperature based on data received from the thermocouple.

An ADC and DAC interface dissimilar signals between the analog nature of the physical world and the digital signals of digital data processing equipment. DACs and ADCs are used extensively in industrial settings as well as in the telephone industry.

Digital-to-Analog Conversion

A digital to analog converter produces an analog signal in response to a binary value. A DAC is described by the number of binary bits used to represent a **discrete** analog value. For example, a 3-bit DAC can represent 2 to the exponent of 3, or 8 points over the range of an analog signal. A 3-bit DAC is illustrated in Figure 2-43.

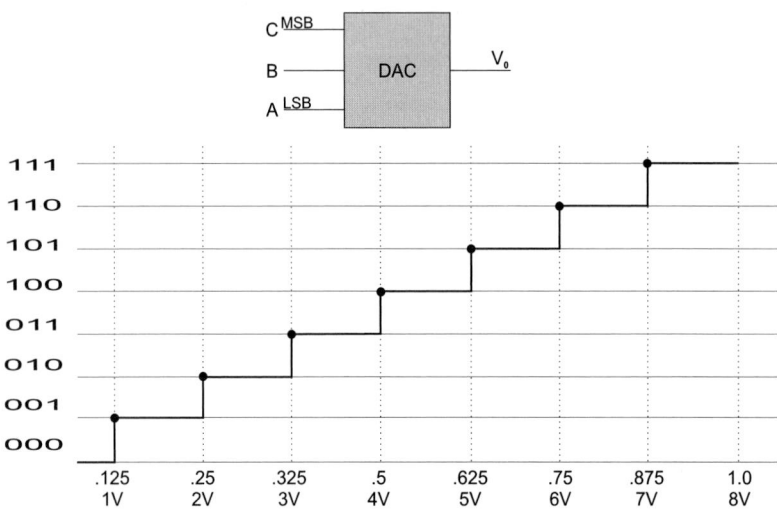

Figure 2-43 3-Bit DAC

The output of the DAC is a **staircase waveform**. Each step of the staircase is equal to the weighted value of binary inputs. Notice that for a 3-bit DAC each input is capable of producing a 12.5% change at the output.

If the peak value of the output were 1V, 001 would indicate .125V, 010 = .25V (.125V + .125V = .25V), 011 = .375V. Each binary value has a resolution of .125V. This means that 000 will be used to represent an analog value of less than .125V. For the range .125V to .25V, 001 is the binary value used. The disadvantage is that 001 = .129V as well as .2V; the 3-bit DAC would not be able to distinguish between the two.

The **resolution** of a DAC is the smallest change in output voltage produced by a change of the binary input. In the 3-bit DAC, each change of binary input produced a .125V change at the output, so it has a resolution of .125V. A 4-bit DAC has 2 to the exponent of 4, or 16 different values for each binary input, and a 16 bit DAC will produce 65,536 values on the output. The resolution is sometimes expressed as a percentage:

$$\% \text{ resolution } = 100 \ (1/2^n - 1)$$

where n = number of different levels produced by the binary inputs. As an example, the percent of resolution of a 16-bit DAC is:

$$\% \text{ resolution} = 100 \ (1/2^n - 1)$$
$$= 100 \ (1/2^{16} - 1)$$
$$= 100 \ (.0000152)$$
$$= .00152\%$$

The percent of resolution of the 3-bit DAC of Figure 2-43 is about 14.5%. The better the resolution, the more accurate will be the analog signal at the output. But a high-resolution DAC costs more and results in greater circuit complexity. For the most part, the resolution of DACs are specified by the number of bits at the input to the DAC. The higher bit value, the better the resolution.

As mentioned earlier, a DAC invariably introduces an error into the reproduced analog signal. In Figure 2-43, 001 is used to represent any value between .125V. and .375V. The error produced by the ranges encompassed by the binary values is called **quantization error**. The quantization error is directly related to resolution and is described as +1 least significant bit or as 1/2 least significant bit.

A DAC is used at the output of a modem to facilitate the transmission of data across the analog phone lines. Since the data flowing out of a computer is digital, and many phone lines are analog, the binary information must be converted to analog before being transmitted through the phone system. It may go through many conversions before it's finally converted back to digital at the receiving computer.

Analog-to-Digital Conversion

In a data communication system, information is converted from analog to digital more frequently than from digital to analog. This is true for applications in which some analog signal (voice through the local loop of the telephone network, many industrial settings, as well remote monitoring of incidental and variable information) is performed. The reason for this is that the analog value needs to be evaluated by digital equipment and once that's done, the data is either stored in memory or replaced with current information.

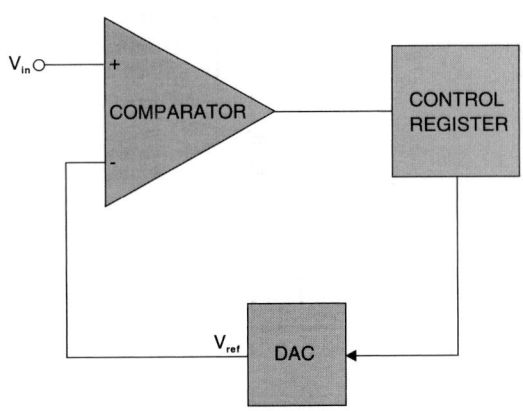

The majority of ADCs include a DAC for referencing the analog input signal. Figure 2-44 illustrates a block diagram of an analog-to-digital converter. The analog input signal is applied to the **comparator** along with the last value of the signal, designated Vref. The output of the comparator is maintained in the **control register** and clocked into the DAC to be converted to a staircase analog signal. The Vin is constantly compared to the previous value of Vin. As Vin changes, the output of the comparator will change, leading to a new value of Vref.

The number of changes represented by the ADC is called the resolution, and is determined in the same fashion as for DACs. The limiting factor in an ADC is the **conversion time**. The conversion time is the time it takes the ADC to achieve full scale and is found by:

Figure 2-44 ADC Block Diagram

$$T_c = (2^n - 1) \, T_{clk}$$

where n = the bit size of the converter, and Tclk = the time used to clock bits to the DAC.

Analog-to-digital converters are available as **IC packages**. The have the same problem of quantization errors as DACs and, like a DAC, can reduce quantization errors by offering higher resolution. It should be pointed out that quantization error is a result of the range of an analog signal embraced by a binary value, but it doesn't provide an indication of the accuracy of the device. Accuracy, in the context of converters, is dependent upon component tolerances, power supply fluctuations and so on.

NETWORK CHANGE CONTROL

Managing a complex network is difficult. Right? Sure it is. Not only do you have to have a reasonable grasp of a mind-numbing number of software packages, you also have to be in possession of a scope of technical details spanning the range from basic electronics and wiring technologies, to complicated—and all too often—customized ICs.

And that's not all. You have to also figure out a labeling scheme for every node wire in the network. Right? Then you have sit in front of a wordprocessor and write a standard operating procedure which describes how to use the scheme you created. Right? And if your boss decides to buy a lightning-fast PC with an ultra-lightning-fast network card, you have to figure out how to implement that change, as well as any other changes and upgrades to the network. Right? And put it all in writing, in a standardized format that's duly approved, dated, and distributed to everyone, particularly those who claim to know the difference between a fiber cable and a rope. Right? Absolutely. Positively. Without a doubt. Because if you don't budget your time and energy to deal with administrative tasks, you're not doing your job. If you don't do it, someone—maybe those claiming to know that difference between fiber and rope—will do it for you.

If you allow that to happen, you're operating the network and no longer managing it. So prepare for, and expect, changes. Decide as soon as possible how changes will be implemented, and commit your plans to documented procedures. An SOP isn't forever. It's a change agent, and should be expected to change as the needs that created it change. However, if you've been instrumental in authoring network procedures, and insist on being on the approval list for all new procedures, along with changes to existing network procedures, you'll retain a credible say-so in the management of the network that you're responsible for.

In this section, several change tasks are described, and an example procedures for each task is given. It's not all-inclusive, and will certainly differ from hundreds of alternate network procedures, but it should provide you with the minimum number of documents to create that will ensure your network grows and changes in a controlled and sensible manner.

NET+ OBJECTIVE
II.2.1

Format for Standard Operating Procedures

A basic format for an SOP was given in Chapter 1. Let's revisit it with an eye to creating several important documents. A procedure format is shown in Figure 2-45. It has a standard header, and the body consists of a Purpose statement and a step-by-step procedure. The required fields are:

- Title: The title should be unique so that the procedure won't be confused by the end-user with another document.

- Revision Control: Some type of revision control is needed. Typically, this consists of alphabetical change increments for each approved revision. Other methods include using date codes as the revision control. For each change, the revision is documented with the approval date, and the user needs only to consult a master list to determine the most current date.

- Approval: At a minimum, the individuals directly responsible for the procedure should approve it. Others may include various management types such as Network Manager, Engineering, Quality Assurance, etc.

- Date: For this field, use the date the procedure was actually approved—not necessarily the date it was written.

- Revision History: A change history is important because the individuals responsible for tasks described in a procedure change frequently. It's good to know that a change that's under consideration has been tried before, and didn't work.

- Distribution List: Maintain a master list of all areas who will receive a copy of the approved SOP. Then, when the document is revised, the same people will be kept current on changes.

- Purpose: Briefly describe the objective of the procedure.

- Procedure: This is the body of the document. It very specifically details the objective as defined in the Purpose. There are no length requirements; say what's needed and try to use graphics whenever possible.

TITLE: Unique name to avoid confusion with other documents	
DATE: Approval date	REV: A
REVISION CONTROL:	
REV A: Initial release of procedure	
REVISION HISTORY:	
REV ?: New employees need to know past actions	
APPROVALS:	
Network Administrator	
Operations Manager	
DISTRIBUTION LIST:	
All Involved Divisions	
PURPOSE PROCEDURE	The objective of this SOP is described. Main body of document includes the specific details on how to meet the objective.

Figure 2-45 Format for a Standard Operating Procedure (SOP)

Networking personnel routinely prepare standard operating procedures (SOPs) to ensure networking duties are consistently applied.

Now, let's look at several areas that should be documented. You'll find that throughout this book, there will be SOPs written for many networking tasks. At this point, the concentration is on simpler and broad-ranging duties.

Cabling SOPs and Conventions

Figure 2-46 shows a rough layout of a small LAN. The LAN consists of a hub, server, printer, and ten client computers. Let's suppose the user of computer 3 has a problem, and the Network Tech suspects the fault lies at the hub. Now imagine standing in front of the hub. Which of the twelve ports should be checked?

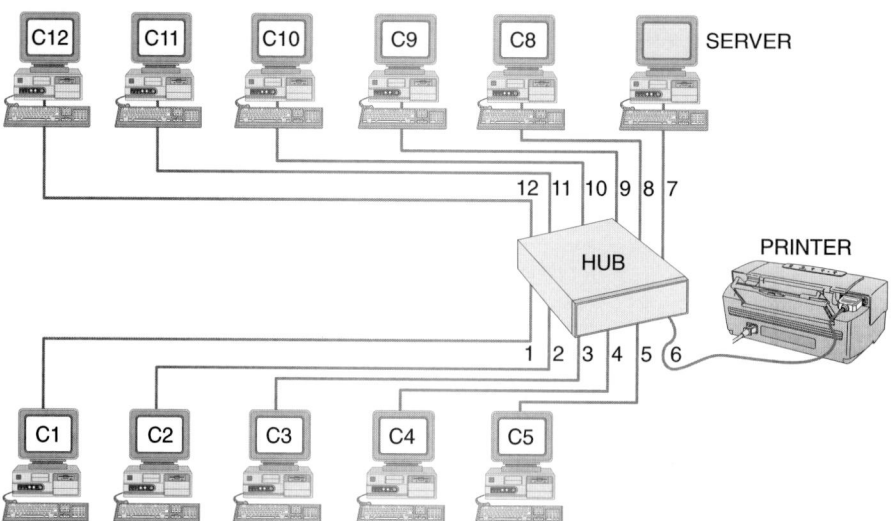

Figure 2-46 Cabling Diagram for a Small LAN

If you have a drawing similar to the one shown, it wouldn't be too difficult to determine that C3 is connected to port 3. But what if you didn't? The Network Administrator could use the server to determine which port C3 is connected to. Or, you could disconnect the ports one-at-a-time staring at port 1, until you've found the offending port—and offended nine other users while doing it.

What if this small LAN is one of a dozen small LANs, and the cable that runs back to twelve hubs in a wiring closet are bundled in groups of ten or twenty wires? What if someone decides to connect a print server to the printer to speed-up access? What if someone else decides the office is just too spacious, and reorganizes the room for twenty nodes?

Do you see the magnitude of the problem? Cabling can quickly amount to thousands of miles of copper wires in a large building. The solution is very simple: wherever a cable connects, label what it connects to. Do so at every connection.

All cables in a network should be labeled at a structural entry and exit point.

Figure 2-47 illustrates one method used for labeling, showing a cutaway of the room. The arrows indicate the location of labels applied directly to the cables. The convention used is source/destination, in which all hubs are considered the source of data, and all other nodes (PCs, printers, servers, etc.) are considered destinations.

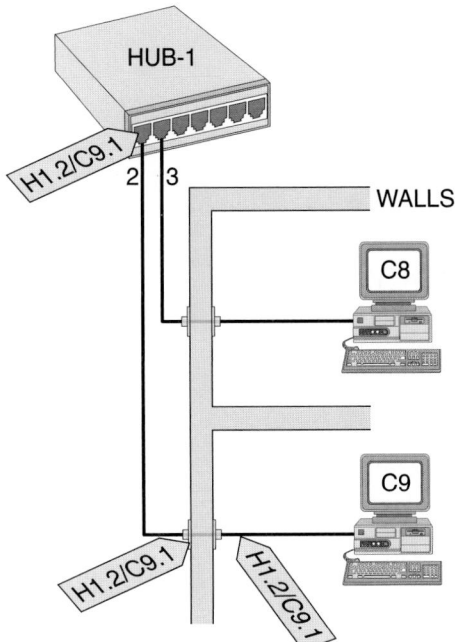

Figure 2-47 Labeling Convention for Network Cables

If a problem occurs at computer 9, the technician will look at the label on the RJ-45 box, mounted to the wall at that computer, and read that Hub 1, port 2 (H1.2) connects to computer 9, RJ-45 jack 1 (C9.1).

If, on the other hand, the technician is sorting through wire bundles in the ceiling, the cable is also labeled at the point it drops into the wall. The same is true if troubleshooting the hub inside a wiring closet (which, not surprisingly, is seldom well-lit or spacious).

There are two main considerations when creating network cabling conventions:

- Label all entry and exit point (walls, ceilings, dividers, patch panels, etc.).

- Decide on a source/destination convention and be consistent throughout the network.

There are other ways to label cables. If a site includes more than one building, room, LAN, or cabling technology (UTP, coax, fiber optic), the label should include enough information to pin-point where a cable goes on either end. Larger networks use logical addresses (IPs) for nodes. The advantage of a logical address is that a node can be moved anywhere, plugged-into a network jack, and still be able to access the network. In this case, it's a good idea to include the IP address along with the physical address. Figure 2-48 is a sample procedure which provides a consistent method for labeling network cables.

STANDARD OPERATING PROCEDURE
NETWORK DIVISION

TITLE: Convention For Labeling Cables	
DATE: June 1, 1999	REV: A
REVISION HISTORY:	
REV A: Initial release of procedure.	
APPROVALS:	
Network Administrator	
Operations Manager	
DISTRIBUTION:	
Network Division	

PURPOSE	The purpose of this procedure is to describe conventions and conditions for labeling networking cables.
ENTRY AND EXIT POINTS DEFINED	All cables are to be affixed with labels at each entry and exit point. Entry/Exit points occur whenever a cable passes through structural impediments such as walls, ceilings, flooring, and electrical connection points such as hub ports, RJ-45 boxes, punchdowns, switches, etc.
LABELING CONVENTIONS	The convention used for labeling cables will be source/destination in which a source is a common connection such as a hub, concentrator, switch, etc., and a destination is a client workstation, printer, server, etc.

Figure 2-48 SOP for Labeling Network Cables

Workorder SOPs

To schedule work performed on a network and to track network expenses, all work performed should be initiated with a workorder.

Back at Figure 2-46, the residents at computers 2,4 and 8 are out of server space, and jointly claim that without additional storage, the entire organization will crumble. Each sends e-mail to the Network Administrator demanding 1GB of server space, to be done during their lunch.

The Administrator, meanwhile, is trying to resolve a crisis between computers 6 and 7 whose users wondered what would happen if they swapped network cables. What should the Network Administrator do—besides go home for the day? The answer is: Don't allow such a situation to occur. Require that all changes, problems, and upgrades be handled through workorders. A sample workorder is shown in Figure 2-49.

COMPLETE THE TOP HALF OF THIS FORM AND SEND IT TO NETWORK OPERATIONS

NAME: _____

DATE: _____

TELEPHONE: _____

LOCATION: _____

SUPERVISOR'S SIGNATURE: _____

DESCRIBE WORK TO BE DONE:
_____
_____

- -

NETWORK OPERATIONS TO COMPLETE THE BOTTOM HALF OF THIS FORM

NETWORK ENGINEER/TECHNICIAN: _____

DATE WORK BEGAN: _____

DATE WORK COMPLETED: _____

TIME WORK BEGAN: _____

TIME WORK COMPLETED: _____

DESCRIBE WORK THAT WAS DONE:
_____
_____
_____

LIST MATERIALS USED (Include quantities):
_____
_____

Figure 2-49 Sample Workorder

This form contains the essential information needed to schedule and complete a job. Note that before Network Operations will accept a workorder, the employee's supervisor must approve the request. There's a couple of reasons for including this. The first is to prevent superfluous requests, and the second is to approve money, which will be charged back to the department receiving the work.

Not all companies track expenses in this manner, but many do, particularly if they contract network maintenance. Even within the same company, a department will often be charged an hourly rate-plus-materials for work performed.

Once the network group receives the workorder, the Administrator will schedule jobs. And it's usually the Administrator who has the last word on when a job will be done. This person is typically in the best position to determine which jobs have priority. As part of a SOP concerning workorders, it's reasonable to require the Administrator to post the schedule and include times and dates when the work will begin, and when it was actually accomplished. This way, the accountability for working efficiently is spread around.

Figure 2-50 is an example of a workorder SOP. The workorder it references is the same one from Figure 2-49.

System Changes and Upgrades

NET+ OBJECTIVE
II.3.2

Not all work is initiated from the user. In a server-based LAN, most software packages reside on the server. E-mail, wordprocessing, spreadsheets, and so on, will be loaded at the server, and clients will access the package as-needed. In many cases, although not all, the server will be brought down when changes are made to it.

> All changes or upgrades to a network should be addressed in a general SOP that is widely distributed.

What's needed is an-agreed-upon specification for making changes that may affect all users. The most convenient time for doing the changeover is during the normally scheduled work hours of networking personnel. Unfortunately, this is the least convenient time for network users. Anticipate network changes that will necessitate interrupting the network, and schedule it during a time which will inconvenience users the least. Usually, this means doing the job before or after the users are at work. This may mean coming to work in the middle of the night.

Figure 2-51 is a template SOP that describes shut-downs for system changes. It specifies that the change will be scheduled twenty-four hours in advance, that it will occur after the nightly server back-up (tape or disk), and it differentiates between changes to a network operating system (NOS) and a computer operating system (OS).

Software revision updates, equipment changes, preventive maintenance, or new installations may all require that network access be interrupted. Create a generic procedure which addresses the possibility of all of these and ensure that it's widely distributed. The specifics of how an upgrade or change is made should be written into separate procedures.

TITLE: Network Workorders	
DATE: June 1, 1999	REV: A

REVISION HISTORY:
REV A: Initial release of procedure, April 1, 1999

APPROVALS:
Network Administrator
Operations Manager

DISTRIBUTION:
All Locations

PURPOSE	The purpose of this SOP is to describe how to complete and submit network workorders.
RELATED DOCUMENT	Workorder Form
CLIENT RESPONSIBILITY	All client work is initiated with a workorder. The client is to complete the top half of the workorder and submit it to network operations. A detailed description of work to be performed (problems, software upgrades, e-mail, server access, Internet, etc.) must be included. All workorders must be signed by the client's supervisor before work will be scheduled.
NETWORK OPERATION'S RESPONSIBILITY	Workorders will be scheduled by the Network Administrator, or designee. The client will receive notification of when work will begin via e-mail. Network Operations is responsible for completing the bottom half of the form and returning it to the Network Administrator.

Figure 2-50 SOP for Workorders

TITLE: Network Changes and Upgrades	
DATE: June 1, 1999	REV: B
REVISION HISTORY:	
REV A: Initial release of procedure, April 1, 1999	
REV B: Initial release didn't specify when upgrades were to be done. Upgrades are specified in this revision to occur between 2:00 AM and 6:00 AM.	
APPROVALS:	
Network Administrator	
Operations Manager	
DISTRIBUTION:	
All Locations	

PURPOSE	The purpose of this SOP is to specify when global network changes will be made, and to differentiate between global and local changes.
RELATED DOCUMENTS	Network Workorder
GLOBAL VERSUS LOCAL CHANGES	Global changes are those which affect all network users.
	Local changes affect only specific users.
	Global changes require that the network service be interrupted, while local changes don't require network interruption.
SCHEDULED NETWORK CHANGES OR UPGRADES	Global changes will be scheduled 24 hours in advance. The network will be brought down after the 2:00AM server backup and will be completed before 6:00 AM.
	If the 4-hour window is too narrow, the work may be scheduled for weekends, consecutive nights, or clients will be advised if the network will be unavailable no later than 6:00 AM.
	Local changes are to be initiated with a workorder. The client or Network Operations may initiate the workorder. In either case, the Network Administrator will schedule local work and the client advised via e-mail.

Figure 2-51 SOP for System Changes

The configuration of a network will change as new users are added, upgrades to existing equipment become available, or new equipment is installed. Ideally, network changes will make the network better. The problem for a network administrator is to define "better". Or, posed as a question: How will you determine the effects of change on a network?

Standardization is one way, and that is achieved using standard operating procedures that cover many of the topics in this book, particularly the titles suggested in Chapter 1. An SOP provides a written blueprint describing the current configuration of a network. It should also direct that all client workstations be documented, as well. The sections to follow contain information that will help you implement a change-control networking environment.

In a well-documented network, any workstation changes will be routinely tracked and recorded. At a minimum, the tracking should include the documentation for the activities listed in Table 2-4.

Table 2-4 Documented Network Activities

REQUIRED STATUS AND CONFIGURATION DOCUMENTATION
Additions and upgrades to network and client operating systems
Additions and upgrades to software systems
Additions or changes to security, including file or directory access
Additions and upgrades to servers
Additional moves or removals of user equipment
Additions or deletions of users
Additions or upgrades of peripherals
Additions or upgrades to client hardware, such as processors, RAM, hard drives, NIC card types, removable media (floppy disks, CD-ROMs), and a listing of IRQ, DMA, and I/O Base Address settings.

However, you may not have the luxury of walking into a situation in which the network has been properly documented. You may, after determining that a workstation is at fault, and not the operator, troubleshoot the client using several different approaches until the problem is corrected. Or you may install a piece of software, say a virus-detection package, and cause conflicts with other software running on the client. In either case, you're left in a situation requiring you to return the system to its original configuration.

You won't be able to do this unless you know what the original configuration was. Therefore, before beginning work on a client's workstation that is connected to a network, take a few minutes and document the status and configuration of certain critical areas.

NET+ OBJECTIVE
II.2.2

This will provide you with a baseline reference upon which to draw if the change creates more problems than it solves.

For example, assume that a client, running Windows 95, is connected into an Ethernet network that operates at 10 MBPS. You get a good deal on NIC cards that support speeds of 10 and 100 MBPS, and even though your network isn't currently 100MBPS-capable, you plan to upgrade it at some future time, so that it will be. The NIC vendor's literature says that the card will automatically fallback to 10 MBPS if the network can't support data rates of 100 MBPS. You don't anticipate problems, so:

    a. You swap NIC cards, and hope the 95 plug-and-play will take care of any problems.
    b. You play it safe, and upgrade all network devices to 100MBPS before making any changes.
    c. You document all server settings in case the card crashes your server.
    d. You document all current NIC card settings, including any static addresses (MAC address).

The correct answer, of course, is **d**. But what about **c**? What if the card caused a problem with the server? First, it's extremely unlikely that the NIC would be capable of crashing the server. Second, this section is focused on establishing a baseline to which a client can be returned if a change doesn't work.

There's an argument that says you can over-document a network. It goes on to say that before changes are made, the common-sense approach is to note all relevant settings before making the change. So, why spend so much time tracking mundane settings, such as the version of software used for word processing, or the interrupt used by a modem? Because it represents good and sound networking practices. Because it's the mark of a professional. Because it allows you to make decisions that are informed, current, and technically accurate.

KEY POINTS REVIEW

This chapter has presented an extensive exploration of the fundamentals of data transmission.

- Digital data is preferred over analog data because noise and distortion is easier to remove, it's in the same format as computer data, and the sharp edges of square waves provide for more reliable bit recognition.

- Digital square waves have the disadvantage of requiring at least five times as much bandwidth as analog.

- Transmission media refers to the channel data travels en route to the receiving station. Transmission media include coaxial cable, twisted wire pairs, fiber optics and microwave.

- Twisted pair is the most widely installed media. It's size ranges form 16 to 24 AWG, and may be found in a single pair cable or up to 6,000 pairs may be encased in a single sheath. Unshielded twisted paid (UTP) is the preferred cabling for LANs. UTP is classified by the EIA/TIA according to categories. Whenever possible, use CAT5 UTP.

- Coaxial cable used in networking has a maximum data rate of 10 MBPS. It offers fair noise immunity. In other applications, it has a maximum data rate of 4,000 MBPS, bandwidths of up to 1,000 MHz and is somewhat more expensive to install than twisted wire pairs.

- Fiber optic media relay data via light waves through a glass or plastic conductor. It offers the best in noise immunity but is the most expensive to install. Data rates may run as high as 200,000 MBPS and bandwidths as high as 1,000 GHz. The disadvantage of fiber optics is the expense, special splicing tools, and need for very careful alignment of splices and connections.

- Microwaves are used with satellites and in the telecommunication's industry. It's used where cable isn't practical such as across oceans. Microwaves are susceptible to solar disturbance and weather conditions. At the LAN level, microwaves and infrared are used in wireless networks.

- Copper cables contain a characteristic impedance of series inductance and parallel capacitance, which gives the cable the properties of a low pass filter.

- The reactive components of cables cause intersymbol interference (ISI).

- ISI is the blurring together of data bits. It's most noticeable in narrow bandwidth channels and increases with data rates.

- ISI can be compensated for by equalizing the data stream. An equalizer separates signal frequencies through filtering and incorporates phase shifts to counter the effects of the channel.

- Data is encoded to represent alphanumeric characters as well as to alleviate ISI and dc drift. Alphanumeric codes include ASCII and EBCIDIC.

- Codes that eliminate ISI and dc drift are non-return-to-zero, Manchester and alternate mark inversion.

- Noise and distortion is expressed in decibels. The decibel results from the ratio of an actual value to a reference value. Reference values for data communications are 1 mW and 6 mW.

- Atmospheric noise results from lightning, solar activity and stellar radiation.

- Impulse noise is sporadic and of short duration, usually caused by electro-mechanical equipment.

- Frequency noise originates from 60Hz wire, system clocks or carrier frequencies.

- Crosstalk is the electro-magnetic induction that results from cables laying in parallel.

- An analysis of noise can be found by calculating the signal to noise ratio.

- Noise factor is another method of analyzing noise. It's the ratio of signal to noise at the input of a system, to the signal to noise at the output of a system.

- Most all data communication systems utilize error control. A common error detection technique is adding a parity bit to a data word. Parity may be even or odd.

- Data is frequently converted from analog to digital, and digital to analog.

- Networking personnel routinely prepare standard operating procedures (SOP) to ensure networking duties are consistently applied.

- All cables in a network should be labeled at a structural entry and exit point.

- To schedule work performed on a network and to track network expenses, all work performed should be initiated with a workorder.

- All changes or upgrades to a network should be addressed in a general SOP that is widely distributed.

At this point, review the objectives listed at the beginning of the chapter to be certain that you understand and can perform them. Afterward, answer the review questions that follow to verify your knowledge of the information.

LAB MANUAL

Lab Exercises

The lab manual that accompanies this book contains hands-on lab procedures that reinforce and test your knowledge of the theory materials presented in this chapter. Now that you have completed your review of Chapter 2, refer to the lab manual and perform Procedure 2, "Network Floorplan."

REVIEW QUESTIONS

The following questions test your knowledge of the material presented in this chapter:

1. If a squarewave with a frequency of 30 kHz is transmitted through a channel with a bandwidth of 10 kHz, how will it be affected?

2. What is the function of a repeater in a network?

3. What type of media is the most commonly installed in local area networks?

4. What is intersymbol interference?

5. Calculate the noise factor of a channel with a SNR at the input of 14.3 mW, and SNR at the output of 21.5 mW.

6. Consider the bit stream 1100100. For even parity, the parity bit is _____.

7. Describe the difference between intrusive and non-intrusive coaxial cable taps.

8. Explain how CAT 5 UTP greatly extends the bandwidth of voice-grade UTP.

9. Why should you know if a cable plant is compliant to EIA/TIA-568A or B?

10. Describe the difference between multimode and single-mode fiber optic cable.

11. What are the advantages/disadvantages of fiber cable?

12. What are the advantages of UTP over STP?

13. An RJ-45 connector is only used with CAT5 UTP cable; True or False.

14. Describe how to establish a baseline reference of the status and configuration settings of a workstation.

15. Why is it necessary to create a cabling scheme for the network cable plant?

MULTIPLE CHOICE QUESTIONS

1. A disadvantage of transmitting digital signals is:
   a. They have narrow bandwidth requirements.
   b. They have wide bandwidth requirements.
   c. It's too difficult to remove noise from them.
   d. They can't be amplified.

2. As seen on an oscilloscope, a digital signal that's been transmitted through a channel with insufficient bandwidth will appear:
   a. Sawtooth.
   b. Rectangular.
   c. Rounded at the corners.
   d. Sharp, ninety-degree corners.

3. In order to transfer the maximum amount of energy in a cable to the load, the cable must be matched with a resistance equal to the _____ of the cable.
   a. Capacitive Reactance.
   b. Inductive Reactance.
   c. Resistance.
   d. Characteristic Impedance.

4. In the Manchester encoding scheme, data bits are represented by:
   a. A logic 1 is the high-to-low transition, a logic 0 is the low-to-high transition.
   b. A positive voltage is a logic 1, 0 volts is a logic 0.
   c. A positive voltage is a logic 1, a negative voltage is a logic 0.
   d. A logic 1 alternates between +V and –V, and a logic 0 is 0Vdc.

5. The type of noise caused by unshielded cables laying in parallel is called:
   a. Atmospheric.
   b. Impulse.
   c. Crosstalk.
   d. Frequency.

6. Determine the SNR of a system in which the signal out of a transmitter is 3.5 mW and the noise level is 20 microW.
   a. 7.52 dB.
   b. 22.4 dB.
   c. 41.7 dB.
   d. 68.2 dB.

7. What is refraction?
   a. The dispersion of light waves.
   b. The bending of light passing through materials of different density.
   c. A narrowing of the light wave as it's transmitted.
   d. A thickening in the intensity of light as it travels further from the source.

8. The path that exists between the transmitter and the receiver is called the:
   a. Data tunnel.
   b. Communication channel.
   c. Staircase waveform.
   d. Glitch.

9. The polyethylene jacket that encloses a coaxial cable is also called the:
   a. Center conductor.
   b. Insulator.
   c. Shielding.
   d. Outer insulation.

10. The proper termination for an RG-58A network cable is:
   a. 50 ohms.
   b. 93 ohms.
   c. 100-120 ohms.
   d. 150 ohms.

CD-ROM

Net+ Practice Test

Additional Net+ Certification testing is available on the CD that accompanies this text. The testing suite on the CD provides Study Card, Flash Card, and Run Practice type testing. The Study Card and Flash Card feature enables you to electronically link to the section of the book in which the question is covered. Choose questions from the test pool related to this chapter.

CHAPTER

3

THE TELEPHONE SYSTEM

Upon completion of this chapter and its related lab procedures, you should be able to perform the following tasks:

1. State four functions of a telephone set.

2. Label a block diagram of a telephone set.

3. Describe the electrical differences between pulse and tone dialing.

4. Describe the structure of the local telephone exchange.

5. Describe each of the BORSCHT functions.

6. Define "IDDD World Numbering Plan".

7. Explain the differences between the telephone exchange classifications.

8. Describe the electrical characteristics of PAM, PDM, PCM and DM.

9. Describe the advantage of companding.

10. State the companding technique used in the United States and Europe.

11. Analyze attenuation, delay, and line conditioning on a voice-channel.

12. Interpret attenuation/ delay charts for conditioned lines.

13. Prepare a brief definition of multiplexing and demultiplexing.

14. Describe the characteristics of SDM, FDM, TDM and STDM techniques.

15. Describe the structure of the analog common carrier hierarchy.

16. Describe the structure of the digital common carrier hierarchy.

17. Explain the services offered through T1, T2, T3 and T4 connections.

18. Label a block diagram of the T1 frame format.

19. Prepare a brief definition of CSU/DSU.

20. State the advantages of T1 and extended superframes over standard T1 frames.

21. Administer change controls by adding new telephone equipment.

22. Design the network by identifying the availability of local T1 access.

23. Describe the electrical characteristics of a T1 signal.

24. State two types of acceptable T1 connectors.

25. Ensure appropriate resources are available for implementing T-Carrier access.

26. Describe the services available with a SONET connection.

27. Describe the frame format of a SONET STS1.

28. Define SONET terms such as virtual tributary, terminating multiplexer, regenerator, and add/drop multiplexer.

29. While planning a customer's job, study technology options, pro and con.

30. Identify the technical capabilities of T-Carrier, SONET, and Multiplexing.

31. Analyze various network training requirements.

32. Design a training needs survey.

33. Determine the training wants and needs of a networked company.

CHAPTER 3

The Telephone System

INTRODUCTION

Alexander Graham Bell shouted, "Mr. Watson, come here, I want you!" And with those words, he launched the world upon a course that would alter the lives of all people on the Earth. As is so often the case with technological breakthroughs, the telephone was discovered by mistake. In March, 1876, Bell was working in his lab attempting to send multiple telegraph signals, when he spilled acid on his trousers. He shouted for Watson, and Watson came running—not only to help his boss, but to also convey his amazement at hearing Bell through the "telegraph."

Telephones spread rapidly. Less than a quarter century later, in 1900, there were 1.3 million phones in the United States. Within a few years, **AT&T** had acquired Bell's original patents, and was rapidly on the way to becoming the dominant supplier of telephone equipment as well as the primary controller of all long-distance systems. AT&T would grow until their payroll consisted of over a million employees. As part of an antitrust settlement in 1982, the behemoth telecommunication company would divest itself of all regional phone companies. The regional companies (large corporations, themselves) would become independent telephone companies and be collectively referred to as "baby bells." AT&T retained the long-distance carrier services as well as its research and development division, **Bell Labs**. The divestiture provided for the development of AT&T computers, noted for their **UNIX** operating system.

From one accidental phone call in 1876, each person in the United States makes an average of 200 calls a year. In the decade between 1970 and 1980, the number of telephones doubled. In 1957, AT&T determined that data rates exceeding 750BPS were possible; in 1989 **Alcatel**, a French telecommunications company, successfully transmitted 600GBPS over a fiber optic network. Ten years later, 1,000GBPS are not uncommon.

The telephone industry has been the heart of electronic communication, accessible to nearly everyone. It continues to dominate communication systems as the most widely installed medium in the world. Today, anyone in the U.S. with a telephone can be connected to 98% of the telephones in the world. And if a telephone can be connected, so can a computer and, so too, can data of all types be exchanged.

In this chapter, telephones and the networks utilized by telephones and DTEs of all types are explored. The signals composing the unique language of the phone system, the interconnection of local and long distance exchanges, the modulation methods used in phone networks, and the digital T-carrier and optical SONET systems are thoroughly discussed.

Expect many changes in the future, and expect to see them crop-up in various areas. The FCC has defined LATAs (Local Access Telephone Areas) which sets the boundaries for the various types of data services to be available.

The telephone system is the key to access outside the local environment—to the Internet, to linking scattered networks, to providing critical real time medical diagnoses to areas that otherwise would do without. The list goes on and on. To successfully master networking, you must have a fundamental understanding of how the phone system is organized, how it works, and how to use the services that are available.

THE TELEPHONE SET

The basic **telephone set** is used to send and receive calls. It contains both a transmitter and a receiver and is more appropriately referred to as a transceiver. Although the basic telephone set is relatively simple in operation, it's responsible for complex and rigid duties.

At a minimum, the telephone set:

1 Initiates use of the telephone system when the handset is lifted.

2 Receives a dial tone indicating the system is ready to be used.

3 Transmits the number to be called to the telephone system.

4 Supervises the status of the set by indicating to a caller if the set is in use (busy), or available to receive a call (ring).

5 Acknowledges an incoming call by ringing.

6 Performs the duties of a transducer by converting audio signals into electrical signals, and electrical signals into audio signals.

7 Compensates for varying power levels supplied to it.

8 Provides an indication to the telephone system that a call is finished when the caller hangs up.

A telephone is responsible for much more than serving as a transceiver for voice calls. It must also manage all line conditions and requests from other telephones as well as notify the central office of its current state.

Most telephones today include additional features, such as **automatic redial**, a switch to turn off the ringer, intercom capabilities, on-board memory for **speed dialing** or **call monitoring**, and facsimile options. These sophisticated data communication devices fulfill the basic requirements of a telephone set, and operate within the strict parameters of the telephone network.

A block diagram of the telephone set is shown in Figure 3-1. The essential functions of the set are the same, whether it be a dial or tone phone.

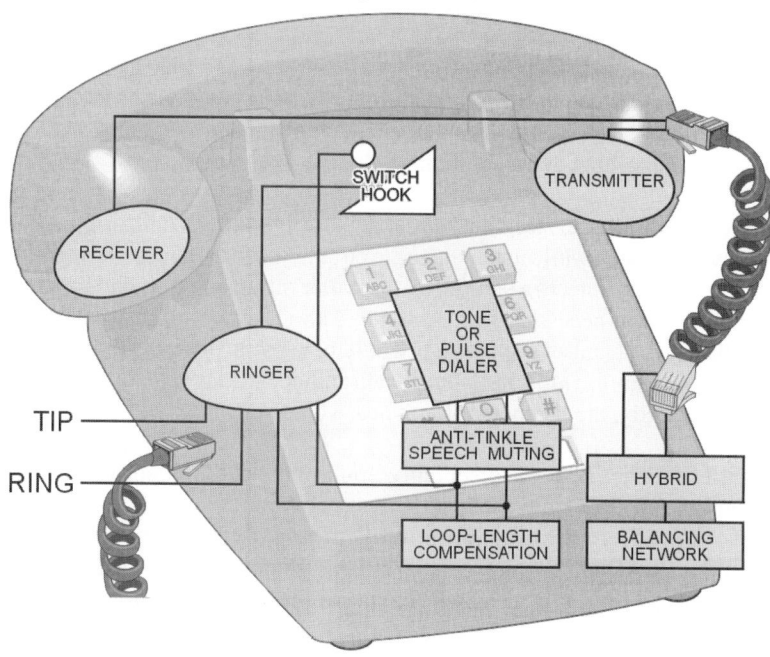

Figure 3-1 The Telephone Set

The block labeled **Switch Hook** corresponds to the handset sitting in the cradle **(on-hook)**, or lifted from the cradle **(off-hook)**. When the handset is on-hook, the telephone is isolated from the telephone system by the open contacts of the switch. When the handset is lifted from the cradle, the telephone is off-hook. Lifting the handset closes a switch which completes a circuit from the telephone through a relay coil at the local office. Current to the circuit is supplied from a battery at the local office. Current through the relay coil will close a set of contacts at the office and energize an **audio generator** which produces the dial tone. The caller may now place the call by pulsing the **loop current** supplied by the local office, or by sending a series of audio tones corresponding to the called number.

When a telephone dialer is rotated, high-voltage spikes are generated by the dial contacts when the local office current is generated. The **Anti-Tinkle and Speech Muting** block of Figure 3-1 prevents these spikes from entering the telephone's speech circuitry. This keeps the dialer from hearing loud clicks in the receiver, and prevents damage in the speech circuits.

The physical architecture of telephones is such that the **Ringer** is connected directly across the two input wires. These same wires also serve as output wires. High-voltage spikes may cause the ringer to tinkle when a number is dialed. A capacitor and a series resister filter the high-voltage spikes in the anti-tinkle circuit, and shunt the spikes from the ringer.

The **Loop-Length Compensation** block of Figure 3-1 is intended to regulate the speech levels of callers, regardless of the distance separating them. Most telephones have a carbon-granule microphone in the handset. The resistance of the microphone varies with the intensity of the caller's voice. In turn, the amount of current drawn from the **local loop** varies. The local loop contains the resistance of the wires from caller to caller. This resistance varies with distance. The voltage in the circuit remains constant at –48 volts dc from the local office.

When a call is made over a short distance, the line resistance is relatively low; consequently, the current is high. If a call is made to the outskirts of the local loop, the line resistance increases substantially, resulting in a low line current. Without loop-length compensation, the voice levels of calls at the edges of the local exchange will sound faint, and the volume of close calls will be loud.

Loop-length compensation is accomplished by connecting a **varistor** across the telephone. The resistance of the varistor increases when loop current increases for short-distance calls. If a call is made to the outskirts of the loop, the varistor resistance decreases. This makes additional current available to the loop to compensate for the increased resistance of the greater distance. Essentially, the varistor serves as a current regulator to automatically maintain a constant volume level throughout the local exchange.

The **induction coil** is an interface transformer. It permits a caller to talk using the telephone circuitry, as well as listen while using the same circuitry. A **balancing network** connected across the transformer detects a sample of the caller's transmission and applies it to the receiver circuits. This is necessary so the caller will know how loud to talk. Without hearing your own voice in the handset's speaker, it would be very difficult to adjust the volume of your voice. If you speak too loud, the listener at the other end may think you're shouting, but if you speak too softly, the listener may not hear you.

The **transmitter** of a telephone is essentially a microphone. It's a transducer that converts **acoustical energy** (speech) into **electrical energy** (current). Several types of transmitters are in use today. The **carbon-granule microphone**, as mentioned earlier, changes resistance at a rate and amount proportional to the frequency and intensity of the audio. Another type of transmitter is the **electrodynamic microphone**. It converts speech to current by causing a thin diaphragm to vibrate. The diaphragm may be a thin sheet of metal or a ribbon containing a length of copper wire. As the caller talks, the diaphragm vibrates. The metal or copper wire cuts the flux lines of a permanent magnet and induces a voltage into a coil wrapped about the magnet. A third type is the **electret microphone**. Its operation is based upon the principle of a capacitor. The electret (a fluorocarbon compound) serves as the dielectric material, and the diaphragm serves as one capacitor plate. As the caller speaks, the diaphragm moves, causing a variation in capacitance. This causes a slight charging and discharging action. The electret material is chosen because it holds a permanent charge. This eliminates the need for a permanent magnet.

The **receiver** of a telephone converts electrical energy (current) into acoustical energy (speech). The receiver is basically a **speaker**, very similar in operation to the speakers used with audio systems. The receiver contains a **permanent magnet** wrapped with coils of copper wire. The wire contains the electrical current representing the received speech. In close proximity to the magnet is a thin **metal diaphragm**. As current in the coil varies at an audio rate, it alternately aids and opposes the **flux lines** of the magnet. The diaphragm is attracted to the magnet when the current aids the flux lines. When the current opposes the flux lines, the diaphragm is released. The vibrating diaphragm causes the relative air pressure near the receiver to change at an audible rate.

The basic telephone just described represents a minimal technological expectation, reminiscent of the good old days when you could throw together a few discrete components and build a working circuit. Now, most of the functionality of a telephone is embedded on a single, integrated circuit. Cordless phones and cellular phones, Internet calling and voice-over-cable are challenging the premise of the telephone as a mere transceiver.

PULSE AND TONE DIALING

Pulse and tone dialing are the two common types of dialers in use today. **Pulse dialing** is associated with the older rotary dials containing ten holes. To place a call, you put your finger in the appropriate hole and rotated the dial. Each number on the dial represented the number of times the local loop current was broken. Circuitry at the local office counted the current breaks and processed the number. The more modern telephones use a method of sending tones to represent the numbers 0 through 9. The primary advantage of tone versus pulse dialing is one of speed. **Tone dialing** takes about one-tenth the amount of time to process a call as does pulse dialing. It is the local telephone company that realizes the savings: more calls can be handled with tone dialing, using less equipment, in a shorter period of time.

Pulse Dialing

> A pulse dialer breaks the line current by the number of times equal to the number dialed. It's a slow dialing method, and unsuited for data communications.

Pulse dialing is mainly found in the older, **rotary dial** type of telephones. It's called pulse dialing because when the dial is rotated, the line current is broken by the number of times equal to the number dialed. When the telephone handset is on-hook, the line back to the central office is broken and no current flows in the line. When the handset is lifted, the line is off-hook. The central office source supplies line current and a dial tone. Figure 3-2(a) illustrates line current as the number 3 is pulse dialed. The on-hook condition shows that the loop is open and there is no line current. When the handset is lifted (off-hook), line current flows from the source. As the dial is rotated from number three, the rotary switch breaks the line current three times—which corresponds to the number dialed.

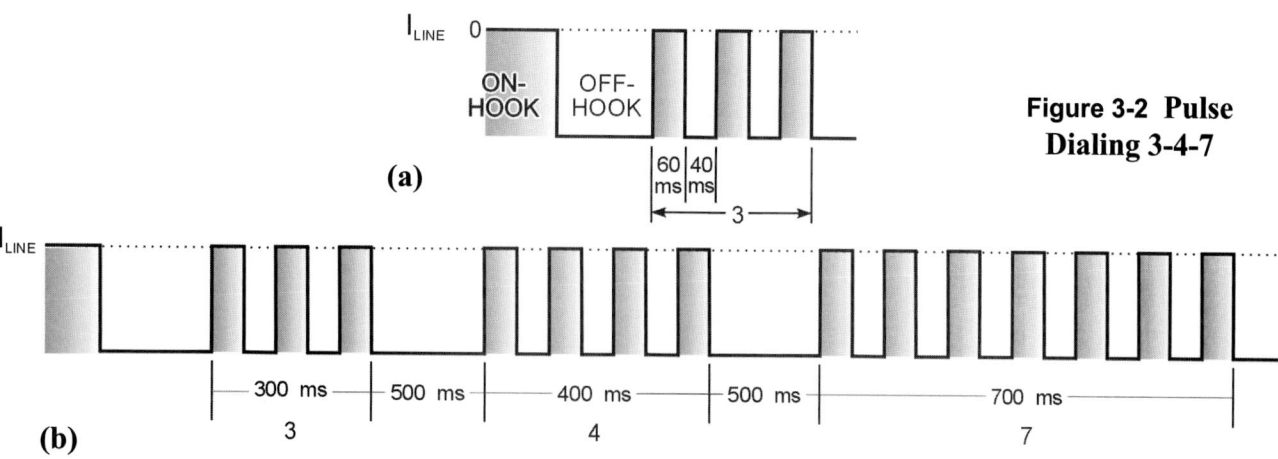

Figure 3-2 Pulse Dialing 3-4-7

The line current is broken for about 60 mS and flows between breaks for about 40 mS. The **pulse period**—the time the circuit is opened and closed—is 60 mS + 40 mS = 100 mS. The total time required to dial the number three is 3 x 100 mS = 300 mS.

Ordinarily, additional numbers are dialed, with the time between dialed digits averaging 500 mS. Figure 3-2(b) shows the exchange number 3-4-7 being dialed. The total time required to pulse dial the three numbers is:

$$(3 \times 100) + 500 + (4 \times 100) + 500 + (7 \times 100)$$
$$= 300 + 500 + 400 + 500 + 700$$
$$= 2,400 \text{ mS}$$

Pulse dialing the three digits of Figure 3-2(b) takes almost 2.5 seconds. This illustrates the severe drawback of pulse dialing for data communications—it requires too much time. Time with the public telephone network and long-distance carriers can be expensive, since the amount of time spent using the facilities constitutes a large amount of the telephone bill. As we'll see shortly, tone dialing is the quick alternative to pulse dialing. Tone-dial phones are quickly replacing the rotary dials.

Tone Dialing

Tone dialing utilizes a twelve-button **keypad** that's used to signal the local exchanges. A combination of **audio tones** is transmitted when the buttons are pushed, instead of interrupting the line current. The first advantage of tone dialing is that once the called party has answered the telephone, the keypad buttons may be further used—for entering a sales order, making a credit card transaction, selecting numbered departments within a large corporation, etc. However, if a caller breaks the current in pulse dialing by rotating the dial, the local exchange may interpret the current break as the end of the call and terminate the connection.

A tone dialer generates a combination of audio tones according to buttons pushed on a keypad, making a tone dialer is much faster than pulse dialing.

The second advantage, then, involves speed. Tone dialing is much faster than pulse dialing. If calls can be dialed faster, then more calls will enter the local exchange in a given time period. The local exchange can then process more calls, more quickly, than with an equivalent amount of pulse-dial equipment.

The time required to send a tone digit is 50 mS, and the time between digits is 50 mS, for a total time of 100 mS a digit. Compared with the earlier example of pulse dialing 3-4-7, the total time required to dial the three digits is 3 x 100 mS = 300 mS.

When the same digits were pulse dialed, it took 2400 mS. Tone dialing the same three numbers represents a savings in dialing time of more than two seconds!

Dual-Tone Multi-Frequency

The most common method of tone dialing uses a technique called **Dual-Tone Multi-Frequency** (DTMF). The use of DTMF is conditional upon the local exchange possessing the equipment to process the tone (nearly all do). The twelve-button keypad has been standardized to include the digits 0 through 9, twenty-four letters of the alphabet (Q and Z are omitted), and the symbols * and #. The DTMF keypad is pictured in Figure 3-3.

The buttons are arranged in a row and column matrix. Each time a button is pushed, a unique tone is generated. For example, when the 7 button is pushed, a combination of 852 Hz and 1,209 Hz is generated. The columns of the keypad have been designated for the high frequencies and the rows have been designated for the low frequencies.

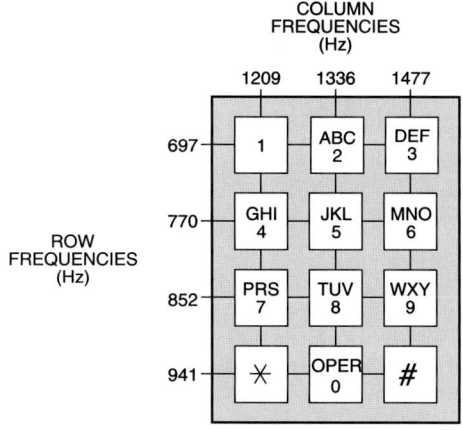

Figure 3-3 DTMF Keypad

The frequencies assigned to the keypad were selected so as to avoid **intertone distortion**. As the tones propagate through the telephone system, the frequencies are invariably acted upon by the system circuitry. Harmonics of the tones may be generated, or the tones may **heterodyne** to produce sum and difference frequencies. For the frequencies assigned to the keypad, none is a harmonic of the fundamental frequency of another, nor are any of the frequencies the sum or difference frequency of the heterodyned combination of any of the other assigned frequencies. As a result, telephone systems can be designed with high reliability factors around DTMF keypads.

LOCAL EXCHANGE LOOPS

The telephones within an area all connect to the local office, or the central office exchange. The **Central Office** (CO) is responsible for connecting callers or subscribers together. Subscriber phones are connected in a loop, to the central office, as shown in Figure 3-4.

> The local exchange loop consists of the telephone, the central office, and a wire pair connecting the two.

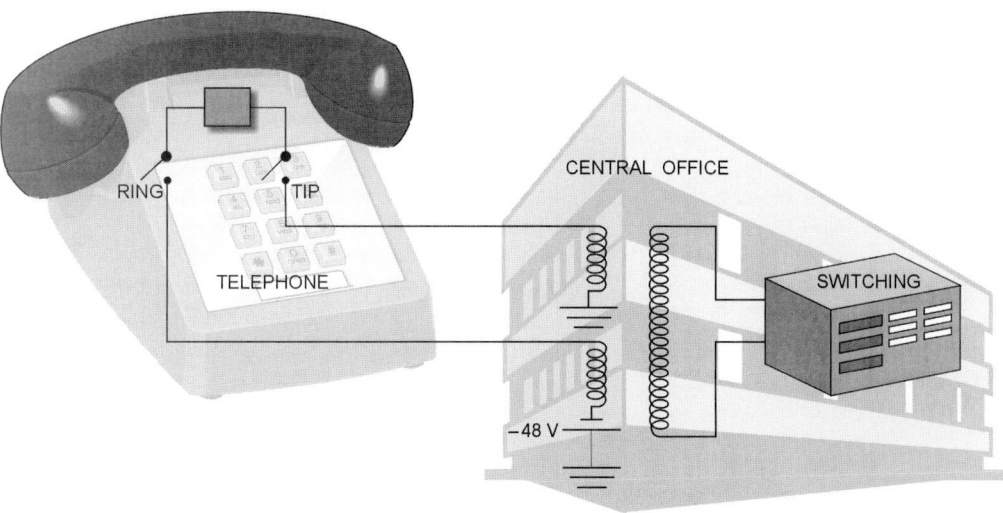

Figure 3-4 Central Office Exchange Loop

Each telephone is connected to the CO by two wires, labeled **tip** and **ring**. The tip and ring terminology is a carry-over from the days when an operator manually switched calls using patch cords. The "tip" wire corresponded to the tip of the patch cord jack that plugged into the socket. The "ring" wire was connected to the actual ring that encased the jack. In modern telephones, the tip wire is always the **green** wire and the ring wire is the **red** wire. This arrangement is used in a standard four-wire telephone cable connector. The other two wires aren't used.

The subscriber phone, via the tip and ring wire, connects to a – 48V dc supply located at the central office. The dc source supplies the current and voltages necessary to operate the telephone.

As shown in Figure 3-4, the telephone handset is resting on the cradle, in the on-hook position. Line current is supplied from the dc source at the central office. The central office dedicates a telephone circuit to thousands of callers as well as provides switching facilities to other exchanges and the long-distance network.

> Each local office is identified by the first three digits of a seven digit, local telephone number.

The CO also provides a supervisory service for the subscriber in addition to supplying switching and line currents. The CO provides **tone** *or* **pulse ring detection**, a **ring signal**, and a **busy signal**. Each local office has a numerical designation equivalent to the first three digits of a telephone number. For example, the number 343-7272 is connected to the 343 exchange. Each exchange has the capability to serve 10,000 subscribers (0000-9999). In the example above, the 343 exchange can service subscribers with phone numbers 343-0000 through 343-9999, for a total of 10,000 subscribers.

> The central office is responsible for switching calls among local subscribers as well as serving as an interface to the long distance network.

The structure of the CO facilities is shown in Figure 3-5.

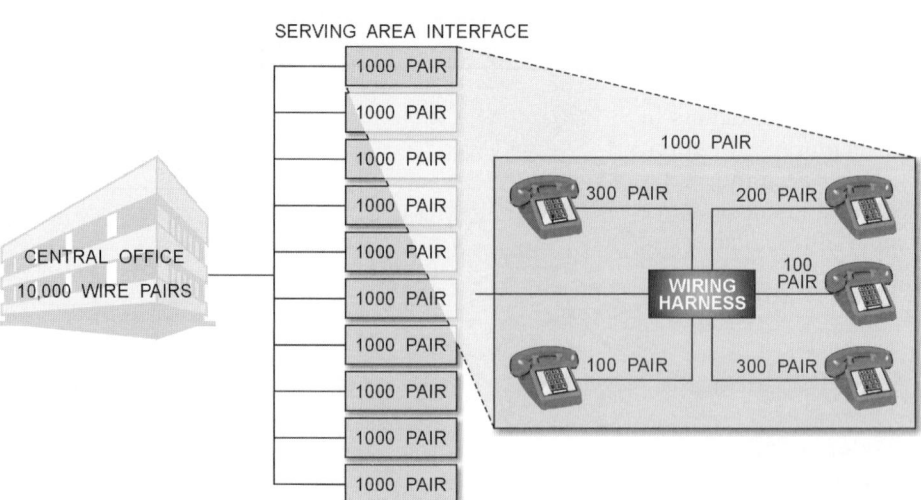

Figure 3-5 Structure of the Central Office

The central office is connected to subscribers through a **feeder network**. The feeder network distributes 10,000 wire pairs to a local area. The local area is divided into 10 serving areas. Each **serving area** is fed 1000 wire pairs from the feeder network. As illustrated, the distribution of wire pairs within the serving area is handled by the **Serving Area Interface**, which distributes wire pairs to actual, as well as expected, subscribers within close geographical areas.

Figure 3-5 details a typical serving area. The serving area interface, a **wiring harness**, distributes wire pairs to concentrations of subscribers. Three-hundred pairs may be distributed to a residential subdivision, while two-hundred pairs may service a cluster of businesses.

Telephone companies are springing up everywhere. And they seldom resemble the model company described above. The reason is that we're discovering methods for utilizing existing wiring infrastructures in unique ways. Cable TV companies—historically offering only video to televisions—are applying technological advances to make better use of the wide bandwidth available in coaxial cables. Not only are they offering Internet access, but they're also providing a wide pipe for businesses to transfer large files. Electric utilities have thousands of miles of wires that have previously carried only electricity, but are now viewed as channels for data that's modulated onto the line frequency.

BORSCHT FUNCTIONS

BORSCHT functions refer to a series of duties handled by the central office. They include Battery, Overvoltage protection, Ring trip, Supervision, Coding, Hybrid and Test.

The tip and ring wires from the subscriber to the central office provide a path for a variety of functions in addition to serving as a communication medium. These functions are commonly referred to as **BORSCHT** functions, an acronym for **battery**, **overvoltage protection**, **ring trip**, **supervision**, **coding**, **hybrid** and **test**.

Battery

As mentioned earlier, the telephone is operated by a -48Vdc source located at the central office. When the handset is on-hook, a voltmeter connected across the red and green wires will read -48 volts dc. When the handset is lifted, the voltage drops to about -6 volts dc.

Overvoltage Protection

The central office is the primary provider of overvoltage protection to the telephone and wire pairs. Protection is provided against lightning as well as incorrect connections. A lowpass filter across the tip and ring wires at the telephone eliminates noisy spikes that may be induced into the wire pairs.

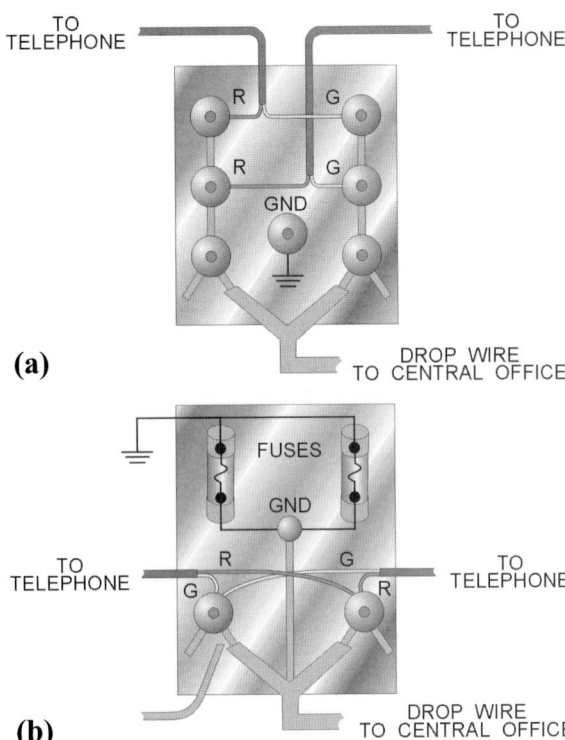

(a)

(b)

Figure 3-6 Overvoltage Protection

Figure 3-6 illustrates typical overvoltage protection devices currently used. These devices are located near or inside a residence or business. They incorporate a fuse connected in series with the ground wire. Other devices may fuse each of the tip and ring wires of the **drop cable**. The **overvoltage protection box** may be located in one of several places. The most common location is to place it at the point where the drop wire enters the structure. This could mean it's in an attic or under the house eaves for aerial connections. Buried drop wires feed back to a **pedestal box**. The device may be found in the pedestal, or mounted to the wall near the point of entry of the dwelling or structure.

Figure 3-6(a) illustrates an older **fuseless protector**. The drop wire provides the connection back to the central office. Each side of the drop wire connects to telephone extensions via a bus. The ring wires connect to the bus on the left, and the tip wires are connected along the bus on the right. Overvoltage protection is provided by a heavy-gauge earth-ground wire. The ground wire should ground high-voltage spikes but this doesn't always happen. If the high voltage isn't shorted to ground, the telephone and anyone who happens to be using it may be severely damaged. Fuseless overvoltage protectors are no longer installed.

A **fused protector** is shown in Figure 3-6(b). The drop cable ground wire has one or more fuses connected in-line. The fuses are then earth-grounded. If a high voltage is induced into the line, the fuse blows. This disconnects the ground of the – 48Vdc supply at the central office, which will make the phone inoperable. Although the phone won't work until the fuses are replaced, it won't be damaged either.

The type of overvoltage protection is important to data communication users. A fuseless protector should be replaced with a fused type. If not, a modem attached to the phone connection can be destroyed or damaged.

Ring Trip

The **ring trip** is a 90Vac (RMS), 20Hz signal sent to a called telephone to activate the phone ringer. It's actually a part of the broader supervisory functions provided by the central office.

Supervision

The central office serves as a supervisor of a local exchange. It controls and directs the electrical details associated with placing a call, answering a call, and notifying the caller if the called number is busy. Since the central office monitors traffic, the various signals you hear on the phone originate at the central office, or are initiated there.

The more common supervisory signals are shown in Figure 3-7.

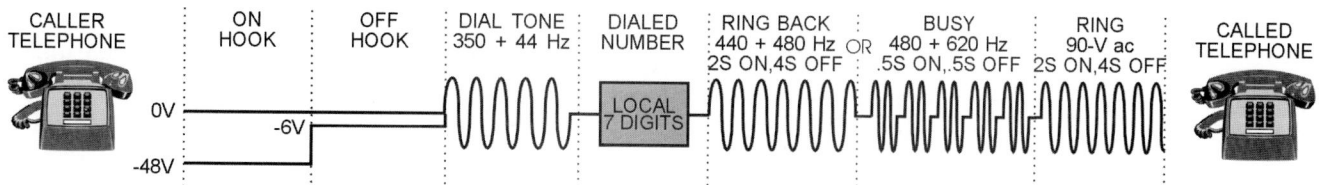

When the phone is on-hook, – 48 volts dc is present across the tip and ring wires. As the handset is lifted, the ring/tip switch is closed and the line voltage drops to – 6 volts dc. With the switch closed, loop current is permitted to flow through the line. The loop current (20 mA) is detected at the central office by energizing a relay. The energized relay enables the **dial tone** oscillator. The dial tone is a continuous 350/440-Hz **dual tone**. Once the first digit of the called number is made, the dial tone is deactivated. When the caller pushes the button on a DTMF keyboard or rotates a dialer, the 20mA current loop is broken momentarily. The loss of current is sufficient to deactivate the dial-tone oscillator.

Operating voltages for telephones are provided by the central office. The on-hook voltage across the tip and ring wire is –48Vdc, while the off-hook voltage is –6Vdc.

The central office counts the dialed tone-pairs or the number of pulse breaks of a rotary dialer to determine when the caller is finished dialing. The central office makes the appropriate connection to the called phone and checks to see if the called phone is on-hook or off-hook. If the called phone is on-hook, the 90Vac, 20Hz **ring signal** is sent. The called phone will ring for 2 seconds, be off for 4 seconds, ring for 2 seconds, and so forth. The caller is informed that the called number is ringing by being sent a **ringback** signal. The ringback is a 440/480Hz dual tone that's on for 2 seconds and off for 4 seconds. This is the ringing signal you hear when you place a call.

The central office checks the called telephone for an on-hook or off-hook condition by sampling the loop current. If there's no loop current, the phone is on-hook. If current is detected, the called phone is off-hook and the central office will send the caller a **busy signal**. The busy signal is a 480/620Hz dual tone that's on for .5 seconds and off for .5 seconds. Occasionally, you may get another type of busy signal. The congestion signal is a 480/620Hz tone that's on for .2 seconds and off for .3 seconds. It sounds like a fast busy signal. If you get a congestion signal, you should hang up and try again a short time later.

Coding

Coding, in the subscriber loop, refers to the manipulation of analog signals to make them suitable for digital switching circuitry at the central office. The signal must then be reconverted back to analog. All of this is done at the central office. Telephone companies have specific techniques for ensuring the integrity of the original voice in the conversion process. Coding is an inherent part of telephone modulation and will be discussed later in the chapter.

Hybrid

The **hybrid** is an interface function handled by the central office. Since telephone communication is conducted through full-duplex operation, the central office provides a 2-to-4-wire interface between the local subscriber loop and the long-distance carriers. The interface is called the hybrid.

A simplified connection scheme illustrating the hybrid is shown in Figure 3-8. Two wires each are provided for the transmit and receive sides of the conversation over the long-distance, and exchange-to-exchange, trunk line. The hybrid itself consists of a multiple winding transformer.

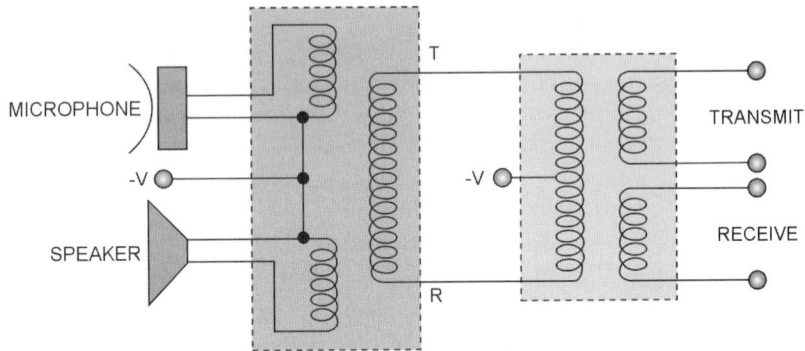

Figure 3-8 Two-Wire to Four-Wire Hybrid

While a central office hybrid is responsible for interfacing to the four-wire circuit, a similar hybrid is found in the telephone. Two wires each run from the **transmitter** (microphone) and **receiver** (speaker). The hybrid interfaces these four wires to the two-wire tip and ring of the local loop.

Testing

Testing is provided by the central office to check for malfunctions in the subscriber loops. Diagnostic access to the loop is provided by relays at the exchange.

The BORSCHT functions are contained in a printed-circuit card at the central office. The card is called a **Subscriber Line Interface Card** (SLIC). The premise of BORSCHT functions dates back to a time when all of telephone communications were analog. Today, the majority of circuitry outside the subscriber loop is digital, and the SLIC is basically an interface between the analog loop and the digital switching circuits. If the subscriber loop was all digital, many of the BORSCHT functions wouldn't be needed—in particular the analog tone signals. Subscriber telephones are gradually following a path similar to that of modems, in that the telephone is becoming much more sophisticated while the cost per function of the telephone is decreasing. This has resulted in the distributed control of many functions that were once the exclusive domain of the central office—call forwarding, **caller number recognition**, speed dialing—to be handled by phones.

PUBLIC INTERCONNECT

In 1955, the first international direct-dialed call was placed between Germany and Switzerland. The call was placed without the assistance of telephone exchange operators. Today, the goal of telephone network subscribers is to have the ability to directly dial any other subscriber, anywhere in the world. While the goal hasn't yet been realized, the time is rapidly approaching when it will be. Fundamental to the goal is the **International Direct Distance Dialing** (IDDD) numbering plan. The IDDD plan is a system which separates the globe into nine regions for the purpose of permitting direct dialing.

> The International Direct Distance Dialing (IDDD) number plan is a world-wide system that permits subscribers to direct-dial any number in the world without operator assistance.

The **world numbering system** is shown in Figure 3-9.

Figure 3-9 IDDD World Numbering System

The number shown in each region is a prefix code required for direct dialing a long-distance call. The prefix provides a means for the public to connect a call to many parts of the world. In the U.S. and Canada, a long-distance call is prefixed with a 1, followed by the **area code**, central office exchange number, and the subscriber number.

As you can see, a call placed to Africa would begin with a 2, and a call placed to South America begins with a 5. Unfortunately, the three-digit **exchange numbers** and four-digit **subscriber numbers** found in North America, aren't followed in many parts of the world. Within North America, the telecommunications system is structured about a well-defined hierarchy.

Network Hierarchy

In the United States and Canada, the telephone system is arranged in a **network hierarchy**. The network is divided into a series of exchanges designated by office class and number. Figure 3-10 shows the classifications.

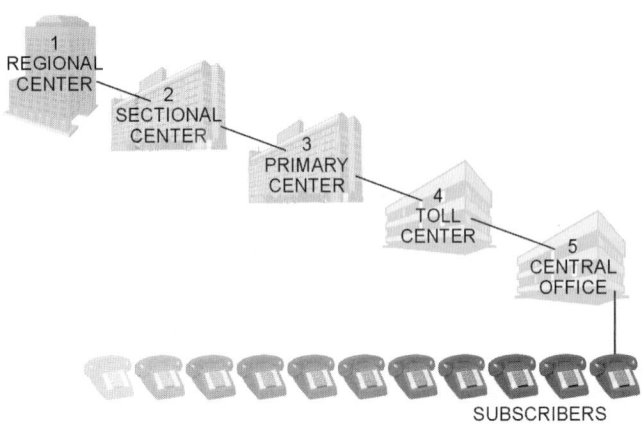

Figure 3-10 Telephone Exchange Classification

Each subscriber is connected to a class 5 exchange, the **central office**. The central office switches subscriber calls to a **toll center**, class 4. The toll center handles only long-distance calls—those calls in which area codes are exchanged. A long-distance call may be routed to its destination by way of any of the **toll exchanges**—class 1 through 4. Once a call leaves a class 4 exchange, it's a part of thousands of other multiplexed calls.

The difference between the toll exchanges is one of switching capability: a class 1 **regional center** has the facilities for switching a far greater number of multiplexed calls than a class 3 **primary center**. The hierarchy describes the ability of an exchange to handle traffic; but it doesn't describe routing patterns of a long-distance call.

> The telephone network is arranged in a hierarchical fashion from the central office (class 5) to four classes of long-distance switching exchanges.

Figure 3-11 shows several paths a long-distance call may make.

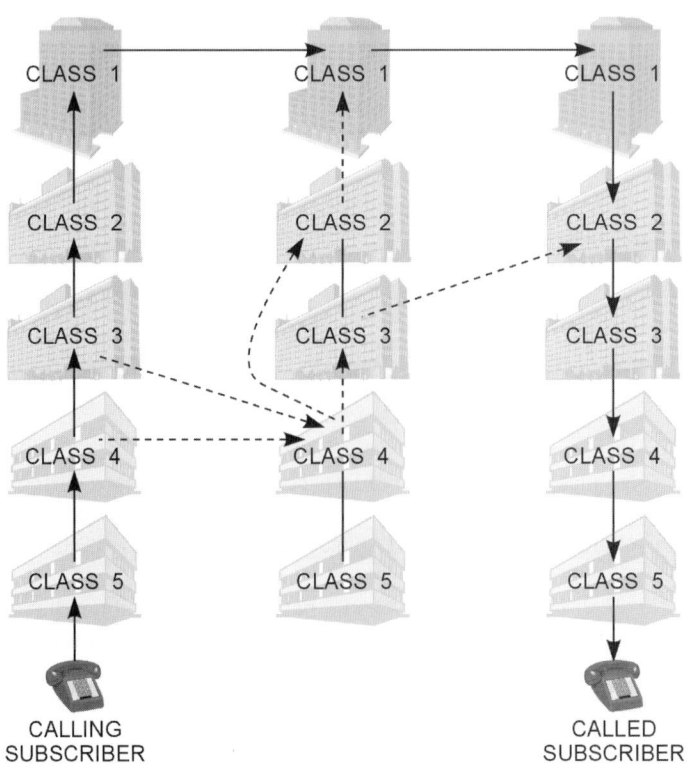

Figure 3-11 Possible Long Distance Routings

The exchanges will look ahead and find the quickest, most-efficient route for a call to travel. This makes sense because the time expended routing and switching a call is time that another caller isn't being serviced. Notice that a call may indeed filter up through the various exchanges, be passed along regional exchanges, and then drop down through succeeding exchanges to the called subscriber. This is the long way around. The alternative paths take a shorter, and quicker, path to the subscriber. Each exchange evaluates the traffic load being switched in upper-level exchanges and determines which exchange has the lightest load. Certain class levels may be jumped or avoided entirely.

Calls within the same area code, but between exchanges, are routed over interoffice trunks. A trunk line is a common pathway between central offices. Figure 3-12 is an example of how central offices may be connected. The **tandem office** shown in the figure is a switching relay. It's used when the interoffice trunks are busy. There are no individual subscribers connected to the tandem office. Although three central offices are shown in Figure 3-12, the size of interoffice connections varies with the traffic patterns of a given area. Large metropolitan areas may have ten or more local offices connected by trunk lines, while a rural area covering many miles may be serviced by one or two central offices.

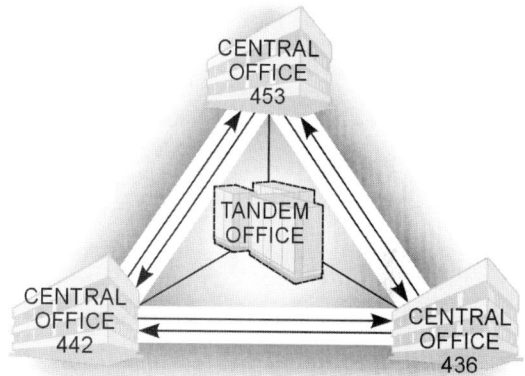

Figure 3-12 Interconnection of Central Office Exchanges

In the United States there are ten class-1 regional centers, seventy class-2 sectional centers, 2,300 class-3 primary exchanges, 1,400 class-4 toll centers, and 20,000 class-5 central offices. The communication medium connecting the centers is frequently microwave transmission. Fiber-optic systems are quite popular as well, due to the low-noise characteristics and very high data rates. An exchange not shown in the figures is the **class-44 toll center**. This is an exchange dedicated only to telephone networks whose switching is accomplished by **all-digital circuitry**. It offers the advantage of speed over the class-4 toll center.

PULSE MODULATION

> Pulse modulation is produced by sampling voice or data at the Nyquist rate.

Modulation in the telephone network has historically been accomplished by opening and closing the 20mA off-hook loop current. This had the effect of creating pulses of current in the line, and the pulses were used to modulate a carrier frequency through the long-distance channel. While the term **pulse modulation** has lingered, the details of modulation have changed considerably.

The type of modulation used in the network may be analog or digital. Analog pulse modulation includes pulse-amplitude modulation and pulse-width modulation. Digital modulation includes pulse-code modulation and delta modulation. Pulse-code modulation is by far the most common method used by the carriers.

As will be seen, no matter if analog or digital modulation is used, the signal must still conform to the original constraints of the voice channel. If a digital technique is used, it must be compatible with analog switching centers. Gradually, analog systems are disappearing and being replaced with the more economical digital network.

Analog Pulse Modulation

The principle of pulse-modulation techniques is to sample a signal and to transmit the samples. Recall from an earlier chapter that the Nyquist sampling rate is equal to twice the highest transmitted frequency. If the signal is sampled at, or above, the Nyquist rate, it can be reconstructed at the receiver with nearly perfect clarity.

Pulse Amplitude Modulation

Pulse Amplitude Modulation (PAM) is illustrated in Figure 3-13(a). The sine wave is sampled with a series of pulses whose amplitude is proportional to the amplitude of the sine wave. The waveform shown in Figure 3-13(a) represents **dual-polarity** PAM since positive pulses are generated from the positive alternation of the sine wave, and negative pulses are taken from the negative alternation of the sine wave.

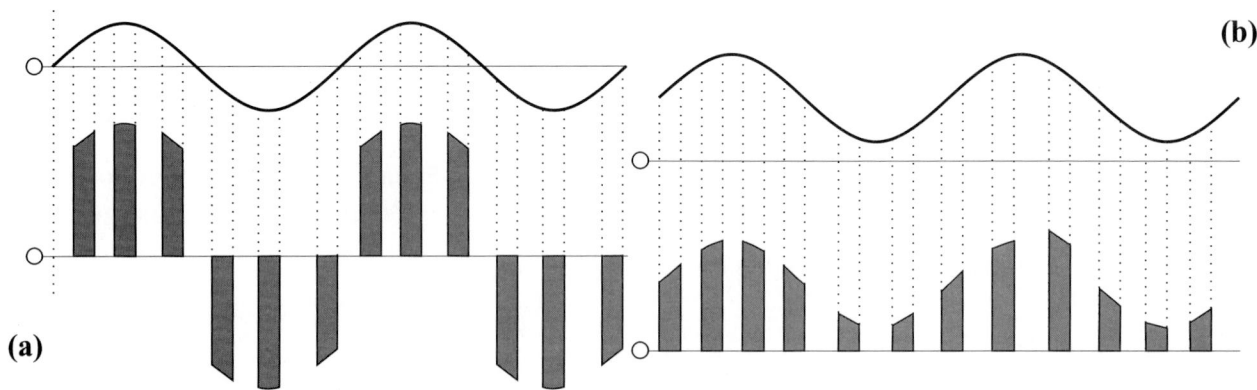

(b)

(a)

Figure 3-13 Pulse Amplitude Modulation

Pulse amplitude modulation is generated by sampling an analog waveform. The amplitude of the pulses is proportional to the amplitude of the waveform.

Single-polarity PAM can also be produced as shown in Figure 3-13(b). A dc bias level is added to the sine wave before it's sampled. PAM closely resembles conventional AM used in broadcast radio. It also has the same disadvantage: noise induced into the modulated signal is very difficult to remove. Single-polarity PAM offers a slightly better noise immunity since only one polarity of voltage is needed; however, it is dual-polarity PAM that's compatible with the positive and negative voltage levels of the EIA/TIA-232 interface.

Pulse Duration Modulation

Pulse Duration Modulation (PDM) is achieved by varying the width of sampled pulses as shown in Figure 3-14(a). The width of the pulse varies in direct proportion to the amplitude of the modulating sine wave. The positive alternation causes the width of the samples to increase and the negative alternation causes the sampled widths to decrease.

The rate, or frequency, of the sine wave is tracked at the 0-degree, 180-degree, and 360-degree **crossover points**. The pulse width at these points is of a constant value equal to 0 volts. The sample's period at the crossovers is proportional to the sine wave's frequency.

> Pulse duration modulation results when the width of a pulse varies in direct proportion to the modulating waveform. Since amplitude doesn't vary, it's not as noisy as pulse amplitude modulation.

A PDM variation appears in Figure 3-14(b). The sample's **trailing edge** remains fixed while its **leading edge** varies with the wave's amplitude. On the positive alternation, the pulse width increases, but on the negative alternation, the width decreases. Since the leading edge varies, this is called leading-edge PDM.

Trailing-edge PDM is shown in Figure 3-14(c). As in the other PDM types, the sampled pulse widens for the positive alternation of the sine wave and decreases for the negative

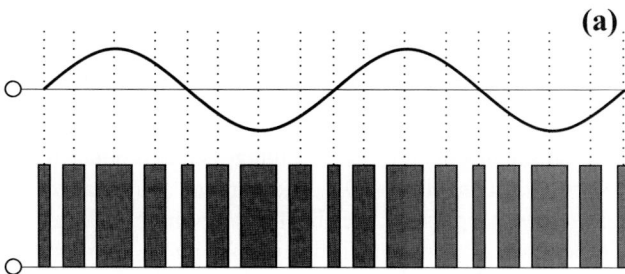

(a)

alternation. The trailing edge creates the pulse-width variance, so this is called trailing-edge PDM. The trailing edge is fixed at the 0-, 180-, and 360-degree crossover points, and is used for calculating the signal modulation frequency.

PDM is less prone to noise distortion than PAM because the amplitude doesn't change. If noise is induced into a PDM signal, the pulse train can be passed through a limiter to eliminate amplitude noise variations.

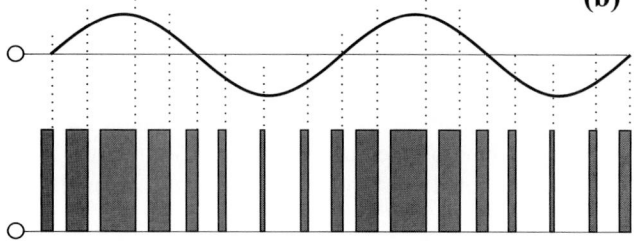

(b)

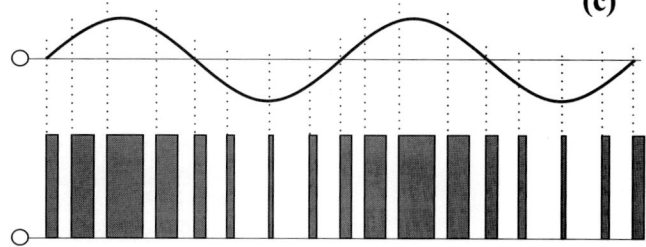

(c)

Digital Pulse Modulation

The analog modulation methods described above are close enough to a digital signal that they can be transmitted through a digital system. PAM has the weakness of noise susceptibility, and PDM can be difficult to transmit because the position of the pulse edges is crucial to recovering the original information at the receiver. It's not uncommon for the pulse to spread apart over long distances, which introduces even more distortion.

Figure 3-14 Pulse Duration Modulation

Digital Pulse Modulation (DPM) is designed to alleviate these problems. With digital modulation, the voice or data is converted to binary square waves, and the amplitude/frequency information is encoded into the bits.

Detection circuits at the receiver are responsible only for determining the presence or absence of the binary bits—specific amplitude, pulse width, and pulse position isn't important for recovering the original information.

The digital signal can be made virtually noise-free at the receiver. Digital signals in the telephone network, as in other applications, require much more bandwidth than do analog signals. The large bandwidth is traded off for lower noise characteristics, compatibility with computers, and lower equipment costs.

Pulse-Code Modulation

Pulse-code modulation is produced by converting an analog waveform into a digital bit-stream.

Pulse-Code Modulation (PCM) is the most widely used digital modulation technique. It's used extensively in the multiplexed hierarchies of the common carriers. PCM is produced by applying the analog signal to an analog-to-digital converter to produce a waveform resembling a **staircase**. The signal from the converter is then integrated to produce pulses with an amplitude equal to the sample voltage of the ADC. The sample voltages are called quantization levels. A **quantization level** represents the absolute amplitude of the analog signal at a particular sampling time. The sampling time is determined by the **Nyquist rate** and is twice the highest frequency of the analog signal. Once the pulse samples are taken, the amplitude of the pulses are converted to a corresponding binary number, or code.

An example of PCM is shown in Figure 3-15. Eight quantization levels are provided from which the sine wave may be encoded. With eight levels, the digitized output will be a 3-bit code, or, the positive alternation of the sine wave can be represented with 16 discrete binary numbers. Figure 3-15(a) shows that five samples were taken of the positive alternation. The samples have been extracted at Figure 3-15(b), and the quantization level representing each sample is noted above the pulse. The quantized samples are PCM-encoded in Figure 3-15(c).

A pulse code modulation sample consists of 8 bits. The first bit represents the sign of the sample (positive or negative), the next three bits specify one of eight sample chords, while the last four bits specify one of sixteen intervals found in each chord.

Coded PCM has no amplitude variation and no dependency on pulse position or width for encoding the signal information. The problem with it is that the quantization levels are fixed, and may not correspond to the actual amplitude of a sine wave at the time of the sample. This is evident in Figure 3-15(a) when the second and fourth samples are taken. The amplitude of the waveform at these times is actually 4.7, but since there's no quantization level at 4.7, it was rounded to 5—the nearest level.

The difference between the actual signal amplitude and the quantized level at the time of a sample is called **quantization error**. (In an analog-to-digital converter, **full-scale error** is analogous to quantization error.) The amount of error is reduced by increasing the number of levels.

Once a PCM-encoded signal is transmitted through the telephone network, it's influenced by noise in the system. The statistical average of noise in a PCM system has been determined to be one fourth the amount of a quantization level. An indication of the quality of a quantizer is the **Signal noise-to-Quantizing Ratio** **(SQR)**. In Figure 3-15, the SQR of the first sample is $1/.25 = 4$, the second sample is $5/.25 = 20$, and the third sample is $7/.25 = 28$. The different SQR values are important—particularly the wide gap between the first sample, and the second and third— because it suggests that those samples taken at higher amplitude levels will be less affected by noise than the smaller amplitude levels. Weak, small signals are much more likely to be found in the PCM system than large, strong signals, so the differing SQRs represent a problem.

The solution is to be found in the coding process. If each quantization level could be encoded so that small signals produce a coded change equal to that of the large signals, then the SQR will be more equal at all quantization levels. The device that does this is called a **compander** (compressor/expander). A compander is found on a monolithic IC called a **codec** (coder/decoder). The codec is responsible for the coding that was mentioned earlier in the BORSCHT functions.

In North America, the most widely used compander is the $\mu=$**255 Law Compander PCM Digital-Coding Standard**, or the μ-Law. The standard specifies the coding method which compresses PCM at the transmitter and expands it at the receiver. Figure 3-16 illustrates the μ-Law Compander.

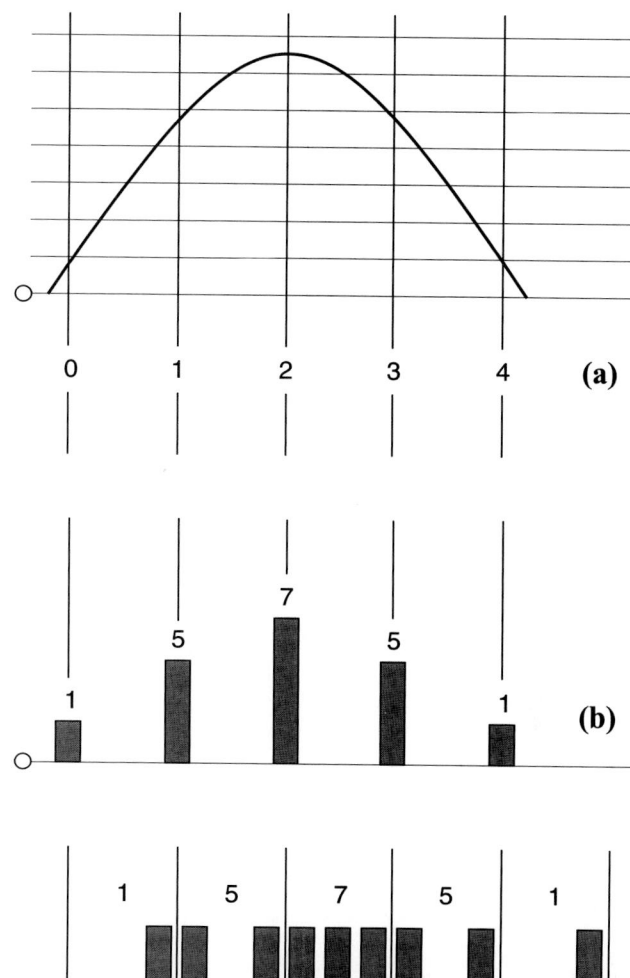

Figure 3-15 Pulse Code Modulation

A PCM signal is companded in order to keep the signal-to-noise ratio equal for small and large amplitude signals. Companding is accomplished by sampling smaller amplitudes at a greater rate than the larger amplitude signals.

The encoder generates an 8-bit code for each sample taken. As an analog signal is input to the compander, it's converted to an approximate of the logarithm of the curve. The slope of the sine wave is restructured so as to rise at a logarithmic rate rather than at a sine rate. The solid line in the figure represents the logarithmic rise of the positive alternation of the input.

Figure 3-16 illustrates the 90- to 180-degree portion of the positive alternation. Notice that as the waveform approaches 0, the binary logarithmic conversion has increased in frequency. This means that the small amplitude signals are being sampled more often than the large amplitude portion of the signal. The smaller amplitudes are at the left of the figure, while the larger amplitudes of the signal are at the right of the figure. If the smaller amplitudes are sampled more often than the large amplitudes, then the smaller amplitudes are occupying a greater portion of time in a data stream. If the amount of time devoted to smaller signals has increased, this is equivalent to making the smaller signals more equal to the larger amplitudes of a waveform. Or, to say it another way, the larger amplitudes have been **compressed** to make them equal to the small amplitudes.

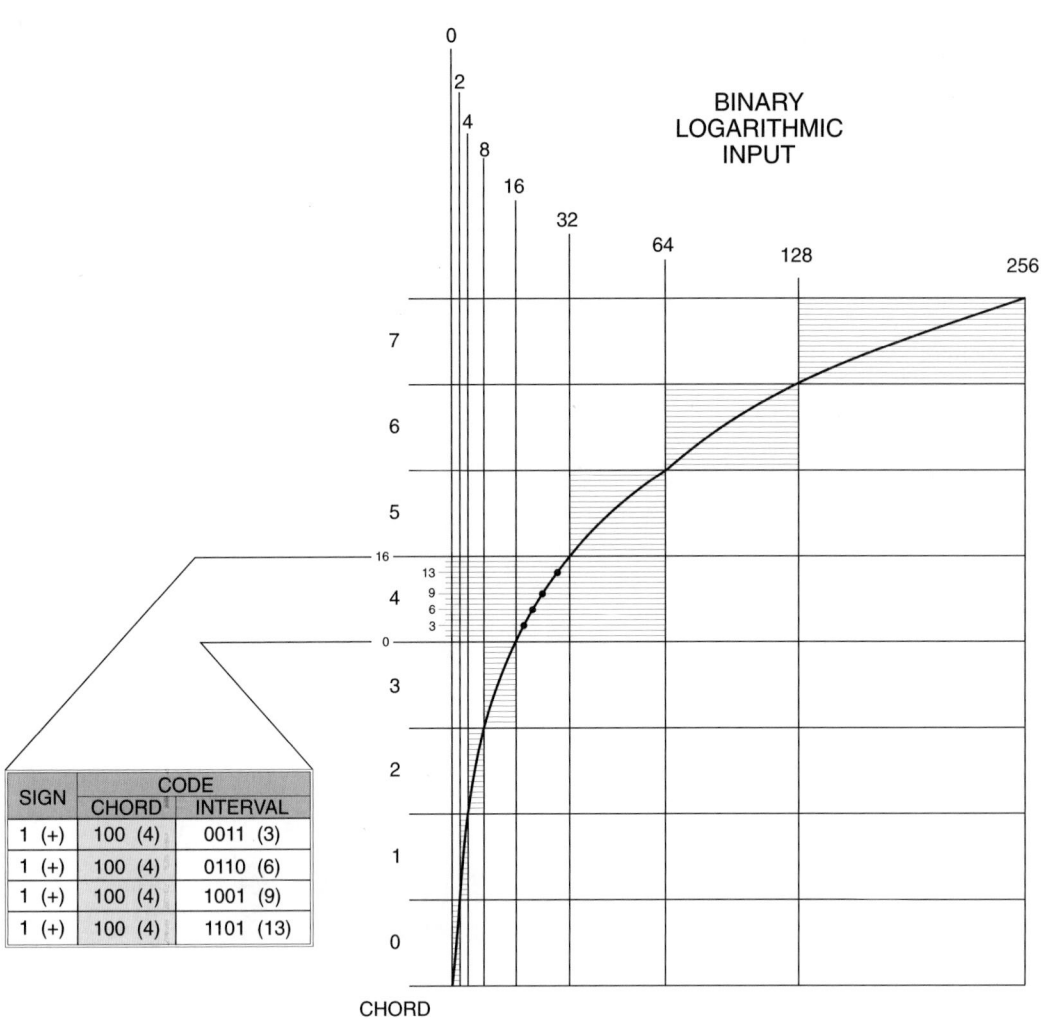

A μ-Law Compander includes sixteen primary quantization levels, eight for the positive alternation and eight for the negative alternation. Figure 3-16 shows the eight levels of the positive alternation. The sixteen levels are known as **chords**. Each of the chords is subdivided into sixteen secondary quantization levels, called **intervals**. Figure 3-16 details the sixteen intervals of the fourth chord.

Due to the logarithmic rise time of the signal, the lower-amplitude samples will indicate a far greater change of amplitude than will the upper levels. Consider the detail in Figure 3-16. The dots indicate PCM samples. For each sample, an 8-bit code is generated, as shown in the box on the left.

SIGN	CODE	
---	CHORD	INTERVAL
1 (+)	100 (4)	0011 (3)
1 (+)	100 (4)	0110 (6)
1 (+)	100 (4)	1001 (9)
1 (+)	100 (4)	1101 (13)

Figure 3-16 The μ-Law Companding Code

The most significant bit in the code (the left-most bit) is a sign bit. It's a logic 1 when the analog signal is positive, and a logic 0 when it's negative. The next three bits are the absolute value of the chord (100). All four samples were taken in the fourth chord. The last four bits are the binary code of the sampled interval within the chord. The first sample is at interval 3, or 0011. The second sample is at interval 6, or 0110. The third sample is taken at interval 9, or 1001. The fourth sample occurs at interval 13, or 1101. The coded data is what's actually transmitted.

Each chord also has a weighted value. The weight is the **binary logarithmic input**. It's needed at the receiver so as to expand the compressed waveform back to its original shape. The weighted base of the intervals within the fourth chord is $(32-16)/16 = 1$. Interval one in the chord is, then, $16 + 1 = 17$, interval two is $16 + 2 = 18$, interval three is $16 + 3 = 19$, and so on.

For comparison, the weighted base in the sixth chord is $(128-64)/16 = 4$. Interval one in the sixth chord is $64 + 4 = 68$, interval two is $64 + 8 = 72$, and so on. A portion of the signal in the sixth chord has an amplitude weight greater than the weight of the fourth chord because the sixth chord contains coded information of a greater amplitude than the fourth. The receiver tracks the chords, and, in the decoding process, provides a greater amount of amplification for data from the sixth chord than the fourth chord.

The actual data transmitted are the 8-bit codes, as shown in Figure 3-16. All samples produce similar 8-bit codes, no matter if a sample is taken in the first or seventh chord. The **weighted value** is implied by the position of the chord. As mentioned above, the receiver counts the chords and decodes the bits based upon their weighted chord positions.

The samples for Figure 3-16 are rough estimates of companding, but they illustrate the benefits of compressing the analog input signal so that small amplitude changes produce a large coding change, while large amplitudes produce a relatively small change. A codec at the receiver reverses the process and expands the signal back to its sine-wave shape. A practical compander is capable of producing nearly equal SQRs across the full range of the analog signal. PCM-encoded data is sampled at twice the rate of the voice-channel frequency. For digital information, the voice channel has a maximum frequency of 4 kHz. The sampling rate is then 2 x 4 kHz = 8 kHz. Since there are 8 bits per sample, 8 x 8 kHz = 64 kHz. The data rate for each PCM digital channel is then 64 kBPS.

> The compander used in North America is the $\mu = 255$ Law Compander, PCM Digital Coding Standard. The European equivalent is the α-law compander.

The μ-Law Compander is used almost exclusively in the United States. In Europe, the α-**Law Compander** is used. It's proven to produce better SQRs at small amplitudes, but has the disadvantage of generating higher noise levels in idle channels.

Companding is an excellent method for increasing fidelity in a voice channel. But it wreaks havoc on data signals, and to a lesser extent, voice signals. The quantization error introduced by the analog-to-digital conversion is...well, an error. Channel distortion has an identical effect as quantization errors, and the remedy for both is the same: boost the signal-to-noise ratio so that distortion (errors) have a minimal effect.

But the FCC limits the amount of radiated power allowed on a phone line (to reduce cross-talk between adjacent channels), and this in turn limits the maximum rate that information can travel across a phone line. More will be said about this in Chapter 4.

Delta Modulation

Delta Modulation (DM) is a low-cost alternative to PCM. It requires a simple circuit to implement at the transmitter, and an equally simple circuit at the receiver detector. The disadvantage of DM is that it doesn't respond well to the fast changes of an analog input. This isn't too much of a problem for voice communication, which seldom has abrupt amplitude changes. However, for data communications with the on/off type of structure, it causes a distorted output. A block diagram of a DM transmitter is shown in Figure 3-17(a).

The analog input signal is applied to an **open-loop gain comparator**.

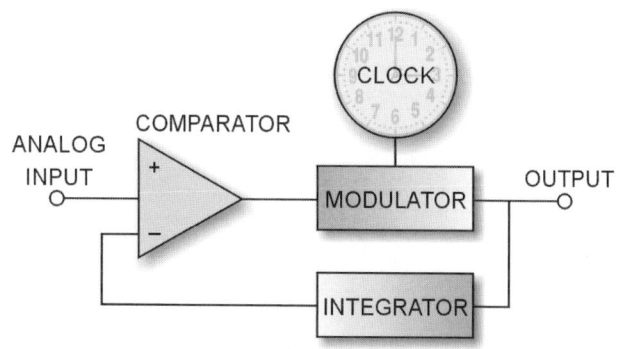

Figure 3-17(a) Delta Modulation Transmitter Block Diagram

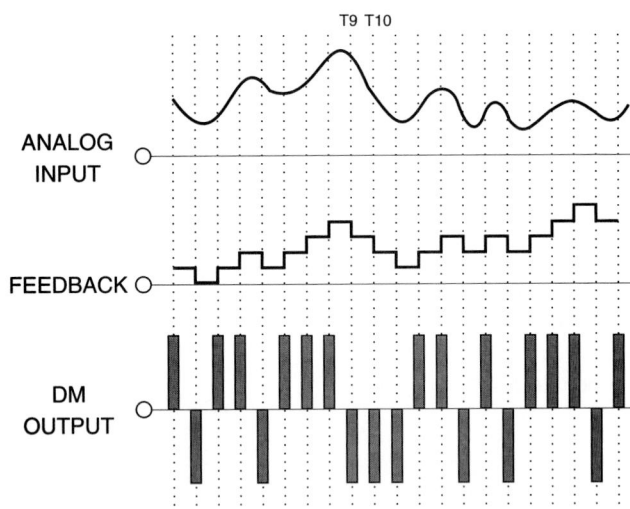

Figure 3-17(b) Delta Modulation Transmitter Waveforms

The saturated output of the comparator is digitized in the clocked, **D-type latch, flip-flop modulator**. The modulator output is sampled and integrated to become a reference signal to the comparator. The comparator output will be in the direction of the largest input: if the analog input is larger than the feedback, the output will go positive. But if the analog input is smaller than the feedback, the comparator will saturate in a negative direction.

Figure 3-17(b) illustrates the analog input to the comparator with the integrated feedback signal. The DM output consists of positive and negative pulses. The modulator outputs a positive pulse by examining the direction of the previous pulse.

If the current sample of the analog signal is more positive than the previous sample, the modulator output will be a positive pulse. For example, in Figure 3-17(b), the DM output is negative at T9. At T10, the analog signal is more negative than at T9. With the feedback ramp applied to the inverting input of the comparator, the comparator saturates in a negative direction since the feedback signal at T9 was greater (more positive) than the analog input at T10.

The effectiveness of DM is determined by the sampling rate. If the samples aren't taken often enough, the detected analog at the receiver will be heavily distorted. On the other hand, a high sampling rate complicates the circuitry and drives up costs—which would offset the advantage of DM. Due to the slow response rate, DM is used at lower data rates and for voice communication, when fidelity isn't particularly important.

VOICE-CHANNEL CHARACTERISTICS

In earlier chapters, the frequency response of speech channels in the telephone system was given as 300 Hz to 3,300 Hz, for a bandwidth of 3 kHz. Speech communication is maintained within this range, but a more precise definition of the telephone channel is now needed because the **voice channel** (VF) extends from 0 Hz to 4 kHz. The **speech channel** occupies the range from 300 Hz to 3 kHz, and is referred to as the **in-band** signaling range. The frequency ranges from 0 Hz to 300 Hz, and from 3,300 Hz to 4,000 Hz are called **out-of-band** signals. Speech communication is not permitted outside the in-band signaling range. Out-of-band signals carry supervisory information. Supervisory information may be as described in the BORSCHT function, or it may include protocol information related to the framing or handshaking of data communications. Out-of-band signals aren't limited to the out-of-band range, and are frequently placed in the in-band range. Figure 3-18 summarizes signaling in the voice channel.

Although voice communications fall within the 3kHz range, data communications utilize the entire 4kHz of the bandwidth. But it's important to understand that the local loop was designed for 3kHz of speech communication.

The width of the voice channel used for data communications is 4 kHz.

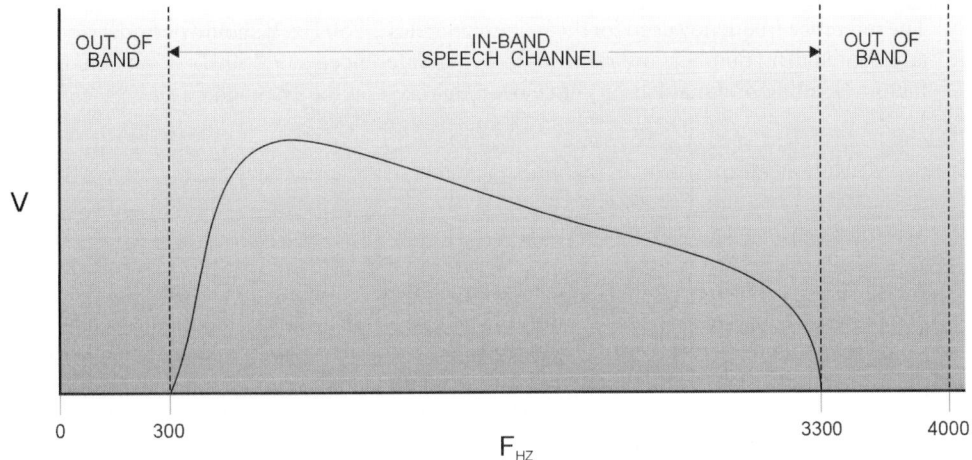

Figure 3-18 Voice Channel Signaling

Two characteristics that are of the most concern in the voice channel are **attenuation** and **delay**. The remedy for phase delay is accomplished at the cost of exasperating the signal attenuation. For example, phase delays increase when a channel is loaded, but loading provides a flatter response across the channel.

Attenuation and Delay

The telephone networks have designated 1 mW as the reference from which to measure amplitude levels. Channel signals may fall above or below the reference, in which case, the ratio between the 1mW reference and the signal level provides an indication of **signal strength**. The ratio is expressed as the logarithmic function of the ratio:

$$dB = 10 \log P1/P2$$

where P1 = signal power and P2 = the 1mW reference.

For example, a signal delivers 50 mW of power at a specified frequency to a load. The power gain is found by:

$$dBm = 10 \log P1/1 \text{ mW}$$
$$dBm = 10 \log 50 \text{ mW}/1 \text{ mW}$$
$$dBm = 17$$

In this example, the ratio is expressed in dBm since the signal power and reference are both expressed in mW. If the power ratio is less than 1, dBm will be negative. For example: a signal delivering .5 mW to a load has a loss of:

$$dBm = 10 \text{ Log } .5 \text{ mW}/1 \text{ mW}$$
$$dBm = -3$$

Decibel levels in the telephone network, and most other applications, are meaningful only at a specified **reference frequency**.

The reference frequency used for the voice channel is 2,250 Hz. It should be understood that any quoted dBm numbers are relevant to 1 mW referenced at 2,250 Hz, if no extenuating factors (loading or equalization) have been imposed on the channel.

> Measurements are made in the voice channel at a reference frequency of 2,250Hz and at a 1mW power reference point.

A typical **attenuation response curve** is shown by the solid line in Figure 3-19. There are two important characteristics of the curve. The first is that the least amount of attenuation is found at about 1.7 kHz. Not coincidentally, the vast majority of voice communication takes place in this area. The second point to note is that attenuation greatly increases below 1 kHz and above 3 kHz. The attenuation **roll-off** is more pronounced for the upper half of the curve.

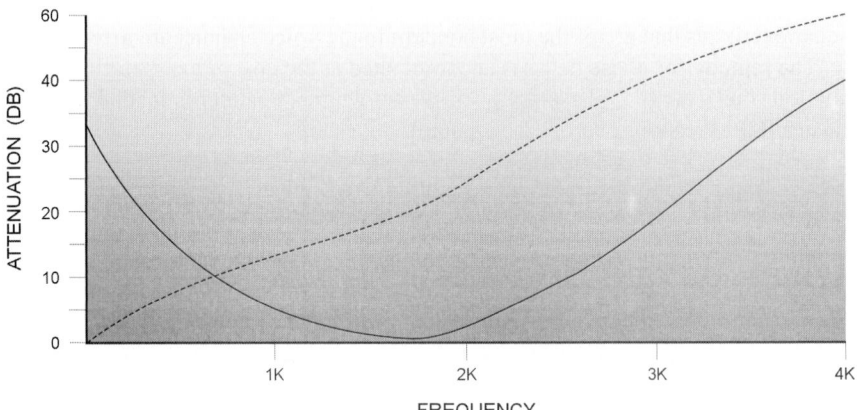

**Figure 3-19
Voice-Channel
Attenuation Response**

This is consistent with the capacitive action of the channel as described in Chapter 2. At the upper frequencies, the signal strength drops because of a smaller capacitive reactance across the channel. The voice channel has the appearance of a lowpass filter.

Figure 3-19 is a normal voice channel, such as you may use when making a telephone call. The telephone company has prepared it for the response shown. Attenuation was minimized at 1.7kHz by loading the channel. "Loading" the channel refers to connecting 88mH coils in series with the channel, repeated every 6,000 feet. The practice is called **H88 loading**.

The dotted line in Figure 3-19 shows the attenuation response of the voice channel without H88 loading. The introduction of the series inductance causes the channel impedance to decrease, which in turn, allows a greater amount of the signal to be available at the load. **Minimum channel impedance** occurs at the resonant frequency of the loading coils and channel capacitance—around 1,700 Hz. As mentioned, the solid-line graph represents a typical voice channel to which your telephone—or, perhaps, modem—is attached. It's sometimes referred to as **3kHz flat weighting**.

The negative effect of H88 loading is increased **phase delays**. Figure 3-20 illustrates with the solid line an H88-loaded voice channel, and the dotted line shows delays without loading. The amount of delay is very much frequency-dependent. Any sort of **channel filtering** also contributes to the delay. As can be seen from the graph, delays aren't very important in voice communication.

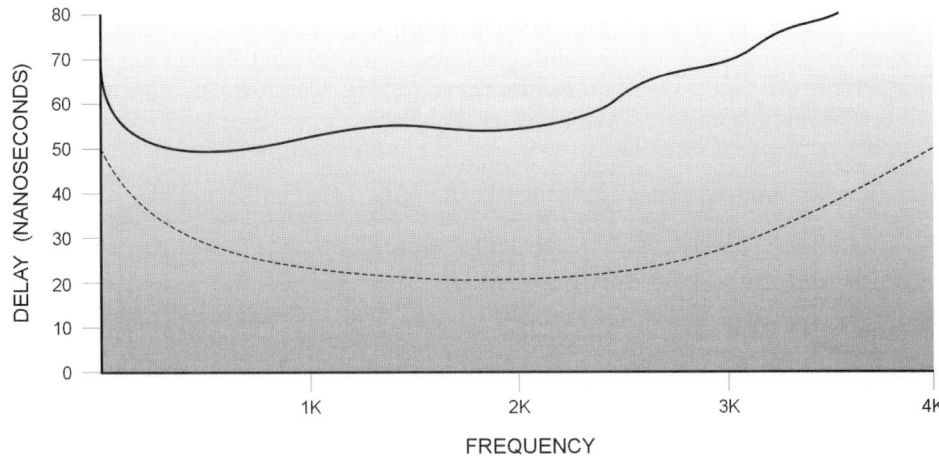

**Figure 3-20
Voice-Channel
Delays**

The ear is not very sensitive to phase delays, but data and video communication can be severely distorted by them. If a digital communication system requires data bits to maintain the sharp corners of the square wave, phase delays will cause the corners to be rounded, and the leading and trailing edges will tend to resemble a **ramp**. This can create false triggering by having a receiver interpret a logic 0 as a logic 1.

Attenuation across the voice channel is controlled by loading the channel with an inductance.

Since **phase distortion** of speech is difficult for the ear to detect but **amplitude distortion** is readily apparent, the voice channel was adapted to provide better attenuation characteristics, at the price of increasing phase distortion. The **adaptive equalizers** in modems are sufficient to offset phase problems for data rates of 4,800 BPS or less. Above this rate, the data bits smear together in intersymbol interference. Telephone companies have made available to data-communication users special lines that have been prepared for smaller delays than are found in the standard voice channel.

Conditioned Lines

Phase delays increase with inductive loading. Phase delay is controlled by line conditioning. Conditioned lines are normally called dedicated channels.

For a monthly fee, the user can gain access to a voice-grade channel, called a **3002**, that's been adapted for data. The channel is Figure 3-21(a) shows the delay characteristics for a 3002 line. The figure shows that if a user pays to lease this channel, the telephone company will provide a maximum phase delay of 1.75 mS from 700 Hz to 2,700 Hz. The attenuation characteristics of Figure 3-21(b) provide a range of signal loss across the voice channel. The 3002 line specifies that at 500 Hz, the loss won't exceed –8 dB. Also, the signal level won't be allowed to rise above –2 dB (which means the signal may receive a large gain hit and still remain at, or below, the –2dB level). The telephone company will guarantee this performance for the channel up to 2,500 Hz. At frequencies less than 500 Hz and over 2,500 Hz, the signal loss may be as high as –12 dB.

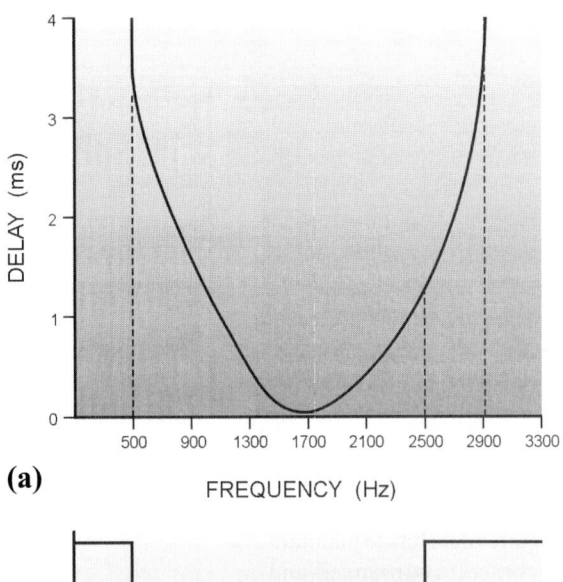

(a)

FREQUENCY (Hz)

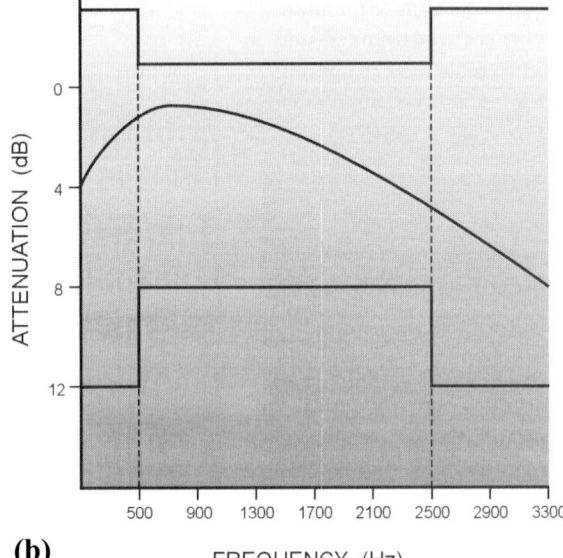

(b)

FREQUENCY (Hz)

Figure 3-21 3002 Leased Line

For additional fees, a data-communica- tions user can lease conditioned lines with improved attenuation and delay properties. The so-called **C-Condi- tioned Characteristics** are depicted in Figure 3-22.

The C1 line in Figure 3-22(a) provides the user with a maximum phase delay of 1 mS from 800 Hz to 2,400 Hz. At frequencies less than 800 Hz and greater than about 2,600 Hz, the delay increases to 1.75 mS. A C2 line provides maximum delays of .5 mS from 1,000 Hz to 2,600 Hz. At frequencies on either side of the range, the delays may increase up to 3 mS for below 500 Hz and over 2,800 Hz. A C4 line (the most expensive) provides a maximum phase delay of .3 mS between 1,000 Hz and 2,600 Hz. As in the C2 line, delays increase below and above this range.

To the right side of Figure 3-22 are the maximum and minimum attenuation ranges for each conditioned line. While a C1 line is erratic at the upper fre- quency limits, C2 and C4 lines offer a generally flat response from 500 Hz to 3,000 Hz. Attenuation is very important in voice communication, but less important when transferring data. High signal-to-noise ratios (low attenuation) mean less distortion and fewer errors. Signal strength can be achieved with repeaters, multiplexers, etc., but phase-delay compensation isn't quite as easily arrived at.

It's important to realize that the delay and attenuation amounts shown in Figure 3-22 are maximum values. A C1 line will have a maximum delay of 1 mS at 1,700 Hz, but it's more likely to be less than .5 mS. The same is true with each of the other lines. The dotted line in the C4 graphs shows the typical delay and attenuation response across the entire channel. The C1 and C2 lines have similar responses within the limits of each conditioned channel.

C-conditioned and 3002 lines are usually referred to as **leased**, or **dedicated**, lines. This shouldn't be misunderstood to mean that a wire pair to a distant location has been reserved for the user. "Dedicated" means that the channel is dedicated to meeting the phase and attenuation requirements of the user. "Leased," as stated earlier, means the user pays a monthly fee for the line. The 3002 voice-grade channel for data communications is the cheapest, while the C4 is the most expensive.

A third type of conditioning, C3, provides improvements similar to C2 lines. The C3 channel is used exclusively for **trunk lines between exchanges**, and isn't available to lease.

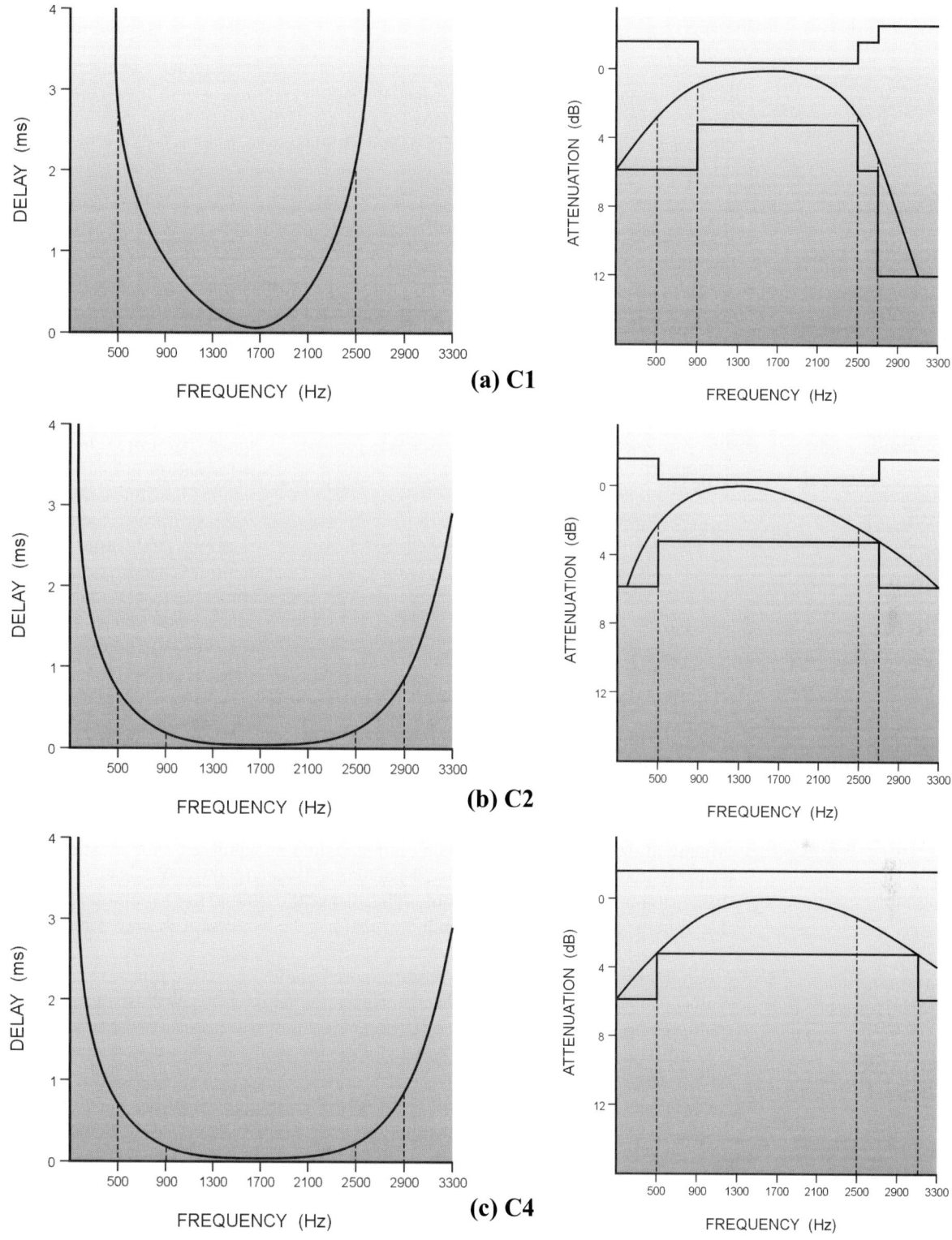

(a) C1

(b) C2

(c) C4

Figure 3-22 C1, C2, and C4 Conditioned Lines

MULTIPLEXING

Multiplexing is done at many levels and at many points in data communications. At the most basic level, it's found within individual ICs in data processing equipment. An address or data bus is a form of multiplexing. As mentioned earlier, the information to be multiplexed may be analog or digital.

It's not unusual for the information to pass through several analog and digital conversions on the way to its destination. In the interest of coherency, the multiplexing information in this chapter is concerned primarily with data multiplexing as it applies to the long-distance telephone network.

Long distance carriers employ a considerable amount of voice-channel

By and large, the carriers use a broadcast form of multiplexing, similar to the 100-station assignment in the broadcast FM band. For the carriers, there's little to distinguish between data and voice communication—any information traveling a long distance is mixed together like a grab-bag of information.

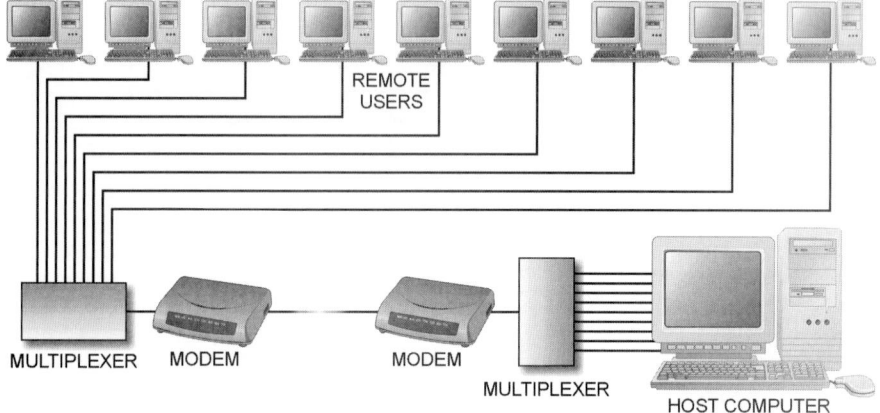

REMOTE USERS

MULTIPLEXER   MODEM   MODEM   MULTIPLEXER   HOST COMPUTER

Figure 3-23 Multiplexing Reduces Hardware

Local multiplexing, on the other hand, occurs before the information is loaded onto the public telephone system. Figure 3-23 is an example of local multiplexing. The device used to multiplex local data is a router. A router, or switch, not only gates blocks of data but it also contains the intelligence to map a complete route to the final destination. Router techniques are described in Chapter 8.

Multiplexing provides an efficient system for transferring large amounts of information from point to point. There are several multiplexing techniques in use today and the best method for an application depends upon several considerations. The first would be the volume of data. Generally, low data volume would be handled by the most economical transmission medium, which is twisted-pair wires. Twisted pairs, you'll recall from Chapter 2, have a limited bandwidth available. This means they would use a multiplexing scheme that either requires a small bandwidth, or that has the bandwidth sharply defined.

CNST OBJECTIVE
I-A

Medium and large data volumes require more bandwidth, so the transmission medium would probably be coaxial cable, fiber optic cable, or microwaves. In many cases, multiplexing systems employ several different techniques. The receiving and transmitting equipment often dictate the technique used, since the equipment may be designed for the use of only one technique.

Today, there are three basic multiplexing techniques in use. **Space-division Multiplexing** (SDM) is the oldest of the three. A separate channel is provided for each device communicating in an SDM system. **Frequency-division Multiplexing** (FDM) is patterned after the broadcast frequency ranges. An FDM system separates a large bandwidth into many narrow-bandwidth channels. **Time-division Multiplexing** (TDM) permits all users access to a large-bandwidth frequency range. The users take turns transmitting into the channel.

The three methods may be easier to visualize by imagining the airline industry in terms of multiplexing. The many passengers on the plane are representative of the data being transmitted. If SDM were to be used, each plane would depart a terminal and travel a separate flight plan to the destination terminal. If the industry adopted the FDM method, a single route would exist to the destination but it would be very wide in order to accommodate all of the planes.

Any terminals between the departure and destination terminal would be accessible by all planes. The TDM technique would require all planes to follow a single flight plan, and the planes would have to follow in order along the path. There would be no intervening terminals enroute to the destination. Once the planes arrive at the destination they taxi to their own terminal to deliver the passengers.

Of course, the commercial airline industry doesn't follow any of the methods just described, but it includes a combination of all three techniques. The same is true of a complete data communication system. A group of communication channels may be time-division multiplexed, and then space-division multiplexed to a group of receivers.

Space-Division Multiplexing (SDM)

Space-division multiplexing calls for a single channel connected to a transmitter and receiver. The single channel is physically isolated from the rest of the communication system. The data bus running on PC boards in a computer is an example of SDM.

The most common example is the local telephone exchange. Each exchange is capable of switching the calls of 10,000 subscribers. Each subscriber is connected to the exchange by a single wire pair, and the wire pairs are sheathed in a thick cable that runs to the exchange.

Figure 3-24 shows a telephone exchange with subscribers connected to it. With the switching shown, each subscriber can communicate with any other subscriber. SDM requires that each channel be physically separated from the other and that each channel have its own receiver and transmitter. The wire pairs feeding the exchange satisfy the channel requirement.

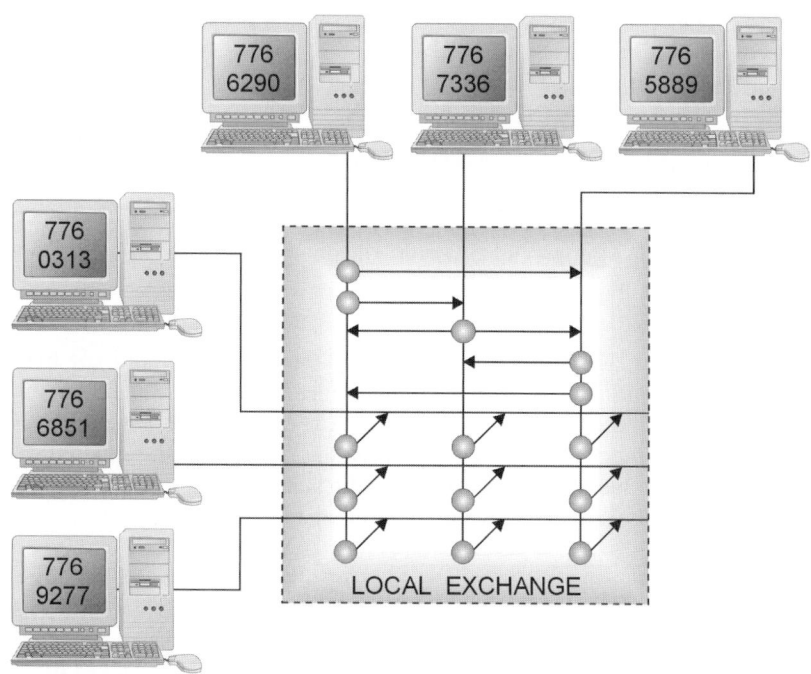

**Figure 3-24
Space-Division
Multiplexing**

The wires in the twisted pairs are insulated from one another and all of the pairs are further insulated by a cable jacket. The telephone—which doubles as a transmitter and receiver—meets the requirement for dedicating a receiver and transmitter to each channel.

In a manner similar to telephone exchanges, the **address bus** in a computer works in an SDM fashion. The microprocessor transmits an address along one of the address lines to the computer memory. Once the address arrives at the memory section, it's gated to the proper address location. If the microprocessor wishes to read from the memory, then the memory assumes the role of transmitter when it sends the requested information. The lines on the address bus comprise a dedicated channel between receiver and transmitter. The microprocessor and memory make up the receiver/transmitter component of the space-division multiplexer.

SDM has the advantage of requiring little to no over-head to frame and transmit data. If one of the channels is disabled, the others are unaffected since each channel has separate receivers and transmitters. Expansion of the system is easy, since all that's required is to run another channel and install the receiver and transmitter. Conversely, it's equally easy to delete a channel.

The disadvantage to SDM relates to the costs of making changes and the lack of resource sharing. If a cable jacket is carrying fifty pairs of twisted wire and a user decides to add another channel, then the additional wire pair will have to be run along with the existing wires. This cost could be considerable.

If, within a cable containing fifty wire pairs, only a few are transmitting and receiving, then the majority of the system is idle. Multiplexing is assumed to increase the efficiency of transporting data, but in this case, SDM would clearly result in a drop in the efficiency. The other side of this situation is one in which all fifty pairs are being utilized, but a few channels have more data than the channel can handle. If those channels could export some of their volume to another channel, the problem would be resolved. Unfortunately, the isolation of channels prohibits **resource sharing** in the channels.

Generally, SDM is a good choice for short distances or when the channels must be isolated. If this isn't an absolute requirement, FDM and TDM offer an alternative that is more efficient.

Frequency-Division Multiplexing (FDM)

> Frequency-Division Multiplexing is used for analog signals. FDM can multiplex up to 10,800 voice channels.

Frequency Division Multiplexing dates back to methods used for broadcast communication, as mentioned earlier. The commercial FM broadcast band covers the range from 88 MHz to 108 MHz, a bandwidth of 20 MHz. An FM radio station is assigned a center frequency within the range and allotted a bandwidth of 200 kHz out of the 20MHz total bandwidth available. This means that 100 FM radio stations can transmit simultaneously across the allotted FM channel bandwidth without disturbing one another.

FDM systems have adopted an identical approach. A single, large bandwidth is divided into many narrow-bandwidth channels. Each of the channels has dedicated receiver/transmitters that send and receive on the assigned channel. It is similar to SDM in that separate receivers/transmitters are required for each channel. But whereas SDM lacked flexibility in rerouting data, an FDM system can send data through a channel and to any receiver that's tuned to the assigned frequency of the channel. It would be difficult and expensive to incorporate the same routing flexibility into a computer address bus or a telephone exchange.

FDM has the same problem with resource sharing as SDM. Illustrated in Figure 3-25(a), are five data channels, each with a bandwidth of 4kHz. The channels are separated one from the other by 500Hz guard bands. The guard bands are needed so that spurious sidebands don't cross into an adjacent channel. The channels are permanently assigned to a transmitter/receiver (called a **transceiver**). The transceiver arrangement is shown in Figure 3-25(b).

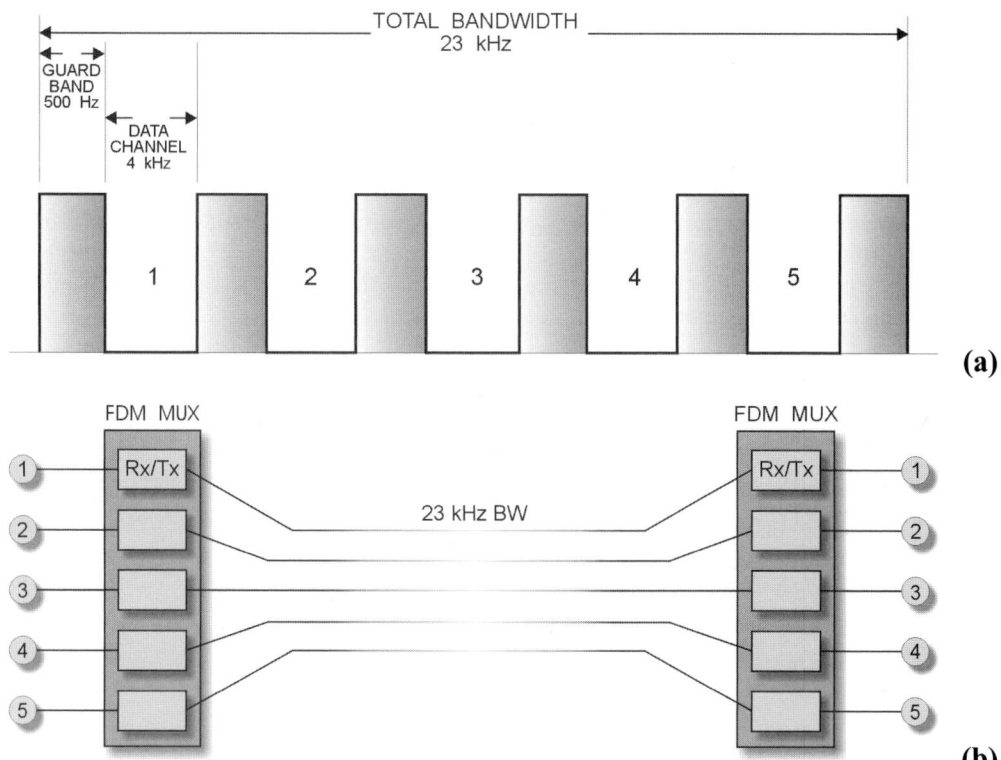

(a)

(b)

Figure 3-25 FDM Frame Formatting

Data to be transmitted is sent to the FDM MUX where it's assigned a channel frequency. The assigned channel is dedicated and won't be used by any other data terminals. An FDM MUX at the other end of the transmission link has receiver filters tuned to the assigned channels. The filters route data to the appropriate receiver, and the receiver sends it on to the terminal that's been assigned to the same channel frequency. This is identical to the FM radio example used earlier. The MUX houses five "radios". If you placed five FM receivers in a room and tuned them to five different local FM radio stations, you would have constructed an FDM multiplexer.

The total package of channels is sent through the **transmission medium**, which could be any of those previously discussed—copper wire, air, or fiber optics. Whatever medium is selected must have a total bandwidth equal to, or exceeding, the sum of the channel bandwidths, including any **guard bands**.

In Figure 3-25(a), how would the total bandwidth be affected if all the channels are carrying data except for channel 3? Would the total bandwidth be reduced? No, it wouldn't. The channels in FDM are permanently allocated to a fixed portion of bandwidth in the frequency time-domain. If channel 3 isn't being used, the channel is wasting valuable bandwidth. This was also the case with SDM.

FDM doesn't permit resource sharing of channels. It proves advantageous over SDM by permitting open routing of the data to any multiplexing receiver tuned to the channel frequency. This technique isn't permitted by SDM.

From a cost view, FDM is generally cheaper to implement, since a single wide-band cable can replace the many wires of SDM. When air is used as the transmission medium, the cabling cost is avoided entirely although the microwave transmitters and receivers offset this advantage. An FDM system is more complex than SDM, which generally decreases reliability. There are no practical distance limitations for FDM, in particular when used with microwaves.

The long-distance carriers have used FDM for a long time, primarily in analog multiplexing. The common-carrier analog hierarchy is pictured in Figure 3-26. The system was originally intended to multiplex thousands of long-distance telephone calls, and as such, transmitted the calls as analog voice messages. The **voice channel** is 3kHz wide, and when used in an FDM multiplexer, includes 500Hz guard bands on each side of the channel. At the **group** level, twelve 4kHz channels are multiplexed together. Five groups are multiplexed to form a **super group** containing 60 channels. A **master group** contains ten super groups for a total of 600 channels. Six master groups form a **jumbo group** containing 3600 channels. At the top of the hierarchy are **multiplexed jumbo groups**. Three jumbo groups multiplexed together carry 10,800 channels. In other words, 10,800 telephone calls are transmitted through a single wide-band channel, at a width of 43.2 MHz.

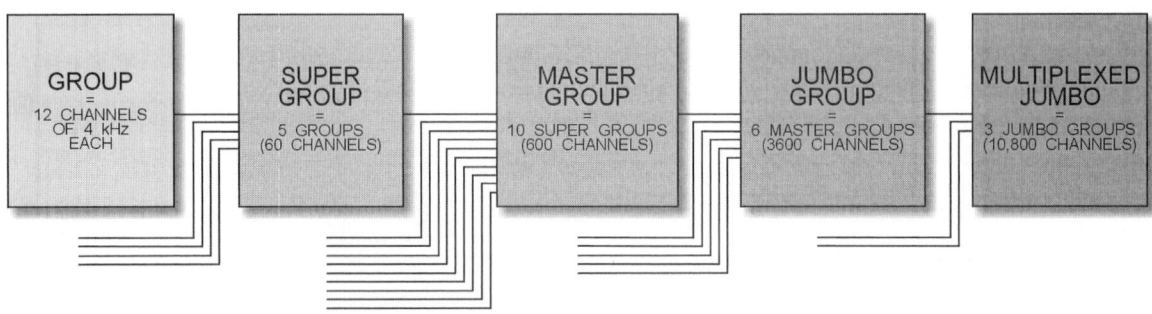

Figure 3-26 FDM Analog Common-Carrier Hierarchy

Since FDM utilizes a carrier within each channel, modems aren't required. When data is to be sent through the dial-up telephone network, the multiplexer packages the information to conform to the voice channel constraints as described above. In this way, a frequency-division multiplexer performs much of the work of a modem. Even though a modem isn't used with FDM, full-duplex operation is easily implemented by assigning each terminal port an originate and answer channel. By doing so, the number of terminal attachments are reduced, since each terminal is now using two channels. Most FDM multiplexers don't have the same capability as modems for symbol baud rates greater than one or two bits per symbol. The reason for this is the narrow width of the voice channel. The low baud rate represents a disadvantage to using FDM.

While FDM is still used in analog carrier systems, it's rapidly being replaced by the much narrower bandwidth time-division multiplexer.

Time-Division Multiplexing (TDM)

Time division multiplexing is used for digital signals. TDM can multiplex up to 4,032 voice channels.

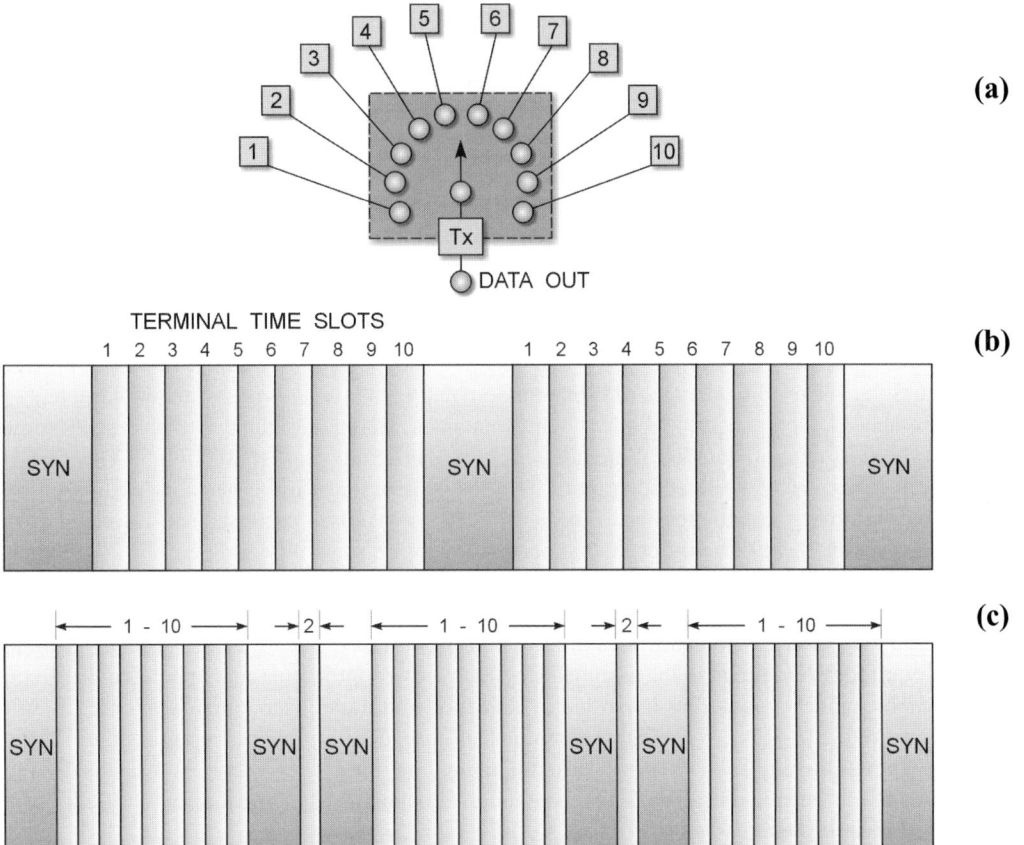

Figure 3-27 TDM Frame Format

A time-division multiplexer (TDM) uses a single transmission path like FDM; however, only one carrier frequency is transmitted. Figure 3-27(a) illustrates TDM as a transmitter switch that connects to ten terminals, one at a time. Each terminal is assigned a **time slot**, during which it transmits information into the channel. When the time of the slot expires, the switch moves to the next terminal and it transmits during its time slot. The process continues until all terminals have transmitted, and then, the switch moves back to terminal one, and the procedure is repeated.

A TDM at the receiver looks identical to Figure 3-27(a). Received data arrives chronologically from the way it was transmitted: the data from terminal one arrives first. The receive switch connects to receiving terminal one for the time of one time-slot. When the time-slot expires, data from transmit terminal two is applied to terminal two through the switch. The switch moves to all ten terminals and then starts back at terminal one to repeat the sequence.

How does the receiver know there are ten terminals at the transmit end? The frame format for TDM is shown in Figure 3-27(b). A **SYN** (SYNchronous Idle Character) begins the frame and is followed by ten time slots, which correspond to the ten terminals. After the tenth time slot, another SYN is inserted and the time-slots are repeated. A SYN is a synchronizing pulse. When the receiver detects a SYN, the switch resets to terminal one. The receiver doesn't "know" if there are 5, 10 or 20 terminals transmitting data. It moves sequentially after each time slot until ordered to start over at the first terminal by the SYN pulse.

The insertion of the synchronizing pulse is **programmable**. If, for example, terminal two tends to send twice as much data as the other terminals, the synch pulse can be programmed to occur after time slot two, and default back to terminal two again. This may happen on alternate frames, as shown in Figure 3-27(c).

The synch pulse shouldn't be confused with data structures such as asynchronous and synchronous. The synch pulse is merely a **flag** that helps the receiver keep track of the time slots. TDM data may be sent in either synchronous or asynchronous formats.

TDM shares a disadvantage of FDM; the time slots are permanently assigned to terminals. If a terminal has no data to send, then no data is transmitted during the assigned time slot (the space is filled with alternating 1's and 0's). This happens quite frequently, since operator activity at a terminal keyboard is of a random nature. The user types in a few characters or sentences, then pauses, and a few more sentences are typed. Each pause represents some time slots with no data to fill them—yet, the slot is dedicated to that terminal. The overall effect is to reduce the efficiency of TDM. The problem can be partially addressed by programming redundancy and fallbacks into the synch pulses, as previously described. But, invariably, the will be times that empty time slots are transmitted.

When FDM was discussed, it was mentioned that each terminal was dedicated to a frequency within the bandwidth of the FDM multiplexer. Each transmit/receive terminal required **filters** tuned to the assigned frequency in order to transmit and receive. In effect, each channel operated as a sub-bandwidth modem, and consequently, modems weren't required with FDM. With TDM, the same can't be said. A single modem is required at the output of the multiplexer to interface it to the phone lines. The multiplexed data is used to modulate the modem carrier. A receive modem recovers the data and it's demultiplexed by a TDM multiplexer.

TDM is nearly always used to multiplex digital data. The narrow time slots can be made to be equal to, or multiples of, the computer's digital clock, making transmitting and receiving a matter of proper timing. Since the computer's clock is used to set time slots, the structure of the slots themselves is digital. Now, they are essentially subdivided with binary data.

TDM requires the use of **buffers** at the receiving multiplexer. A buffer is used to hold over-flow data from the transmitter. Data may be received faster than the time-slots can be delivered to the terminals. The buffer stores the data and delivers it to the multiplexer switch at each synch pulse. Buffering isn't required in FDM because the transmit and receive terminals are considered to be directly connected by an assigned carrier.

TDM offers to users slightly better efficiency, a single carrier frequency, no guard bands, and less distortion with the use of digital modulation. It seldom offers much in the way of bandwidth savings, primarily as a result of the use of digital data. As previously mentioned, square waves occupy much more bandwidth than do sine waves. The total bandwidth of the TDM channel is equal to the sum of the bandwidth of the transmitting terminals. Information requires bandwidth in order to be transmitted, and the TDM channel may carry data from many terminals.

The long distance carriers have been reconfiguring their networks to carry digital voice and data. The multiplexing scheme chosen to handle the thousands of long-distant calls is time-division multiplexing, and is called T-Carrier by the long-distance companies.

The **T-Carrier** multiplexing scheme used by the common carriers is depicted in Figure 3-28. As with the analog multiplexing techniques used with FDM, the T-Carrier is hierarchical. The first level of the hierarchy is called T1. The T1 level contains 24 channels (either data or voice) transmitting at a frequency of 1.544MBPS.

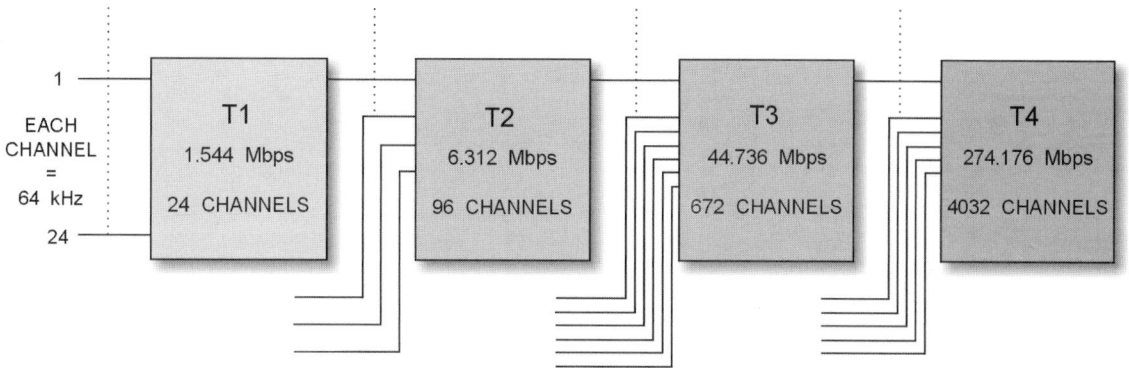

The channels are composed of digitalized information sampled at a rate of 8KBPS. Four T1 carriers are multiplexed together to form the 96-channel T2 level, transmitting at 6.312MBPS. The T3 level is composed of seven T2 carriers, and handles 672 channels transmitting at 44.736MBPS. The highest level of the hierarchy is the 274.176MBPS T4. It contains six T3 carriers multiplexed together, for a total channel count of 4,032 channels.

Figure 3-28   T-Carrier Multiplexing Scheme

A simplified frame format for the 24 channels in a T1 system is shown in Figure 3-29. Each terminal feeding the T1 TDM multiplexer has an 8-bit time slot in which to gain access to the 1.544MBPS carrier. There are 24 channels multiplexed together to form 192 bits (24 channels X 8 bits = 192 bits) transmitted in the frame. A single synch bit precedes the data frame to give a total frame length of 193 bits. The full length of the frame (with synch bit) is sampled 8,000 times per second, or: 193 bits x 8,000 samples per second = 1.544MBPS.

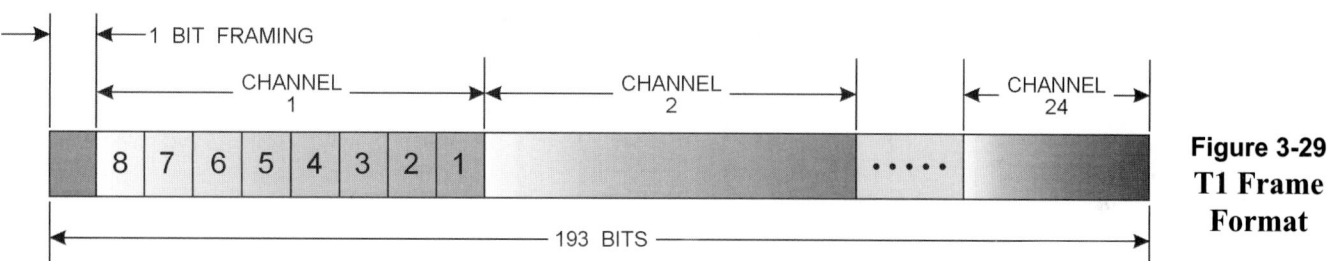

Figure 3-29 T1 Frame Format

Recall from Chapter 2 that Nyquist determined data may be sampled at a rate of at least twice the highest transmitted frequency, and the original data can be recovered at the receiver. The T1 carrier takes 8,000 samples per second. The reason for this is that a digital voice channel is 4kHz wide. An analog voice channel is at least 3kHz wide; the digital channel contains extra space for control information, or it contains a **fallback** channel, and may require a guard band. According to Nyquist, the 4kHz digital data must be sampled at least 2 x 4,000BPS = 8,000BPS. Each of the 24 channels has a time-slot of 8 bits; or, in other words, each channel has a bit rate of 8 bits x 8,000 samples per second = 64kBPS. All channels comprising the T-carrier system are 64kBPS channels. However, not all of them transmit user data at 64k; in some cases, the data rate is 56k.

TDM doesn't require guard bands, and is composed of digital information. As such, it is a significant improvement over FDM. A modified version of TDM, **Statistical Time-Division Multiplexing** (STDM), vastly improves upon TDM.

Statistical Time-Division Multiplexing (STDM)

In a statistical time division multiplexer, data rates have an aggregate rate higher than the line speed.

Statistical multiplexers can collect data from terminals at a rate exceeding the data rate of the channel. Imagine an STDM transmitting at a channel rate of 2,400BPS. Feeding the multiplexer are four terminals that send at 300BPS, 1,200BPS, 4,800BPS, and 9,600BPS, respectively. The STDM will collect and store in memory the terminal data at an **aggregate rate**. The aggregate is the statistical, or sum-total, of the terminals. As long as the average terminal rates don't exceed 2,400BPS, the STDM will be able to transmit the 9,600BPS data as well as the 2,400BPS data. The trick is for the multiplexer to allocate the time slots so that the average speed of data it receives from the terminals doesn't exceed the channel speed.

STDMs are quite similar to TDMs in their approach. The main difference is that dedicated channels (as in FDM) or dedicated time slots (as in TDM) aren't required. Dedicating time slots is usually an option of STDM. Another difference between STDM and the other techniques is that the size of the time slot (channel) is variable—from 7 to 127 bytes long. A simplified STDM is shown in Figure 3-30.

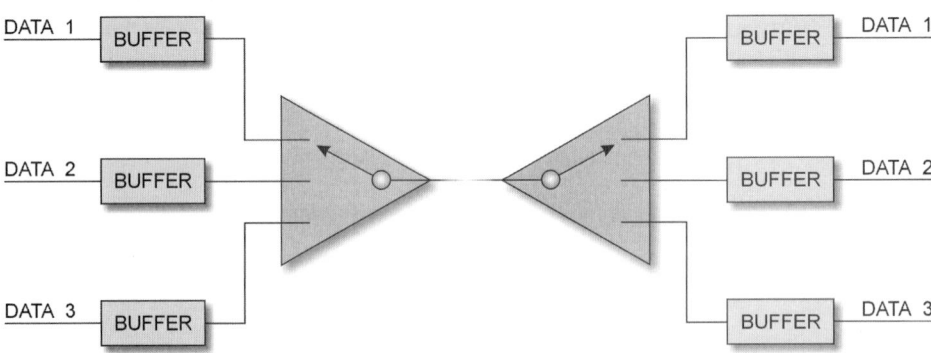

Figure 3-30 Simplified STDM

Notice that it's quite similar to the TDM shown earlier, except the STDM is illustrated with buffer memory. In practice, all time-division multiplexers contain buffers to hold overflow data from the input terminals, but statistical TDMs utilize the buffers in ways unique unto themselves. These applications will be discussed shortly. The multiplexer portion of Figure 3-30 is identical to TDM. The switch moves from terminal to terminal and data is transmitted during time-slots. The output of the STDM is a single, wideband carrier modulated by the terminal data. The demultiplexer at the receiving end extracts the data and routes it to the appropriate receive terminal.

The basic operation of STDM is identical to TDM, but there are vast differences in frame formats, speed, efficiency and flexibility between the two. The frame format for STDM is shown in Figure 3-31.

Figure 3-31 STDM Frame Format

A single frame contains control and address bits, data error and flags bits. The **control field** is one to two bytes in length and serves to identify the type of frame being transmitted. It contains sequencing information that tells the receiver which frame—of the many frames transmitted—is being received. The **address** is one to three bytes in length. At a minimum, it contains the address of the receiving terminal, and may include the address of the transmitting and receiving multiplexers, and the address of the transmitting terminal.

The **data field** used with STDM is variable in length, from 7 to 127 bytes, and in some cases may contain no data at all.

The **error field** is a 16-bit error-detecting code that checks the entire frame for errors. Instead of correcting errors, it asks the transmitter to send the frame again if an error is detected.

One-byte **flags** are appended to both ends of the frame, and are intended to mark the beginning and end of a frame, so the receiver can properly track each frame received.

The STDM frame format of Figure 3-31 is based upon protocols found in level 2 of the OSI model. It's called **high-level data link control** (HDLC) and is widely used in data communication systems. Due to the widespread use of HDLC, it's frequently adapted to STDM for frame formatting the multiplexed data. HDLC is discussed in detail in Chapter 5.

The single frame described above is equivalent to a single time slot of TDM. Recall a TDM time slot contains 8 bits (1 byte). An STDM frame can contain up to 1,016 bits, but at a cost of including lots of overhead. Overhead decreases efficiency, consuming bandwidth and requiring time to transmit, but contains no actual data. As mentioned before, the data field is variable in length. An effort should be made to fill this field with the maximum amount of data in order to keep the efficiency (throughput) high. Since the overhead is of a fixed length, efficiency decreases when the size of the information field is small. STDM multiplexers can be configured to avoid much of the overhead. Before looking at an alternate configuration, we'll examine methods for loading data into the multiplexer frames.

FDM and TDM dedicate discrete portions of the channel to a terminal. The terminal is assigned a channel whether or not it has data to send. This results in a considerable amount of waste. If a terminal has no data to send when the multiplexer switches to it, the data frame is terminated with a flag. Some multiplexers require a 7-bit code in an empty time slot to tell the receiver no data was sent; other types of multiplexers contain a code in the control field instructing the receiving multiplexer to ignore the frame.

Data is loaded into the multiplexer in a manner similar to Figure 3-30. The buffers contain any overflow information that the terminal is sending. The terminal may send data quicker than the multiplexer can transmit it. The buffers prevent the data from being lost. There are three arrangements used with buffer memory.

The first type involves **discrete buffers** dedicated to each input port of the STDM. The semiconductor memory (RAM) is of sufficient size (several thousand bytes) so that the worst nightmare of multiplexers is avoided: **buffer overflow**. If the buffers are allowed to fill up, data will be lost, and the receiving multiplexer will receive a string of gibberish. The problem with discrete buffers is that it's often difficult to predict how much memory will be needed—if the multiplexer contains too much memory, there will be wasted space and added costs; if not enough memory is provided, the buffer will overflow.

The second method of buffer arrangement eliminates the guess work inherent in discrete buffers. It's called **buffer pools**. In a pool system, all terminals compete for desired amounts of the memory. If one terminal is sending large amounts of data, there will be sufficient memory space available to park the information until the multiplexer can transmit it. It's possible that with a pool system, a single terminal can acquire the entire pool, thereby disabling all other terminals. Or, if there's an electrical problem in the pool memory, the multiplexer is shut down, since the buffer serves as the gate to the multiplexer.

The third buffer combines the advantages of discrete and pool buffers. It's called **user-defined buffer allocation**. With this technique, terminals are assigned dedicated buffer space based upon their estimated need for the space. The total memory is held in a pool and the terminal operator (or network manager) monitors the flow of data out of the terminals, and allocates memory according to the amount of data leaving each. In this type of system, each user is assured buffer space. No single terminal is permitted complete control of the buffer. Once a block of memory is dedicated to a port, it provides a gateway to the multiplexer in the event that the remainder of the memory fails.

No matter which of the buffer arrangements is used, all require some form of flow control. An STDM is a microprocessor controlled device unlike FDM and TDM systems. Microprocessors are required to handle variable frame lengths, addressing assignments, insertion of codes in the control fields, and so forth. They are also used to control the flow of data into the buffers. If the data arrives more quickly than it can be allocated memory space, the flow control disables Clear-To-Send on the EIA/TIA-232, or it sends a "transmit-off" code to the terminal. Flow control is discretionary software, meaning it's only called upon when needed. In most multiplexers, when the buffers reach a capacity of 80%, flow control begins to monitor each terminal individually to determine which ones are driving the buffers toward an overflow condition. Once the buffer capacity has been reduced to 60% of the available memory, flow control is disabled.

The use of buffers, along with the microprocessor control, provides the STDM with a distinct advantage not found in TDM and FDM. A statistical multiplexer permits the average input data rate to be equal to the capacity of the multiplexer output. The peak input data rate can actually exceed the capacity of the channel for short periods of time. This means that for brief periods, more data flows into the multiplexer than flows out of it. This is accomplished by a combination of buffer memory and the variable frame format of STDM.

The STDM assumes that there will be idle channels at any one time. If a terminal is sending data into the buffers exceeding the **channel rate**, it's a good bet that the idle channels will permit the time slot of the busy terminal to cycle around quickly enough to transmit the data.

This characteristic of STDMs provides them with tremendous flexibility. With the dedicated channel sizes of FDM and TDM, it is impossible to exceed the data rate of their respective channels. An STDM system has the capability for processing data at very high data rates for short periods of times. Imagine an office in Chicago sending a group of fifty personnel files to an office in Dallas. This heavy concentration of information can be sent much more quickly with STDM than with the other multiplexing techniques.

Clever uses of the buffer memory, in conjunction with the STDM microprocessors (there are several), can increase the efficiency of STDM up to 100% greater than TDM. The greatest efficiencies are achieved with asynchronous data, since the asynchronous frame contains only a start, stop and parity bit. These can be stripped entirely, and replaced with several bits for the entire 1-kilobit frame. With the incorporation of microprocessors into STDMs, manufacturers have delegated more duties to them. Many STDMs today utilize the power of microprocessors to incorporate **data concentrators**.

> Data concentrators utilize compression techniques to increase data throughput.

Data concentrators reduce the number of bits required to represent data. One technique is the **Huffman method**. The Huffman method samples data to determine which bit sequences occur more often than others. Those sequences with higher occurrence rates are given a shorter, or abbreviated, bit representation than sequences rarely occurring. For example, consider the phrase:

THAT CAT

The letters A and T occur twice as frequently as the H and C. Consequently, it can be assumed the probability rate of the letters at occurring is high, and they can be assigned only a few bits. The Huffman code could also examine the pairing of A, T and conclude that it will occur 100% of the time in the above phrase. It will then represent A T with a few bits. The letters H and C occur rarely in comparison to the other letters, so they might be assigned the full 7- or 8-bit ASCII code. The Huffman code typically compresses English text from the 7 to 8 bits of ASCII, or EBCDIC, to 4 or 5 bits.

Another compression technique is the dictionary method. The dictionary is composed of the words contained in the data to be transmitted. For example,

THAT CAT ATE THAT RAT

may be filed alphabetically in the dictionary. Once all of the redundancies in the phrase are deleted, the above phrase would look like:

ATE, CAT, RAT, THAT
1   2   3   4

Each word is then assigned a numerical representation as indicated directly beneath the previous phrase. The original sentence is shown below in parenthesis, and directly above it are numerical representations of each word. The numbers are encoded into a 3- or 4-bit format and transmitted in the sequence shown.

4   2   1   4   3
(THAT) (CAT) (ATE) (THAT) (RAT)

The dictionary method improves upon the Huffman method by representing each character by 3 to 4 bits.

The most effective compression techniques predict a character by examining the previous characters. For example, when the letter "Q" is encountered, the next letter to occur will probably be "U". Predictive compression techniques are capable of representing an English character with 2 or 3 bits.

The examples of data compression given were only for the data that's being transmitted. But buffer addresses and control information may also be compressed. In fact, when the Huffman method is implemented, the address and control overhead of Figure 3-31 is eliminated entirely and only block terminators (2 bits, representing the Flags shown in Figure 3-31) are retained. This is possible when the buffer memory is pooled so there are no memory allocations, or addresses.

Another reason it's possible to eliminate the headers is that as each block of data from each terminal is compressed, the resulting encoded data is unique for the given terminal. That is, if one terminal is transmitting data composed primarily of scientific data, it will be encoded much differently from another terminal sending a routine business letter from a word processor.

Statistical multiplexers routinely compress data. This is another reason that the peak data rate can exceed the line rate.

LONG-DISTANCE CARRIER SYSTEMS

Long-distance carriers transmit voice and data by analog or digital methods. For the most part, toll facilities are digital although a few analog systems are still used in the United States and are common in other parts of the world. While digital transmission consumes a considerable amount of precious bandwidth, it's the favored technique because of better noise properties, greater reliability, high data rates and lower costs.

At the long-distance level, transmission is described in terms of multiplexing schemes and choice of analog or digital signals. The multiplexing schemes used are FDM and TDM. FDM is used for analog systems, while TDM is the choice for multiplexing digital signals.

We'll quickly review the analog hierarchies, then shift into a detailed examination of the digital system. The reason for this is that digital communications dominates the telephone network. In addition, deregulation has made digital data transmission available as an end-to-end technology in most areas of the United States.

Analog Hierarchy

The analog carrier hierarchy consists of twelve channels.

Figure 3-32(a) is the FDM multiplexing hierarchy used with analog signals. Twelve voice channels, each with a bandwidth of 4 kHz, are multiplexed to form a **group**. Five groups make up the 60-channel **super group**. Ten super groups form a 600-channel **master group**. A **jumbo** consists of six master groups, or, 3,600 channels. A **multiplexed jumbo** combines three jumbo groups for a total of 10,800 voice channels.

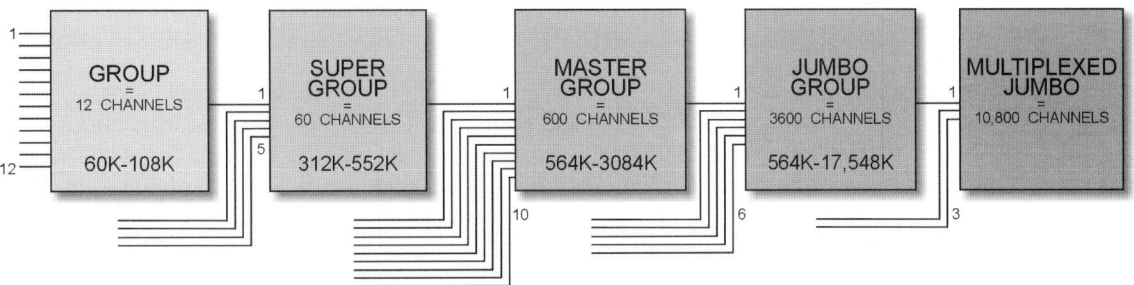

Figure 3-32(a) FDM Common-Carrier Analog Hierarchy

Figure 3-23(b) illustrates a typical modulation method used in producing a 12-channel group. If a 4kHz signal amplitude modulates a carrier at 64 kHz, the upper and lower sidebands at 60 kHz and 68 kHz will appear. Now, if the carrier is suppressed along with the upper sideband **(single-sideband, suppressed carrier)**, the first channel of the group is produced. It's extended from the frequency domain graph by dashed lines and placed in the group. The second channel represents the lower sideband of a 68kHz carrier. The process of suppressing the carrier and upper sideband continues through twelve channels. The twelfth channel consists of the lower sideband of a suppressed 108kHz carrier. A synchronization signal at 104.8 kHz is included in the group to track it through other multiplexing levels.

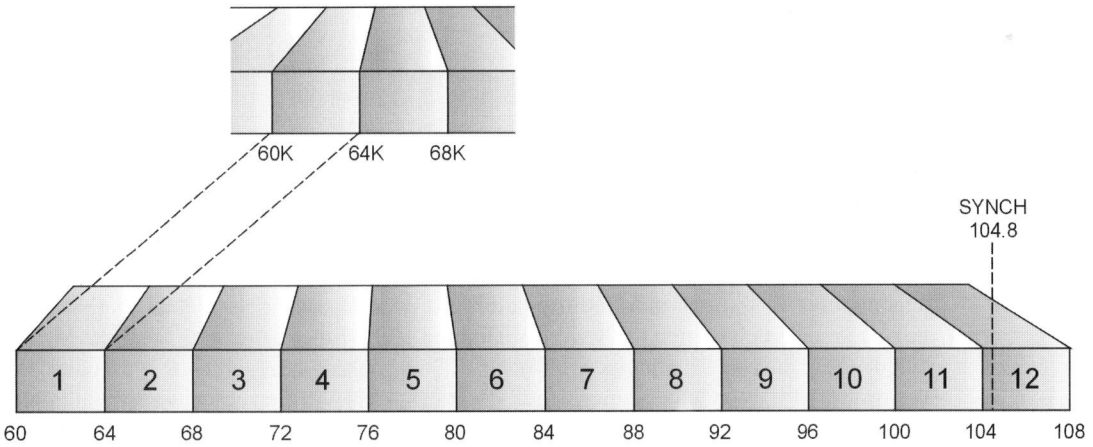

Figure 3-32(b) FDM Typical Modulation Method

Analog FDM multiplexing uses any of the media discussed in earlier chapters—twisted pairs, coaxial cable, fiber optics, and microwaves. There are many subcategories of analog carrier systems in addition to the groupings shown in Figure 3-32. For example, high-quality coaxial systems can multiplex up to 108,000 calls on a cable containing ten coax-cable pairs.

Digital T-Carrier Hierarchy

Digital TDM, used by a common carrier, is referred to as a **T-Carrier**. The most common T-Carrier group is the T1. A T1 facility multiplexes 24 voice channels. Each channel is transmitted at 64 kBPS for a total T1 data rate of 1.544 MBPS.

The T-Carrier, digital technology has been around for over thirty years. In that time, it has evolved from a trunk-to-trunk transmission method to a fully-implemented solution. This means that there are no analog portions from source to destination for digital signals that originate in a computer. The effect is a very reliable, low-distortion link. Data is transmitted at either 56 kBPS or 64 kBPS, in both directions, as opposed to rates in which there is an analog portion. In the case of the analog local loop, the upstream rate is fixed at a maximum of 35 kBPS, while the downstream rate (using V.90 modems) is about 48 kBPS maximum.

T-carriers aren't the only way to achieve fast, digital connections over a long distance. ISDN, described in Chapter 8, is an alternative. Another approach is to use **Frame Relay**, a distant cousin of X.25 packet switching. Frame Relay and X.25 are normally associated with wide area networks (although not always) and are discussed in Chapter 8, while T-carrier is normally associated with dial-up connections.

A T-Carrier system multiplexes digital data using TDM techniques. The T-Carrier digital hierarchy is pictured in Figure 3-33.

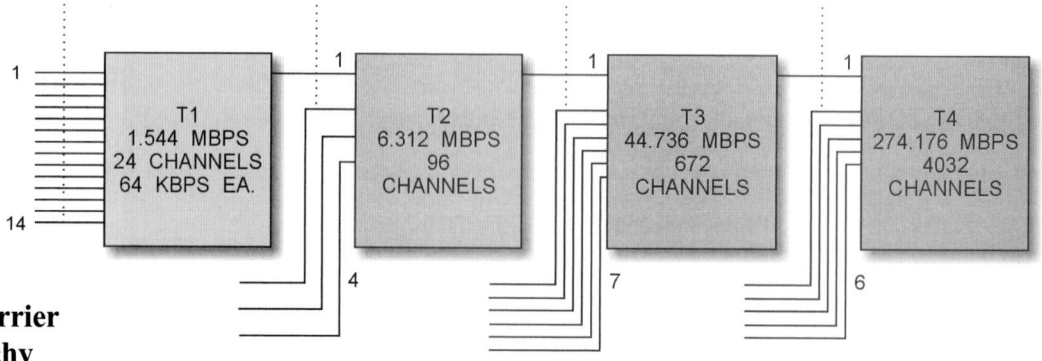

Figure 3-33 T-Carrier Digital Hierarchy

The popular T1 transmission facility combines 24 voice channels. Recall that when an analog signal is converted to PCM, it's sampled 8,000 times a second, since the highest frequency of the voice channel is 4,000Hz. A PCM signal contains eight bits in the code. The data rate of a PCM-encoded signal in the T-Carrier system will then be 8 bits x 8,000 samples = 64 kBPS. Each of the 24 PCM-encoded voice channels has a BPS rate equal to 64 kBPS. The data rate of the T1 system supports the channels at 1.544MBS. Within the T1 system, the channel signals are referred to as DS0, for digital service. A T1 channel is often called DS1.

A T1 multiplexer may transmit data from the twenty-four channels by alternating bits from each channel, in which case it would be utilizing **bit-interleaved** TDM. Or, it may alternately transmit 8-bit samples from each chord, and then be referred to as **word-interleaved** TDM.

DS and Tx are often used synonymously, but this isn't technically correct. DS refers to the physical digital signal, while T (for Transmission) refers to the type of carrier.

A T2 carrier contains 96 PCM channels (DS-2 signals) at 6.312MBS. Seven T2 facilities are multiplexed at the T3 facility to produce the 672 channel DS-3 signal. Six, T3 groups are multiplexed to form the 274.176MBS T4 carrier. The T4 facility produces 4032 voice channels.

Table 3-1 presents the hierarchy in a table format.

CNST OBJECTIVE
VI-B

Table 3-1 T-Carrier Digital Hierarchy

T-CARRIER	DIGITAL SIGNAL	LINESPEED	T1 MULTIPLE	CHANNEL CAPACITY
	DS0	64 kBPS	1/24 of a T1	1 Channel
T1	DS1	1.544 MBPS	1 T1	24 Channels
T1C	D1C	3.152 MBPS	2 T1's	48 Channels
T2	DS2	6.312 MBPS	4 T1's	96 Channels
T3	DS3	44.736 MBPS	28 T1's	672 Channels
T3C	DS3C	89.472 MBPS	56 T1's	1,344 Channels
T4	DS4	274.176 MBPS	168 T1's	4,032 Channels

Notice that there are subdivisions at T1C and T3C, due to advances in channel bank technology. A channel bank is the terminating equipment used to format each channel. As the technology improved over the years, more channels could be framed within a channel bank, which filled some wide gaps from T1 to T2, and from T3 to T4. In practice, T1 and T3 are the normal carrier implementations.

T-Carriers are replacing most analog systems. In some places, the only remaining analog portion of the telephone system is the subscriber loop. Soon, the analog loop signals will be converted to digital as well. At this time, there are thousands of T1 facilities.

A large corporation may lease T-Carrier facilities from the common carrier, or install their own. The corporation is given direct access to the facility from a local network, called a **Private Branch Exchange** (PBX), so that data from computer equipment need not go through the analog local loops. The result is a high-speed, all digital path to a remote location. At the time of this writing, a T1 lease from Washington D.C. to Los Angeles costs about $1,000 a month. With a T1 connection, you pay based on distance, unlike Frame Relay where you pay a flat rate each month. A corporation with a large amount of data traffic can lease the facility for about the same cost per channel as an unconditioned voice-grade channel. Dedicated T1 facilities have made sense only to users with high volumes of data traffic. But what about a medium or small corporation?

Until recently, there was little cost justification to a small company in leasing a 24-channel T1 facility. If the company's average channel use was only half the capability of the facility, it would be paying for a large amount of unused bandwidth. The common carriers now recognize that many potential customers were shut out of leasing a T-Carrier system because they had to lease the entire 24-channel bandwidth. To open up these markets, the common carriers have created **Fractional T1** (FT1).

Now, a small- or medium-size company can lease portions of a T1 facility as their needs require. The significance of FT1 is that digital communication is now available to nearly any size corporation, and is particularly beneficial to organizations with hundreds of regional offices—of which no single one transmits enough information to utilize a full T1 facility, but collectively, may use many facilities.

Installing T1 requires some careful thought, and a fundamental understanding of the technology. This is particularly true when you consider that there are alternatives such as Frame Relay and X.25. Later in this chapter, you'll see how to implement a T1 line and to weigh the pros and cons of committing an organization to T-Carrier.

T-Carrier Frame Format

A T1 frame consists of 24, PCM encoded channels.

The frame format of T1 was shown back in Figure 3-29. As previously described, twenty-four PCM-encoded 8-bit channels are carried in the frame. A single framing bit precedes the 192 data bits to give a total frame length of 193 bits. The frame is sampled 8,000 times each second, or once every 125 µS (1/8,000 = 125 µS). Since there are 193 bits in the frame, the time of each bit is 125/193 = .647 µS. This translates to a data rate of 1.544 MBPS.

The **framing bit** serves as a marker to identify the beginning of the frame. As the frame is transferred through various switching facilities, and at the final receiver, it allows the equipment to synchronize to small differences in bit times so that the frame won't be lost.

The frame format shown in Figure 3-29 is only for T1. All other higher-order carrier facilities frame the channels differently, and treat a T1 frame as nothing more than a series of bits. This is why a T1C carrier with 48 channels transmits at 3.153 MBPS rather than the expected 2 x 1.544 MBPS.

T-Carrier framing has been through numerous changes. With each change, more data was sent faster. The changes are the direct results of chip technology and channel bank advances. There are five different channel banks in the system, and they are referred to as D1, D2, D3, D4 and DCT (Digital Carrier Trunk), which is only used between T-Carrier facilities, and therefore, not available to subscribers.

The **channel banks** are the equipment responsible for combining the channels at the T-Carrier facility. The channel banks for T1 use a D4 (digital) bank. They're responsible for gating the 24 channels into the facility, companding (compression at the transmitter), PCM-encoding, and interleaving onto the T1 channel. A simplified block diagram of the D4 channel bank is pictured in Figure 3-34.

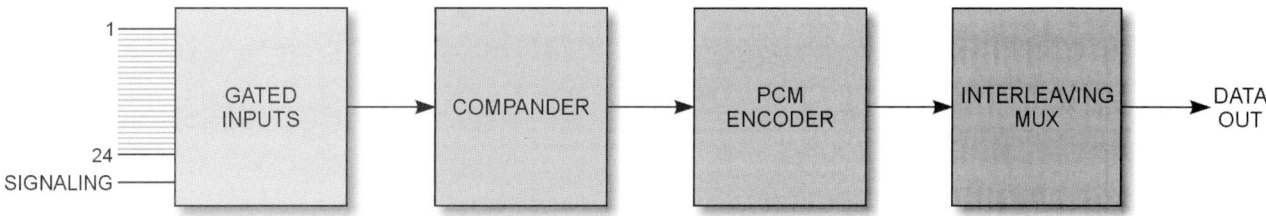

The original D1 banks (DIA, B, and C) sampled 8-bit voice channels at 8,000 times a second. However, one of the eight bits was used for signaling information such as on-hook, off-hook, etc. This left seven bits to actually carry the voice information, and resulted in a voice signaling rate of 56 kBPS. This is why, if you live in an area that uses older channel banks, the telco can only provide you with 56 kBPS on a T1 line.

Figure 3-34 Simplified D4 Channel Bank

With signaling data being sent every eighth bit, the frames were synchronized by alternating 1's and 0's in the 193rd bit position. The receiver synchronized to this bit sequence by searching for the pattern across all frames received. The idea was that it was unlikely that random data sent would ever produce this bit pattern at each 193rd bit time. This is the way it worked until the frames were transmitted, and the system locked up each time a 1kHz test tone was sent through the network. It produced alternating 1's and 0's every 193 bits. The tone has since been changed to 1,004 Hz.

D1 channel banks may still be used around the country, but it's difficult to send data through them because of the 7-bit user data restriction, unless a modified codec is used at the source. Instead, you're more likely to encounter channel banks which use all eight bits for data.

This was implemented in the next channel-bank iteration called D2. A D2 bank has 96 channels packaged into the bank, while a D1 has 72. D3 and D4 banks have 144 channels in the same bank. Channel density increased for each bay of channel banks, but so did the amount of user data, from 56 kBPS to 64 kBPS.

In a D1 channel bank, losing a bit in each channel for signaling couldn't be detected in voice communications, but when digital data was sent through the same system, the results were disastrous. Starting with D2, all eight bits of the sample were reserved for user data. Well, not quite all; the system still needed to transfer signaling information, but it turned out that it wasn't necessary to send it with each channel. Instead, it was sent every sixth frame—and this led to the use of superframes.

Table 3-2 shows the frame format for a D4 channel bank, called a superframe. A superframe contains twelve, T1 frames. Each frame has 193 bits. Except for the sixth and twelfth frames, all eight bits contain user data. In the sixth and twelfth frames, one bit is designated for carrying signaling information that contains the status of the connection.

The 193rd bit in each frame is still used for frame synchronization. Beginning with D2, synchronization was divided between terminal framing and superframe synchronization. **Terminal synchronization** is used by the terminal equipment at the ends of the link to ensure channel synchronization, while **superframe synchronization** ensures the full twelve T1 frames are tracked through each switching facility along the route to the destination.

Table 3-2 Superframe Format

FRAME NUMBER	TERMINAL SYNC BIT	SUPERFRAME SYNC BIT	INFORMATION BITS	SIGNALING BIT
1	1	-	1 through 8	-
2	-	0	1 through 8	-
3	0	-	1 through 8	-
4	-	1	1 through 8	-
5	1	-	1 through 8	-
6	-	1	1 through 7	8
7	0	-	1 through 8	-
8	-	1	1 through 8	-
9	1	-	1 through 8	-
10	-	1	1 through 8	-
11	0	-	1 through 8	-
12	-	0	1 through 7	8

Each synchronization technique uses a specific 6-bit code that's interleaved within the superframe. The bit codes are as follows:

Terminal: 101010
Superframe: 001110

Once the two codes are interleaved at bit position 193 in each of the T1 frames, they generate the following 12-bit code:

100011011100

As you can see in Table 3-2, the terminal synchronization bits are placed in each of the odd numbered frames, while the superframe synchronization bits are placed in each of the even numbered frames.

With this code, the transmit and receive stations will know if a frame is lost and will be able to correctly track channel data within ± two frames. Keep in mind that in a superframe, twelve, 12-channel T1 frames (144 total channels) are being transmitted.

A superframe contains twelve, T1 frames. The extended superframe contains twenty-four, 12-channel T1 frames.

T-Carrier frame formats enlarged with AT&T's **Extended Superframe Format** (ESF). The format is illustrated in Figure 3-35.

Frame Number	Fe Bit	Data Link Bit	CRC-6	Information Bits	Signaling Bit
1	-	m	-	1 through 8	-
2	-	-	C1	1 through 8	-
3	-	m	-	1 through 8	-
4	0	-	-	1 through 8	-
5	-	m	-	1 through 8	-
6	-	-	C2	1 through 7	8
7	-	m	-	1 through 8	-
8	0	-	-	1 through 8	-
9	-	m	-	1 through 8	-
10	-	-	C3	1 through 8	-
11	-	m	-	1 through 8	-
12	1	-	-	1 through 7	8
13	-	m	-	1 through 8	-
14	-	-	C4	1 through 8	-
15	-	m	-	1 through 8	-
16	0	-	-	1 through 8	-
17	-	m	-	1 through 8	-
18	-	-	C5	1 through 7	8
19	-	m	-	1 through 8	-
20	1	-	-	1 through 8	-
21	-	m	-	1 through 8	-
22	-	-	C6	1 through 8	-
23	-	m	-	1 through 8	-
24	1	-	-	1 through 7	8

Figure 3-35 Extended Superframe Format

The ESF contains 24, 12-channel T1 frames (288 total channels). Bit 193 is multiplexed to serve three distinct purposes:

- The Fe bit provides frame synchronization at every fourth frame using the bit pattern 001011. Fe serves the same purpose as the S and T bits in the D4 format.

- The Data Link (DL) bit carries line performance information at every other frame.

- The CRC-6 is a 6-bit cyclic redundancy check that inspects all 4,632 bits of the frame for errors.

Signaling data is retained at every sixth frame as it is for a D4 superframe. The data rate for both D4 and ESF approaches 64 kBPS. Due to the sixth frame signaling bits (sometimes called "robbed bit", or 7 5/6 coding, since 5 of 6 frames contain eight user bits and one frame contains seven user bits) the data rate (user information rate) will never reach a full 64 kBPS.

If you install a T1 connection today, expect to use D4 channel banks. Your data will be sent using the D4 superframe, or it may use the Extended Superframe Format. With ESF, more information will be sent more quickly, since fewer overhead bits will be sent.

T-Carrier Signals and Connectors

A DS1 pulse has a positive amplitude of 3.0 volts, and a line rate of 1.544 MBPS.

Each T-Carrier DS pulse is defined for the carrier type. The specifications for a DS4 will be different than for a DS1, for example. Since most T-Carrier signaling occurs at the fundamental T1 level for end users, this section will be limited to DS1 signal characteristics and connector types. Table 3-3 lists the criteria for DS1 pulses that are imposed on T1 lines.

Table 3-3 DS1 Signal Characteristics

PARAMETER	VALUE
Line Rate	1.544 MHz ± 75Hz
Cable Length	6,000 Feet
Signal Amplitude	+ Voltage: 3V, ± .3V
Attenuation at Receiver	1.5 to 22.5 dB

PIN	SIGNAL
1	Send Data (tip)
2	Reserved for Network
3	Receive Data (tip)
4	Reserved for Network
5	Not Defined
6	Not Defined
7	Not Defined
8	Not Defined
9	Send Data (ring)
10	No Connection
11	Receive Data (ring)
12	No Connection
13	No Connection
14	No Connection
15	No Connection

Figure 3-36 AT&T T1 Connector Pinout

The line rate is at the expected 1.544 MBPS. The cable length is limited to 6,000 feet with losses at the receiver falling between 15 and 22.5 dB. T1 uses solid 24AWG UTP, Category 2 cabling, that has a characteristic impedance of 100Ω.

T1 uses **Alternate Mark Inversion** (AMI) as the coding scheme. Logic 1's are alternately inverted, while logic 0's are 0V. The original AT&T specification (contained in publication 62411) states the a positive voltage will be 3.0V ± .3V. The negative voltage is stated in absolute values; that is without a − sign. Instead, the specification says that the negative alternation of the AMI code will be within .2V of the positive alternation, but will not be less than 2.7V or more than 3.3V.

There are two connectors used with T1 lines. The AT&T specification calls for a subminiature female connector with the pinout shown in Figure 3-36. As you can see, the connector appears to represent a bit of overkill, since most of the pins aren't used. They were originally intended for future applications, when connecting remote LANs via T1.

The **American National Standards Institute** (ANSI) has published a T1 specification using a CAT2-compliant RJ-48 connector with only four wire pairs. The pinout of the ANSI connector is depicted in Figure 3-37.

PIN	SIGNAL
1	Transmit (ring)
2	Not Used
3	Not Used
4	Receive (ring)
5	Receive (tip)
6	Not Used
7	Not Used
8	Transmit (tip)

Figure 3-37 ANSI T1 Connector Pinout

T-Carrier Multiplexing

Earlier, it was stated that the T-Carriers use time-division multiplexing at the switching facilities. There are two formats the carriers use with TDM—**word interleaving** and **bit interleaving**. Word interleaving is illustrated in Figure 3-38(a).

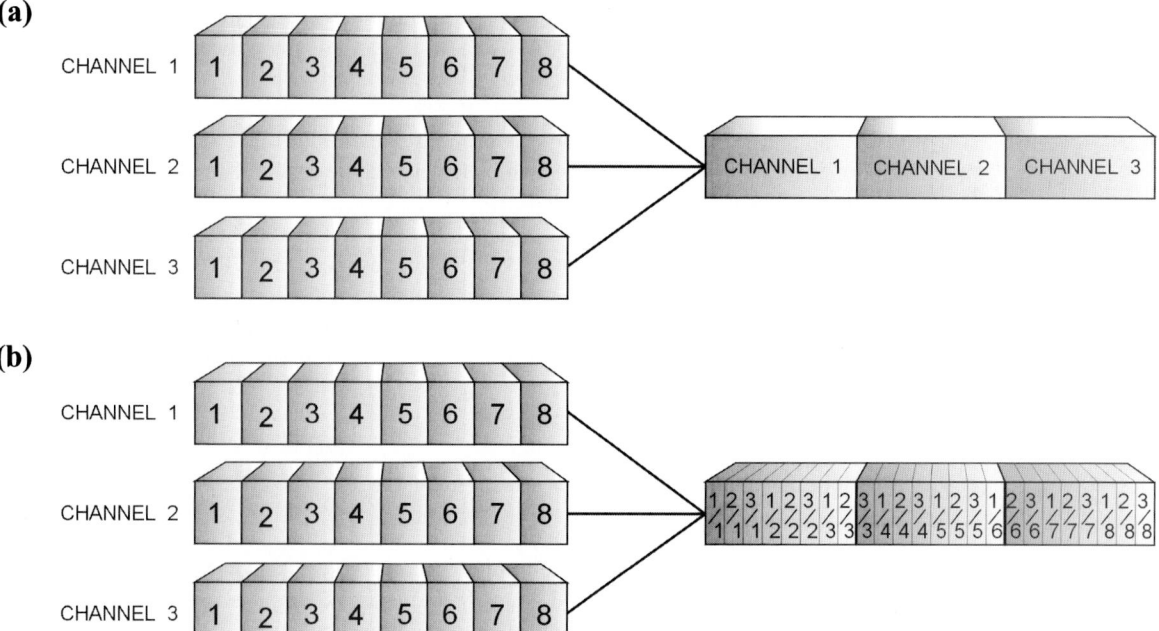

On the left, three 8-bit channels are shown. These are time-division multiplexed as complete 8-bit words, one after the other. Typically, this is the method used at T1 facilities. If you have a full T1 line available at your location, this is how the data will be treated from users who access the connection. Once the data leaves your site, it will be multiplexed across trunk lines at the higher levels. The approach at these levels is a bit different.

Figure 3-38 Word and Bit Interleaving

Figure 3-38(b) shows bit interleaving. Instead of complete words being interleaved, bits from the channel are alternately transmitted. The figure shows the left-most bit as channel 1, bit 1 (1/1). In the next bit position, channel 2, bit 1 (2/1) is sent. Channel 3, bit 1, is next to be transmitted. Since there are only three channels in Figure 3-38, the rotation starts back at channel 1. Now, bit 2 of channel 1 is interleaved (1/2). The process continues with each channel taking a turn at placing a bit on the line, until all eight bits of each channel are sent.

Bit interleaving is done at the upper levels of the T-Carrier hierarchy, because data traffic is complex to the point that the high-speed facilities are concerned only with switching streams of bits. A T1 carrier, on the other hand, can attach **address identifiers** so that common frames can be directed to a particular location.

Getting a T1 Connection

First, check with your local telco to see if you can. If so, decide if you actually need one. A T1 line is beneficial for companies that need to send large amounts of data between geographically separated locations. (This is equally true of other wide area connections, as well.) If your needs are limited to fast Internet access, even a fractional T1 is a bit much. There are simpler and cheaper approaches (See ISDN in Chapter 8 and V.90 and cable modems in Chapter 4.). Compare the benefits of using a simple dial-up to the Internet using PPP. The upload data rate will be about 33.2KBPS while downloads will travel at about 48KBPS.

As a rule of thumb, you need a T1 if you have at least thirty telephone lines. The voice/ data communication in and out of your business will be faster, and the cost will be slightly more than thirty discrete dial-up lines.

With T1, expect data rates approaching 64 kBPS. If you have a full T1, the primary advantage is that many users can transmit at these rates using the multiplexing capabilities inherent in T1. The justification that one or two users have a lot of data to send probably isn't enough. Again, if many users are communicating at remote locations at a steady rate, then a T1 line will make more sense.

> There are four basic levels of T-Carrier service available.

Once a decision is made to implement T1, determine the level of service you want to pay for. There are four basic levels available, and a nearly endless mix of these four with other options. These are all marketed uniquely by local and long distance carriers, as well as companies which sell access to line bandwidth, such as electric utilities.

The four levels of service are:

- Customer may change location of terminating equipment with carrier's assistance.

- The use of multiplexing to allow the customer to connect up to 24 channels to switched or dial-up services.

- The use of multiplexing to allow two T1 lines that each carry up to 22 channels on a single T1 connection.

- The customer controls all configurations which allows dynamic allocation of circuits—all without assistance from the carrier.

Now, be prepared to do some leg work. It will save you money to do much of the ground work yourself, but you must be prepared to play the middleman between various parties such as the T1 provider, equipment vendor and the Internet Service Provider, as well as coordinate on-site training for local support.

Before any user equipment is connected to a DS1 facility, a **Channel Service Unit/ Digital Service Unit** (CSU/DSU) must be installed at the user premises. In a CSU/DSU, the Channel Unit recovers multiplexed data, while the Digital Unit removes encoding that was used to package the data.

CNST OBJECTIVE
I-A

The channel specifications are setup in the CSU/DSU. These include the channel rate (64 kBPS), frame type (Extended or Superframe), number of channels (1 for 64 kBPS and 24 for 1.544 MBPS), and so forth.

Figure 3-39 shows a typical T1 connection. In the Figure, a LAN is using the connection to communicate with another LAN. Data from the LAN nodes is first sent to a router. The router switches the data into the CSU/DSU in what is essentially time-division multiplexing. The CSU/DSU then formats the data into T1 frames and sends them, through a V.35 cable, to the T-carrier facilities.

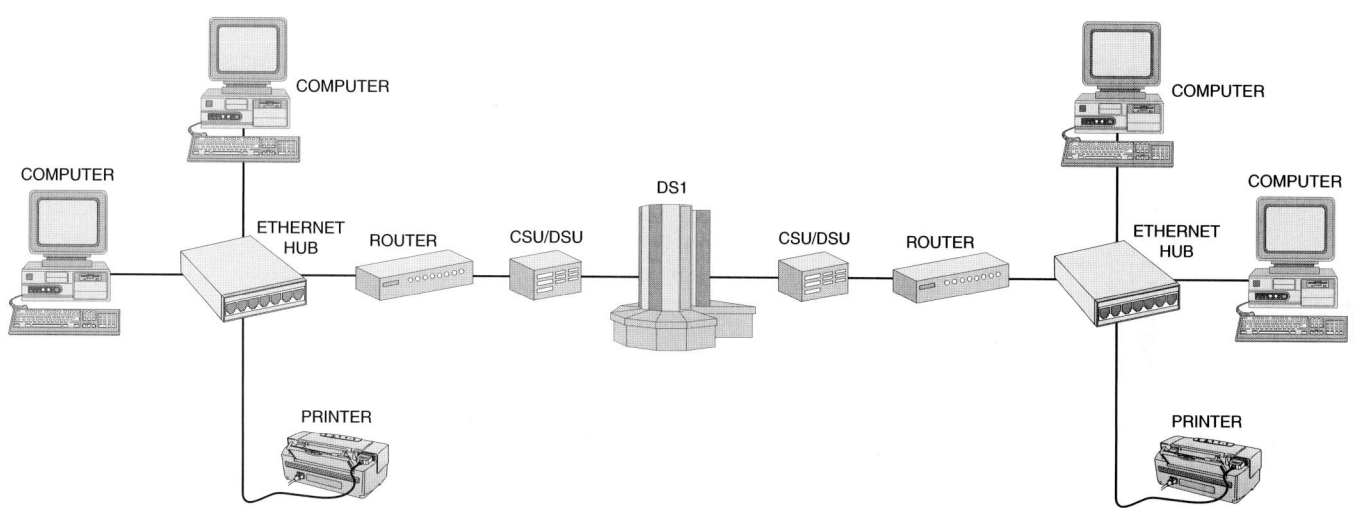

At the remote LAN, the CSU/DSU accepts T1 frames through another V.35 cable, strips the T1 encoding and demultiplexes the frames. The router selects the correct LAN node based on the node addresses encapsulated in the LAN's data frames. Notice that in order to implement a T1 line, you must buy a CSU/DSU unit along with a router. This is why you need to do your homework before setting up a T1 line. Setting up and maintaining a router is formidable in itself.

Figure 3-39 Typical T1 Interconnection

Even though you may not have access to T-carrier technology in your location, you may be able to utilize DDS instead. DDS (Digital Data Service) offers similar advantages to a T1 line. An important difference between the two is that DDS operates at 56KBPS, while T1 operates at 64KBPS.

SONET

> The Synchronous Optical Network is the fiber optic alternative to digital carrier systems.

SONET (Synchronous Optical NETwork) is the optical-based transmission standard for telecommunications. Data in a SONET network is transmitted through fiber optic cables and may consist of voice, data, graphics or video.

SONET networks are tasked to provide the following services:

- Reduction in copper-based equipment costs and increased reliability.

- Frame lengths of sufficient size to carry management information about the link and the pay-load carried in the frame.

- The establishment of accepted standards which permit networks to be built that are vendor independent.

- The ability to format lower speed frames such as DS1, and multiplex these using a synchronous structure.

- The creation of an architecture that promotes future development at varying transmission rates.

Only within the past ten years has SONET been deployed to any extent. Prior to this, there were only competing and proprietary implementations. However, with the deregulation of the telecommunications industry in 1982, it became advantageous for common carriers to develop a single standard (begun in 1984) that would be used to transparently pass optical signals from one company to another. The benefit to those carriers was that it increased traffic through their networks, thereby increasing their revenues.

Today, SONET is widely embraced. It is the optical cousin to the T-Carrier system, but one which runs much faster and with considerably more flexibility.

SONET Signals

> The basic SONET signal is called STS1. It propagates at 51.84 MBPS through an OC1 channel.

SONET was designed to carry multiple optical signals by **byte interleaving** the frames. At the lowest level is the **Synchronous Transport Signal-1** (STS1), which has a frame length of 6,480 bits and operates at 51.84 MBPS. STS signals are transported by an **Optical Carrier** (OC) that corresponds to the bit rate of the STS. Therefore, STS1 will be transmitted through an OC1 channel.

What if three STS signals (STS3) need to be transmitted? They will be carried through a channel with a bandwidth of 3 x 51.84 MBPS = 155.520 MBPS, or through an OC3 channel.

Notice that in the SONET channel hierarchy, succeeding levels are direct multiples of the base STS-1 rate. In a T-carrier system, this wasn't the case because above T1 the channels used bit stuffing (bit stuffing is a method used to offset timing differences) for synchronization. Table 3-4 illustrates the SONET signaling hierarchy.

Also, for comparison, the equivalent T-Carrier channels are shown. At the lowest level of STS1, an OC1 channel can accommodate a T3 line. And at OC192, 192 T3 lines can be carried through the channel. This is due to the very high bandwidth capability of fiber-optic cables. Since the signals are multiplexed, they are carried on a single fiber-optic cable.

Table 3-4 SONET Signaling Hierarchy

SONET SIGNAL	BIT RATE	T-CARRIER CAPACITY
STS1 (OC1)	54.84 MBPS	28 DS1's or 1 DS3
STS3 (OC3)	155.52 MBPS	84 DS1's or 3 DS3s
STS12 (OC12)	622.08 MBPS	336 DS1's or 12 DS3s
STS48 (OC48)	2488.32 MBPS	1344 DS1's or 46 DS3s
STS192 (OC192)	0053.28 MBPS	5376 DS1's or 192 DS3s

All data on a SONET network is synchronized to a master atomic clock that resides at the OC3, or higher, level. An OC1 channel for example, is synchronized, but a SONET requirement is that the synch pulse must originate at OC3 or above.

A T1 line is **asynchronous**. Each terminal provides its own means of clocking bits—by tracking the 193rd bit position. As you may expect, when a T1 frame is sent through several terminals on its way to a destination node, the timing will vary somewhat due to minor differences in equipment tolerances, environmental changes, and so forth. And, since each terminal is providing its own clocking pulse, the clocks can be expected to be off by some amount. This means that a T1 signal probably won't ever be exactly 1.544MBPS, but could vary above or below that amount by a couple of hundred BPS. When the T1 signal is multiplexed to T3, the errors propagate so that a 44.736MBPS T3 rate may be off by as much as 2,000 bits. These tolerances are provided for, and corrected in the T-Carrier system, by stuffing extra bits in a frame that is off-frequency. That's why a T3 line isn't some direct multiple of a T1 line. The extra bits cause it to operate at a different data rate and even then, this rate can't be precisely nailed down. SONET doesn't have this problem, since all frames are synchronized to stable master clocks.

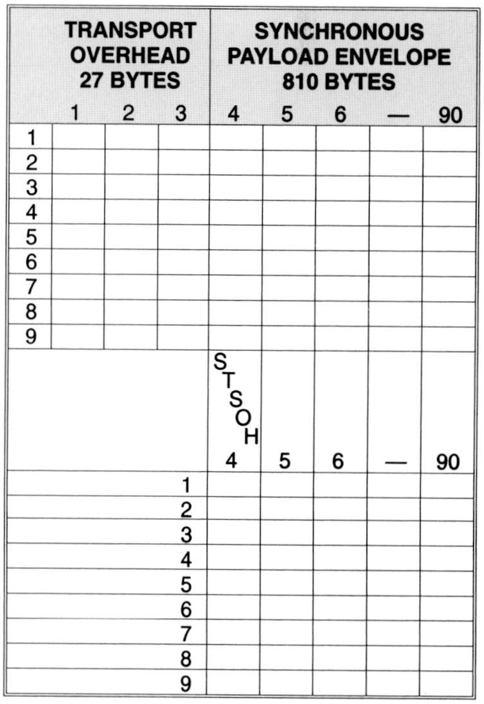

Frame Format

A SONET frame has a length of 810 bytes.

The frame format for SONET is shown in Figure 3-40. The frame consists of 27 bytes of transport overhead, and 783 bytes of payload, called the **Synchronous Payload Envelope** (SPE). The SPE is further subdivided into the STS path, and the actual payload.

SONET frames are byte interleaved through a SONET network so it's convenient to depict the frame as a serious of bytes that occupy rows and columns. The frame consists of nine rows and ninety columns. With nine bytes in each column, there are 9 bytes x 90 columns = 810 bytes in the frame. With 810 bytes in the frame, there are 8 bits/ byte x 810 bytes = 6480 bits in the frame. 8000 frames are transmitted/ second, so 8000 frames/s x 6480 bits/ frame = 51,840,000 BPS, or 51.840MBPS.

Figure 3-40 SONET Frame Format

The transport overhead occupies the first three columns of the frame, and contains information pertinent to source-to-destination communication. This includes framing bytes to mark the beginning of the frame, low-level error-checking, a 192kBPS channel for **Operations, Administration, Maintenance and Provisioning** (OAM&P) messages, pointers used to indicate the location of the first byte of the STS1 in the SPE, and alarm and defect signaling.

As mentioned, the SPE is sub-divided into STS (**Synchronous Transport Signals**) **path overhead** (PO) and the actual payload of the frame. The STS path overhead consists of nine bytes that occupy the first column of the SPE. The path overhead is tasked to provide performance information concerning the SPE, to label the contents of the SPE, to provide status information of the SPE back to the originating terminal, to transmit a signal ahead to the receiving terminal that's intended to ensure the connection continues. This means that in a full-duplex line, the transmitting node should always be aware of any problems with the frame it transmitted, and the frame will always know in advance of problems with the receiving destination. This is one reason that SONET is extremely reliable as compared to the WAN protocol TCP/IP which transmits on a best-guess effort (In practice, it's the IP portion of the protocol suite which sends using "best-guess." Best-guess means that the receiving node doesn't return an acknowledgment that a packet was received.) that a data packet will actually arrive at its destination.

The STS path overhead also contains a byte called the **Virtual Tributary** (VT) **Multi-frame Indicator Byte**. The byte contains an indicator to so-called **tributary payloads**. A tributary payload (all of which are commonly, if not quite correctly, referred to as VTs) is non-SONET information, such as a T1 frame. SONET will encapsulate a T-Carrier frame within the SPE as a virtual SONET tributary, by modifying the T-Carrier data rate. It does so by converting the electrical signal to optical, synchronously clocking T1 data at a basic rate of 1.728 MBPS; then single-step multiplexing this rate thirty times, until it's at the OC1 rate of 51.84 MBPS.

Once the DS signals are clocked into the SONET network, they can be multiplexed to any of the higher OC levels. Because they are encapsulated within the STS frame, they need to be labeled and tracked. This is what the VT Multi-frame Indicator Byte does. Since they're easily identified within the SPE, they can be dropped at any point and converted back to the original DS rate by demultiplexing the SONET rates.

Network Elements and Configuration

There are several physical elements in a SONET network that are unique to the technology and they come with their own terminology. Before reviewing common SONET topologies, you need to have a basic idea of the types of SONET elements, or the physical devices used in a SONET network.

A terminating Multiplexer is a concentrator placed at the entrance of a SONET network and is shown in Figure 3-41.

It's used to multiplex various STS signals up to a higher OC level, as well as to convert DS signals to VT and above levels. Notice that several inputs consisting of SONET and T-Carrier signals are applied to the input ports of the multiplexer. The T-Carriers are converted to VT rates, then multiplexed to the basic STS-1 rate, and finally multiplexed to the OC rate at the port output. This figure shows two ports at the output, but one is for transmit and the other is for receive (it's a full-duplex connection).

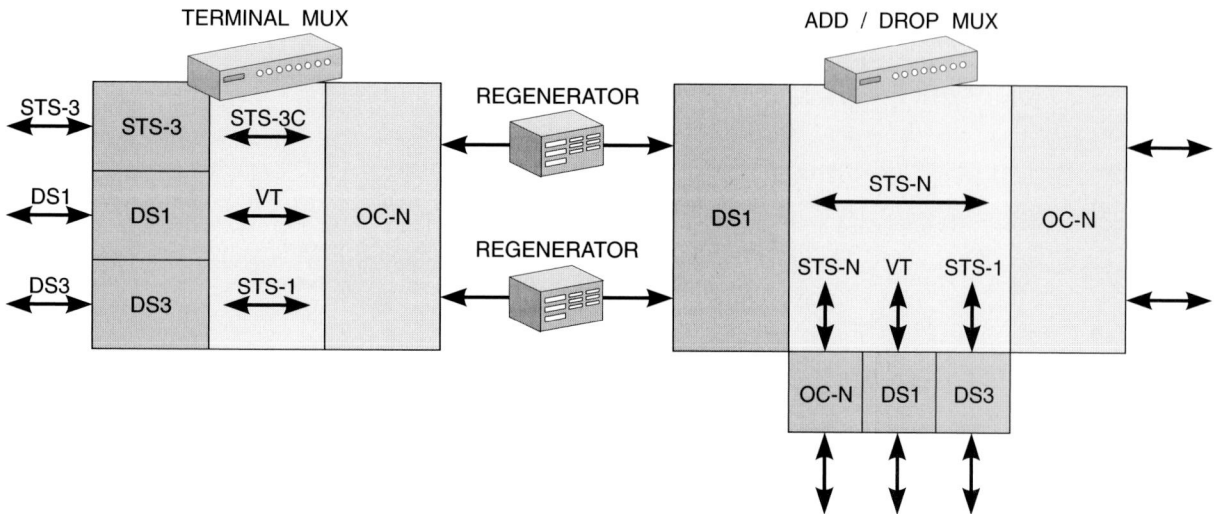

Figure 3-41 SONET Terminating Multiplexer

Optical signals lose signal strength with distance. Regenerators are inserted in-line with the fiber cable, and serve the same purpose as a repeater in a copper-based network—they restore the amplitude and shape of the signal.

An **add/drop multiplexer** is used to multiplex various inputs into an OC channel. Notice that it's inserted in-line with the OC channel. A typical application of an add/drop multiplexer is the convergence of T-Carriers from many areas. These are coupled onto the OC channel at the add/drop. Existing traffic on the OC channel isn't affected by the new data, since it's treated as multiplexed frames that are added to the new, converted frames.

The add/drop will also demultiplex VT frames within the STS frame, and convert them back to their original T-Carrier frequency. Then, they are routed out of the SONET network and back to a T-Carrier line.

There are three basic configurations used with SONET:

- **Point-to-Point**.

- **Hub (Star)**.

- **Ring**.

All are illustrated in Figure 3-42, although the ring architecture is the most widely deployed.

> SONET networks may be configured in a point-to-point, hub or star topology.

A point-to-point topology uses terminating multiplexers at each end, and one or more regenerators between them. Typically, this arrangement is used to link DS signals across long distances, thereby boosting the data rate of the DS signals while still retaining asynchronous compatibility at both ends of the optical link.

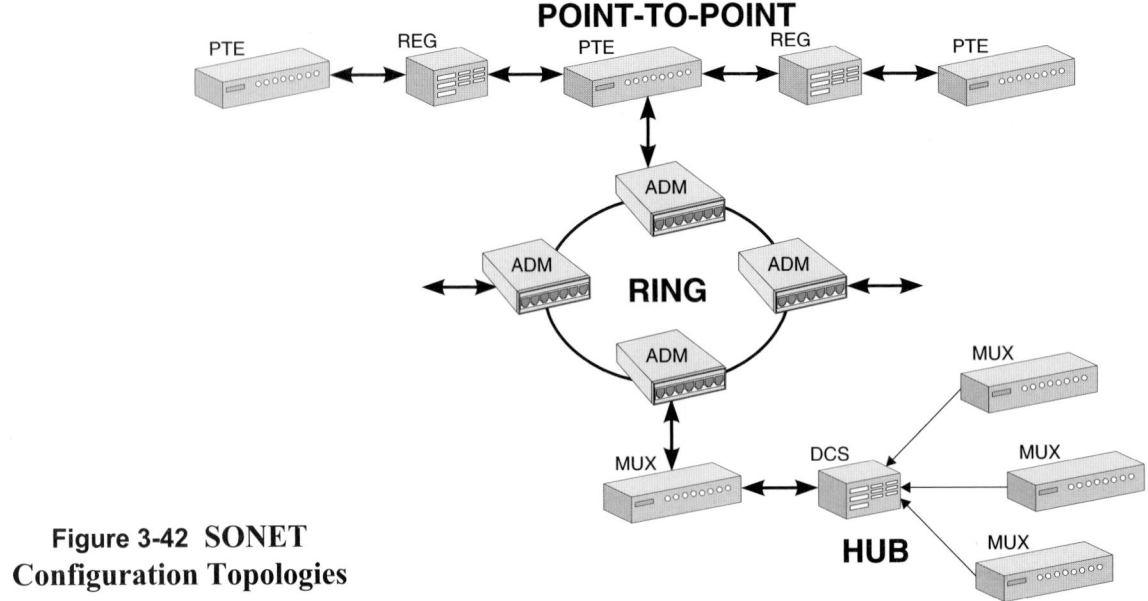

POINT-TO-POINT

RING

HUB

**Figure 3-42 SONET
Configuration Topologies**

In a hub network, a **broadband cross-connect** is installed as the hub. The cross-connect is used to switch SONET and T-Carrier data rates. In the figure, all signals entering and exiting the hub are SONET optical. The blocks labeled MUX are actually add/drop units used to convert the T-Carrier tributaries and STS frames to a common OC rate. The DCS hub then becomes a high-speed optical switch. Since all information in this segment of the network flows through it, the hub is in a perfect position to manage all aspects of the network, from changing logical port connections to monitoring and reporting performance data.

In the ring topology, Add/Drop Multiplexers serve as an interface to the SONET network. The ADM converts all inputs to a common ring speed and couples them onto the network. Rings have the advantage of survivability by including redundant, fall-back rings that will wrap around a cut fiber cable. This allows the ring to operate even when the primary transmission path is broken. Typically, the fall-back, or secondary, ring is geographically separate from the primary ring, so that if the primary is lost due to a thunderstorm, earthquake, etc., the secondary isn't likely to be broken by the same event.

NETWORK ENGINEERING

Training helps employees to become more efficient and productive in their jobs. Increasingly, corporations are turning to experts to supply the training.

For average end-users, networking "just works". They're not sure how, and most couldn't tell the difference between a protocol and an avocado. Networking is difficult, complex and, in many cases, highly specialized. Yet, in all sizes of organizations we're expected to use the network—a small peer-to-peer LAN, Internet logon, e-mail, global server distributions, and so on—as if each of us know what we're doing.

Corporations spend millions installing and upgrading networks because it helps them to be more competitive, leaner, productive, profitable; only to moan when the guy in cube 14/C.23-B1 (Refer to Figure 2-55) hits CTRL-ALT-DEL, crashes the entire infrastructure, bankrupts the company and puts thousands out of work. Maybe he was having a bad day, maybe his bad chemicals were acting up, or maybe he didn't have a clue as to what he was doing.

It's the same old dilemma that management encounters when faced with employees who aren't doing what they're supposed to be doing: Is it a performance problem or a training problem? The only way to know for sure is to train the affected employees. Then, if they aren't doing the right thing, it's a performance problem. Training is particularly important in networking because we've become dependent on networks, as we've become dependent on computers and calculators. Our job is to enhance end-user skill levels to a plateau equivalent to computer literacy. That is, we now expect new employees to have a basic understanding of how to operate a personal computer. They need to have the same skill in manipulating the local and wide area networks that they routinely use in their jobs.

Who does the training? Typically, we first turn to so-called subject matter experts—you. You're responsible for the continuing operation of the network, so you should have a significant say in the training of users. More and more corporate training departments are becoming fragmented and populated with specialists. This is necessary because we expect more and more of our employees, and arm them with increasingly complex tools to do their jobs. These days, no one can know it all—so we turn to specialists.

Employee training is a profession. It consists of few absolutes and many gray areas. Throughout this book, basic principles are divulged. These should be sufficient to prepare you to prepare other employees. The principles have been broadly divided into three arenas:

- Developing a Training Program

- Delivering a Training Program

- Coordinating Training

These topics represent a huge investment in thought and planning. But the payoff is better informed users who, when trying to describe a problem, will be in a position to accurately state the symptoms as they perceive them.

Developing a Training Program

There are several steps involved in designing a training program. You have to establish a need for training, identify the audience to be trained, perhaps conduct a "needs" survey, develop a training task analysis, and specifically define the broad content of the program.

Let's assume a new network will be installed, and you're responsible for making sure users are proficient in its operation. As a networking pro, you know what they should know to be reasonably self-sufficient. But you're not sure of their networking literacy. Even worse, after some casual snooping, you determine that the range of their technical skill goes from expert to none. To get a handle on where to begin, write a **Training Needs Survey**. Write the survey as if you were the individual expected to be reasonably self-sufficient in using the network. The survey criteria should advance from simple to difficult. If you set it up so that it covers the gamut of expected skill levels, you'll avoid having to distribute it multiple times.

A Training Needs Survey compares expected to actual skill levels.

Figure 3-45 is a sample Training Needs Survey. Notice that the questions at the beginning of the survey are directed at novices, the middle of the survey is directed to intermediate users, while the last part of the survey includes higher-level skills. The survey is easy to understand, and it takes little time to complete. The survey target is given only three choices in which to describe their competency: (1) Little to none, (2) Intermediate, (3) Advanced. It's unlikely that you'll have the time or resources to develop a training program that will respond to competencies other than these, so base your survey upon them.

TRAINING NEEDS SURVEY

The results of this survey will be used to develop training on network use and operation. For each competency, check the appropriate column as to how well you can perform the competency. Use the following to judge your skill level:

1: Little to no skill.
2. Intermediate skill.
3. Advance skill.

Department Name: _____

COMPETENCY	1	2	3
1. Logon to network.			
2. Print to a shared printer.			
3. Email a file attachment.			
4. Internet Proficiency			
5. Share files or directories with a workgroup.			
6. Password protect shared files.			
7. Perform daily file back-ups.			
8. Restart network operating system.			
9. Allocate space on a local file server.			
10. Connect a remote server.			

Figure 3-45 Training Needs Survey

Notice the survey is department-specific but user-anonymous. This is optional. Some companies require employees to state their name and the name of their immediate supervisor. This is risky because, by nature, we don't like to admit our ignorance—even when it's justifiable. Remember, the goal in a needs survey is to determine what level of training the user needs to use the network. Make it easy for them to convey their needs to you.

Once you collected the survey—and you should require that all employees complete one—you have the basic information necessary to determine the training wants and needs. It's a matter of tabulating the results of the survey against the survey criteria. Figure 3-46 shows the average score in each category of the original survey.

COMPETENCY	AVERAGE
1. Logon to network.	2.6
2. Print to a shared printer.	1.8
3. Email a file attachment.	1.7
4. Internet Proficiency	2.4
5. Share files or directories with a workgroup.	1.4
6. Password protect shared files.	2.7
7. Perform daily file back-ups.	2.0
8. Restart network operating system.	0.6
9. Allocate space on a local file server.	0.3
10. Connect to a remote server.	1.2

Figure 3-46 Training Needs Survey Results

Depending on your situation, you may decide to ignore any averages over 2.75. This score indicates a relatively high skill level; probably high enough that there will be adequate support in the local environment to the few who are weak in the particular competency.

On the other hand, any score below 2.0 is a statistical weakness, and must be addressed through training. These scores will ultimately guide you in focusing in on the attributes of your audience, and the broad elements of the training.

What about the scores between 2.0 and 2.75? These are a toss-up. Analyze the effect on network usage. For example, the score on Internet Proficiency is 2.4. More than likely, many of the employees have spent some time on the Internet, but if you're installing a new corporate intranet and all employees will need to know how to find their way around it, company specific intranet training is indicated.

The results of the training survey indicate the "wants and needs" of training.

As you'll see later, the training time spent on the Intranet category won't be nearly the time spent on Connecting to Remote Servers, since this category averaged a 1.2.

Again, consider the effects of not training in a particular category. If it would have a negative impact on important, required skills, then include it as a training topic. But be prepared to defend your decision, since training is expensive, and takes employees away from their jobs.

KEY POINTS REVIEW

This chapter has presented an extensive exploration of the telephone system.

- A telephone is responsible for much more than serving as a transceiver for voice calls. It must also manage all line conditions and requests from other telephones as well as notify the central office if its current state.

- The telephone set is a transceiver responsible for receiving and transmitting voices, supervising its status, monitoring activity on the telephone network such as in-coming ring and busy signals, and providing compensation for varying power levels.

- A pulse dialer breaks the line current by the number of times equal to the number dialed. It is slow and unsuited for data communications.

- A tone dialer generates a combination of audio tones according to buttons pushed on a keypad. A tone dialer is much faster than pulse dialing.

- The local exchange loop consists of the telephone, a central office, and a wire pair connecting the two.

- The central office is responsible for switching calls among local subscribers, as well as serving as an interface to the long-distance network.

- A local office is identified by the first three digits of a seven-digit, local telephone number.

- BORSCHT function refers to a series of central office duties. It stands for Battery, Overvoltage protection, Ring and trip, Supervision, Coding, Hybrid, and Test.

- Operating voltages for telephones are provided by the central office. The on-hook voltage across the tip and ring wire is –48VDC, while the off-hook voltage is –6VDC.

- The International Direct Distance Dialing (IDDD) number plan is a world-wide system that permits subscribers to direct-dial any number in the world without operator assistance.

- The telephone network is arranged in a hierarchical fashion from the central office (class 5) to four classes of long-distance switching exchanges.

- Pulse modulation is produced by sampling voice or data at the Nyquist rate.

- Pulse amplitude modulation is generated by sampling an analog waveform. The amplitude of the pulses is proportional to the amplitude of the waveform.

- Pulse duration modulation results when the width of a pulse varies in direct proportion to the modulating waveform. Since amplitude doesn't vary, it's not as noisy as pulse amplitude modulation.

- Pulse code modulation is produced by converting an analog waveform into a digital bit-stream.

- A pulse code modulation sample consists of 8 bits. The first bit represents the sign of the sample (positive or negative), the next 3 bits specify 1 of 8 sample chords, while the last 4 bits specify 1 of 16 intervals found in each of the chords.

- A PCM signal is companded in order to keep the signal-to-noise ratio equal for small and large amplitude signals. Companding is accomplished by sampling smaller amplitudes at a greater rate than the larger amplitude signals.

- The compander used in North America is the $\mu = 255$ Law Compander, PCM Digital Coding Standard. The European equivalent is the α-law compander.

- The width of the voice channel used for data communications is 4 kHz.

- Measurements are made in the voice channel at a reference frequency of 2,250Hz and at a 1mW power reference point.

- Voice channel attenuation is controlled by loading the channel with an inductance.

- Phase delays increase with inductive loading. Phase delay is controlled by line conditioning. Conditioned lines are normally called dedicated channels.

- Long distance carriers employ a considerable amount of multiplexing of voice channels.

- Frequency-division multiplexing is used for analog signals. FDM can multiplex up to 10,800 voice channels.

- Time-division multiplexing is used for digital signals. TDM can multiplex up to 4,032 voice channels.

- When digital TDM is used by a common carrier, it's referred to as a T-Carrier. The most common T-Carrier group is the T1. A T1 facility multiplexes 24 voice channels. Each channel is transmitted at 64kBPS for a total T1 data rate of 1.544MBPS.

- A T1 multiplexer may transmit data from the 24 channels by alternating bits from each channel, in which case it would be utilizing bit-interleaved TDM. Or, it may alternately transmit 8-bit samples from each chord, and then be referred to as word-interleaved TDM.

- In a statistical time-division multiplexer, data rates have an aggregate rate higher than the line speed.

- Data concentrators utilize compression techniques to increase data through-put.

- The analog carrier hierarchy consists of 12 channels.

- A T1 frame consists of 24, PCM-encoded channels.

- A superframe contains 12, T1 frames. The ESF contains 24, 12-channel T1 frames.

- A DS1 pulse has a positive amplitude of 3.0 V and a line rate of 1.544MBPS.

- There are four basic levels of T-Carrier service available.

- The SONET is the fiber optic alternative to digital carrier systems.

- The basic Synchronous Optical Network signal is called STS1. It propagates at 51.84MBPS through an OC1 channel.

- A SONET frame has a length of 810 bytes.

- SONET networks may be configured in a point-to-point, hub or star topology.

- Training helps employees to be more efficient and productive in their jobs. Increasingly, corporations are turning to experts to supply the training.

- A Training Needs Survey compares expected to actual skill levels.

- The results of the training survey indicates the "wants and needs" of training.

At this point, review the objectives listed at the beginning of the chapter to be certain that you understand and can perform them. Afterward, answer the review questions that follow to verify your knowledge of the information.

Lab Exercises

The lab manual that accompanies this book contains hands-on lab procedures that reinforce and test your knowledge of the theory materials presented in this chapter. Now that you have completed your review of Chapter 3, refer to the lab manual and perform Procedures 3, "Network Cabling," and 4, "Modem Installation."

REVIEW QUESTIONS

The following questions test your knowledge of the material presented in this chapter:

1. What is DTMF?

2. On average, how long does it take to tone dial the numbers 692?

3. What are the BORSCHT functions?

4. State the voltages present on the line when a telephone is on-hook and off-hook.

5. What is the purpose of companding a PCM-encoded signal?

6. What signal characteristics are controlled through line conditioning?

7. What is the data rate of a T1 channel?

8. Describe the difference between FDM and TDM.

9. What is the bit rate of an OC1 data signal?

10. What is a SONET virtual tributary?

11. A superframe contains how many T1 frames?

12. What is the difference between pulse and tone dialing?

13. What components does the local exchange loop consist of?

14. Describe the basic configurations capable of being used in a SONET.

15. At what point does it make sense to consider installing a T1 connection?

MULTIPLE CHOICE QUESTIONS

1. The device in a telephone that allows full-duplex operation is:
   a. Hybrid.
   b. Speech Muting.
   c. Ringer.
   d. Loop length Compensation.

2. A busy signal originates from:
   a. The called telephone.
   b. The central office.
   c. The calling telephone.
   d. The Borscht functions.

3. The output of a PDM modulator.
   a. Varies in phase.
   b. Varies in amplitude.
   c. Varies in pulse width.
   d. Varies in polarity.

4. A PCM modulator samples data at quantization levels 3, 4 and 8. The PCM encoded output is:
   a. 011, 100, 111.
   b. 1111.
   c. 1100.
   d. 011, 0100, 1000.

5. The output of a PCM micro-Law compander is 10101001. Select the statement below that is true.
   a. The code is from the sixth chord, ninth interval.
   b. The code is from the second chord, thirty-second interval.
   c. The code is from the second chord, ninth interval.
   d. The code is from the tenth chord, eighth interval.

6. How are attenuation and phase delays affected by loading of the voice channel?
   a. Attenuation is decreased while phase delays are increased.
   b. Attenuation is increased while phase delays are not affected.
   c. Phase delays are decreased while attenuation is not affected.
   d. Attenuation is increased while phase delays are decreased.

7. The T1 frame format includes _____ PCM encoded channels.
   a. 8
   b. 193
   c. 24
   d. 12

8. What format is used when T-Carrier data is TDM multiplexed?
   a. Data streaming.
   b. Word or bit interleaving.
   c. Fractional.
   d. Jumbo MUX.

9. Describe how delays are affected in a telephone line when attenuation is increased.
   a. Delays decrease.
   b. Delays increase.
   c. Delays cause reflective waves.
   d. Delays oscillate.

10. What is the advantage of companding?
    a. High-amplitude signals are over-amplified.
    b. Low-amplitude signals are over-amplified.
    c. Low-amplitude signals are encoded more often that high amplitude signals.
    d. High-amplitude signals are encoded more often that low-amplitude signals.

CD-ROM

Net+ Practice Test

Additional Net+ Certification testing is available on the CD that accompanies this text. The testing suite on the CD provides Study Card, Flash Card, and Run Practice type testing. The Study Card and Flash Card feature enables you to electronically link to the section of the book in which the question is covered. Choose questions from the test pool related to this chapter.

CHAPTER

4

MODEMS

LEARNING OBJECTIVES

Upon completion of this chapter and its related lab procedures, you should be able to perform the following tasks:

1. Describe the parameters of modem performance specified in the ITU "V-dot" series of standards.

2. Differentiate between analog and digital modem transmission methods.

3. Describe the sequence of events that occur between modems.

4. Calculate channel bandwidth for a given carrier frequency and symbol rate.

5. State several features that may be found in a modem.

6. Install and configure a modem.

7. Locate an unused port and IRQ to be used by the modem.

8. Using appropriate equipment, choose the correct IRQ.

9. Modify modem configuration settings using appropriate software.

10. Explain the meaning of "Hayes compatible" as it relates to modems.

11. Explain the steps to follow for setting up and using Hyper Terminal.

12. Describe a method for measuring actual modem performance.

13. Name several types of modulation used in modems. Name the most common modulation type used in modern, high-speed modems.

14. Provide a general description of FSK.

15. Provide a general description of PSK.

16. State the difference between baud and bit rate.

17. Describe DPSK, and interpret a DPSK constellation map.

18. Provide a general description of QAM.

19. Interpret a QAM constellation map.

20. Use a chip-set block diagram to describe data flow and major chip functions.

21. Why does the operation of V.90 modems represent a significant departure from earlier modems.

22. Explain the attributes, advantages and disadvantages of the PSTN (POTS).

23. Use Shannon's Theorem to calculate the data rate of a channel.

24. Give maximum vs typical V.90 modem data rates for uploading/downloading.

25. Explain why voice channels are data rate limited to 35 kBPS.

26. Describe three types of common loop back tests.

27. Set up an SOP to gain approval for system changes and upgrades.

28. Track system additions and upgrades.

29. Locate vendor's upgrades on the Internet.

30. Test software upgrades downloaded from the Internet.

31. State several advantages to network group accounts.

CHAPTER 4

Modems

INTRODUCTION

A **modem** converts digital data into a format suitable for transmission over a long distance. It also accepts transmitted data and reconverts it back into digital data. The term, "modem", is an acronym for **modulator/demodulator**. A modem is a vehicle used for sending and receiving data. For the most part, a modem is needed to transmit and receive data when the communicating devices are separated by up to 50 feet. This distance may be extended to 100 feet in environments relatively free of electrical noise.

> Modem is an acronym for modulator/demodulator.

By far, the single largest application of modems is to interface computers to the telephone network.

Modems always work in pairs, as shown in Figure 4-1. Typically, they handle data transfer over telephone lines. The phone lines were originally intended to pass analog voice signals within a bandwidth containing the fundamental frequencies of most voices. These frequen- cies occur in the range of 300 Hz to 3,300 Hz. This means that in order for a computer user to make use of the extensive telephone network, any data transmitted through it must be mani- pulated to fit the tight constraints of the phone system. The individual channels allocated by phone companies to subscribers have a bandwidth of 3,300 Hz – 300 Hz = 3,000 Hz.

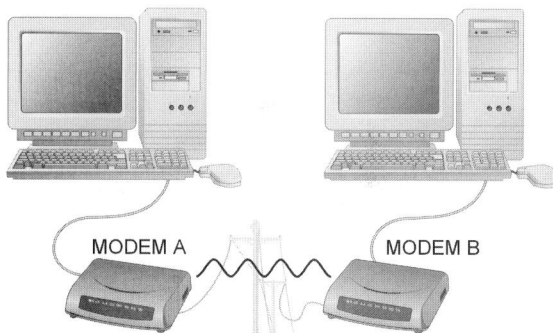

Figure 4-1 Modems Work in Pairs

In practice, the available bandwidth beyond the local loop extends to 4,000 Hz, as mentioned in Chapter 3. Conditions in the voice channel have improved significantly over the past decade. For computers, this translates to extra bandwidth, so that the full 4kHz channel width is routinely used to send data. The modem is used to modify data in such a way that it fits the bandwidth limitations of phone channels without degrading the original information.

> A modem can receive as well as transmit data.

A modem is a transceiver in that it has the ability to transmit as well as receive. As you'll recall from Chapter 1, data traffic may take one of three forms: simplex, half duplex and full duplex. Simplex is one-way-only communication. A television receiver is a simplex device since it receives, but can't transmit, information. Half-duplex traffic occurs in both directions between communicating devices; however, the two-way traffic is forbidden to occur simultaneously. Citizen band radios are half-duplex devices. Full-duplex means data is allowed to travel simultaneously between communicating stations. Telephones are common full-duplex devices. A modem can be configured to work as simplex, half-duplex or full-duplex. In this chapter, all discussions on modems are centered around full-duplex transmissions.

Primarily, modems serve as an interface to the public telephone network. Modems always work in pairs. The pairs must be compatible in terms of speed, frame format, word length and parity.

Modem pairs must be compatible. In the case of modems, compatibility refers to speed (BPS), frame format (synchronous or asynchronous), word length, parity, etc., as well as interface protocols. For the most part, modems in the United States use the EIA/TIA-232 interface standard for signaling conventions. When the modem is fitted into a PCs expansion slot, it will include a Universal Asynchronous Receiver-Transmitter (UART) parallel interface.

In Figure 4-1, modem A may accept data from the personal computer, and frame format it as synchronous or asynchronous, determine the type of parity, and then modulate a carrier for transmission over the phone lines. The data is then transmitted. At the receiving modem (modem B), the **message frame** is demodulated from the carrier, and parity is checked. The data is then converted into binary logic levels and passed into the receiving computer.

Once data leaves a modem, it's treated just like a telephone call by the phone companies. In fact, to send a message through a modem, you must supply the phone number of the receiving modem. Circuitry within modems handles the telephone interface and operation.

A modem provides a computer user with a tremendous amount of access. Literally, a good modem makes the difference in working at an isolated PC (even if it's part of a network) and accessing the great, wide-open spaces of the Internet.

Nearly all of data communications utilize modems—from the single user at home with a PC, to internationally distributed networks of conglomerate corporations. In the past decade the price of modems has dropped so significantly that a good-quality, 56kBPS modem can be purchased for under $200. The World Wide Web, which, for most of us, is accessible only via a modem, remains an amusing curiosity without a modem.

This chapter takes a thorough look at all aspects of modems, from the universally-used Hayes AT command set, to modulation methods, to installing and setting up a modem, to figuring out how it's possible to achieve 56kBPS data rates, when the fastest data rate possible through a voice channel is about 35 kBPS. First, we'll start with modem standards, commonly called the V-Series, or "V-dot", standards.

V-SERIES RECOMMENDATIONS

The V-Series Recommendations for modems are published by the **International Telecommunication Union** (ITU), formerly called CCITT (**Consultative Committee for International Telephony**). The ITU, headquartered in Geneva Switzerland, is "an international organization within which governments and the private sector coordinate global telecom networks and services". In short, the ITU is composed of representatives from industry and government who try to hammer out a standard that will encourage interoperability between vendors and manufacturers.

Interoperability is the key, if somewhat extravagant, word. It's intended to encourage competition without giving any single company a technological advantage due to deep pockets of a few large vendors. It also provides a measure of flexibility for the user since the buyer isn't tied to one company's product line.

> Characteristics of modems are described in a series of ITU recommendations called the V Series.

While the recommendations cover many aspects of telecommunications, at a minimum they will tell you the following information directly related to modems:

- The highest data rate of the modem.

- The type of modulation used in a modem.

- The communication method between modems (simplex, half-duplex, full-duplex).

- The telco connection between modems (point-to-point 2-wire, switched, etc.).

CNST OBJECTIVE
VI-D

The ITU V-Series recommendations are important to networking personnel because they define attributes such as data rates, modulation methods, encoding methods, connections, and so on. As with other protocols, the V Series doesn't attempt to dictate to manufacturers how to implement the recommendations, but instead specifies outcomes. Table 4-1 lists several ITU-Series Recommendations.

Table 4-1 ITU-Series Modem/Telephone Network Recommendations

Series A	Organization of the work of the ITU
Series G	Transmission systems, media, digital systems and networks
Series I	Integrated Services Digital Networks (ISDN)
Series L	Construction, installation, and protection of outside cable and elements
Series P	Telephone transmission quality, telephone installations and networks
Series V	Data communication over the telephone network
Series X	Data networks and open-system communication

Table 4-2 lists selected V-Series recommendations for data communications over the telephone network. Prior to acceptance of standards, the only broadly embraced guidelines were proprietary from AT&T. These were called the Bell Standards, and have been included in parenthesis next to their equivalent V-Series.

Table 4-2 V-Series Modem/Telephone Network Recommendations

V.2	Power levels for data transmission
V.17	2-wire fax modem with rates up to 14.4kBPS
V.21	300BPS standard
V.22	1,200BPS standard for use on a point-to-point 2-wire leased line
V.22bis	2,400BPS FDM standard for use on point-to-point 2-wire leased lines
V.23	600/1,200 baud standard
V.24	Definitions for interchange circuits between DTE and DCE
V.25bis	Synchronous/asynchronous auto-dialing procedures on switched networks
V.26bis	2,400/1,200BPS standard
V.27bis	4,800/2,400BPS standard
V.29	9,600BPS standard for use on 4-wire leased lines
V.32bis	9,600BPS duplex standard for use on phone networks and leased lines
V.33	14.4kBPS standard for use on 4-wire leased lines
V.34	33.6kBPS standard for use on phone networks and leased point-to-point 2-wire lines
V.42bis	Data compression procedures for DTE using error-correction

As you can see, the Bell Standards only cover lower-speed modems. The reason is that shortly after modems became accessible to the general public, AT&T embraced the standards which were published at that time by the CCITT.

Standards change frequently. At the time of this writing the standard for 56kBPS (V.90) modems had been finalized but not approved. Even older standards change over time, so you should check frequently with the ITU to make sure you remain current with the latest technological trends.

OPERATIONS BETWEEN MODEMS

A modem connects to the port (serial or parallel) of a computer on one side and the telephone line on the other side. The modem may be internal (meaning it connects to the parallel bus of the host computer), or it may be external (meaning it connects to the serial bus via a EIA/TIA-232 interface). Neither type has a particular advantage over the other, although external modems are slightly more expensive.

Historically, modems have been classified as analog or digital. The distinction is evident: an analog modem converts digital data from a computer to analog, in order to send it across the analog local loop to a central office, while a digital modem works exclusively in the **Public Switched Telephone Network** (PSTN) in which all data is digital (for the most part). With the V.90 recommendation, the distinction between analog and digital is blurring, as you'll see later in this chapter.

Figure 4-2(a) illustrates the use of a modem in a typical environment.

NET+ OBJECTIVE
I.8.1

CNST OBJECTIVE
I-A

(a)

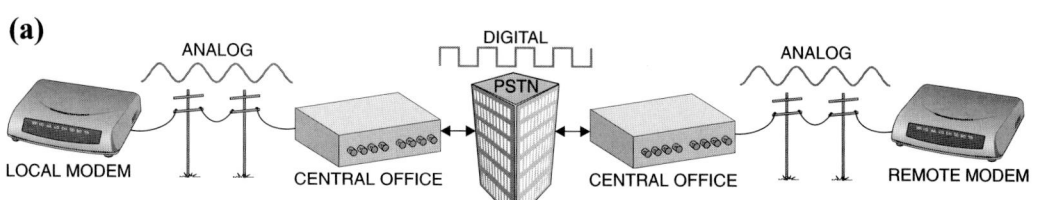

(b)

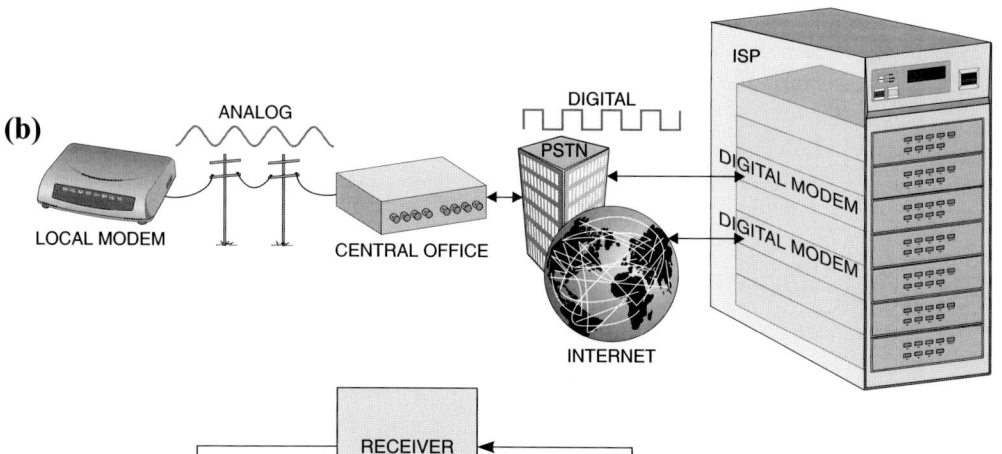

(c)

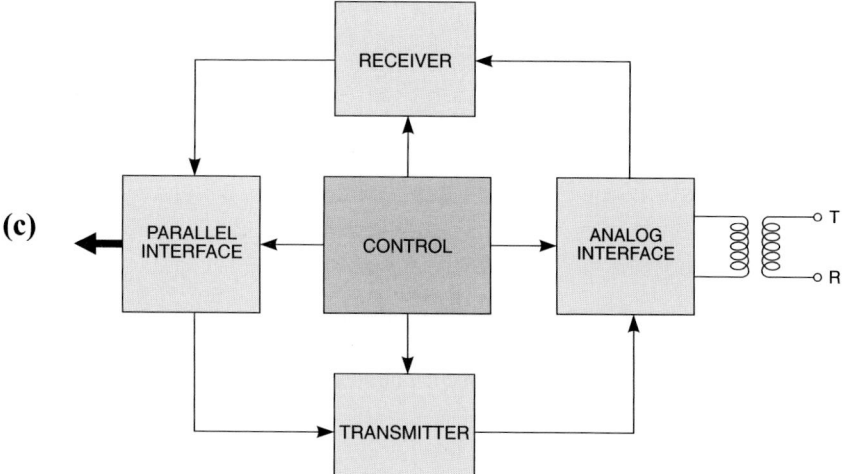

Figure 4-2 (a) Typical Local to Remote Modem Connection, (b) Modem Used to Access the Internet, (c) Simplified Block Diagram of a Modem

A source modem is sending data to a remote modem. Notice that the connection on both ends from the modem to the central office is an analog loop, but once the signal enters the PSTN it's converted to digital. Both modems must be capable of converting transmitted data from digital to analog, and received data from analog back to digital. In addition, the modems have a very narrow bandwidth to work within; a bandwidth that was designed for voice communications, and not data communications (text, video, graphics).

In the past ten years or so, the voice channel characteristics have improved to the point that a full 4,000 Hz of the channel can be used for data messages. Better modulation methods such as PCM and companding have also contributed to improving the channel for data. Still, it remains a voice-intended channel. So the modem must carry the data across the analog loop on a carrier that falls somewhere within the 4kHz bandwidth, and for full-duplex transfers, has to provide different transmit and receive carriers.

In addition to all of that, a local modem transmitting to a remote modem has to be able to manipulate data in way that the remote will understand, or at least to emulate the distant modem. Manipulating the data means matching the data rate abilities of the two, formatting data the same way with parity and stop/start bits, using the same modulators/demodulators, and so on.

Of course, we expect the remote modem to receive the data that is sent, so a modem will also anticipate noise and distortion characteristics of the link between them, and compensate for it with pre-equalization before it's transmitted. A modem is a complex device and shouldn't be taken for granted.

Figure 4-2(b) illustrates a familiar scenario for a modem. This time, the modem is in a home and is used to access the Internet. Notice the difference here is that modems used at the **Internet Service Provider** (ISP) are digital. The PSTN and the Internet are digital entities, so there's no need for an analog conversion; it only occurs on the down-stream side from the central office to the residence.

So, why is that significant? The analog-digital and digital-analog conversions in Figure 4-2(a) create noise in the form of quantization errors (refer back to PCM and convolutional coding in Chapter 3). In the second figure, the analog-to-digital and digital-to-analog conversions don't occur on the remote side, since the home-based user only accesses digital data. Consequently, the amount of quantization error is greatly reduced.

Remember that when data is μ-Law encoded, small signal amplitudes were represented by more bits than the large signals. This was done to normalize the amplitude difference and resulted in a relatively flat signal-to-noise ratio for all amplitudes. If this isn't done, then small signals may be obscured by noise that has the same or greater amplitude. A low signal-to-noise ratio results in a high number of errors.

There is a relationship between errors and data rates on a telephone channel. Recall from Chapter 1 that bandwidth and capacity are directly related. Well, since the voice channel is bandwidth-challenged, the capacity that data can be sent across it will be limited. What is the limit? It turns out to be about 35 kBPS. For the scenario shown in Figure 4-2(a), data rates will be limited to V.34 speeds of 33.6 kBPS.

For the situation shown in Figure 4-2(b), the user will still access the Internet at V.34 data rates, and will be able to receive data at much higher speeds. But we're getting ahead of ourselves. First, let's take a look a some broad capabilities of modems.

Modem Parameters

A block diagram of a simplified modem is shown in Figure 4-2(c). As shown, the modem has a telephone line connection, depicted as T and R. T and R stand for **tip** and **ring**, a carry-over term from the telephone industry. In a 4-wire telephone cable, ring is the red wire and tip is the green wire. For access to the public network, these are the only wires needed. A signal received from the telephone line will be accepted by the analog interface and switched to the receive section. In the receiver, the carrier is demodulated and converted from analog to digital data. The digital data is sent to the parallel interface, where it is converted from serial to parallel data and sent to a computer along a parallel data bus.

Information to be transmitted is converted to serial data in the parallel interface. The transmitter section converts the logic levels to analog in one of several modulation methods. The modulated carrier is then coupled to the public telephone network by the analog device.

When an actual modem is analyzed later in this chapter, you'll agree that Figure 4-2(c) is a highly simplified model. But it serves to point up several general observations about modems.

In Figure 4-2(c), the modem can either transmit or receive, but can't do so simultaneously; therefore, it's a half-duplex modem. All modems are actually full-duplex so they send and receive at the same time. To do so, each requires a transmit carrier and a receive carrier. Modulation creates frequency changes centered around the carriers. The total amount of carrier change equates to the bandwidth of the transmit and receive channels.

How does the internal circuitry determine if a signal is a legitimately received signal? A transmitting modem is designated as the originate modem and must transmit at a carrier frequency specified for various types of modems. The receiving modem is designated the answer modem. It responds to the originate modem at a specified frequency as well. For example, a modem that uses **Frequency Shift Keying** (FSK) modulation transmits at 1,170Hz in the originate mode, and the answer modem responds at 2,125Hz. The answer and originate frequencies are fixed within modems and depend upon the data rate and type of modulation used. Of course, the answer modem may work in the originate mode, and the modem that was formally in the originate mode would now respond in the answer mode. A modem only responds to legitimate answer and originate frequencies.

> A modem may operate in an originate or answer mode. The originate mode initiates the data exchange while the answer mode responds to an originate modem. Modems have specific originate and answer carrier frequencies.

Table 4-3 shows carrier frequency rates for a 33.6BPS 3Com/U. S. Robotics modem. In this modem, two carrier rates are available for each symbol rate (See section Quadrature Amplitude Modulation for more information on baud and BPS rates.) The symbol rate is the amount of user data sent and is a different number than the bit rate because more than one bit of user data is contained in a symbol bit (the baud). For example, assume the modem chooses a carrier frequency of 1,800Hz. The symbol rate for this carrier is 3,000 baud. The amount of bandwidth needed in the 4kHz voice channel is:

$$BW \text{ Required} = F_{ul} - F_{ll}$$

where F_{ul} is the **Upper Limit** of the frequency BW, and F_{ll} is the **Lower Limit**. The frequency limits are determined by:

$$F_{ul} = F_{carrier} + (Baud/2)$$
$$= 1,800 + (3,000/2)$$
$$= 3,300 \text{ Hz}$$

$$F_{ll} = F_{carrier} - (Baud/2)$$
$$= 1,800 - (3,000/2)$$
$$= 300 \text{ Hz}$$

The channel bandwidth is then calculated as:

$$BW \text{ Required} = F_{ul} - F_{ll}$$
$$= 3,300 - 300$$
$$= 3,000 \text{ Hz}$$

Table 4-3   Carrier Frequencies Available for a 33.6kBPS Modem

SYMBOL RATE	MINIMUM BIT RATE	MAXIMUM BIT RATE	CARRIER FREQUENCY	BANDWIDTH REQUIRED
2,400 Baud	2,400 BPS	21,600 BPS	1,600 Hz 1,800 Hz	400-2,800 Hz 600-3,000 Hz
2,743 Baud	4,800 BPS	24,000 BPS	1,646 Hz 1,829 Hz	274-3,018 Hz 457-3,200 Hz
2,800 Baud	4,800 BPS	24,000 BPS	1,680 Hz 1,867 Hz	280-3,080 Hz 467-3,267 Hz
3,000 Baud	4,800 BPS	26,400 BPS	1,800 Hz 2,000 Hz	300-3,300 Hz 500-3,500 Hz
3,200 Baud	4,800 BPS	28,800 BPS	1,829 Hz 1,920 Hz	229-3,429 Hz 320-3,520 Hz
3,429 Baud	4,800 BPS	28,800 BPS	1,959 Hz	244-3,674 Hz

Another general observation concerning the simple modem of Figure 4-2(c) relates to the actual interface. On the tip and ring side, modems are equipped with a standard **RJ-11 modular telephone jack**. This is a female connector identical to the wall jacks used with an ordinary telephone. The modem plugs directly into the wall jack via a cable with suitable male telephone jacks.

On the computer side, the modem connects to an **EIA/ITU-232** serial port (for an external modem). EIA/ITU-232 signaling conventions are universally installed in commercial modems. The handshaking protocols associated with the interface are also common to modems. The interface is designed to be compatible with 16650 UARTs (**Universal Asynchronous Receiver Transmitter**).

Before examining the functions and parameters of modems, one other aspect of Figure 4-2(c) is noteworthy: it doesn't contain a complex arrangement of the blocks of data flow. This is true of most modems. The demand for the product has been such that ICs are available to perform all functions of a modem with a minimum amount of support chips. This has the added feature of making high-quality, fast modems available to the general public at reasonable prices.

A modem may be packaged as an independent device that is situated near the computer. It connects to the computer with an EIA/TIA-232 cable, and to the telephone network with a conventional telephone jack. **Stand-alone** modems have the advantage of being portable—they're easily moved for connection to other computers. In addition, they usually have status indicators that inform the operator of the status of the message transmission as well as providing information in the event there's a problem.

Another type of modem is the older **acoustically-coupled** variety. A telephone handset rests on a cradle packaged with the modem. The modem monitors the line with tone-detection circuitry. When a distant modem wants to send data, the acoustical modem will decipher the incoming tones through the telephone-handset microphone. The disadvantage to these types of modems is the additional equipment that's needed—handset and cradle, and tone-detection circuits. Some people prefer acoustical modems since they usually double as a telephone.

> A modem may be packaged as a stand-along device, as a board that plugs into a computer expansion slot, or as an acoustical modem that doubles as a telephone.

A third, and increasingly popular type of modem is the **internal** modem. An internal modem plugs directly into an available expansion slot of a computer, or it may be a part of the computer interface adapter. In either case, internal modems offer the advantage of savings on cable and connector costs, as well as a reduction in noise that may be induced into the cables. An internal modem truly makes a computer a mobile system and they are quickly becoming standard features in personal computers.

To initiate the transfer of data with a modem, you simply use the Touch Tone pad on the modem, or if it's equipped appropriately, dial the number of the receiving modem. In newer modems, dialing is done with software from the host computer. The modem, when the handset is lifted or a software command is initiated, will be placed in the **command state**. The command state is equivalent to the dial tone you hear when you lift the handset. In fact, it's the presence of the dial tone that places the modem in the command state. Once the call is made, the answer modem will respond with an acknowledgment for the originate modem to send a message. Once the originate modem gets the approval to transmit, it enters the **on-line state**. The on-line state is equivalent to gaining access to the public network when you make a call. Once the modem is in the on-line state, it transmits the data message.

What if a distant modem wants to send you a message but you're not there to answer a call? A modem normally has an **auto answer** feature that can respond to tone signals from push-button phones or pulses from rotary-dial telephone exchanges. The ability to respond to either type of call makes the modem compatible with nearly all the telephones and switching equipment in the United States. When the tone detectors in the modem detect a call, the originate modem is signaled that the connection has been successfully completed.

In addition to auto answer, most modems are equipped with **auto dialing**. The example given earlier of a call placed from the keyboard is an example of auto dialing. A modem may contain onboard **Random-Access Memory** (RAM) in which you can store telephone numbers and initiate the call with the system software at the keyboard.

Modems also contain all the necessary circuitry so that the modem has voice-call capabilities. That is, you use the same modem chip to place a voice call as you do a data call. Since it handles voice and data, why not graphics, as well? Most modems also have fax capabilities, but the data rate is currently limited to 14.4 kBPS.

INSTALLING AND CONFIGURING A MODEM

In a Win 95/98 or NT setting, the operating system may already have drivers for the modem you're installing. Then again, it may not. If the system doesn't have them, make sure you have a companion disk for your modem, so that you can install it yourself. Even better, check the chip-set used with your modem. Make sure it's manufactured by a company you recognize, that has a Web site, so you can download drivers and upgrades to the software.

Typically, installation and configuration for a modem is easy. When it doesn't work, however, you may reach a point where you want to just sit down and gnash your teeth. There are two areas which commonly cause problems—interrupt and port setting conflicts. We'll take a look at these after setting up a modem that installs the way it's supposed to.

Figure 4-3 shows a modem being installed into an available expansion slot of a PC. The printed circuit board may have components which are sensitive to **electrostatic discharge** (ESD), so be sure to handle the board by the edges. Ideally, you should purchase and use an ESD wrist strap, connecting it to an actual earth ground such as a water pipe.

To install the modem, exit all programs and shut the system down. Turn the power off to the computer. Remove the chassis cover. Locate an available expansion slot, and firmly press the board into the slot.

> Internal modems are installed in an available expansion slot of a personal computer, and software installed using the PC or Network operating system software.

Once the modem is securely installed into an expansion slot, replace the chassis cover and turn the computer on.

Before installing the modem, review the following hardware resources. The information is necessary for installing modems, network interface cards, sound card, etc. The key-point to hardware resources is that they must be unique for each device. If not, a conflict will disable the device.

IRQ: Interrupt Request is a setting assigned to each device in a computer that's used to get the attention of the microprocessor. All devices must be assigned unique IRQs so the processor will be able to tell which device it's servicing. Common IRQs are shown in Table 4-4.

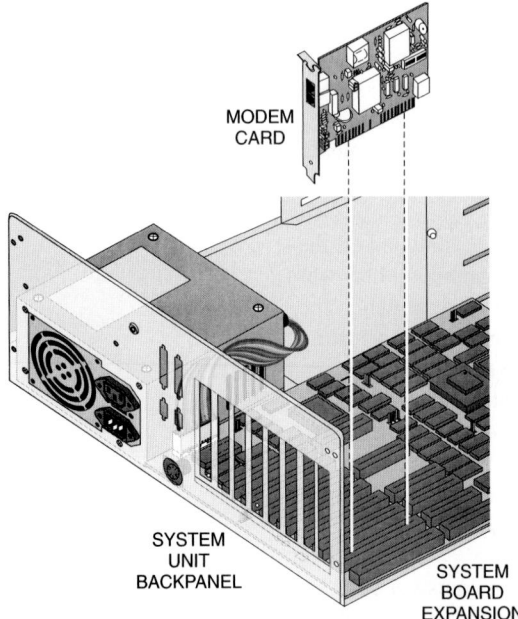

MODEM
CARD

SYSTEM
UNIT
BACKPANEL

SYSTEM
BOARD
EXPANSION
SLOTS

Figure 4-3 Install an Internal Modem into an Available Expansion Slot

Table 4-4 Interrupt
Requests and
Corresponding Device

IRQ	DEVICE
0	System Timer
1	Keyboard
2	Secondary IRQ controller, or video adapter
3	Unassigned (May be specified for COM 2 or COM 4)
4	Serial Ports COM 1 and COM 3
5	Unassigned (May be used for LPT2 or sound card)
6	Floppy Disk Controller
7	Parallel Port LPT1
8	Real-time Clock
9	Unassigned (May be used for redirected IRQ2, sound card, or third IRQ controller)
10	Unassigned (May be used for primary SCSI controller)
11	Unassigned (May be used for secondary SCSI controller)
12	PS2 Mouse
13	Math Coprocessor (If used)
14	Primary Hard Drive Controller
15	Unassigned (May be used for secondary hard drive controller)

Table 4-5 Common I/O Assignments

I/O Port	Device
200	Game Port
230	Bus Mouse
300	NIC Card
310	NIC Card
270	LPT3
2F0	COM2
370	LPT2
3B0	LPT1
3C0	EGA/VGA Video Adapter
3D0	CGA Video Adapter
3F0	COM1, Floppy Disk Controller

Base I/O Port: The hexadecimal address that a microprocessor in a computer uses to communicate with a device in a computer. Base I/O assignments must be unique. Common I/O assignments are shown in Table 4-5.

Base Memory Address: Buffer area in a computer's RAM memory where data coming in on a computer's parallel bus is stored while being converted to serial data to be transmitted from a serial port.

DMA: A Direct Memory Address controller is used to transfer data in the NIC (Network Interface card)card buffers directly into system memory. This relieves the microprocessor from devoting time and resources to the task.

For peripheral devices installed in a computer (NIC card, modem, sound card, etc.), the IRQ, DMA and Base I/O must be unique. If not, there will be a resource conflict. To resolve the conflict, assign unique parameters to each device.

As Windows boots, it may detect the presence of the modem and generate a message saying that it's found new hardware, asking you if you want to install it. Click on YES, and if it doesn't initially find the modem, do the following to get to the configuration boxes:

- Click the Start button in the lower-left corner of your screen.

- Highlight Settings in the Start Menu selections, and click on Control Panel.

- Click the Modem icon. The Modem Properties box, shown in Figure 4-4 will open.

- Click the Add button, and the Install New Modem box, pictured in Figure 4-5, will open.

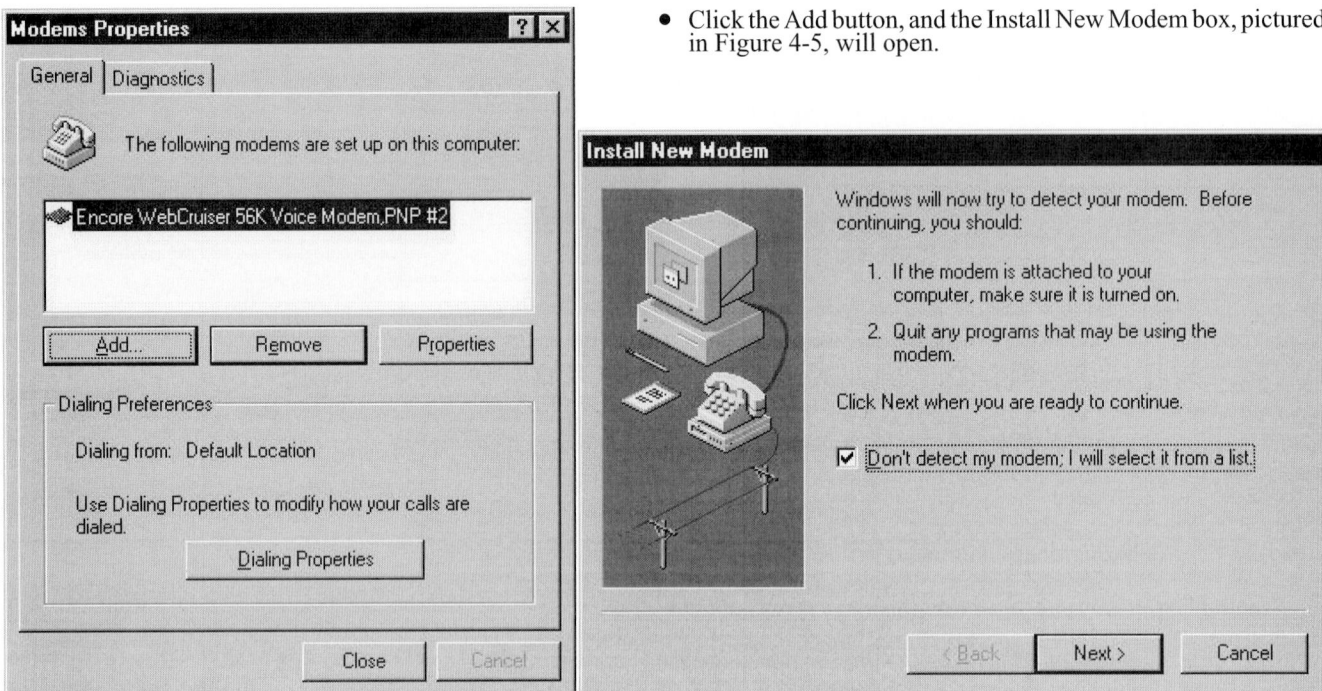

Figure 4-4 Modem Properties Dialog Box   **Figure 4-5 Install New Modem Dialog Box**

You have two options here; let Windows detect your modem, or select it from a list. Leave the field unchecked and see if it will correctly detect it. This may save you time, but if your modem is relatively new and has drivers which weren't installed with Windows, you'll have to install them yourself from the disk.

- Check the field labeled "Select from a list."

The dialog box will change to Figure 4-6. Now, you'll need to scan through the list to see if your modem is listed. If it is not, press the Back button and remove the check from the "Select from a list" box, and let Windows try to detect it. If it doesn't, go back to the screen shown in Figure 4-6, and click on the Have Disk button. A box will open telling you to place the disk in drive A and press the OK button. The installation files will be on the disk, and you should follow the instructions as they open.

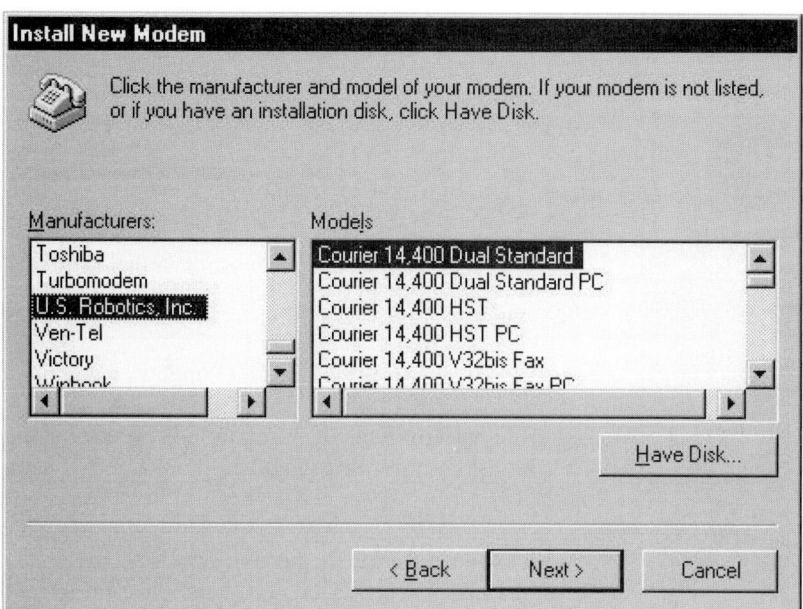

Figure 4-6 Select the Modem from the List

Once the drivers are installed, or Windows accepts your selection from the list of modems, a box will open, shown in Figure 4-7, prompting you to select one of the serial COM ports for your modem. For example, COM1 or COM3 would normally default to **Interrupt Request** (IRQ) 4, and be used for a serial mouse.

- Choose COM2. Along with COM4, these ports will normally default to IRQ3.

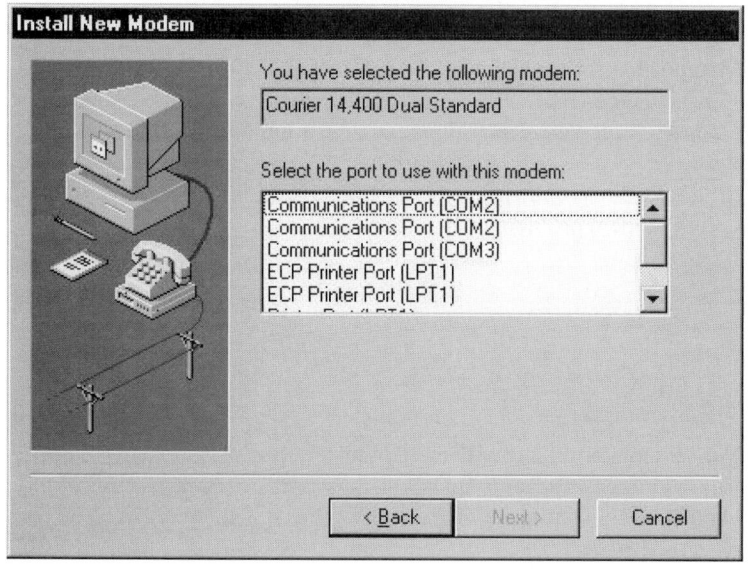

Figure 4-7 Select the COM Port Settings

The software will now complete the installation and you're almost finished with the installation. A final step is to make sure the modem works.

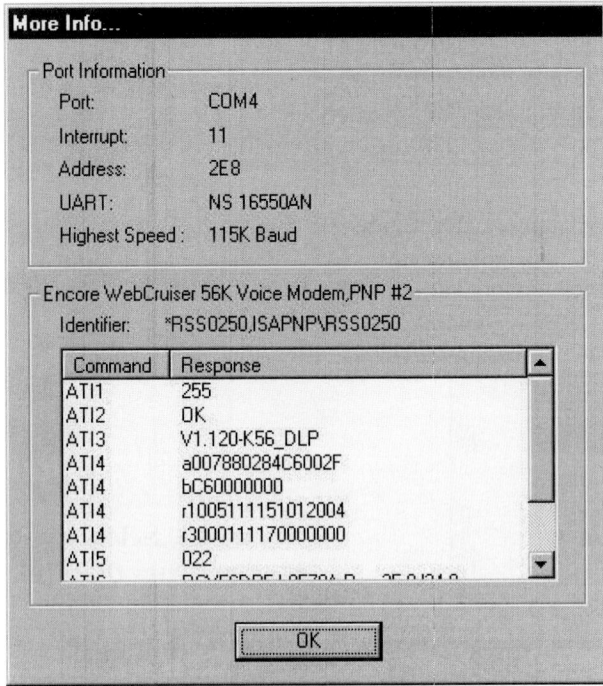

Port Information
Port: COM4
Interrupt: 11
Address: 2E8
UART: NS 16550AN
Highest Speed : 115K Baud

Encore WebCruiser 56K Voice Modem,PNP #2
Identifier: *RSS0250,ISAPNP\RSS0250

Command	Response
ATI1	255
ATI2	OK
ATI3	V1.120-K56_DLP
ATI4	a007880284C6002F
ATI4	bC60000000
ATI4	r1005111151012004
ATI4	r30001111 70000000
ATI5	022

OK

Figure 4-8 Modem Diagnostics Test Results

The quickest way to do this is to communicate with another modem, however, the most common method is to engage the Internet. If you're not yet hooked-up to cyberspace, all's still not lost. You can use Window's diagnostics by doing the following:

- From Control Panel, click the Modems icon. The Modem Properties dialog box (Figure 4-4) will open.

- Click the tab labeled Diagnostics. A dialog box will open listing all com ports. Highlight the port that your modem is on; then click More Info.

You'll receive a message telling you Windows is communicating with the modem. In a couple of minutes, the results of the diagnostic test will be shown in a dialog box called More Info. The box will display information about you modem, as depicted in Figure 4-8.

Of particular interest are the commands listed at the bottom of the box. These are Hayes AT commands for your modems. The AT commands control the functionality of modems. Notice that next to each command is an assortment of information that was generated. This means that the modem passed the diagnostic test since the computer software can communicate with the modem hardware.

A Hayes-compatible modem uses the Hayes AT Command Set to control modem functionality.

Windows diagnostics for modems isn't a full test since it doesn't test the ability of the modem to send and receive files to a distant modem. But it sometimes detects discrepancies such as port and IRQ conflicts as well as faulty seating of the modem card.

If a modem doesn't respond, it's time to get serious. The next section is devoted to troubleshooting modem problems.

Modem Troubleshooting

Earlier it was said that problems with modem installations result from COM port and IRQ conflicts. A modem may appear to install and configure properly, as well as appear to be working when the diagnostics are run. Yet, when you connect a phone line to the modem, it may neither send or receive.

You—and many others—may think that Windows should warn you if you blew the installation. Typically, though, the only hints you get are when you try to dial out, and receive messages such as "No dial tone" or "Can't detect modem". This will seem strange, since the modem was detected when you installed it. Why could there now be a problem?

Actually, the telephone line connection is the real acid test for a modem, and Windows can't test this function until you actually attempt to dial out. When you do, and the modem doesn't work, you get those cryptic messages. Now what?

Let's take a closer look at the COM port and IRQ settings. By the time you install a modem, many other sub-systems have already been installed in the computer (mouse, floppy drive, hard drive, CD-ROM, etc.). There's a good chance that the port and interrupt you assigned to your modem is being used by another device. So you have to find an unused port and IRQ for the modem.

There are two ways to do so:

- For Win95, click the System icon in Control Panel.

- Click the Device Manager tab. Highlight the Computer icon at the top of the list of devices.

- Click the Properties button. A listing of IRQs and their assigned devices will be displayed.

- For Windows NT, click Run. Type "WINMSD". A similar listing will be displayed.

- For Windows 3.x, exit windows and at the DOS prompt, type "MSD". Again, look for the IRQ/COM port listing.

The box will display all IRQs in your system and the devices they're assigned to. Look for the COM ports. For Plug-and-Play devices, Windows will attempt to assign COM 2, IRQ 3 to your modem. That's fine as long as these selections are not being used by another device. However, if you're getting conflicts, that's probably the case.

Usually, you can assign COM 4 to the modem along with an unused IRQ. However, you should be somewhat cautious about choosing COM 4. Video cards typically use some of the memory locations assigned to COM 4, and because of this, many modem manufacturers don't recommend using this port.

Any unused IRQ will work. However, check your modem literature, and if possible, use an IRQ between 1 and 7. Many serial devices, including modems, won't work at interrupts above 7. If the modem documentation doesn't say one way or the other, all you can do is try assigning one of the higher IRQs.

> A common problem during installation is conflicts between COM ports and interrupt requests (IRQs).

COM port and interrupt settings are configured on the hardware as well as the computer software, unless you have a Plug-and-Play modem. If so, all assignments are handled through software. If it's not Plug-and-Play, you'll have to manually change switch settings on the modem. These are usually black shunt switches which slide over vertical pins, or they may consist of a ganged DIP switches. The settings for IRQ and COM ports will either be marked directly on the modem card, or the documentation will instruct you about how to set them.

To change the software settings, do the following:

- For Win95/ NT, click the System icon in Control Panel.

- Click the Device Manager tab. Highlight the device you want to change.

- Double-click and/or press the Properties button. A properties dialog box will open.

- Select the Resources tab. If the field marked "Use Automatic Settings" is checked, remove the check.

- Highlight the resource you want to change (IRQ for modems) and press the Change Settings button.

- An Edit box will open. Change the IRQ setting and click OK.

- For Windows 3.x, double-click the Ports icon in Control Panel.

- Highlight the port used with your modem, then click Settings, and then Advanced.

- Select the IRQ you want to use for your modem.

COM port and interrupt conflicts are resolved by making sure the settings on the modem card (for non-Plug-and-Play devices) match those setup in the software. Once that's done, resolve any other conflicts by checking to see if the port and IRQ you're using is being used by another device. Windows 95 and NT will tell you at the Resources tab in Device Manager if there's a conflict. If so, you must make a change.

HAYES AT COMMAND SET

The functionality of a modem is contained in the Hayes Command Set. These are software commands used to configure the modem. In Windows-based software, much of the configuration is implemented within dialog boxes. For example, when you click the modem icon in Control Panel, the Modem Properties box opens. Highlight your modem in the list, and press the Properties button.

**CNST OBJECTIVE
VI-D**

Another dialog box opens which contains configuration data about you modem. Com port, speaker volume, word length, maximum speed (See the section labeled How's our Modem Doing? for an explanation of what maximum speed means.), word length, number of stop bits and so on. The information you see in these boxes is normally contained in the NVRAM (non-volatile random access memory) chip on the modem card. AT commands allow you to access the NVRAM to see what you're currently using. A modem that uses the Hayes AT Command Set is said to be Hayes Compatible.

A modem that uses the Hayes AT Command Set is said to be Hayes Compatible.

AT Commands can tell you quite a bit about your modem. Unfortunately, not all modem manufacturers give you access to them, and those who do don't always make it easy. It takes a little experimenting. Be cautious when nosing around the AT Commands, since any changes you make will affect how your modem works.

Table 4-6 shows a partial list of AT Commands. While these are typical, they may differ from your modem since each manufacturer implements the commands a little differently. The next section explains how to view the command set.

Table 4-6 Sampling of Hayes AT Commands

COMMAND	DESCRIPTION
&$	Help
A/	Repeat Last Command
A>	Continuously Repeat Command
AT	Command Mode Preface
A	Answer Call
B0	V.xx Mode
B1	Bell Answer Sequence
D0	Dial Telephone Number
D$	Help Dial Commands

SETTING UP AND USING HYPER TERMINAL

AT Commands are entered using Hyper Terminal with Windows 95.

You can learn quite a bit about your modem from AT commands. To do so, you first need to setup Hyper Terminal in Windows 95 (or Terminal in Windows 3.x). To start Hyper Terminal, click the Start button in the lower-left of your screen. Choose Programs/Accessories, then click on Hyper Terminal.

In the icon window which opens, click HYPERTRM.EXE. The Connection Description box, shown in Figure 4-9, opens. Enter a name for the terminal session such as Test Term.

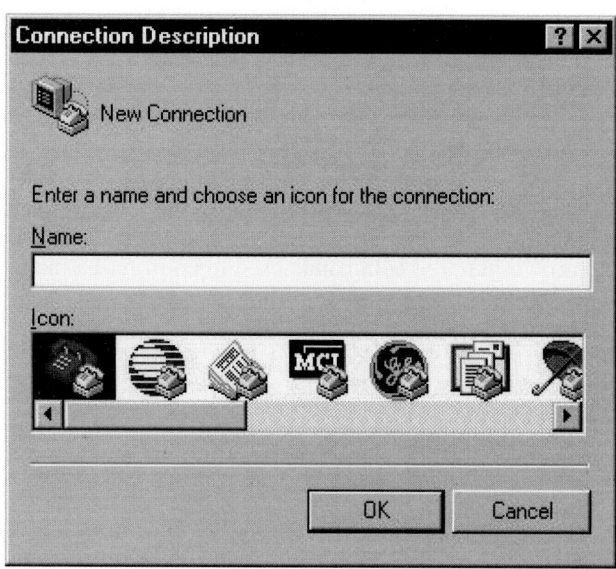

Figure 4-9 Hyper Terminal Connection Description Box

Figure 4-10 Hyper Terminal Phone Dialer

The Phone Dialer box will now appear. As you can see in Figure 4-10, it contains telephone numbering information. Enter 555-5555 for a telephone number, since you won't be dialing out.

Once the numbering information is entered, Windows will ask you if you want to connect, as shown in Figure 4-11. Click the Cancel button, and a blank terminal screen will be on your monitor.

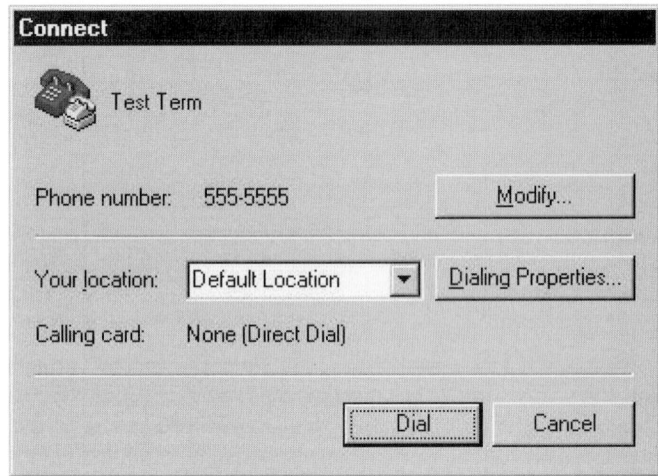

Figure 4-11 Hyper Terminal Connection Pop-Up

Type "AT", and press ENTER. The screen should respond with OK. This is a quick test that checks to see if the computer can communicate with the modem. If you get an OK, it means the communication software is able to communicate with the modem hardware.

If, when typing the command AT, you weren't able to see the letters, the Echo command has probably been turned off. Try typing "ATE1" and pressing ENTER. Remember to press ENTER after each command set.

The letters you type should now appear on the screen.

If, after entering AT, the screen responds with "ERROR", it's telling you the test failed. Or, in other words, Terminal can't find your modem. Either the COM port you've selected for the modem is incorrect, or some other device is currently using it.

Currently, three vendors manufacture 56k modem chips—Rockwell, Lucent Technologies, and 3Com/U. S. Robotics. They all use Hayes AT Commands, and all three implement them differently. Before using them, you need to know the chip manufacturer of your modem. Read the modem documentation, or look at the modem card to see who made the chip.

There are more than two-hundred commands used to configure a modem if it includes data/fax/voice capabilities. Most of these you'll never need, but some are very useful in learning about your modem and in troubleshooting it.

Table 4-7 lists several basic commands for each of the three modem chip vendors. Determine which modem you're using and try them out. For a complete listing of all AT commands, go to the Web site of each vendor and download data sheets for the respective chips.

Table 4-7 Implementations of Hayes AT Commands

ROCKWELL	
COMMAND	**DESCRIPTION**
AT	Switch from data mode to command mode.
AT/	Re-execute the last command.
ATEI	Turn on the command echo.
ATI0	Report the product code.
ATI1	Compute and report the checksum.
ATIX2	Report basic call progress codes and connection speeds.
AT&V	Display the current configuration.
AT$V1	Display the statistics on the last connection.

3COM/U.S. ROBOTICS	
COMMAND	**DESCRIPTION**
AT	Switch from data mode to command mode.
ATI2	Perform a RAM test.
ATI4	Show the current settings.
ATI5	Show the NVRAM settings.
ATI6	Display the statistics on the last connection.
ATI7	Display the product configuration.
AT$	Display the Help list of AT commands.

LUCENT TECHNOLOGIES	
COMMAND	**DESCRIPTION**
AT	Switch from data mode to command mode.
ATI3	Show the firmware version.
ATI11	Display the statistics on the last connection.

CHECKING YOUR MODEM

To test the speed capabilities of a modem, download a large file from an FTP site, and use AT commands to check the transfer rate.

If you've ever watched transfer rates of files downloaded from the Internet, you may be confused with the rated specifications on your modem. Some downloads are fast—42 kBPS with a 56k modem—while others are painfully slow—22 kBPS with the same modem.

Or, you may have tried to speed-up your modem by clicking the modem icon in Control Panel, and then, Properties from Modem Properties. There's a field that says Maximum Speed. You may set it for 115 kBPS, but when you actually connect, you discover you're transferring data at only 31.2 kBPS.

Why so many data rates from the same modem? There's several reasons, but let's take them one at a time. First, the Maximum Connect speed referred to in the previous paragraph has nothing to do with the speed that you transfer data to or from a distant modem; i. e., the Internet. When you set this field, you're instructing the software to transfer files to and from the computer and modem. That is, this speed is the maximum DTE/DCE speed. Set it high in your computer, then forget about it; but note that to utilize the feature at the maximum of 115 KBPS requires a 16xxx UART in the computer.

Typically, there will always be varying download rates from the Internet. When you cruise the wide-open-spaces, you're passed from server to server, across many hops, along channels that vary in speed and through hardware that varies in capability. For an explanation of how that's possible, refer to Chapter 8.

The telephone voice channel has a maximum data rate of about 35 kBPS. Using your telephone company to access your local Internet service provider ensures you will never connect any faster.

In fact, it could be much slower depending on the capability of the telco. If it can't support higher data rates, then your modem will fallback to the fastest rate that it can support. If it's any comfort, you're guaranteed a minimum of 9,600 BPS. An exception is that 56k, or V.90, modems download data much faster than the upper voice channel limit of 35 kBPS. Typical download rates, through a channel which can support V.90 technology, vary from 42 kBPS to about 48 kBPS. The FCC, due to limits placed on the radiated power in telephone channels, actually ensures you won't download any faster than 53 kBPS. Why are they called 56k modems? Who knows? But the important point is they manage to slip by the 35k limit. When uploading with a V.90 modem, however, you're using V.32 rates at 33.6 kBPS.

So how can you determine how fast your modem is actually uploading and downloading data? The most accurate way is to check transfers between your modem and a known, distant modem. An easy way to do this is to upload and download a file from the FTP (**File Transfer Protocol**) server of an **Internet Service Provider** (ISP). Most of them provide downloadable files on a server at an address which contains the name of the ISP. For example, assume that there is an ISP called Internet Provider. The name of the server is likely to be called ftp.internetprovider.com (check with your ISP to be sure of the conventions being used).

Choose a file that's large (+100kB or more). Look for files that have been archived, and that contain a .ZIP extension. The reason for this is that modems routinely compress files, unless they are already compressed. By choosing a compressed file, you know exactly how many bits are being sent. Download the same file at different times during the day and night, because congestion affects transfer rates. Traffic will be heavier during the day and lightest in the middle of the night. Note whether your downloads are reported as bits or bytes. If bytes are reported, multiply the number by 9 to convert to bits. There's an error correction protocol in the modem, called V.42, that removes the stop/start bits, but adds some overhead of its own. Therefore, 9 bits-per-byte is a reasonable estimate.

You'll need an FTP client if you don't already have one. Web browsers aren't particularly accurate when reporting downloads, since they're updating graphical changes. It's difficult to extract actual file transfer rates with them, and they'll surely vary among different servers. There are many FTP programs out there. For example, Figure 4-12 shows WS_FTP95, a shareware FTP program. Whatever you choose, set it up, then connect to your ISP and download a file to a temporary directory in your computer.

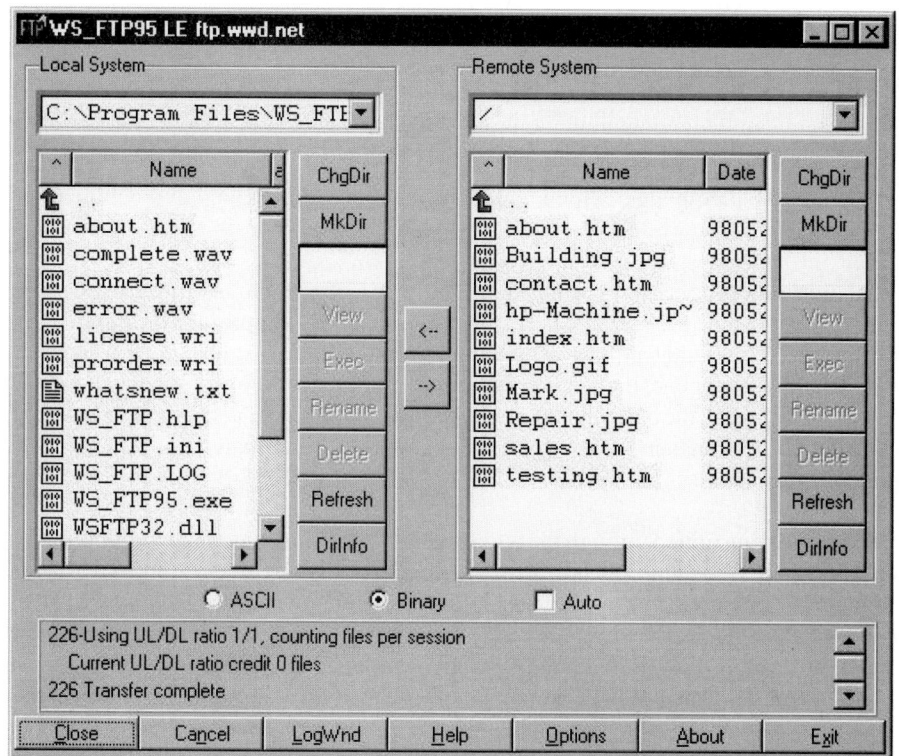

Figure 4-12 FTP Client Program

Once you've finished, disconnect from the Internet and start Hyper Terminal. Choose an AT Command for your modem chip that displays the statistics of the last connection. Figure 4-13 contains typical upload and download statistics for a modem. Speed is displayed as TX/RX where TX is the transmit, or upload rate and RX is the receive, or download rate.

```
OK
ati6
Texas Instruments RK 33600 Fax Link Diagnostics...

Chars sent            6383      Chars Received      18576
Chars lost               0
Octets sent           3328      Octets Received      6050
Blocks sent            189      Blocks Received       128
Blocks resent            0

Retrains Requested       0      Retrains Granted         0
Line Reversals           0      Blers                    0
Link Timeouts            0      Link Naks                0

Data Compression      V42BIS 2048/32
Equalization          Long
Fallback              Disabled
Protocol              LAPM
Speed                 31200/28800
Last Call             00:02:48
```

Figure 4-13 FTP Download Transmit and Receive Statistics

MODULATION IN MODEMS

> Data to be transmitted is modulated onto a carrier. Common modem modulation techniques are FSK, PSK, DPSK and QAM.

Modulation is the process of superimposing data upon a carrier. Modulating a carrier may be necessary for a couple of reasons. The distance between **Data Terminal Equipment** (DTE) may be several thousand feet, causing the signal-to-noise ratio to drop below an acceptable level. When this happens, high error rates are likely to occur. For these longer distances (exceeding 100 feet), the data signal is modulated onto a carrier. The carrier is operated at a frequency that will sustain the energy losses in the cable, thus maintaining an acceptable signal-to-noise ratio.

If data is to be transmitted through the telephone network, modulation is a requirement. As mentioned earlier, the limited bandwidth (4 kHz) of a telephone voice channel is the primary reason for this requirement. In addition to this, a large segment of the telephone system is analog, whereas the data leaving the computer is digital. The digital data must be converted to analog to be transmitted into the telephone network and modulated onto a carrier in such a way that the intelligence of the original data is retained across the analog phone lines.

Modulation used with modems is a variation of AM, FM, and PM. Four types of modulation will be examined in this section: **Frequency-Shift Keying** (FSK), **Phase-Shift Keying** (PSK), **Differential Phase-Shift Keying** (DPSK) and **Quadrature Amplitude Modulation** (QAM). Keep in mind that when data leaves a modem and arrives at the Central Office of the telco, it will be subjected to other signal manipulations such as pulse amplitude modulation, encoding, and a wide range of multiplexing techniques.

A basic understanding of modulation remains important, even though modems can be purchased containing a single modem chip and only a few support components. The reason is that the type of modulation has a significant impact of how fast data can be exchanged between modems.

Frequency-Shift Keying (FSK)

Frequency-Shift Keying (FSK) is a modulation method in which the carrier frequency is shifted higher or lower to represent a logic 1 or 0. It's generally reserved for low-speed modems of 300 BPS. As will be shown shortly, it utilizes an extravagant amount of the precious voice-channel bandwidth. On the positive side, FSK is easy to implement and demodulate.

Figure 4-14 shows digital data modulated onto a 1,170Hz carrier. The carrier frequency is well within the voice-channel bandwidth. A logic 1 modulated onto the carrier shifts the carrier forward to 1,270 Hz, while a logic 0 shifts the carrier back to 1,070 Hz, for a nominal bandwidth of 200 Hz.

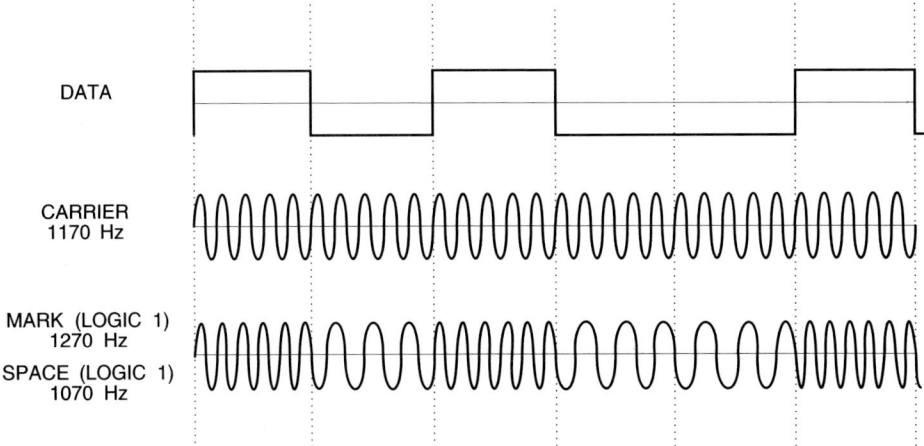

Figure 4-14 FSK Modulation

However, with each frequency change, harmonic sidebands will be generated at 2 x BPS = 2 x 300 BPS = 600 Hz. This means that in order to superimpose a 300BPS square wave using FSK, 600 Hz of the voice channel must be reserved. Keep in mind that over a communications channel, two modems are used. The transmitting modem is called the **originate** or **calling modem** and the receiving modem is called the **answer modem**. There must be sufficient space in the voice channel to permit the modems to operate in either mode.

> FSK represents bit changes by shifting the carrier higher and lower for logic 1's and 0's. FSK modems require plenty of bandwidth and are restricted to low speeds.

Figure 4-15 illustrates the bandwidth allocation for an FSK modem. The originate modem is centered at 1,170 Hz and the answer modem is centered at 2,125 Hz. A mark, logic 1, is shifted to 2,225 Hz in the answer mode while a logic 0 shifts the carrier back to 2,025 Hz.

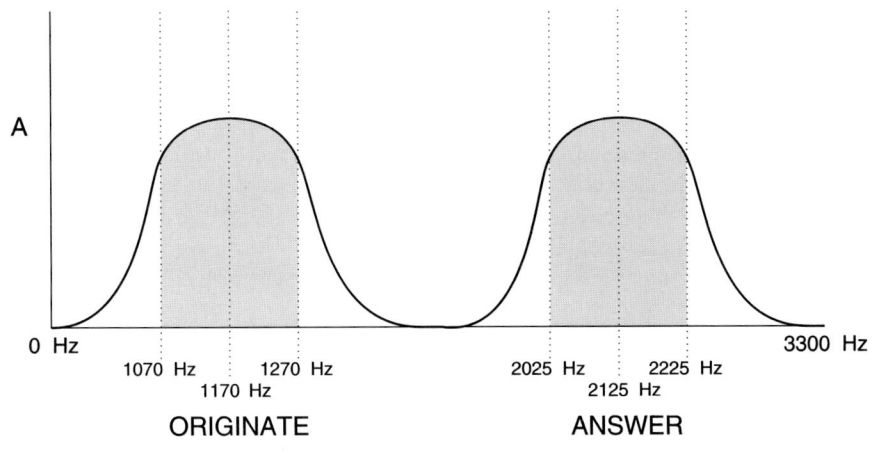

Figure 4-15 Bandwidth Allocation for an FSK Modem

Due to **harmonics** contained in the 300BPS data, the effective bandwidth required in the answer mode is also 600 Hz. The large bandwidth requirement of FSK is the reason that the answer and originate carriers are located so far apart.

What if the data rate increased to 600 BPS? The answer and originate modes would both require 1,200 Hz of bandwidth each, for a total of 2,400 Hz of the 4,000 Hz available in the voice channel. This leaves very little room left and, in fact, approaches the maximum data rate at which information can be considered to be reliably transmitted. While FSK modems are unacceptable at higher data rates, the simplicity of FSK modulators and demodulators resulted in low-priced modems becoming available to many users and, in turn, spurred the development of higher-speed modems that could be purchased at reasonable prices.

Phase-Shift Keying (PSK)

The concept of **Phase-Shift Keying** (PSK) is shown in Figure 4-16. For each change of logic level, the phase of the carrier is inverted 180 degrees. The receiver detects logic level changes only when it detects the phase inversion. PSK, as shown in the figure, suffers from the same bandwidth problems of FSK. It also has another problem. If a long string of logic 1's or 0's arrive at the receiver, synchronization between transmitter and receiver may be lost. To keep the receiver clocked to the transmitter, there should be a change of carrier frequency at the end of each bit, even if there's a logic level change.

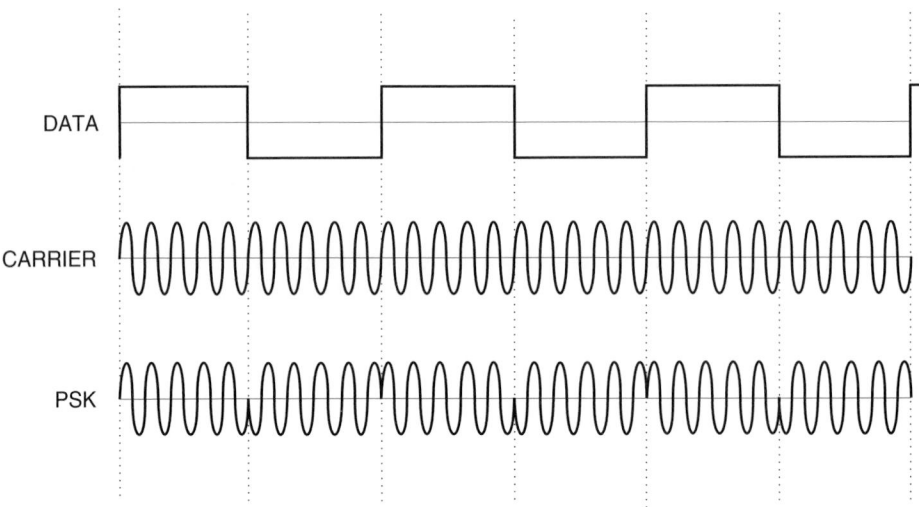

Figure 4-16 PSK Modulation

PSK represents logic 1's and 0's by inverting the phase of the carrier for each bit change.

Since the bandwidth of the voice channel restricts the data rate at which information can be transmitted, it's necessary to use more bits to express a change of the voice-channel carrier. FSK represented a single bit change by shifting the carrier. As we saw in Figure 4-14, four frequency changes (two each for answer and originate) were enough to consume a large amount of the bandwidth. An alternative to this technique is to have two or more bits produce a carrier change. In this way, the voice-channel bandwidth is more efficiently utilized. The process of having multiple bits, or symbols, produce a carrier change, refers to **baud**. If a symbol contains two bits *(a **dibit***) and modulates a 1,200BPS carrier, then the baud rate is:

$$Baud\ Rate = BPS/N_s$$
$$Baud\ Rate = 1200/2$$
$$Baud\ Rate = 600$$

where N_s is the number of bits per symbol.

It's important to note that baud rate has been degraded within the industry through incorrect usage. It's often used synonymously, and incorrectly, with BPS (**Bit Per Second**). The two are only equal when the bits per symbol is one, as in FSK. Modem manufacturers specify data rates only in BPS.

Baud rate is actually a measure of how much information (the user data which modulates the carrier) a given frequency can carry. It's meaningful only when the BPS rate is known. For example, a modem may have a baud of 600. Is this good or bad? If the BPS rate is 4,800, then the number of bits per symbol must be eight; but if the BPS rate is 2,400, the bits per symbol is four. The 4,800BPS modem is transmitting at twice the rate as the 2,400BPS modem, but at the same effective data rate—which is also called the baud rate. In other words, both modems will deliver user data at the same rate.

PSK readily lends itself to multiple bits per symbol. When the data phase modulates a carrier in such a way as to make more efficient use of the channel, it's referred to as differential phase-shift keying.

PSK is a marginal improvement over FSK. But, once it's modified to address the two problems described above, it delivers much superior results. The improved version of PSK is **Differential Phase-Shift Keying** (DPSK).

Differential Phase-Shift Keying (DPSK)

DPSK represents data bits by phase shifting the carrier in increments that are smaller than is available with FSK. This allows a greater number of bits per symbol.

DPSK is an extended version of the PSK described in the previous section. DPSK permits the symbol encoding to cause the phase to change based upon the phase position of the previous symbol. Using this approach, there's no need to transmit a portion of the carrier to be used for phase demodulation at the receiver. The receiver will look for the signal to fall within predetermined boundaries. The assumption that the phase-modulated data will drift due to jitters and ringing makes DPSK more fault tolerant than straight PSK.

DIBIT	PHASE SHIFT	ALTERNATE PHASE SHIFT
00	0^0	45^0
01	90^0	315^0
11	180^0	225^0
10	270^0	135^0

(a)

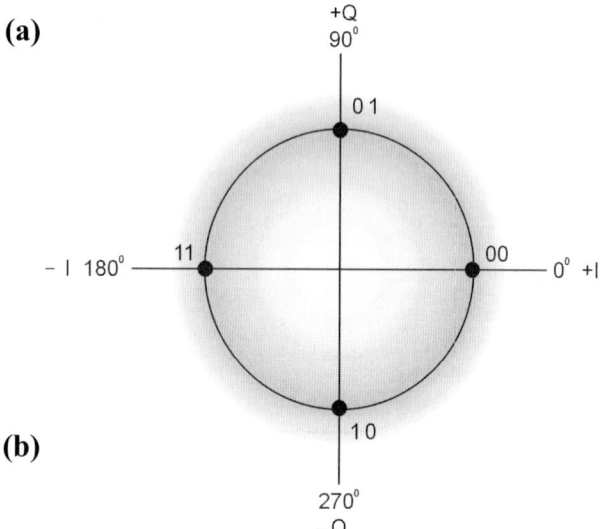

(b)

Figure 4-17 DPSK Truth Table and Constellation Map

DPSK derives its name from the fact that the information symbols are located at some phase- shifted point which is established by the first symbol of a word. The phase location of succeeding symbols will differ from the reference point based upon encoding. The **truth table** for 2-bit DPSK is shown in Figure 4-17(a). The phase shifts shown in the figure represent four phase positions, and are shown graphically in the constellation map of Figure 4-17(b).

A constellation map is nothing more than a vector representation of phase angles. Recall that signals have amplitudes and exist in time. When several points (representing signal amplitudes) are plotted (according to their phase relationship to the reference signal), the vectors appear to look like a constellation of stars—hence, the name constellation map.

The truth table is that of a 2,400BPS, V.26 modem. Since four positions of the 360-degree constellation are used, it's usually called DQPSK, with "Q" referring to quaternary or **quadrature**, in deference to the four phase positions. You may also see it referred to in literature as 4-PSK, or simply QPSK. When PSK was introduced in the previous section, only two phase changes were described—so, it would aptly be called 2-PSK.

Symbol rates of 4 and 8 are common with DPSK (referred to as 4-DPSK or QPSK, and 8-DPSK). Symbol rates beyond 8 bits per symbol are difficult, because phase jitters make the separation between symbols difficult to interpret. For 8-DPSK, there are 3 bits per symbol *(tribits)*. The encoded bits are separated by 22.5 degrees, so phase jitters may cause the 3-bit symbol groupings to blur across the narrow separation, making demodulation at the receiver impossible. The maximum number of bits per symbol for DPSK is 16.

DPSK is used extensively in 1,200BPS and 2,400BPS modems. An examination of a typical modulator will help to clarify how the modulation method is implemented in the modem. A 4-PSK (QPSK, DQPSK) modulator is shown in Figure 4-18(a).

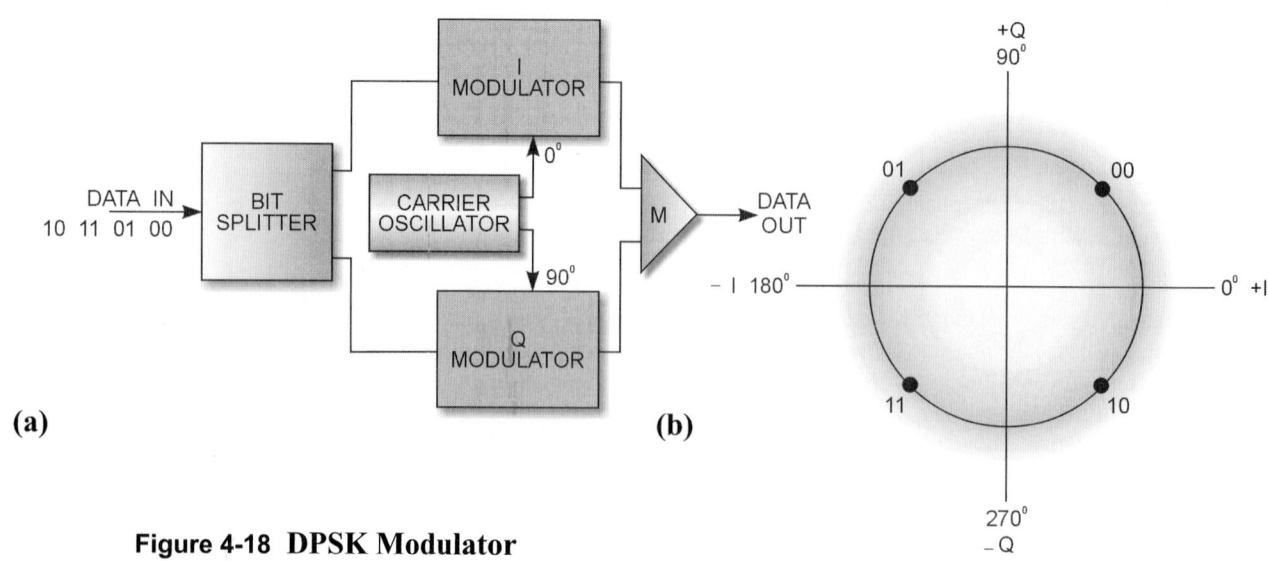

(a)

(b)

Figure 4-18 DPSK Modulator

Serial data is clocked into the **bit splitter** in dibit pairs. The first bit is designated the **Least Significant Bit** (LSB) and the second bit is the **Most Significant Bit** (MSB). A logic 0 from the bit splitter is a positive voltage while a logic 1 is a negative voltage. The bits are sent to a **balanced modulator** from the bit splitter.

A carrier is generated from a **crystal oscillator** and applied to both modulators. The carrier applied to the **I modulator** is in phase with the crystal oscillator. The carrier applied to the other modulator (the **Q modulator**, for quadrature or quaternary) is first shifted 90 degrees. The output of the I modulator will be in phase with the carrier, while the output of the Q modulator will be phase-shifted 90 degrees. The two modulator outputs are combined in the **summing amplifier** and their vector sum will be the **output data**.

Now, an 8-bit data word can be modulated. We'll select the bit pairs from the truth table of Figure 4-17(a): 00 01 11 10. The 00 dibit will be the first applied to the modulator. The bit to the right of each dibit is the **Least Significant Bit** (LSB) and will be applied to the Q modulator, while the left bit is the **Most Significant Bit** (MSB) and will be applied to the I modulator. Logic 0's are converted to positive voltages in the bit splitter. The I modulator output will be positive and is designated $+I$. The Q output is also positive, and is designated $+Q$. These two positive signals, separated by 90 degrees, are added vectorially in the summing amplifier to produce a positive voltage that's phase-separated by 45 degrees from the I carrier.

The position of the 00 dibit is plotted on the constellation map of Figure 4-18(b). Note that it's located at 45 degrees, between $+I$ and $+Q$. This point will be the location from which all other phase shifts will be referenced.

The next dibit is 01. The logic 1 is the LSB. A logic 1 is converted to a negative voltage in the bit splitter. It's applied to the Q modulator and will be phase-shifted 90 degrees. The positive-voltage logic 0 is applied to the I modulator. The $+I$ from the logic 0, and the $-Q$ of the logic 1 are summed. Their position on the constellation map is a 90-degree phase shift from the 00 dibit reference.

The next dibit is 11. Logic 1's are converted to negative voltages and will appear at the summing amplifier as $-I-Q$. The truth table calls for a 180-degree phase shift, and the $-I-Q$ location is 180 degrees from the reference set by 00 (the first dibit).

The last dibit is 10. The LSB is 0. It will be output from the Q modulator as $+Q$. The logic 1 will be output from the I modulator as $-I$. This is a 270-degree phase shift from the original 00 reference.

The disadvantage to the DPSK modulator just described is the 0-degree phase change for the 00 dibit. If a long string of 0's are transmitted, the carrier wouldn't be shifted. A communicating modem may lose synchronization. Alternate phase shifts are 45 degrees, 135 degrees, 225 degrees, and 315 degrees for 00, 01, 11, 10, respectively. Using the alternate change, the carrier will be shifted for each symbol, ensuring that the modems won't lose carrier synchronization.

DPSK solves both of the problems of FSK—timing of the carrier synchronization, and more bits are available. In fact, a 2,400BPS data rate with 2-bits-per-symbol modulation will propagate through the voice channel at a baud rate of 1,200, effectively doubling the utilization of the channel.

As mentioned earlier, 16 binary levels per symbol have successfully phase modulated a carrier. Unfortunately, each bit increase per symbol raises the noise and distortion levels at the receiver. This is due to **phase jitter**.

Phase jitter is the unavoidable delay in arrival times of the symbols created by harmonic distortion of the logic levels carried by the symbol. As the bits-per-symbol increase, so does the noise. The remedy is to increase the channel **Signal-to-Noise Ratio** (SNR). How- ever, for each doubling of the bits-per-symbol, so must the SNR be doubled. The additional circuitry and power consumption may not justify the higher baud rates.

Quadrature Amplitude Modulation (QAM)

CNST OBJECTIVE VI-D

A modulation technique that responds to the symbol limitations is **Quadrature Amplitude Modulation** (QAM). QAM specifies amplitude as well as phase changes to modulate the carrier. A 4-bit-per-symbol constellation map of QAM is shown in Figure 4-19(a). In this arrangement, 16 symbol points, or locations, represent the carrier modulation scheme. In other words, Figure 4-19 illustrates the constellation of 16-point QAM. QAM transmitters are used to modulate data rates at 2,400 BPS and higher. The 33.6kBPS modems use QAM on transmit and receive sides, while 56k modems use QAM only on the transmit side.

> QAM represents bit changes by varying the carrier amplitude as well as shifting the carrier phase.

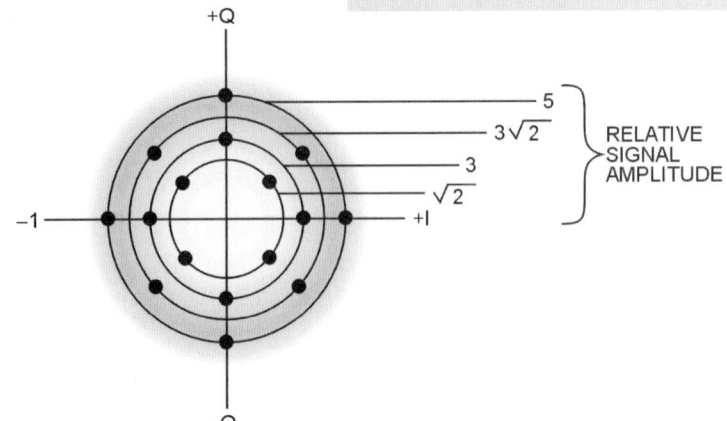

(a)

QAM is the most commonly used modulation method for higher speed modems.

Consider the advantage of using multiple bits per symbol. In Figure 4-19, a baud rate of 2,400 yields a BPS rate of 2,400 baud x 4 bits-per-symbol = 9,600 BPS. A 9,600 BPS data rate can be transmitted at 2,400 baud through the voice channel using QAM. Now, if the symbol rate increased to 14 bits-per-symbol, the effective data rate will be 2,400 baud x 14 bits-per-symbol = 33,600 BPS.

(b)

Q_1	ABSOLUTE PHASE		RELATIVE AMPLITUDE	Q_2	Q_3	Q_4	PHASE CHANGE
0	$0°$	$90°$	3	0	0	1	$0°$
1	$180°$	$270°$	5	0	0	0	$45°$
0	$45°$	$135°$	$\sqrt{2}$	0	1	0	$90°$
1	$225°$	$315°$	$3\sqrt{2}$	0	1	1	$135°$
				1	1	1	$180°$
				1	1	0	$225°$
				1	0	0	$270°$
				1	0	1	$315°$

(c)

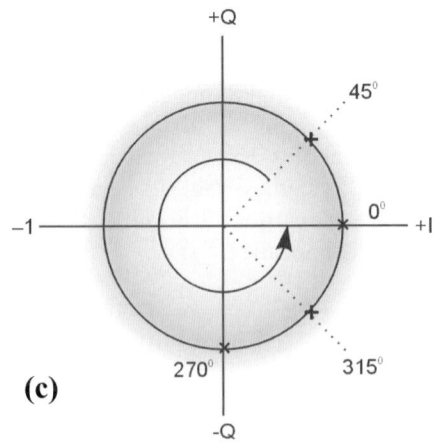

Figure 4-19 QAM Signal Amplitude and Phase Constellation, Truth Table, and Constellation Map for the Quad Bit 0101

In addition to shifting the carrier phase, QAM makes use of the available power level spectrum within the voice channel. Since **Bit Error Rates** (BERs)—which are caused by noise—decrease with high signal-to-noise ratios, it's advantageous to transmit data at several factors above the 1mW reference. QAM simply uses that available power to combine amplitude modulation with phase modulation.

The level of the amplitude is not as strictly constrained as it is within the commercial broadcast radio industry. Transmitted messages in data communications may vary over several decibel decades. Rather than prescribe specific power levels, QAM amplitude variations are described as the ratios between various amplitudes. In the example of Figure 4-19, the four amplitudes are referenced to the first quad bit.

The truth table of the QAM **constellation map** is shown in Figure 4-19(b). The first bit, or LSB, is designated as Q1. It serves to anchor the remaining three bits in the quad by serving as a base from which amplitude levels and phase changes for the quad are referenced. The four amplitude levels are shown as $\sqrt{2}$, 3, $3\sqrt{2}$, and 5.

These are relative amplitudes whose absolute value in watts, voltage, or current depends on the channel parameters. It's the job of the modem transmitter to establish power levels and scale the amplitude variations accordingly. The Q1 bit also establishes an absolute phase reference. The other three bits will be sourced to this reference to shift the carrier phase. The amount of phase change is determined by the combination of bits Q2, Q3, and Q4.

As an example, the quad bit 0101 will produce the constellation map of Figure 4-19(c). The 0 bit is the LSB. From the truth table, with Q1 equal to a logic 0, the absolute phase may be referenced at 0 degrees, 90 degrees, 45 degrees, and 315 degrees from the +I carrier. We'll select 45 degrees. At an absolute 45-degree phase angle, the amplitude of this quad will lie in the $\sqrt{2}$ plane. Now, the bit arrangement of Q2, Q3, and Q4 (which is 101) is found on the truth table. This bit arrangement produces a 315-degree phase change from the point established by Q1. It also lies in a concentric circle in the $\sqrt{2}$ amplitude plane as determined by Q1. The quad's bit positions are marked on the constellation map of Figure 4-19(c). Literally, then, when the carrier is phase-shifted 315 degrees, and the amplitude of the carrier is equal to $\sqrt{2}$ times the available channel power, the receiver will detect a 0101 bit stream.

A next set of quad bits will then be shifted into the transmitter in a manner similar to the DPSK transmitter discussed earlier. The transmitter assigns the new Q1 bit an absolute phase position and relative amplitude. The bit pattern of the next three bits would be examined to determine the amount of phase change required.

Single-amplitude QAM is also an option as well as 2-, 4-, 8-and 16-bit symbols. If the single-amplitude option is selected, the operation is identical to DPSK.

What if, in the example of Figure 4-19(c), the next quad bit was identical to our example? The transmitter may select the same absolute phase and relative amplitude as before. If a long string of this bit pattern was transmitted, the transmitter could continue to send at the same phase change and amplitude. This is a potential problem for several reasons. One reason involves the level of transmitted power. If the modem transmits continuously at a relative amplitude of 5, it is delivering the maximum power level to the channel. Continuously transmitting at this level decreases the efficiency of the channel.

Another problem is that of intersymbol interference. Generally, the modem converts the digital levels to analog for transmission over the voice channel. The analog symbols resemble normally distributed sine waves. If all symbols are transmitted at similar power levels and at the same degree of phase shift, the symbols are sure to overlap and appear to smear together. This blurring together of the symbols describes ISI.

A modem addresses the problems above in two ways. An **adaptive equalizer** is included in the modem to compensate for channel-induced ISI. To avoid the problem of repetitive selection of the same phase and amplitude (a common occurrence for long strings of 1's and 0's) the modulated data is **scrambled**. Scrambling is not done for any reason of security, but rather to ensure the signal power is consistent across the voice channel.

> Modems routinely scramble data in order to reduce intersymbol interference as well as to evenly distribute the signal power.

The scrambler consists of a series of shift registers into which the symbols are clocked. At selected points on the shift registers are taps, as shown in Figure 4-20. The data is sampled at the taps and summed together using two exclusive-OR gates. The number of registers and the placement of taps is derived from the **generator polynomial** shown in the figure. The result is that the repetition described earlier is avoided, since the scrambler ensures a different bit arrangement due to the cyclical movement of data through the registers, and the redundant summing of the bits. For an in-depth explanation of cyclic redundance encoders, see Chapter 10, Error Control and Data Security.

$$D_s = D_{IN} + D_s X^{-14} + D_s X^{-17}$$

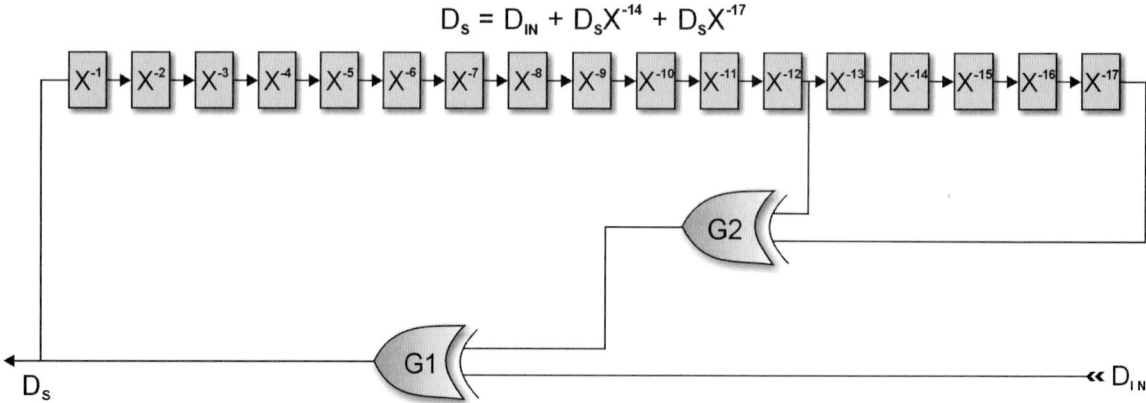

Figure 4-20 Modem Scrambler

A **descrambler** in the receiving circuitry of the answer modem provides an inverse operation. Data scramblers are incorporated into all modern modems. They're an integral part of the initial exchange of bits between the transmit and receive modems, used to establish synchronization.

MODEM CHIPSET

The operation of modern modems can best be understood by analyzing an actual modem. In this section, we'll examine data exchanges between 2,400BPS modems. In terms of current technology, 2,400BPS is slow; yet the underlying principles remain current. Higher-speed modems achieve high data rates by virtue of improved voice-channel characteristics, the inclusion of improved error-correction techniques in the pre-equalization stages, and a more robust implementation of modulation methods which were described in previous sections. Its operation is based on the operation of the Rockwell R2424DS chip set pictured in Figure 4-21.

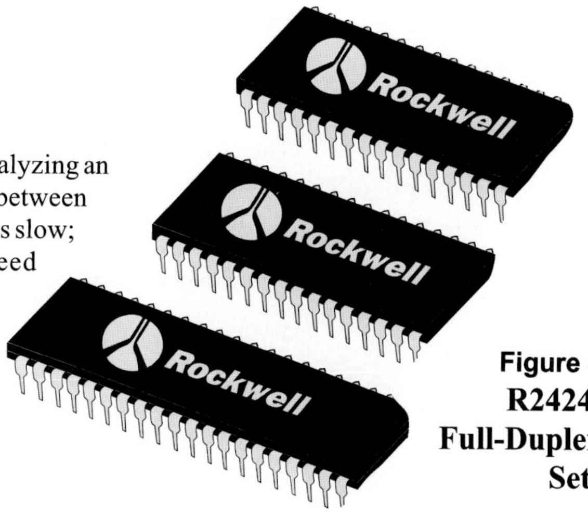

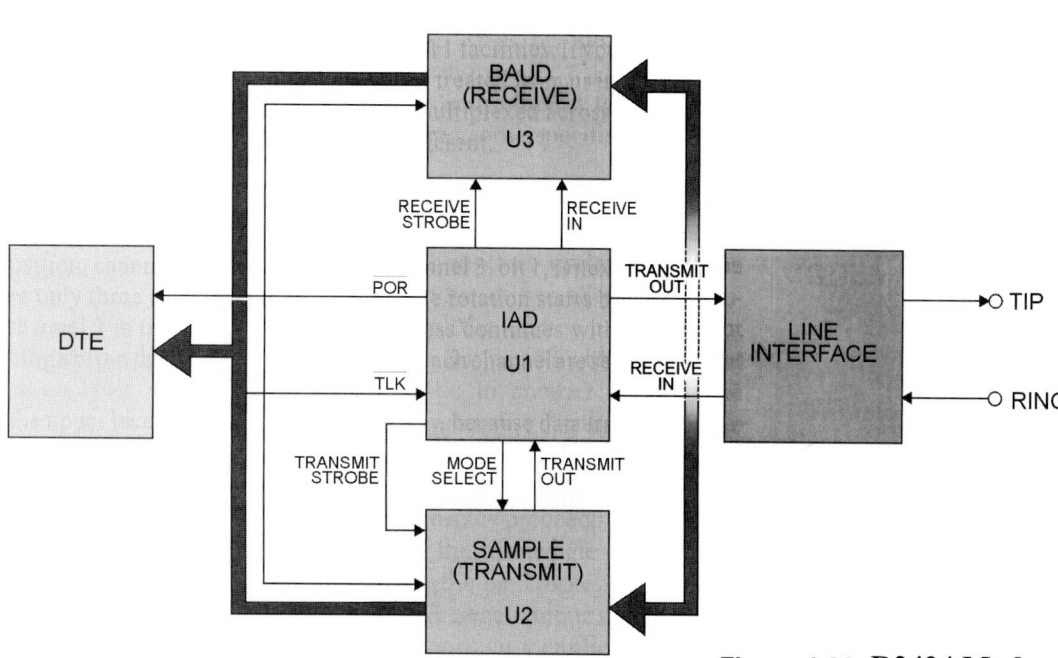

**Figure 4-21
R2424DS
Full-Duplex Device
Set**

The three ICs shown use **Very Large Scale Integration** (VLSI) technology to provide synchronous or asynchronous data rates of 2,400, 1,200, and 600 BPS.

The modem is compatible with ITU V.22 bis, Bell 212A, and Bell 103 standards. The DTE interface is EIA/TIA-232 and the particular configuration that the modem will operate in (2,400, 1,200, 600 BPS) is controlled via a microprocessor bus. It is a full-duplex modem that contains fixed, and adaptive, error-correction equalization to reduce channel noise and signal distortion.

A block diagram of the chip set hardware is illustrated in Figure 4-22. It consists of two signal processors (U2 and U3) and an integrated analog device (U1). The **Integrated Analog Device** (IAD) contains the telephone line interface, the analog-to-digital and digital-to-analog converters, and the telephone channel filters. The IAD is under host microprocessor control, but communicates with the signal processors through a one-way internal bus. If it's determined that the modem is to transmit and receive data at 1,200 BPS, the **signal processors** (SPs) will configure the IAD for 1,200 BPS. The host microprocessor places the modem on-hook and off-hook by enabling TLK. On-hook is a term describing the termination of a call; when you "hang-up" the phone after finishing a call, you are going on-hook. Conversely, off-hook means the handset has been lifted from the cradle; it's the same as answering a call.

**Figure 4-22 R2424 Modem
Set Block Diagram**

POR is a signal generated by the IAD. It is a reset signal, and when energized by the IAD or host microprocessor, the signal processors will be reset in order to prepare for a new configuration.

The IAD monitors the telephone channel for receive and transmit data. When a distant modem calls, the IAD selects the proper **filters** to receive the ring tone, as well as filters for answering a call. It informs the DTE of the channel status and makes sure the received and transmitted data is handled properly. Essentially, the IAD serves as a general clearinghouse for the modem data.

The **Signal Processors** (SPs) have the responsibility for manipulating the data to prepare it for transmission and for recovering information from the received signal. Generally, the **baud rate device** (U3) works as the receiver while the **sample rate device** (U2) serves as the transmitting section. This is a bit of an oversimplification since the R2424DS is noted for its quick response, which is due to the parallel processing capabilities of the two SPs. This means, for example, that when a signal is received, some tasks of receiving the data are run on one SP, while other tasks are handled by the other SP. The internal parallel bus running between the two processors is designed for keeping each SP abreast of what the other is doing. However, in an effort to present a coherent model of how a practical modem operates, we'll designate U3 as the receive section of the modem, and U2 as the transmit section.

The R2424DS can be configured for the various operating modes by commands held in 1k ROMs in each SP. Each processor also has a 256-word by 16-bit RAM. Typically, many parameters held in RAM are set by default functions contained in the SP ROMs. For example, modems continuously monitor channel conditions for noise, and equalize the data to compensate for it. The ROM contains instructions for various degrees of equalization, and sends the commands to the RAM, as required, to control the equalizers.

Each SP also has 128 bits of interface scratchpad memory. The host microprocessor may request that the SP read the RAMs and write data from them into the interface memory. This permits the host to monitor channel conditions, as well as provides a system of manual overrides for the host operator.

The modem provides an EIA/TIA-232 port to the DTE. Many of the operations associated with modems are dictated by the EIA/TIA-232 standard and the R2424DS is no exception. It offers an excellent opportunity to observe the sequencing of protocols implied by the standard and readily lends itself to the interaction of the modem's hardware, the standard, and the transfer of data.

The EIA/TIA-232 standard implements protocols described by Level 1, the Physical layer, of the OSI model (refer to Chapter 1). The logical structure of the Level 1 protocols are described by Level 2, the Data Link Layer, of the OSI model. Usually, when data flow between devices connected by EIA/TIA-232 cables is discussed, it's described as handshaking. Handshaking is synonymous with the protocols, or set of rules, describing information content and structure of the OSI levels. An EIA/TIA-232 connector and cable simply implement those rules.

The handshaking sequence for the EIA/TIA-232 standard requires a calling modem to send a **Request-To-Send** (RTS) signal to the called modem. After a short delay, both the called and calling modems inform their hosts they have detected a carrier by enabling **Received Line Signal Detect** (RLSD). RLSD is usually referred to as **Carrier Detect** (CD). The called modem then sends a **Clear-To-Send** (CTS) to the calling modem, telling it that it's ready to receive data. The calling modem is now free to transmit on pin 2, **Transmitted Data** (TD).

The sequence described above is typical of descriptions of EIA/TIA-232 handshaking but it is severely abbreviated, in particular in the area referred to as "a short delay." It is within this delay that the intricacies of the handshaking protocols occur. Figure 4-23 expands upon the abbreviated version of the handshaking.

The calling or **originate** modem, at the right of Figure 4-23, initiates the sequence when RTS is energized by the DTE. The calling modem places the call. The called or **answer** modem tells its DTE a call has arrived by enabling **Ring Indicator** (RI). The called DTE asserts **Data Terminal Ready** (DTR) to tell the modem to go off-hook. The called modem sends an answer tone of 2,100 Hz for a few seconds to the calling modem. The answering tone is equivalent to saying "hello" when answering a call.

Once the called modem has sent the answer tone, it asserts **Data Set Ready** (DSR). DSR is a signal sent to the DTE saying the connection has been made. When the call is finished, the modem disables DSR to tell the DTE the call is finished.

The calling modem also asserts DSR to its DTE. The calling modem listens for the answer tone from the called modem and, once it determines the answer tone is valid, enables DSR. As with the called modem, DSR tells the calling DTE that a connection has been established.

At this time, the modems transmit a series of data signals back and forth. This is the delay shown in Figure 4-23, and is called the training time of the modems. During training, the modems agree upon a data rate, ensure synchronization, and fine tune their equalizers to the conditions of the channel. Modem training may last several seconds.

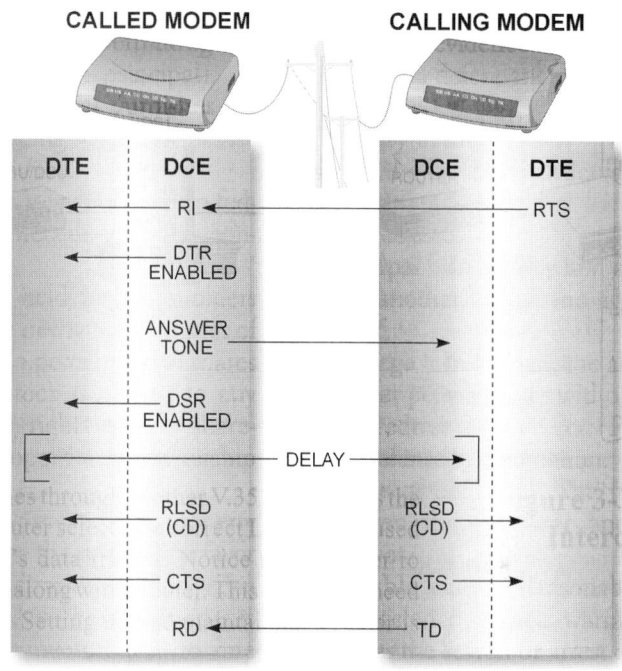

Once the modems have trained each other, they both send a **Received Line Signal Detect** (RLSD) to their DTEs. As mentioned before, RLSD is commonly referred to as Carrier Detect. This isn't a good practice because the Electronic Industries Association abbreviates pin 20 of the EIA/TIA-232 as CD—for Data Terminal Ready.

Finally, the modems will send CTS to their DTEs. The calling modem will now send data and the called modem will receive it.

As the Rockwell R2424DS chip set is analyzed, you may find it helpful to refer back to Figure 4-23. The handshaking sequence described is typical of most modems.

Figure 4-23 R2424DS Modem Handshaking Sequence

Transmitted Data

A detailed block diagram of the modem is shown in Figure 4-24. In this figure, the modem is configured to operate at 2,400 BPS, full-duplex. Each block will be discussed, and then, the timing of the modem handshaking sequence will be described.

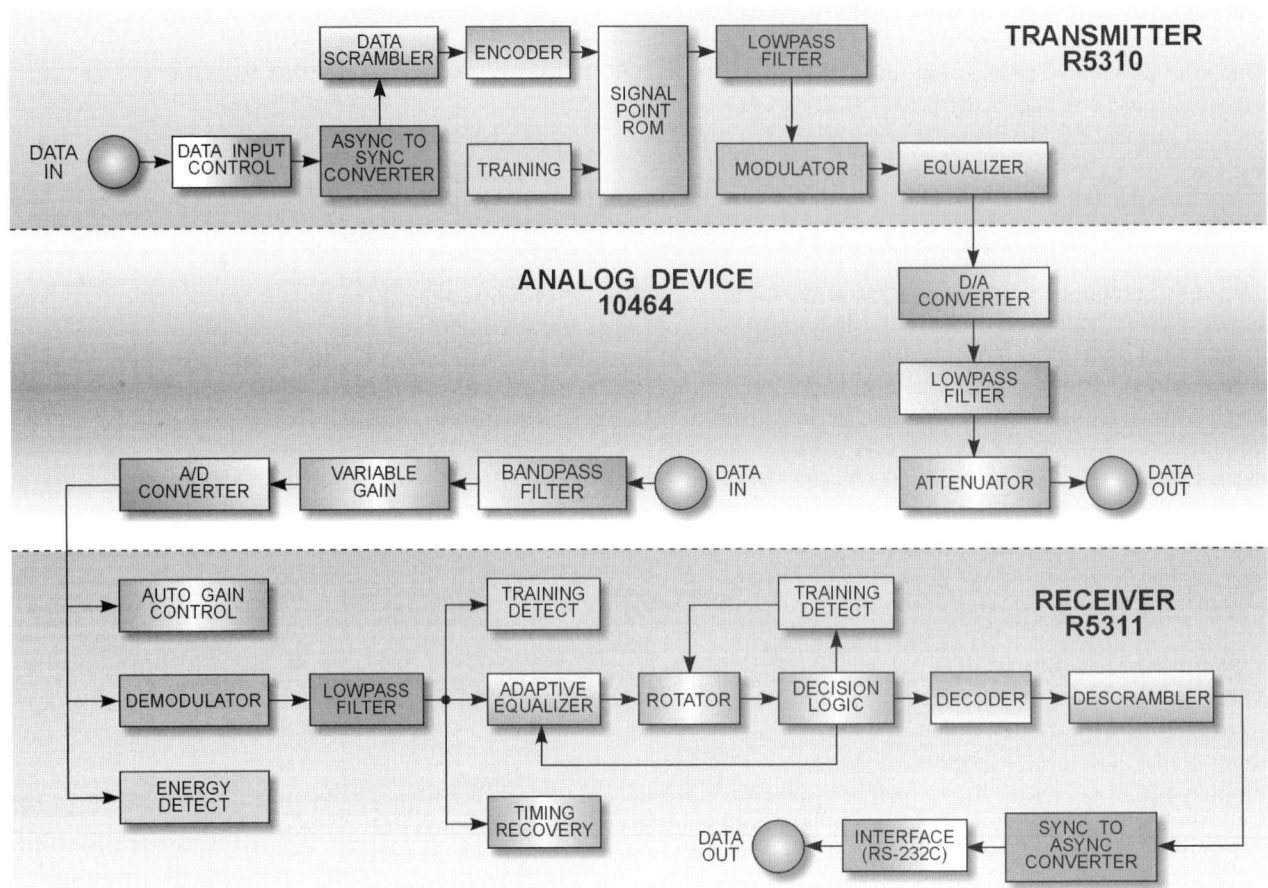

Figure 4-24 Rockwell Chip Set Block Diagram

Data to be transmitted is applied to the 5310 IC (U2 in Figure 4-22) via the EIA/TIA-232 port. The CTS signal has been enabled and the transmitting modem is now ready to transmit.

Digital data from the host is applied to the **data input control**. The data input control is a selectable shift register that simply gates the data in. Following the input control is the **asynchronous-to-synchronous converter**. In the 2,400BPS mode, the two modems in the system synchronize themselves so as to prevent data from being lost. A base reference for synchronization occurs here. In this modem, the reference is established by referencing the phase position of a previous bit, as described in the section on modulation.

Once synchronization has been established, the data is applied to the **scrambler circuitry**. The scrambler examines the data bits and reorganizes their sequence so that long strings of 1's or 0's aren't transmitted. This is done for a couple of reasons. Intersymbol interference and other noise (described in Chapter 2) is reduced by avoiding long runs of a single logic level. Also, the radiated power in the channel is kept at a higher and more predictable level when the sequence of transmitted bits has been preordained. This allows the modem's adaptive equalizers to respond to true channel changes without the added confusion of tracking the power levels of individual data bits.

A simplified **scrambler** is illustrated in Figure 4-25. The exclusive-OR gates are representative of a **full-adder** with data-in serving as a carry-in bit. The scrambler is a closed-loop system, fed by taps from a series of clocked shift registers. The inputs to the adder are taken after the fourteenth and seventeenth shift register. These inputs are ex-ORed together in G2. The output of G2 is ex-ORed at G1 with the input data.

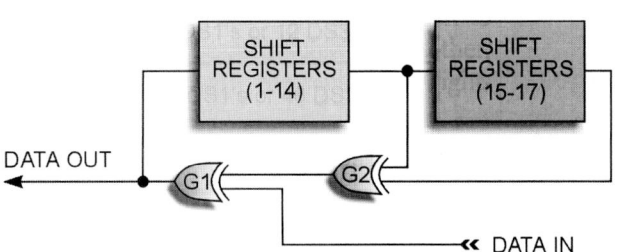

Figure 4-25 Simplified Modem Scrambler

Each of the **shift registers** implement a one-bit delay to data fed through the system. The selection of taps at the shift registers ensures the output of G2 will resemble a subtraction process (ones complement addition). Since the input is continually fed through the system, the subtraction is successive, and **successive subtraction** defines division.

The combination of exclusive-OR gates and shift-register delays used in modems to scramble data involves a coding process called **convolutional coding**. This means that the output is constantly fed back upon itself, so that the data out is based upon a predetermined state of the registers. This state is described by the generator polynomial given in Figure 4-25:

$$D_{OUT} = D_{IN} + D_S X^{-14} + D_S X^{-17}$$

As arranged, the polynomial describes the location of taps and exclusive-OR gates. The complete circuit performs binary division. The polynomial represents the divisor, the data in represents the dividend, and the data out is the division quotient and remainder.

At the receiving modem, the process is reversed. The received data—which is the quotient and remainder from the transmitter—is successively added (using twos complement addition) to a generator polynomial identical to that of the transmitter. **Successive addition** is equivalent to multiplication. A simplified example would be $22/7 = 3.14285$. The quotient and the remainder, 3.14285, are transmitted. At the receiver, 3.14285 is successively added, or multiplied, by 7. This is equivalent to the same generator polynomial used at the transmitter. It describes the organization of logic gates at the receiver, as it did at the transmitter. The product of 3.14285 and 7 is 22. The 22 represents the original data at the transmitter.

Convolutional codes are used extensively in error-detection circuitry. The derivation of generator polynomials, and the corresponding gate circuitry, is addressed in Chapter 8.

The output of the scrambler is organized into data symbols in accordance with ITU recommendations for V.22 bis modems in the **encoder section**. The encoder separates the bits into groups of four bits. This means the symbol, or baud, rate is 2,400 BPS/4 bits per symbol = 600. The ITU recommends sixteen distinct values for 2,400BPS modems. The first two bits of the quad determine the absolute phase position, while the second two bits determine the amplitude of the quad.

Figure 4-26 illustrates the phase and amplitude positions of encoded data. For example, to encode the quadbit 1101, the encoder would examine the phase position of the previous quadbit. Assume it was located at signal point 1 in Figure 4-26. The encoder now looks at the first two bits (11) of the quadbit, which represents a 270-degree phase shift (counterclockwise in this modem) to quadrant four. The second two bits (01) specify the amplitude of the quad, or position 13 in quadrant four. Symbol 1101 will then be encoded to lie in the fourth quadrant of the signal plane with an amplitude equal to quadrant position 13.

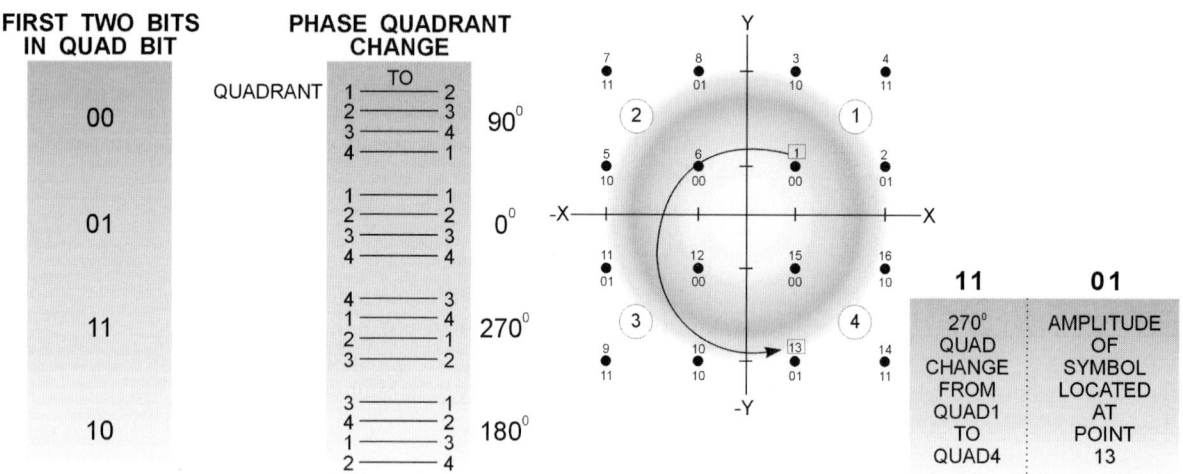

Figure 4-26 Phase and Amplitude Encoding

The encoding is necessary so that both the transmit and receive modems will be in agreement as to the interpretation of the modulated carrier. Consistent encoding and modulation is important between transmitting and receiving modems so that the data will be accurately recovered; hence, the ITU recommendation describing the phase and amplitude positions. The process described here is quite similar to the quadrature modulation described earlier in this chapter.

Each point in the signal constellation is stored in the **signal point ROM**. The encoder selects the proper address in the ROM, based upon the phase position of the previous quadbit. The ROM provides two identical outputs separated by 90 degrees.

The two ROM outputs, selected by the encoder, are sent to a **lowpass filter**. Although a single lowpass filter is shown in Figure 4-24, there is actually a filter for each of the outputs of the ROM. The filter is needed to eliminate the high-frequency harmonics contained in the digital data generated from the ROM. Keep in mind that the modem's first priority is to condition digital data for transmission through the narrow bandpass of the telephone channel. If the higher-order harmonics are permitted to become a part of the modulation process, a nearly infinite signal bandpass will result by the multitude of sum and difference frequencies generated for all fundamental and harmonics applied to the modulator. The lowpass filter is intended to restrict the bandpass of signals being modulated.

The **modulator** outputs a signal with a frequency of 1,200 Hz (originate mode) and 2,400 Hz (answer mode). The waveform is modulated with data as previously described for Quadrature Amplitude Modulation (QAM).

The **equalizer** incorporates an inverse delay to the modulated data proportional to that of the communication channel. Equalization reduces intersymbol interference and offsets the reactive delays found in the channel.

The equalized data is then sent to a **Digital-to-Analog Converter** (DAC) in the integrated analog device. The DAC provides a sinusoidal representation of the digital modulation. In the process of conversion, the many high-frequency harmonics of the square wave are multiplied to sinusoidal waveforms. These harmonics aren't passable through the telephone channel and are eliminated by a **lowpass filter** following the ADC. But since they collectively constitute the components of the digital data, those that are transmitted must be treated equally well before transmission.

In short, this means that the power levels out of a modem must be set high enough to ensure that small-amplitude signals are boosted without over-amplifying larger signals, which don't need as much amplification. It's somewhat of a catch-22 since the power out is restricted, but errors will increase if the signal-to-noise ratio for small signals isn't maintained high enough to discriminate noise from the signals. Notice that if it weren't for the ADC conversion at the receiving end, this problem wouldn't occur. In an ISDN link, for example, data rates run much higher (128 kBPS) because the transmitted data is digital—it isn't transformed to analog in DACs.

The filtered data is sent to an **attenuator** that caps the output signal level to 6 dBm. The data is now fully conditioned for transfer through the public telephone switching system. The last element to handle the data is a standard **line interface** that couples it through a conventional RJ-11 telephone jack to the tip and ring wires of the phone cable.

Received Data

The receiver is found on the baud-rate device, the R5311 chip. As shown in Figure 4-24, it's configured to receive data at 2,400 BPS.

Data is coupled through the **line interface** from the tip and ring wires of the RJ-11 connector. The received data is applied to a **bandpass filter** that rejects channel noise and spurious sidebands. The output of the filter is gain-controlled by a **variable gain amplifier**.

The amplifier is used to boost the level of weak signals, helping the receiver circuitry provide a better response across the spectrum of the telephone channel. Frequencies toward the low and high ends of the channel tend to be weaker than those in the 1,500Hz to 2,000Hz range.

The actual amount of amplification of the variable gain amplifier is controlled by the **Automatic Gain Control** (AGC) circuit. Once the received analog data is converted to digital by the **Analog-to-Digital Converter** (ADC) in the integrated analog device, the AGC samples the digital information and provides a response back to the amplifier that instructs it to increase or decrease the gain.

An **energy detector** also samples the ADC output. The energy detector is used by the receiver to determine if the modem threshold has been exceeded, indicating the presence of data signals on the line. The level detector in this modem will place the receiver in an active state (the demodulator is enabled) if the channel energy exceeds −43 dBm for about 5 ms.

The **demodulator** extracts the digital data and applies it to a **lowpass filter**, which eliminates the harmonics generated in the demodulation.

A **training detector** samples data from the filter. In the handshaking sequence, the receive and transmit modems exchange data to establish synchronization, speed compatibility, etc. The training detector is responsible for establishing compatibility during handshaking.

Correct synchronization between receiver and transmitter is measured by the **timing recovery element**. The energy level is measured at the midpoint of each baud symbol and then measured slightly ahead and behind the midpoint. The timing recovery circuit seeks the point in the baud where the level is greater than the early sample, but less than the late sample. Half the level between the late and early sample represents one-half baud. Once the circuit achieves the proper midpoint, the receiver has been timed. The timing recovery circuit continues to check for the proper timing by measuring signal levels for every other baud.

An **adaptive equalizer** eliminates most of the effects of intersymbol interference. An adaptive equalizer is a variable tuned filter. It consists of a series of filters that delay the received signal in inverse proportion to those found in the channel. The amount of delay is the variable factor, and is set by the block called **decision logic**. It receives an error signal from the **rotator** and converts the signal to a binary code. The code specifies a specific amount of time delay. The time delay is fed back to the equalizer filters. This closed-loop system continuously tracks errors calculated by the rotator and **carrier recovery**, and feeds them back to the adaptive equalizer to change the delay of the filters.

The baud symbols were encoded at the transmitter to fall within well-defined points in the signal constellation map, as shown in Figure 4-26. At the receiver, the signal points are defined by boundaries, as shown in Figure 4-27.

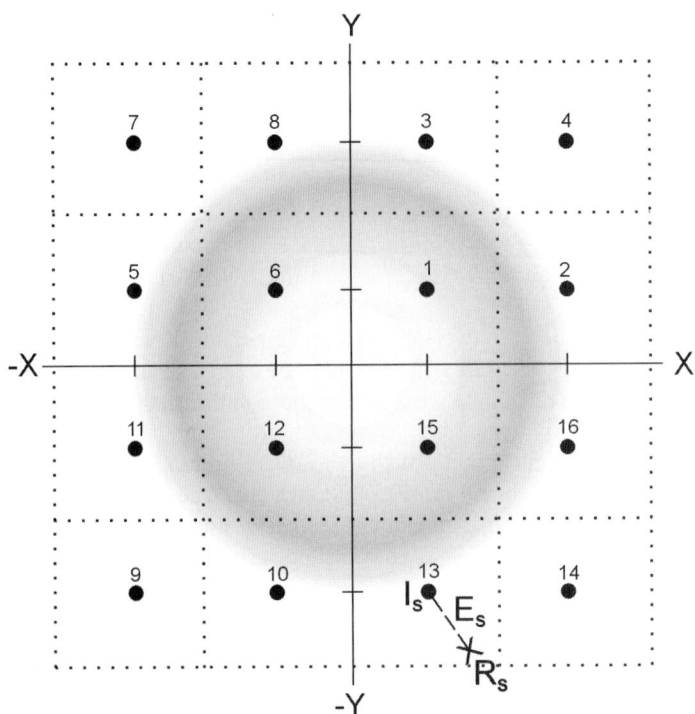

Figure 4-27 Signal Boundaries

Any signal falling within the boundaries will be determined to be the ideal point in the decision logic and forwarded on to the **decoder**. For example, in Figure 4-27, a **received signal** (R_S) in the fourth quadrant falls within the boundary of the encoded **ideal signal point** (I_S). The decision logic will decide R_S actually represents the ideal signal position, and it is this position that's sent to the decoder. The **error signal** (E_S) is the phase and amplitude difference between the received and ideal signal. E_S forms the basis for the error signal sent back to the adaptive equalizer.

E_S is also fed to the carrier recovery. The carrier recovery calculates the precise amount of phase error, and directs the rotator to compensate for it.

At this point, the adaptive equalizer has compensated for channel conditions that cause the data to ring and generate ISI. An error signal is sent to it from the decision logic to offset this distortion in time. The decision circuit sends the same error signal to the carrier recovery, where a value proportional to any phase error is calculated. The rotator then adjusts the equalized data to eliminate the phase distortion. Within these feedback systems, frequency and phase errors are detected and corrected.

Corrected data from the decision logic is phase and amplitude decoded in the decoder. The decoder looks at the first two bits of a quadbit with respect to their position relative to the previous symbol, and the last two bits are examined in order to decode the amplitude level. However, the output data of the decoder remains scrambled.

The receiver **descrambler** reassembles the data into the original sequence by multiplying the scrambled data stream by a generator polynomial identical to the one used at the receiver. The product is identical to the original data. Recall that at the transmitter, the data was divided by the polynomial and the quotient and remainder were transmitted. At the receiver, the quotient and remainder are multiplied by the polynomial, and the resulting product is the original data.

The descrambled data is then converted by the **synchronous-to-asynchronous converter**, and data bits are sent to the host on the **Receive Data** (RD) line of the EIA/TIA-232 port, or to a UART.

The chip set of the modem represents a typical example of data flow for 2,400BPS modems. As is the case with many advances in today's technology, the configuration of the modem lies in the software capabilities built into the VLSI chips. The configuration for 300BPS, 600BPS and 1,200BPS modems is similar to the 2,400BPS modem. The major differences are in the coding and modulation. For example, the baud rate of a 1,200BPS device is 600, meaning the symbol rate is two bits per symbol. The dibits represent phase changes but amplitude variations aren't incorporated.

Handshaking Sequence

Earlier in the chapter, an abbreviated example of EIA/TIA-232 handshaking was described. The heart of the sequence–the actual "handshake"–was briefly referred to. The R2424DS chip set offers a good opportunity to examine the exact nature of modem handshaking for a real-world application. The handshaking used with the R2424 is typical of modems in general, and it follows the recommendations of the EIA/TIA-232 standard, as followed in the United States.

Figure 4-28 shows the timing of the handshake sequence, along with the activation of pertinent EIA/TIA-232 data and control signals. The calling modem (shown in the top half of the figure) has dialed the number of the answer modem. The answer modem has responded to the **Request-To-Send** (RTS) from the caller by enabling **Ring Indicator** (RI). RI tells the answer host there's an incoming call. The answer host indicates it will accept the call by enabling **Data Terminal Ready** (DTR). DTR travels from the answer host to the answer modem. It tells the modem to go **off-hook**, or to answer the phone. It is at this point—the answer modem going off-hook—that the handshaking in Figure 4-28 begins.

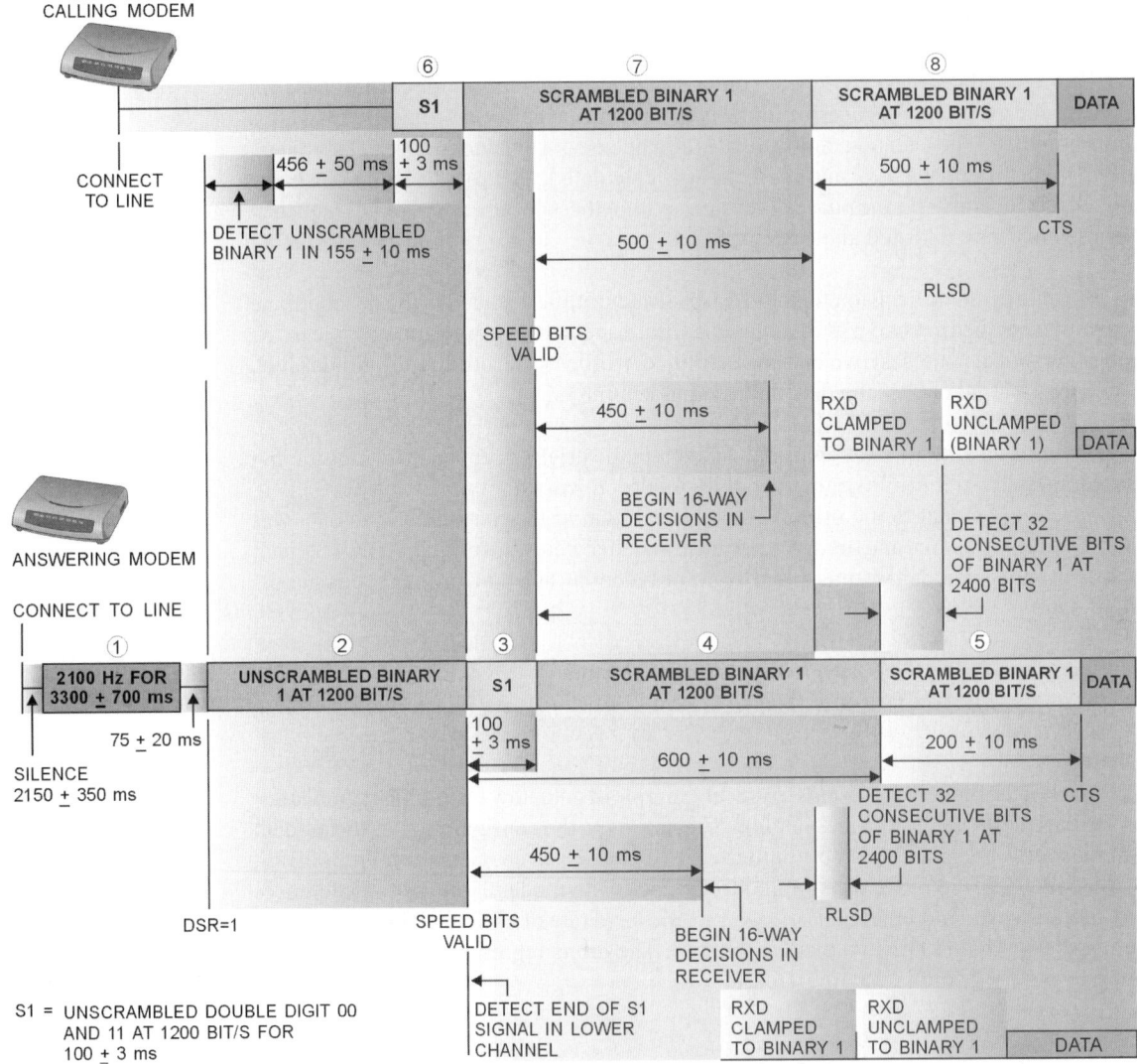

Figure 4-28 2,400 BPS Handshake Sequence

The answer modem goes off-hook for about 2 seconds before generating the 2,100Hz answer tone for 3.3 mS. The answer tone tells the calling modem that its call has been answered. After sending the answer tone, the answer modem enables **Data Set Ready** (DSR). DSR tells the answer host that the connection has been made.

It is at this point that a "delay" occurred when EIA/TIA-232 handshaking was described in Figure 4-23. The calling and answering modem now begin a training period in which they establish a case of compatibility necessary for the data transmission to take place.

The answer modem will transmit a string of alternating logic 1's at 1,200 BPS for 711 ms. A quick check back to Figure 4-26 shows the dibit 10 will produce a 180-degree phase change. The redundancy of the transmission allows the calling modem to coarse-tune its equalizer, and establish synchronization with the called modem.

The calling modem must detect the unscrambled logic 1's within 155 mS. Once it's done so, it activates DSR to tell the calling DTE that a valid connection has been made. After setting DSR, the calling modem remains silent for 456 mS, and then sends S1 to the answer modem.

S1 is transmitted to the answer modem for two reasons. First, it tells the answer modem that the calling modem is a 2,400BPS modem. If the answer modem is capable of receiving at 2,400 BPS, it will respond with S1, and the two modems will soon extend the training to include 2,400BPS data. If the calling modem doesn't receive S1 from the answer modem, it will configure to the 1,200BPS mode. Second, it allows the answer modem to conduct coarse timing adjustments at its equalizer.

The calling modem now transmits a scrambled binary 1 for 600 mS. During this time, the answer modem sends back S1 to tell the calling modem it can configure for 2,400 BPS. Upon receiving S1, the calling modem activates **Data Signal Rate Selector** (DSRS), which is shown as "SPEED BITS VALID" in Figure 4-28.

The answer modem previously activated this pin on the EIA/TIA-232 connector when it received S1 from the calling modem. Data Signal Rate Selector is used in modems that have the ability to automatically shift to various data rates. It's designated as pin 23 on the connector. In this modem, enabling the pin tells both calling and answering DTEs that the data rate will be 2,400 BPS.

After sending a scrambled logic 1 at 1,200 BPS for 600 mS, the calling modem transmits a scrambled logic 1 at 2,400 BPS. Once the answer modem has detected 32 consecutive logic 1's at 2,400 BPS, **Received Line Signal Detect** (RLSD) is enabled. RLSD tells the answer host that the signal energy of the carrier meets the criteria of the answer modem.

The answer modem continues to receive scrambled data at 2,400 BPS. The adaptive equalizer now fine-tunes itself, since all 16 points of the signal constellation map of Figure 4-27 are being transmitted by the calling modem. Once the answer modem has received the scrambled 2,400BPS data for 200 mS, **Clear-To-Send** (CTS) is activated and the modem is said to be in the data mode.

The calling modem also receives scrambled data at 2,400 BPS. When 32 consecutive bits of the 2,400BPS data have been received, RLSD is energized at the calling modem. The calling host is informed that the answer modem is capable of communicating at a power level sufficient to meet the criteria of the calling modem. The calling modem fine-tunes its equalizer on the remainder of the 2,400BPS data. It then enables CTS, placing the modem in the data mode. It will now begin sending data to the answer modem.

The entire handshaking sequence, as described, takes a maximum of seven seconds. This is fairly typical of modems of this caliber. In practice, modem training is often completed in a much quicker time. The communication taking place is in full-duplex; if half-duplex is used, the training time would take considerably longer.

The handshaking for lower-speed modems can be accomplished in half the time of the 2,400BPS mode. But the trade-off is that the data being transmitted is done so at a much slower rate.

V.90 MODEMS

V.90 modems mark an important stride in modem development because they exceed the so-called Shannon limit during downloads.

V.90 modems changed the way we perceive the analog portion of the telco local loop. Prior to V.90, full-duplex data rates peaked with 33.6kBPS V.34 modems. However, so-called 56k modems changed that perception. A V.90-compliant modem transmits data at 33.6 kBPS (maximum) and receives at 53 kBPS (maximum).

Before describing how a V.90 modem downloads data so fast, let's take a look at Figure 4-29 (A). This figure shows the situation in which V.34 modems are exchanging data through a typical dial-up telephone line. The local modem internally converts digital data from a connected computer using a digital to analog converter (DAC). The modem then uses QAM to modulate the signal and sends it through the analog local loop. At the Central Office, the analog data is converted to digital using an analog to digital converter (ADC) to be sent across the (mostly) digital public switched telephone network (PSTN). When the data arrives at the remote central office, it's converted back to analog using a digital to analog converter (DAC) so it can be sent across the remote analog local loop.

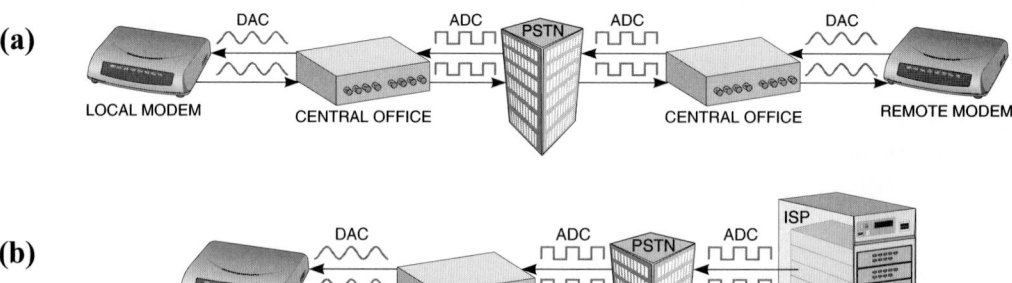

Figure 4-29 (a) V.34 Modem Exchange (b) V.90 Modem Exchange

When the remote modem responds, it converts digital data from its host computer to analog, using QAM, and sends it across the remote local loop to the central office. The remote central office converts the analog data to digital to send it through the digital PSTN. When the data arrives at the local central office, it's converted back to analog and sent through the local loop. That's the sequence of events in a normal, 33.6kBPS data exchange.

Now consider Figure 4-29(b), which shows the same local modem. Instead of a distant V.34 modem, the local client is accessing an **Internet Service Provider** (ISP). The ISP connects directly to the digital PSTN. The modems used at the ISP are digital because they receive digital data from the local office, and upload/download from the Internet over the PSTN (which is nearly all digital data). There's no need for an analog-to-digital conversion, since none of the data at the ISP is analog.

A V.90 modem, as shown in Figure 4-29(b), sends data through the local loop on a QAM analog carrier. Once the data arrives at the local office, it's converted to digital. The ISP receives the digital data from the central office, or from any other point in the PSTN. When a Web site is downloaded from the Internet to the local modem, it's sent as digital data to the local office. But, instead of using QAM to modulate a voice-channel carrier, the ISP digital modem uses PCM encoded **Pulse Amplitude Modulation** (PAM). The digital modulation is then converted to analog at the central office and sent to the local modem.

There are two particularly important points to emphasize in Figure 4-29. The first is that when V.34 modems are used, an analog-to-digital conversion occurs twice in the process: the first at the local central office, and the second at the remote central office. The second point is that downloads with V.90 modems use PAM to modulate a carrier, and the modulation is then PCM encoded. These two points constitute the reason why V.90 modems can download so much faster than a V.34.

In fact, before V.90 technology it didn't seem possible to send data through the local loop faster than 35 kBPS. That was the theory, anyway—and not just any theory. It was developed by Claude Shannon, in 1948, and was pretty much left unchallenged until the mid 90's. Before developing a case for the points mentioned above for 56kBPS downloads, let's throw ourselves into the Shannon Theory debate, and see what sticks.

Shannon's Theory and the Upstream Rate

Shannon's theory predicts the maximum capacity, or data rate, of a voice channel. His formula for channel capacity is:

$$CC \text{ (BPS)} = BW \times (\log(1 + SNR)/\log_2)$$

where CC is channel capacity in BPS, BW is the bandwidth of the channel, and SNR is the absolute signal-to-noise ratio.

Recall that BPS is approximated by:

$$BPS = baud \times N$$

where baud is the signaling rate (the actual data transfer), and N is the number of information bits-per-symbol.

The more bits used to represent a symbol, the greater the BW needed to carry the symbols. This is true because in **Amplitude Modulation** (AM):

$$BW = F_{usb} - F_{lsb}$$

where F_{usb} is the upper sideband frequency, and F_{lsb} is the lower sideband frequency.

QAM is used in the upload direction of a V.90 modem, and it shares general sideband characteristics of conventional AM. With QAM, the more points placed in a constellation map—the more symbols-per-bit—the more sidebands will be generated, and the more BW will be needed to carry the modulated signal.

Intuitively, both formulas are telling us that the data rate of a channel is directly affected by the modulation method, and that with QAM, there will ultimately be a point where trying to modulate bits with more information symbols will require a lot of bandwidth.

But BW in the voice channel is severely restricted. In the worst case, it's 3 kHz in the analog loop portion of the telco network. A single information bit is modulated onto a single carrier frequency Hertz. QAM reserves many phase and amplitude positions to represent information bits, but there will always be a one-to-one relationship between the two. The reason is that if two or more information bits were used to modulate a carrier Hertz, the sidebands would exceed the BW limits of the voice channel.

The QAM baud is one factor that restricts data rates in V.34 modems, and the upstream rate of V.90 modems.

The second factor is the signal-to-noise ratio in the channel. Again, if you look at Shannon's formula, you can see that BPS is directly related to SNR. The higher the SNR (absolute power gain, and not the gain in decibels), the higher the channel capacity. So why not make it infinitely high and transmit megabit data rates?

If we did, the signal power would be so high that it would interfere with adjacent channels and produce crosstalk. Crosstalk would likely garble data bits. The SNR is predictable; the codecs used in modems produce a maximum of 39.5 dB, but a more realistic value is 35 dB. The SNR_{dB} in a voice channel is 35 dB in the typical case.

Now, we can calculate the maximum capacity of a voice channel since the BW is known at 3 kHz, and the SNR is known at 35 dB. Since the SNR in Shannon's formula is in absolute values, the 35 dB must be converted by:

$$dB = 10 \times \log_{10}(P_s/P_n)$$

where P_s is the signal power in watts and P_n is the noise power in watts, and $(P_s/P_n)=SNR$.

$$dB = 10 \times \log_{10}(P_s/P_n)$$
$$35dB = 10 \times \log_{10}(SNR)$$
$$3.5dB = \log_{10}(SNR)$$
$$10^{3.5} = (SNR)$$
$$3,162 = SNR$$

Substituting the SNR back into Shannon's channel capacity formula:

$$CC\ (BPS) = BW \times (\log(1 + SNR)/\log2)$$
$$CC = 3kHz \times (\log(3,163)/\log2)$$
$$CC = 3kHz \times (3.5/.3010)$$
$$CC = 3kHz \times 11.63$$
$$CC = 34,890\ BPS$$

This is the maximum data rate of a voice channel. The upstream rate of V.90 modems is fixed at this level, and you shouldn't expect to see significant increases in the near future. However, the inexorable march of technology has been known to exceed man's expectations time and time again.

Downstream Rates

A V.90 modem transmits at V.34 speeds and downloads at rates near 48 kBPS.

The downstream rate of V.90 modems may reach a theoretical high of 56 kBPS, although it's limited to about 53 kBPS by power restrictions placed by the FCC. The restrictions are intended to avoid crosstalk among voice channels.

V.90 achieves faster downloads by avoiding QAM as the modulation method, and by boosting the SNR by eliminating a portion of the noise. The modulation method is **Pulse Amplitude Modulation** (PAM) that is then PCM-encoded in a manner that's identical to the PCM described in the previous chapter.

With PAM, an analog waveform is sampled in an ADC so that the modulated waveform looks like a series of pulses whose amplitude corresponds to the amplitude of the analog signal. The PAM signal is then PCM encoded. Figure 4-30 reviews the process. Each pulse is converted to binary, the value of which corresponds to the pulse amplitude.

Once the analog signal has been digitized, it's companded in the modem codec. The purpose of companding is to normalize the SNR of all signal levels. This is done by representing small signal amplitudes with more digital bits than with larger signal amplitudes. In a μ-Law compander, a total of 256 levels are possible.

When the PAM signal is sent through the PCM encoder, the digital codes will round the actual value of the sample (either up or down, but not both). For example, refer to Figure 4-30. Notice that sample 1 is interpreted as a 5, when it's actually 4.5. The encoder rounds the actual value up to 5. This results in a **quantization error** of .5. Quantization error is also called **quantization noise**, since the effect of the error is identical to the effects that a noisy channel would produce—it distorts the actual signal.

You may remember that decibel noise tends to be cumulative. Add all losses in a system for an approximation of the total system loss. PCM encoded PAM introduces inherent noise into a channel that can't be eliminated while using codecs standardized for the telephone network. The SNR remains a problem in Shannon's formula and limits the maximum channel capacity.

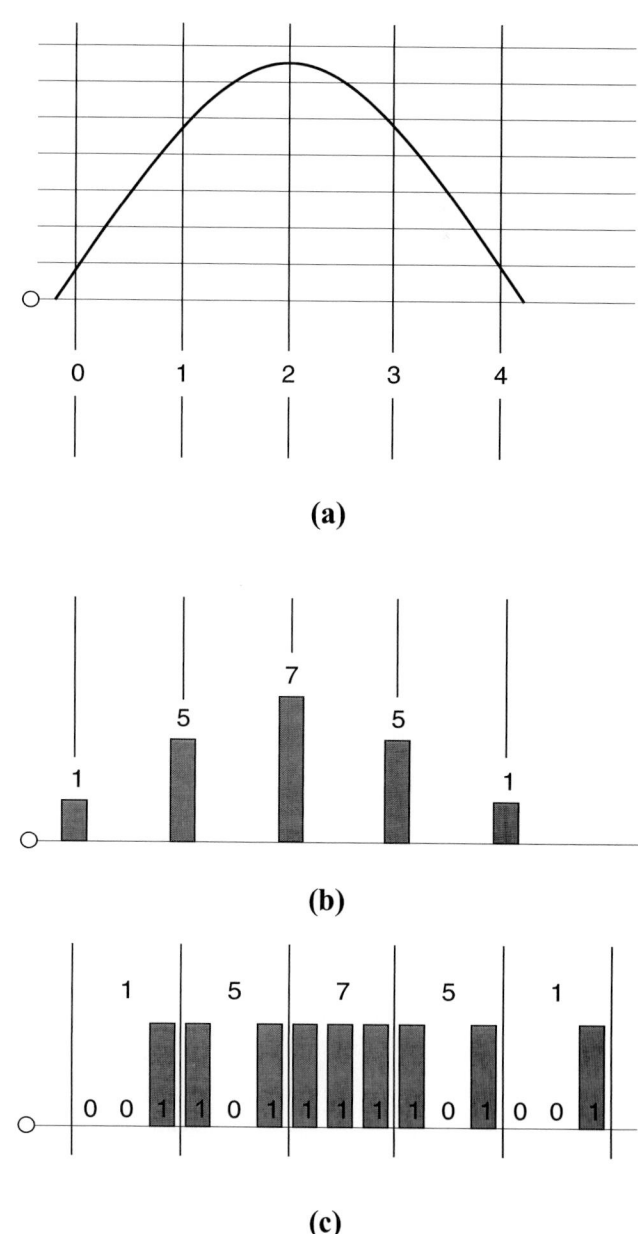

Figure 4-30 PAM and PCM Encoding

The SNR remains a problem in Shannon's formula and limits the maximum channel capacity.

Quantization noise can't be eliminated but it can be reduced. The best way minimize a problem is to go to the root-cause of the problem, and that occurs whenever there's an analog-to-digital conversion. Referring back to Figure 4-29 (a), the data is subjected to two ADCs. In Figure 4-29 (b), the data goes through an ADC only once. Since the analog data is converted to digital once instead of twice, it seems reasonable that the cumulative losses in the channel due to quantization noise will be less. The effect is to raise the SNR in Shannon's equation which will then increase the channel capacity.

Note that the downstream signal needn't be QAM-modulated, because the data is already in a digital format. It wouldn't be advantageous anyway because PCM has twice the symbol rate as QAM. Remember that the Nyquist sampling rate must be a minimum of twice the signaling rate. In the digital portion of the PSTN, the channels offer much better quality to data signals, so that the full 4 kHz of the channel are used. With a maximum channel rate of 4 kHz, the data is sampled at 8 kHz. That means, two information bits are assigned to each hertz of the 4kHz channel frequency. With PAM, we're literally sending more data, faster, than with QAM.

If you use a V.90 modem to communicate with a distant analog modem as in Figure 4-29 (a), the data rates will fallback to V.34 speeds. But for communicating with a fully digital modem as shown in Figure 4-29 (b), the uploads will occurs at V.34 rates while downloads will travel at V.90 rates.

Why not use PAM in the upstream direction and achieve higher than V.34 rates? It's certainly possible, but from a cost/complexity standpoint, it isn't practical. Switching equipment at the local office expects to convert an analog signal to digital, and if it arrives as a digital waveform, the central office equipment will have to be modified to accept it and simultaneously accept any data or voice analog signal. If faster uploads than V.34 are needed, it would be best to look into an ISDN connection.

NET+ OBJECTIVE
II.5.7

LOOPBACK TESTS

Modems incorporate tests that allow the user to verify the operation of the modem, to check the communication path to a remote modem, as well as allowing a remote user to check the data channel. These tests are called **loopback tests**, and they're subdivided to make **analog loop** and **digital loop** tests.

Loopback tests are initiated with AT commands. You may or may not be able to implement them from Hyper Terminal. The only way to know for sure is try.

Modems incorporate circuitry to make analog and digital loopback tests. An analog loopback test checks a local modem to see if it will transmit and receive an analog signal. Figure 4-31(a) shows the data flow for analog loopback checks. The telephone interface (the RJ11 connection) is disabled, placing the telephone network out of the circuit. The modem generates an unscrambled analog test signal at the transmitter, and the signal is checked by receiver circuitry. Basically, analog loopback tests check to see if the modem will generate an analog carrier, and simulate reception and detection of an analog carrier.

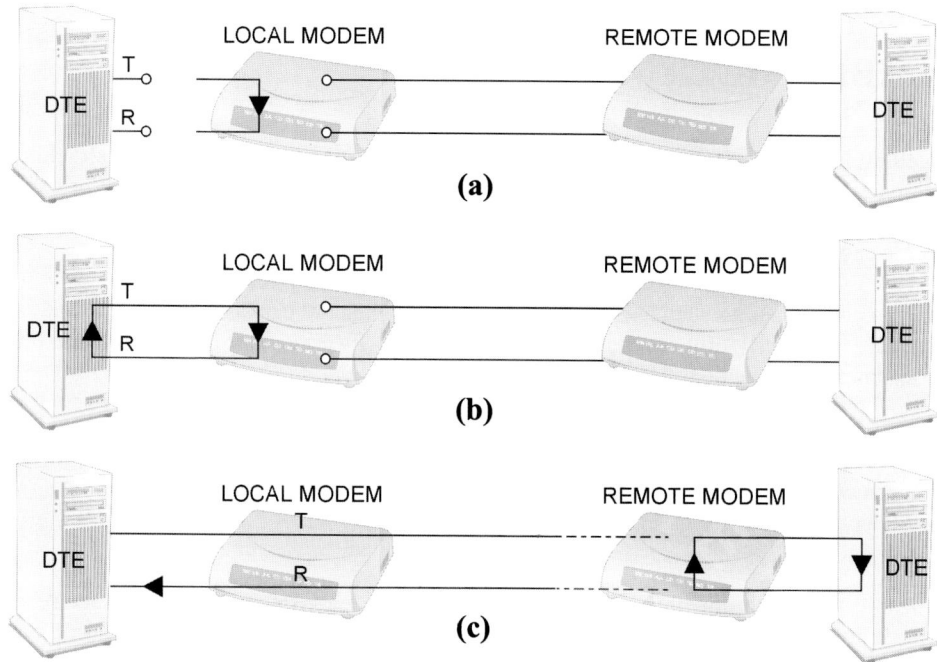

Figure 4-31 Analog, Digital, and Remote Loopback Tests

Digital loopback tests are used to determine if the DCE side of the modem is working properly. A local digital loopback test is illustrated in Figure 4-31(b). When making a digital loopback test, the local DCE is disabled. The modem transmits unscrambled digital data and loops the data back. Note that the modem is simulating actual conditions. The direction of data flow shows it moving from the receive wire to the transmit wire. This is consistent with the modem's actual operation, since data is received from the remote modem at this pin under normal conditions. The data flow shows information flowing into the transmit pin, but this is the direction data flows from the DCE to the modem when the DCE has data to transmit.

Most modems provide the user with loopback tests that will verify the proper operation of the local modem, telephone channel between local and remote modem, and the remote modem.

Most modems also have the capability to conduct remote digital loopback tests, as shown in Figure 4-31(c). Here, the local modem has instructed the remote mode to perform a digital loopback test and to provide the local modem with the results. The remote modem performs the check as if it were a local digital loop. It then transmits the results to the local modem. The advantage of remote digital loopbacks is that both modems are checked, along with the telephone systems connecting the modems.

Loopback tests are generally done by the operator entering an AT code corresponding to the specific loopback test to be done. Once in the appropriate loopback mode, several test characters are typed in. The operator checks the characters on the monitor to see if they match the tests characters. If they do, then the loopback test has been successful.

CABLE MODEMS

Cable television providers are the newest entrants into the networking business. It shouldn't come as too much of a surprise since many homes and business are now wired for cable TV. The promise of cable (In this context, "cable" refers to coaxial or, more likely, a fiber optic cabling infrastructure.) is very wide bandwidth capabilities.

If you check back to Claude Shannon's formula for channel capacity, you'll see that the capacity is directly proportional to bandwidth. Cable TV has a lot of bandwidth and this translates into very fast speeds for data.

> A cable modem uploads/downloads data using the existing cable television wiring infrastructure, or it may upload at V.34 rates using the analog portion of the local telephone loop.

A cable modem up/downloads data using existing cable television wiring infrastructure, or they may upload at V.34 rates using the analog portion of the local telephone loop.

The idea behind a cable modem is to use the wide bandwidth all ready available form cable companies to download at very high speeds. Typical applications include Internet access, distance learning or medical diagnoses to rural areas, and local telephone access (which will compete directly with regional telephone companies). The obstacle to implementing access to computers is that the current system is primarily simplex in nature. At the cable headend, cable television is piped to homes and business via a point-to-multi-point configuration. The multi-point cables lead to boxes which attach to television sets. A television receives information; it doesn't transmit back any information, so there hasn't been much of a need to incorporate transceivers at the headend.

But in order to access and communicate with distant modems such as the Internet ports, full-duplex communication is a requirement.

The solution to the problem appears to be a hybrid system. Figure 4-32 (a)shows an implementation of a cable modem system developed by Zenith.

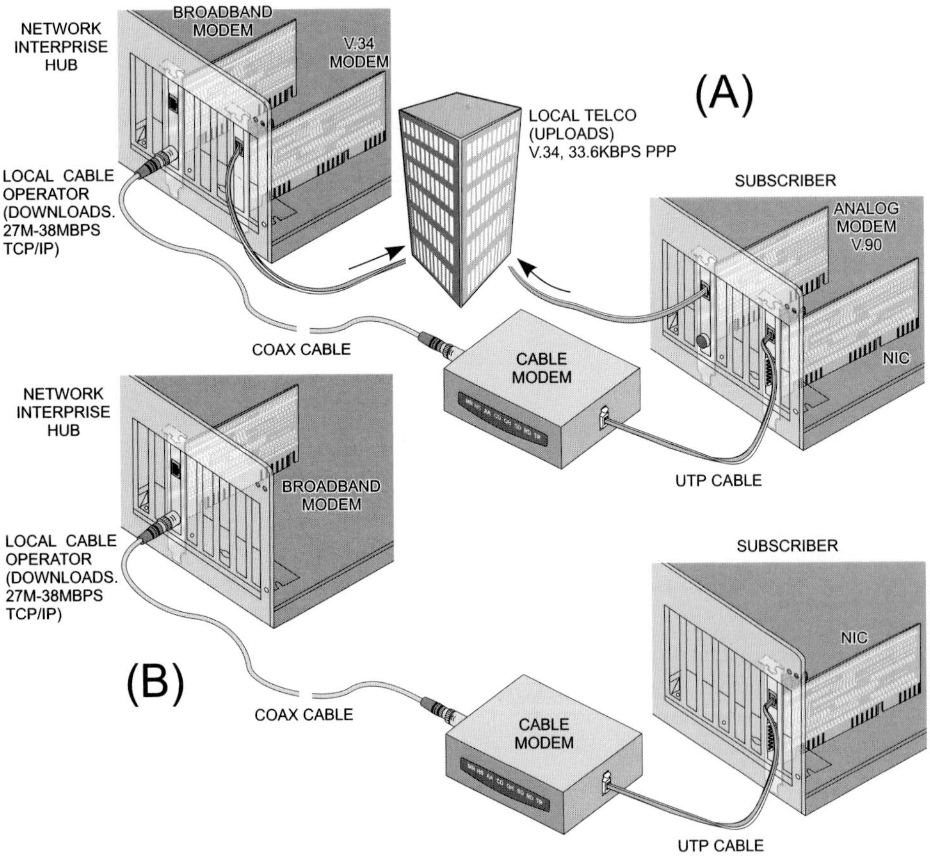

Figure 4-32 Cable Modem System

The system consists of an enterprise hub at the cable headend which includes the PSTN and cable interface components. These include V.34 modems for analog modem connections, a broadband modem for the RF downloads, ISDN interface if the subscriber has an ISDN connection, and a router to switch between the cable and analog telephone connections.

At the subscriber end is a cable modem which has a coaxial cable connection to receive data. The cable modem connects to the subscriber computer through a conventional RJ-45 connector to a standard Ethernet (10Base-T) network interface card. For cable plants that lack headend equipment needed to transmit and receive, an analog modem is also required. The V.34 modem connects to the local telco via a standard RJ-11 jack.

Data from the cable headend is downloaded at rates between 27M and 38MBPS. This is fast. Compare it to V.90 speeds of 48KBPS or ISDN rates of 128KBPS, and there is no comparison. The upstream, or transmit, side of the connection is at V.34 speeds. The reasoning for the lower upstream rates is similar to that for V.90 modems—the down stream infrastructure is in place but not a similar upstream infrastructure, so we utilize what we have available which is the analog loop with its bandwidth and SNR limits. Note that during an Internet session, most of the data that's transferred consists of downloads; uploads are mainly mouse clicks or Internet address entries.

There are a couple of other aspects of cable modem systems. The standard analog modem at the PC is included so that upload data has a return route to the cable operator. The existence of the cable system will be transparent to the computer; it will see the cable modem as nothing more than a load. This is important because it implies that the computer won't require specialized—and, perhaps, proprietary—software to communicate with the cable system. The up stream channel will be managed by point-to-point (PPP) protocols which is the same protocol running most access channels to Internet Service Providers. The down stream channel will be under control of TCP/IP which is installed as the internetworking protocol in nearly all larger networks.

The system shown in Figure 3-32 (a) is appropriate for cable operators who can't invest in the costly headend equipment needed for full-duplex transfers across the coaxial cable. Expect it to be used by smaller operators. For those operators who invest in headend equipment which allows two-way transmission across the cabling infrastructure, there's the two-way RF (Radio Frequency) system shown in figure 4-32 (b). In this system, data travels up and down from the cable operator. No analog modem is needed. This is the preferred method but may not be available if you live in a small community.

Data over cable is well-suited for business applications because it's fast. To connect more than one computer to the system, a hub would be placed at the UTP output of the cable modem. The multiple users would then connect to the cable modem via hub ports. Although the cable modem shown in Figure 4-32 is an external modem, there are internal modems available as well. They remain less common than the external variety.

For larger companies using two-way RF systems, there is the **Data Over Cable Service Interface Specification** (DOCSIS), which was established by the **Multimedia Cable Network Systems** (MCNS), a consortium of cable companies. This is a consortium within the cable television business that sets cable-based standards. The DOCSIS standard is currently being implemented by the majority of chip and system vendors who sell to cable operators. After all, it was the operators who established it as a standard that was approved by the ITU in March of 1998.

Pertinent specifications of the DOCSIS standard are:

Downstream

- Modulation: 64 and 256 QAM
- Carrier Rate: 6MHz
- Data Rate: 27 or 36MBPS

Upstream

- Modulation: QPSK or 16QAM
- Carrier: Variable, 200KHz to 3.2MHz
- Data Rate: 320KBPS to 10MBPS

Subscriber Interface

- 10Base-T

Network Interface

- 10Base-T
- 100Base-T
- ATM
- FDDI

In a nutshell, the DOCSIS standard specifies that the subscriber connection will be to a network interface card (an Ethernet card) in the user's PC. This cable from the NIC card will be routed to the cable box sitting on the top of a television set.

The data rates quoted above may be misleading; these are maximimum rates, not necessarily typical rates. Many factors will influence the actual transfer in both up and down stream directions—the number of subscribers connected to the channel, the capability of the subscriber-side modem (if one is used), the integrity of the channel, etc. But if the down-stream rate were to fall to 1.5MBPS, this is a T1 data rate and still much faster than ISDN (128KBPS).

If the user is accessing the cable operator through a network, there are more options available—100MBPS Ethernet, FDDI, or ATM. In this configuration, a single cable modem at the subscriber sight will be used to connect the network users (which can range in number from four to a maximum of sixteen).

A competing standard is IEEE802.14 (not approved at the time of this writing). This standard has been in the works for quite some time, long enough that cable operators became impatient with its progress and developed DOCSIS in the interim. There's one significant difference between 802.14 and DOCSIS. The IEEE standard specified ATM at the user interface. All data formatted to the ATM protocol is separated into 53 byte frames, or cells as they're called. The cell size is fixed and predictable. Ethernet (10Base-T), on the other hand, is a variable frame length with a maximum size of about 1500 bytes.

The huge advantage of using ATM is that because of the small cell lengths, the cells can be passed through nearly any type of network on their way to a final destination. This isn't always true with Ethernet. Because of the almost guaranteed routability of ATM, it's used for multi-media applications. Cable television, for example.

While cable operators have included ATM in the DOCSIS standard, don't expect to see it widely implemented for some time to come; the operators feel it adds an unnecessary level of complexity to the system (which is true) and increases the time to market for cable modems. The IEEE would specifically require that subscribers interface to the operator using ATM.

The IEEE 802.14 standard is the better one because it looks to the future and anticipates bandwidth demands on the coax that the DOCSIS standard won't be able to handle. Unfortunately, it also increases the cost of implementing cable modems. At least fifty vendors are marketing, or plan to in the near future, products compliant to the DOCSIS standard.

Stay tuned. Great things are expected of cable modems.

NETWORK CHANGE CONTROL SYSTEMS

Once a system change has been decided upon and receives the support of appropriate management levels, it must be implemented. In this section, we'll look at several key change areas—Requests and Approvals, Add and Upgrades, and Security Changes.

Requests and Approvals

The latest version of everyone's software is now available for beta testing. All that's required is to go to the vendor's Web site, download and install it. Why not? It costs nothing, and may very well be free of troubling bugs.

A network exists so that a company can be better at making money. It's a business tool before it's a neat piece of software or hardware. Corporations are quite serious about remaining profitable, and they may loose the edge it takes to make money if their network crashes because someone in a remote cubicle decides to experiment with system changes. The only way to maintain network reliability is to control change.

Write a procedure dictating the steps to requesting a change. Require a one-over-one signature process. That is, anyone who requests a change must have the approval of (generally) their supervisor. Include a statement to the effect that the Network Administrator must also approve the change.

NET+ OBJECTIVE
II.2.1

Networks should have a specific SOP detailing how requests for upgrades are handled.

Normally, the change request follows the format of a work order. The difference is that a change request should contain detailed information on the change, who will perform it, and an analysis of expected outcomes. Figure 4-33 is an example of a change request form.

NETWORK CHANGE REQUEST	
Name:	Date:
Telephone:	Location:
Describe the proposed change in detail:	
Materials Required:	
What are the expected outcomes of the change?	
What risks have been identified for this change?	
Who will perform the change?	
When will the change begin/ be completed?	
Signature:	Signature:

Figure 4-33 Change Request Form

Create a standard operating procedure to describe how to complete the change request. This is important because it ensures that the change control system is widely supported.

Upgrades

Upgrades are a fact of life in the fast-changing network business. An upgrade offers a chance to improve the network, and should be tracked and documented for all devices on the network. This is no easy task because it's time-consuming and meticulous.

All hardware and software is revision controlled. It is for the same reason that SOPs are revision controlled; because when a change is made, it's intended to be an improvement on an earlier version. All of our work should be a system of continuous improvements. Embrace upgrades, but control them as normal changes and document the changes extensively.

NET+ OBJECTIVE
II.2.1

Throughout this book, you'll see many references to software upgrades and patches. There are many varieties, and we'll take each as they come. Here, we'll begin with upgrades to modems. It's important to understand that you can't really perform an upgrade if you don't know some specific information about the product you are upgrading. You need to know the particular version of the software or hardware you want to upgrade before doing so. This means getting to know the devices on a network. Get to know them well enough that, in the case of a modem, you can use Hyper Terminal, with the proper AT commands, to see what version of software you're using or the product code for the modem hardware.

All V.90 chip vendors have promised a software upgrade from 56K to V.90. Software upgrades are routinely made available for modems as well as most networking products. However, you can only upgrade a product that can be upgraded. Does that make sense?

> Many modems are software upgradable by locating and downloading the upgrade file from the vendor's Web site.

The software used to configure a modem is programmed onto a PCB in one of two ways—by placing it into **Read Only Memory** (ROM), or into **volatile memory**. Volatile memory includes EPROM, NVRAM, FLASH, etc. If you have a ROM chip on your modem card which contains the software for your modem, you can't upgrade. If the software is contained in volatile memory, then you can upgrade.

Each modem, and each modem vendor, has a unique procedure for upgrading. But they all follow a general pattern. Go to the Web site of the company that sold you your modem. Locate the download area of the site. From a list, choose your modem. You'll need to know a few details about your modem (or modem card) such as the product number, software version, etc. Check the site requirements. Download the upgrade to a floppy disk, then disconnect from the Internet.

In the Control Panel, go to Modems and Remove your current modem. Then, choose Add/ Have a disk. From there, Windows will treat your upgrade as a new installation. Once you're finished, reconnect to the Internet, and check the performance by repeating the FTP test as described previously.

If your modem chip was made by Lucent, can you go to their Web site and download the upgrade, even when your modem card was made by a company who recently went out of business? Probably not. Some manufacturers buy the software license from the chip vendor and use it as-is; others tinker with it, or create their own code.

The only way to know for sure is to do the upgrade. But if it doesn't work, you're out of luck and a modem, because the software you've installed won't work your modem. And since the company you bought it from is gone, there's no easy way to re-install the original software. This is the reason you should be willing to do a little research on a product—even one as inexpensive as a modem—before buying it.

Security Changes

The U. S. military has an excellent security attitude. Not only do you have to have a "clearance", you also have to have a "need-to-know". This type of mind-set works equally well for network security, and should serve as a basis for deciding who gets access to what.

There are four elements to maintaining a secure network. These four elements or categories, when properly addressed and maintained, will guard a network against intentional or unintentional intruders. The four categories to be addressed are:

- Physical

- Logical

- Procedural

- Personnel

Network operating systems tend to focus on the logical category with mechanisms such as logons, passwords, read-only access, and so forth. This is an important area, but the other areas are equally important, and will be examined in detail in the chapter on Data Security and Error Control. For now, we'll focus only on logical security, with an emphasis on creating and implementing changes.

By far, security-related requests center on access. Typically, this requires giving individuals access to servers (or portions thereof) that they don't currently have access to. Most network operating systems handle security, in the larger sense, by organizing individuals into related groups, all of whom have a general need to a specific class of information.

CNST OBJECTIVE
V-A

There are several advantages to group accounts. It's much easier to track access within small groups than it is within an entire organization. A security program should begin, then, by logically dividing personnel into groups according to their job functions. They are then given access to servers that they need in order to do their job. If you aren't familiar with the job duties of other departments (Purchasing, Accounting, etc.), you need to talk with individuals in these respective departments to determine what information they need access to.

Another advantage involves organizing server data to match the needs of the group accounts, and matching their needs to the available data. Once that's done, you have a reference for establishing **across-the-board-access** to the logical group. Personnel within the group will have special needs, and these should be approved using a **one-over-one signature system**.

There are several ways to approach the initial setup. A good idea is to send a questionnaire to department managers asking them to list the information that their employees routinely need. Then, maintain another list that documents the contents of the servers on your network. If departments within your organization are internally billed for server access, the department managers needs to know this, because it will certainly affect their decisions.

KEY POINTS REVIEW

This chapter has presented an extensive exploration of modems.

- Modem is an acronym for modulator/demodulator.

- A modem can receive as well as transmit data.

- Primarily, modems serve as an interface to the public telephone network. Modems always work in pairs. The pairs must be compatible in terms of speed, frame format, word length and parity.

- Characteristics of modems are described in a series of ITU recommendations called the V Series.

- A Hayes Compatible modem uses the Hayes AT Command Set to control the functionality of a modem.

- Internal modems are installed in an available expasion slot of a personal computer, and software installed using the PC or Network operating system software.

- A common problem during installation is conflicts between com ports and interrupt requests.

- AT Commands are entered using Hyper Terminal with Windows 95.

- To test the speed capabilities of a modem, download a large file from an FTP site and use AT commands to check the transfer rate.

- Data to be transmitted is modulated onto a carrier. Common modem modulation techniques are FSK, PSK, DPSK and QAM.

- FSK represents bit changes by shifting the carrier higher and lower for logic 1's and 0's. FSK modems require a large amount of bandwidth, and are restricted to low speeds.

- PSK represents logic 1's and 0's by inverting the phase of the carrier for each bit change.

- DPSK represents data bits by phase shifting the carrier in increments that are smaller than is available with FSK. This allows a greater number of bits per symbol.

- QAM represents bit changes by varying the carrier amplitude as well as shifting the carrier phase.

- Modems routinely scramble data in order to reduce intersymbol interference as well as to evenly distribute the signal power.

- A modem may operate in an originate or answer mode. The originate mode initiates the data exchange while the answer mode responds to an originate modem. Modems have specific originate and answer carrier frequencies.

- A modem may be packaged as a stand-alone device, as a board that plugs into a computer expansion slot, or it may be an acoustical modem that doubles as a telephone.

- V.90 modems mark an important stride in modem development because they exceed the so-called Shannon limit during downloads.

- A V.90 modem transmits at V.34 speeds and downloads at rates near 48 kBPS.

- Most modems provide the user with loopback tests that will verify the proper operation of the local modem, telephone channel between local and remote modem, and the remote modem.

- A cable modem uploads/downloads data using existing cable television wiring infrastructure, or it may upload at V.34 rates using the analog portion of the local telephone loop.

- Networks should have a specific SOP detailing how requests for upgrades are handled.

- Many modems are software-upgradable by locating and downloading the upgrade from the vendor Web site.

At this point, review the objectives listed at the beginning of the chapter to be certain that you understand and can perform them. Afterward, answer the review questions that follow to verify your knowledge of the information.

LAB MANUAL

Lab Exercises

The lab manual that accompanies this book contains hands-on lab procedures that reinforce and test your knowledge of the theory materials presented in this chapter. Now that you have completed your review of Chapter 4, refer to the lab manual and perform Procedures 5, "Modem Commands," and 6, "Measuring Modem Speeds."

REVIEW QUESTIONS

The following questions test your knowledge of the material presented in this chapter:

1. Determine the baud rate for a 9,600BPS carrier modulated with 2-bit symbols.

2. Explain the difference between baud and BPS.

3. A DPSK constellation map depicts the following phase shifts: 90, 0, 270, 180. What bits are represented by the phase shifts?

4. The 4-bit word 1110 is to be modulated in a QAM modulator, with 1=Q1, 1=Q2, 1=Q3, 0=Q4. Assume an absolute phase shift of 180 degrees from +I and determine the phase angle and amplitude of the modulated word.

5. What is the purpose of loopback tests?

6. What is a "Hayes compatible" modem?

7. Describe a method to measure actual modem speeds.

8. What is the practical send/receive rates for V.90 modems?

9. How do cable modems differ from analog modems?

10. How do V.90 modems exceed the so called "Shannon Limit"?

11. What is the purpose of the Ring Indicator in a handshake sequence?

12. Is it true or false that a V.90 modem transmits faster than it receives?

13. What is the reason for a V.90 modem's inability to reach its theoretical maximum downstream rate?

14. What is the major obstacle in the implementation of a cable modem system?

15. What is the advantage to a software-upgradable modem?

MULTIPLE CHOICE QUESTIONS

1. _____ is the process of superimposing data on a carrier.
   a. Space marking
   b. Mark spacing
   c. QAM
   d. Modulation

2. In a 4-bit/symbol QAM modulator, how many signal points will be represented on the carrier?
   a. 4
   b. 8
   c. 16
   d. 20

3. Why is data scrambled in a modem?
   a. To avoid ISI and dc-drift problems.
   b. To avoid security breaches.
   c. To increase the bit/symbol rate.
   d. To decrease the SNR.

4. Which loopback test checks the line connection and the remote DCE/DTE?
   a. Remote digital loopback.
   b. Digital loopback.
   c. Analog loopback.
   d. Local DTE.

5. When the signal energy of the received carrier meets the criteria of the answer modem, _____ is enabled.
   a. CTS
   b. RI
   c. RTS
   d. RLSD

6. When a high-speed modem communicates with a low-speed modem, the high-speed modem must use a _____ frequency.
   a. varying
   b. signal level
   c. phase
   d. fallback

7. What are the V-dot series of standards?
   a. Protocols for local area networks.
   b. Descriptions of parameters used with modems.
   c. Explainations of multiplexing techniques.
   d. Protocols that are synonymous with the OSI Reference Model.

8. What does a typical modem "upgrade" refer to?
   a. Removing and replacing the modem.
   b. Removing and replacing critical integrated circuits in the modem.
   c. Downloading software enhancements for the modem.
   d. Performing preventive maintenance on the modem.

9. ITU modem recommendations include all of the following, except the:
   a. Purchase price of the modem.
   b. Highest data rate of the modem.
   c. Communication method between modems.
   d. Connection medium between modems.

10. A modem may be packaged as a/an:
    a. Stand-alone device.
    b. Expansion board.
    c. Acoustic device.
    d. All of the above.

CD-ROM

Net+ Practice Test

Additional Net+ Certification testing is available on the CD that accompanies this text. The testing suite on the CD provides Study Card, Flash Card, and Run Practice type testing. The Study Card and Flash Card feature enables you to electronically link to the section of the book in which the question is covered. Choose questions from the test pool related to this chapter.

CHAPTER
5

PROTOCOLS

LEARNING OBJECTIVES

LEARNING
OBJECTIVES

Upon completion of this chapter and its related lab procedures, you should be able to perform the following tasks:

1. Define Protocol.

2. State the difference between a protocol, and interface.

3. Define handshaking, virtual communication path, and data packaging.

4. Describe the hierarchical nature of the OSI Reference Model.

5. State the benefits of the OSI Reference Model.

6. Define the layers of the OSI model, and identify the protocols, services, and functions that pertain to each layer.

7. Match specific applications to the layers.

8. Describe the functions of the MAC and LLC sublayers.

9. State specific applications that the MAC and LLC sublayers govern.

10. Describe the Data Link layer concepts in the 802.2 specs.

11. Describe the function of the LLC sublayer Service Access Point (SAP).

12. State the difference between a Type I and Type II LLC frame.

13. Define connectionless and connection-oriented protocols.

14. Draw and label a block diagram of the LLC sublayer frame format.

15. Discuss the purpose of each of the fields in the LLC frame.

16. State the difference between character-oriented and bit-oriented protocols.

17. Label a block diagram of the asynchronous frame format.

18. Describe the user-selectable parameters of an asynchronous protocol.

19. Describe a typical asynchronous exchange.

20. Calculate throughput given the overhead and information field sizes.

21. Label a block diagram of the BSC frame format.

22. Describe text transparency used with BSC.

23. Describe a typical BSC exchange.

24. State several protocols that are implementations of HDLC.

25. Discuss differences between normal, asynchronous, and balanced modes.

26. Label a block diagram of the HDLC frame format.

27. Identify the HDLC frame in the extended mode.

28. Discuss information, supervisory and unnumbered control field formats.

29. Discuss the HDLC method of text transparency.

30. Describe a typical HDLC exchange in the normal mode.

31. Given two LAPB nodes, describe the link setup and data exchange.

32. Prepare a Training Plan, and create an accompanying format.

33/ Design an effective instructional strategy for a given training solution.

34. Given a scenario, select the appropriate instructional strategy.

CHAPTER 5

Protocols

INTRODUCTION

Protocols are the set of rules governing the organization and transmission of data. In many cases, the rules are written as recommendations, or descriptions, of how data should be packaged and transmitted. Individual vendors are responsible for designing and building equipment that will actually implement the protocol. This has resulted in a multitude of "exceptions to the rule". Many of the standard protocols have roots in large computer and office automation companies. What has become a standard protocol was once a proprietary protocol belonging to a company. IBM's **Synchronous Data Link Control** (SDLC) is the forerunner of the standard protocol **High-Level Data Link Control** (HDLC). The Zerox/Intel/Digital **Ethernet** is the foundation of the IEEE **Carrier Sense Multiple Access/Collision Detection** (CSMA/CD) standard. IBM uses SDLC extensively, and many other vendors support HDLC. Both protocols are very similar, but they're not the same. The same holds true for Ethernet.

> **Protocols** are the set of rules governing data communications.

Within this chapter, the emphasis is placed upon protocol standards written by respected standard's organizations. Even within these standards, many liberties by vendors are taken—and often encouraged—by standards organizations. In this way, precautions have been taken that won't make data communications inflexible to technological developments.

For the most part, the intent of a protocol is software-oriented. But, as we'll see shortly, this directly affects the actual movement of data. To have a clear understanding of data transfer, it's necessary to study the force driving the data—the data communication protocols.

PROTOCOL FUNCTIONS

Most of the information presented so far in this book has evolved from a wide-ranging set of rules that attempt to make the exchange of data between computers an orderly process. Those rules are collectively called protocols.

A protocol is a logical concept. It does not consist of any physical devices, but describes how data can be exchanged between computers, or other devices of similar architectures.

CNST OBJECTIVE
I-A

For example, there are protocols related to **asynchronous data**, and **synchronous data**; but not a protocol for transferring asynchronous data to a synchronous device. For that to occur, a **protocol converter** would be required.

Protocols shouldn't be confused with **interfaces**. An interface is the physical connection between dissimilar devices. Figure 5-1 shows the difference between a protocol and an interface.

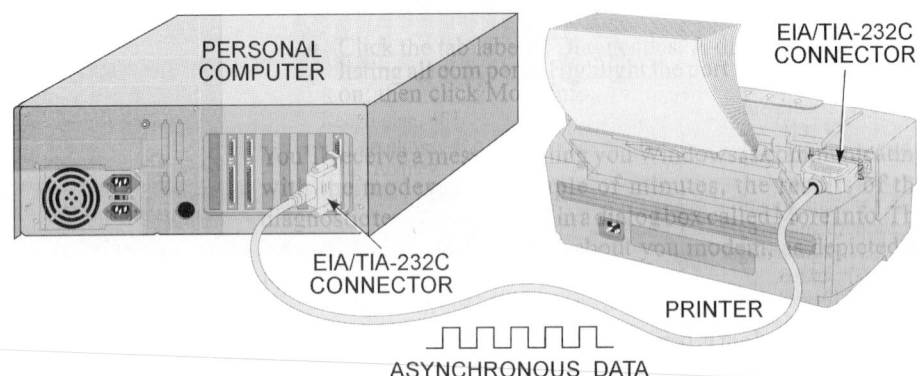

Figure 5-1 Implementing an Asynchronous Data Protocol with the EIA/TIA-232 Interface

The printer is an **asynchronous** device. It's connected to the asynchronous port of the personal computer. The printer needs to know when a character begins and ends so it can print the character. An asynchronous protocol dictates how the printer will be informed of the start and end of each character. The EIA/TIA-232 connector provides the physical interface between the computer and printer.

The three functions of a protocol are:

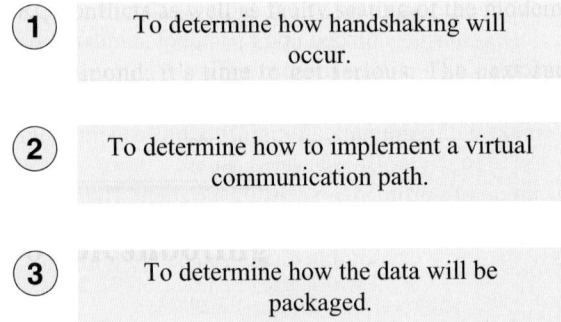

1	To determine how handshaking will occur.
2	To determine how to implement a virtual communication path.
3	To determine how the data will be packaged.

In Figure 5-1, both the computer and the printer are involved in the same process of manipulating data. A protocol sets the rules for insuring that the manipulation doesn't degrade the original **message**. On the other hand, the computer and the printer perform entirely different functions. The EIA/TIA-232 interface is the physical means of implementing the constraints defined by the protocol.

There are many protocols in use today, and they are always expanding to respond to technological developments. As changes in the industry occur, the protocols themselves will change. But data communication protocols will always have three basic functions:

- To determine how handshaking will occur.

- To determine how to implement a virtual communication path.

- To determine how the data will be packaged.

The process of setting up an exchange of data is referred to as **handshaking**. Handshaking occurs when the transmitter and receiver engage in a dialogue to let each other know that there's a message to be sent, that the line is free to transmit, and that the message was—or wasn't—received. Figure 5-2 demonstrates the process as it occurs for a personal computer and printer.

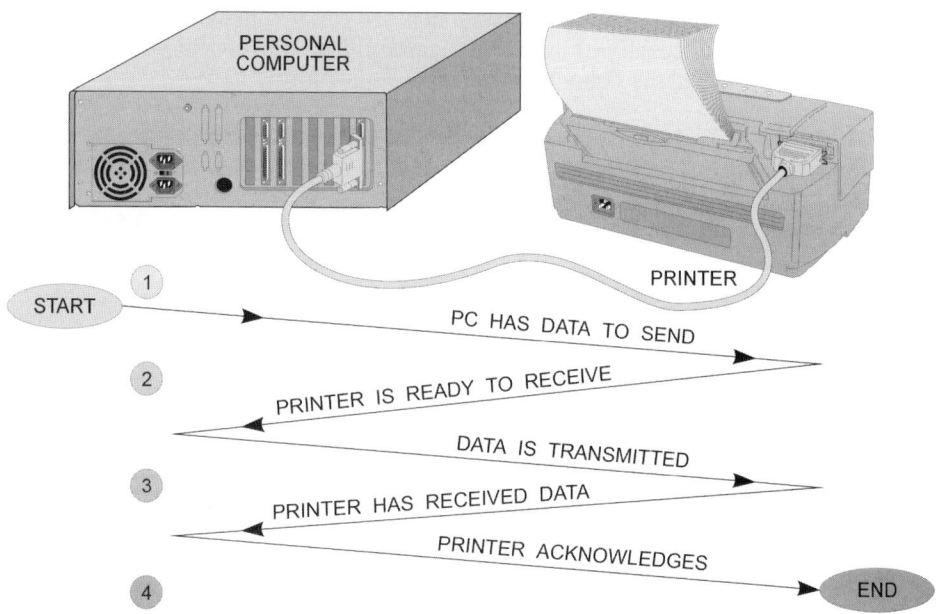

Figure 5-2 Handshaking Between a PC and a Printer

A **virtual communications path** is a medium that appears to exist but actually doesn't. A long distance telephone call is a virtual communications path. A caller in Miami talking to someone in Los Angeles appears to be connected by a wire, but in reality there are central offices, switching centers, and perhaps microwave links between the two telephones. A protocol establishes the same illusion between computers. The protocol anticipates problems and directs that the data be prepared accordingly. In order to accomplish this, protocols establish procedures for error detection and correction.

Computers must know before sending any data how to package the data. Will they communicate a bit at a time, a character at a time, a hundred characters, or a hundred pages? Most protocols can be classified as bit or character oriented. Each has its advantages and disadvantages as we'll see later in the chapter. The main point to keep in mind is that the computers must be compatible. A bit-oriented computer cannot directly send data to a computer that accepts only character-oriented data.

The functions of a protocol can be related to the PC and the printer of Figure 5-2. Handshaking occurs when the PC requests to send data to the printer, and the printer acknowledges the request. The protocol includes a start and stop bit with each message sent.

A virtual communications path is established with the EIA/TIA-232 connector and the software conventions used with the connection. As far as the computer (or user) is concerned, there's a wire that lets data move from the PC to the printer when a print command is initiated. The protocol recognizes the differences between the PC and the printer, and realizes that problems may arise. Consequently, it requires that the communicating devices be informed of problems by including error detection. In this case, a parity bit is included.

The data in Figure 5-2 is packaged as character-oriented messages. A character is sent and printed, then another character is sent, etc. If the printer was designed to accept only a bit of data, rather than characters, the devices would be incompatible.

Moving information to various places around the globe would be an impossibly confusing task, if not for some sort of guidelines. The designers of data communications systems more or less follow a model developed by the **International Standards Organization**. The reference model is called the **Open System Interconnection** (OSI).

OPEN SYSTEM INTERCONNECTION MODEL

In 1975 the International Standards Organization began work on the Open System Interconnection (OSI) reference model. Their work was completed three years later, in 1978. The final structure of the model is shown in Figure 5-3.

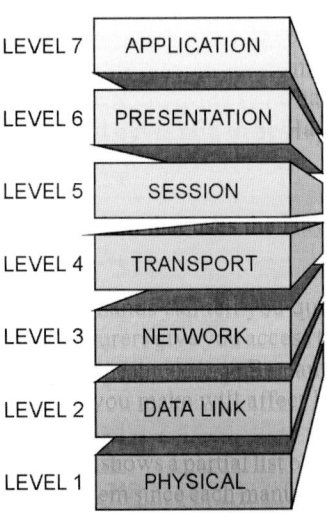

Figure 5-3 OSI Reference Model

At first glance, it may seem like three years was a long time to develop a simple block diagram. But the organization had the very difficult job of deciding what constitutes a data communications system, and determining what its major functions would be. The OSI model provides designers and users of data communications a logical structure for defining protocols for a variety of network configurations.

The time was ripe for a widely respected organization to advance a model to which vendors could refer when developing data communications products. In 1974 IBM had pioneered their own model, called **System Network Architecture** (SNA). The purpose of SNA was to bring a sense of organization and compatibility to the IBM product line. The SNA model was proprietary to IBM, meaning it was designed for their current products, as well as those products still on the drawing board. And while SNA did (and does) provide a blueprint for IBM networks, it also had a significant impact on the product development of smaller, less influential data processing vendors. These smaller organizations were in business, in many cases, to fill product gaps of IBM. Their products tended to address a particular weakness of some aspect of the IBM line. Effectively, SNA placed IBM in a position to dictate to smaller companies the specifics of their products.

Other, larger vendors were quick to see the value of SNA. For example, **Digital Equipment Corporation** (DEC) and National Cash Register (NCR) produced their own models. In those days, data communications was an emerging industry, and incredibly confusing due to a lack of standardization and compatibility among vendors. The danger to smaller companies and users was that the proprietary communication models would restrict the development of the industry to a few major players—based upon their past and present products, as well as their future plans. As you can probably surmise, what was good business for IBM, DEC or NCR wasn't necessarily good for the data communications user.

The impact of computers in general was having the effect of exceeding the corporate bounds of large companies, and to their credit, the major vendors were sensitive to the negative aspects of proprietary models. Their models would ultimately regulate growth, inhibit new developments, and restrict information access to a few of the key companies. The OSI model was intended to provide all vendors with a blueprint of data communications.

The OSI model specifies the function of exchanging data over seven levels, or layers. It does not state how the functions are to be implemented. This is left to vendors. Within the functions are protocols describing the specifics of the functions. This is an important part of the model. If the vendors themselves are left to determine how to implement a protocol, then a reasonable sense of standardization will be achieved without sacrificing opportunities for developing and using new technologies. The idea here is similar to using 120Vac for households. The houses may be required to provide 120Vac at the outlets, but how the voltage is produced is determined by a vendor, the local electric company. If a new technology is developed, the electric company needs to have the flexibility to change the method used to produce the 120Vac.

Why use a layered approach in a data communication model? Examine the simple network of Figure 5-4(a). A point-to-point network is illustrated. Imagine that the data exchange is taking place between two compatible computers. In order for the exchange to occur, there must be rules governing the program tasks to be done. This includes procedures for how a dialogue is initiated and stopped, error detection, how acknowledgments are made, etc. Before the program tasks can be done at all, there also has to be an agreement between the two computers about the electrical structure of the data, and how the two com- puters will be physically connected.

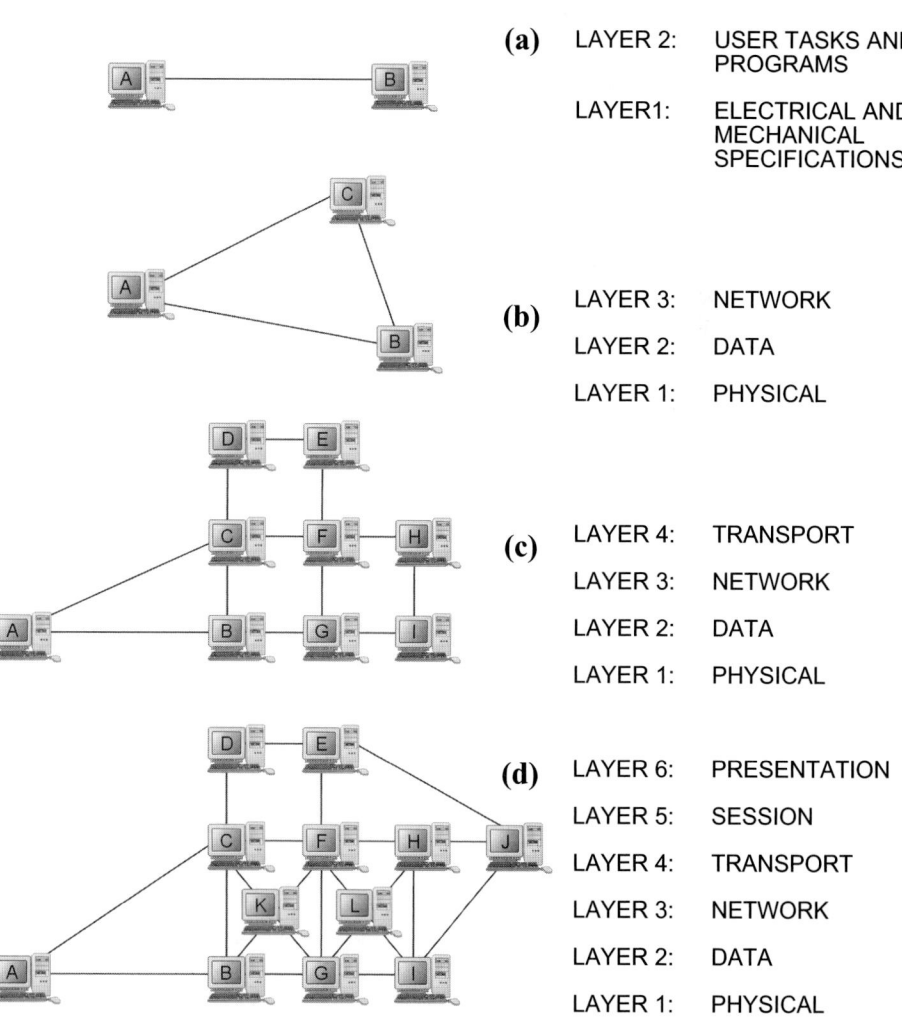

**Figure 5-4 Developing a
Layered Approach to Protocols**

The user tasks and programs (software) can be lumped together as a single unit, and labeled layer 2. The electrical and mechanical specifications (hardware) can be organized under the label, layer 1. Notice that layer 2 describes the data and layer 1 transfers the data. Layer 1 will transfer any data—it doesn't matter if it's a computer instruction or a sentence in a report. Conversely, it's not the job of layer 2 to figure out the **amplitude** of a bit, but it is concerned if the proper number of bits are successfully received. The two layers are separate entities but are bound with the common purpose of transferring data.

Now, imagine we decided to expand the simple network by adding another computer, as shown in Figure 5-4(b). The third computer (or node as it's commonly called) provides a new dimension. In the simple point-to-point network, a single layer was dedicated to all software tasks. The three-node network presents complications that require careful decisions to be made. If computer "A" sends a message to "B", how will it ensure it's not sent to "C" instead? And if "B" wants to acknowledge receipt of the message, what's to prevent the acknowledgment from being sent to "C" rather than "A"? Clearly, layer 2 will need to be subdivided. It will retain its original job of seeing that data moves through the network in an organized manner. However, the complexity of including the third computer will be attended to at the **network layer**. This layer will assign each computer a unique address so as to avoid the confusion described above.

The network layer may also establish the **routes** that data may take. For example, if a message is to be sent from "A" to "C", the network layer could contain a fallback route of "A" to "B" to "C" in the event that the "A" to "C" link were to be disabled.

Many more nodes can now be added, since the third layer is involved with organizing the network as a whole, the second layer is responsible for describing the structure of the data, and the first layer specifies the electrical and mechanical specification.

In Figure 5-4(c) more nodes have been added, bringing more options for selecting data routes. If node "A" sends data to node "I", there are quite a few paths the data can travel. And if all of the nodes would like to transmit and receive at the same time, the number of wires connecting each to the other would be unmanageable. Due to the sheer volume of available nodes and routes, an opportunity exists for expanding our network layer by providing a new layer with some additional functions. Since this new layer is concerned with transporting data across a complex network, it'll be called the **transport layer**.

The transport layer has the primary purpose of seeing that the network operates efficiently. Efficiency in data communication means multiplexing and switching, so the transport layer will ensure that the links between nodes can carry many messages by multiplexing the data. As the network layer assigned each node a unique address within the network, the transport layer will address the nodes, too. But in order to prevent the functions of the transport layer from straying from the purpose of maintaining network efficiency, we'll assign the **transport addresses** with no thought as to where a node actually is in the network. In fact, we won't even be concerned if a specific node is in our network, or not!

The transport layer is a cavalier concept, but consider the possibilities by referring to Figure 5-5. Node "J" falls outside the network, but a user at "A" has decided to send data to it anyway. The fact that "J" isn't in the network is no problem to the transport layer. Since it's involved in end-to-end communication, it assigns "J" a transport address. Now that "J" has a transport address, will the data get there? It's the responsibility of the network layer to determine a path to "J". If the network layer determines there is no route, it will inform the transport layer.

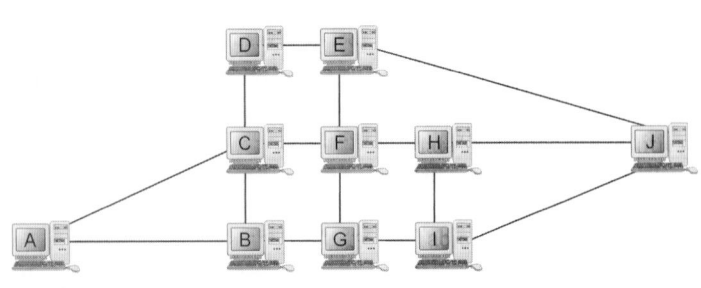

**Figure 5-5 Node
Arrangement Requiring a
Six-Layer Approach**

The transport layer would be particularly helpful if "J" belonged to a network in another area, and the network layer could route data through the long distance telephone network. If this were the case, our network would now have worldwide access.

As the sophistication of our network grows, it may be time to determine particular features of the data exchange sessions among nodes. For example, will the sessions resemble the full-duplex convention of a telephone call, will the nodes take turns sending data in a half-duplex mode, or will some nodes be the recipients of broadcast data (as in simplex)? If the network contains many paths, or links, it may be multiplexed along different routes. A feature the **session layer** may incorporate would be a system of recovering when a link malfunctions. A node sending a long message to another node should have a way of recovering from a problem that pops up near the end of the message, without losing the complete message.

It may become necessary to also regulate communications among nodes, so that certain nodes are forbidden to engage in a communication session with other nodes. Or, certain nodes may be permitted to communicate only with an assigned host, and the host is permitted to communicate only through other hosts. Therefore, the session layer establishes the conventions to be followed by the various nodes of the network.

Our simple network has grown and become sophisticated to the point that the original software layer has been divided several times. Throughout the growth, it's been assumed that all the nodes have been compatible in the way data is presented to the user. Now, we'll add two new computers, "K" and "L", in Figure 5-4(d). Let's assume these new computers are **personal computers** and they convert data into ASCII for displaying on CRTs, while all other computers in the network code data in EBCDIC. If computer "A" sends an EBCDIC encoded message to the PC at "K", how will "K" display it, since it handles only ASCII?

This new challenge hasn't previously been encountered in the network. All of the layers thus far have been involved in the management of the network itself, and little thought has been given to the presentation of the data messages. What if terminal "K" was located in a faraway country—like Korea? Or suppose this network was involved with national defense, and the data needed to be encrypted? Obviously, we need a layer that's involved in data interpretations, because data bits are coded in many ways, sometimes many times over.

This layer is christened the **presentation layer**, since it's involved in the manipulations needed to present data to the nodes in a manner each recognizes.

There is, of course, a final layer: the **application layer**. It's name correctly implies the functions of this layer. What does our network do? What is it's purpose? The applications of the network are user-defined, and determine the implementation of the lower layers. For example, the network may have one function—to transfer files back and forth between the nodes. If so, then a file transfer protocol will need to be defined at this level.

Once the application of the network is decided, then the presentation layer can determine how data will be presented at each end node. The session layer can decide the back and forth conventions to be followed in the communication dialogue, while the transport layer sees that the end-to-end communication is done in an efficient manner. The network layer determines the node-to-node route data will take through the network, while the data layer organizes the information into manageable units. Finally, it's the **physical layer** that actually transports the data.

Perhaps now you can see why it took several years to complete the OSI model. It's indeed difficult to determine what constitutes a sophisticated system, and then separate the system into logical areas. The layered approach was taken to allow both simple and complex networks an opportunity to implement standard protocols. It's common to have networks similar to Figure 5-4(b), but if the network is implemented with the OSI protocols it can be interfaced to a network like the one shown in Figure 5-4(d), using the same set of protocols.

Not all layers of the model are used, or even necessary, in all applications. If the personal computers hadn't been added to our network, the presentation layer may not have been necessary. On the other hand, a future product may be developed that includes a new encoding scheme. The OSI model is versatile enough so that this development can be incorporated into the presentation layer without affecting any of the other layers.

Each layer is subordinate to the above layer. Recall that the transport layer in our network assigned the "J" node a logical address, and the network layer had to determine a route over to "J". The higher, adjacent layer is referred to as a **user**. The transport layer made use of the network layer's ability to route the data. The lower adjacent layer is called a **provider**. The network layer provides a route to the address specified by the transport layer.

> The OSI model consists of seven levels: Application, Presentation, Session, Transport, Network, Data Link, and Physical.

The model provides for a hierarchial relationship as discussed above within a network. But the model also provides a **peer-to-peer** relationship for end users, as illustrated in Figure 5-6. From transmitter to receiver, data messages filter through successive layers of the model. In order to ensure consistent compliance to the model protocols, the end users must have a way of communicating with one another.

CNST OBJECTIVE
VIII-A

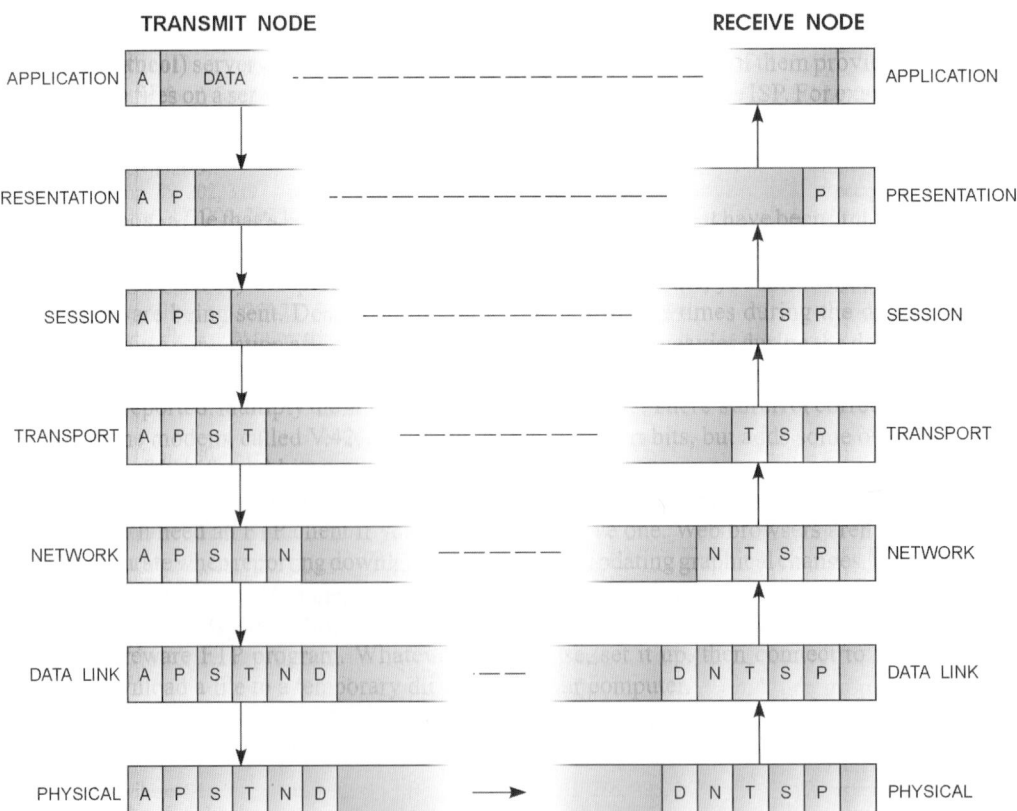

**Figure 5-6
Peer-To-Peer
Communication
Within OSI
Layers**

The OSI model accomplishes this through **logical connections** in the application, presentation, session and transport layers. These layers are involved in end-to-end communication, designated by the dotted lines in Figure 5-6. The network and data link connection is also logical, but these two layers include all points between the end stations. The physical layer is the only level at which data is actually transmitted or received.

How is a logical connection made? First of all, a logical connection doesn't actually exist in a physical sense. The only "real" connections are found at the physical layer. The logical connections are facilitated through the communication software, and can be found in the **headers** preceding the data message. In Figure 5-6, a header is added to the message, at each level, down to the physical layer. A header isn't needed here, because the physical layer isn't a logical connection. The receiving node successively strips the headers as the data percolates up through the layers of the model.

What is in the header? Adding headers at the various levels is similar to the telephone numbers dialed when you make a phone call. They precede your message and contain not only routing information, but information needed at telephone exchanges for processing the call. The same is true for the OSI model. A network header contains the route that data is to take through the network, but it may also contain a message to the network layer at the other end. For example, the network layer is responsible for regulating the rate at which data moves through a network. Within the header there may be a message providing the receiving network layer pertinent information regarding data rates. With the use of headers appended to the application message, a logical peer connection is made between each layer at both ends of the communication link.

While Figure 5-6 shows all layers being used, keep in mind that it's not always necessary or desirable to include them all. However, the standards committee sought to develop a model that would accommodate present and future developments. Without restricting new technologies, it also facilitates the implementation of the protocols for communications systems at all levels of complexity.

The benefits of the layered approach to the OSI model can be summarized as follows:

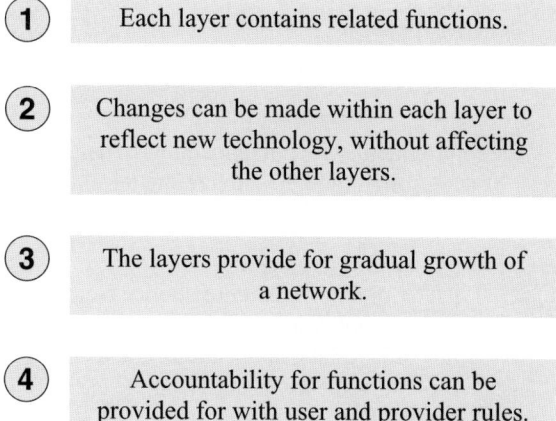

1. Each layer contains related functions.

2. Changes can be made within each layer to reflect new technology, without affecting the other layers.

3. The layers provide for gradual growth of a network.

4. Accountability for functions can be provided for with user and provider rules.

The following sections provide a more detailed overview of the seven layers of the OSI model. It's important to understand that the model is incomplete, in particular in the upper layers. While the OSI has had broad acceptance in the industry, many vendors advertise their products as "look-alikes" or "similar to OSI". Before a look-alike is selected to implement the OSI protocols, it would be wise to thoroughly research the product under consideration.

The OSI model describes the scope of data communications and the various functions of a data communication system.

Application Layer

The application level provides support to those functions that are necessary to initiate the application. This is the only level at which the user has direct contact with the model. The specific application functions that are used obviously depend upon the application itself, and are often a part of its reason for existence.

The Application layer is implemented with user specific software.

It's the final check for ensuring the quality of the lower layers and does so by forming the proper environment to initiate the data transfer.

More and more, this level is being associated with software packages since they contain the components needed to use the software—and this is synonymous with application level functions. For example, airline reservation software requires password IDs for security purposes. The **sign-on procedure** would be an application function since it's a procedure necessary to implement the application of making an airline reservation.

Functions of the application level are:

1. To provide a facility for serving end users.

2. To authenticate user Ids and passwords.

3. To provide for file requests or file transfers.

4. To provide for downline loading (transfer of data from remote host to remote terminal, and vice versa.

5. To determine the quality of service from lower layers. If a problem occurs at a lower layer, the application should incorporate a means of notifying the user, such as an error message.

6. To provide for remote job entry. A remote terminal would be given access to the application maintained in the host, which could be located thousands of miles away.

To provide for utilizing user applications, such as off-the-shelf software for work processing, database management, and spreadsheet preparation.

Examples of specific Application layer protocols include:

- DNS: The Domain Name System (database system used to map host names, IP addresses and e-mail routing).

- FTP: File transfer Protocol (transfers files by copying file from one system to another).

- BootP: bootstrap Protocol (defines how to determine the IP of a diskless system when bootstrapped).

- SNMP: Simple Network Management Protocol (defines packet exchanges).

- TelNet: Tel Net Protocol (provides access to differing nodes or host types).

- SMTP: Simple Mail Transfer Protocol (e-mail).

- NFS: Network File System (Provides for file access to servers).

Presentation Layer

At the Presentation layer, the syntax and format of information is determined.

The Presentation layer ensures that data messages are received in a format that's understood. In order to accomplish this, the Presentation level has to retain the content of a data message while modifying the **syntax** of the data for the end user.

In the earlier example, an EBCDIC message had to be converted to an ASCII message. A **virtual terminal circuit** must be in place to make such a conversion. A virtual terminal circuit describes how data is to be displayed on CRT screens despite coding differences.

The Presentation layer defines fields for **remote data entry** work such as may be found in an inventory system. The operator is required to enter quantities of various items and the presentation layer describes where the data entry fields are located on the screen.

The presentation layer is also responsible for managing special events such as **data encryption** and **foreign language translation**.

NET+ OBJECTIVE
I.1.5

CNST OBJECTIVE
VIII-A

The functions of the Presentation layer are:

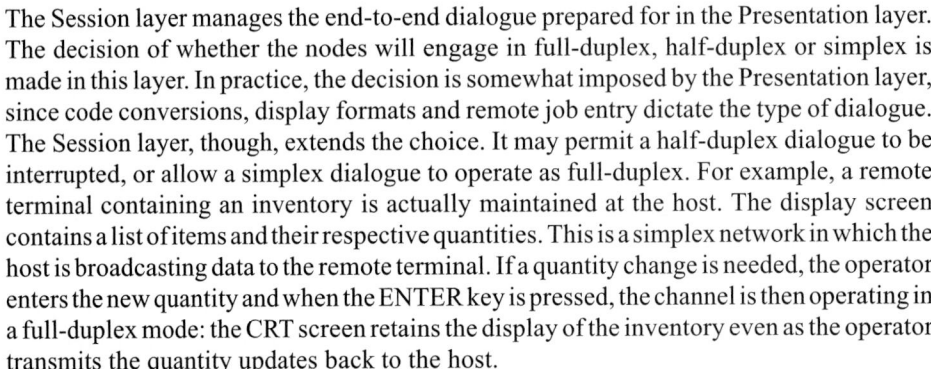

1 To change data syntax in order to meet the needs of the source and destination of the message.

2 To provide for data compression, encryption, and coding.

3 To inform the session layer when to establish a session, as well as when to terminate the session.

Session Layer

The Session layer will determine if the exchange is half-duplex or full-duplex.

NET+ OBJECTIVE
I.1.5

CNST OBJECTIVE
VIII-A

The Session layer manages the end-to-end dialogue prepared for in the Presentation layer. The decision of whether the nodes will engage in full-duplex, half-duplex or simplex is made in this layer. In practice, the decision is somewhat imposed by the Presentation layer, since code conversions, display formats and remote job entry dictate the type of dialogue. The Session layer, though, extends the choice. It may permit a half-duplex dialogue to be interrupted, or allow a simplex dialogue to operate as full-duplex. For example, a remote terminal containing an inventory is actually maintained at the host. The display screen contains a list of items and their respective quantities. This is a simplex network in which the host is broadcasting data to the remote terminal. If a quantity change is needed, the operator enters the new quantity and when the ENTER key is pressed, the channel is then operating in a full-duplex mode: the CRT screen retains the display of the inventory even as the operator transmits the quantity updates back to the host.

As the Presentation level is partly responsible for decisions made in the Session layer, the Transport layer is forced to map the session layer decisions for each session. That is, the Transport layer will be required to know the mode of dialogue of each session.

The Session layer also manages a process called **checkpointing**. A checkpoint is inserted into data messages to allow the session to recover from network failures without losing the complete message. This saves time when large amounts of data have been transmitted and the connection fails near the end of the message.

Since the mode of transmission is determined at this level, **synchronization** must also occur. Synchronizing headers are necessary so that complete messages are received. If the synchronization (which is often the checkpoint) is lost, the Session level can determine that a problem exists. While direct error control isn't a function of the Session level, it is nonetheless implied through checkpointing and synchronizing headers.

The functions of the Session level are:

1 To start and stop data transfer.

2 To provide dialogue control via full duplex, half duplex, simplex, or a combination of these.

3 To provide for the recovery from network failure without losing the complete message.

4 To provide mapping functions to the transport layer for each session. The transport layer may then provide identical destinations via multiplexing for sessions whose address lay in similar routes.

Transport Layer

The transport layer is concerned with end-to-end communication across the network. It is the last of the upper layers to be concerned with only end users. It establishes a **virtual path**, from transmitter to receiver, by assigning end users an address without regard to their position in the network. The end-user address is supplied to the Network layer, where the actual route to the address will be determined.

The quality of data transfer is determined at the Transport layer.

Since this layer is involved with making sure that data messages are accurately received, there's an implied quality-control function of the transport layer. The original intent of the layer was to establish a virtual channel from user to user, but this has proved to be difficult. In addition, the specific protocols for the Transport layer were written in 1984, then revised in 1986. The explosion of computer networks since then took the standards organization by surprise, and the protocols were written after they were already needed in the industry. Without specific protocols, data communications users implemented what they had, which were Network, Data Link and Physical layer protocols. This was unfortunate, because the Transport layer has very powerful capabilities. The 1986 revisions provided for choices that permitted many functions that were being handled by the Network layer to be a formal component of the Transport layer.

These functions are called **classes of service**, and they allow data to be sent over a network with varying degrees of quality. They are, strictly speaking, Transport layer functions. However, as previously stated, network users implemented them in the Network layer as they were needed, at a time before the established protocols were specifically written.

NET+ OBJECTIVE
I.1.5

CNST OBJECTIVE
VIII-A

The Transport layer also assigns end-user addresses in the header, appended to data messages. These end-user addresses are mapped onto machine addresses in the network layer. The Transport layer doesn't care where the end user is, because the Network layer is left the job of finding the user. The implication of the network address is that networks are permitted to change in structure and topology without a consequent software change in this layer. Many networks require a **user password**, and a **user ID**, before access to the network is granted. This is an example of a Transport address mapped onto a Network layer address.

Don't let Transport layer addressing confuse you, because it may or may not be used in a network. What is used though, almost universally, are Network and **Data Link** layer addresses. A Network layer address is a logical convention. An IP address is a Network layer address. On the other hand, a network node also has a physical address, or Data Link address. This is typically called the MAC address (from the MAC sublayer of the Data Link layer), and it specifies the physical location of a node.

In establishing a virtual path between end users, the Transport layer has been given the function of determining if multiplexing is called for. This is done by evaluating each dialogue session established in the Session layer.

Data rate flow control is handled by the Transport layer. Data rates between networks may be much slower than within a network. The **gateways** connecting networks are composed of relays, and the switching time of the relays contribute to the time it takes data to arrive at the destination. The Transport layer regulates **flow control** by allocating data amounts. Data **allocation** is initiated by the transmitting station, and provided for in the Transport header. The sending station will send a message to the receiver asking it how much data should be sent. The receiver responds—through a transport header tacked-on to a message traveling back to the sender—by specifying the amount of data it can receive in a future time period.

The Transport layer provides for **negotiation** concerning flow rates. In the discussion of allocating data rates, the transmitter asked the receiver the amount of data it could handle. The negotiated function begins with the transmitter offering a data rate to the receiving station. The receiver may accept the offer, or it may send back a counter-offer. The counter-offer must be less than the original offer from the transmitter. In most Transport level services, negotiations don't extend beyond the counter-offer. If the transmitter won't accept the counter, it disconnects the channel.

Data rates may be allocated by the receiver, or negotiated between the transmitter and receiver. In practice, negotiation is the more efficient of the two since the initial proposal may be acceptable, whereas allocation will always require the receiver to respond to the request from the transmitter. This means that, at a minimum, the allocation method will require three exchanges, while the negotiated method will require two exchanges.

Once the data rate is agreed upon, the Transport layer has to ensure the data will be delivered at this rate. Consider, if the data rate of the transmitting station network is 10 MBPS and the data rate of the receiving station network is 1 MBS, how will the Transport layer reconcile the data rates? If messages are allowed to flow continuously from the high-speed network into the low-speed network, the receiving buffers of the slower network are sure to overflow, and much of the message will be lost. The answer lies in blocking messages into smaller units, and timing the release of the blocks through the network. Messages from the slow receiving end back to the high-speed transmitter can be **concatenated**.

A concatenated network is one in which message blocks are transmitted over various links that may run in parallel. The effect is to speed the arrival time of the data. Once the messages are blocked, they're arranged in **packets** at the network layer. A data packet contains link addresses within a network, whereas the **data block** contains only the end-user address.

The functions of the Transport layer are:

(1) To assign **end-user addresses**.

(2) To regulate data flow using allocation or regulation.

(3) To provide message blocking and concentration.

(4) To evaluate the need for multiplexing.

(5) To provide for the sequencing of blocked messages. This provides the receiver with a way of checking to see if all messages have been received.

(6) To provide for error detection and recovery. This is provided for in sequencing and service classes.

(7) To provide five classes of service intended to match the needs of the user to network characteristics.

Class 0

Class 0 fulfills the minimum requirements of the Transport layer: Message **block segmentation**, end-user addressing, error detection, **block sequencing**. If a problem occurs in the Network layer, the Transport layer has no method for recovering; consequently, the connection will be lost. The ability of a network to recover from problems is described in terms of "**robust**". A class 0 network is not very robust, since it can't recover from problems easily.

Class 1

Class 1 is somewhat more robust than class 0. Recovery from problems is accomplished by adding a sequencing header to each block of data. If a problem causes the transmission to be interrupted, the end receiver notifies the end transmitter about the last block received (identified by the **block sequence number**), and the transmitter resumes with the next block in the sequence.

Class 2

Class 2 is primarily concerned with flow control. It allows multiple transport layers to be transmitted through a single channel. This is done by multiplexing the various layers. As in class 0, the class 2 has no provision for recovering if the network crashes.

Class 3

Class 3 is identical to class 2, except that a recovery capability is added. A class 3 Transport layer recovers from a problem by reestablishing the connection, and by adding sequencing headers, as in class 1.

Class 4

Class 4 is the same as class 3, except it's more tolerant to problems such as a lost data block, out-of-sequence blocks, or received blocks that are heavily distorted. Any of these problems can cause a network failure in the previous classes, but a class 4 includes the capability of resolving the problems and continuing the transmission. A class 4 Transport layer is the most robust of the five classes.

Examples of Transport layer protocols are:

- TCP: Transmission Control Protocol (used to establish a reliable connection between client and server).

- UDP: User Datagram Protocol (simple TCP implementation, without the reliability).

Network Layer

CNST OBJECTIVE
IV-A

NET+ OBJECTIVE
I.1.5

The Network layer implements the virtual path created in the Transport layer. It determines the actual route the data will take. As the Transport layer separates data into blocks, the Network layer organizes the blocks into **data packets**. The number of packets are negotiated by inter-network nodes. There may be from 1 to 4,095 packets, or more.

> Routing to the correct network node occurs at the Network layer.

Routing techniques in the network layer may be **fixed**, **stochastic** or **adaptive**. A fixed route will be carefully mapped, and won't change. A stochastic route carries the promise of eventual delivery. These routes are usually selected for short messages, called datagrams, sent between two stations that frequently communicate. An adaptive route is a concatenated path, and it's based upon the performance of the network. The routes described above are determined by the class of service selected in the Transport layer. For example, Class 4 service would probably be sent along an adaptive route, since it contains capabilities for recovering from out-of-sequence data blocks.

The Network layer also implements link multiplexing when called for in the transport layer. This marks a departure from the end-to-end functions of the higher levels. It's the first layer to become directly involved in the links connecting end-to-end users, serving as an interface. It must provide a virtual path to the upper layers across multimedia networks and various data rates, and incorporates means of detecting and recovering from errors, if called for in the upper layers. Many of the details of these functions are delegated to the Data Link layer, but the Network layer implies the tasks to be conducted at the Data Link layer by its selection of routes, packetizing data, etc.

Since this layer is responsible for forwarding packets onto other stations, it includes a logical addressing scheme. The most common one is called **Internet Protocol** (IP), and it consists of a logical address that may be assigned to a node, or to an entire network. The address is logical, meaning that the location of a node with an assigned IP can be moved anywhere, or transferred to another node as needed. This frequently occurs with Internet service providers when they assign so-called "dynamic" IPs to their subscribers. Each time you log onto the Internet (logons occur at the Transport layer), you're assigned a different IP, although your physical address remains unchanged.

CNST OBJECTIVE
VIII-A

Routing data packets across a network is the responsibility of the Network layer. To achieve this, we use routers. A router contains huge libraries of logical addresses, as well as the next "hop" needed to get to a logical address. The widespread use of routers has spawned many routing protocols, and these will be described later in this book.

NET+ OBJECTIVE
I.4.1

It may be of some (possibly confusing) interest to you that the functionality of the Transport and Network layers was blurred for many years, and the confusion carries over to the present. The original intention of the Transport layer was to assign logical addressing, while the Network layer was to route data packets from a physical address, assigned at the Data Link layer, to the Transport layer's logical address. Note that this is in contradiction to the functions of these two layers as described above. Remember, networking vendors needed the functions of the Transport layer before it was finalized, so they did the best with what they had—which was the Network layer. Consequently, many Transport layer functions were designed into equipment that, technically, operated at the Network layer.

By the time the Transport layer was finished, the need for it was in full swing. This is unfortunate, because the Transport layer is the most useful of all the layers in the OSI model for wide area networking, such as Internet applications. At present, the accepted functions of these two layers are as previously described.

The functions of the Network layer are:

(1) To establish which routes the data will take.

(2) To provide for multiplexing of data channels.

(3) To separate data into packets.

(4) To detect and recover from errors.

(5) To establish, maintain and terminate connections.

Examples of Network layer protocols include:

- IP: Internet Protocol (used in conjunction with TCP, UDP but has no reliability).

- IGNP: Internet Group Management Protocol (used to multicast hosts or routers).

- BGP: Border Gateway Protocol (used to communicate between systems with different underlying protocols, and routers).

CNST OBJECTIVE
IV-B

- RIP: Routing Information Protocol (most widely implemented router protocol).

- ARP: Address Resolution protocol (allows mapping of 32-bit IP addresses to other types of addresses).

- RARP: Reverse Address Resolution Protocol (allows mapping between some other address type and 32-bit IPs).

- OSPF: Open Shortest Path First (a newer and better version of RIP).

- ICMP: Internet Control Message Protocol (communications network control information such as errors within an IP frame).

Data Link Layer

The Data Link level contains two sublayers: **Logical Link Control** (LLC) and **Medium Access Control** (MAC).

NET+ OBJECTIVE
I.1.5

The purpose of the Data Link layer is to provide for the accurate exchange of data between nodes. A node refers to communication equipment that receives and/or transmits. A data message may be shifted through many nodes enroute to the destination, but the Data Link layer is concerned only with point-to-point communication between nodes. A final, Data Link layer will be appended to the message frame, along with a Start Of Frame (SOF) header (or, flag, as it's commonly called), End Of Frame (EOF) header, and a field dedicated to detecting errors of the entire frame. This includes the headers from the various layers.

When discussing data communications protocols, the functions of the Data Link layer are most frequently described. One of the reasons for this is that this layer is heavily documented, and its protocols are widely adhered to within the industry. In fact, sublayers of the Data Link layer form the foundation for the majority of local area networks in place today. This section offers general information concerning this layer, and later sections in this chapter and the next provide detailed information.

CNST OBJECTIVE
IV-B

CNST OBJECTIVE
VIII-A

The Data Link layer contains two major subdivisions: the **Medium Access Control** (MAC) protocols, and the **Logical Link Control** (LCC) protocols. The MAC sublayer refers to techniques the workstation uses to gain access to a network. For example, in a Ethernet network, it's forbidden for two stations to have access to the network simultaneously. But how do the two stations "know" that their data is about to collide? The MAC protocols specify that a **disallowed voltage** (1.5V) will appear across the network if this occurs. Channel monitors will read the voltage, and both stations wait awhile before trying again.

The MAC sublayer is a logical convention, but it's closely, and inseparably, involved in the Physical layer implementation. Chapter 6 includes detailed descriptions of the MAC sublayer protocols.

The LLC protocol describes conventions to be followed by the sender and the receiver to ensure that the link's communication is reliable. The LLC provides for a distinct interface to the Network layer.

The functions of the Data Link layer are:

1 To provide for frame formatting.

2 To provide error detection and recovery.

3 To provide access methods for networks.

4 To provide for transmission between nodes.

Examples of Data Link protocols include:

- PPP: Point-to-Point Protocol (an improved version of SLIP).

- IEEE 802.2: IEEE protocol for the Logical Link Control sublayer.

- SLIP: Serial Line Internet Protocol (provides for serial encapsulation of IP frames).

- CSLIP: Compressed Serial Line Internet Protocol (an improved version of SLIP).

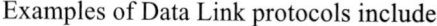

Physical Layer

The Physical layer is the only layer at which actual data bits are encountered.

The purpose of the Physical layer is the actual transmission of data. It includes the physical connection of stations to the network, and the parameters of electrical signals such as the amplitude and **polarity** of data bits. The processes of full-duplex, half-duplex and simplex are accounted for at this layer with the proper selection of channel media, and the formatting of data flow that may travel as synchronous or asynchronous, as well as serial or parallel.

The OSI physical layer is quite detailed in its description of the acceptable mechanical and electrical parameters. Unfortunately, the protocol hasn't been widely accepted in the United States. Instead, the standard implementation of the physical layer has been the EIA/TIA-232 **Electronic Industries Association** (EIA) standard. It's similar to the OSI protocol, and because of it's widespread use in the United States, is recognized as an OSI alternate.

The functions of the physical layer are:

1 To transmit data between connections.

2 To provide electrical and mechanical parameters for data connections, and channel media.

3 To activate and deactivate physical connections.

The Physical layer has been implemented with a combination of Data Link and Physical layer protocols, most notably the IEEE 802 series of protocols. The reason these are included as a Physical layer protocol—since they're typically referred to as Data Link protocols—is that they include many physical characteristics. The correct way to describe the IEEE protocols is as a combination of logical Data Link attributes and Physical layer attributes, since they cross the boundary between the MAC sublayer and the Physical layer.

Physical layer protocols are:

CNST OBJECTIVE
IV-B

- ISO 2110: which defines the encapsulation of IP datagrams for Ethernet.

- IEEE 802.x: which defines the structure of frames in an IEEE 802 network.

The OSI reference model is a blueprint for data communications. It competes for acceptance with IBM's **System Network Architecture** (SNA), and Digital Equipment Corporation's **Digital Network Architecture** (DNA). Both are displayed, along with the OSI model, in Figure 5-7. IBM has indicated a gradual support for the OSI protocols. This won't be too difficult because the OSI and SNA are quite similar. Digital's DNA model is considerably different. It lends itself more to local area networks than to large distributed systems.

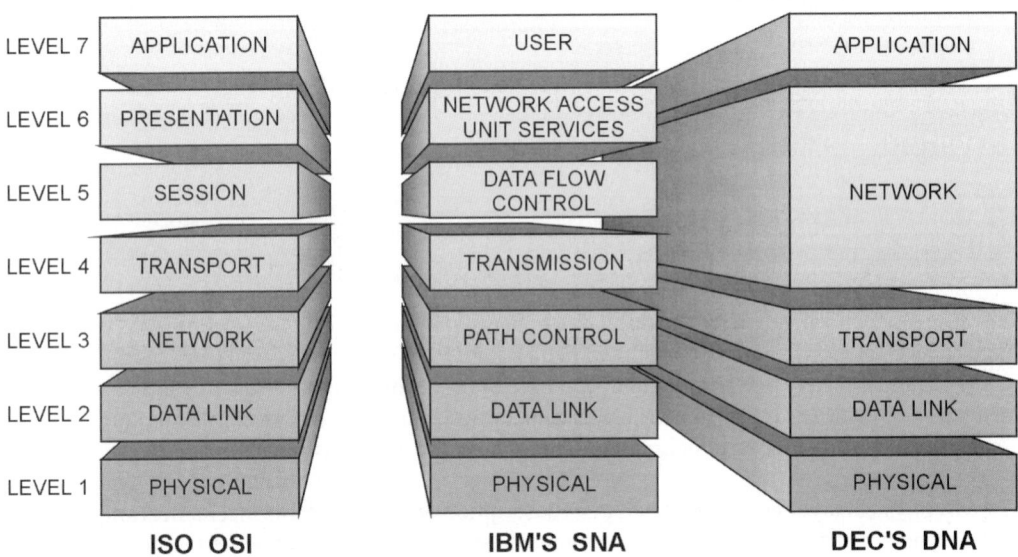

Figure 5-7 Comparison of OSI,SNA and DNA Data Communication Reference Models

The Data Link protocols of DEC are full-duplex character-oriented whose frame format is significantly different than HDLC or SDLC (framing methods used at the Data Link layer). There has been widespread support for the intent, if not the specific implementation, of the OSI model. But as far as DEC is concerned, it's not likely to grow since the company was bought by Compaq and Cabletron Systems, and now doesn't exist. Even if large vendors such as IBM never comply with all OSI requirements, its proprietary model still serves to present a logical framework for pursuing the broader issues of data communications systems.

DATA LINK PROTOCOLS

As mentioned previously, the lower levels of the OSI reference model have been the most widely documented, and have been implemented on a broad scale. There is considerable standardization at the Data Link layer, and in those cases where differences exist among vendors, they tend to be slight, particularly for protocols noted for high speed and efficiency.

The Data Link layer is responsible for detecting errors, packaging data into frames, and seeing to it that the data is reliably transmitted between nodes of a network. The network may be a simple, point-to-point arrangement involving a PC and printer, or it may be quite sophisticated and involve thousands of computers sharing information across the public telephone network. As the complexity of a network increases, so does the probability of errors, delays, mis-routed data, and so forth. Protocols at this layer have evolved with the growth, and needs, of various network configurations.

In the particular case of local area networks, the Data Link layer must frame data as well as deliver the frames to the network in a systematic and organized manner. This has led to a subdivision of the Data Link layer, as shown in Figure 5-8.

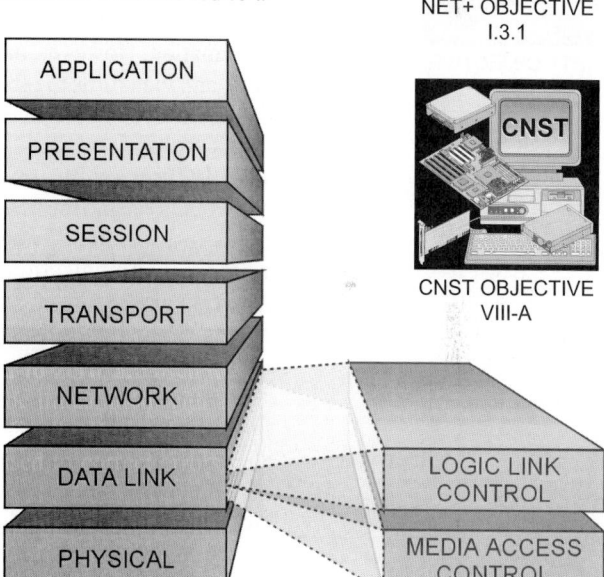

The **Medium Access Control** (MAC) sublayer is involved with the techniques that network stations employ in gaining access to the network. A MAC protocol describes a specific type of network. There are MAC protocols for Ethernet, Token ring, etc. Each protocol requires that specific frame formats and conventions be followed before a station will be permitted to use the network.

The MAC sublayer has a physical implication, since its function revolves around accessing the physical network. The IEEE 802.x protocols, while conventionally described as if they were Data Link layer protocols, are actually Physical layer protocols. Ethernet (IEEE 802.3), for example, is a MAC Protocol. But the IEEE standard is quite specific about physical characteristics such as cabling, signaling parameters, and so forth. It's difficult to separate the MAC sublayer from the Physical layer, and it's not unusual to see it represented as crossing the interface between Data Link and Physical layers. This is, in fact, proper and correct.

Figure 5-8 Data Link Sublayers

The Medium Access Control level describes methods stations use to gain access to a communication channel.

The MAC layer is subordinate to the Logical Link layer (LLC). It can, and sometimes will, operate independently and without the need for the LLC network interface. However, in any network larger than a small, peer-to-peer topology, the LLC will manage the flow of frames in and out of a node. The MAC sublayer will ensure that the frames are properly formatted, have a means of checking for errors, and will see that the source and destination nodes have a valid—and physical—address. Since the MAC sublayer is bound in the protocol literature of standards organizations, such as the IEEE for local networks, it will be discussed in Chapter 6, Local Area Networks.

The other sublayer—the **Logical Link Control** (LLC)—describes the specific conventions that a sender and receiver must follow when exchanging data. Essentially, the LLC is a description of frame formats, the content of frames, and the dialogue that has to be exchanged between the sender and the receiver in order to exchange messages. The Logical Link Control sublayer of the Data Link layer will be described in detail in this chapter.

LOGICAL LINK CONTROL PROTOCOLS

The Logical Link Controls describes the conventions a sender and receiver follow to ensure the data flow is orderly. They correspond to the IEEE 802.2 standards.

NET+ OBJECTIVE
I.3.1

The LLC is a software interface that is situated between the software that controls network interface hardware, such as the **Network Interface Card** (NIC), and the communication software running on a network such as IP, or NetBIOS. The NIC is where the MAC controls—Ethernet, Token Ring—are found. LLC information will be encapsulated in a MAC frame, but the MAC function will remain unaware of the LLC, or any other layer information. However, once an exchange is initiated between nodes, the MAC frames its data, and then turns the frame over to the LLC, where the LLC information is placed in the MAC frame (in the **Information field**).

The LLC uses a software structure, called a **Service Access Point** (SAP), that interfaces the Network layer and the MAC sublayer. The SAP is responsible for communicating the MAC frame to a specific communications software, such as IP, NetWare, NetBIOS, etc. In this way, the communications software is made aware that a frame will be sent across the network, and the MAC layer will be made aware of the type of software running on the network. Figure 5-9 lists several vendors and their assigned SAP values.

Vendors who want to be compliant to the Data Link layer of the OSI model (and most do at this level) must have a SAP value assigned to their Network layer software. As you'll see shortly, the SAP is a formal field in the LLC frame.

CNST OBJECTIVE
IV-B

Before examining the intricacies of the LLC, let's clarify some LLC terminology.

- Type I LLC: In a Type I LLC, frames from the MAC sublayer pass through the LLC SAP, and the only service they receive is to differentiate them for the particular communications software running at the Network Layer.

- Type II LLC: Type II LLC also differentiates MAC frames for the Network Layer software, but the frames are also given sequence numbers so that the receiving node can track individual frames, and send back an acknowledgment that they were received. This creates a level of network reliability not found in a Type I network.

- Connectionless Service: A connectionless protocol doesn't track the sequence of frames or packets of frames. A connectionless service, at the Data Link layer, is Type I LLC. Connectionless frames may also be referred to as Datagrams, a carryover from IBM.

- Connection-Oriented Service: A connection-oriented protocol assigns sequence numbers to frames passed into the LLC, and tracks them at the receiving node. At the Data Link layer, it's the same as Type II LLC. Because the frames are tracked, connection-oriented protocols are also called reliable.

SAP VALUE	VENDOR
00	Null LSAP
02	Individual LLC Sublayer Management Function
03	Group LLC Sublayer Management Function
04	IBM SNA Path Control (individual)
05	IBM SNA Path Control (group)
06	ARPANET Internet Protocol (IP)
08	SNA
0C	SNA
0E	PROWAY (IEC955) Network Management & Initialization
18	Texas Instruments
42	IEEE 802.1 Bridge Spanning Tree Protocol
4E	EIA RS-511 Manufacturing Message Service
7E	ISO 8208 (X.25 over IEEE 802.2 Type 2 LLC)
80	Xerox Network Systems (XNS)
86	Nestar
8E	PROWAY (IEC 955) Active Station List Maintenance
98	ARPANET Address Resolution Protocol (ARP)
BC	Banyan VINES
AA	SubNetwork Access Protocl (SNAP)
E0	Novell NetWare
F0	IBM NetBIOS
F4	IBM LAN Management (individual)
F5	IBM LAN Management (group)
F8	IBM Remote Program Load (RPL)
FA	Ungermann-Bass
FE	ISO Network Layer Protocol
FF	Global LSAP

Figure 5-9 Vendor
SAP Values

LLC Frame Format

The frame format for the LLC sublayer is shown in Figure 5-10. Keep in mind that the LLC frame will be imbedded in the information (also called data) field of a MAC frame. Shortly, we'll look at frame exchanges at the LLC layer, but keep in mind it's assumed the LLC content is embedded in a MAC frame.

- Information Field: The Information Field contains user data as well as frames from any of the seven layers of the OSI Reference Model. Remember that lower layer frames are encapsulated by upper layer frames. But in the case of the LLC sublayer, it's encapsulated by the MAC sublayer frame. The maximum size of this field is determined by the MAC protocol; 1,500 bytes for Ethernet.

- Destination Service Access Point contains the Network Layer identifier used to differentiate between communication software types.

- SSAP: Source Service Access Point contains Network Layer identifier used in differentiating the type of communication software.

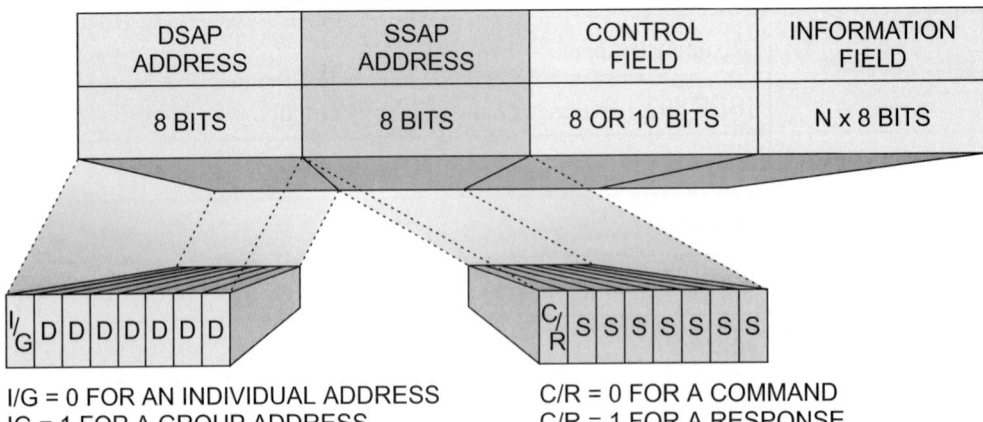

Figure 5-10 LLC Sublayer Frame Format

CNST OBJECTIVE
I-A

Notice in Figure 5-10 that a single SAP is listed for each of the network software vendors. But the LLC frame contains both a Source field, and a Destination field, which implies different logical locations. The reason for this is that the same value is used in both the DSAP and SSAP fields. How, and why, would a destination and source identifier be the same value? There are two ways to look at it.

First, consider the network from the viewpoint of a MAC frame. A user on the network has gained access to the network using a MAC protocol (Ethernet), placed data in the information frame, and is now ready to send that framed data to another user. The MAC frame contains the physical address of the destination user, but the frame doesn't know how to get there. Fortunately, we have a Network layer protocol to get the frame to the physical address contained in then MAC frame.

Let's assume that the network protocol is NetWare (Novell). The DSAP makes any necessary changes to the MAC frame so it can be sent across the Novell network. That is, the source/identity of the network software (NetWare) is specified by the SAP value.

Now, when a frame is returned from the distant user, the NIC card (in the local computer) needs to know what type of communication software was used to send the frame to the physical address assigned to it. Since it's a Novell network running NetWare at the Network layer, the destination node is informed about this by an SAP identifier for NetWare.

This may seem silly, but you have to understand the problem. The LLC sublayer, as with all other layers of the model, is supposed to be independent of subordinate layers, and the Network layer is supposed to be independent of the LLC sublayer. In other words, it's not the Network layer's responsibility to figure out how to tell the LLC what type of software it's running. It's responsible for getting frames to the right address. Therefore, the destination and source SAP values are the same in the LLC frame.

However, the LLC does need to know what type of MAC frame is being used. Technically, a standard LLC frame can be placed inside any type of MAC frame—Ethernet, Token Ring, etc. The type of frame is indicated in the **Control field** of the LLC. This field also tracks frames that are sent and received, as well as provides link administrative information to the LLC and Network layer.

The length of the Control field may be one or two bytes, depending on the size of the **address fields**. The longer the address, and the more frames sent without an acknowledgment, the longer the control field needs to be.

The 8-, or 16-bit Control field is the heart of the LLC functions, so we need to take a detailed look at how it works. But, before doing so, let's distinguish between character, and bit-level, protocols.

CHARACTER AND BIT-LEVEL PROTOCOLS

Character, and bit-level, protocols refer to the information content of a frame of data. Character protocols divide data into **alphanumeric** characters, and send the letters (or numbers) one-at-a-time, in a frame. Or they may block the characters into a group, and send the block in a single frame.

A bit-level protocol doesn't distinguish between alphanumeric characters. It's concerned only with streams of data. All modern, high-speed networks use bit-level protocols.

The significance of using character, or bit-level, protocols is one of efficiency and speed. When data is sent through the long-distance telephone network, the time required to send information translates to money. If data can be sent quickly, and with a minimal amount of overhead, using the telephone system will be cheaper. Bit-level protocols offer much greater efficiency than do character protocols. This means that data can be sent more cheaply using bit-level frames, and the long-distance switching facilities will be able to handle more information, since they won't have to spend as much time switching individual calls.

Character-oriented protocols such as Asynchronous and BSC, and the bit-level protocol HDLC, are three very different types of Data Link protocols. This chapter will describe each one in detail. As with many aspects of data communications, one type is not necessarily better than another. The user application is the best indicator for deciding which type is appropriate for a given situation. For example, HDLC would represent overkill, if used with a PC and printer.

Character-Oriented Protocols

There are two types of character protocols: asynchronous and **Binary Synchronous Communications (BSC)**. Asynchronous is the simplest in structure and practice. It's the protocol followed by most personal computers and printers. BSC is an improved version of asynchronous. The efficiency is higher in BSC because **throughput** (the ratio of header to information content) is higher. BSC is an older, IBM protocol. It may be found in distributed networks as well as local area networks.

Asynchronous Character Protocols

Asynchronous protocols usually have high over-head, low efficiency, and are typically found in PC environments.

The frame format for asynchronous data is shown in Figure 5-11. When no data is being sent, the line is in the idle state. The idle state for asynchronous communication is a logic 1. The EIA/TIA-232 specification defines a logic 1 (or **mark**) as a voltage between –3V and –25V. A logic 0 is defined as the voltage between +3V and +25V. The 6V region between –3V and +3V is ambiguous, and may result in the receiver interpreting it as either a logic 1 or 0. The **ambiguous region** permits about .5V of noise to be included with the data without interfering with data detection at the receiver. For this reason, it is preferable that the broadest range be used between a mark and a **space**.

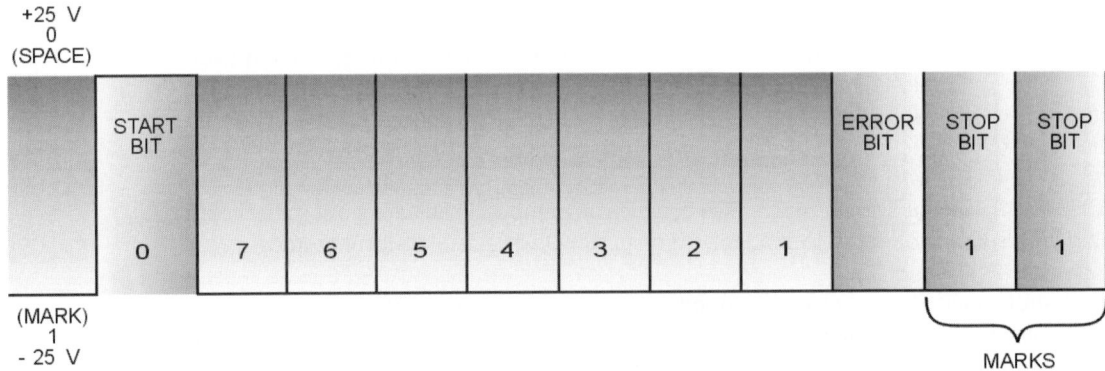

**Figure 5-11
Asynchronous Data
Frame Format**

When the receiver is ready to transmit, a **start bit** is sent, and the line goes to a logic 0—the space condition. Immediately following the start bit are 7 or 8 data bits. Typically, the data being sent is an ASCII character, which requires 7 bits. If 7 bits are sent, an error bit immediately follows the data. The method of error detection for asynchronous protocols is usually odd or even parity. After the error bit-or eighth data bit-one or two **stop bits** are added. Occasionally, one and a half bits are used to indicate the end of the character. The stop bits place the line in the mark state. This tells the receiver the transmission is over. If another character is to be sent, it will be initiated with the mark to space transition of a new start bit.

Standardization of asynchronous communications is achieved through equipment selection. Both the sender and receiver must agree on the following:

(1) The status of an idle line; mark or space.

(2) The number of character bits; 7 or 8.

(3) The number of bits to indicate stop; one, one and a half, or two.

(4) The voltage levels used to represent logic 1 and logic 0, and the bit time.

It is possible for two devices to communicate, even if they don't agree on the parameters listed above, but the exchanges will probably be erratic, and prone to errors. Of all the data link protocols, asynchronous is probably the least standardized. For this reason, the parameters described above are usually user-selectable. An example of asynchronous communication is shown in Figure 5-12.

(1) STX ————————————————————▶

(2) ACK ◀————————————————————

(3) TEXT ————————————————————▶

(4) EOT ————————————————————▶   **(a)**

(5) ACK ◀————————————————————

(1) STX 000 0010

(2) ACK 000 0110

(3)

TEXT	START	7	6	5	4	3	2	1	EVEN PARITY	STOP	
W	0	1	0	1	0	1	1	1	1	1	1
A	0	1	0	0	0	0	0	1	0	1	1
I	0	1	0	0	1	0	0	1	1	1	1
T	0	1	0	1	0	1	0	0	1	1	1

(4) EOT 0000 0100

(5) ACK 0000 0110   **(b)**

A computer is shown communicating with a peripheral using ASCII code. The precise dialogue will follow the conventions of the actual equipment used. The computer is transmitting the word "wait" to the peripheral. The dialogue is composed of ASCII symbols, and an EIA/TIA-232 connection is assumed to exist between the devices, with the appropriate interface pins being utilized.

Figure 5-12 Communications Dialogue Between a PC and Printer

The computer may initiate the transfer by sending a **Start of Text** (STX) to the peripheral. The peripheral is ready to receive the text, and returns an **Acknowledge** (ACK) signal to the computer. This tells the computer to send the data.

The actual binary representation of this protocol is shown in Figure 5-12(b). As each letter is sent, a start bit is transmitted followed by seven ASCII data bits. In this example, error detection has been included with the use of the even-parity format. Each character is ended by adding two stop bits.

Immediately following the "w", the "a" is sent, beginning with another start bit. Each letter, or character, of the word "wait" is transmitted to the peripheral. Each letter contains its own header—start, parity, stop bits. Since each character is segregated, asynchronous is classified as a character protocol.

The computer tells the peripheral it's finished transmitting by sending an **End of Transmission** (EOT) signal. The peripheral responds with an ACK signal, and the line returns to the idle state.

A close examination of Figure 5-12 will illustrate the inefficiency of asynchronous communications. A single frame of text has 11 bits, 4 of which comprise the header and trailer (start, parity, 2 stop bits) for a text throughput of 64%.

The throughput is found by:

$$TP = ((\text{total bits} - \text{header})/\text{total bits}) \times 100$$

$$TP = ((\text{total bits} - \text{header})/\text{total bits}) \times 100$$
$$TP = ((11 \text{ bits} - 4 \text{ bits})/11 \text{ bits} \times 100$$
$$TP = (7 \text{ bits}/11 \text{ bits}) \times 100$$
$$TP = 64\%$$

Even if we elect to dispense with the parity bit, and use only one stop bit, the text throughput is only $7/9 = 77.7\%$. But to present a more accurate picture, the protocol dialogue needs to be included. In Figure 5-12, 65 bits are exchanged in order to send the word "wait" which has a total of 28 bits. This means the total throughput is only 43% (28/65).

Binary Synchronous Communications

Synchronous protocols offer higher efficiencies and lower overhead. BSC is a synchronous protocol.

Binary Synchronous Communications (BSC) protocols are an improvement over asynchronous, by increasing the efficiency. BSC was first formulated and implemented on a wide scale by IBM. Much of the syntax and convention used with BSC has roots in IBM networks. As you may have guessed, BSC is widely used by IBM.

In asynchronous communications, the receiver and transmitter achieve synchronization with the start and stop bit sent with each character. BSC achieves synchronization for a much longer time. Several thousand bits may be sent before the sender and receiver check their synchronization. A longer bit stream results in lower overhead and higher throughput rates; consequently, the efficiency of BSC is higher than that of asynchronous.

The frame format of BSC is illustrated in Figure 5-13. BSC is a variable frame format, which means that there is no minimum or maximum word length in the data field. In practice, restrictions may be imposed by the receiver. If the receive rate is slower than the transmit rate, the transmitter limits the size of the data field so the receiver has a chance to catch up. In some networks, the data field size is specified—say, at 128 bytes—to allow for error correction and precise synchronization.

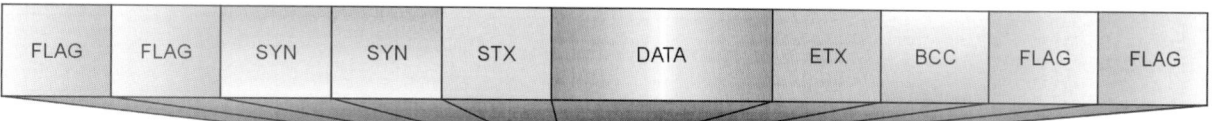

Figure 5-13 BSC Frame Format

The first two fields of the frame are identified as **flags**. The purpose of the flag is to establish bit synchronization between sender and receiver. The flag consists of alternating 1's and 0's. For example 10101010 is common, as is 01010101. Each flag is 1 byte (8 bits). The BSC flag may also be referred to as a **Packet Assembly/Disassembly** (PAD).

The PAD isn't always needed. In modern data processing equipment, **SYN characters** may be adequate for synchronizing transmitter and receiver. The SYN field establishes character synchronization between sender and receiver. The SYN characters are sent as 0010110. At this point, the receiver has captured bit synchronization of the transmitter, and it achieves character synchronization by counting 8 bits of the SYN characters. This process is similar to modem training.

Next to be transmitted is the STX signal (0101000 ASCII). The STX tells the receiver that the header information has ended, and a block of text is beginning. Following the data field is the **End of Text** (ETX) character, which signifies the end of the data field. The binary ASCII for ETX is 1100000. As mentioned earlier, there are no maximum or minimum length requirements in the data field.

Once the receiver detects the ETX, it performs a **Block Character Check** (BCC). The BCC is an error-detection algorithm. If the receiver finds a discrepancy in the BCC (one or two bytes in length), it will ask the transmitter to send the frame again. Once the frame has been transmitted, two more flag fields are transmitted.

One of the goals of the more powerful protocols is **text transparency**. The transmitter must have the flexibility to send any character or bit sequence in the **information field**, without crashing the transmission. The information field may contain a control character as a part of the text. For example, a frame of data may include the phrase "A BSC frame includes an ETX field". ETX is a control character, and tells the receiver when the information field is finished. The receiver will then do a **block check** for errors. In fact, there may be hundreds of characters to follow the sentence in the above example, but they wouldn't be received since the receiver interpreted ETX as the end of the field. The bit pattern for an ETX is 1100000. If this same bit pattern were to occur in the text, even in another context, the receiver is likely to read it as an ETX.

BSC provides for text transparency as an option. That is, an operator may or may not want to use it. Obviously, if it's not initiated, the likelihood of errors will increase. If it is selected, a technique called **character stuffing** is used.

Synchronous protocols provide virtual communication with the use of byte stuffing.

Character stuffing provides the text transparency for BSC. Within the frame, all control characters are prefaced with a **Data Link Escape** (DLE) character, as shown in Figure 5-14. All control characters (STX, ETX, BCC, etc.) have a DLE placed before them. By stuffing the DLE character in the frame, the receiver interprets the control character as a true control instruction, rather than simply another text element.

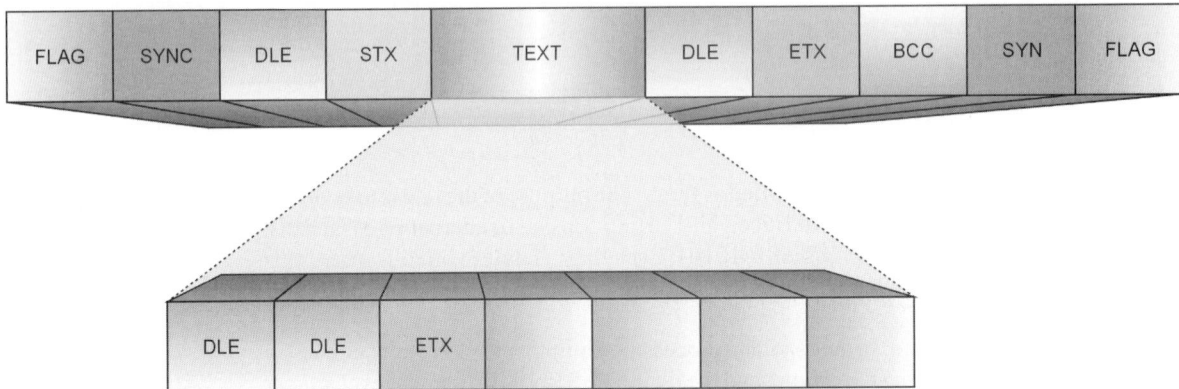

Figure 5-14 BSC Text Transparency Using Character Stuffing

If, in the data field, a character or bit stream identical to a control character is included, the transmitter places a DLE before it as well. But, in order to separate it from true control characters, two DLE's precede control characters in the text. In this way, the sentence from the previous example would read:

"A BSC frame includes a DLE DLE ETX field."

Once the receiver reads the two consecutive DLE characters, it will properly interpret the characters as a part of the text, and not as an instruction. The receiver strips the extra DLEs from the text so that the message reads as originally intended. The receiver determines text transparency has ended when it stops receiving consecutive DLE's. A portion of text from the data field has been expanded in Figure 5-14 to illustrate character stuffing.

An example of data transfer using the BSC protocol is shown in Figure 5-15(a). The sequence of events are shown as follows:

 The sender sends an 00000101 in ASCII to the receiver, the **Enquiry** (ENQ) control character. The sender tells the receiver it has something to transmit and asks if the receiver will participate.

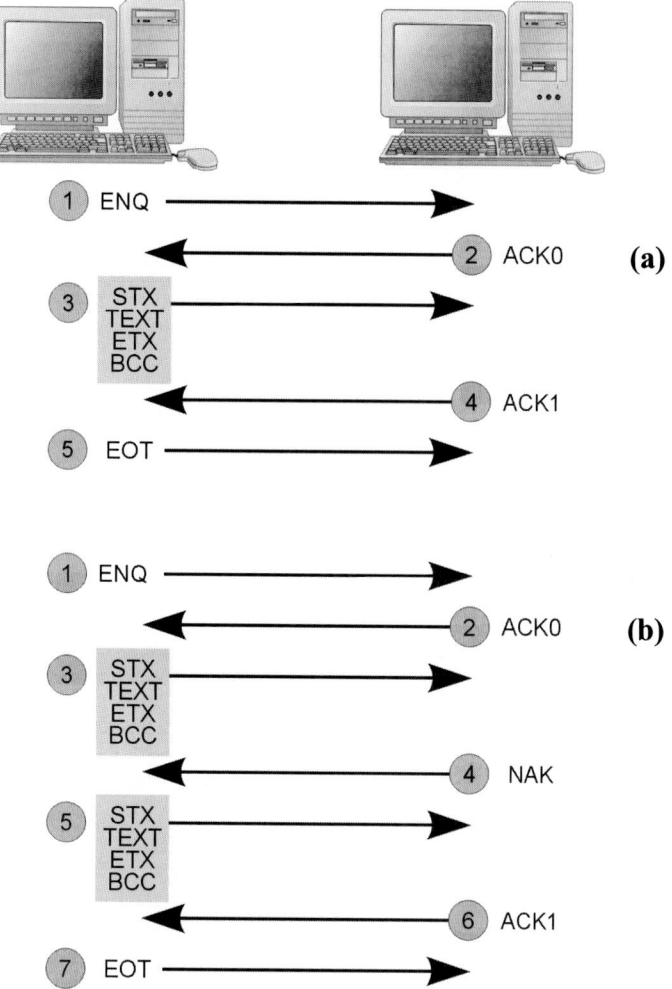

(a)

(b)

Figure 5-15 BSC Communication Dialogue Between Two Computers

(2) The receiver responds with an **Acknowledge (ACK)**, which is 00000110 in ASCII. The receiver is telling the sender it has received the request to transmit and it can receive data. There's not a direct corresponding mnemonic in ASCII to ACK0 or ACK1. In BSC, an extra bit is added to acknowledgments. The extra bit is either a 0 or 1. If a 0 is added, even acknowledgment has been used; if a 1 is added, odd acknowledgment has been used. ACK0 and ACK1 are used alternately at the end of message blocks and are incorporated in error detection.

(3) Upon receiving ACK, the transmitter sends the data frame. Typically, the DLE sequence isn't shown, but you should assume DLE precedes the STX field and the ETX.

4 The receiver does a block check to determine if the frame contains any errors. No errors are discovered and the ACK is transmitted to tell the sender the message was received. Notice the acknowledgment is ACK1.

5 The sender receives the ACK and transmits an **END of Transmit (EOT)** character, which is 00000100 in ASCII, to tell the receiver it has nothing more to transmit at this time. The line now returns to the idle state.

What would happen if the sender transmitted an ENQ, and the receiver was occupied? The receiver would send back a **Wait Before Transmit Affirmative Acknowledgment** (WACK). This means the receiver is temporarily unable to accept new data, but has received the sender's request. The sender will continue to transmit ENQ until an ACK is received.

Each protocol provides for handshaking through the use of dialogues. Examples of handshaking dialogue are command/response, primary/secondary, and ACK/NACK.

Figure 5-15(b) illustrates the sequence of events when the receiver does a block check and finds an error.

1 The sender transmits an enquiry to the receiver.

2 The receiver acknowledges the enquiry.

3 The message is transmitted.

4 The receiver does the block character check and discovers an error. A **Negative Acknowledgment** (NAK) is sent to the transmitter, telling it the last block of data was incorrectly received, and to transmit it again.

5 The sender complies with the receiver's request and retransmits.

6 This time the message is correctly received, and an ACK is sent back to the transmitter.

7 The transmitter sends an EOT and the line is placed in the idle condition.

BSC offers about a 20% efficiency improvement over asynchronous. For the amount of data sent by either, a considerable number of overhead bits are needed to get the data to the final destination. Both of these protocols are half-duplex. BSC may be transmitted over a four-wire, full-duplex channel, but it remains half-duplex, requiring an ACK or NAK after each frame. Although the data field has no length restrictions, it is in practice usually a multiple of 8 bits, with 128 bytes common for IBM machines. If a frame of this length is sent, the transmitter has to wait for a response from the receiver before continuing. In the more versatile protocols such as BSC, the transmitter must retain the data frames sent to a receiver until it receives an ACK. It may then discard the data and transmit a new frame.

From this you can see that transmitting BSC over a full-duplex channel saves time, since an ACK or NAK can be sent back over the second channel. However, the receiver and transmitter aren't communicating in a full-duplex fashion, since the exchanges aren't simultaneous. The more common BSC **mnemonics** are listed in Table 5-1, along with a description of their use. **Bit-oriented** protocols, discussed in the next section, are full-duplex protocols that incorporate text transparency within the design of data frames.

Table 5-1 Common BSC Mnemonics

BSC MNEMONIC	DESCRIPTION	ASCII CODE
SOH	Start of Heading	0000001
STX	Start of Text	0000010
ETX	End of Text (indicates the end of a series of character blocks)	0000011
EOT	END OF TRANSMISSION (indicates the sender has completed the transmission)	0000100
EMG	Enquiry	0000101
ACK	Acknowledge	No Corresponding ASCII Character ACK0 = DLE0 (001000 0) ACK1 = DLE1 (001000 1
DLE	Control Character Delineator	0010000
NAK	Negative Acknowledgment	0010101
SYN	Synchronous Idle	0010110
ETB	End of Transmission Block	0010111
WACK	Wait Before Transmitting	No Corresponding ASCII Character DLE = 0010000 0111011
DISC	Mandatory Disconnect (the sender terminates the link)	No Corresponding ASCII Character DLE EOT = 0010000 0000100
TTD	Temporary Text Delay (the sender isn't ready to transmit but wants to keep the link)	No Corresponding ASCII Character STX ENQ = 0000010 0000101

Bit-Oriented Protocols

Bit-oriented protocols have the highest efficiency and lowest overhead. SDLC, HDLC, and LAPB are bit-oreinted protocols.

Asynchronous and BSC are character-oriented protocols. Transmitter and receiver synchronization is dependent upon synchronizing the characters. The character synchronization occurs for each character in asynchronous, and for blocks of characters in BSC, making it the more efficient protocol. Data transparency is an option with BSC, rather than a feature designed into the protocol.

The bit-oriented protocols improve upon the efficiency of BSC as well as incorporate text transparency into the frame—that is, transparency is an integral part of bit protocols. The BSC user has the option of not using text transparency, which reduces overhead, but at a cost of increasing errors.

In 1968, the CCITT (now the ITU) developed the bit protocol, **High-Level Data Link Control** (HDLC). Many dominant vendors of the time worked closely with CCITT in developing the protocol. The result has been the evolution of several protocols that are very similar to HDLC. In addition to HDLC, the following are the major bit protocols in use today. They're functionally the same as HDLC.

1   Normal Response Mode (NRM): HDLC grew out of IBM's SDLC protocol, and NRM was, and still is, used in many point-to-point (PPP) topologies.

2   Link Access Protocol (LAP): An early implementation, it's been replaced by LAPx series protocols.

3   Link Access Protocol-Balanced (LAPB): LAPB is common in X.25 telecommunications networks, as well as local area networks.

4   Link Access Protocol, ISDN D-Channel (LAPD): The HDLC-equivalent framing for ISDN and Frame Relay networks.

5   Link Access Protocol for Modems (LAPM): Referenced in ITU's V.42 standard for error-correcting in modems.

6   Synchronous Data Link Control (SDLC): IBM stand- ardized Data Link protocols, and the CCITT used SDLC as the basis for HDLC.

We'll take a look at two implementations of the bit-level protocol HDLC: In the normal response mode, and LAPB which is a peer-to-peer technique.

> There are three types of LLC sublayer protocols; asynchronous, synchronous, and bit oriented.

HDLC

In 1979, the **International Standards Organization** formally adopted **High-Level Data Link Control** (HDLC) as the protocol for the Data Link layer of the OSI reference model. It should be considered the dominant Data Link protocol, and those protocols mentioned in the previous section should be considered as subsets of HDLC. In actual operation, the differences are slight.

As previously mentioned, HDLC is a full-duplex protocol, but it's not restricted to full-duplex channels. It was designed to accommodate a broad range of paths from sender to receiver, so that if a receiver is located at the end of a multipoint network, HDLC can still be used. This is true even for low speed, broadcast (simplex) networks.

Text transparency was achieved with BSC by stuffing characters into the data stream to notify the receiver of true control characters. As will be shown shortly, HDLC provides for transparent text by incorporating it directly into the frame and does so with a single bit, which saves considerable overhead. This system of integrating text transparency makes HDLC a very efficient protocol.

Recall that BSC depends upon sending an ACK or NAK between each frame (half-duplex operation) to ensure proper sequencing and reception of frames. HDLC has the capability of transmitting seven, and in some cases 128, frames without an acknowledgment. On a full-duplex channel, acknowledgments are often "piggybacked" onto data frames between transmitting stations. HDLC-formatted data travels considerably quicker than BSC on channels of the same bit-per-second rate.

The ISO has provided for two modes of HDLC operation. Stations on a network may be configured for a **Normal Response Mode** (NRM), or an **Asynchronous Response Mode** (ARM). The normal-mode stations are designated as **primary** or **secondary**. Within a network, only one primary is permitted, but there may be many secondaries. Before transmitting, the secondaries must first have permission from the primary, and in addition, they are forbidden to transmit to one another. The primary may transmit at any time to any, or all, of the secondaries. Each of the secondaries has a unique address that's provided for in the HDLC frame format. The address of the primary is implied. Since the secondaries may only transmit to the primary, their frame addresses are their own. In this way, the primary is able to determine which secondary data frame has been received.

In the asynchronous response mode, the primary/secondary designation is followed, but the secondaries may transmit to the primary without the express permission to do so. However they're still forbidden to exchange data among themselves. An alternative form of this mode is the **Asynchronous Mode-Balanced** (AMB), which is commonly implemented as LAPB. A network configured in the balanced mode disregards the primary/secondary terminology. Stations on the network are **peers**, and may communicate with one another, as well as initiate and stop exchanges.

Of the three modes, the normal response mode is common in distributed networks where nodes are supplying collected data to a host. A data acquisition network, used in an industrial setting that monitors process control variables, may use NRM. Some older server-based LANs used the ARM mode. Most modern LANs use the LAPB version as well as many wide area protocols, such as Frame Relay and X.25.

The frame format for HDLC is shown in Figure 5-16. Notice that the LLC frame has been singled out for clarity. HDLC is a layer 2 protocol, so it's inclusive of the MAC and LLC sublayers. It's worth mentioning that layer 2 is a logical level of the OSI model, so it doesn't specify physical network parameters, such as connector pin-outs, signal levels, data rates, and so on. These are found elsewhere, in the IEEE 802 standards for example. As you'll see in the next chapter, the frame format for Ethernet is almost identical to HDLC. This is as it should be, because the 802 protocols include physical characteristics which are subordinated by the logical characteristics at layer 2, and defined in HDLC.

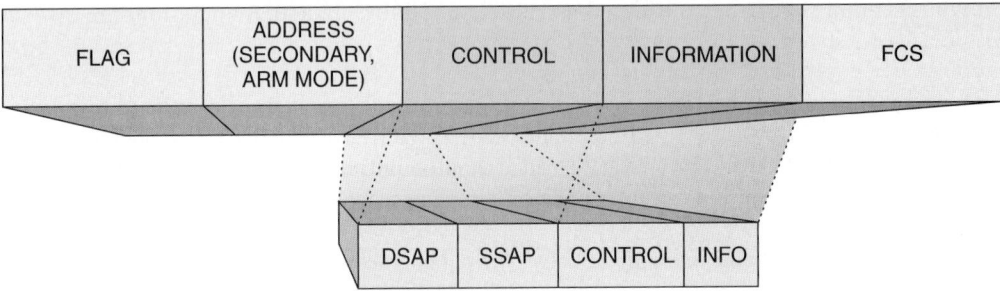

Figure 5-16 HDLC Frame Format

The frame is bound by flags with a fixed bit pattern of 01111110. This pattern tells the receiver that a data frame is to follow. The ending flag has the same pattern, and when consecutive frames are transmitted, the same bit pattern is used to signify the beginning of the next frame. This means that the Start and End fields of consecutive frames use the same bits. HDLC also contains an abort flag which has the bit pattern 01111111. If for some reason, a sending or receiving station wanted to disconnect a link, it would send the abort flag, and the seven consecutive 1's would tell the receiving station to disconnect.

The next field in the frame is the Address field. In the balanced mode, the frame contains a address field for the source node as well as the destination node. It's 1 byte in length, and in the figure, only the address of the secondary station is shown. The length of the address can vary up to six bytes in length in the balanced mode, depending on the implementation. Ethernet, for example, permits a 6-byte address.

The Control field, which is actually a portion of the LLC sublayer, is also 1 byte long, and is the heart of HDLC. The Control field identifies the type of frame being transmitted. It contains a sequencing scheme so that the primary and secondaries can track those frames that were received error-free, and it includes a method of polling, used between stations, that identifies the last frame sent. The actual length of the Control field can vary up to two bytes. More will be said about the Control field shortly.

The Information field contains user data. The length of the field isn't specified; that's left to the communicating stations. While its length is indirectly a function of the Data Link layer, it is formally determined by the Transport layer. The reason for this is that error-free, end-to-end communication is partly determined by machine capabilities. The receiving station contains buffers that store data while it's being fetched into a computer. If the Information field is made too long, the buffers will overflow, and parts of the message will be lost. In practice then, the Information field has some predetermined length. Actual sizes may vary from less than a hundred bytes, to well over ten-thousand bytes.

The **Frame Check Sequence** (FCS) field, also called the **Cyclic Redundancy Check** (CRC) field, is used for detecting errors. The field is two bytes in length, typically. However, it may also be longer. For a large frame of, say, 16kB, a 32-bit CRC field is needed to ensure all errors are caught. The IEEE 802.3 standard for Ethernet stipulates a 4-byte CRC field.

At a minimum, an HDLC frame contains 32 bits between flags—8 in the address, 8 in the control field, and 16 in the Frame Check field. Any frame less than 32 bits between flags is considered invalid, and will produce a NAK response from the LLC sublayer. In Chapter 6, you'll see a distinct difference in IEEE 802 frames regarding the minimum length. In all fields, except for the FCS and the Information field, the **Least Significant Bit** (LSB) is the first to be transmitted. The order of transmitting in the Information field is left to the user. For reasons that will be explained in the chapter on Error Control, the use of significant bits in the FCS field is misleading.

With 8 bits in the address field, 256 stations can be assigned unique addresses. If there are more than 256 stations, HDLC has an extended mode which allows any number of stations to be addressed. The extended mode is identified with a logic 0 in the LSB of the Address field. Remember, the LSB is the first bit of the Address field to be transmitted. The number of address bits are usually extended by **octets**, or by 8 bits at a time. If the LSB of the address field is a 1, the frame will be in the basic format of 8 bits in the Address field. When the **extended addressing mode** is used, the Control field is also extended. An additional 8 bits are added to the basic length, to give a total Control field length of 16 bits.

There are three types of HDLC frames: **information**, **supervisory** and **numbered** frames. These are identified by the bit configuration of the Control field, as shown in Figure 5-17. The Information frame is used to carry user data from primary to secondary, or from secondary to primary, or, in the balanced mode, between any two stations. Supervisory frames are used to acknowledge correctly received frames, as well as to inform stations of various operating conditions such as a busy station, a station that's not busy, and to reject bad frames. **Unnumbered frames** contain special link functions, such as initiating the link between stations, disconnecting the link, setting the frame mode (normal, asynchronous, balanced synchronous) or for tracking nonsequenced frames.

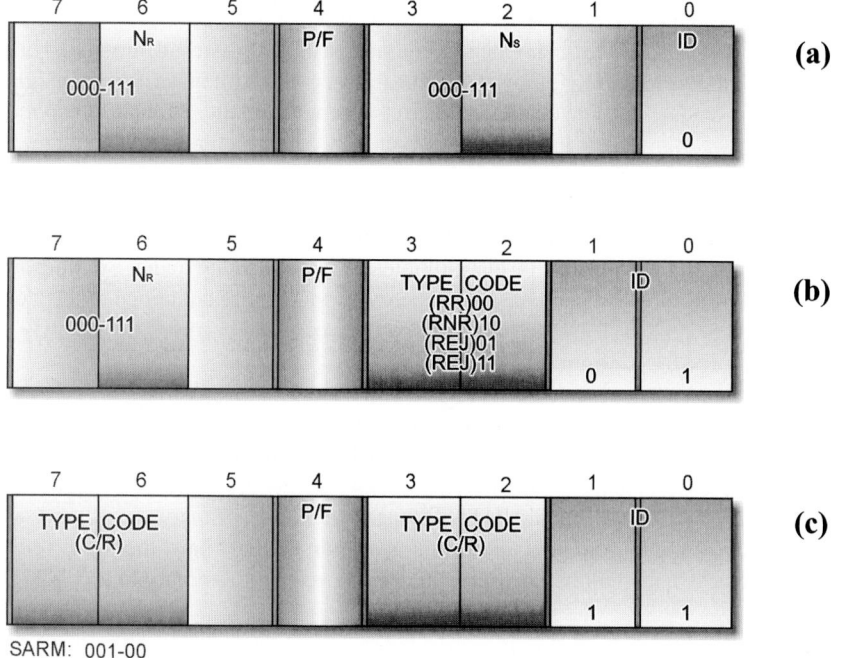

Figure 5-17 HDLC Control Fields

The Control field of the Information frame is shown in Figure 5-17(a). The LSB of the field is the frame identifier. A logic 0 in this bit identifies the frame type as Information. The receiver will expect user data to be contained in the frame. In bit place 4 is the P/F, or **Poll/Final bit**. The purpose of the P/F bit depends upon the usage. When a primary sends a frame to a secondary, and sets the P/F to 1, it's a poll to the secondary. Another way to say it is that if the P/F bit is set to Poll, the secondary must make a response. For example, if the primary were to ask the secondary if it has data to send, and the primary had set the P/F bit, the secondary would have to respond as to whether or not it had data to send.

If the primary sends data to the secondary and required an acknowledgment that the data was received, it would set the P/F bit. The secondary would then send a frame back to the primary to say it had received the frame. The foregoing illustrate the polling function of the P/F bit. But note that the terminology of "primary" and "secondary" means the same as source and receiver in the balanced mode.

It's also used to indicate the final frame of data sent. For example, if a secondary had five data frames to send, it would transmit the first four frames with the P/F bit set to 0. In the fifth frame, the secondary would set the P/F to 1. This tells the primary that the fifth frame is the last frame to be transmitted from the secondary. In this case, the P/F bit is used to tell the receiving station which frame is the final frame. In either a poll or final situation, a P/F bit set to a logic 0 is ignored.

The NS and NR fields of the Information frame are used to maintain proper sequencing between primary and secondary stations. **NS** refers to the **number of frames sent**, while **NR** refers to the **number of frames received**. The HDLC system of frame sequencing ensures that no frames are lost between stations. For example, if a primary has three frames to send to a secondary, it would sequentially number the frames sent in the NS field. The first frame to be sent would have a count of 000, the second frame to be sent would have a count of 001, and the third frame would have a count of 010. The count sequence permits the receiving secondary to check each frame. If a frame is lost, the primary will be able to tell because it won't be able to account for the frame in the sequential count. The NR field has a similar function, except it's sent to the transmitter from the receiver, telling it the number of frames received.

The 3-bit send and receive fields means that up to eight frames can be sent, until the field reaches the maximum count of 111. Once the maximum count is reached, the fields rollover to 000. HDLC allows for seven frames to be sent and received without an acknowledgment. A primary can send seven consecutive frames of data without the secondary responding. This represents a significant improvement over BSC, in which an acknowledgment is required after each frame of data.

The bit configuration for the Control field of a Supervisory frame is shown in Figure 5-17(b). Supervisory frames don't have Information fields. They're used to manage conditions on the link. The conditions of a primary or secondary encounter are contained in the Control field of the Supervisory frame. The first two bits of the Control field identify it as Supervisory by the 01 configuration.

As with information frames, a P/F bit is contained in the Supervisory Control field. The P/F bit is set to 1 when a Supervisory frame is used to ask a secondary if it has data to send. The secondary must respond to the command. Supervisory frames are also used to acknowledge receipt of data frames. If a secondary had sent four frames to the primary, the primary would acknowledge with the NR count equal to four. The frame would have the P/F bit set to 1 because, in this case, it would indicate the final frame sent from primary to secondary.

The Supervisory frame also contains a Type field in bit position two and three. The type of Supervisory frame describes several conditions of the link between stations on the network. The **Receive Ready** (RR) is used when stations—usually the primary, or source of data—sends polls asking if there's any data to be sent, or to tell the destination node that it has data to send. It's a general indication that conditions on the network are normal. **Receive-Not-Ready** (RNR) is a busy response from a polled station. Most of the time, RNR is sent because the polled station's buffers are filled, and it's unable to accept new data. The polling station will continue to poll (using an RR Supervisory frame) until the busy condition is cleared. A **Reject** (REJ) is sent when a **data error** is found in the CRC field. When a problem is discovered by the receiving station, it ignores any frames received after the bad frame. It sends a REJ frame back to the transmitter with the NR count set to the last good frame that was received. For example if the third frame received by a secondary contained an error, it would send an REJ frame, with the NR reading a count of two, back to the primary. This tells the primary that the first two frames were received successfully, so it retransmits beginning with the third frame.

Another type of Supervisory frame is the **Sequence Reject** (SREJ). If, after the third frame, a secondary received an Information frame with NS=5, it would generate a SREJ to the primary. The SREJ would contain NR = 4. This tells the primary that the frames received after the third frame were out of sequence, and the primary would retransmit, beginning with the fourth frame. If this doesn't clear the problem, the secondary would respond with an REJ.

The Control field for Unnumbered frames is shown in Figure 5-17(c). An Unnumbered frame is used to start the link exchange, as well as to disconnect links. The first two bits of the field identify the frame as Unnumbered. The fifth bit is called a **Poll/Final** bit, and is used in the command/response methods of Information and Supervisory frames. If a station sends an Unnumbered frame with the P/F bit set to 1, a response is expected. As with Supervisory frames, there are several types of Unnumbered frames. The particular type of frame is given in a 5-bit **command/response** code (also called modifier function bits). For example, to initiate a link exchange, a series of Unnumbered frames are sent, back-and-forth, between two stations. The following text describes the procedure.

A station initiates the exchange by sending an Unnumbered Command frame (P/F =1) to a receiver. The initiator contains a **Set Asynchronous-Response Mode** (SARM). The SARM is a command asking another station to set up a link. The receiving station sends back an **Unnumbered Acknowledgment** (UA). At this point the link has been established. Supervisory frames will now be sent, with RR in the Type field, and Information frames containing the user data will be exchanged. If the initiator wishes to terminate the link, a **Disconnect** (DISC) Unnumbered frame is sent to the receiver. HDLC allows for up to 32 commands and 32 responses for Unnumbered frames. The type of frame depends on the network mode—asynchronous response mode, normal response mode or asynchronous balanced mode.

The SARM or **Set Normal Response Mode** (SNRM) are from IBM's SDLC. As local and wide area networks proliferated, IBM extended the number of frames that could be transmitted, up to 128, without requiring an acknowledgment. This mode is called **Set Asynchronous Balanced Mode Extended** (SABME), which is pronounced sa-bim-ee. The IEEE incorporated SABME directly into the 802.2 protocol, and it should be considered the standardized implementation of HDLC.

The Information field must be free to transmit any bit sequence in order to achieve data transparency. Recall that the header and trailer flags are 01111110. For HDLC to be truly transparent, it must be able to include in the Information field bit streams containing 6 consecutive 1's without a receiver interpreting the 1's as a trailing flag. HDLC uses a technique called **bit stuffing**, or **zero insertion**, as shown in Figure 5-18. When the sender finds 6 consecutive 1's in the Information field, a bit generator inserts a 0 after the fifth bit.

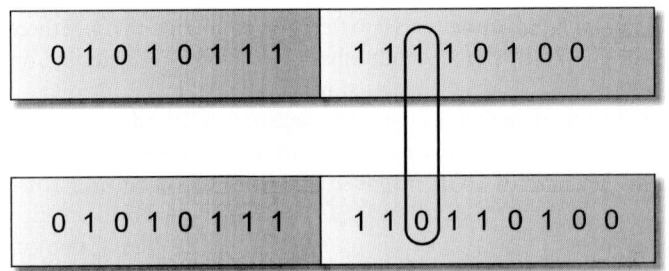

Figure 5-18 HDLC Text Transparency Using Character Stuffing

| 0 1 0 1 0 1 1 1 | 1 1 1 1 0 1 0 0 |

| 0 1 0 1 0 1 1 1 | 1 1 0 1 1 0 1 0 0 |

Bit-oriented protocols provide virtual communications using bit-stuffing

At the receiver, the 0 is deleted. Bit stuffing ensures that any number of consecutive 1's greater than five will be a flag, or an error.

The last field is the **Frame Check Sequence** (FCS). The FCS is analogous to the BCC of BSC. It's used to detect errors.

The HDLC Control field, DSAP and SSAP all constitute the LLC sublayer information, while the remainder of the HDLC frame comprises the MAC sublayer information. Together, the two form a Data Link frame. Now, we're ready to look at data flow using HDLC. The first example shows HDLC in the normal response mode, and is illustrated in Figure 5-19.

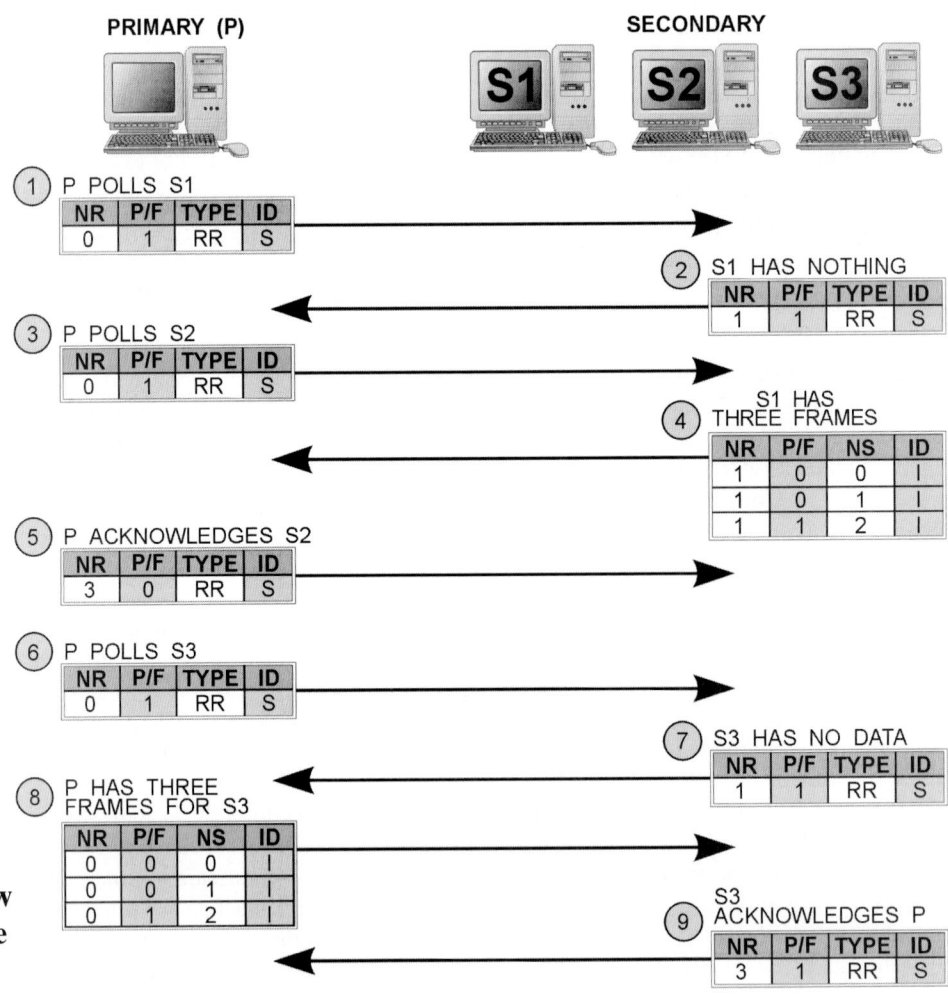

Figure 5-19 HDLC Data Flow Between Primary and Three Secondary Stations

A single primary (P) is communicating with three secondaries (S1, S2, S3). The Control field is the only portion of the frame shown, but you should assume that each exchange includes flags, address, FCS, and an Information field for Information frames. The Address field contains the address of the secondary station, and the primary address is implied. If a secondary sends data to the primary, the Address field is the address of the secondary. The devices in Figure 5-19, then, are operating in the normal response mode.

The data flow sequence is as follows:

1 The primary polls S1, to determine if the station has data to send. The primary has transmitted a **Supervisory frame**—the I/D field would read 01. The NR field reads 0 because the primary has received no data from the secondary. The **P/F** bit is set to 1. Recall that when the P/F is set in a Supervisory frame from a primary, a polled secondary must respond. The Type field is set to **RR**. This means the primary is asking the secondary if it has data to send.

2 S1 has no data, and replies to the primary demand for a response with a Supervisory frame. Notice the NR field is set to 1. This tells the receiver S1 received one frame of data. The Type field is set to RR, telling the primary it acknowledges the poll, and is ready to transmit data—but the P/F bit is set to 1, meaning this frame is the final frame from S1, and, by inference, S1 has no data to send.

3 The primary polls S2. Again, a Supervisory frame is sent. The **Control field** is identical to the poll in step 1. Keep in mind, the **Address field** will differ since S2 has its own address.

4 S2 has three Information frames to send. In each frame the NR field is set at 1, acknowledging receipt of the polling frame from step 3. In the first two frames, the P/F bit is off, but in the third frame, it's been turned on, telling the primary the third frame will be the final frame sent. The secondary knows it will send three frames, and numbers the frames sequentially in the NS field. The frames are transmitted one after another. The primary doesn't acknowledge the transfer until it reads the P/F bit set in the last frame.

5 The primary acknowledges receipt of the data by sending a supervisory frame to S2. The NR field reads a count of 3. This tells S2 that the receiver accepted three frames, and detected no errors. The P/F bit is turned off, because it has no function in an acknowledgment. The type of supervisory frame is RR.

6 The primary polls S3.

7 S3 has no data to send.

8 The primary has three frames to send to S3 and transmits three information frames. Note that the NS field indicates the number of the frame sent, not the number of frames sent.

9 S3 acknowledges the correct receipt of three frames by returning a Supervisory frame to the primary. Here, the NR field shows the actual number of frames received (3), not the number of the last frame received (2).

There's some variation in the actual implementation of HDLC. For example, a secondary reply to a primary poll may not update the NR field (Figure 5-19, step 2). In some cases, a primary will acknowledge receipt of secondary data in an Information field. If, in step 5, the primary had data to send to S2, it would send Information frames with the NR field set to 2. The set NR field would acknowledge that the primary had received two frames from S2.

An example of a **data error** is shown in Figure 5-20. In this example, the primary is communicating with a single secondary.

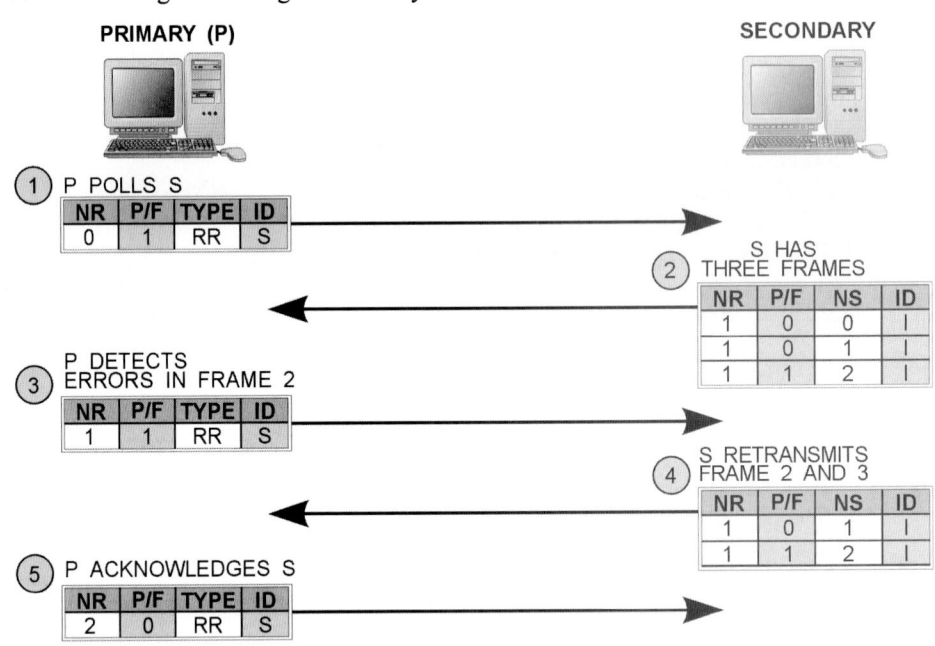

Figure 5-20 HDLC Error Control

The data flow is as follows:

1 The primary sends a Supervisory frame to poll the secondary.

2 The secondary sends three frames of data to the primary.

3 The primary detects an error in the second frame during a frame sequence check. The primary doesn't stop the secondary from transmitting; it simply ignores any data received after the error frame. In the last frame, the P/F bit is turned on, and the secondary waits for an acknowledgment.

4 The primary transmits a Supervisor RR frame with an NR count of 1. The secondary interprets the frame as a positive acknowledgment that the first frame was received, but not the second and third.

6 The primary sends an acknowledgment with the NR counter set to 2, indicating the last two frames were received correctly.

5 The secondary retransmits frames 2 and 3. Frame 2 has NR=1 to acknowledge the primary's step three frame. P/F=0 since frame 2 isn't the last transmitted frame. NS=1 since this is the second frame, and ID=I because it's an Information frame. The third frame has the P/F bit=1 because it's the last frame, and the NS=2, since it's the third frame.

In order to avoid confusion, the number of frames transmitted without an acknowledgment is seven—the maximum count of the NR field. But keep in mind, HDLC allows up to 128 frames to be sent. Sending so many frames without an acknowledgment might not be a good idea. Suppose an early frame, perhaps the third, was corrupted. The receiver wouldn't get an acknowledgment that the remaining 125 frames had been ignored until after they were sent. HDLC may also use REJ rather than using an RR, or an **unnumbered frame** may be used to convey link problems.

In the LAPB mode, the connection must first be set up before any data is sent. To do so, the source station sends an unnumbered SABME frame to the destination node. Figure 5-21 shows the sequence as viewed from a **protocol analyzer**. In order to make it easier to follow events, the data has been placed in a tabular format. The setup occurs in the first four lines. The remaining lines show data exchanges between two nodes.

Line #	Source	Dest.	Sub-layer	C/R	DSAP	SSAP	Type	P/F	NR	NS
1	Node_A	Node_B	LLC	C	FO	FO	SABME	P	--------	--------
2	Node_B	Node_A	LLC	R	FO	FO	UA	F	--------	--------
3	Node_A	Node_B	LLC	C	FO	FO	RR	P	0	--------
4	Node_B	Node_A	LLC	R	FO	FO	RR	F	0	--------
5	Node_A	Node_B	LLC	C	FO	FO	I	F	0	0
6	Node_A	Node_B	LLC	C	FO	FO	I	P	0	1
7	Node_B	Node_A	LLC	R	FO	FO	RR	F	2	--------
8	Node_B	Node_A	LLC	C	FO	FO	I	P	2	0
9	Node_A	Node_B	LLC	R	FO	FO	RR	F	1	--------
10	Node_A	Node_B	LLC	C	FO	FO	I	P	1	2
12	Node_B	Node_A	LLC	R	FO	FO	RR	F	3	--------
13	Node_B	Node_A	LLC	C	FO	FO	I	P	3	1
14	Node_A	Node_B	LLC	R	FO	FO	RR	F	2	--------
15	Node_A	Node_B	LLC	C	FO	FO	I	F	2	3
16	Node_A	Node_B	LLC	C	FO	FO	I	P	2	4
17	Node_B	Node_A	LLC	R	FO	FO	RR	F	5	-------

Figure 5-21 HDLC LAPB Data Exchange

A protocol analyzer will show specific layers of data, or all layers. You select the level of detail, typically from a list of menu options. In Figure 5-21, the LLC sublayer has been selected. The DSAP and SSAP are FO, which is Novell NetWare. In other words, NetWare is running at the Network Layer during this transaction. Since these fields remain constant throughout the exchange, no more will be said about them.

1 Node_A sends a SABME frame to Node_B. This sets up the link as LAPB. Node_A has sent a command (C) frame which means it expects a response from the destination node. To reinforce this, the Poll (P) bit is set. Node_B must acknowledge the command from Node_A.

2 Node_B sends back a response (R) in an Unnumbered Acknowledgment (UA) frame. Node_B, by sending the UA, is telling Node_A that it's not busy and that the link between the two of them is consistent—they're both using FO at the Network Layer. Although Node_A expects to see the P/F bit set to F, it's irrelevant. Node_B wouldn't set it to P because that would instruct Node_A to send back a response (R), which it couldn't do because it hadn't received a command (C) from Node_B.

3 Node_A sends a Receive Ready (RR) command (C) to Node_B, with the Number Receive (NR) field set to 0. It's telling Node_B that it is ready to send data, and that its NR field should be set to 0, because no frames have been sent yet.

4 Node_B responds (R) with a RR frame that has NR=0. This is an acknowledgment that its NR field is indeed set to 0. This exchange is like synchronizing watches in the LLC sublayer.

At this point, the link has been set up, and the two stations can send data frames back and forth. The remaining lines do just that. But one station will send a couple of frames before getting an acknow- ledgment from the destination. Although it could send as many as 128, this isn't likely to occur except in very slow WANs, and LANs in which the server is overloaded. In fact, if a destination node doesn't send back an acknowledgment every four or five frames, you should suspect a problem. You'll want to know why it's taking so long for the destination to respond.

5 Node_A sends an Information frame to Node_B with C set. This frame contains user data in the Information field. Notice that the P/F bit is set to F. This means that Node_A doesn't expect an acknowledgment to this frame. Node_B could acknowledge it, anyway, although in this example it doesn't. NR=0 means it has received no frames from Node_B. NS=0. This tells the destination the **number of the frame that it's now sending**. This is important because although Node_A is sending frame number 0, Node_B would indicate that it has received 1 frame.

6 Node_A sends another Information frame to Node_B. This time the P/F bit is set to P, so Node_B must return an acknowledgment. NR=0 because Node_A still hasn't received any frames from B. NS=1 because this is the number of the frame it's sending.

7 Node_B responds (R) with an RR frame. NR=2. It does because Node_B has received two frames.

8 Node_B has some data of its own to send to A and does so by sending a command (C) in an information (I) frame with the poll (P) bit set. This is telling A that it expects an acknowledgment. NR=2 because it has received two frames from A, and NS=0 because the number of the frame it's sending is 0.

9 Node_A responds (R) to the command with an RR frame, and has NR=1 since it received one frame from B.

10 Node_A sends back some data in an Information frame. NR=1 and NS=2. It's received one frame from B, and is sending frame number 2, which is the third frame it has sent.

11 Node_B responds to the command with an RR frame that has NR=3. Although the final (F) bit is set, it means nothing.

12 Node_B now wants to send data. It does so in an Information frame with the P/F bit set to P, so it expects an immediate acknowledgment from A. NR=3 because it has still only received three frames from A, but NS=1 because the number of the frame it's sending is one.

13 Node_A acknowledges in an RR frame with NR=2 since it has received two frames from B/.

14 Node_A also takes an opportunity to send data in an information frame. With the P/F bit at F, it doesn't require an immediate acknowledgment. NR=2 because it has received two frames, and NS=3 because three is the number of the frame it's sending.

15 Node_A, being a bit of a network hog, sends another frame. Notice NR=2 remains unchanged, but NS=4 since this is frame number four. It has the P bit set so B must acknowledge receipt.

This scenario could go on and on, but these data exchange steps should be enough to give you an idea about the activities occurring in the Data Link layer. You may have wondered how it was possible, not only for computers to find one another on a large network, but to ensure that the information sent actually got to the right computer. Reliability, as designed into the NS and NR fields, is an assumption in Data Link protocols. This extends to the IEEE 802.x protocols, because they use an identical logical implementation of HDLC. As mentioned earlier in this chapter, Data Link protocols are well documented and widely implemented—because they work, and work reliably.

16 Node_B responds (R) as instructed in an RR frame. NR=5 because it has received a total of five frames from Node_B.

HDLC offers the widest versatility of all bit-oriented protocols, because it imposes fewer restrictions on users. IBM's SDLC, which is very similar to HDLC, requires information fields to be a multiple of 8-bits in length. HDLC has no length limitations in the information field. SDLC, on the other hand, contains many more commands/responses in unnumbered frames than does HDLC. For example, IBM has incorporated a **test command** that checks the integrity of a link. HDLC must depend upon the initial dialogue between stations to ensure that the link is workable. LLC Type I has a command called TEST. Technically, any command found in Type I is included in Type II. But note that it's not needed, since in LAPB, the link is tested when the two stations set up the initial ink. This is a Type II test.

The practice of bit stuffing—also used in SDLC—decreases the efficiency of HDLC. But, for the most part, the extra bits are worth the true transparency found in HDLC. Unfortunately, it complicates the hardware at each end of the link, since bit insertion and removal circuitry is required.

TRAINING

Prepare a Training Plan

Network engineering calls for the creation of a Training Plan. This plan should follow a prescribed format consisting of a Program Description, Program Content, Terminal Objectives, Time Required, Student Materials, Classroom Equipment and Supplies.

Training in the workplace should ideally be implemented from a broad, top-level map—some sort of master plan designed to increase employee effectiveness. The master plan would be based upon establishing the requirements as described in the previous section. These included:

- Determining training wants and needs.

- Conducting a task analysis (or use another appropriate instructional strategy).

- Designing a needs-based survey.

- Analyzing the results of the survey.

- Defining training content based on the needs survey and task analysis.

- Determining the training target population.

Ultimately, this leads to a general list of topics which need to be learned, and these are defined in the training content. The content of a training program is typically broad, and depending on the scope of the needs analysis, may have a few, or dozens, of listed items.

For example, consider a company with a thousand employees, versus a company with twenty employees. The first company has employees at all levels—from non-skilled to professional. The second company has only professional employees. Obviously, the scope of training between the two companies will differ, with the first offering many more lower-level topics, while the second will train employees across a specialized, higher-level range. What won't change between these two examples is the method used for planning the training.

Training plan formats vary widely between companies. It may be a thin document, consisting of several overall outcomes, or it may be a thick guide, detailing the day-to-day activities in a training program. Usually, the plan will fall somewhere between these two extremes. Note that a training plan is only prepared once you've determined a need for training. This seems obvious, but it's often overlooked in corporate training departments, where the need for training is assumed. Training discussions among managers and supervisors often culminate in the creation of a plan to justify the development of unit lessons, resulting in a situation where employees attend classes they don't need, or are unprepared for.

Figure 5-22 illustrates a fundamental format to use for preparing a training plan. It contains the essential information needed to convey the overall outcomes of the training, along with the time needed to complete the training. This is essential to users and department managers, since they must know what training their employees will get during time spent away from the job, and how much time will be needed to acquire the new skills.

FORMAT FOR PREPARING A TRAINING PLAN	
1) Program Description	
2) Program Content	
3) Terminal Objectives	
4) Time Considerations	
5) Student Materials	
6) Equipment and Supplies	

Figure 5-22 Format for a Training Plan

We'll take a close look at each heading in the illustration, then apply it to a training situation.

Program Description

The program description should answer the following questions:

- What is the purpose of the training?

- Who will receive the training?

- What are the general goals of the training?

- What will the student do with the training?

- Where will the training occur? (in a classroom, at the student's worksite, etc.)

- Who will deliver the training? (A third-party, corporate training, supervisor, mentors, subject experts, etc.)

- What is the cost of the training?

- What skill level is expected at the completion of training?

Optionally, you may include needs and task analysis information in the program description, since this is the best justification for cost.

"What" signifies a task, or portion of a task, for which an employee will be held responsible. For example, assume you're addressing a need to show employees how to connect to a remote server; the purpose of the training is to illustrate the steps involved in doing so. What will they do with this skill? Hopefully, they will upload, download, start application software, and so on. What is the expected skill level? It may be to locate remote servers to which they're attached, and have access to, and to locate specific information on the server.

"Who" refers to the student-employee in the class, as well as the individual delivering the training. When associated with a student-employee, you can gain insight into the appropriate skill level to be expected at the completion of the training, as well as the approximate time needed to complete the training. Normally, which the student would be suited for a particular program is alluded to in the target description.

When "who" refers to the trainer, it also is indicative of costs. The trainer may be an outside consultant, an employee with specialized knowledge, or a specific trainer/mentor/supervisor. It can also include references to course materials, such as computer-based training, in which the employees work on their own, without a direct trainer.

"Where" the training occurs will be a major indicator of the cost. If all training is to take place off-site, then airfare, motel accommodations and meals are a direct cost of training. But if training will occur in an on-site classroom, these types of costs will be reduced. However, you must now ensure access to the room (local scheduling and timing will certainly become an issue).

"When" the training is to begin, and end, is important to conveying the overall scope of training. It also helps in avoiding conflicts with other events such as the launch of a new project, employee vacations, seasonal production rushes, and so on.

How much does training cost? There are two aspects to the cost: direct and indirect value. Direct costs are the instructor's hourly rate, the total hourly rates of employees attending the training, the travel costs, the costs of materials—that is, the concrete and measurable costs. Indirect costs involve using a conference room for several hours each day for the training, the utility costs while training, the time needed to research training materials, and so on.

Intuitively, most of us understand that, in the long run, the lack of adequate training costs a company far more than the money needed to train. The problem is, the training appears to have little immediate impact. Or, as the bean counters say, "the return on investment doesn't justify the expenditure." And it doesn't, and never will, if you don't very specifically quantify the costs and outcomes.

Here's a way to specifically quantify costs for on-sight training. Determine the total expenditures (the cost of goods + the costs of selling), and divide this amount by 2,080 (the number of hours in a normal, 40-hour/week work year). This tells you the hourly cost of a business. For example, assume a business with costs of $1,000,000, and total number of employees of 20. The amount needed to run the business each hour is:

$$\text{Cost} / 2080 =$$
$$\$1,000,000 / 2080 = \$480$$

Express the costs in terms of the total number of employees by dividing the hourly cost by the number of employees:

$$\text{Hourly Cost} / \text{Total Employees} =$$
$$\$480 / 20 = \$24$$

This means that for each employee to attend one hour of training will cost the company $24. If ten employees attend the training session, it will cost $240.

Even if the business operates normally for this hour, when half the employees are in training, the remainder are expected to pick up the slack, and it's reasonable to assume that it will cost money ($240) for them to do so. This amount is directly attached to the total cost of the business, so that now it's $1,000,240 for the year.

This may not seem like much until you assume that 15% of the amount of time an employee spends at work will involve some type of training. In our example, 15% of 2080 is 312 hours each employee will be participating in training. At a cost of $24 an hour, the total cost to train is $24 x 312 x 20 = $149,760. And the actual costs of the company have now swelled to $1,150,000.

This represents about a 7.5% increase in costs. When you begin to quantify the cost of training, you can see why many companies don't invest into it as they should.

Now, assume that the training isn't made available. How much will it cost not to train? Estimate the amount of time employees will be spending on their newly acquired skills (if they had received the training). Average this by the total number of employees, and multiply by the hourly labor rate.

For example, assume the same training scenario in which half the employees need to learn how to connect to a remote server. Apparently, the company is receiving a significant upgrade to their networking hardware, since all employees will now need to be able to make the connection. One way to estimate the time spent on the skill is to estimate the amount of time employees will be involved in an activity which requires them to connect to a server. We'll assume an estimate of 20 hours each week. Since ten employees don't know how to connect, the direct impact will be that their productivity will be cut in half, or:

20 hours x 10 employees x 52 weeks x $24 per hr. = $249,600

The cost of not training is $249,600, while the cost of providing training is $149,760, for a difference of $99,840. That is, the company will save nearly $100,000 a year by training the employees than by not training them.

The above method of calculating training costs is somewhat simplistic. Alternatively, you can calculate training costs as a function of actual labor cost, if you know the total amount spent on salaries. Regardless of which approach you take, the ratios will remain the same as long as you accurately determine the number of employees who need training, and the amount of time they'll be required to utilize the new skill.

Program Content

The content of a training program consists of a list of tasks to be mastered. These are typically derived directly from a task analysis. Occasionally, you'll see the list expressed in terms of topics to be taught. Whenever possible, commit yourself to using the task analysis result method. The reason is that it shows very specifically what the student employees will get from the training—and it's supported by your task analysis.

It also forms the basis for evaluating the success of the training along with the effectiveness of the instructor and/or training materials.

Figure 5-23 shows a typical example of the content of a training program. Notice that the items listed are terminal. They describe the outcomes of training (the tasks the employees are expected to be able to perform once they return to the job), but they don't specify how to do anything. Resist the tendency to over-detail the content; this will be done later, when you design the actual method for delivering the training—which is where you'll include the how-to information.

Program Content: **Connecting To A Remote Server**
1. Locate all servers connected to your computer. 2. Determine the servers you have access to. 3. Access directories or files at a remote server. 4. Upload/ download files to the remote server. 5. Start application software residing on a remote server.

Figure 5-23 Format for a Training Plan

Terminal Objectives

A terminal objective defines the major competency to be acquired. Don't confuse them with program content. The items listed in the content section are occupational; they describe what the employee must do. Learning objectives are inclusive of a task (a single task may generate more than one terminal objective), but they also set the stage for performing the task. For example, in order to locate all of the servers connected to your computer, you need to know what software will be running on your computer—Windows 95/ 98/ 3.x, Unix, Novell, or NT. The required steps, and the screen presentations, will differ with each software package.

Typically, terminal objectives are stated:

- In terms of a given condition.

- An action to be performed.

- And an expected result of the action.

First, state the condition under which they employees will be performing the task.

Using Network Neighborhood in Windows NT,

The employee is given the software package they'll be using, and the specific command associated with the software. Next, state the action to be performed.

identify servers by clicking the Entire Network icon,

The employee is expected to take some action. Therefore, this part of an objective should always contain an action verb. Finally, express the objective in terms of the expected result. This will provide the employee with a means to evaluate their own success in meeting the terminal objective.

so that a list of servers are displayed on your screen.

In the Program Content, we said that the employee will be able to locate all servers connected to their computer. Now we have a specific objective to which they'll be held accountable:

Using Network Neighborhood in Windows NT, identify servers by clicking the Entire Network icon, so that a list of servers are displayed on your screen.

If another software package is used, the terminology changes, but not the actions to be performed or the results.

Terminal objectives are frequently delineated into a series of secondary, or supporting, objectives. This depends on the target population and their level of competence. For example, if Windows NT is replacing 3.11, a secondary objective may need to be included that leads the employee through the task of locating the proper icons and commands. However, this isn't the place for it. Supporting objectives, or interim steps, are communicated at the point-of-instructional-delivery, which is the training setting.

Time Considerations

How long (one minute, five minutes, fifteen minutes?) does it take to teach someone how to find the servers their computer is connected to? It depends on the target audience and your experience in performing the task. If it takes you one minute, it'll take a beginner two or three minutes. This is an educated guess, but you can be certain that the time required for a student employee to master a task will be longer than it takes you to perform it. There are other factors to consider when estimating the time of a training session. These include:

- Introducing the training topic (Locating Servers).

- Stating learning objectives.

- Showing/demonstrating/explaining how to locate the servers.

- Providing time for all students to perform the objective.

- Evaluating the success/failure of each student

- Summarizing the task they've mastered.

A reasonable estimate of the time needed to teach this simple learning objective, in a class of ten students, would be about fifteen to twenty minutes. There are no fast and hard rules for estimating training times. Some of us learn more quickly than others, and it's those who have a difficult time mastering a concept or task that we are truly trying to reach. The quick learners will probably master it with or without us. Don't be stingy with training time.

Student Materials

What materials will the student need in order to complete the objectives? Should they bring something with them, or will you supply them with all they need? Student material refers to books, handouts, paper, pencil or pen, tests or quizzes, and questionnaires (for feedback on the class and instructor).

Make a list of all materials they need, then indicate which, if any, will be supplied by the trainer. Figure 5-24 shows an example of a worksheet used to list the materials, along with the costs of supplying the student with the material.

Figure 5-24 Student Materials Worksheet

STUDENT MATERIAL	SUPPLIED BY	COST
3.5 in. Floppy Disk	Instructor	.25 ea.
Ink Pen	Student	.50 ea.
Networking Handout	Instructor	.75
Notepad	Instructor	1.00

The reason you determine the needed materials beforehand is so that you and the employees will be prepared for the class. Valuable, and expensive, time is wasted simply because no one has a pencil with which to take notes.

Equipment And Supplies

What equipment will a trainer need to conduct the class? Typically, a class has a whiteboard or chalkboard, erasable markers or chalk, an overhead projector, perhaps a paper flip-chart, a television and VCR, tables and chairs for the students, and any objective-specific equipment such as computers, printers, network hardware and software, etc.

It needs to be listed so that the cost can be budgeted and the equipment purchased or acquired. In many cases, a company will make specialized equipment available for the length of a training session, then return it to normal use. Someone has to arrange for it to be delivered, connected, set up and running, then return it once the training is done. This requires considerable coordination, time, and resources. Figure 5-25 is a listing of needed equipment that differentiates items that are specialized for the class and those that are on-going.

CLASSROOM EQUIPMENT LIST		
ITEM	ONGOING / SPECIALIZED	COST
OVERHEAD PROJECTOR	ONGOING	$400.00
TELEVISION/ VCR, 30 IN.	ONGOING	$1000.00
FIVE, 8 FT. TABLES	ONGOING	$800.00
TWENTY PADDED CHAIRS	ONGOING	$1600.00
TWENTY PERSONAL COMPUTERS	ONGOING	$25,000.00
ETHERNET HUB, SOFTWARE AND CABLING	ONGOING	$5000.00

Figure 5-25 List of Classroom Equipment

Figure 5-26 is a sample, and incomplete, training plan for the Connecting To A Remote Server training.

SAMPLE TRAINING PLAN: Connecting To A Remote Server

I. PROGRAM DESCRIPTION:

> Connecting To A Remote Server is a one hour class intended for all users who's primary responsibility is to upload and download software from a remote server. The course is available only for those who have;t received training on this subject but have a basic proficiency with personal computers and graphical interface software (Windows), or with permission from their Supervisor and the Instructor.
>
> The class will be scheduled during normal business hours in the Training Center. Each employee will be required to bring a pen for note taking. All other materials will be provided.
>
> At the end of the training class, each student will be required to demonstrate the competency in connecting to an actual remote server, uploading a text file, then downloading the same file.

II. PROGRAM CONTENT:

> At the conclusion of Connecting To A Remote Server, the you will be able to:
>
> 1. Locate all servers connected to your computer.
> 2. Determine the servers you have access to.
> 3. Access directories or files at a remote server.
> 4. Upload/ download files to the remote server.
> 5. Start application software residing on a remote server.

III. TERMINAL OBJECTIVES:

At the conclusion of this class, you will be able to:
- Using Network Neighborhood in Windows NT, identify servers by clicking Entire Network icon so that a list of servers are displayed on your screen.
- (As many Terminal Objectives as needed are listed which satisfy the topics in the Program Content)

IV. TIME CONSIDERATIONS

> Length: 1 Hour (50 to 60 minutes)
> Competency Evaluation: 10 to 15 minutes
> Total Class Time: 1 hour 15 minutes

Figure 5-26 Sample Training Plan

Designing Effective Instructional Strategies

Considerations for choosing a strategy include cost, time required to implement, reliability of data, and objectivity of data.

Earlier, a hypothetical training situation was given in which a new network was installed, and workers were polled to determine what they did and didn't know. The results of the poll were used as the foundation for providing the training which would bring their skills up to speed. Ultimately, the results would be used to determine the content of a training program.

In other words, a strategy was selected to aid in the design of the employee training. In that example, the strategy selected was to conduct a task analysis of the employee's skill levels. A strategy describes the approach you intend to take in achieving a goal. Once the strategy is determined, you then develop methods, or action plans, which contain steps for implementing the strategy.

In this section, we'll look at several common instructional strategies used to aid in developing an outline of a training program. Each has its own merits as well as disadvantages, but typically, the best approach involves using two or more strategies. This helps to offset any disadvantages that each may have.

There are four factors which will influence the selection of an instructional strategy:

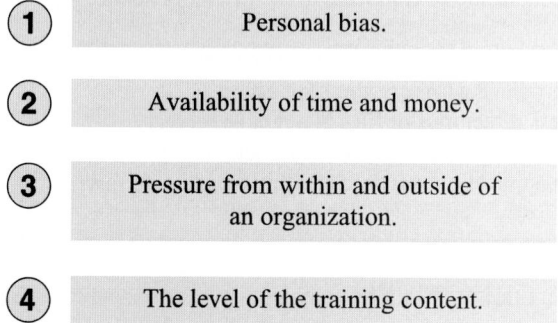

1. Personal bias.

2. Availability of time and money.

3. Pressure from within and outside of an organization.

4. The level of the training content.

Personal bias refers to your particular views about employee training. If you feel that it's a necessary evil, and someone else feels it's absolutely essential, then the two programs that are suggested for the same situation are going to be considerably different. One will probably be more time consuming, expensive, thorough, and effective. Yours is more likely to be short, inexpensive, contain only essential information, and produce mixed results. There are benefits to either approach, but the point is that personal philosophies can, and do, affect the type of training plan that is designed.

Is there a specified amount of money allocated to the training? How much time is available to pull employees away from their job to train them? These are practical considerations that will influence the strategy you choose. Some strategies are quick and inexpensive while others are time-intensive and expensive.

Consider not only hourly wages when choosing a strategy. A content determination process may involve travel to various locations if training needs to be delivered throughout a large corporation. Professional printing, the use of educational consultants, specialized software to analyze the results of the process—all factor into the expenses.

As our personal thoughts affect training outcomes, so they do with others. Don't be surprised if each employee you talk with, each supervisor, manager and bureaucrat has his/her own ideas about what should be taught to employees. The same is true within your own department, particularly if you're involved as a subject matter expert, because in your department, you work with similar experts. The pressure from within and without can be significant, and at times, beyond your resources to do anything about it.

> An instructional strategy is the specific approach taken to training.

If you see this scenario as likely to develop, choose a strategy that contains little in the way of subjective analysis. That way, you can always quote "just the facts."

The greater the complexity of the task, and the lower the skill level of the target audience, the more extensive the content of the training. In this case, choose a strategy which will provide you with an abundant amount of data from which to develop an outline of the program. You'll need a great deal of information because your training plan will be extensive, time consuming, and expensive.

Think through the factors described above before choosing a strategy. Try to determine which are likely to be significant, and let them guide you when selecting specific strategies.

There are many instructional strategies available. We'll examine those which have been proven as effective through their use. Strategies used to determine the content of a training program can be broadly classified according to their level of subjectiveness and objectivity. Predictably, the more objective a strategy is, the more time and money it takes to complete. Subjective strategies can often be completed very quickly, and at a low cost. Objective strategies are noted for their use of hard data, while subjective strategies are often based on the opinions and preferences of an individual or group.

We'll look at several strategies, then apply them to several training situations.

> Examples of instructional strategies include Introspection, DACUM and Task Analysis.

Introspection

The introspection process involves asking yourself what the content of a training program should consists of. It assumes you're knowledgeable in the tasks to be learned, that you're competent to perform them, that you have a broad understanding of the associated tasks to be performed, and that your decisions will be reliable.

Many employee training programs are developed using the introspection process. Typically, it begins by studying literature related to the desired task to determine information which may exist that may be helpful in making decisions.

Once the literature has been studied, the process continues by considering what's best for the company and the employee for achieving the desired results of the training. The process may grow into a group effort as supervisors and department managers become involved. The advantage of introspection by group is the increase in the reliability of the results.

However, this doesn't mean that they are reliable. For example, if a group of computer experts decides that all employees should learn how to format 5.25-inch diskettes, notwithstanding the fact that the employee workstations are equipped with 3.5-inch disk drives, then the strategic decision isn't valid. This is the danger of utilizing only subject matter experts, or corporate trainers, to determine training content. Too often, they "know what's best for us", even if it isn't.

One way to avoid the risk of invalidating introspection decisions is to use a diverse group of people when determining content. If you have access to individuals in similar jobs outside the company, ask them to jot down content headings, then pull the group together and jointly determine an outline. The assumption is that these individuals are close to the work, have experienced most of the problems firsthand, and they'll be able to distinguish between what's actually needed and what isn't.

Once the group is together, delete any redundant topics or headings. What's left will be the rough outline of a training program.

The advantage to introspection is that it's quick and inexpensive. It may take as little as a day or two, or a couple of weeks, to complete. It may be the best strategic choice when the proposed training is simple, informal, and non-critical to the operation. It's a highly subjective choice, though. This means that the training may not succeed to the level you expect. Figure 5-27 lists the steps involved when the introspection approach is selected.

STEPS REQUIRED FOR INTROSPECTION STRATEGY
The strategy is initiated by one individual, or a small group with vested interest in outcome (i.e., a supervisor).
(1) Study/ research relevant material related to job/ tasks. •   Identify current skills for the same or related jobs and duties.
(2) Develop a topical list based upon: •   Personal Experience •   Knowledge of subject •   Perceived skills needed on the job
(3) Convene group of similar subject matter experts.
(4) Group determines final training topics.

Advantages to the introspection strategy:

(1) Data collection is quick and easy.
(2) Strategy designers are usually well informed of working conditions.
(3) Costs are low.

Figure 5-27 Steps for Implementing the Introspection Instructional Strategy

Disadvantages to the introspection method:

(1) Data may be unreliable.
(2) The training topics lack objectivity.

DACUM

DACUM is an acronym for **Developing A CurriculUM**. It's essentially an introspection strategy that avoids much of the subjectiveness by imposing a systematic approach as a guide in determining the training content.

DACUM is easily recognizable as consisting of skills profiles that are used as both a training outline and as an evaluation instrument. Typically, the skills are displayed on a single sheet of paper in a tabular format that's organized as blocks of related skills. Figure 5-28 is an example of a DACUM profile.

Network Installation

Student Name _____

Instructor _____

Date _____

Identify and select network cabling	Idetify and select CAT 5 UTP	Identify and select CAT 2 UTP	Identify and select thicknet coaxial cable	Identify and select thinnet coaxial cable	Identify and select multi-mode fiber optic cable	Identify and select single-mode fiber optic cable
Design a network cabling floor plan	Prepare a node floor plan	Draft a cable labeling procedure	Determine locations of plenum-rated cabling	Locate areas of adverse interference.	Prepare a materials list of all cabling components	Using graphics software, create the floor plan
Install network cabling	Interpret and follow installation specifications	Select tools and equipment	Select, order and store cabling and components	Schedule installation according to specification	Run cabling to termination points	Prepare and make cable terminations
	Label terminations according to SOP	Bundle wire runs to prevent stress	Inspect installation for compliance to spec.	Account for wages, equipment and tool costs	Prepare billing or invoice	Reconcile change orders to original floor plan

Ratings:

4. Can perform all skills satisfactorily and can lead others in the tasks.
3. Can perform satisfactorily without assistance from supervision.
2. Can perform satisfactorily but requires occasional assistance from supervision
1. Can perform portions of this skill satisfactorily but requires assistance from supervision.

Outcomes are listed in the first column at the left. These outcomes are then organized as a series of skills that, when mastered, demonstrate competence in achieving the outcome. A DACUM profile usually contains a rating system, as well. The rating system has a two-fold purpose—it provides a record of achieving the skills for both the student and instructor, or in the case of an employment setting, to the employee and supervisor.

Figure 5-28 Example of a DACUM Profile

By listing the required skills in an easy-to-read format, the student is able to track his progress through the training. He/she is able to tell at a glance exactly where he/she is, where he/she is going, and what he/she has completed satisfactorily.

A DACUM strategy is implemented by selecting a group who are experts in a particular field. These may be employees, or supervisors, who have mastered related tasks and routinely perform them in their jobs. It begins with the group meeting together and familiarizing themselves with written descriptions of tasks and duties the employees will be expected to do. The group then identifies broad areas of competence the employee should be able to perform in their job. This will eventually become the first column in Figure 5-28. These broad competencies are then described in terms of specific skills needed to master the competency, shown in the remaining columns. The skills are then organized into a logical sequence. Finally, the group assigns levels of competence typical of the work place setting. This is shown in the system of ratings.

The DACUM approach allows the content of a program to be reasonably relevant while avoiding significant costs or time consummation. The costs may be no more than reimbursement of group member's time, and the associated copying or printing costs. When the group is organized by a facilitator who is not an active member of the group, the entire process can be wrapped up in a day. What's left is a documented blueprint from which detailed performance objectives can be developed.

The disadvantage of DACUM is the same as for introspection. The reliability of the data is suspect, and only as good as the group members' contributions. In a traditional academic setting, a DACUM profile is created with no input from instructors. This serves to avoid academic biases that tend to flaw an introspection strategy. The instructor is introduced to the DACUM profile once it's completed, and will then develop lesson plans around the skills specified in the profile. Figure 5-29 summarizes the DACUM approach.

STEPS FOR IMPLEMENTING A DACUM STRATEGY
DACUM is initiated with a group of subject matter experts competent in the occupation. A facilitator, usually from outside the occupation, keeps the group focused.
(1) Group reviews a written description of the job.
(2) Group determines broad areas of competence.
(3) Group identifies specific skills related to each area of competence. •   Areas of competence and related skills are organized in tabular form on a single sheet.
(4) Areas and related skills are organized into proper learning sequence.
(5) Scales showing level of accomplishment for skills are determined. •   The scales may be used by both employee and instructor as a means of evaluating progress.

Figure 5-29 Steps for Implementing a DACUM Instructional Strategy

Advantages:

(1) Due to forced documentation, DACUM is considered an objective strategy.
(2) The reliability of DACUM is much higher than introspection for the same reason.
(3) Since the training outline is limited to a single page, the strategy isn't time consuming.

Disadvantages:

(1) The reliability of DACUM may be suspect since only experts are involved in the document.
(2) Academics often prepare DACUM profile which skews the objectivity and reliability.

Function

The function approach focuses on the skills necessary for the total job performance. For example, a networked database may be used for data entry input, but the same individual who inputs the data may also be responsible for analyzing that information as well as information input by others. Not only must this person need to understand the menus available in the database, but he/she also needs to know how to enter data, check for errors, cross reference the data to other's information, draw correlations between the two, and present valid findings. This process includes a meshing of skills that apparently have little to do with mastering a complex database. The employee will need a gestalt understanding of the available information. He/she will need to know how to use a wordprocessor, save, copy or print reports, be able to present a talk and answer questions about the report.

A function strategy looks at the complete set of skills necessary to perform a role in an organization. It typically works best when applied to a general category of jobs rather than to specific job titles. The information garnered from the function approach is particularly relevant when a company wishes to prepare employees to "wear many hats." A function strategy is initiated by defining the purpose of a job in an organization. The functions (purposes) needed to perform the job are then identified. Once the functions are identified, a list of activities needed to perform the function are listed. The activities are quantified by specifying the level of competence required to master the activity. The competencies are logically grouped, and organized into related areas. The final product is scrutinized for appropriateness before being released.

The function approach is time-consuming, and somewhat expensive. It's best implemented when its proponents are willing to abandon traditional approaches to training, and when resources are adequate. The most important resource is versatility within the group involved in the strategy, since these individuals will have varied, and unrelated, backgrounds, and they all must be able to submit expert recommendations. The steps needed to implement the function strategy are listed in Figure 5-30.

STEPS FOR IMPLEMENTING THE FUNCTION STRATEGY
(1) Define the purpose of a job or occupation.
(2) List the functions needed to perform the job.   • Functions are defined as general areas which aren't directly related but when taken together, describes the occupation.
(3) Create a list of activities needed to perform the job functions.
(4) Competencies (activities) are then organized into related areas.
(5) Final product is reviewed for appropriateness.

Advantages:

(1) When a variety of resources are used to identify functions, it's a reliable strategy.
(2) The function approach is also considered valid for describing the occupation.

Disadvantages:

(1) Generally time consuming due to the broad resources that must be brought together.
(2) Costs may escalate rapidly.

Figure 5-30 Steps for Implementing the Function Instructional Strategy

Task Analysis

Task analysis is the most widely used instructional strategy. This is because the results are reliable, and the costs are reasonable. However, task analysis is time consuming, and it depends on participation from many sources.

In essence, task analysis is the process of identifying and verifying the tasks that are performed in a job. There are two components of a job. We have **duties** we're expected to perform, and these duties consists of a series of **tasks** that must be completed. Duties refer to a broad category, while tasks specify the activities performed. For example, one of the duties of a Network Engineer may be to create **Standard Operating Procedures** (SOPs) that standardize changes to a network. To perform this duty, the engineer must:

- Use a wordprocessor.

- Be able to write technical documents.

- Create forms as needed.

- Identify network components (hardware and software) that may be changed, and distinguish those that won't change.

- Schedule work on the changes.

- Evaluate the effect of the change, and so on.

You can see that a task is a discrete unit or activity, self-contained, with a beginning and an end. It's considered to be a valid task if it consumes a considerable portion of an individual's time on the job. The validity is reinforced by polling the individual to determine which tasks he/she actually performs, and having he/she rate themselves on their competency.

A task analysis is initiated by first researching any related literature to see if an analysis has been done before for the same, or closely related, job. Since task analysis has been widely deployed, you're likely to find information which will shorten your analysis. Next, a list of competencies are generated, along with any equipment used in performing the tasks. The equipment list is as important as the task list, because it will guide you in selecting equipment needed for the training session.

Once the task and equipment lists have be prepared, they're reviewed by a sampling of employees and supervisors before being formally distributed. This is an essential element of a task analysis, since it validates the preliminary work done—usually—by one individual or a small group. Note that the preliminary lists may not necessarily be compiled by an expert in the job to be evaluated. However, this individual must be well versed in gathering appropriate and relevant material.

When the lists have been reviewed and validated by field workers, it's distributed to the field. Figure 5-31 shows a simplified task analysis survey that was used earlier. Note that it includes a system of scales, so that recipients can evaluate their competency in the indicated task.

Depending on the size of a training project, it may not be feasible to survey all employees. If this is the case, choose a sampling plan that reflects the targeted population. Contact the National Education Association for appropriate methods for determining sample sizes. Obviously, the field feedback will be more meaningful and valid when as many respondents as will be involved in the training return the survey.

TRAINING NEEDS SURVEY

The results of this survey will be used to develop training on network use and operation. For each competency, check the appropriate column as to how well you can perform the competency. Use the following to judge your skill level:

1: Little to no skill.
2. Intermediate skill.
3. Advance skill.

Department Name: _____

COMPETENCY	1	2	3
1. Logon to network.			
2. Print to a shared printer.			
3. Email a file attachment.			
4. Internet Proficiency			
5. Share files or directories with a workgroup.			
6. Password protect shared files.			
7. Perform daily file back-ups.			
8. Restart network operating system.			
9. Allocate space on a local file server.			
10. Connect a remote server.			

Figure 5-31 Sample Task Analysis Survey

You may need to solicit help from management to ensure a high return rate.

A considerable obstacle to task analysis is that many surveys are long, and take a lot of time and thought to complete. One way to avoid this is to categorize the skill sets and equipment lists, and distribute the survey a piece at a time. The downside to this approach is that it lengthens the time to complete the analysis.

It's not unusual to solicit personal information from respondents. This may include the job title, years or months in their occupation, general and specialized education, age, sex, etc. If the results are anticipated to be murky, you may want to also ask for telephone numbers, names, and addresses. This can be helpful if you need clarification on comments they include, or inconsistencies in the responses. But as mentioned previously, you run the risk of receiving skewed data, particularly from employees who don't want to appear "dumb."

Often, originators of a task analysis complain of low return rates. Twist whatever arms you need to twist to get the rate high—at least above 50% of the total surveyed. As a final and time-consuming alternative, you may have to go to the field and personally interview the sample respondents.

Figure 5-32 shows the step-by-step implementation of a task analysis.

STEPS FOR IMPLEMENTING A TASK ANALYSIS
A task analysis may be initiated by anyone but the individual must be knowledgeable in research, sampling and analysis methods.
(1) Research literature for relevancy to target group. There's considerable information available on task analysis results.
(2) Generate a trial list of competencies.
(3) Generate a trial list of equipment used in the tasks.
(4) Competency and equipment list is reviewed for appropriateness by small sample before final distribution.
(5) Correct trial lists as necessary.
(6) Distribute final competency and equipment list to field. For large populations, use a sampling plan to reduce time and costs.
(7) Analyze the results.

Respondents of a task analysis are to rate their competency (or time spent) according to some scale such as Above Average, Average, Below Average, etc.

Advantages:

(1) An objective approach due to direct feedback.
(2) Results are reliable due to direct feedback.

Disadvantages:

(1) Data collection is time consuming.
(2) Total costs can be considerable for a large task analysis; but for small populations, they may be minimal.

Figure 5-32 Steps for Implementing a Task Analysis Instructional Strategy

KEY POINTS REVIEW

This chapter has presented an extensive exploration of data communications protocols.

- Protocols are the set of rules governing data communications.

- The three functions of a protocol are: to determine how handshaking will occur, to determine how a virtual communications path is implemented, and to determine how data will be packaged.

- The OSI model describes the scope of data communications, and the various functions of a data communication system.

- The OSI model consists of seven levels: Application, Presentation, Session, Transport, Network, Data Link, and Physical.

- The Data Link level contains two sublayers: Logical Link Control (LLC), and Medium Access Control (MAC).

- The Logical Link Control sublayer describes the conventions that a sender and receiver follow to ensure the data flow is orderly.

- The Medium Access Control level describes methods stations use to gain access to a communication channel.

- There are three types of LLC sublayer protocols: asynchronous, synchronous, and bit-oriented.

- Asynchronous protocols usually have high overhead, low efficiency and are typically found in PC environments.

- Synchronous protocols offer higher efficiencies and lower overhead. BSC is a synchronous protocol.

- Bit-oriented protocols have the highest efficiency and lowest overhead. SDLC, HDLC, LAPB are bit-oriented protocols.

- Synchronous protocols provide virtual communication with the use of byte stuffing.

- Bit-oriented protocols provide virtual communication using the bit-stuffing technique.

- Each protocol provides for handshaking through the use of dialogues. Examples of handshaking dialogue are command/response, primary/secondary, and ACK/NACK.

- A training Plan should follow a prescribed format consisting a Program Description, Program Content, Terminal Objectives, Time Required, Student Materials and Classroom Equipment/Supplies.

- An instructional strategy is the specific approach taken to training.

- Considerations for choosing a strategy include cost, time required to implement, reliability of data, and objectivity of data.

- Examples of instructional strategies include Introspection, DACUM and Task Analysis.

At this point, review the objectives listed at the beginning of the chapter to be certain that you understand and can perform them. Afterward, answer the review questions that follow to verify your knowledge of the information.

REVIEW QUESTIONS

The following questions test your knowledge of the material presented in this chapter:

1. Define protocol.

2. What is the purpose of the OSI reference model?

3. Which OSI layer is responsible for ensuring that the syntax of the data is acceptable to the receiver and transmitter?

4. List several responsibilities of the Data Link layer.

5. What is the purpose of the LLC sublayer?

6. Determine the throughput of a frame with 96 bytes in the data field and 18 bytes of overhead.

7. When an HDLC station must receive permission from a primary station before transmitting, it's configured in the _____ mode.

8. Exchanges between two HDLC stations involve a primary sending five frames to a secondary. When the last frame is sent, what will the P/F field read?

9. Refer to question 8. When the sending station transmits the fifth frame, what will the Nr and Ns fields read?

10. List the minimum headings that would be required for a Training Plan.

11. State the seven layers of the OSI model.

12. What are several protocols that are used in the Application layer?

13. What do the five Classes found in the Transport layer represent?

14. What does the IEEE 802.2 specification describe?

15. What is an instructional strategy?

MULTIPLE CHOICE QUESTIONS

1. A protocol is defined as:
   a. A hardware entity.
   b. The transfer of data between dissimilar devices.
   c. Rules describing the exchange of data between similar devices.
   d. Rules for implementing network hardware.

2. An example of virtual communication is:
   a. The telephone system.
   b. The address bus in a PC.
   c. A FDM mulitplexer.
   d. Fiber optic cable.

3. In addition to a hierarchial relationship between layers of the OSI model, the layers also have a _____ relationship.
   a. Adversarial
   b. Proportional
   c. Unstable
   d. Peer

4. Which layer of the OSI model would be responsible for ensuring that a message sent in Spanish is displayed in English at the receiving terminal?
   a. Application layer.
   b. Presentation layer.
   c. Transport layer.
   d. Data Link layer.

5. The purpose of the MAC sublayer is:
   a. To package data into frames.
   b. To provide a virtual path across coaxial cable.
   c. To describe how stations gain access to the network.
   d. To check for bit errors.

6. When asynchronous data is sent, the user can configure its:
   a. Location of the start bit.
   b. Type of parity and number of stop bits.
   c. Number of data bits and number of start bits.
   d. Frequency of mark.

7. BSC protocols are classified as:
   a. Character-oriented.
   b. Bit-oriented.
   c. Level 3.
   d. A physical interface.

8. When HDLC is configured for asynchronous balanced mode:
   a. Transparency is turned off.
   b. HDLC reverts to a character-oriented protocol.
   c. All stations on the network are peers.
   d. The primary is in receive-only mode.

9. The type of HDLC frame that carries user information is called:
   a. Information frame.
   b. Supervisory frame.
   c. Unnumbered frame.
   d. Balanced frame.

10. Which of the following bit streams illustrates bit stuffing?
    a. 01011111 01010101
    b. 01001111 01111000
    c. 11110111 11100011
    d. 11111110 11111110

CD-ROM

Net+ Practice Test

Additional Net+ Certification testing is available on the CD that accompanies this text. The testing suite on the CD provides Study Card, Flash Card, and Run Practice type testing. The Study Card and Flash Card feature enables you to electronically link to the section of the book in which the question is covered. Choose questions from the test pool related to this chapter.

CHAPTER
6

LOCAL AREA NETWORKS

LEARNING
OBJECTIVES

Upon completion of this chapter and its related lab procedures, you should be able to perform the following tasks:

1. Define a LAN and a WAN in terms of geographical coverage.

2. Discuss the use of baseband vs broadband technology on the network.

3. Sketch several LANs communicating over a baseband and a wide area network.

4. State several responsibilities of a network and examples of network interfaces.

5. Describe the types of physical media and access protocols used with networks.

6. Draw simple sketches of mesh, star, ring and bus topologies.

7. State advantages and disadvantages for mesh, star, ring and bus topologies.

8. State two major areas of LANs covered by the IEEE 802 series of standards.

9. List the IEEE 802 series protocols for Ethernet, Token Bus, Token Ring.

10. Relate IEEE 802.3, .4 and .5 to the ISO OSI Reference Model.

11. Label a block diagram for the frame format for CSMA/CD.

12. State the purpose and length of each field of the IEEE 802.3 CSMA/CD frame.

13. Describe how Ethernet MAC addresses originate.

14. Define slot time, interframe gap, SQE, jam, backoff delay, and segment.

15. Discuss the procedure used with CSMA/CD for detecting collisions.

16. Sketch/design a typical/compliant Ethernet LAN using the IEEE 802.3 specs.

17. State the data rates and cabling types for several BaseT systems.

18. Describe how several BaseT data rates are achieved.

19. State several characteristics of 100VG-AnyLAN.

20. Sketch a typical migration plan from 10BaseT through 1000BaseT.

21. Label a block diagram for the IEEE 802.4 Token Bus frame, and describe the purpose and length of each field.

22. Discuss token passing and token recovery on a Token Bus network.

23. Label a block diagram of the IEEE 802.5 Token Ring frame.

24. State data rates available for Token Ring LANs.

25. Describe the purpose and length of each frame for the Token Ring.

26. Design/sketch a typical Token Ring LAN using IEEE 802.5 specifications.

27. Describe the process of token passing on a Token Ring network.

28. State the purpose, topology and specification for the ANSI FDDI protocol.

29. Label a block diagram of the FDDI protocol stack.

30. Discuss the functions/specifications of the Physical Medium Dependent layer, the Physical layer Protocol and the Media Access Control layer.

31. Label a block diagram of a FDDI token, frame, and state each field's purpose.

32. Describe the process of wring-wrapping a fault condition using FDDI.

33. Identify the Microsoft WFW, Windows NT, Novell NetWare, and UNIX OS's, their specific clients and resources, and their directory services.

34. Demonstrate the knowledge of NIC configuration, use of NIC diagnostics, and the ability to resolve hardware resource conflicts.

CHAPTER 6

Local Area Networks

INTRODUCTION

A network often crosses vendor boundaries by allowing different types of computers—and users—to communicate. The public telephone system is the largest network. Telephone system users have access to the system, and to nearly all parts of the world. Many devices (telephones, facsimile, computers, modems) are able to utilize the telephone system media. The telephone system media includes everything between the separate telephone jacks—cables, microwaves, protocols, switching centers, software, multiplexers, etc.

> A data communications network is a system of media allowing independent users to share information.

Since about 1980, computers have been systematically networked together to such an extent that the life of nearly everyone has been dramatically affected. The "911" emergency calls are a result of networks. Law enforcement agencies need only access codes to compare fingerprints at a rate of 80,000 comparisons per minute. The money machines offered by financial institutions allow you to make a withdrawal from your checking account, post the withdrawal to your account, and receive a hardcopy of the transaction—all done at 2:00am and a thousand miles from your bank. Network applications are nearly endless, but several examples will give you a feel for the diversity found in networks.

A company may occupy several floors of an office building. As is increasingly the case, computer power is being distributed among many of the company's departments. The distribution has tended to focus on many personal computers. With the distribution of computer work comes a logical tendency to share information from one PC to another. A network can be used in this situation to tie the many PCs together. Each PC remains an independent work station, and a peer to any other station in the network. The user still has a PC to work with, but also has access to work being performed, or residing in, the memory of another PC.

This same company may have offices at various locations around a city. Each office is equipped with PCs that the employees use as a part of their daily duties. As in the case of the PCs in located in one office building, the PCs located in different parts of a city may be connected together. In this case, the efficiency of the company is increased because of less work duplication.

Point-of-sale terminals are used in many retail and grocery chains. When a product is sold, an inventory adjustment is made to reflect the sale. This vastly improves the efficiency of managing the store, and the company inventories. Large chains are increasingly networking their stores.

Networks may also be distributed around the country. A business with a thousand offices, or stores, scattered over a wide geographical area, may network their offices to a central computer. Typically, the central computer updates inventory records, tracks sales/financial data, and employee records.

There are networks that tie together other networks. A network of PCs in a building may be networked to PCs in other buildings throughout a city. These PCs may be connected to a network of PCs in another city, and so on.

The ultimate trend of networking is to provide users access to any location in the world. The technical, logistical, and political concerns of such an endeavor are considerable. However, the technology exists today, and the logistics are becoming more feasible as hardware and software prices decrease. It is the political issues, from the ideologies of various countries, to user acceptance of standard protocols and interfaces, that have yet to be resolved.

TYPES OF NETWORKS

There's more information available describing the intricacies of networks than there is describing types of networks. One reason for this is that the type of network is heavily dependent upon usage. For the purposes of this book, networks will be generally divided into local area networks and wide area networks. As we'll see, the boundary between the two is vague, and crossovers frequently occur.

NET+ OBJECTIVE
I.1.7

CNST OBJECTIVE
I-A

Local Area Networks

A **Local Area Network** (LAN) shares the broad definition of networks in general: a system of sharing information. We'll specify the definition to the sharing of information of many users, from those in a single room, to users within a metropolitan area. This includes networks in a building, networks from building-to-building, and networks combining users throughout a city and surrounding communities.

Local-area networks may be operated as **baseband** and **broadband** networks. Typically, a baseband network is used when users are in close proximity—in a single room, from floor-to-floor in a building, or between adjacent buildings. Baseband networks don't require modems because of the short distances between users.

> A local area network shares information between users in a single room, to users within a metropolitan area.

A broadband network is usually required when the users are dispersed throughout a city. A modem couples the computer data to the telephone lines, and recovers it at the other end. A baseband network may be installed in a building, and communicate across a broadband network to other buildings, as shown in Figure 6-1.

Baseband networks restrict users to only one on the network at a time. In order to avoid having one user dominate the network, users are permitted access through **Time-Division Multiplexing** (TDM) of the network. Broadband networks, on the other hand, are essentially broadcast networks. Broadband users have access to a specified amount of bandwidth (frequency range) of the total available. This is achieved through the **Frequency-Division Multiplexing** (FDM) of a carrier frequency.

Local Area Networks (LANs) are one of those great ideas that caught on, and won't let go. What is so good about them? A LAN provides small-system users the ability to share resources in a way that was once only possible with larger computers. As an example of LAN benefits, imagine a car maker that decided to develop a new car model, and the development was done sequentially. The front bumper was designed, then the headlights, the parking lights, the front fenders, the hood, and so on. The process would be painfully slow and tedious. By the time the car maker got around to designing the engine and electronics, the car may very well be obsolete. For the small computer user, this was essentially their state ten years ago.

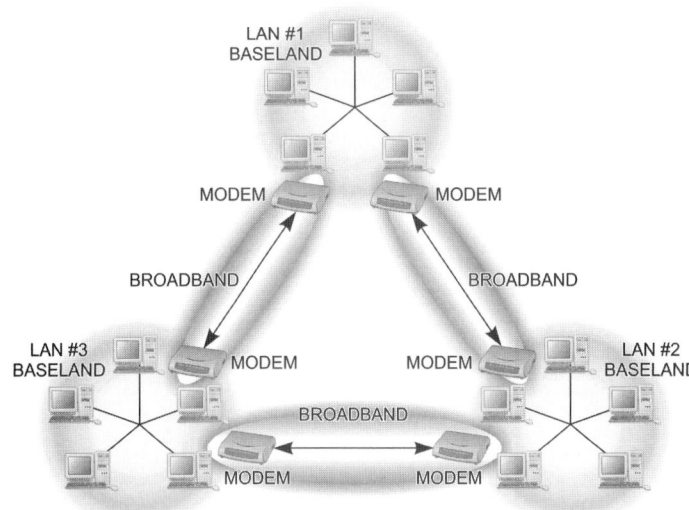

Figure 6-1 Baseband Networks Communicating Over a Broadband Network

Typically, when a LAN is considered, a business will have a number of stand-alone personal computers (10 to 1000 PCs). The LAN is installed to link the PCs together. It provides an efficient and manageable interconnected network for sharing, or distributing, a large amount of work among the attached PCs.

If the car maker in the previous example had a LAN, the design of the car could be distributed among engineers working with PCs. The body and frame could be handled by one PC, the engine by another, the transmission by a third, and the electronics by still another group. With the LAN, each group can design the car in parallel with other groups. If the engine design resulted in a last-minute body modification, the body engineers would simply request the new engine design, and incorporate the change into their ongoing work.

This example of distributed processing was once possible only with large computers. Now, with competitively-priced PCs and LANs, smaller businesses can become major players.

Wide Area Networks

> A Wide Area Network (WAN) is the sharing of information by users separated by a long distance. A long distance is the area beyond the metropolitan regions of a city.

A **Wide Area Network** (WAN) is the sharing of information by users separated by a long distance. A long distance is the area beyond the metropolitan regions of a city. Wide area networks are often called long-haul networks, a carry-over term from the telephone industry to describe long-distance calls. The Internet is a WAN as are corporate intranets that span across geographical regions.

NET+ OBJECTIVE
I.1.7

CNST OBJECTIVE
I-A

Some wide-area networks use a technique called **packet switching**. The data to be sent is disassembled by a **packet assembler/disassembler** (PAD) to be transmitted over the network. At the receiving end, another PAD reassembles the data, being careful to maintain the original packet sequence. A packet switching network is shown in Figure 6-2. This shows a mesh topology in which there are redundant links between nodes. Much of the public switched telephone uses a similar technique, while the Internet employs a mesh topology and uses logical addressing rather than a PAD.

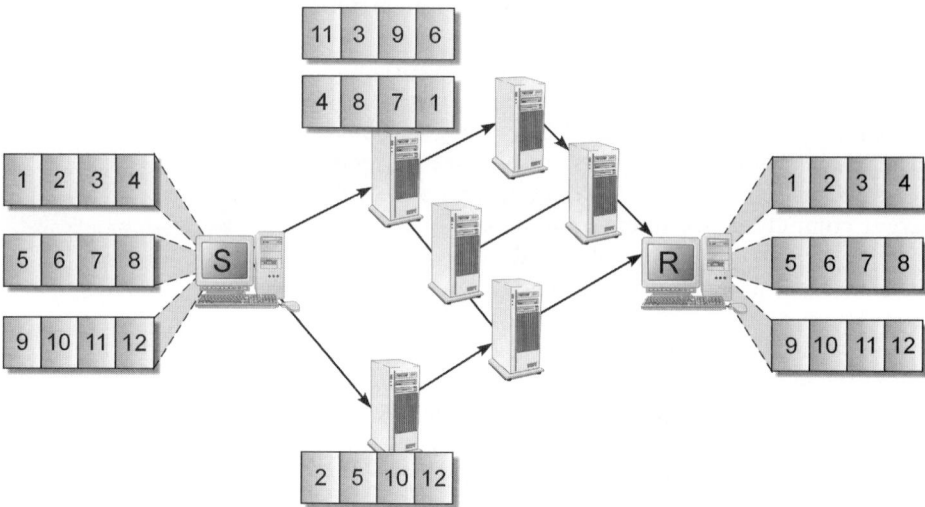

Figure 6-2 Packet Switching Network

Wide area networks are frequently used to connect local area networks. An example is a series of offices, each containing a LAN, but connected by a wide area network. This is shown in Figure 6-3. Each of the offices are in different cities, and each has a local area network. A wide area network, utilizing the long-distance telephone companies, connects the LANs. At the junction of the LAN and WAN is a **gateway**. A gateway is an interface between different types of networks.

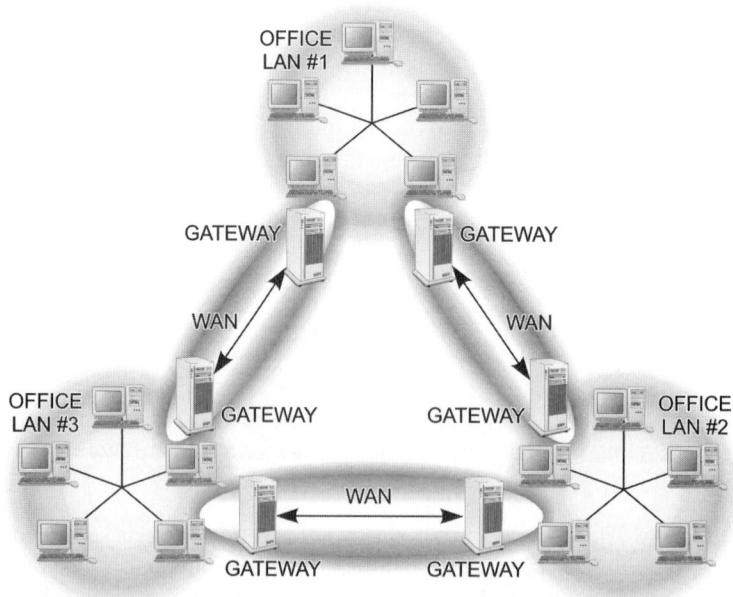

Figure 6-3 Gateways Interfacing LANS in a Wide Area Network

Wide area networks will be explored in detail throughout Chapter 10.

NETWORK CLASSIFICATIONS

Networks are classified by **transmission medium**, **access protocols**, **topology**, **type of modulation**, and **data rate** or **bandwidth**.

To describe a network as local, or wide, provides an indication of the geographical coverage of the network, and, by inference, the general capabilities of the network. Most networks are classified in further detail based upon performance criteria—how well they actually transfer data.

All networks, no matter what their particular advantages and disadvantages, have certain responsibilities to users. Before describing the particular classifications, it's worth mention- ing the fundamental user expectations of networks. It then becomes a matter of application to determine how well a particular type of network meets the overall purpose of the user.

At a minimum, a network should be **reliable**. If too much time is spent on data detection and correction, the network may not be **cost-effective**. The network should cost less than a competing method of data transfer (the U.S. mail or overnight express services, for example). The network should be **quick**, and offer a **sufficient amount of channel bandwidth** for the application. The network should offer **growth opportunities**. Finally, a network should be **easy to use**.

Networks are classified by **transmission medium**, **access protocols**, **topology**, **type of modulation**, and **data rate** or **bandwidth**. Once again, there is no definitive separation in the classifications. Two networks, using different access protocols, may use the same type of medium and topology. At the local area network level, the particular access protocol being used provides more insight than the other classifications into the capabilities and limitations of a network. The emphasis changes slightly when the LAN utilizes Network layer software (most do) because this layer is more concerned with node-to-node communication, and doesn't care how the network was actually accessed.

Interface

The interface refers to the hardware and signal parameters on the physical level. This includes EIA/TIA-232, EIA/TIA-422, EIA/TIA-423, EIA/TIA-449, and X.25 (packet switching), among others. In addition, interface is a reference to the Physical layer parameters. Examples of these include the IEEE 802 protocols, ANSI (American National Standards Institute) for fiber optic connectors and protocols, ISO, ITU for T-Carrier, SONET and others.

To describe a network in terms of physical parameters alone doesn't provide much information. One or more upper-layer logical protocols are directing the action at the physical level. And these, in turn, may use one or more physical interfaces.

NET+ OBJECTIVE
I.1.6

Transmission Medium

Media is the physical path along which the data travels from node to node. Twisted-pair wiring, coaxial cable, fiber-optic cable or microwaves are the transmission mediums. Twisted pair is usually associated with baseband LANs, and coaxial cable with either baseband or broadband. Fiber-optic cable can be used in either, but its use is limited by the topology selected. Microwaves are employed in wireless networks.

The mechanics of the various media were described in Chapter 2, but in this chapter, we'll revisit some of those specifications as they apply to standards used in the industry.

To say that a network uses CAT5 UTP, as opposed to thinnet coaxial, provides some insight into the performance of the system—CAT5 UTP can operate at higher data rates than coaxial (using common LAN protocols), so the network may be fast. However, if it's using fiber optic cable, it's not only fast, but it's not a bus topology either.

It may be in a star configuration, or a ring. It may be using Ethernet, or Token Ring, as the access method. To accurately describe a network, more information is needed.

Access Protocols

Recall from Chapter 5 that the Data Link layer protocols were subdivided into Logical Link Control and Media Access Control protocols. The LLC protocols were described in Chapter 5. In this chapter, the common MAC sublayer protocols will be described. The MAC sublayer actually extends to the Physical layer, and in the case of the IEEE 802 protocols, is specified as a Physical layer protocol.

You can't realistically separate protocols at this level from the physical interface that implements them, and there is an interface for just about any protocol that you can name. Because this chapter focuses on LANs, we'll examine those type of interfaces. In this context, interface will refer to the connectors used to attach a node to the network media, using one of the following protocols:

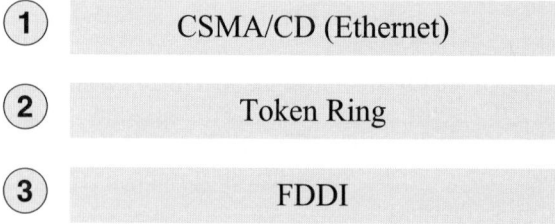

The sections to follow in this chapter will involve a detailed analysis of the access protocols. Interfaces which are associated with WANs will be examined in Chapter 8.

But before discussing network access methods, it's important to understand a couple of fundamental truths:

- A LAN will have multiple users.

- Errors (collisions, lost data, garbled data etc.) will occur on a network.

- In order to give all users a reasonable opportunity to use the network's resource, the information sent by each user will be limited. The method used to do so will involve framing the data, or by limiting the amount of time the user may access a network.

- Separating user data into frames also allows recovery from problems that will occur. Rather than loose all data sent, a user will only loose that data which was sent in a frame that encountered a problem.

Topology

Network topology is the physical arrangement of nodes. A node refers to any DTE—a computer, workstation, switching unit, etc. Network topologies are significant because they affect the network reliability, flexibility, cost of adding nodes, future growth, and the disruption of data flow when adding or deleting nodes.

> You can't realistically separate protocols at the MAC sublayer from the physical interface that implements them.

Originally, the purpose of formulating network topologies was to reduce the workload of workstations spent in routing data. If the routing workload is reduced, then more time can be spent shuttling data frames that carry user data. The basic idea of networks, then, is to more or less distribute the work among all the nodes. Topologies—the method chosen to physically connect nodes—directly affects the total time the network system manages itself. While great strides have been made in this area, there's remains much to be done. When considering the GHz speed of microprocessors, any attempt to send a packet of data with this same throughput will result in failure. It doesn't happen, even in the fastest networks.

The speed capabilities of end users have far out-paced speed developments in networking.

No one topology is best. Some have more advantages than others, and as such, have come to dominate the topology market. But networking changes in a blink, and what was discarded last year may very well be resurrected this year, clothed in a new technology. As with most of electronics in general, and data communications in particular, the best topology is the one that best fills the needs of the user.

It's significant to point out that a formal network isn't always necessary or desirable. A topologically defined network is only needed when production costs, and the consumption of time required to add and manage links, exceeds the costs of a network. In the purest implementation, a peer-to-peer topology (and by extension, a point-to-point topology) is the best network because at any one time, only two nodes are communicating. Visualize a personal computer connected to an ISP (Internet Service Provider), for example. Although this connection only directly involves two nodes, it's a full-fledged network in a point-to-point topology.

NET+ OBJECTIVE
I.1.1

CNST OBJECTIVE
VII-A

How will you know when it's time to network beyond the peer-to-peer relationship? By factoring sheer numbers and production costs. The most basic type of topology is the mesh, shown in Figure 6-4. This represents five computers that have been connected together. In a pure mesh network, each node has a physical link (coax, twisted pair, microwave, fiber optic) connection to all other nodes. Ten links are required to connect the five computers. If a sixth node is added, fifteen links will be required; if a seventh node is added, twenty-one links will be needed.

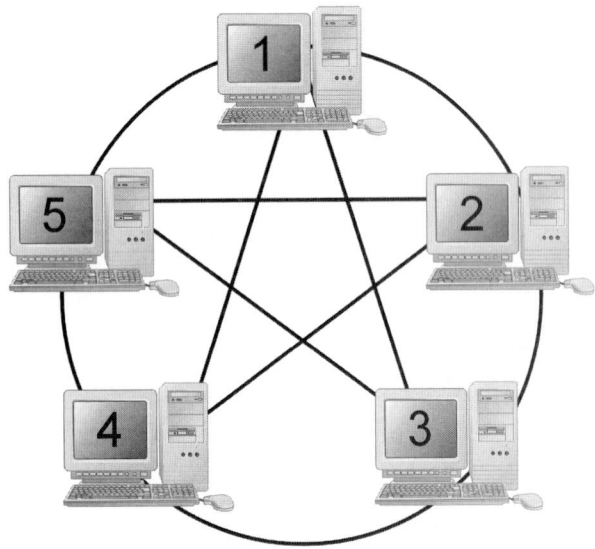

Figure 6-4 Mesh Network

The number of links required to service a specified number of nodes in a mesh network is found by:

$$Ln = [Nn(Nn-1)]/2$$

where Ln = number of links required, and Nn = number of nodes in the network.

If an office building has 99 PCs and the network administrator decides to add another, an additional 99 wires will be needed to tie the PCs together, for a total of 4,950 links! Somewhere, in those thousands of links, will be a point at which the cost of purchasing a more efficient network will make a lot of sense. And if we think about the arrangement, there will be a better way to physically organize the nodes, using one or more hubs, for example, that can simplify the thousands of wires needed.

Wireless LANs are basically mesh networks even though they share a common communication channel, or frequency range—unlike the above example in which multiple wires are needed for the common connection. Wireless systems have been around for a long time and have proven very effective in broadcast communications. Wireless networks have been around for some time, too. But only in the last couple of years has there been renewed interest in them, no doubt due to the explosive growth in cellular technology.

Mesh networks have their place. As mentioned, the Internet and public telephone system are both examples of mesh networks. However, the technologies used to manage the connections differ radically for these two examples as opposed to local area networks.

There are many topologies available. A few structures have come to dominate the market and these are well supported by hardware and software vendors. The three main topologies (at the LAN level) are the star, ring, and bus. Frequently, these topologies are combined to become hybrids. The topologies are protocol independent—CSMA/CD is usually run on bus and star networks, but also works well on ring networks. Each of the three will be discussed in terms of how the topology affects the operation of a network.

Star

The star topology consists of a central hub with spokes extending out from it and terminated in nodes, shown in Figure 6-5. The hub is essentially a complex switch used to connect the nodes. The star is one of the older topologies. In the early days of its use, it tended to be used inappropriately; that is, over long distances of many miles. If limited to the distance in a building, or adjacent buildings, and if the central hub retains the original intent as a switch—then it performs well.

> The star topology consists of a central hub with spokes extending out from it, and terminated in nodes.

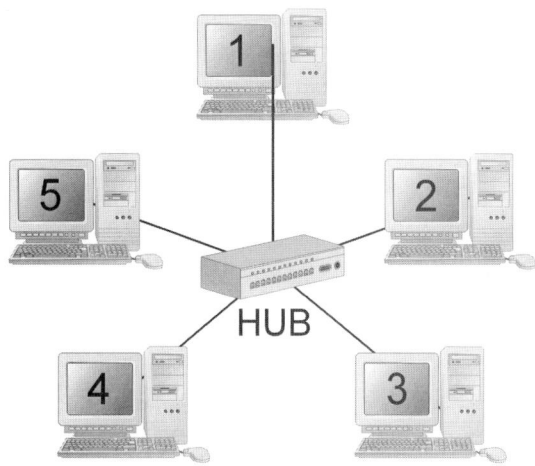

Figure 6-5 Star Topology

The performance factors of a star are paradoxical because for each advantage it has, a drawback is uncovered. It's one of the lowest cost-per-node topologies. All that's required is to add another node to a hub port. This sounds easier than it is. The addition of a node may require a long and awkward wire run, which means it's an expensive expansion. The relative ease of adding nodes makes the star a good contender for networks with good growth opportunities. However, a hub must be installed with the ports ready to be plugged into. In other words, you have to initially pay for a performance level you aren't utilizing.

Star topologies usually have low overhead and high throughput. But this depends on the hub. If the hub can switch only one message at a time, the hub may act like a bottleneck. If the nodes transmit data at a faster rate than the hub can switch it, then the hub buffers may overflow, and data from the nodes may be lost. The hub is the critical network component Many central hubs incorporate parallel switching for use in high-volume environments.

Since all traffic passes through a hub on the way to its destination, the hub is a useful point for regenerating signal levels. Noise that's acquired from a copper cable run can be eliminated by having the hub work as a repeater in a network. Then, as a repeater, it can also be used to segregate—or extend—the length of a LAN.

Notice that each node in a star topology is connected in a point-to-point arrangement with the hub. A node need only know the physical address of a hub in order to communicate with any other node. The hub, however, needs to know the physical address of all nodes, so that when it receives a data frame it can forward it on to the correct physical location. In other words, the hub may also work as a router in a LAN.

It's typical to have Ethernet running on a star LAN. If a hub is also used as a router or bridge, it can be configured to connect the Ethernet LAN to a Token Ring LAN. In this case, the topology is of a hybrid nature (meaning that two or more physical topologies comprise the network) and nodes on the different types of networks will be able to communicate.

NET+ OBJECTIVE
I.1.1

CNST OBJECTIVE
VII-A

Hubs do all of the above and more. The options available are almost endless, with some hubs having stackable capabilities so that you can add additional ports at a rate equal to the growth of your network. Other hubs consists of circuit cards which slip into slots of a chassis, so you can add functionality—router or gateway capabilities—as needed. And there's no need to bring the network down to add the electronics, since the chassis upgrades are "hot swappable", which means you add or remove the circuit cards without removing power. This keeps the network running while you do the upgrade.

Hubs come in several varieties. The following reviews the most common types:

- Passive Hubs: A passive hub requires no power and is used to organize wiring in a room or building. A patch panel is a passive hub.

- Active Hubs: Active hubs regenerate data signals. They are used to link coaxial cable segments, or to sub-divide larger UTP-based LANs. The require power and typically come with multiple-ports for node connections.

- Switching Hubs: Allows any port on the hub to be logically connected to any other port on a hub. This allows greater use of the available bandwidth on the network by assigning ports their own Ethernet segment.

Finally, the hub requires some sort of management as it grows. The more sophisticated hubs allow you to configure ports on the fly; that is with software. This saves the time of having to actually go to the wiring closet and move an RJ-45 connector from one port to another.

The reliability of the star is directly related to the hub. It's not unusual for several layers of switching redundancy to be built into the hub. This saves the entire network from crashing. A recent trend in star topologies has been to reduce complexity of the hub by distributing some of the work to nodes. This degrades an otherwise simple topology by complicating the nodes (and increasing cost), and requiring a more complex routing protocol.

Any of the physical media is suitable for star topologies, and any of the common character and bit-oriented protocols work well.

Ring

Ring topologies offer much versatility. The nodes are con- nected into a continuous loop, and data is passed from node to node, usually flowing in one direction (see Figure 6-6). Message transmission can use one of two techniques. The transmitting node gains access to the ring and sends it to the receive node, and the receive node removes the message. In the second technique, the sender transmits the message and the receiver makes a copy of the message, rather than rem- oving it from the ring. The message returns to the transmitter and serves as an acknowledgment that it was received.

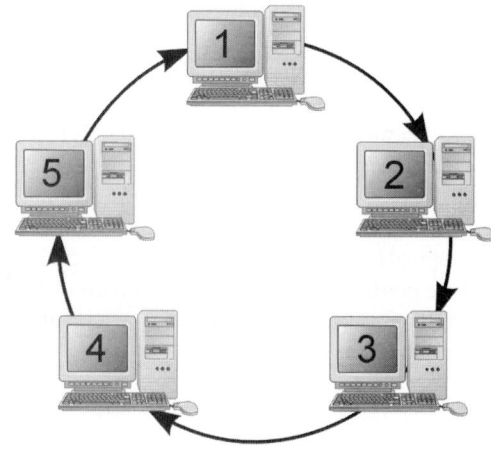

Figure 6-6 Ring Topology

> Ring topologies are connected into a continuous loop, and data is passed from node to node.

Rings have a high future-growth potential. To add another node, simply break the ring, and plug in the node. The ease with which changes can be made makes it a very flexible topology.

Speed and throughput are a function of the nodes. This network will only work as well as the poorest performing node. Assuming all nodes are of similar integrity, efficiencies run quite high, with +90% throughput common. Routing decisions are quite simple since data travels in only one direction. The nodes—which monitor routing—can be made simpler, and dedicated to the primary task of transmitting and receiving data.

The major disadvantage of ring topologies is one of reliability. If one node fails, the whole system may fail. In anticipation of this, ring designers use data-path redundancies. In Figure 6-7, the link between nodes 1 and 2 is broken. Data is rerouted around the break, and onto the spare ring. Once the break is bypassed, data returns to the primary ring.

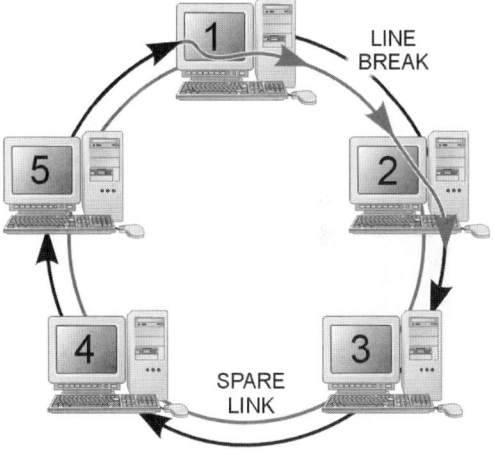

Another drawback of ring networks is that if a node is added, the ring must be broken. Network message flow can continue by bypassing the node, but eventually the node will have to be actively wired into the network to ensure its operational status, etc. During this time, the network is down.

Three basic techniques are used for gaining access to a ring network: **token passing**, **fixed slots**, and **delay insertion**. In token passing, the token presents control of the network to the node holding the token. The token may be offered to each node sequentially, or the nodes may contend for it.

The fixed-slot technique calls for dividing the ring channel into fixed slots that circulate around the ring. If a slot arrives at a node that has data to transmit, it fills the slot; or the node may remove data from the slot. If the data is addressed to that node, it removes the data and the now-empty slot moves on to be filled by a node with a message to send.

Figure 6-7 Spare Ring Topology

The delay-insertion technique calls for incoming messages to be delayed. During the delay time, a node can transmit data. Once the delayed messages arrive at the node, the transmitter is turned off and data that didn't get transmitted is stored in a transmit buffer. The node also contains a receive buffer. If the node is unable to process the received messages before the transmitter is turned back on, they are stored in the receive buffer.

Token passing is easy to implement and widely used. Unfortunately, if not carefully monitored, throughput can nosedive with a corresponding increase in overhead. Delay insertion is very efficient, but requires more complex, and expensive, nodes.

Token Ring topologies are attributed to IBM. They have used them successfully for years, and the main reason for that success is that they were used appropriately; that is, in a small environment in which there was a need for predictability and control of which nodes had access to the network. The topology fell out of favor for some years because network managers tried to replace Ethernet LANs with Token Ring (Token Ring LANs were running at 16MBPS, while Ethernet ran at 10MBPS) with the intent of speeding up their networks.

NET+ OBJECTIVE
I.1.1

It didn't work. On a bit-by-bit basis, a 16M Token Ring LAN will have higher delays than a 10MBPS Ethernet LAN. On the surface, then, the Token Ring solution didn't make sense. But you have to look a bit deeper than simply speed and delays. The access methods used with Token Ring offer advantages that Ethernet will never have—but things change.

Ring topologies are now an important part of distributed LANs. Typically, several Ethernet LANs connect to the ring and it's used as a backbone for connecting the Ethernet networks. The ring media is fiber optic and runs at a speed of 100MBPS (FDDI), much faster than 10MBPS Ethernet "nodes" connected to its ports—and equal to the 100MBPS data rates of Fast Ethernet.

Any physical media can be used with rings. They lend themselves particularly well to fiber optics systems.

CNST OBJECTIVE
VII-A

Bus

Of all networks, the bus is the predominant topology, though its use in networking is used less and less. A bus topology may be inches long, or miles long. It's the favored architecture for routing data and address information in computers, and by extension, was one of the first topologies used in networking.

CNST OBJECTIVE
VII-A

> A bus topology may be inches long or miles long.

A typical bus topology is illustrated in Figure 6-8. Nodes are attached to the network bus through interface units. Data are transferred and received through specified node addresses. The most efficient bus networks will decentralize the routing decision workload among the nodes. In some networks, a node is assigned to be a centralized network controller, or server. Many of the routing decisions and protocol implementations are performed by the central work station. The controller may be fully dedicated to managing the network (and no longer available as a work station), or it may serve as controller, while retaining workstation functions. The mode of the controller in centralized bus topologies is determined by network vendors. Originally, network control was centralized, but as mentioned in Chapter 1, user demands have caused the trend to shift away from this concept, and to distribute control among the user nodes.

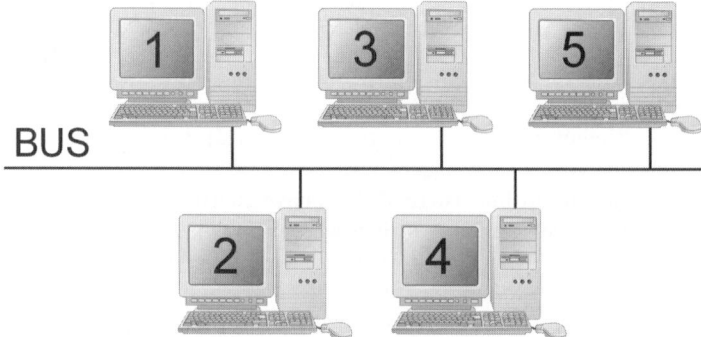

**Figure 6-8 Bus
Topology**

With the proper protocol, bus topologies can be one of the best performers. It's easy to add nodes by simply plugging them into the bus, and the reliability of the bus is very high. However, an electrical fault may render a portion of the bus inoperable. If a bus opens, or a short occurs, the entire network could crash, or a node may be damaged.

As in ring structures, there are three common technologies associated with transporting data across the bus: **polling**, **time slots**, and **contention**. With the poll technique, a transmitting station may be asked by the controller if it has a message to send. If the node has nothing, the poll moves on to the next node. In many bus networks, the user can prioritize nodes so that if a node midway along the bus declines to transmit, the poll is reset and the first node on the network is polled. Each time the poll is declined, it's reset and polls the first node. The first node has been assigned the highest priority to transmit.

A simpler technique for granting nodes access to the network is the time slot. A master oscillator in the controller begins a counting sequence, and when the count matches a node's assigned ID count, that node sends a message to the controller to transmit. The master oscillator is turned off, and the node has the network to itself. When combined with a fast switch or router, this method is extremely effective.

The most common access method is the contention-based technique. Nodes that have messages to send compete for control of the channel, and eventually, a winner emerges.

Data communications over cable systems (used to access the Internet using cable television fiber/coaxial media) use bus topologies with the coaxial cable serving as a backbone to subscribers. As in any bus topology, the subscribers share the backbone's bandwidth using one of the methods described above, resulting in Internet access that is much faster than through dial-up telephone lines. Prior to the demand for cable modems, bus topologies had been relegated to specialized applications or small LANs, out of mainstream networking. But, things change.

The bus topology isn't without drawbacks. It's the only network that can't easily use end-to-end fiber optics, since the bus taps make for an awkward connection. The length of the bus may create problems. The nodes furthest from a server (if used) may be ignored occasionally. The length of the bus creates opportunities for noise to distort control messages, and the cumulative voltage drop can cause messages to be lost altogether. Long buses require that repeaters be selectively placed to boost the signal strength and restore its shape.

NET+ OBJECTIVE
I.1.1

Since all users share the bandwidth, speeds are related to the number of users. The more users on a bus topology, the slower it operates. One solution to this drawback has been to avoid MAC-layer protocols such as CSMA, and employ only Network layer protocols. ATM shows the most promise because of its small cell size and low frame overhead.

IEEE 802 FAMILY OF LAN STANDARDS

The IEEE 802 standards consist of specifications of the **Media Access Control** sublayer of layer 2, the **Data Link** layer; and descriptions of the electrical and physical characteristics at the **Physical** layer.

CNST OBJECTIVE
IV-B

Perhaps one of the reasons LANs have been so widely embraced by users is the existence of well-documented standards. In 1985, the IEEE approved a series of LAN standards describing several recommendations for implementing LANs at layers 1 and 2 of the OSI reference model. Since then, the ISO has adopted the standards, exactly as approved by the IEEE, in ISO 8803 series of standards. The recommendations are referred to as the IEEE 802 standards. The 802 standard describes two major portions of LANs:

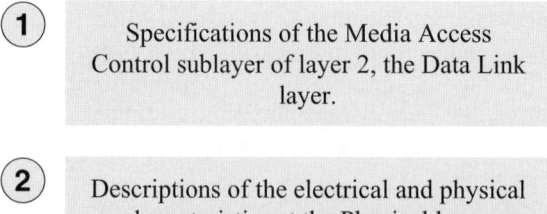

1 Specifications of the Media Access Control sublayer of layer 2, the Data Link layer.

2 Descriptions of the electrical and physical characteristics at the Physical layer.

Figure 6-9 details the Data Link level. The LLC was dealt with in Chapter 5. As described by IEEE 802.2, it's identical to the Type field used with HDLC. In the sections to follow, the specifications of frame format, addressing, and control fields will be described in the context of specific access methods.

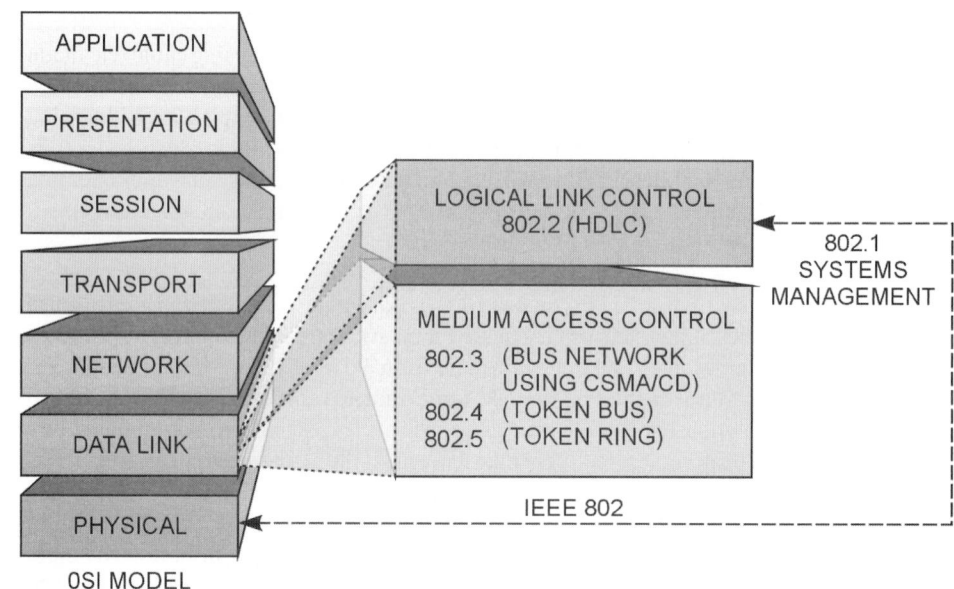

Figure 6-9 IEEE 802 Standards

The Media Access Control is the lower sublayer of the Data Link level. The 802 standards for this sublayer describe how various techniques are used to gain access to a network.

IEEE 802.1 describes the system's management between the logical link, the medium-access methods, the Physical layer, and a network with the upper OSI levels. Essentially, it describes the architecture of the system manager. Areas of involvement include protocol initialization, and parameters for error control or security. This standard won't be discussed further.

In practice, protocol 802.2 is confined to the Data Link level, as shown in Figure 6-9. But the MAC sublayer protocols (802.3, 802.4, 802.5, etc.) actually cross the boundary to the physical level in their scope of operation, and as such, are more correctly referred to as Physical layer protocols. As we'll see in the following sections, there are two main access methods: **contention** and **token passing**. Each of the methods will be explored in detail. The IEEE 802 standards are summarized in Table 6-1. Many have been adopted by the ISO for the OSI Reference Model.

Table 6-1 Description of IEEE 802 Standards for LANs

IEEE 802 STANDARDS	
802.1	Systems standard for local and metropolitan area networks.
802.2	Logical-Link Control (LLC) sublayer.
802.3	CSMA/CD access, including MAC sublayer and Physical layer signaling (10Base2, 10Base5, 10BaseT, 100BaseT, 1000BaseT, 10Broad36).
802.4	Token bus. Included in the Manufacturing Automation Protocol suite (MAP).
802.5	Token Ring.
802.6	Metropolitan Area Networks. Specifies a dual fiber optic bus with time slots.
802.7	Broadband technology.
802.8	Fiber optic technology.
802.9	Integrated Voice and Data. Describes use of ISDN devices with LANs.
802.10	LAN security.
802.11	Wireless LANs.
802.12	100VG-AnyLAN.

Most vendor specifications will refer to one of these standards when describing their LAN product. This chapter emphasizes 802.3, 802.4, and 802.5. A thorough understanding of LAN protocols is essential to evaluating networks, and they will be discussed in detail in the next three sections. Protocols aren't static. They change because there's always a better way discovered to network. Also, users want more speed and bandwidth, and vendors want more market share—because we simply aren't content to limit our achievements. You can keep abreast of LAN-level changes by visiting the IEEE Web site at www.ieee.org/.

IEEE 802.3 ETHERNET

The 802.3 standard for bus networks is founded upon the joint efforts of Digital Equipment Corporation, Intel and Xerox. The original standard was called Ethernet, and the name has been retained although the current versions are not the same as the original. The original is now called Ethernet I, or simply "the DIX standard" after the founding companies.

Based upon experimental works performed in Xerox laboratories, the three companies sought commercial applications of Xerox research. The result, in 1980, was a data communications network called **Ethernet**. Ethernet represented the first non-proprietary network, and vendors were encouraged to design equipment geared toward Ethernet. Many vendors did indeed do so. In 1985, the DIX version was revised, and this version, called Ethernet II, was submitted to the IEEE. The IEEE used Ethernet II as the foundation for bus network standards called IEEE 802.3 Carrier Sense Multiple Access with Collision Detection Access Method and Physical Layer Specifications. Whew! If you try to say all that a few times, you'll quickly realize why the standard is simply called Ethernet.

There are four basic variations of Ethernet in use today. The distinguishing factor from one to the next is subtle differences in the frame format—the manner used to package data so it can be sent onto the network. None are compatible with the other. Table 6-2 lists the types and includes brief differences and typical applications.

Table 6-2 Ethernet Frame Types

Ethernet Frame Types		
Frame Types	**Features**	**Applications**
Ethernet 802.3	Also called *raw Ethernet*, the frame begins with a 7-byte Preamble which is followed by a 1-byte Start Frame Delimiter. Along with source and destination address fields, a 2-byte length field is included that specifies the length of the data field. Ethernet 802.3 is not in compliance with IEEE 802.3	Used in NetWare version 2.2 and 3.x networks
Ethernet 802.2	This frame type includes three fields from the LLC-sublayer and is in full compliance with IEEE 802.3.	Used in NetWare version 3.12 and 4.x networks.
Ethernet SNAP	Ethernet SNAP (Sub-Network Address Protocol), is similar to Ethernet 802.3 except the length field is replaced with a Type field. The Type field specifies network layer protocol in the Data (Information) field.	Used in AppleTalk networks.
Ethernet II	The preamble and start frame delimiter are combined into a single 8-byte Preamble field. A 2-byte Type field is included (but not a length field) which contains Network layer information and LLC-sublayer information.	Typically used in TCP/IP networks. Ethernet running across the Internet is likely to use Ethernet II.

Although not technically correct, IEEE 802.3 CSMA/CD is referred to as Ethernet.

The basis of the standard, at the logical level, is the medium-access technique known as **Carrier-Sense Multiple-Access/Collision** (contention) **Detect** (CSMA/CD). It's operated in both baseband and broadband modes.

The IEEE 802.3 standards specify that the protocol used is Ethernet, while the access method used is CSMA/CD. When CSMA/CD is operating in a baseband mode, it doesn't use a carrier, so the acronym is a little misleading. The terminology derives from using Manchester encoding with CSMA/CD. Recall from earlier chapters that data are frequently encoded to prevent the build-up of a dc component when long strings of 1's and 0's are transmitted (intersymbol interference). The positive and negative transitions of the Manchester code are a continuous event, so the constant repetition is similar to the predictability of a carrier. A CSMA/CD node samples (or senses) the channel for Manchester data. From this process, the "carrier sense" is derived.

All nodes have access to the media; i.e., "multiple access." In a network operating in the baseband mode, only one node can transmit at a time (half-duplex). If two nodes attempt to transmit at the same time, the messages will collide. When a collision occurs, it's detected in the first 64 bytes of a transmission. Detection occurs before the signal has had time to be received by any stations on the channel. The terminology "collision detect" comes from this.

The data frame format for CSMA/CD is depicted in Figure 6-10. The 7-byte preamble is a series of alternating 1s and 0s used for synchronization. The start frame delimiter consists of the bit pattern 10101011. The last bit in the preamble is used to designate the start of the frame. It tells the receiving node that the synchronization time is completed and the next bit begins the start of critical frame information. Depending on the type of Ethernet frame used (See Table 6-1) the preamble and start frame delimiter fields may be combined into a single 8-byte field.

PHYSICAL LEVEL		MEDIUM ACCESS CONTROL DATA LINK LEVEL					PHYSICAL LEVEL
7	1	2 OR 6	2 OR 6	2		4	4
PREAMBLE	START FRAME DELIMITER	DESTINATION ADDRESS	SOURCE ADDRESS	LENGTH	DATA 46-1500 BYTES	FCS	END FRAME DELIMITER

Figure 6-10 CSMA/CD Data Frame Format

When a frame tries to send data, the preamble and delimiter are sent first. If a collision is going to occur, it will be during this period of time. Since the first two fields of the frame don't contain critical data, the collision must be detected within this 64-byte window, because if an Ethernet frame collision occurs past this point, the frame will be lost. If there's no collision, the two communicating nodes use the fields for bit synchronization. The end frame delimiter formally ends the frame. This is physical activity occurring on the network. Because it's actual bits being discussed, the IEEE 802.3 is a Physical layer protocol. Remember, implementing the 802 standards results in a crossover between the Physical and Data Link levels.

All nodes, or stations, on the network have a unique address. A 6-byte length is permitted. The original version of Ethernet specified a 6-byte address; IEEE 802.3 permits a 2-byte alternative that is seldom used. At this time, the first three bytes of an address field are assigned by the IEEE, while the last three bytes are assigned by the user (network administrator). The first three bytes tend to be vendor-specific, since vendors reserve blocks of addresses for their products. A partial list of the addresses for various vendors is shown in Figure 6-11. The reason the addresses are assigned is so that the address will remain unique for any Ethernet port. Originally, XEROX supplied the addresses, but has since delegated the responsibility and control to the IEEE. Any addresses assigned prior to the change-over were retained.

NET+ OBJECTIVE
I.3.1

Sample Vendor MAC Addresses	
Hex Address	**Vendor**
00000C	Cisco
00001D	Cabletron
00003D	AT&T (One of several.)
00005E	US Department of Defense
000062	Honeywell
00608C	3COM
00C0BE	Alcatel
080006	Apple
080009	Hewlett Packard
08005A	IBM (One of several.)
1000D4	DEC

Figure 6-11 Vendor MAC Address

Ethernet addresses are commonly called "MAC addresses", or "physical addresses". This is used to differentiate them from logical addresses assigned at the Transport layer (in Network layer software). Since a MAC addresses is hard-wired into the circuitry of a node, it must go wherever the node goes. The usual implementation occurs in a **Network Interface Card** (NIC) containing transceiver and frame-formatting electronics. If you remove an NIC card from one PC, and place it in another PC, you have to tell the Network layer software (NetWare, NT, etc.) that you've done so, or run the risk of blocking the node from the network. In larger LANs, this is a requirement.

Ethernet addresses are commonly called "MAC addresses", or "physical address".

Ethernet (the IEEE 802.3 version) includes a source and destination address, which means it's assumed to be operating in the LAPB, HDLC-like mode. Nodes are peers, so they need to specify where a frame is being sent, and where it came from. The receiving node will acknowledge a frame receipt in an LLC frame, within the Data field of an Ethernet frame. In order to do so, it needs to know which node sent it the frame. The destination address is needed so that the sending node can communicate the destination of its frame to the LLC and Network layers.

NET+ OBJECTIVE
I.3.1

In a small LAN, consisting of nodes sharing the same cable infrastructure, getting a frame to its destination is rather straightforward. Each node compares the destination address to its own address and, if they match, reads it into the buffers of its own NIC card. If it doesn't, the frame is ignored. But in larger networks, in which a bridge or router is used to link several LANs, finding the destination address isn't so easy. For example, assume that a new computer is attached to the network, and you want to send an e-mail welcoming the new user. How does your computer know that the new PC is attached? How does it know the MAC address of the user, since it's burned into the hardware of the NIC card? In a nutshell, the network may use one of several approaches, ranging from receiving a simple "Hello"! from the new node, to checking a lengthy user-name address map contained in the memory of a router. We'll take a detailed look at these routing protocols in a later chapter.

The Length field contains 2 bytes to indicate the amount of data that's contained in the data field. This includes any frames from the upper layers, as well as all user data. In short, the Length field indicates the size of the data field. What isn't counted are bytes that may be placed in the Data field—called pads—that are used to pad the frame size, so that it's a minimum of 64 bytes.

Some versions of Ethernet (Ethernet II, for example. See Table 6-1.) omit the length field and replace it with a Type field. This is the same type field described in the previous chapter for the LLC-sublayer. It contains addressing information for the Network layer software.

The CSMA/CD Data field may contain many bytes of information from the upper layers. For example, the entire LLC frame is embedded in the CSMA/CD Data field. Remember that the LLC communicates the type of software running at the Network layer, and includes several types of (HDLC) frames—information, supervisory, or unnumbered. The logical-link message also reserves space for information data.

Following the Data field is a 32-bit frame-check sequence, using the **Cyclic Redundancy Check** (CRC) algorithm. The FCS is used to detect errors in the frame.

The CSMA/CD frame function is constructed from information supplied by the Logical-Link Control sublayer. In turn, the LLC receives its information from Network layer software (IP, NetBIOS, etc.). The functionality is apparent in the addressing scheme, and may include broadcast frames sent to all nodes, or the network can be stipulated as Type I or Type II. Recall from the last chapter that a Type I network is connectionless, and a Type II is connection-oriented. In Type I operation, the LLC sublayer is nothing more than a pass-through to the MAC sublayer. Stations don't send acknowledgments, there's no need for flow control, and Network layer addressing can be either individual, or broadcast to all stations. In Type II networks—the type of LAN usually associated with Ethernet—there is a need for flow control and error-recovery procedures.

The CSMA/CD protocol operates by continuously monitoring the channel for other transmitting stations. If the channel is being used, the station waits until it's cleared. Once the station detects no carrier, it waits 9.6µS and then transmits. This is equivalent to 96 bits on a 10MBPS LAN, and is called the **InterFrame Gap** (IFG). The delay is necessary to give the other stations time to reset after receiving or transmitting a message.

Once a station begins transmitting, if there's to be a collision, it will happen in the first 512 bits (64 bytes) of the transmission. This bit time is called the **slot time** (or collision window), and is related to the round-trip propagation delay on the network, which is 51.2µS. The receive and transmit circuitry in the station detects the collision by measuring the average dc voltage on the network. On the network, a logic $0 = 0$ volts, and a logic $1 = –2.05$ volts; the average of the two conditions equals 1 volt [$(0 + 2.05)/2 = 1$ volt]. When two stations transmit at the same time, the average voltage rises to about 1.5 volts, and the collision-detect circuits inform the transmitter that there's been a collision. The IEEE defines a collision as a **Signal Quality Error** (SQE), which has created some confusion.

The Ethernet II used a mechanism called a **heartbeat** which served the same purpose of the SQE, to check for proper media functioning. However, the two mechanisms aren't compatible, and the IEEE 802.3 standard stipulates that, when the two versions of Ethernet are mixed, the heartbeat from Ethernet II must be turned off.

Once the collision occurs, and is detected by the transmitting stations, the transmitter continues to transmit for 32 bits. This bit time is called a **jam**. A jam is necessary to make sure each transmitting station has had time to detect the collision, and 32 bits is the maximum time it takes data to travel the length of a **segment**, 25.6µS. At the end of 32 bits, the station will stop transmitting.

The nature of a CSMA/CD network is to create collisions.

When a station has stopped transmitting, it backs off from further transmitting by a randomly selected time interval, based on its MAC address. The **backoff delay** varies slightly with each station, since each one has a different address. At the end of the backoff delay, each transmitting station tries again. If there's another collision, the backoff times will be doubled. After sixteen attempts to transmit, the station generates an error, and stops trying. Because of the exponential binary algorithm used with backoff delays, it's extremely improbable that any two stations will continue to create a jam over the full sixteen tries. However, if this occurs, any data that was in the attempted frame is lost at the MAC layer. Collision detection is shown in Figure 6-12.

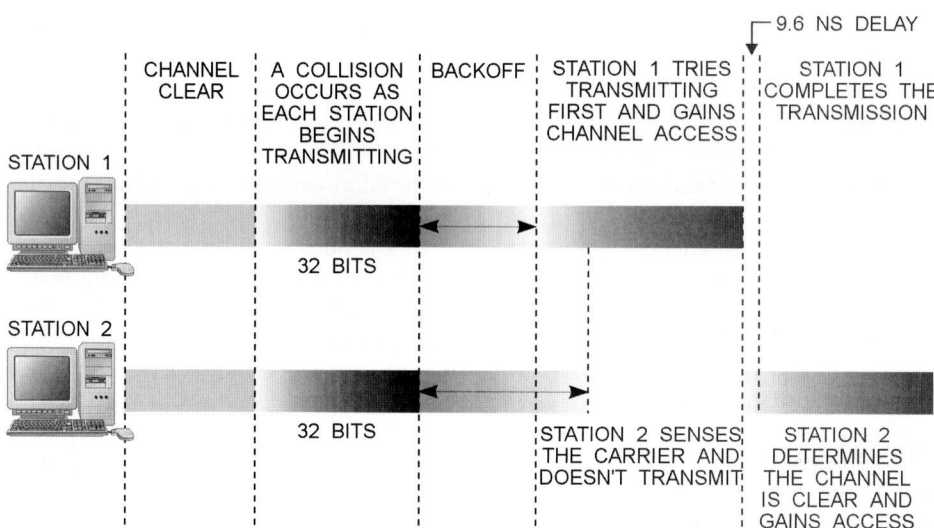

Figure 6-12 CSMA/CD Collision Detection

Note that the nature of a CSMA/CD network is to create collisions. The more nodes on the network, the more collisions. This is why the number of stations on the link segments are limited. The same is true for the volume of traffic running on a network. Network traffic is measured as **utilization rates**.

This is the ratio of the amount of time the network is used, to the amount of time that it's idle. The time is surprisingly small, averaging between 20% to 40%. But it tends to peak at certain times such as the mornings, when e-mail is checked, and responded to. As the utilization rises, collisions will increase non-linearly—that is, a doubling of the utilization rate will create more than a doubling of collisions. As you might imagine, the network slows down in the same fashion as delays increase. As a rule of thumb, a utilization rate of about 75% is the maximum for networks.

As mentioned earlier, the IEEE 802.3 CSMA/CD protocol is very similar to the original Ethernet. However, there are exceptions. Ethernet contains a Type field prior to the Data field. The Type field specifies the type of frame as information, unnumbered or supervisory. It serves an identical function to the LLC frame that's encapsulated in the Data field of an 802.3 frame. In its place, 802.3 has a Length field, and as mentioned previously, it gives the length of the data field.

IEEE 802.3 CSMA/CD is a mouthful. It should come as no surprise, then, that the term "Ethernet" has been retained in the networking industry even when Ethernet is actually obsolete. For the purposes of this book, consider "Ethernet" to mean the IEEE 802.3 protocol, and not the original DIX, Ethernet I or Ethernet II versions. Table 6-3 shows specifications for IEEE 802.3a-t. (The specifics of the 802.3 variants are described in the sections to follow.) These specifications are valid for Ethernet running at 10MBPS or less.

Table 6-3 IEEE 802.3a-t Specification

Attempt Limit	16
Backoff Limit	10
Insertion Loss	11.5dB at 5-10MHz
Interframe Gap	9.6μS
Jam Size	32 bits
Maximum Bridge Hops	7
Maximum Propagation Delay	21.6μS one-way, 51.2μS round trip
Maximum Repeater Hops	4
Maximum Segments	5 (3 with nodes; 2 as link segments)
Maximum Stations on Network	1024
Maximum Frame Size	1514 bytes
Slot Time	512 bits (64 bytes)
Minimum Frame Size	64 bytes

	10Base5	10Base2	10BaseT (STP)	10BaseT (UTP)	AUI	Fiber	
Attenuation	Max 8.5dB at 10MHz Max 6.0dB at 5MHz		8-10dB at 20ºC		3dB over frequency range	50/125μm	≤13dB
						62.5/125μm	≤16dB
						100/140μm	≤19dB
						8-12/125μm	≤10dB
Impedance	50 ± 2Ω		150Ω	85-111Ω			
Jitter	≤ 8.0nS		≤ ± 5.0μS		1.5nS at receiver		
Limits	≤ 2.5km between receivers					5 segments max: link segment ≤ 500m, w/4 segments and 3 repeaters, max segment is 1000m	
Max Propagation Delay/Link Seg	2165nS	950nS	1000nS		257nS	5000nS	
Maximum Cable Length	500m	185m	200m	100m	50m	1000m	
Minimum Cable Length		.5m					
Min Separation Between MAUs	2.5m	.5m					
Stations/Segment	100	30	2	2	1DTE/ 1MAU	2	

A typical Ethernet installation is shown in Figure 6-13. In this configuration, three 24-port repeater/hubs are running Ethernet in a star topology to 72 nodes. According to the 802.3 standard, this is a small LAN because it could support up to 1,024 nodes.

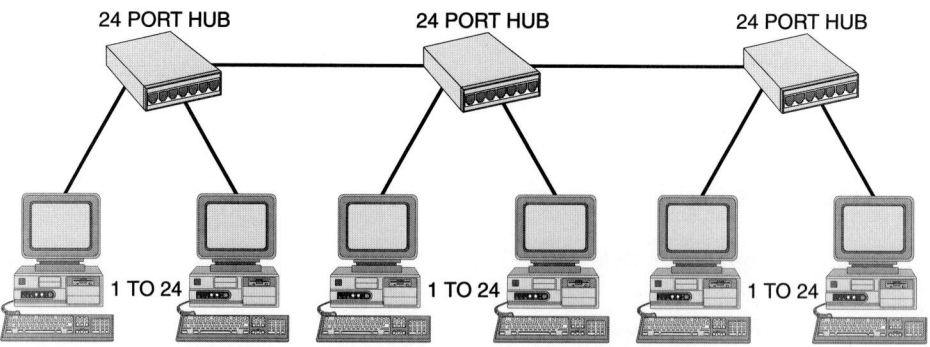

Figure 6-13 Typical Ethernet Installation

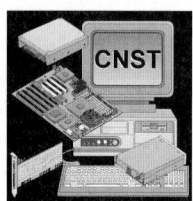

CNST OBJECTIVE
VII-A

The entire LAN as you see it in the Figure is a network. A **network**, in the context of Ethernet, means that if a collision occurs, it will be sensed by all nodes. The LAN could also be called a segment if it was a part of a larger, interconnected network. Figure 6-14 illustrates this scenario. Two identical LANs (A and B) have been linked by a bridge. A collision on LAN A will not be sensed by any of the nodes on LAN B since the router filters traffic between the two **networks** which consists of two **segments** in an **internetwork**.

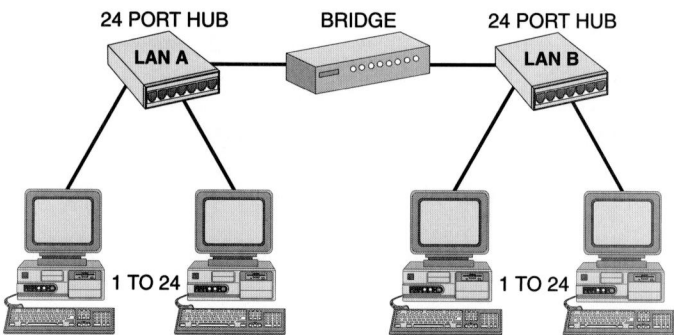

**Figure 6-14
Interconnected Ethernet
LANs**

Note that in a star topology using 10Base-T Ethernet, a **segment** is understood to mean the wire from hub port to node. A single node may be connected on a segment. For Ethernet LANs using a different media—coaxial—more than one node is permitted on a segment.

Another scenario is pictured in Figure 6-15. This time, four 48-port repeater hubs (IEEE 802.3 permits a hub size of up to 132 ports) are stacked, presumably in a wiring closet. The four hubs have a total of 192 nodes connected them. Since the hubs are nothing more than signal regenerators, all nodes are in the same **network**. Because this is a 10Base-T LAN running UTP cable, each connection from node to hub port is a **segment** and is limited to a maximum length of 100 meters.

If, on the other hand, the LAN shown in Figure 6-15 were cabled with coaxial instead of UTP, we have a different situation. The hubs may still be linked (stacked) together, but the nodes could be daisy-chained together in a bus arrangement (making it a star-bus topology). Coaxial media topologies are driven by the 5-4-3 rule which states that Ethernet networks can have *five segments*, connected to *four repeaters*, with only *three of the segments populated* with nodes connected in a bus.

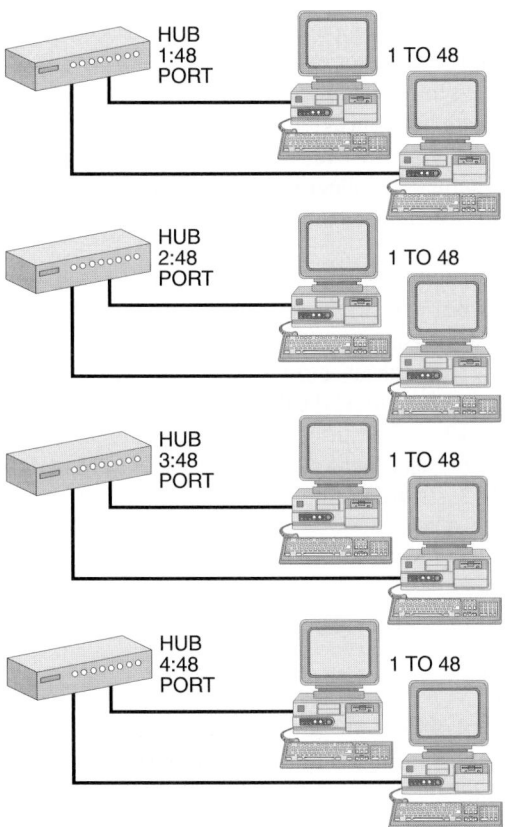

Figure 6-15 Ethernet LAN with Repeater Hubs

CNST OBJECTIVE VII-A

The three Ethernet LANs in the above example are using CAT5 UTP in the cabling infrastructure. At least one, (probably two or more) of the nodes is a server. A Network layer software package such as Windows NT or Novell NetWare is managing the flow of packets, as well as providing a level of reliability in the form of acknowledgments at the LLC sublayer. The nodes are all communicating in half-duplex; that is, one gains access to the media bandwidth, sends a packet, then vies for access again. If a receiving node has a response to the sending node, it has to wait until it gains access to the media. Or, in other words, 10MBPS Ethernet—at the node level—is a half-duplex protocol.

It doesn't have to be. Recall that HDLC is a full-duplex protocol, and Ethernet shares an identical LLC frame format, where the Ns and Nr count fields are located. At the time the standard was being determined, though, the predominate media was coaxial, and full-duplex operation on coax was cost-prohibitive. Since then, technology has changed, prices have dropped, and full-duplex is a reality for Ethernet. However, at 10MBPS data rates, it remains half-duplex.

The IEEE 802.3 maximum data rate (20 MBPS) is full-duplex, but it's rarely implemented at the end-user node. Full-duplex is routinely run at the Network layer, and above, for Ethernet frames. Routers and switches, for example, send and receive simultaneously.

IEEE 802.3u Fast Ethernet

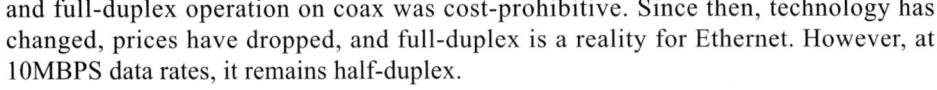

IEEE 802.3u Fast Ethernet runs at 100 MBSP.

Fast Ethernet is very similar to the 10MBPS variety, except it uses a modified physical interface, and it runs ten times as fast at 100MBPS. Why do we need to get faster?

NET+ OBJECTIVE
I.1.6

CNST OBJECTIVE
IV-B & VII-A/B

Comparatively speaking, networks are slow when compared to their silicon colleagues in the nodes they connect. A modern microprocessor, for example, runs hundreds of times faster than the data that it generates can be sent to another computer. This means that the servers connected to a LAN or WAN, such as an intranet or the Internet, are prepared to serve users faster than the network technology can bring them the information. A database file, a voice or video file, complex and very graphical engineering or simulation applications, real-time medical images—all of these may be bottle-necked by the network.

Higher-speed technologies are easing the network throughput strain, and Fast Ethernet is one that has been widely accepted. Approved by the IEEE as a subgroup of the IEEE 802.3 standards, it has the same frame format, access method (CSMA/CD), and is backwards compatible with 10MBPS, 10BaseT LANs (through an auto-negotiation mechanism). The cabling infrastructure may be UTP, fiber, or a 40-pin AUI cable (an option, rather than an implementation for copper-based systems) when the transceiver circuitry's not on the NIC. For each of the physical connections, there are Fast Ethernet specifications. These determine the particular method used to achieve the 100MBPS data rate. They include the following:

- 100BaseTX: CAT 5 UTP

- 100BaseT4: CAT 3 UTP

- 100BaseFX: multimode fiber optic

- 100VG-AnyLAN (IEEE 802.12): Token access

100BaseTX and FX are the most widely used. 100VG-AnyLAN was given its own 802 subgroup heading because it may also be used in Token Ring topologies. However, since it resembles Fast Ethernet in all aspects other than the access method, it's included in the section. 100BaseT4 is a low-cost version of 100BaseTX that allows for the use of voice-grade, UTP cabling.

100BaseTX uses a coding scheme called 4B5B coding. This means that for each four bits entering the NIC card (during transmit), a 5-bit symbol is encoded. The encoded data is then subjected to MLT3 signaling. In MLT3 encoding (Manchester), a line transition is represented by a logic 1, while no-changes (consecutive logic 1's or 0's) are represented as a logic 0. Data is transmitted at 100 MBPS on two transmit wires (Tx+ and Tx–) and received on two receive wires (Rx+ and Rx–).

NET+ OBJECTIVE
I.1.6

This occurs over CAT5 UTP, and the pinout of the RJ-45 connector is shown in Figure 6-16 (for STP wiring, a sub-D9 connector is used). Since it's CAT5, the +/– polarities of the transmit and receive wires provide excellent noise immunity. Notice that with two wire pairs, the 100BaseTX is configured for full-duplex operation, although this is typically reserved for 100MBPS switching hubs or routers. When a hub or router is operating in full-duplex, the exchange between them runs at 200 MBPS. The nodes connected to the hubs or routers still send only when they have access to the network, which means they operate at half-duplex, 100MBPS rates.

**Figure 6-16
100BaseTX
Connector**

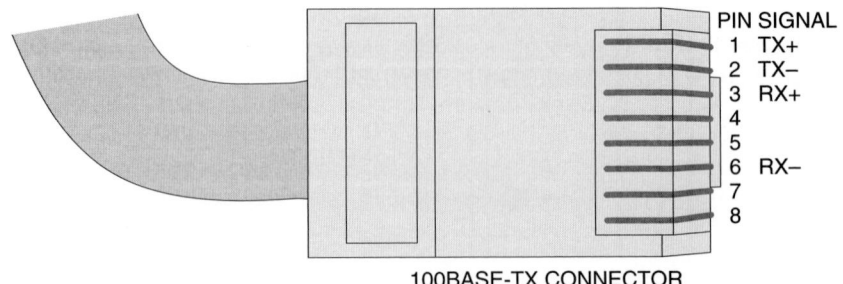

100BASE-TX CONNECTOR

Since 100BaseTX utilizes most of the characteristics of 10BaseT, it's not uncommon to include both options in node NIC cards. The reason is twofold. First, 100BaseTX is a painless upgrade for 10BaseT networks. The most apparent change is in routers, switching hubs or repeaters. Each of these need to be physically and logically compatible to the 100M standard. The NIC card will use the same RJ-45 connector to attach to either type, but will be software configured for either 10M or 100MBPS operation.

The second reason is that, with relatively little hardware change, both 10M and 100M nodes can be connected to the same repeater. Many vendors offer an option to 10BaseT hubs that includes one or more 100BaseTX ports.

100BaseTX uses the full bandwidth capabilities of CAT5 cable to achieve 100MBPS data rates. Notice in Figure 6-17 that the specifications are very similar to 10BaseT.

CNST OBJECTIVE
VII-A/B

IEEE 802.3u 100Base-Tx Specifications	
Wire Speed	100 MBPS
Cable Type	CAT 5
Connector	RJ-45
Maximum Segment Length	100m
Maximum Taps/ Segment	2
Maximum Stations/ Network	1024
Maximum Number of Repeaters	2
Typical Topology	Star

Figure 6-17 100BaseTx Specifications

10BaseT4 is an alternate version of 100BaseTX. It uses category 3 (or better), voice-grade twisted pairs for cable links to hubs. Unlike 100BaseTX, T4 must use all eight wires that are attached to a RJ-45 connector. The pinout is shown in Figure 6-18.

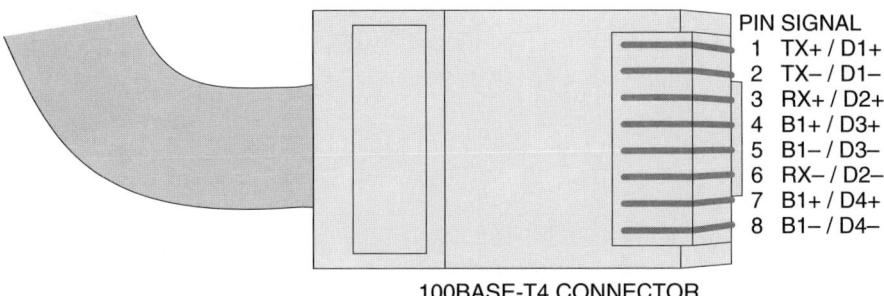

PIN SIGNAL
1 TX+ / D1+
2 TX– / D1–
3 RX+ / D2+
4 B1+ / D3+
5 B1– / D3–
6 RX– / D2–
7 B1+ / D4+
8 B1– / D4–

100BASE-T4 CONNECTOR

Figure 6-18 100BaseT4 Connector

NET+ OBJECTIVE
I.1.6

Shown are two transmit and two receive wire pairs. Also, there are two pairs of bidirectional wires (BI–D3 and BI–D4). The bidirectional pairs are shared during transmit and receive. When a node wins access to the network, the data bits are organized into 8-bit bytes. Using 8B6T coding, the eight bits are coded so that each byte is converted into a group of six, three-level symbols. Each symbol is then sent to the transmit and two bidirectional pairs in a round-robin manner.

CNST OBJECTIVE
VII-B

The data rate of each wire pair of 100BaseT4 is 33.33MBPS. Since three pairs are sending one byte of data (encoded into six symbols) one-after-another, the data is being transmitted at 3 x 33.33MBPS = 100MBPS. If you do the math, you will see that sending eight bits of unencoded data would take more than one pass across each wire pair. But each symbol is carrying an average of 1.33 data bits (eight data bits are used to create six symbols), so a full byte is delivered to the receiving station at a 100MBPS rate.

100BaseT4 was created so that having installed a base of CAT3 cabling, a company wouldn't have to pull it all out and replace it with CAT5 in order to run 100MBPS Ethernet. For a new installation, it makes sense to spend a little extra and install CAT5 to run 100BaseTX. The specifications for 100BaseT4 are shown in Figure 6-19.

IEEE 802.3u 100Base-T4 Specifications	
Wire Speed	100 MBPS
Cable Type	CAT 3 or Better
Connector	RJ-45
Maximum Segment Length	100m
Maximum Taps/ Segment	2
Maximum Stations/ Network	1024
Maximum Number of Repeaters	2
Typical Topology	Star

Figure 6-19 100BaseT4 Specifications

100BaseFX is the fiber optic version 100MBPS Ethernet. It uses any of the common fiber optic connectors illustrated in Figure 6-20. The connection between devices includes only two fiber strands, a transmit and receive strand. Both are running at 100MBPS.

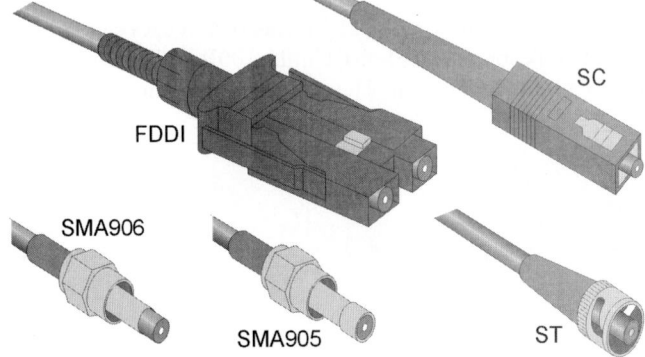

Figure 6-20 100BaseFX Connectors

Data to be transmitted is first separated into 4-bit groups, then encoded into a 5-bit symbol (a 4B5B coding scheme). Next the data is encoded using unipolar NRZ. Recall that unipolar NRZ assigns a positive voltage to logic 1's, and 0 volts to logic 0's. Since a fiber channel isn't affected by distributed reactances that cause intersymbol interference, this simple encoding method is all that's needed.

The IEEE specified 62.5/125μm multimode fiber at a wavelength of 1,300 nm for 100BaseFX. Singlemode isn't in the specification, but if it's used, it will increase distances to around 20 km. Figure 6-21 lists the specifications. Notice that when it's run full-duplex, allowable distances are far greater. Typically, full-duplex operation will occur between switching hubs or routers, and not from the node to the hub.

IEEE 802.3u 100Base-Fx Specifications	
Wire Speed	100 MBPS
Cable Type	Fiber, 62.5/125µm multimode
Connector	ST, SC, SMA, FDDI
Maximum Segment Length Half-Duplex	412m
Maximum Segment Length Full-Duplex	2000m
Maximum Taps/ Segment	2
Maximum Stations/ Network	1024
Maximum Number of Repeaters	2
Typical Topology	Star

CNST OBJECTIVE
VII-A/B

Figure 6-21 100BaseFX Specification

100VG-AnyLAN is described in the IEEE 802.12 protocol. It operates at 100MBPS but uses an access method totally different than CSMA/CD. In a 100VG network, a hub determines which nodes transmit by using a **demand priority** access scheme.

Demand priority consists of a poll issued from the hub to each of the nodes asking them if they have frames to send. If they do, the node has full access to the network bandwidth and sends its frame. If not, the poll goes to the next port and does the same. In this way, each node connected to a port hub is given an equal chance to transmit, and there should never be a situation in which one node dominates the network by winning access (a remote, but possible occurrence in CSMA/CD access methods).

A network manager may configure access (through software) so that some ports have a higher priority than others. For example, assume node 1 sends large, graphical files on a routine basis, while nodes 2 and 3 primarily send text files. Node 1 may be given higher priority to access the media than nodes 2 and 3, so that it's not penalized for sending large files across the LAN. Now, access may be extended as node 1, node 2, node 1, node 3, node 1, etc. Obviously, if all nodes have a high-access priority, the advantage is lost.

100VG-AnyLAN is very similar to Token Ring access methods, except it operates at 100 MBPS and can be used on star topologies (as well as rings), which have historically been reserved for Ethernet. A huge disadvantage to CSMA/CD is that network managers can't prioritize access for bandwidth-intensive users. They compete for access just like a user who sends out one, 4-line e-mail message a week.

The downside to 100VG-AnyLAN is that users who don't have priority may complain about a slow connection, because high-priority users will be serviced before them. This situation can get to the point that a high-priority user can appear to dominate the network. It's up to the network manager to set the priorities so that this doesn't happen.

One way IEEE 802.12 deals with scaling priorities is to set a maximum time that any node has network access. 100VG contains a timer that can be set from 200–300 mS, limiting the amount of time that a normal-priority request can be kept waiting. If a high-priority node has the media for an amount of time exceeding this, the hub will reset the priorities, giving the normal node a high priority. It then starts accessing ports beginning at port 1. When it gets to the normal port, it's permitted to continue sending frames until it's either finished, or the 200–300ms timer once again expires. In this way, the protocol tries to ensure that no one port is allowed to dominate the network.

As mentioned earlier, 100VG-AnyLAN can be used with star and ring topologies, making it independent of the physical infrastructure. CAT5 UTP or fiber cables are used to connect nodes to the hub.

IEEE 802.3z Gigabit Ethernet

IEEE 802.3z Gigabit Ethernet runs at 1,000 MBPS.

Gigabit Ethernet means that data is sent at one-billion bits a second. The technology uses CSMA/CD as the access method, and is typically installed in a star topology. It's backwards compatible with Fast Ethernet, so that a network can be reasonably upgraded from Fast Ethernet to Gigabit Ethernet.

The standard specifies fiber or coaxial cabling with CAT 5 UTP expected to be added late in 1999. Typically, the technology isn't run to desktop computers but is used between switching hubs or routers, and from hubs to farms of super-servers.

The servers contain a 100/1,000MBPS NIC card to interface the cable and hub. The 100M option is made available so that existing Fast Ethernet systems can be migrated to Gigabit systems, the same way as many Ethernet cards include a 10/100MBPS option. There are four physical implementations available with Gigabit Ethernet:

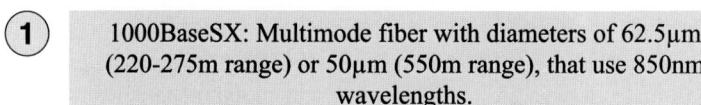

(1) 1000BaseSX: Multimode fiber with diameters of 62.5μm (220-275m range) or 50μm (550m range), that use 850nm wavelengths.

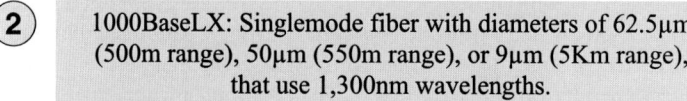

(2) 1000BaseLX: Singlemode fiber with diameters of 62.5μm (500m range), 50μm (550m range), or 9μm (5Km range), that use 1,300nm wavelengths.

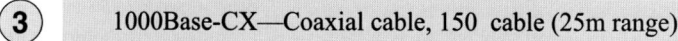

(3) 1000Base-CX—Coaxial cable, 150 cable (25m range).

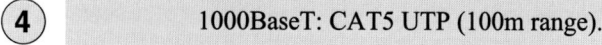

(4) 1000BaseT: CAT5 UTP (100m range).

Although 1000BaseT isn't yet approved, you should expect it to be, because the wiring infrastructure of all networks is 75% CAT5 UTP. While some details remain to be resolved, we can get a good idea of how it will work by examining what we do know of the standard.

1000Base-T uses all four wire pairs in a CAT 5 cable to send and receive. This provides two pairs for transmitting and two pairs for receiving. Send and receive may occur simultaneously during full duplex operation. When data is transmitted, it's organized into groups of eight bits that are then separated into 4-bit nibbles. The nibbles are encoded using a 4B5B scheme. The encoding is done with 5-level Pulse Amplitude Modulation (PAM). The relative modulation levels used are -2, -1, 0, +1, +2. (Refer to Chapter 4, Figure 4-19 for a review of PAM) Four of the levels are used to represent two bits of data with the fifth bit is used for forward error correction. In other words, a single symbol contains two bits of frame data. Since there are four pairs, then 2 bits x 4 pairs = 8 bits which is the size of the group that was originally encoded.

Data on each wire is sent at 125M baud. There are eight wires in the CAT5 cable, so 125M x 8 = 1,000 GBPS. Note that 125M is necessary, because 5-amplitude PAM is used with the fifth bit, or amplitude, for error correcting.

In order to operate at full-duplex so that send and receive occurs at the same time, a hybrid is used at each wire port, to separate send and receive signals on each wire pair. In essence, the transmit signal on the receiving end is eliminated.

Figure 6-22 shows a typical Ethernet installation which includes many of the Ethernet variants discussed. Notice it illustrates the practical uses of the faster technologies. The scenario shown is a reasonable migration from 10BaseT to Gigabit Ethernet.

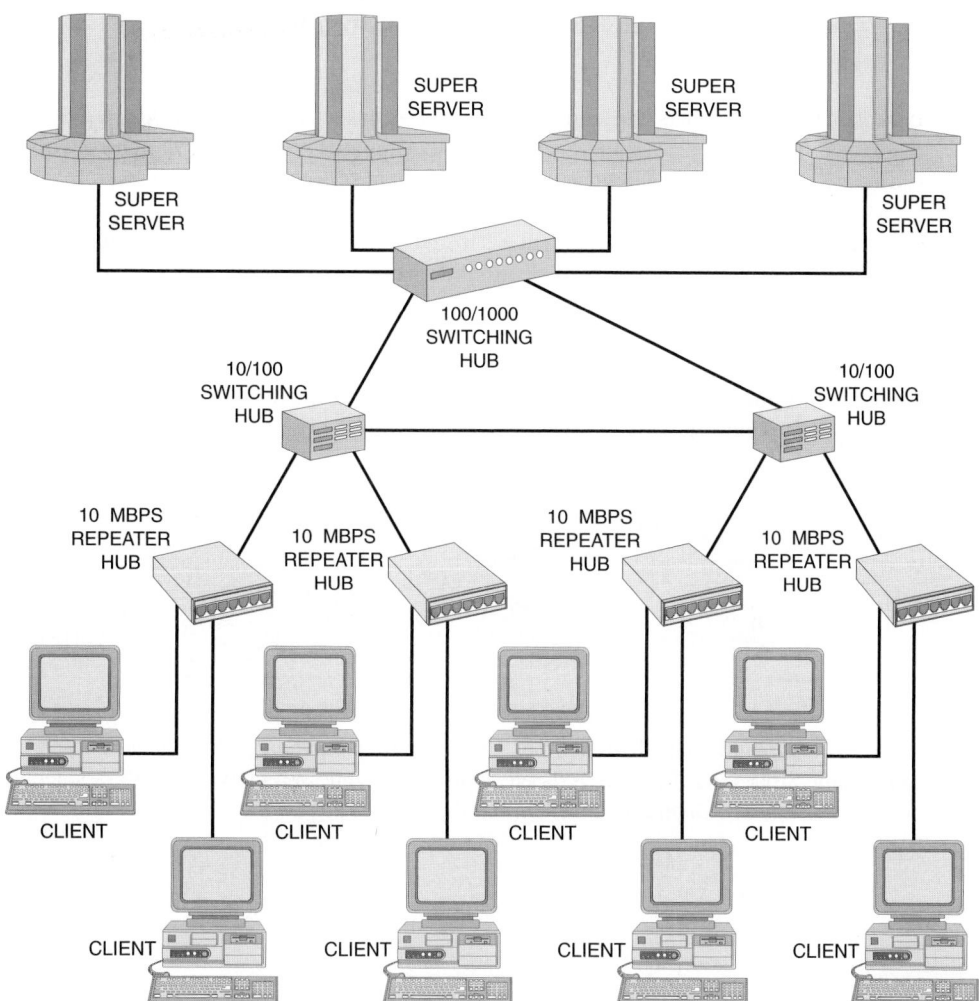

Figure 6-22 Ethernet Migration Strategy

IEEE 802.4 TOKEN BUS

A token-passing network sends a signal to each station, providing it access to the network. The access signal is commonly referred to as a **token**. The token bus access method differs from CSMA/CD by directly ensuring that a station has time on the network, rather than through a contention method.

The token bus method has several similarities to CSMA/CD. Only one station may transmit at any one time. The network taps are passive, allowing easy station addition or deletion. The token bus doesn't readily lend itself to fiber-optic cable, due to the bus taps. No bus network does. However, it should be noted that although there are many products that facilitate fiber optics in a bus, none are straightforward.

> The token bus access method differs from CSMA/CD by directly ensuring that a station has time on the network, rather than through a contention method.

There are also several differences between a token and contention bus. The first is that with each being a bus network—with its general pros and cons—a contention system is less complicated, and generally more reliable. From an applications standpoint, most of the advantages found in a token bus are also found in a token ring, without the bus disadvantages, as will be shown shortly.

In a token bus, the token is transferred to each station based upon **priority tables** contained in the network software, and there is little competition for the token. Stations with heavy traffic are permitted to transmit more frequently than stations with a light work load.

If a station in the token-passing sequence is lost, there are fallback measures to reconfigure the network, but during the reconfiguration, the network is basically at a standstill. This doesn't occur on the CSMA/CD bus.

CNST OBJECTIVE IV-B

The frame format for token bus is shown in Figure 6-23. The **preamble** is used to establish station synchronization. The Start Frame Delimiter marks the formal beginning of the data frame, and the End Frame Delimiter marks the end of the frame.

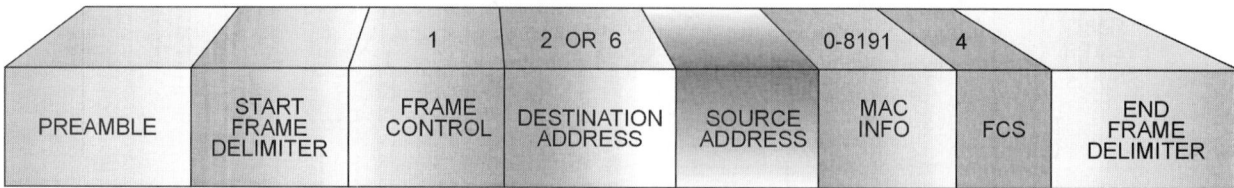

Figure 6-23 Frame Format For Token Bus

As in the CSMA/CD bus, the token bus has destination and source addresses. These are 6 bytes long. IEEE 802.4 allows a 2-byte option, as well. Whichever length is selected, consistency must be maintained throughout the network.

The Frame Control field determines the type of data contained in the **Media Access Control** (MAC) Info field. The Frame field is 1 byte long, and specifies if the MAC field contains logical-link control data, management instructions for the media-access control sublevel, or station-to-station (user) data. The MAC Data field, containing one of the above, is 0 bytes to 8,191 bytes long. The Frame-Check Sequence, following the Info field, examines the frame for errors.

A token-bus network operates by identifying a station as a **predecessor**. In Figure 6-24, station 5 receives the token from station 6. To station 5, station 6 is its predecessor. Station 4 is the **successor** to station 5. To say it another way: the station receiving the token from the transmitter is a successor, and the transmitter is the predecessor to the receiving station.

The token usually passes down in a numerically descending order. Although it's shown to pass sequentially in Figure 6-24, the token-bus software contains **table arrays** for selecting which station is first to receive the token, which is second, and so on.

For example, the token route may be programmed for an initial pass of the following stations of Figure 6-24:

11, 7, 5, 3

on the next pass:

11, 9, 5, 1

on the third pass:

10, 8, 5, 4

on the final pass:

10, 6, 5, 2

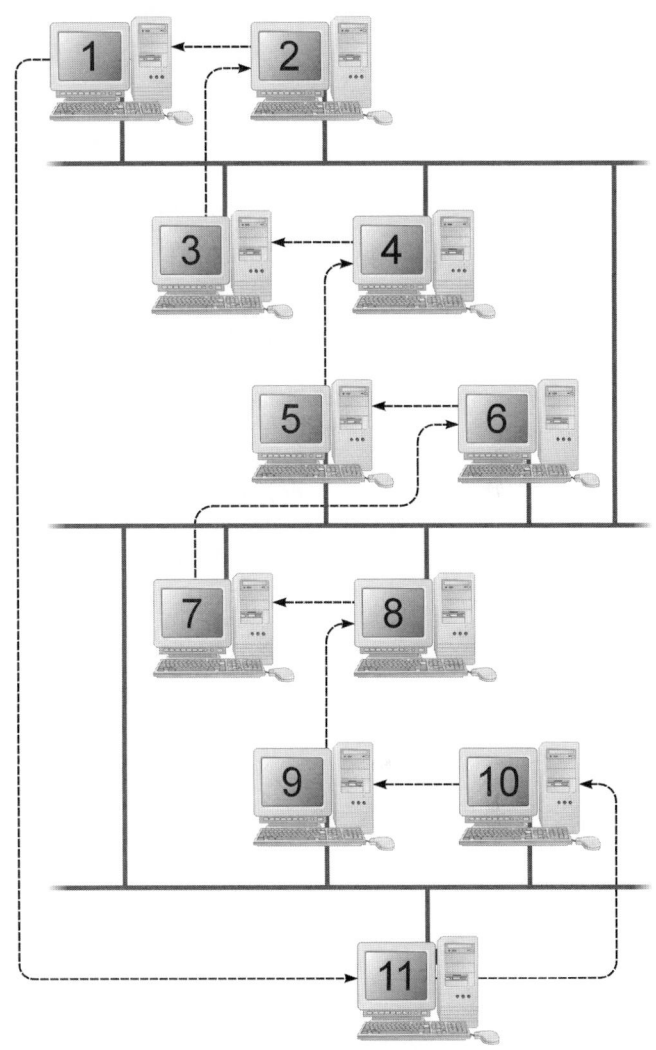

Figure 6-24 Successor and Predecessor

In this example, station 10 and 11 have two opportunities to transmit, whereas station 5 transmits with each pass of the token through the network. All other stations are permitted time to transmit on every fourth pass of the token. The network may be configured in this fashion because station 5 has a heavy workload, as do stations 10 and 11. The other stations, relatively speaking, aren't expected to transmit as much.

The simplified network of Figure 6-25 illustrates the **token recovery** in a situation where one station in the network has become inoperable.

A transmitting station (station A) monitors the channel after sending the token (step 1) to its successor (station B), and if the successor transmits, it assumes the token pass was successful. If the successor doesn't transmit, it tries a second time (step 2).

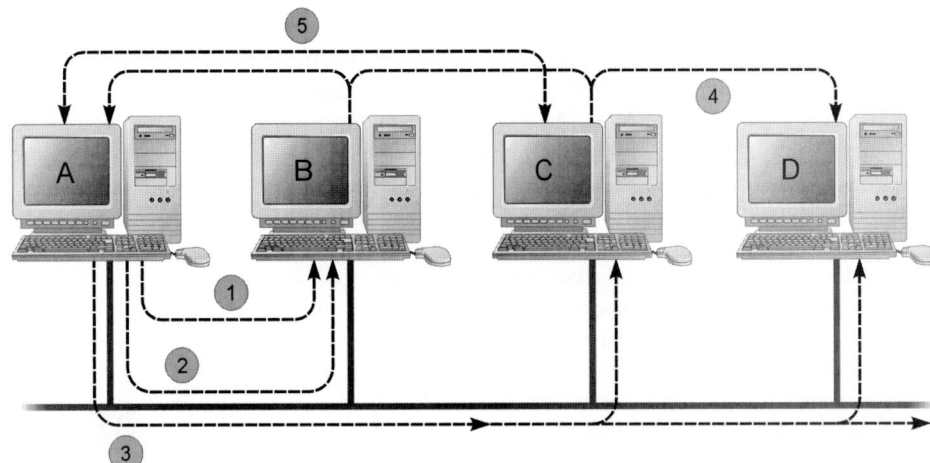

Figure 6-25 Token Bus Fallback Token Recovery Procedure

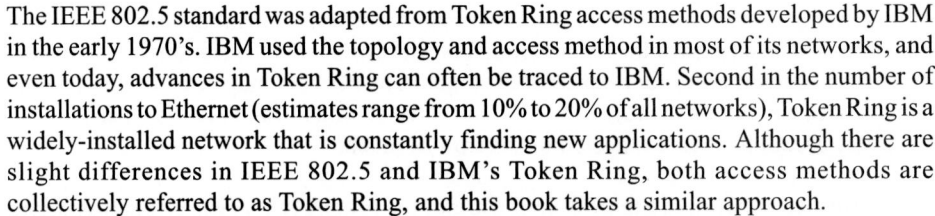

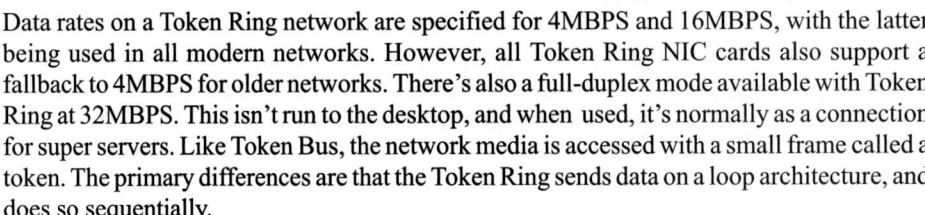

If the above fallback doesn't work, the transmitter sends a **who-follows** across the network (step 3). The who-follows has the address of the transmitter's successor in the data frame. The network stations compare the address in the frame to see if it is their predecessor's.

Once a match is made, the station who makes the match (station C) sends its address to the original transmitter (step 4). The transmitter reconfigures the **routing table** to make the matching station (station C) its successor. The station loading the token (station B) is cut out of the network, under the assumption that it contains a fault that requires operator attention.

The example token bus utilizes a continuously shifting FSK carrier, at a data rate of 1 MBPS, using Manchester encoding. The bus cable is 750-ohm coaxial. A multiple bus network is often connected by regenerative repeaters. Stations connect to the bus via a 50-ohm coaxial cable, no more than 35 cm long. The 1MBPS data is modulated onto a 5MHz carrier. Other token-bus networks are available with data rates of 5 and 10 MBPS, at carrier frequencies of 10 MHz and 20 MHz.

IEEE 802.5 TOKEN RING

IEEE 802.5 Token Ring runs at 16 or 4 MBPS.

The IEEE 802.5 standard was adapted from Token Ring access methods developed by IBM in the early 1970's. IBM used the topology and access method in most of its networks, and even today, advances in Token Ring can often be traced to IBM. Second in the number of installations to Ethernet (estimates range from 10% to 20% of all networks), Token Ring is a widely-installed network that is constantly finding new applications. Although there are slight differences in IEEE 802.5 and IBM's Token Ring, both access methods are collectively referred to as Token Ring, and this book takes a similar approach.

Data rates on a Token Ring network are specified for 4MBPS and 16MBPS, with the latter being used in all modern networks. However, all Token Ring NIC cards also support a fallback to 4MBPS for older networks. There's also a full-duplex mode available with Token Ring at 32MBPS. This isn't run to the desktop, and when used, it's normally as a connection for super servers. Like Token Bus, the network media is accessed with a small frame called a token. The primary differences are that the Token Ring sends data on a loop architecture, and does so sequentially.

CNST OBJECTIVE
IV-B & VII-A/B

The token is a 3-byte data stream passed from node to node. When the token is in transition from one station to another, it's known as an **idle token**. When a station with data to send receives the token, its mode changes to busy. During the **busy mode**, no other stations have access to the channel.

All Token Ring networks are structured in a similar manner by connecting nodes to hubs in a star configuration, then interconnecting hubs in a ring fashion. Token Ring hubs are called **MultiStation Access Units** (MSAUs). Figure 6-26(a) illustrates a MASU with nodes attached. Note that the MSAU-to-node connection is via a Token Ring NIC card.

CNST OBJECTIVE
VII-A/B

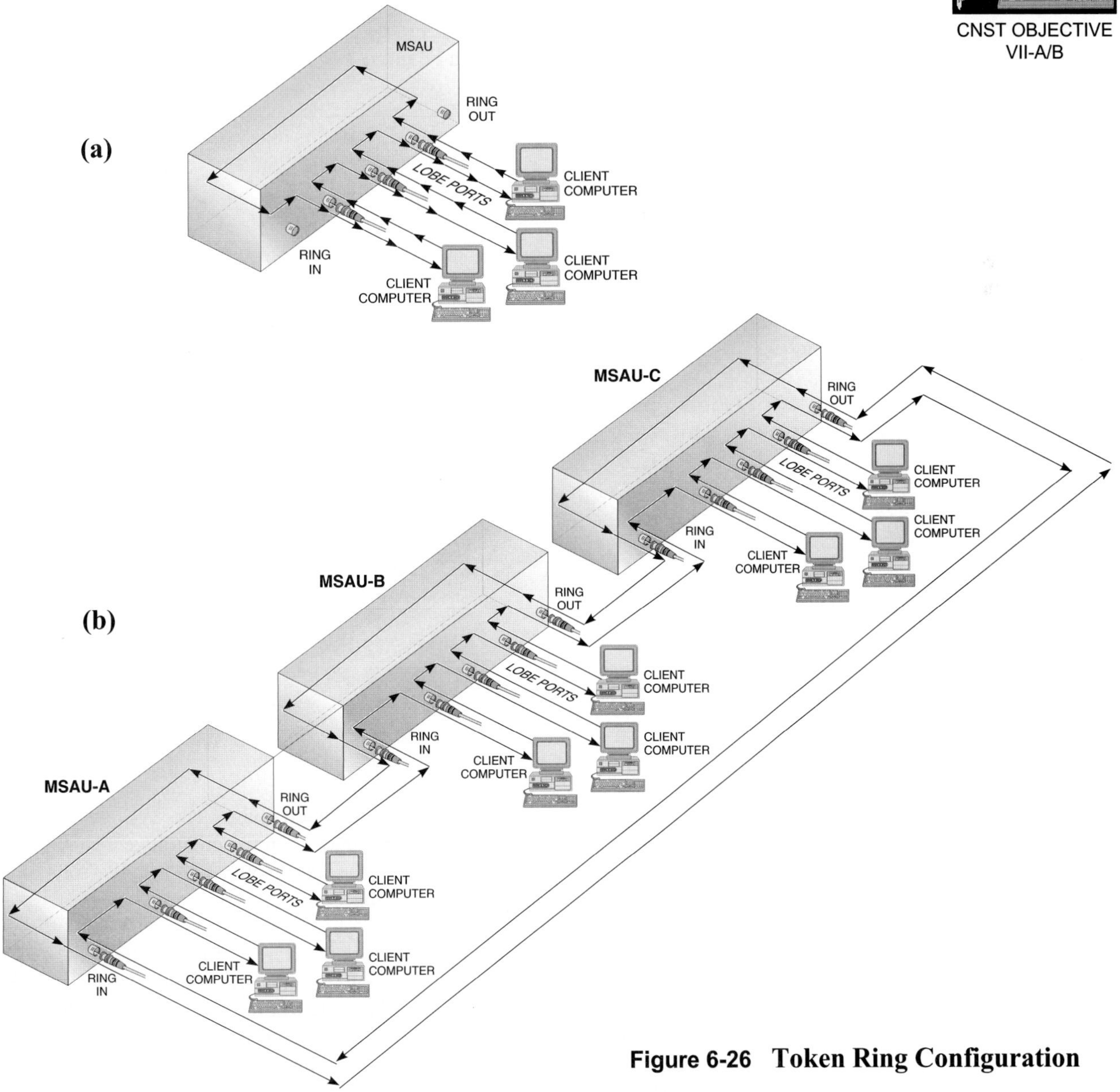

(a)

(b)

Figure 6-26   Token Ring Configuration

Ports on the MSAU are labeled Ring In, Ring Out, and Lobe. The lobe ports attach to nodes on the ring. The ring ports are only used to connect to other MSAUs, and can't be used to connect nodes to the ring. In Figure 6-26(a), there are no other MSAUs, so the ring ports simply loop signals back through the ring as shown. This occurs without any intervention from users or network administrators.

Figure 6-26(b) shows the same MSAU, but it's now connected to two other MSAUs. You can see the ring ports are used to interconnect MSAUs, while lobe ports have nodes attached.

You should notice an outside ring that doesn't connect to any of the lobe ports. This is a secondary ring that's used if a node were to fail, causing a ring break. If that happened, the failed node would be wrapped out of the ring, and the secondary ring used in its place. You can see an example of ring-wrapping in Figure 6-27.

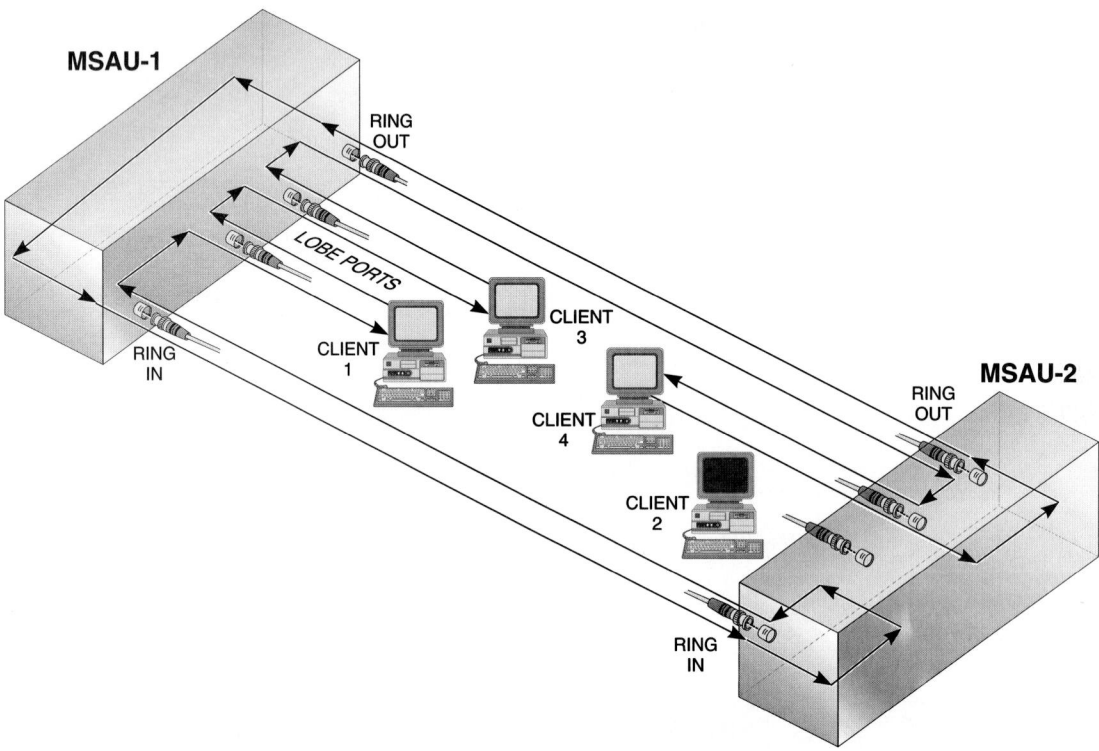

Figure 6-27 Ring-Wrapping a Failed Node

The outer ring is the secondary ring, and client node 2 has a failure. The problem may be in the cable connecting the node and MSAU2, or it may be in the client node. The MSAU detects the problem, and wraps the client out of the ring. Notice that in order for this to happen, data on the rings must be counter-rotating.

Token Ring networks wrap a node from the network by using a process called *beaconing*. Every seven seconds, a test frame is sent around the ring (it starts with the first node to be powered-up) that includes the address of the sending node. The next node to receive the frame strips the address of the previous node from the frame and replaces it with its own; then sends it to the next node. If a node doesn't receive the frame within the seven second time limit, it sends a beacon. The beacon contains the address of the sending node, the address of the up-stream node that didn't send the test frame, and a beacon type. The beacon travels around the ring and if the node that didn't initially respond still doesn't respond, it's wrapped out of the ring.

On a Token Ring, the cable is physically broken at the node. The data-in is said to enter the receiver on the **downside**, and exit via the transmitter on the **upside**. Once a station transmits, the token is returned to the idle state until it's received by the next station. The usual arrangement in a Token Ring is to have the sender's message rotate around the network, be removed by the receiver, and be regenerated around the loop until it arrives back at the original transmitter. Once it arrives back, the transmitter checks the frame for errors, and if none are discovered, assumes it was received, error-free, by the receiving station.

The physical interconnections may take one of three forms:

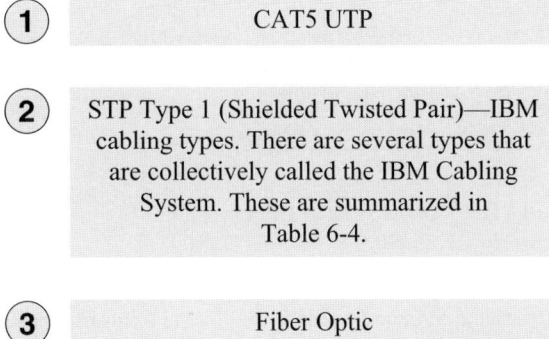

(1) CAT5 UTP

(2) STP Type 1 (Shielded Twisted Pair)—IBM cabling types. There are several types that are collectively called the IBM Cabling System. These are summarized in Table 6-4.

(3) Fiber Optic

CNST OBJECTIVE
VII-A/B

Table 6-4 IBM Cabling System

TYPE	AWG/STRAND	IMPEDANCE	SHIELDING	DATA RATE	COMMENTS
1	22 AWG	150Ω ±10%	Overall shield applied.	16 MBPS	Between MAU and wall plate.
2	22 AWG	150Ω ±10%	Two pair shielded, then shielded together; additional four pair.	16 MBPS	To carry data through walls; also carries 10BaseT.
3	22/24 AWG	100Ω ±10%	Minimum two twists/foot.	16 MBPS	Token Ring UTP.
5	62.5/125μm	3.75dB/km w/850nm source 1.5dB/km w/1300nm source		100 MBPS	FDDI equivalent.
6	26 AWG	150Ω ±10%	Two pair twisted, then shielded.	16 MBPS	From wall plate to station.
9	26 AWG	150Ω ±10%	Two pair twisted, then shielded.	16 MBPS	From wall plate to station; accepts RJ-45 connector.

UTP and STP shouldn't mixed in the same ring network because they have different characteristic impedances, and may cause the ring to crash. The IBM cables have the advantage of supporting up to 250 nodes on a single ring. UTP can support a maximum of 72 nodes. While IBM Type 1 cable supports more nodes, it's also more expensive, and not compatible with CAT5 UTP.

If you install a ring architecture, think carefully about what will happen to the ring in the future. Typically, UTP infrastructure—due to the small node limit—generates the creation of several small rings consisting of 50 to 70 users. The multiple MSAUs needed to interconnect the rings may offset the higher cost of the Type 1 cable. The frame format for Token Ring is shown in Figure 6-28.

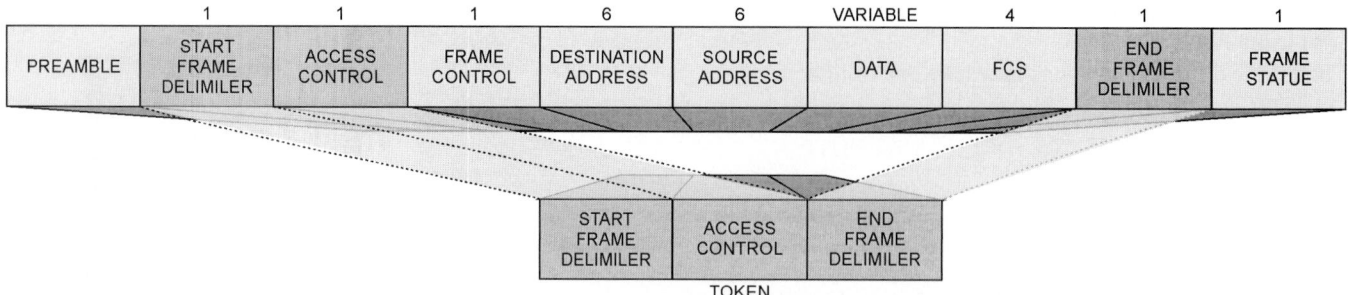

Figure 6-28 Token Ring Frame Format

CNST OBJECTIVE
VII-A/B

It closely resembles the format for the token bus. The Start Frame Delimiter is one byte, and is used to alert nodes to the arrival of a token, a full frame of commands, or user data. The actual token is formed by the Start Delimiter, Access, and End Delimiter Fields.

The Access-Control field designates the frame as a Token or Command/Data frame. It also includes Priority and Reservation fields (used for demand priority scheduling), and a monitor bit. The monitor bit is examined to determine if a frame is endlessly circling the ring (which may happen if a node sends a frame that gets wrapped out before it returns, due to a failure).

A Token Ring frame is designated as a Data or Command frame. A Data frame contains node data, as well as information to upper-layer protocols. A Command frame contains no user data or upper-layer information. It's used only to carry control information for the ring.

The Frame Control field is used to indicate if the frame is data or command. IEEE 802.5 contains a source and destination address, and as in Ethernet, these are six bytes each.

In Figure 6-28 you can see the portion of the frame that constitutes the token and which is the complete frame. When a station receives a token, it must first remove any messages addressed to it. It does so by examining the destination address field. Notice that the token will also be used to form the first two fields of the frame that's delivered to the node, along with the last byte if the token contains user data.

Since the transmission times of nodes can be predicted, Token Ring has a huge advantage over Ethernet.

Token Ring has a huge advantage over CSMA/CD networks in that it's deterministic. This means that the nodes transmit at specific, predictable times. Since the transmission times of nodes can be predicted, so can the delivery times. Without contention on the network, there are no collisions. Ultimately, this has led to a general consensus that Token Ring networks offer a higher degree of reliability, and integrity, than Ethernet networks.

FIBER DISTRIBUTED DATA INTERFACE (FDDI)

> An FDDI network transmits data at 100 MBPS on a ring, with a maximum distance of 100 km.

The expectations of network users over the last several years has changed from one of enormous amounts of computing power, to one of speed and volume. This is particularly true with the wide-spread use of available screen presentation software—Windows, Presentation Manager, large, memory-intensive applications that accompany engineering applications, and multi-media programs. Computer users have come to expect the same high level of screen enhancements for all the work they do on computers. The problem with conventional LAN technologies is that they lack the bandwidth required to handle a large base of users who are exchanging graphics-intensive work.

A CSMA/CD, Ethernet LAN has a bandwidth of 10 MBPS, while a Token Ring network operates at 4, or 16 MBPS. Ethernet is available at 1,000 MBPS, but only with a contention access method. 100VG-AnyLAN operates on ring topologies, but isn't widely deployed. Although Token Ring only runs at 16MBPS, the good thing about it is that node access can be made deterministic, an option not available with Ethernet. What's needed is a technology that offers the access advantages of Token Ring, and the speed of Ethernet.

The solution is the **Fiber Distributed Data Interface** (FDDI). FDDI is a 100MBPS fiber-optic network that's specified in the standards of the **American National Standards Institute** (ANSI), as well as the ISO. This standard, as will be shown shortly, corresponds to the first two layers of the ISO **Open System Interconnection** (OSI) model for data communications. FDDI networks can coexist with common mid-speed systems, such as Ethernet and Token Ring, and are, in fact, typically installed to interconnect other LANs.

Before beginning a discussion of FDDI, it's important to distinguish it from a related system—the **Synchronous Optical NETwork** (SONET). SONET networks, described in Chapter 3, were developed primarily by the common carriers as a fiber optics-based system for interconnecting high-speed networks, with reasonable compatibility. It begins at speeds of 54.840 MBPS, and increases in increments to 2.5 GBPS. SONET isn't acceptable for LANs, because it doesn't address Physical layer access methods. A SONET network, then, is applicable to wide area networks, while FDDI is associated with local area networks.

CNST OBJECTIVE
VI-B

Specifically, FDDI is finding a larger range of user applications in the areas of real-time applications, distributed applications, client/server-based systems, and as mentioned previously, graphics applications. Real-time applications include the process control industry, in which the mixture of volatile chemicals must be monitored continuously. Distributed applications include those tasks accomplished in tandem, among users with multiple systems. In a client/server system, the network connects the user to a database that contains the memory-resident programs holding print, scan, graphic, directory, and other network services. FDDI can offer quick access to servers, so they can handle the many requests they receive.

In each of these examples, the user gains access to data, and it is routed on a shared network cable. The cabling is shared among many users, and must have the bandwidth necessary to accommodate the requests. Fiber-optic systems, when compared to twisted pair and coaxial cable, have very wide bandwidth and speed characteristics. As you'll see later in this section, FDDI is a versatile technology, allowing network administrators to use their existing twisted-pair cabling for transmitting 100MBPS data from a fiber backbone.

FDDI is characterized by a **dual-ring** topology, as shown in Figure 6-29(a). The outside ring is known as the primary, or **active ring**, while the inside ring is called the **secondary ring**. Stations gain access to the active ring through a token-passing arrangement that allows equal network time for all nodes. If a node should fail, or lose power, the ring reroutes data around the station onto the secondary ring. In Figure 6-29(b), node two has failed. Notice that the failed station has been bypassed, taking it out of the network, while permitting the other stations to continue operating. When this happens, the network is said to have "wrapped" the failed node. A loopback route on the secondary ring creates a single, **virtual ring**.

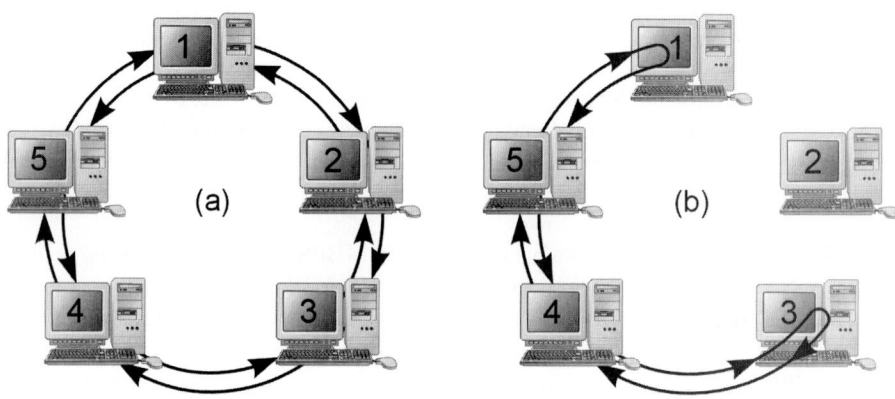

Figure 6-29
FDDI Dual-Ring

In networks where the loading is exceeding the current technology of the departments, FDDI is used as a **backbone** for feeding other LANs. The LANs are connected to the fiber backbone in a star configuration, and are considered to be conventional local area networks connected to a FDDI network, as shown in Figure 6-30. Notice that the LANs are independent networks, connected to one another by the fiber backbone. The cable media in the LANs may be fiber, twisted pair, or coaxial cable.

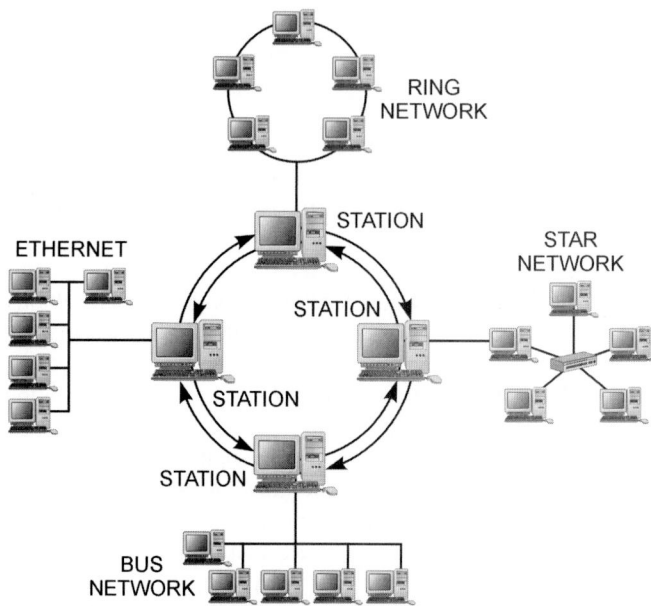

An FDDI network transmits data at 100 MBPS on a ring with a maximum distance of 100 km. The distance between stations, called the **link distance**, is 2 km for multimode fiber, and 60 km for single-mode cable. The maximum distance may be

Figure 6-30 Backbone Connectivity For LANs

extended to 200 km by utilizing both rings in the network, but doing so eliminates the fallback channel if there's a station fault. When both rings are used in a single ring, the maximum number of stations increases to 1,000.

CNST OBJECTIVE
VI-B

FDDI Protocol Stack

FDDI is patterned after the first two layers of the OSI model, and is comprised of four ANSI standards: the **Physical Medium Dependent**, **Physical Layer Protocol**, **Media Access Control**, and **Station Management**.

The standards are shown in Figure 6-31 along with the corresponding layers in the OSI model. The Physical Medium Dependent describes the type of optical interface, connectors, and characteristics of the cable. The Physical Layer Protocol discusses the encoding and decoding of data on the ring. Media Access Control provides for token transmission on the ring, framing of data, and symbol management. Station Management monitors the network for faults, recovery, and station configuration.

Physical Medium Dependent

The **Physical Medium Dependent** (PMD) layer contains specifications for cable and connector types, as well as the designation of receive and transport on the connectors. Devices attached to an FDDI ring are described by a single- or dual-ring attachment.

Devices attaching to both rings are called Class A devices, while those only attached to the active ring are called Class B devices. Normally, a "Device" is a generic term referring to the stations on the ring (computers, concentrators, bridges, or routers). Keep in mind that the usual topology used with FDDI is a dual ring of trees, with the trees branching off the ring as self-contained LANs. These LANs interface to the rings via a **concentrator**.

Figure 6-32 shows several devices attached to the ring, along with the correct class designation. The dual-attached station may represent a mainframe computer, or large file server, containing engineering drawings. The same is true of the single-attached station. On the right side of the ring are two concentrators, one dual-attached, while the other is single-attached. Typically, concentrators serve as an interface for conventional mid-speed LANs, providing data encoding and the necessary frame formatting.

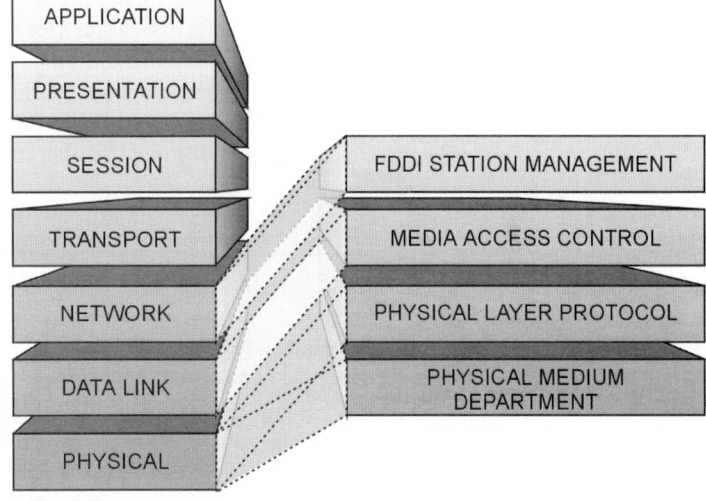

Figure 6-31 FDDI Protocol Stack

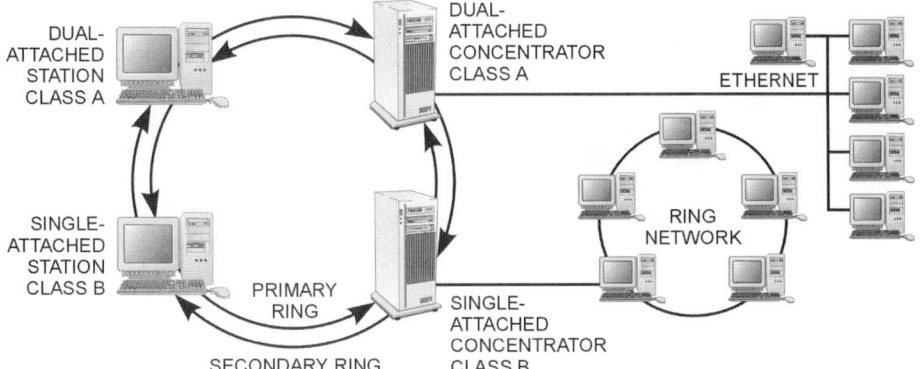

Figure 6-32 FDDI Device Classifications

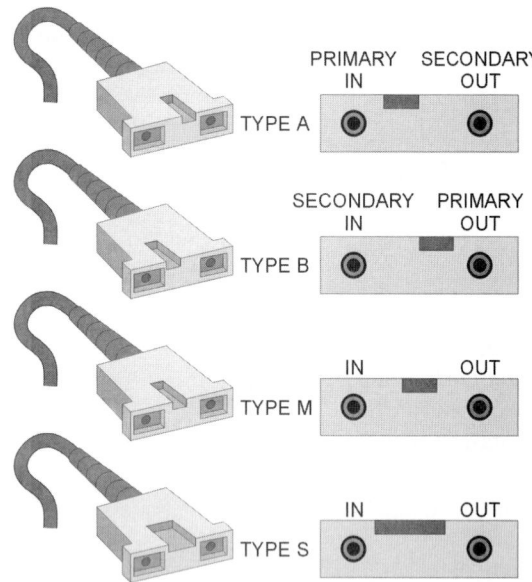

Each device attachment includes a uniquely-keyed connector. The connector types are illustrated in Figure 6-33, along with their respective pinouts.

Figure 6-34 is the physical connection for a dual-attached device.

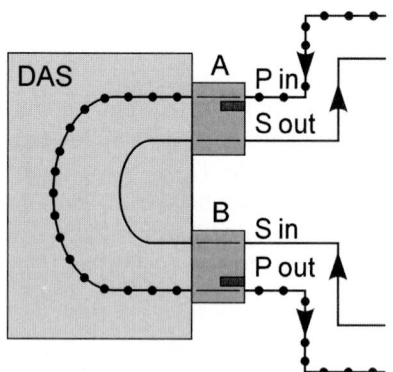

Figure 6-33 FDDI Connectors and Pinouts

Figure 6-34 Connecting a Dual-Attached Station

The ANSI standard describes the characteristics for fiber-optic cabling used in the FDDI ring. You may refer to Chapter 2 for an in-depth description of fiber optic transmission techniques. The cables may be multimode, or single-mode. Multimode cable refers to light that enters the cable at various angles and reflects along the cable in many directions. In a single-mode cable, the light tends to travel in parallel lines for the length of the cable. Laser light is often single-mode, while the light emitted from LEDs is generally multimode.

A single-mode cable will have less dispersion of the light wave, and consequently, less distortion of data bits. Because there is less dispersion, single-mode light travels further along the cable than multimode before repeaters are needed, although at a higher cost.

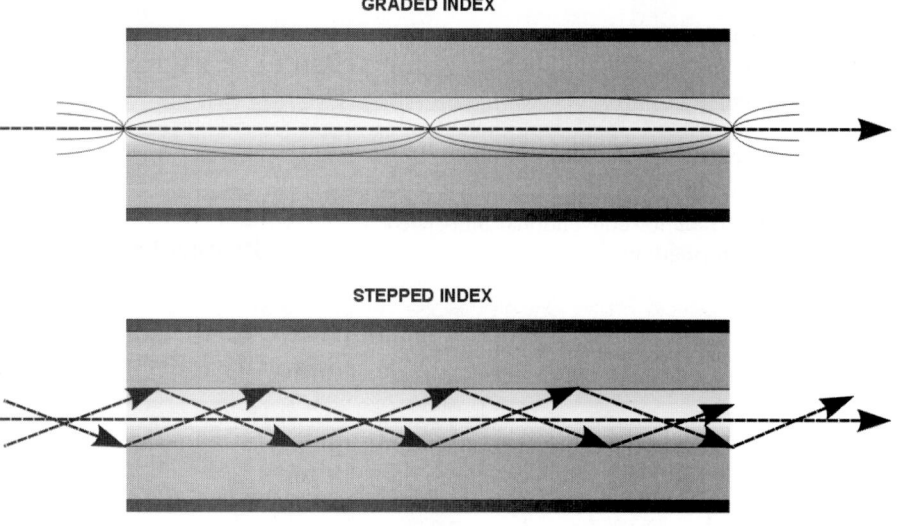

In addition to being single- and multimode, the cable may be stepped-index or graded-index. A stepped-index cable refracts at the junction of the core and cladding in a sharp index, as shown if Figure 6-35. Graded-index cable includes layers of cladding material, with smaller refraction indexes relative to the distance from the core. The graded nature of the core results in the light waves traversing the cable with fewer refractions, and far less dispersion of the light. It is the choice fiber cable for handling high data rates. The precise specifications for multimode and single-mode cables are detailed in Table 6-5.

Figure 6-35 Indexed Fiber Cable

Table 6-5 Multimode
and Single-Mode
Fiber Specifications

MULTIMODE		
Nominal Core Diameter	**Cladding Diameter**	**Nominal Numerical Aperture**
50 microns	125 microns	0.20
50 microns	125 microns	0.21
50 microns	125 microns	0.22
62.5 microns	125 microns	0.275
85 microns	125 microns	0.26
100 microns	140 microns	0.29
SINGLE-MODE		
Nominal Core Diameter	**Cladding Diameter**	**Nominal Numerical Aperture**
8 microns	125 microns	0.20

In addition to standards for fiber cable, ANSI has a similar set of standards for transmitting 100MBPS data over CAT5 UTP. The standard is referred to as the Copper Distributed Data Interface (CuDDI). Table 6-6 provides the CuDDI UL rating specifications for a 24 AWG twisted pair cable.

Table 6-6 CuDDI UL Ratings for 24AWG Twisted-Pair Cable

EIA/TIA Category	Underwriters Laboratories	Industry Standard Application	Attenuation @ 1 Mhz dB/1,000 ft	Attenuation @ 4 Mhz dB/1,000 ft	Attenuation @ 16 Mhz dB/1,000 ft	NEXT dB @ 1,000 ft	Maximum Data Rate
	Level 1	Voice, RS232	Not Specified	Not Specified	Not Specified	Not Specified	Not Specified
Similar to IBM Type 3	Level 2	ISDN, 120kBPS	8.0	Not Specified	Not Specified	Not Specified	Not Specified
Category 3	Level 3	LAN, 10BaseT	7.8	17	40	23	10 MBPS
Category 4	Level 4	Super, IEEE 802.5	6.5	13	27	38	16 MBPS
Category 5	Level 5	TPDDI	6.3	13	25	44	100 MBPS

Physical Layer Protocol

The Physical Layer Protocol is involved with clock rates, repeat functions, and symbol encoding and decoding. In order to achieve the high data rates that fiber is capable of, FDDI encodes the data into groups of symbols, using a modified version of Nonreturn-To-Zero. Unipolar NRZ is used for FDDI, where a logic 1 is represented by a positive voltage, and a logic 0 is represented by 0 volts. In a light-based system, there are no voltages, so the encoding must be modified. Figure 6-36 shows an example of FDDI encoding.

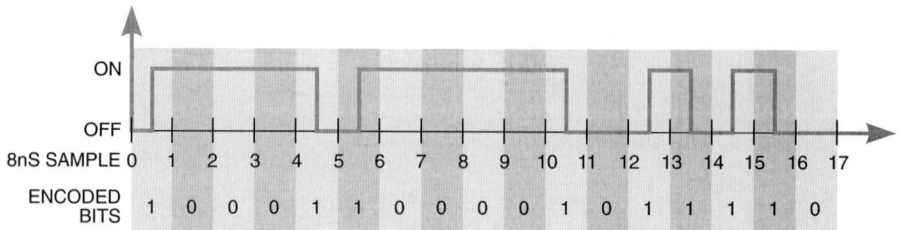

Figure 6-36 FDDI Encoding Scheme

In an FDDI system, a bit is defined as a change of state in the light, such as the presence or absence of light. A node samples the light (every 8ns) coming from another node. If the light has changed states, it's a logic 1. If the light hasn't changed states, it's a logic 0.

CNST OBJECTIVE
IV-B

From sample 0 to 1, the light changes from off to on. This change of state is represented by a logic 1 bit. During the next three samples, the light doesn't change states (it remains on) so the state is encoded as three logic 0s. At sample 5, the node will detect that the light has changed states, so it encodes the change as a logic 1. The next transition doesn't occur until sample 11 is taken. The light goes from on to off, so this is encoded as a logic 1. This goes on and on with a logic 1 generated for each change in the status of the light. The NRZ-encoded data is then separated into 5-bit symbol groups. The symbol groups and their assigned functions, are listed in Table 6-7.

The reason for organizing the bits into groups of five is that the FDDI clock rate is set at 125 MHz—a multiple of five. The fifth bit in the symbol is used as a synchronizing bit, so that the receiver can properly track the symbols as they arrive. Once the symbol arrives at the receiver, the fifth bit is stripped from the group. This means that although the FDDI clock rate is 125 MHz, the actual data is transmitted at eighty percent of that rate, or 100 MHz, because the fifth bit is stripped from the symbol.

The Physical Layer Protocol also is responsible for ensuring that all of the attached stations serve as repeaters for frames that are intended for another station. This is accomplished by examining the station address in the data frame. If the frame contains an address other than the station possessing it, it is copied and sent to the next station. There may be times when the next station is busy, and unable to receive a frame that's being repeated. In this case, the station holds the frame in an **elastic buffer**, until the next station is free to receive the frame. An elastic buffer is simply an area of RAM set aside to handle overflow frames.

ETHERNET

00 -

00000000

00000000

00 -

CANONICA

Following the
there is no mi
length of the f

The Frame Ch
the source an
including the
network. FDL
Control fields
some faulty fi
increase in sp

The final field
stations with
example, a rec
Frame Status
shortly, this is
network, until
indicator set,
Other uses of
that the frame
that the statio

The Media-A
illustrated in l
two-symbol s
delimiter. In t
set, the token
station.

NUMBE
SYMBC

Once the dat
network. Bef
The process

DECIMAL	BINARY	ASCII	MEANING
LINE STATE SYMBOLS			
00	00000	Q	Quiet
31	11111	I	Idle
04	00100	H	Halt
STARTING DELIMITER			
24	11000	J	1st of Seq SD Pair
17	10001	K	2nd of Seq SD Pair
ENDING DELIMITER			
13	01101	T	Terminates Data Stream
CONTROL INDICATOR			
07	00111	R	Reset (Logical 0)
25	11001	S	Set (Logical 1)
INVALID CODE ASSIGNMENTS			
01	00001	H or V	H = Halt
02	00010	H or V	V = Violation
03	00011	V	
05	00101	V	Used for consecutive code-bit zeros or duty cycle requirements
06	00110	V	
08	01000	H or V	
12	01100	V	
16	10000	H or V	

Table 6-7 FDDI NRZ Symbol Coding

The process begins with all stations issuing a **claim frame**. The claim frame contains a randomly generated number called a **target token rotation-time value**. The stations with the shorter rotation time values repeat the claim frame. Stations with a longer rotation time value are excused from the competition. The issuance of claim frames continues, with the time parameter set shorter and shorter, until ultimately, a station emerges with the shortest rotation time value. This is the station that wins the token.

The specific, winning target token rotation-time value is also the time that the token will complete a cycle around the ring. All losing stations will set their transmission times in accordance to the target rotation time. For example, if the value is one second, this means that the token will complete a trip around the ring in a second. Each station then knows the exact amount of time it has access to the token for transmitting or receiving data.

In addition to sending and receiving data frames, the stations connected to a ring network must also serve as repeaters for frames intended for other stations. You may wonder, if a station repeats frames, when does it have time to transmit? The repeater function is handled independent of the token. For example, assume that Station A is sending to Station C. Station A, possessing the token, transmits the frame to B. Since the frame is not addressed to B, it sends the frame on to station C. When Station A is finished transmitting, or the rotation time value expires, the token moves to Station B, which has already received the frame destined for Station C, and sent it on. Now that it has the token, Station B transmits its own data.

Can a station that is repeating a frame send it at the same time that a station in possession of the token is transmitting? No. Only one station has access to the ring at any time. What happens to repeat frames while another station is transmitting? They are held in elastic buffers until the network is free. This occurs in the time between a frame being transmitted, and the expiration of the rotation timer.

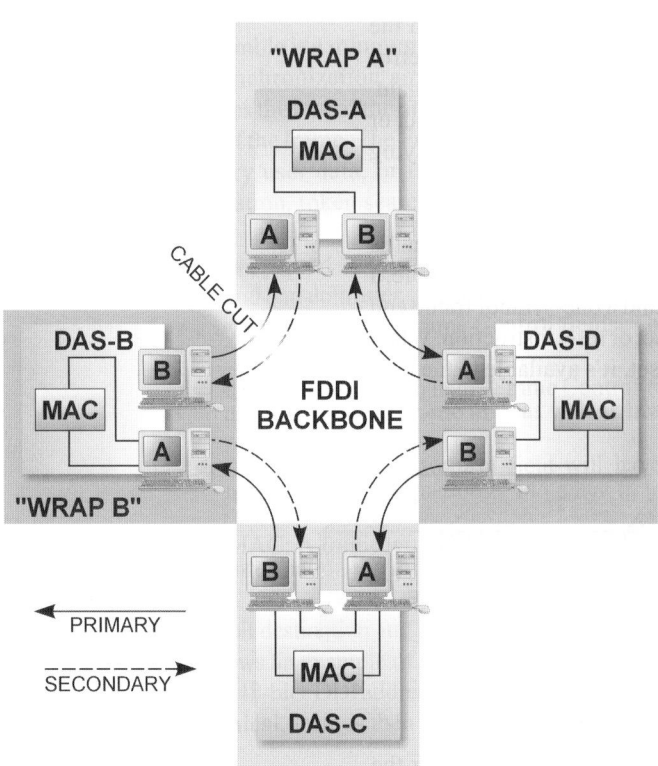

Figure 6-40 Ring Wrapping a Fault Condition

Timing considerations don't always fall into place as neatly as just described. A station may use the entire time available to send a long frame, and the frame may be cut short due to the timer expiring. Then the token goes to the next station and it sends a frame. In the meanwhile, the elastic buffers of the stations are filling with frames to be repeated. In the worst case, the ring crashes. Usually, this situation does not occur because the frame lengths are limited to 9,000 symbols, and the rotation time is set slightly higher. This should allow time for repeating frames, as well as time for sending the maximum frame length.

Suppose Station A finishes transmitting a frame, and releases the token to Station B. But B does not receive the frame from A. Any station failing to receive a frame generates a **beacon**. A beacon is a Token frame the sender transmits to itself. If it does not receive its beacon, it declares a broken ring, and forces a **wrap condition**.

A ring wrap is shown in Figure 6-40, where the frame was lost between Station A and Station B. By wrapping around the cable between the two stations, the ring continues to operate using the **counter-rotating redundancy** of the primary and secondary rings. It's important to mention that single-attached stations may be cut out of the ring if they are located in the section that has been eliminated.

Symbol management, which refers to the generation and monitoring of network-control instructions, originates in the Media-Access Control layer. The software examines data frames for invalid symbols, link conditions, and ensures the symbols generated are appropriate to a particular situation.

Station Management

The Station Management layer provides for individual station control of the FDDI system. Note that Station Management is not centralized in an FDDI network, but is delegated to each device attached to the ring. The stations are responsible for managing the lower layers, as well as coordinating events among all stations. In this respect, the devices are management peers on the network.

NETWORK OPERATING SYSTEMS

CNST OBJECTIVE
III-A

A **Network Operating System** (NOS) consists of software running at the Network layer (for LANs) that controls and directs activity on the network. There are many available and their function is to ease the administrator and operator tasks. What differentiates one from the other is the degree of transparency they provide.

Consider that an Ethernet LAN is an Ethernet LAN—no matter what software is at the Network layer. The MAC sublayer is unaware of Microsoft, or Novell. Typically, the NOS will implement the Data Link and Physical layer protocols, as well as offer a slew of options and enhancements that make for a more powerful network. This includes station-to-station protocols such as IP.

Windows for Workgroups

The demand by IBM computer users for a graphics-based environment, similar to what Macintosh users had been enjoying for years, led Microsoft Corporation to develop the Windows series. With the advent of Windows version 3.0, its popularity skyrocketed.

Software developers all over the world eagerly jumped on the Windows bandwagon.

CNST OBJECTIVE
III-A

With the introduction of Windows version 3.1 in 1992, software applications previously found only in the Macintosh format began appearing in Windows versions. The addition of Windows **MultiMedia Extensions** (MME), accelerated this pace further, including the introduction of applications within the previously Mac-dominated domain of music software. Windows-based applications are easy to learn, because once a user has mastered the essentials of one Windows application, he or she is already prepared to use other Windows-based applications as well. The capability to run DOS-based and Windows-based applications side-by-side, with information sharing between them, has created another strong motivation for users to work in the Windows computer environment.

The growing trend towards networking among corporate and business users, as well as numerous government and military interests, prompted Microsoft to offer its clients a networking alternative, Windows for Workgroups, which virtually superimposed a network environment over the Windows 3.1 framework. Sharing resources and exchanging data among the members of a workgroup were greatly simplified, and quickly accomplished.

New Applications

When existing Windows systems were upgraded to Windows for Workgroups, several new applications were introduced to users. One of these was **Mail**. This is an electronic mail application with which users can send files or electronic messages to, or from, each member of the workgroup. These messages can be printed, organized, stored in folders, or searched for according to specific user-selected criteria.

Another new application introduced to Windows users in Windows for Workgroups was **Schedule+**, a personal scheduling tool used to keep track of various appointments to attend, or tasks to perform. Meetings with others in the workgroup could be set up from the desktop. In fact, the user could share his or her schedule with others in the workgroup, and have them update it as required. Schedules could be printed in regular, or organizer, size for portability.

This was even a network version of **Hearts**, a popular card game, that could be played by up to four users, simultaneously. This game was added to the regular fair of Solitaire and Minesweeper, usually located in the Games Group in Windows version 3.1. How badly production suffered during these data-sharing sessions is difficult to ascertain.

To allow users to share parts of documents with the workgroup, another new application called **Clipbook Viewer** was included. When combined with the **Object Linking and Embedding** (OLE) tool, the Clipbook Viewer allowed shared information (called an object) to be updated across the workgroup, in any linked document sharing the updated object. Updated information could originate from any linked workgroup member.

Windows for Workgroups also added several applications to the Accessory Group. The **Chat** accessory application allowed the user to converse with other members of the workgroup. After dialing the other member's computer, the user simply typed the message. Any return message appeared in the user's Chat window as it was typed.

To check on how other individual's shared resources (files, directories, or printers) a user could run **Net Watcher**. Information, such as who has used the resources, how long they had been connected, or how much time has elapsed since the last time they used your resources, was readily available. The user could also disconnect someone from using his or her resources if necessary, or close any shared files.

To check on how well a user's CPU was performing, **WinMeter** could be run. The time required by the user's CPU in accomplishing personal tasks and network tasks was reported.

Application Enhancements

Applications with which Windows users had gained prior experience were upgraded significantly. One of these applications was the Windows **File Manager**. File Manager allowed the user to select which files and directories to share with others in the workgroup. The user could also gain access to files, directories, and applications shared by others.

Many commands could be executed by using buttons located on the **toolbar**. This made file sharing, connecting to directories, sorting files, and changing the type of displayed file information quick and easy to perform. The toolbar could be customized to fit the requirements of the individual user.

A special icon was used to indicate which directories were being shared. Information about shared directories, menu commands, and the usage/availability of disk space was displayed on the **status bar**. The names of people using your shared directories were available.

The **Print Manager** application was also upgraded to allow a network printer to be accessed by every user in the workgroup. The Print Manager window was enhanced to provide more information, in columns which can be resized as desired. Icons were selected to differentiate between printers reserved for individuals, and those set up for network use. Various documents from each user were listed in the cue, by name and size.

Print Manager also used a toolbar to run various commands quickly. The buttons allowed a user to share his or her printer, or to connect to any network printer. The user could easily pause, resume, or cancel the printing of any document(s) in the print cue.

The Windows **Control Panel** contained additional features that allowed the user to change his or her computer name, change the workgroup he or she belonged to, describe the features of his or her computer to other users of the workgroup in a list of workgroup computers, change of modify his or her logon password, allocate how much of his or her CPU time would be spent on running applications, or sharing resources with the workgroup, and set up network cards and software.

Network Connectivity

An important feature of Windows for Workgroups was its ability to connect to other network types, such as **Novell Netware**, **Microsoft LAN Manager**, and **Windows NT**.

For instructions on the installation, setup, and operation of Windows for Workgroups, please refer to a Microsoft Windows for Workgroups User's Guide.

Windows For Workgroups was a very effective solution for networking, and remains one. It still runs on many networks.

Windows NT

Windows NT is a follow-on to Windows For Workgroups 3.11.

> It would seem that someone at Microsoft must have a made a long list of all the things that they didn't like about other NOS's and addressed them in NT.

It has become hugely popular for several reasons. It's easy to setup and use. It works with other popular NOS's. It was specifically made for powerful network servers that have several microprocessors. It also works with **Hardware Abstraction Layers** (HALs), that allow for a large number of microprocessors. It supports hard drives larger than 2 GB. It permits you to run Windows 95 on clients, or you can install the NT Client instead.

In a pure installation, a Windows NT server uses the Windows NT operating system for both server, and client, operations. This means it's a self-contained operating system, and in particular, a system designed for business applications. It's equally at home in a small LAN, or a globally distributed network.

Windows NT was designed for 32-bit applications; consequently, it won't support 16-bit device drivers found in older PCs. This has allowed a considerable amount of flexibility for Microsoft designers, since they don't have to worry about backwards-compatibility issues. The server and workstation versions of Windows NT are modular components, and are added to the basic operating system to make the package complete— they both run across a common source code.

Windows NT competes directly with Novell NetWare. Versions earlier than NT 4.0 addressed many NetWare weaknesses with the intent of luring customers from Novell. Unfortunately for Microsoft, most network administrators were quite happy with NetWare, and didn't take the bait. With the release of NT 4.0, Microsoft altered it's strategy by permitting side-by-side compatibility with NetWare. This strategy has delivered results, and given NT a segment of the networking market which had been reserved for desktop operating systems.

Windows NT is relatively easy to install. A basic installation can be performed in two hours, and it works! It works in a small LAN consisting of a dozen PCs, and in a large, distributed network containing hundreds of computers, connected by sophisticated routers.

All client computers on an NT network participate in either a **domain**, or a **workgroup**. A workgroup consists of computers that maintain a list of user accounts on each machine. All passwords and access rights reside in the individual computers. Members of a workgroup utilize the same network protocol, and share the same workgroup name.

Administering a workgroup is difficult if the users move frequently; that is, if they move from one workgroup to another. The reason is that, as mentioned above, all user account information resides in each computer. If a change is made, all members of the workgroup must be updated to reflect the change. However, for a small LAN in which user changes aren't likely to occur frequently, a workgroup may be a very good organizational tool.

In workgroup situations, an NT server is a stand-alone server that's primarily used for file sharing, and perhaps, as a print server.

A domain is a collection of servers that may be organized according to some function, such as accounting, or sales. Alternately, the domain may be organized according to geography such as North, South, etc. The idea behind a domain is that when you log on, you do so to a domain, and consequently, to all servers (and the resources that they make available) with one logon, rather than separately logging on to a dozen related servers.

Since client computers are a part of a domain (one or more servers), you also have access to the client machines when you log onto the domain. File and directory sharing are a big part of a NOS, and NT is no exception. But just because you can get to a machine doesn't mean you've been given access to its contents; that's one of the jobs of a network administrator, to determine who has access to what.

There are three types of domains used with NT. You must specify the domain type during the installation. The three types are summarized in Table 6-8. A primary domain controller may also be used as a file, print and application server. A backup domain controller, while a wise addition to a network, isn't required. The BDC contains mirror copies of information on the PDC.

NET+ OBJECTIVE
I.1.2

Table 6-8 Windows NT Types of Domains

Windows NT Server Types
Primary Domain Controller
The Primary Domain Controller (PDC) is the server designated as containing master user account information. These are files which describe rights and profiles of all users in a domain. There can only be a single PDC in a domain. If, when a server is first installed, it's designated as a PDC, you must provide a unique domain name for it. The name can't be used in any other servers on the network. Since the domain is created with the installation of the PDC, it will always be the first server installed in a network with multiple servers in the same domain.
Backup Domain Controller
A Backup Domain Controller (BDC) is installed into an existing domain that has a PDC installed in it. When additional servers are needed in the network, they will be installed as BDCs. The advantage of a BDC is that it provides fault redundance since user accounts are copied from the PDC to the BDC. If the PDC fails, the BDC can be elevated to a PDC with a minimal loss of data--only the information changed in the PDC since the last copy to the DBC. There can be multiple BDCs in a network.
Stand Alone Server
A Stand Alone Server (SAS) is primarily used when the server will double as a workstation. In a small LAN, it may not make sense to dedicate the resources of a computer to managing the network. In this case, application programs can be installed into the FAT partition of the hard drive and it can be used in a dual role. The drawback to creating a SAS is that it can't participate in an existing domain, although you can create a domain consisting of only the server and the attached workstations.

Note that a print server is used to queue print jobs. A print server uses a print spooler, which is temporary memory, to store impending print jobs. The idea is that a printer may not have sufficient memory to store all print jobs until the printer can print them, so a print server allows the jobs to be queued without losing the documents to be printed. A file server, contains assigned directories or sub-directories where users can store their work. A application server contains application software such as Microsoft Word or Excel that a user launches to work with.

In a domain, client logons are authenticated at the server. The domain controller is the central site for user account information. If a change is made in a domain, the account residing at the server is updated once, and all clients are then informed of the change. In terms of simplifying client access and organization, a domain is far superior. However, in terms of implementation, it's somewhat more difficult.

> Normally, the best choice between a workgroup and a domain, when using NT, is to choose a domain. The reason is that once the choice is made, it's difficult to reverse.

Users are assigned to **groups** on a NT network. The network administrator will assign rights (NT makes this fairly easy, as you'll see in the paragraphs to follow) and permissions for users and groups. A **right**, by the way, is an activity users perform, such as where they may log on, or changes they can make. A **permission** refers to the logical concepts they can do, such as their file access, or read-and-write access. A right involves a physical activity, while a permission is a data activity.

CNST OBJECTIVE
III-A

Groups of users are assigned to domains of servers. If you're wondering about how this is done—that is, what rules are there to guide you—the answer is: not many. That's not to say that there aren't a plethora of tools available for creating domains and groups. However, you must **carefully plan for the logical organization of an NT network** before you install the software. During installation, NT will prompt you for the group names, and the computer names, for example. Plan who's going to be where, what rights and permissions they'll have, whether a user needs to belong to more than one group, and so on.

Windows NT supports two file structures, FAT and NTFS. FAT is short for **File Allocation Table** and is the type of file system used with DOS, Win 3.x, Win 95, and OS/2 (along with HTFS). Because there is such a huge base of installed operating systems which employ FAT, you may feel compelled to setup the hard disk on an NT server with it. FAT is a 16-bit structure that, in earlier versions, didn't support long file names. However, when installed with NT after 1996, long file names are supported (up to 255 characters) in a FAT32 version. FAT may or may not be a good choice, but it depends on a couple of factors that we'll take a look at shortly.

NTFS originated with the HTFS file structure that Microsoft, and IBM, developed for the OS/2 operating system. It's the recommended choice for Windows NT, because NTFS is more secure than FAT, and NTFS is not limited by the FAT 4GB partition limit. NTFS, also utilizes the disk space far more efficiently than FAT, especially for larger file sizes.

In effect, it supports unlimited partition sizes, and will attempt to restore good data (and remove bad data), in the event of a power loss. As already mentioned, the security features of NTFS are superior to FAT. File- and directory-level security allows you to specify the access permissions to individual files and directories.

There are not many good reasons for installing FAT on an NT server. However, you have the option of installing both FAT and NTFS in separate partitions. If, after the software is installed, you decide to convert all partitions to NTFS, NT will permit this. However, in order to convert from NTFS to FAT, the reformatting of disk partitions, and the reinstalling of Windows NT, is required—in effect, there's no practical way of doing it.

There are, however, two reasons why you'd want to consider setting up a FAT partition on an NT server. The first is if the server microprocessor is RISC-based. In this case, FAT is a requirement. The second reason is if you have another operating system, besides NT, installed on the hard disk—such as DOS, Windows 95 or Windows for Workgroups. This is called dual-booting the computer, and isn't a recommended practice. None of these operating systems can access an NTFS partition.

NT NTFS supports most (though not all) application software used with other Microsoft operating systems. If you have clients running an unsupported program, then you'd want to include a FAT partition. Resolve this during the planning stage, and if you don't need FAT on the server, choose NTFS for all partitions.

NET+ OBJECTIVE
I.1.2

There are several NT features that will be reviewed in this section. We'll take a look at the basic desktop of NT, locate some basic, but important, wizards, examine how users are organized, and finally, see how you can use NT to monitor a network.

The Windows NT desktop is very similar to the Windows 95 user interface, and is a considerable improvement over the 3.1 interface, since the user has total control of the icons.

To access other programs, you click the start button, and as each directory is high-lighted, any existing subdirectories are listed. Some important directories you'll find under Programs include:

CNST OBJECTIVE
III-A

 Windows NT Explorer

This program is equivalent to the File Manager used in Windows 3.x. Notice that it includes a list of directories and subdirectories on the hard drive. From the File menu, you can share drives and folders. NT uses a convention for inserting parameters into dialog boxes, called **property sheets**. A property sheet is equivalent to a dialog box, and refers to the tab at the top of each folder. For example, if you choose Shared Properties, a series of tabbed folders will open. These folders are property sheets. Typically, the sheet contains fields for you to enter information. The mechanics are identical to using dialog boxes, but the look is different.

 **Administrative Wizards
(See Figure 6-41)**

Administrative wizards are programs that simplify the installations of new or updated hardware and software. They also aid in the management of the various network responsibilities in Windows NT.

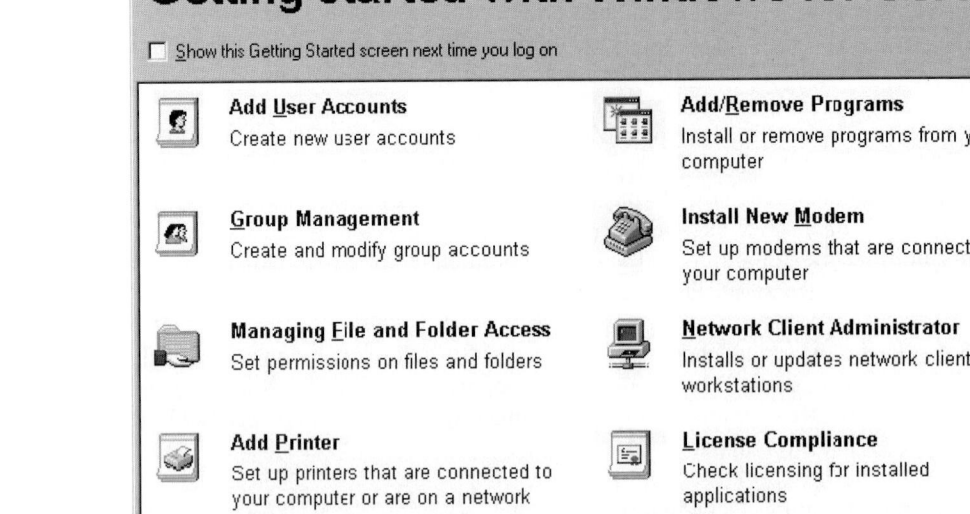

NET+ OBJECTIVE
I.1.2

Figure 6-41
Administrative Wizards

CNST OBJECTIVE
V-A/B

- Add Printer Wizard: Used to set up local or network printers. Appropriate printer drivers are downloaded to the server, then to the clients when a printer is configured as a shared resource.

- Network Client Administrator Wizard: Used to automatically load software to client computers. This is also used when software upgrades are needed.

- Add/Remove Programs Wizard: This is identical to the Add/Remove tool found in Control Panel. As a wizard, however, it's used as a shortcut. It's used when software is added to, or removed from, the network.

- License Wizard: This is a simple database used to track licensing agreements for software running on the server and clients. Essentially, it makes it tough to claim ignorance if you're caught using pirated software.

- Install New Modem Wizard: Used to detect and install a new modem added to the server. Along with the Add/Remove Program wizard, it operates in an identical manner to the '95 Plug and Play feature.

- Add User Account Wizard: Used to add new users to the network. The process includes identifying the new user by his/her full name, as well as a login name. Access and sharing rights are prescribed as well.

- Group Management Wizard: Used to organize users into groups with similar rights. This minimizes the work required when a new user is added.

- Managing File and Folder Access Wizard: Used to set up shared drives and folders among groups.

Server Manager

This is a tool used to manage computers, collections of devices and users (domains) by monitoring their activity, and by modifying it as needed. This may include setting permissions, sharing directories, adding or removing computers from a domain, sending broadcast messages to domain members, and so on.

 Network Client Administrator

This is used to install or upgrade client workstations. It is particularly useful for performing software upgrades to NIC cards located in client computers.

 Performance Monitor

This feature lets you monitor the performance of your own computer, or others on the network. You have the option of viewing all client computers simultaneously, then logging the data for specified times. Being a Microsoft product, you can then export the statistical data to Excel for interpretation.

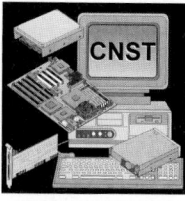

CNST OBJECTIVE
V-B, IX-A & XI-B

 User Manager

This is a tool for setting up and managing user accounts. This includes creating the account, determining who has access to group accounts, who belongs to a group account, specifying logon hours, deleting or renaming user accounts—in short, this is where the network administrator manages client-users on the network.

7 **Windows NT Network Monitor**

This is a software-based network analyzer that runs on each segment of an NT network. Information captured from the network is displayed on the screen in realtime. This means you see detailed traffic information as it occurs. Since the information is realtime, you have an excellent tool to observe problems which are inconsistent, or random in nature.

Some important features of Network Monitor include:

- Can be run over any LAN segments, including Ethernet and Token Ring.

- Decodes traffic in realtime, and displays it using several layers of detail and format.

- Calculates common network statistics, such as number of frames transmitted, number of frames dropped, and the status of the network.

- Determines the utilization rate of the network, along with the number of frames or bytes sent each second.

- Lists Session layer parameters, which show end-to-end source and destination addresses.

- Allows you to set filters for specifying information you want to see.

- Displays captured traffic for all layers of the OSI model.

- Provides cumulative levels of detail for each captured packet.

NET+ OBJECTIVE
I.1.2

Network Monitor provides you with information, as it occurs, and in absolute numbers. The Filter option permits you to conduct an in-depth analysis of traffic targeted to a specific node, or segment, of a network.

Network Monitor is an excellent tool for situations when you want to know what's happening on a network, at any particular time. In this experiment, and the next, you'll practice using some of the common elements of Network Monitor.

The Windows NT Task Manager folders include Applications, Processes and Performance of the computer/server on which NT is installed. To access it, position the cursor on the taskbar located at the bottom of the screen. Click the right mouse button. Choose Task Manager from the menu listings, and the Windows NT Task Manager window will open. Figure 6-42 shows a typical example.

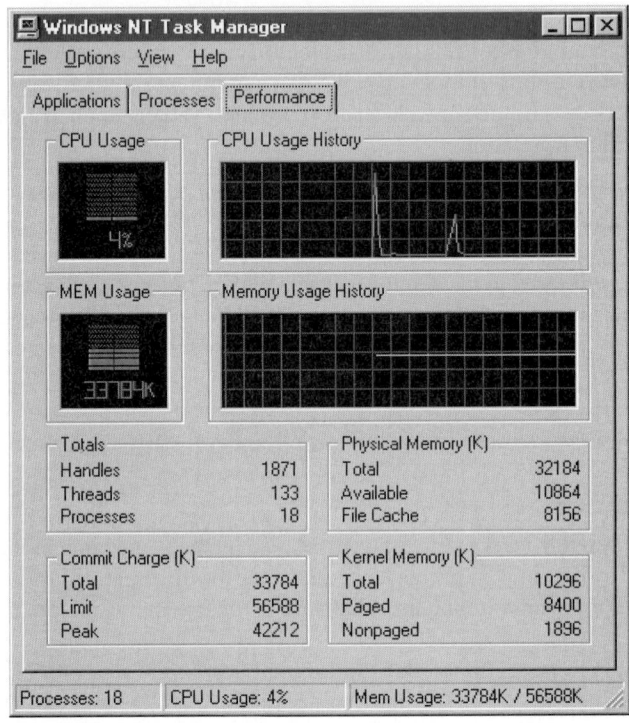

Figure 6-42 NT Processor Performance

You can instruct NT to present three types of information by clicking on the appropriate tab:

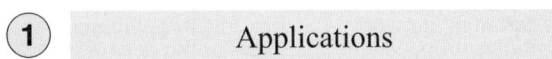

1   Applications

If any applications are currently running, they are listed in the folder along with the status of each application. You can terminate a selected application by right-clicking it, then disabling the application in the pop-up dialog box.

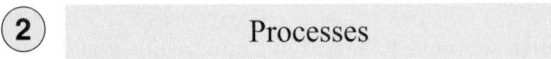

2   Processes

Processes shows any executable files which are running. In addition, the columns display the percentage of CPU time each process is using, along with the amount of memory consumed by the process.

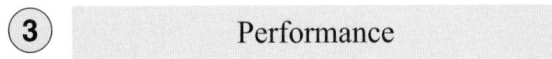

3   Performance

Performance presents you with graphical information on the basic performance of the system, the CPU, and the memory usage.

Windows NT 4.0 has limited **security** options, although it's a considerable improvement from previous versions of NT. Security is limited to assigning rights and permissions to directories and files. The problem with a system such as this is that it's all based on passwords, and user IDs. If these are compromised, a logon could occur from anywhere. Security at the server, however, is far superior than at any client with access. When an NT server boots, the administrator must perform a second (warm) boot before any clients can actually log on. This forces the administrator to be physically present at the booting server, and prevents a remote client from booting the server, then logging on using a stolen password.

In addition to the tools described above, there are several other important tools available with NT. They are:

- NT Disk Administrator: Shows logical partitions of a hard drives as well as multiple hard drives on the server. It lists the type of file structure as well as the size of partitions. Disk Administrator is also where you use RAID-software (RAID is **Redundant Array of Inexpensive Disks**; see Chapter 10) for fault tolerance to backup hard drive data.

- Event Viewer: A tool used to mange system, security and application events on a network. For example, it can be used to determine when a user logged on and off the network, or to see print jobs sent to a print server.

- HCL: HCL is an acronym for **Hardware Compatibility List**. Microsoft publishes the guide to show hardware types that have been tested to be compatible with Windows NT 4.0. Before installing a new NIC card, for example, check the HCL to make sure it can be used with NT. It's also a good idea to check the guide when upgrading from an earlier version of NT to 4.0 to ensure the same hardware is compatible.

- GroupWare: Groupware is a set of software solutions designed to help members of workgroups work together. Typically, groupware contains e-mail, some type of database tool, meeting planner and scheduler, and so on. Microsoft Exchange and Lotus Notes are both examples of groupware.

- SMS: A tool available with Back Office, **Systems Management Server**, is used to configure a network based upon information about each computer on the network. Typically, SMS is used for larger networks as a centralized administrative tool for organizing the network.

- Auditing: Provides information that's targeted to a particular resource. The auditing function is located on the Security tab of the share Properties folder of a directory or file. To use it, logon to the server as Administrator and open User Manager for Domains. Choose Policies, then Audit. The Audit Policy dialog box will open.

NT **network administration** has other tools in addition to those described with NT Wizards. The system supports **Dynamic Host Configuration Protocol** (DHCP), which allows the server to assign IP addresses dynamically. **Domain Name Server** (DNS) is a tool that reconciles Internet domain names to IP addresses. The Internet site, microsoft.com, is located at IP 207.68.137.35. When the domain name is entered, DNS will convert to the IP. Windows NT supports a wide array of protocols, and the major ones are listed in Table 6-9.

Table 6-9 NT Protocols

NET+ OBJECTIVE
I.1.2

CNST OBJECTIVE
IV-B/C & V-A/B

Network Protocols Supported by Windows NT	
NetBEUI	NetBIOS Extended User Interface, a non-routable Microsoft protocol developed by IBM.
NWLink	NWLink is a Microsoft version of Novell IPX/SPX (Internetwork Packet Exchange/ Sequenced Packet Exchange) which is a routable protocol and the default choice when NT is setup.
TCP/IP	Transmission Control Protocol/ Internet Protocol is a routable protocol and used in most wide area networks. Noted for its reliability, TCP/IP is the best protocol for larger or interconnected networks.
Apple Talk	Apple Talk is the network protocol used by Macintosh computers. Windows NT allows Macintosh users to share MAC-files in NT server space and to share printers.
Remote Access Service	Remote access includes dial-up services that include SLIP (Serial Line Internet Protocol). PPP (Point-to-Point Protocol), ISDN, and PPTP (Point-to-Point Tunneling Protocol).

In addition, the **Point-to-Point Tunneling Protocol** (PPTP) is available for secure, remote connections that use the Internet as the communication medium between the remote user, and an NT server.

NET+ OBJECTIVE
I.1.2

CNST OBJECTIVE
XI-A

Novell NetWare

Currently, NetWare is at Version 5. This is the most robust implementation that Novell has ever marketed, and in many respects, it is superior to version 4.0 of Windows NT.

As networks grew from several computers that needed a more efficient way to share files and printing, no other network operating system has evolved with the need like Novell NetWare. Although Windows NT may eclipse NetWare in the years ahead, NetWare is a testament to the versatility of software developers who have the ability to meet the demands of the marketplace year after year. Based upon the original international CCTT standard x.500 for directory services, NetWare is a stable and reliable network operating system.

NetWare performs the same basic functions of all network operating systems. It manages connectivity at the local- and wide-area level, allows file, directory and print sharing, and provides security for authorized access, and against unauthorized access. NetWare also includes network management tools that allow you to troubleshoot and fine tune the installation, as well as manage the network resources. In addition, it provides methods for data backups, and includes database access and replication tools.

How these services are presented and implemented varies from one NOS to the next. The previous section previewed those services available with Microsoft's Windows NT, and Workgroups. In this section, we'll examine the methods used by Novell with NetWare.

An important requirement of NetWare is that a NetWare Client software must be installed on client computers. These include any Microsoft client operating system. Before the client can access a NetWare server, the NetWare client software must be installed on the client.

The NetWare directory services are based on the **Novell Directory Service** (NDS) scheme. NDS specifies a network element as an **object**. An object is any network resource, including printers, client computers, routers, bridges, software applications—anything that a client may use. Once all objects are identified, they're arranged in a tree structure. There are two types of objects—a **container** and a **leaf**. A container allows you to manage objects as a set, rather than manage them individually (individual management is an option with leaf objects). You can specify a change—access to a printer, for example—to a container, and all objects within the container will be affected.

As an alternative to containers, Novell offers a **leaf object**. A leaf represents information about system resources such as a printer, computer, user, application, etc. With a leaf, you can manages individual characteristics, and properties of a single object.

The structure begins with a **root**. A root is the primary object from which the tree is built. This is normally named after a company, a department within a company, or by departmental group. The root branches to an Organization, which is a delineation of the root. For example, there may be Organization headings for Sales, Accounting, Production and so forth. These could also be organized by cities, states, or whatever makes sense for a company. Branching from the Organization level is an Organizational Unit. This may refer to individuals within a department, or cities within a state.

Figure 6-43 shows an example from the NetWare online documentation.

Notice that the NDS structure begins with the ROOT DIRECTORY, and branches to the organization level YOURCO. From YOURCO, there are two organizational units, East and West. Each of these contain two organizational units. Branching with NDS can continue as long as necessary, but Novell ships with a recommended default structure for networks with fewer than 1,000 objects. For most applications, you shouldn't have to spend an excessive amount of time designing the organizational structure.

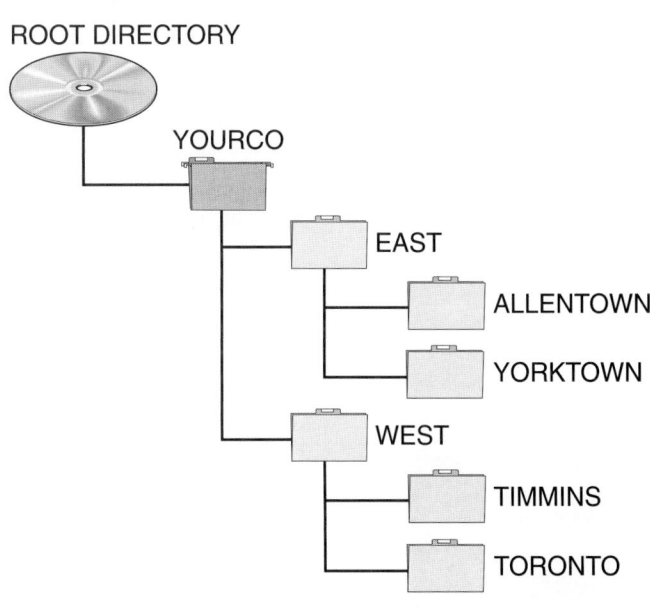

Figure 6-43 NetWare NDS Structure

The advantage of NDS is the ease of management of the objects in a tree. Since each container is linked logically, you can apply the same rights and permissions to all objects within a container. This includes logon scripts, file and directory access, and printer sharing. Or, through a process called **inheritance**, rights "flow-down" the tree containers. For example, in Figure 6-43, if a user is granted rights to WEST, he can manage all objects in WEST, TIMONS and TORONTO. If a user has rights to YOURCO, she can manage objects in EAST and WEST.

Administering NDS can occur from any workstation having the NetWare client installed. It may be running any Windows software, including Windows NT Workstation, and the Administrator can add, delete, move, rename, or setup printer services.

> Since an NDS container can have global rights, a single logon can provide a user access to all relevant resources. There's no need for multiple passwords.

Security of files and directories has been well established in Novell networks. The implementation is considerably different than in Windows NT, however. NetWare uses a public key cryptography mechanisms to safeguard files. The subject of cryptography is described in detail in Chapter 10. In a nutshell, a public key system generates two keys, one public and one private. The encryption and decryption keys are related, but can't be derived from one other. The public key—which is a complex algorithm—is made available to one or more, and sometimes all, nodes on a network.

The private key, however, is unique for each node, and is used to decode the message that's encoded with a public key. The system is effective when one, public key-encoded message, can be decrypted by many private keys. In this way, the intricacy of an already complex system is manageable. But what if a coded message is sent to the wrong node? If it possesses a private key for the published public key, it can decode the message. Before the message it sent, the sender transmits an encoded message to the receiver asking for its private key. The receiver responds with a message encoded with its private key. If the sender can decode it, it does so, and sends a response. The receiver acknowledges the response, and then the transaction occurs.

Note that a receiver will reject a coded message if the sender hasn't been authenticated. This means that the system relies on both authentication, and the possession of related public and private keys.

The advantage to incorporating public key encryption in NetWare is that it's similar to encryption schemes used in many other electronic transfers, such as credit card transactions on the Internet.

File structures refers to the physical and logical characteristics of files and storage devices (i.e., hard drives). The Novell file system consists of **volumes**, and **partitions**. A partition is used to separate operating systems. For instance, a hard drive may be separated into two partitions, with one containing the NetWare OS, and the other containing DOS. Up to four partitions may be placed on a single disk.

A volume is used to sub-divide partitions into smaller units. With four allowable partitions on each disk, you can have up to eight volumes. Whereas a partition is limited to a physical disk, a volume may span multiple disks. A volume is organized into logical groupings, such as user directories, for various departments such as sales, production, etc. A volume may also be created to contain the application software made available across the network.

Partitions and volumes are managed by two types of available file services: **Novell Storage Services** (NSS), which is available only on version 5.0, and **NetWare File System** (NFS), which was used on earlier versions of NetWare, and is still available on version 5.0.

With either service, directories and files are stored in the volumes described above. You specify which objects can access other objects, along with the level of access: read only, read/write, print. With NSS, space on all server hard drives is efficiently utilized. NSS collects all free space, as well as any space not used by a volume, and pools it. From this pool, you can create additional volumes, and you will always know how much actual hard drive space remains available. Table 6-10 lists pertinent features of NSS.

CNST OBJECTIVE
XI-A

Table 6-10 NSS Features

Novell Storage Services (NSS) Features	
Feature	Capability
Number of Files/ server	8 trillion
Maximum File Size	8 terabytes
Maximum Simultanously Open files	one million/ server
Time Ti Open Files	All file open immediately
Maximum Volume Size	8 terabytes
Maximum Number of Volumes On A Single Server	255 mounted
Volume Segments	Unlimited
Directory Tree Depth	None, except as by client
RAM Required	Minimum 4 MB

When users on a NetWare network write to the server, there's a chance that database information may be corrupted during the process. NetWare prevents this with a process called **transaction tracking system**. Essentially, the system makes a copy of the database before the write is executed; then, if all goes well during the update, destroys the copy.

File backup with NetWare is accomplished by adding a tape reader, optical reader, or similar device. NetWare doesn't directly support RAID, as Windows NT does. In effect, the backup system used with NetWare is analogous to Raid level 1, since it involves copying data to a tape backup, or another hard drive. You have the option of specifying full, differential or incremental backups. A complete discussion of RAID can be found in Chapter 10.

Wide area connectivity with NetWare will meet most users needs. You have the option of installing:

- Routing between local LANs.

- Remote access for mobile or home users, who access the server through a modem.

- Remote service management of wide area connectivity from any desktop.

Table 6-11 lists routing protocols supported by NetWare.

Table 6-11 Routing Protocols

NetWare Routing Protocols	
IPX	Novell's proprietary network protocol.
TCP/IP	TCP/IP is a routable protocol and the most widely deployed for large and interconnected networks.
Apple Talk	Apple Talk allows Macintosh clients to share files and printing on a NetWare server.
Source Route Bridging	Proprietary Novell routing protocol for connecting Token Ring networks.
NetWare Link	Novell's remote access protocols supported by NetWare include PPP, ATM (Asynchronous Transfer Mode), X.25 packet switching protocol, and Frame Relay.

There's a great deal of interoperability available between NetWare and Windows NT. Although the two remain competitors, don't expect either to disappear anytime soon. Novell remains the dominate network operating system. There are still thousands of older versions of it running on small LANs, and for many of the administrators of those LANs, it meets their current needs, and they have no reason to change.

The operating system has long relied on **Internetwork Packet Exchange** (IPX) as a proprietary Data Link and Network layer protocol. However, just as Windows NT uses NetBEUI as a proprietary protocol at the same level, you should keep in mind that both of these protocols are encapsulated within a normal 802.3 frame; these networks are, after all, Ethernet LANs. What's missing in the implementation is an SAP interface at the LLC sublayer. It's not needed, since both NOS's stipulate the Network layer interface.

For a smaller LAN, or intranet, that will not connect outside a corporate or local environment, IPX has the same advantages as NetBEUI does for Windows NT—it eases the setup and configuration of the network. IPX has an advantage over NetBEUI in that it's a routable protocol, and can be used for Internet connections. But if the users will be connecting to the Internet, or communicating across a WAN using public switched facilities, another protocol is recommended. In the case of both operating systems, TCP/IP is supported and used for these situations.

Windows NT is the easier of the two to set up and manage. It has less of a proprietary feel, since many of the conventions used with NT were derived from UNIX. With Microsoft's dominant position in workstation operating systems, NT receives far more third-party attention, in the area of add-on development, than NetWare.

UNIX

UNIX has been around for thirty years. It began as an experiment, commissioned by the U.S. government, to find a way of keeping military information systems running in the event of an attack. You have to keep in mind that at that time, an "information system" consisted of a large mainframe computer, with terminals connected to it. All of the data resided in the mainframe. And although the computer had an endless number of security precautions installed, if a nuclear warhead was dropped anywhere in the vicinity of the computer—it was smoked, and the data it contained would go with it.

The problem was compounded due to the many different types of mainframe computers in use, with very few of them being compatible with one other. In 1969, four computers successfully exchanged data, using what would eventually become the TCP/IP protocol suite for internetworking. While the information exchange was a huge stride forward, it lacked a critically important element—a network operating system. Back to the drawing board went the engineers, and academics, and they created an operating system specifically designed for internetworking, calling it UNIX.

UNIX was officially designed by AT&T's Bell Laboratories. Not realizing that UNIX would become such a powerful force in networking, Bell Labs freely gave the operating system, along with its source code, to academic institutions. By the late 70's, UNIX was in full swing and AT&T had second thoughts. Since the operating system was so widely used, they reasoned, it had commercial value. Now it was no longer free, and academic institutions, as well as everyone else, would have to pay for it.

Not so, claimed the University of California at Berkeley. In full possession of the UNIX source code, they rewrote UNIX from the ground up, and christened the new operating system UNIX **Berkeley Software Distribution** (BSD). The AT&T version of UNIX came to be called Sys V. The result, and the point of this little history lesson, is that there were now two versions of UNIX available, and nearly all implementations in use today can be traced back to one of these two.

This lends some insight into why there are so many types, or "flavors", of UNIX. When Sys V UNIX was converted into BSD UNIX, it was obvious that the operating system was portable. This means that it's adaptable to different situations, particularly machine types and file structures. Windows 95 isn't a portable operating system, since it can't run on a Macintosh computer. Table 6-12 lists some of the more common UNIX flavors on the market.

The strengths of UNIX are considerable:

- It supports 32 or 64 bit applications.

- It's multiuser (a small, Intel-based server can support several hundred users).

- Comes with complete TCP/IP suite for servers and clients.

- Hierarchical file system that's multitasking.

- Supports logical partitions.

- It's the most widely used NOS with the Internet.

- Many versions of UNIX are free/inexpensive, when downloaded from the Internet.

NET+ OBJECTIVE
I.1.2

CNST OBJECTIVE
XI-C

Table 6-12 UNIX Versions

Common UNIX Flavors	
UNIX Derivative Protocol	Proprietary Development
A/UX	Developed by Apple Computer and designed to run on MAC-II systems.
AIX	Developed by IBM and rigidly follows standards established by the federal government such as POSIX.
BSD	BSD was developed at the University of California at Berkeley. Variants are called BSD/ OS, BSDI, FreeBSD, OpenBSD and NetBSD. The latter runs on many PC-based operating systems.
Digital UNIX	Digital UNIX is 64-bit UNIX that is extremely reliable and robust. It's used on many large--enterprise--networks.
HP-UX	A Hewlett-Packard version of UNIX that was designed for workstation use and includes HP-Vue, which is a proprietary GUI.
IRIX	Silicon Graphics, Inc. version of UNIX that's primarily used for sophisticated graphics in two and three dimensions.
SunOS and Solaris	Developed by Sun Microsystems, Inc. SunOS runs on RISC-based processors while Solaris runs on both Intel processors. Used extensively by ISPs because it can withstand sustained hits of resource-intensive requests such as video, music, graphics.
UNIXWare	Currently owned by SCO (Santa Cruz Operation), it was designed to run on Pentium and x86 processors.
Linux	Developed by Dutch programmer Linus Torvalds, Linux has been subsequently strengthened by many programmers. Due to the large number of hardware devices it supports, it's becoming a favorite for servers.

NET+ OBJECTIVE
I.1.2

CNST OBJECTIVE
XI-C

Note that Windows NT and NetWare only support 32-bit applications. Because UNIX has far superior performance in creating intense applications such as graphics and mathematical computations, it will invariably be used before either NT or NetWare. It's a true multiuser system. When a UNIX user logs-in to the system, he can run any application. On an NT network, a user can run any client/server application. This is why Windows 95 or DOS applications can be stored on an NTFS server, but not run on one.

All commercial versions of UNIX ship with TCP/IP. That shouldn't come as a surprise, since it's the most effective protocol for intranets and the Internet.

The directory structure used with UNIX resembles a tree cluster, similar to a DOS system. Figure 6-44 illustrates a typical example.

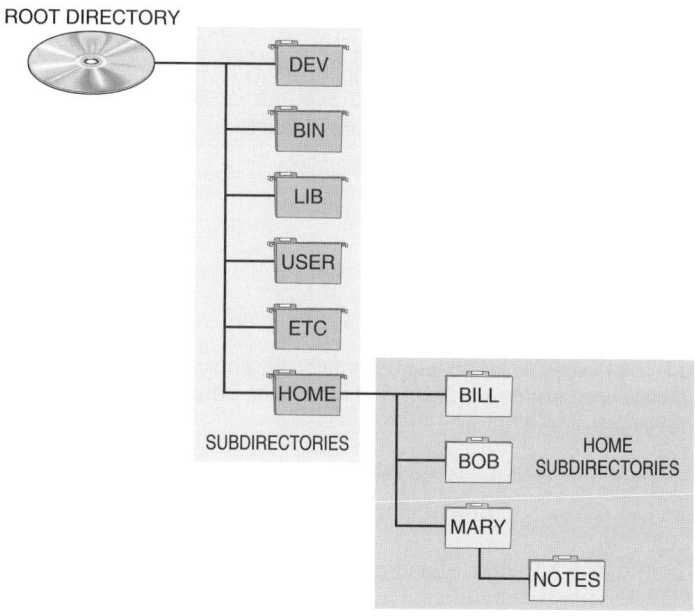

**Figure 6-44 UNIX
Tree Cluster**

At the top level is the Root Directory, symbolized by the / symbol. Directories which branch from the Root are called Subdirectories. Subdirectories may have their own subdirectories, as well. As shown, the subdirectories **/bill**, **/bob**, and **mary** are subdirectories of **/home**, which is a subdirectory of /. When written on a command line, the **/notes** subdirectory appears as:

/home/mary/notes.

The file structure described above is an example of an absolute path. Another way to specify files is to use a relative path. A relative path is specified at the time of login, and will start at a specified file name. For example, a relative may appear as:

/mary/notes.

Otherwise, the user, Mary, would be required to execute the proper UNIX commands that would place her in the appropriate directory.

Files on an UNIX system are organized into **user**, **groups** and **all other users**. This convention is helpful in applying security to files and directories. Mary, in the above example, may want to give permission to other users in her group, so they'll be able to read her notes. If so, she can specify the level of access. Or, she may want to specify that other group members can read and write to her notes.

NET+ OBJECTIVE
I.1.2

However, she may want to restrict access to only her group members, and forbid read or write access to any other user. Figure 6-45 shows the typical listing of a file contained in the **mary** subdirectory. Let's look at each field in the listing.

1	2	3	4	5	6	7	8	9	10
-	rwx	rw-	r--	2	mary	students	1200	Apr 6, 1999	notes

Figure 6-45 Typical File Listing

-/d: - is a file, and d is a directory
r: Read Only
w: Write, modify files
x: Run executable files

- Field 1: This one-character field designates the entry as either a file or a directory. A – (hyphen) represents a file, while a **d** represents a directory. Since the first character is a hyphen, it's a file.

The next nine characters (fields 2, 3 and 4) specify the permissions that the user, Mary, has applied to this file. There are three file permissions available:

Read (r): The file may be accessed and read.
Write (w): The file may be modified.
Executed (x): The file may be run if it's an executable file.

NET+ OBJECTIVE
I.1.2

If permission is denied, it's represented by the - symbol. These permissions are designated as follows:

- Field 2: Specifies the user (in this case, Mary) permissions. Because field 2 contains **rwx**, this means that the user, Mary, has read (**r**), write (**w**) and executable (**x**) access to this file.

- Field 3: Designates the user group permissions. Because field 3 has **rw-**, this means that users in her group may read and write to the file, but won't be able to execute it, even if it's an executable file.

- Field 4: Designates permissions for everyone else. Because field 4 has **r--**, this means that all other users may read the file, but can't modify, or run it.

- Field 5: Indicates how many links, or subdirectories, away from the root directory the file being referenced is located. Because field 5 has **2**, the subdirectory, **Mary**, is two links away (through **Home**) from the root directory, which is designated as **0**.

- Field 6: Indicates the name of the user, **Mary**.

- Field 7: Indicates the name of the user group, **Students**.

- Field 8: Indicates the size of the file, in bytes.

- Field 9: Reveals the most recent date that the file was modified.

- Field 10: Indicates the name of the file, **Notes**.

While the user has total control over setting permissions for files in his/her directory, the administrator of the network is the only one who can assign users to the system, and create, delete, or change user groups.

With UNIX, there are two options available for interacting with the screen. The first is a command line interface, similar to what Microsoft DOS users became accustomed to, prior to the release of Windows. The second is with a graphical interface, approaching the ease of use that we've become accustomed to with Windows and Apple computers. HP-UNIX, running on HP9000 machines, is actually more versatile and configurable than the GUI found in Windows.

The basis for a graphical interface using UNIX is found in the X protocol. Originally developed as a client/server networking tool, X allowed clients to connect to any server, gather information from that server, and then make it available to other clients. In effect, X permitted a client to operate in a dual role, as client and server.

X is platform independent. It runs on Windows NT, Windows 95, Mac OS and of course, UNIX. Of interest to programmers is that X is written in C, the same language that UNIX is written in. Until recently, the graphics available with X weren't spectacular. Since X is fully user-configurable (maybe too much so), there may be many different configurations of it running on UNIX workstations.

CNST OBJECTIVE
XI-C

UNIX is experiencing a renaissance in the networking industry, for several good reasons. It can be freely downloaded from the Internet, or purchased for a nominal fee (less than $100) on a CD. It ships with many of the tools that you must pay extra for when buying NT or NetWare. Table 6-13 lists the basic tool set available with UNIX. It supports true multi-user access to the server resources, and was specifically designed for intranets and the Internet—that is, large, homogenous networks. Contrary to perception, the command line interface used with UNIX is neither difficult, or required. And it requires fewer and cheaper hardware components than either Novell NetWare, or Windows NT. UNIX, due to its longevity in the marketplace, is more reliable under extreme conditions than its competitors.

Table 6-13 Basic UNIX Tools

UNIX has two strong qualities going for it. As mentioned earlier, it has a thirty-year history, and has had far more time to stabilize than either NetWare or NT. What this means is that a UNIX system is perceived to be more reliable that NT, or NetWare (and, it seems, there's empirical evidence supporting this), and when information systems are a critical component of a corporate business plan, reliability becomes equally critical.

Also, UNIX is non-proprietary, and is not bound to address-quirky aspects of a network operating system. For example, Novell makes it difficult to run any other networking protocol other than IPX (although it does offer NetWare/IP, a scaled-down version of TCP/IP), while Microsoft tried for years to push NetBEUI, which works only with LANs.

UNIX Tools and Services	
FTP	FTP is the File Transfer Protocol used to copy files.
Email	Email is native to UNIX and easy to implement.
Gopher	Gopher is used to organize data in large databases.
Finger	Finger is used to identify other users by email address.
HTTP	HTTP is the HyperText Transfer Protocol and is used in all Internet applications.
Telnet	Telnet allows you no logon to a remotely computer as if your computer was physically attached to it.
News Reader	A news reader is required to access the many USENet bulletin boards on the Internet.
Utilities	UNIX utilities include ping, tracert, ipconfig, and many others. They're used for troubleshooting networking problems.
Network and Transport Layer Protocol	TCP/IP is the networking protocol used with UNIX systems. It's the most reliable of all network protools.

UNIX, in a more realistic streak of stubbornness, supports only TCP/IP. Neither Microsoft or Novell support a full implementation of TCP/IP, but an NT or NetWare server uses TCP/IP as a machine-independent networking protocol, because it is the best there is.

NETWORK CLIENT SERVICES

Microsoft is noted for client operating systems. Virtually all of the Microsoft OS's run on a NetWare network, as well as an NT network. A UNIX system, on the other hand, is a bit different. Both Microsoft and Novell support implementations of UNIX, generally with the TCP/IP protocol suite. In the case where multiple clients reside on a network, the universal solution is to install TCP/IP for those clients that don't natively support it (early versions of Windows for Workgroups, for example).

The trick (one of many) of connecting a client to a server, is to be able to see the file that's on a server from a client machine. So far, the underlying elements have been accounted for such as MAC-layer functions and a Network layer operating system. So, using a MAC access method and network operating system, you can get to the server file and connect to it; but then what? You need to be able to see as it appears on the server (or in manner that you're accustomed to seeing it in). In other words, a Presentation layer protocol is needed. This is handled by two components: A **requester** and a **redirector**.

- A requester is a software object sent from a client computer to the server to send a particular item; a file or directory, for example.

- A redirector is a software object that receives a request, then sends it to the client computer that made the request.

But notice it's one thing to connect to the server file and have it presented to you on your screen, but another thing to maintain the connection until you terminate it. Sounds like we need a Session layer parameter to handle this chore. This is accomplished with the **Server Message Block** (SMB). On a Windows NT network, SMB runs on top of a NOS (such as TCP/IP) using a NetBIOS session. Once the session between client and computer is setup, SMB sends packets between the two to maintain the connection. In addition to file requests, SMB is also used to handle print requests from a client to print server.

In this section, we'll preview client operating systems, and the types of service each offers, as well as their short-comings in a networking environment. The major client operating systems supported by NT and NetWare include:

- Windows NT Workstation.

- Windows 95/98.

- Windows for Workgroups 3.1x.

- Windows 3.1+.

- MS-DOS Clients.

- OS/2 Clients.

- Apple Macintosh Clients.

- UNIX Workstations.

Theoretically, any client operating system will interact successfully with NT—or any other NOS, for that matter. The deciding factor is the Network layer protocol running between the client and server. For example, TCP/IP is designed to be machine-independent, and should allow any machines to connect. In practice, and particularly at the LAN level, the ability to use a client/server relationship in which the client is a workstation, using the server to manage its place on a network, is determined by the resident features of both machines.

All of the client operating systems listed above can be used with NT, or NetWare, for their designated purpose of providing a workstation for users. Not surprisingly, NT works seamlessly with its partner, **Windows NT Workstation**, which uses the same 95 graphical interface as NT Server. At first glance, NT Workstation is difficult to distinguish from NT Server and Windows 95, and was designed to work in any of the following environments:

- As a stand-alone workstation.

- As a member of a workgroup in a peer-to-peer network.

- As a client in a Windows NT domain.

As a stand-alone, Workstation supports far more processors than does 95, as well as multiple processors (up to 32, but only two processors out-of-the-box, and only four without performance degradation). Although probably not needed as a stand-alone, Workstation has far superior security capabilities than Windows 95 workstations.

Workstation allows clients to run any of the networking protocols supported by NT Server. Unlike Windows 95, it also permits clients to operate in multiple-access, peer-to-peer workgroups, independent of the server. In a workgroup setting (with or without the server), up to ten clients can access another Workstation member simultaneously. The disadvantage to using Workstation in a peer-to-peer configuration, however, is that the powerful security features of Windows NT aren't utilized. With all of the workgroup's members having access to one another's directories, security becomes a moot point.

A natural implementation of Workstation is a smaller LAN, in which security isn't a concern. The clients may be peers, with file and directory access between them. When Window's NetBEUI is selected as the networking protocol, the network becomes easy to set up, configure and maintain.

Coupled with NT Server, Workstation has many of the advantages of 95, with the additional benefit of extensive file, access, and directory security. As with NT Server, Workstation has limited backwards compatibility to earlier Windows operating systems. The reason is one of security. No applications software is permitted to directly access the client hardware, which means that MS-DOS applications may not run on an NT Workstation (or server).

As the predominant client operating system, **Windows 95** is more likely to be found in a Windows NT-based server LAN. As with Windows NT, and Workstation, it supports 32-bit networking protocols, and may be used in any of the following environments:

- As a stand-alone workstation.

- As a member of a workgroup in a peer-to-peer network.

- As a client in a Windows NT domain.

An important advantage of Win 95 is its Plug-and-Play (PNP) feature, which isn't available in NT Server and NT Workstation. From a production standpoint, PNP simply makes it easier to work with client computers. Win 95 provides out-of-the-box drivers for hundreds of devices, while NT provides relatively few. Windows 95 supports FAT and FAT32 file systems, but FAT32 isn't supported by NT.

Win 95 doesn't provide for a central server; it only networks in a peer-to-peer arrangement. However, when a server is needed, the Win 95 client can be used in a Windows NT domain-based server. In addition to the low-level security built into Win 95, network logons can be administered and controlled from NT, thereby enhancing the security of the client.

Win 95 and Windows Workstation are both compatible with Novell NetWare.

The precursors to Windows 95/NT are **Windows for Workgroups 3.1x, Windows 3.1**, and **MS-DOS** clients. Workgroups, because it was released later than the other two, supports more networking protocols. It may or may not have TCP/IP installed. If a Workgroup computer has been in a network at some point, and if it has a NIC card installed, the networking protocol stack will be there. Even if the computer hasn't yet seen any network duty, the stack may still already be installed, since later versions of Workgroups shipped with Winsock DLLs and TCP/IP.

A computer running any of these operating systems can be connected to an NT, or NetWare, server. Windows 3.1+ and MS-DOS clients will need the Winsock DLL (available from Trumpet software) and TCP/IP installed. The Windows NT Server CD contains the necessary setup files to connect any of these clients to an NT server. Once you copy the files to a diskette, you install them from a command prompt, and during the installation, you will be offered the following choices for networking protocols:

- IPX (Novell).

- IPX/SPX (Microsoft's version of NetWare IPX).

- NetBEUI (Microsoft).

- TCP/IP.

In a peer-to-peer network, Win 95 clients permit a single access, compared to NT Workstation, which allows ten simultaneous accesses. Unfortunately, a Windows 95 network lacks the extensive security features that NT Workstation provides.

Novell IPX/SPX is the default choice, but you can switch to Microsoft's NetBEUI for a small LAN (that's not connected to other LANs, or the Internet, since this protocol can't be routed) or the recommended, TCP/IP. The latter requires more memory than the others, but provides you with the flexibility for wide-area applications, and IP-based addresses.

When using NetWare, a NetWare client is installed on machines running any of these operating systems. The Network layer protocol that's installed may be either TCP/IP, or IPX.

Older operating systems, like Windows 95, will run MS-DOS applications as well as older software that NT can't run. It's hard to make a case for using them, unless they're already installed in an entire group of computers, and there's no justifiable reason to upgrade the operating system, or to create a needless expense.

IBM's OS/2, developed jointly with Microsoft, was designed to run on Intel PCs. With each release of the operating system, IBM provided increased support for networking. There are multiple versions and flavors of OS/2 now on the market, so you need to check the documentation to determine if a protocol stack, and Winsock, are installed on a specific machine. If the OS/2 client has been connected to a network in the past, they will be there.

The CD of the NT Server contains setup files for OS/2, as it does for the other operating systems described above. During the client installation, you're prompted to select a network protocol, and you can choose any of the following:

- IPX (Novell).

- IPX/SPX (Microsoft's NetWare IPX).

- NetBEUI (Microsoft).

- TCP/IP.

It's a good idea to remove support for a network protocol that won't be used. If you chose to install TCP/IP, remove the others to conserve system resources.

Apple Macintosh clients running System 6.0.7, or higher, can be connected to an NT/NetWare server. The NT Server CD contains Services for Macintosh, that permit users to access folders and printers in Windows domains. This service must first be set up on the server, then the client must be configured.

An advantage to connecting Apple computers to an NT or NetWare server is the increased security made available to users. In addition to a logon name, the Macintosh client will now have an NT logon that's appended to the user logon.

A Macintosh computer uses AppleTalk as the network protocol. The AppleTalk protocol suite consists of the following layers:

- AppleShare: Similar to the Application layer of the OSI model, it initiates network applications.

- AppleTalk Filing Protocol (AFP): Used to create and manage file sharing between Macintosh computers. Network security and logon authentication are handled by AFP. In addition, it provides services for translating file requests.

- AppleTalk Transaction Protocol (ATP): Provides a reliable connection between nodes. This is similar to the Transport layer of the OSI model.

- Datagram Delivery Protocol (DDP): Allows data packets to be delivered across a network, similar to methods used with IP and IPX.

AppleTalk uses the term **LocalTalk** to refer to the cabling system and access method used on AppleTalk networks. The **access method** is **CSMA/CA** (Carrier Sense Multiple Access / Collision Avoidance). CSMA/CD is similar to CSMA/CD except that before a station sends data, it transmits a broadcast message to all nodes telling them it's going to send a packet of data. When another node receives the broadcast, it waits until the transmitting node sends before sending a broadcast packet of its own. CSMA/CA is suitable for smaller LANs because collisions aren't likely to occur with it. However, since each node sends a broadcast packet before sending data, the broadcasts make it unsuitable for larger LANS because they require much of the network's time. It limits the data rate on an Apple network to about 240K BPS.

To address the speed limitations, **EtherTalk** was released in AppleTalk Phase II and can be used over a IEEE 802.3, 10MBPS Ethernet LAN. Similarly, **TokenTalk**, released at the same time, allows AppleTalk to be sent over a IEEE 802.5, 4 or 16MBPS LAN.

A **UNIX** workstation communicates using TCP/IP. If a UNIX client is connected to a Windows NT/NetWare server, there may be problems. The same is true for connecting Microsoft clients to a UNIX server. The TCP/IP that comes with NT/NetWare includes the **File Transfer Protocol** (FTP), and this may work for exchanging files between client and server. Problems may arise, however, because the file formats that these operating systems use all differ.

This isn't to say that Windows OSs shouldn't be connected to a UNIX server; in fact, the network may actually run better when they are. What's needed is more technical expertise at the administrator level, since command-line interface configurations will be required in some instances, even though there are GUIs available for UNIX. SAMBDA is a free product that runs on UNIX hosts, and emulates the Microsoft LAN Manager. It allows a Microsoft client to access UNIX host files as if they were residing on an NT server.

Another interesting product is Linux, created by a Dutch programmer (Linus Torvalds) who was trying to improve the UNIX flavor that he was using (Linus; hence, the name Linux). Linux is unique in that programmers around the world took an interest in it, and developed hardware drivers for many devices that were used with it. Soon, the volume of platforms that Linux was able to cross became quite extensive. Now, less that ten years after Torvalds first released his version of Linux—free of charge on the Internet—it's being used in many commercial applications as a replacement for Windows NT, and Novell NetWare. Microsoft clients can be connected to Linux servers, and users typically have no idea that they're not running on an NT server.

NETWORK INTERFACE CARD (NIC)

NET+ OBJECTIVE
I.2.1

The NIC card must be installed and configured in a client or server using Plug-and-Play software, or by manually setting the parameters. Once it's installed, the card needs to be checked to determine if it's working properly. If it's not, you need to be able to select an appropriate course of action that will fix the problem. This may involve changing configuration settings, resolving interrupt conflicts, or using software tests and diagnostic tools to determine the problem.

The basic hardware in this section is limited to those devices that connect to NIC cards, or to a similar interface in the client computer. In the material to follow, each of these devices will be summarized. You should be able to state the differences between them, as well as identify what they're used for.

A network interface card (NIC) contains a transceiver for sending and receiving data frames on and off a network, as well as the Data Link layer hardware needed to format the sending bits and to decipher received frames. A NIC card slips into an expansion slot of a personal computer (or server) and, in an Ethernet installation as well as many Token Ring LANs, will connect the computer to a hub.

NIC cards contain a driver interface that allows the network card to be bound. "Bound", or binding order, refers to the order that an operating system runs a protocol. When a network protocol (TCP/IP, NetBEUI, etc.) is configured on a computer, you specify (bind) the protocol that you want to run first. In the bad old days, you could only bind one protocol to a NIC card. Since this made it difficult and cumbersome to run more than one network protocol at the same time (you had to install a NIC for each protocol), a solution was developed to allow a NIC card to be bound to more than one network layer protocol. The protocols have emerged and they are:

- NDIS: Network Driver Interface Option Defines the interface between the MAC-sublayer and protocol drivers. It was developed by Microsoft and mainly used on Microsoft networks.

- ODI: Open Driver Interface allows multiple network protocols to be run on a network. It was developed by Novell and Apple. It's used primarily on NetWare networks.

A **Network Interface Card** (NIC) contains a transceiver for sending and receiving data frames on and off a network, as well as the Data Link layer hardware needed to format the sending bits, and to decipher received frames.

An NIC card slips into an expansion slot of a personal computer (or server), and in an Ethernet installation, as well as many Token Ring LANs, it will connect the computer to a hub.

Figure 6-46 shows a typical installation. In this example, the computer is a client in a server-based Ethernet LAN. The NIC has a single port for an RJ-45 connector, and the cabling is CAT5 UTP. Normally, the NIC also has indicator LEDs which will tell you if it's receiving. But these have limited value, since they're only visible from the back of the machine. Generally, they're helpful when you install the card, map a connection and nothing happens. If the receive/transmit remains red, it means your card is not working properly.

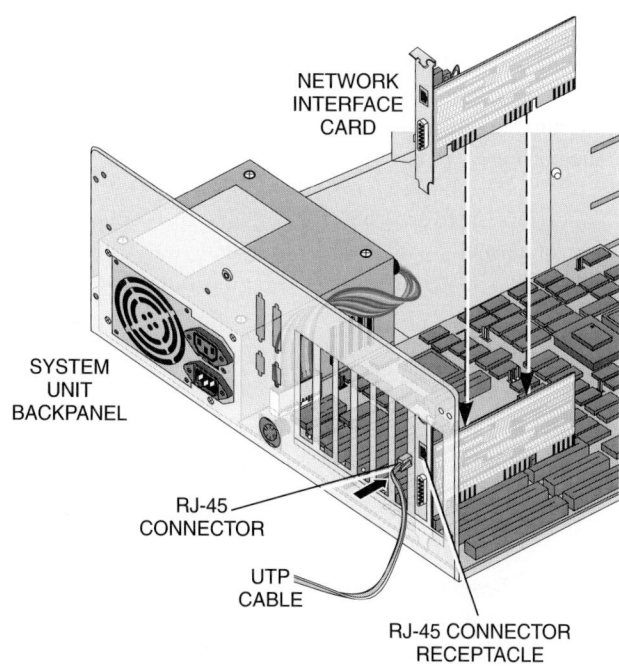

NETWORK INTERFACE CARD

SYSTEM UNIT BACKPANEL

RJ-45 CONNECTOR

UTP CABLE

RJ-45 CONNECTOR RECEPTACLE

Figure 6-46 NIC Card Installation

I/O ports and interrupt settings are configured on the hardware, as well as with computer software. For Win 95 clients, Plug-and-Play (PNP) will configure a card that supports it. If so, all assignments are handled through software. If it's not Plug and Play, or if the card is an older NIC, you'll have to manually change the settings. These are black, shunt switches, which slide over vertical pins, or they may consist of ganged DIP switches.

Manually configuring a card is accomplished with jumper and DIP witches. Figure 6-47(a) shows jumper settings while Figure 6-47(b) illustrates DIP switch changes. To change a jumper setting, remove the plastic hood over the pins on the jumper block. Place the hood on the pins, as indicated in the network card documentation. Figure 6-47(a) shows jumper setting changes for positions 2 through 5.

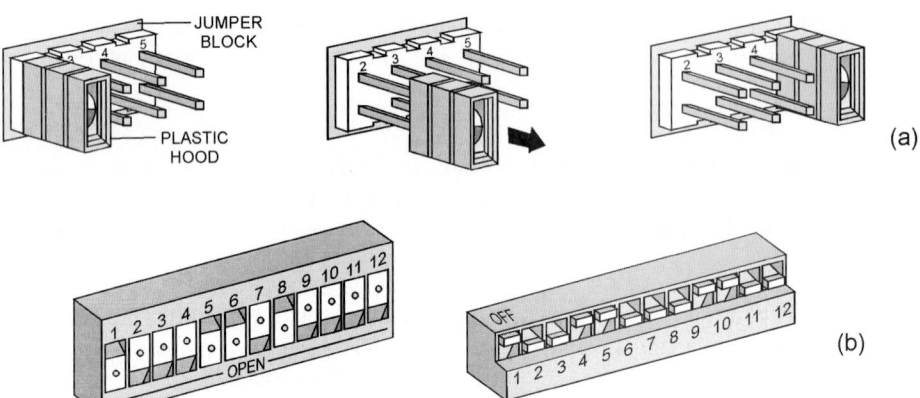

(a)

Figure 6-47 Configuration Jumpers and DIP Switches

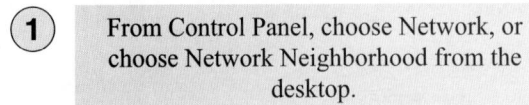
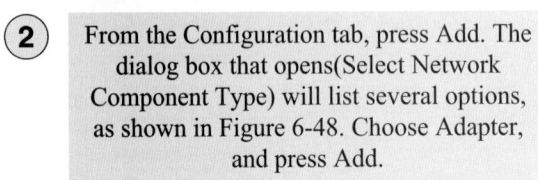

(b)

To reset a DIP switch setting to an alternate setting (on to off, open to closed, etc.), move the switch to the settings indicated in the network card documentation.

The IRQ settings for NICs and COM ports (for modems) will either be marked directly on the card, or the vendor documentation will instruct you as to how to set them.

Circuit cards in computers aren't hot-swappable, so turn off the machine before opening the cover. Once the machine is off and the cover removed, locate an available slot, and remove the NIC card from its anti-static bag. **Be sure to ground yourself using an anti-static wrist strap.** Press the card into the slot, and replace the cover. Connect the RJ-45 connector to the port, and turn on the machine.

Depending on the network software you're using, one of two things may happen. The computer may come up normally with no indication that you've made a change, or it may detect the card upon boot-up. **Consult your NOS User Manual for procedures unique to your environment.**

The following describes the procedure for installing an NIC card using Windows NT.

(1) From Control Panel, choose Network, or choose Network Neighborhood from the desktop.

(2) From the Configuration tab, press Add. The dialog box that opens(Select Network Component Type) will list several options, as shown in Figure 6-48. Choose Adapter, and press Add.

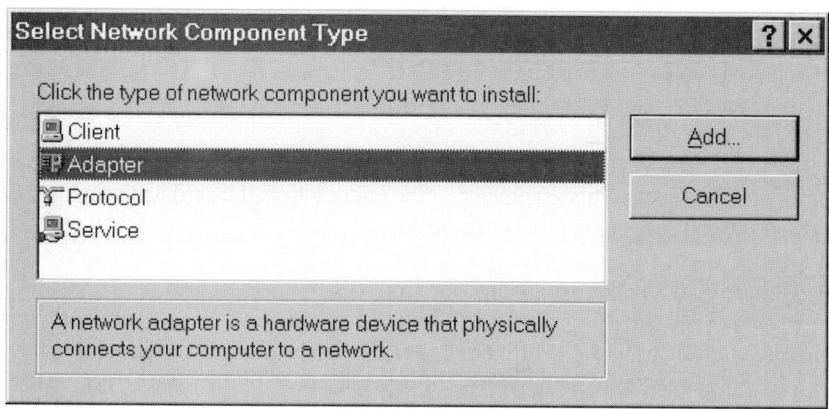

Figure 6-48 Types of Network Components to Install

(3) Select Network Adapters (Figure 6-49) will open, and this box lists NIC card drivers that Windows has pre-installed. Select from the list.

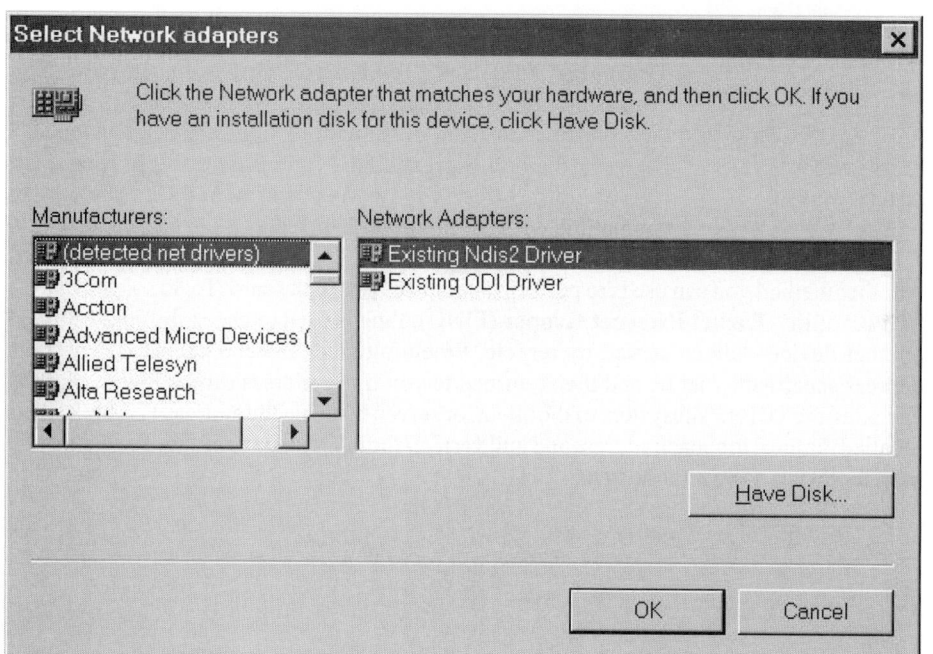

NET+ OBJECTIVE
I.2.1

Figure 6-49 Network Adaptor Dialog Box

If your card isn't listed (but it is listed on the NT Compatible Hardware list) click on have disk. It's usually a good idea to load drivers that come with your hardware because they may be more current that the ones installed in NT.

(4) Once the drivers are installed, click Add. The card is now installed.

NIC Testing

Once the card is installed, how do you determine if it's working? The easiest way is to access a directory on the server. This assumes that the client where the card has been installed is configured for network connectivity. To do so:

- Double-click the Network Neighborhood icon on the desktop.

If things are working properly, you'll be shown the names of servers, other computers, and printers that are connected to the network. However, it's possible that you'll receive the error message shown in Figure 6-50.

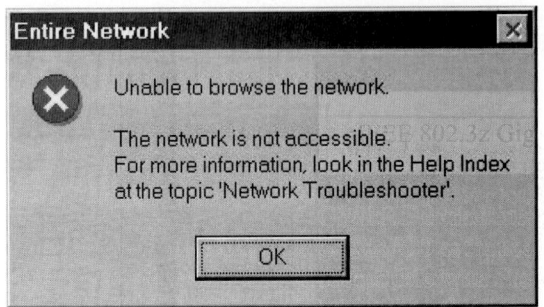

Figure 6-50 NIC Error Message

The message means that you can't get out to the network, and there are many possible reasons. You can follow the Windows troubleshooter to determine the problem. It takes you through a physical test of the cabling from NIC card to hub, then gravitates to software settings for the card and network.

A very basic test is to see if the link light on the NIC card is lit. Typically, this is a green LED (But consult your NIC documentation to be sure.) that glows when the card is installed and connected to a hub. A similar link light will be lit on the hub. Between the hub light and NIC light, this test tells you if the connection between the two is working and that the card is compatible with the hub type.

Another method you can use is to perform a loopback test to the card. To do so, you use the TCP/IP utility, **Packet INternet Groper** (PING). Ping is used to check the connection to another device—client, server, router, etc. When initiated, an echo packet is sent to an address specified by its IP, and then returned to you if the address can be found. Start by checking the TCP/IP subsystem of the client, or server, by using the address 127.0.0.1. This is called the local loopback address and will verify if the NIC card is working. To perform the ping loopback, follow these steps:

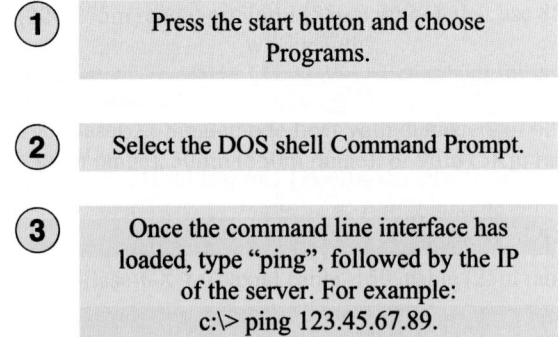

One of two messages will appear on the screen. The first will indicate that the server has been found and the second that the server hasn't been found. Figure 6-51 shows an example of a successful ping.

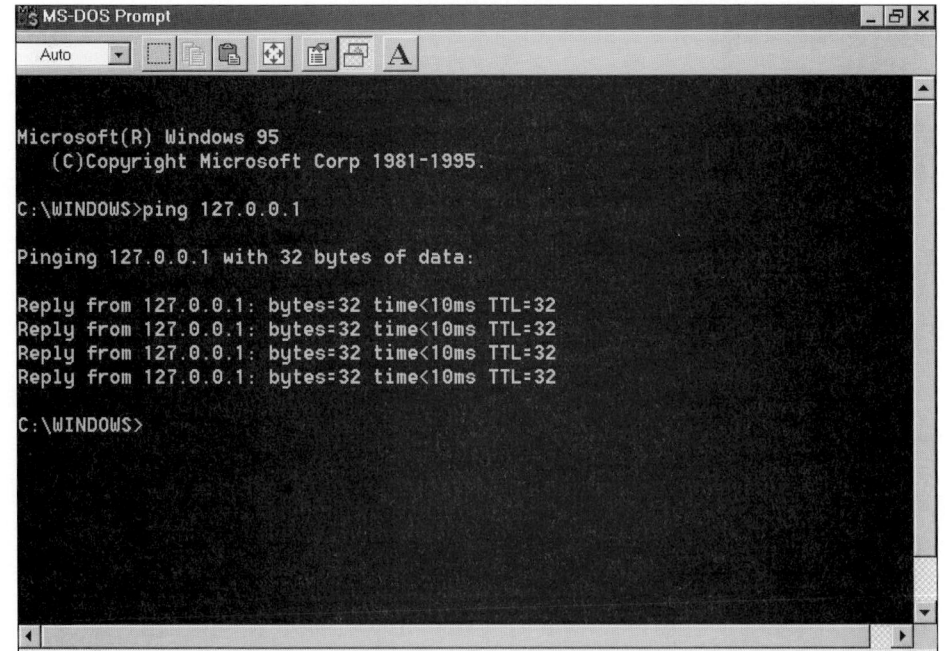

**Figure 6-51 A
Successful Ping**

4 If the local loopback is successful, ping the
IP of the local machine.

5 Ping the IP of another client on the
network.

6 If that's successful, ping the IP of the
server/default gateway. If you can't ping
the server, this means that there's not a
connection from the client to the server.

Some NICs are shipped with diagnostic routines that assist you in troubleshooting
connectivity problems. If the NIC that's installed has diagnostics, read the vendor literature on
its operation and run them. Be sure to check the physical connection between the NIC and hub.
An inexpensive cable tester can help eliminate cables as the source of connectivity problems.

An NIC may not be able to communicate because the PNP configuration has set it up so that it
conflicts with other devices. With client computers, you'll probably get an error message if
this occurs (although not always). But if Windows NT is installed on a server, you may not
get an immediate message indicating a problem. Since NT doesn't support PNP, an NIC
installed in the server may require some manual intervention.

Take a closer look at the IRQ and I/O addresses settings. By the time you install an NIC, many
other subsystems have already been installed in the computer (mouse, floppy drive, hard
drive, modem, CD-ROM, etc.). There's a good chance that the I/O address and/or interrupt
assigned to the NIC is being used by another device. If this is the case, you will have to locate
an unused IRQ for the card. There are several ways to do so.

NET+ OBJECTIVE
I.2.1

For Win 95:

1 Click the System icon in Control Panel.

2 Click the Device Manager tab. Highlight the Computer icon at the top of the list of devices.

3 Click the Properties button. A list of IRQs and their assigned devices will be displayed.

For Windows NT:

1 Click Run.Type WINMSD.

2 The Windows NT Diagnostics window will open. Click the Resources tab.

Figure 6-52 shows the window which opens. Notice that IRQs for all devices are listed and you can see the assigned range of I/P address by clicking I/O Port at the bottom of the screen.

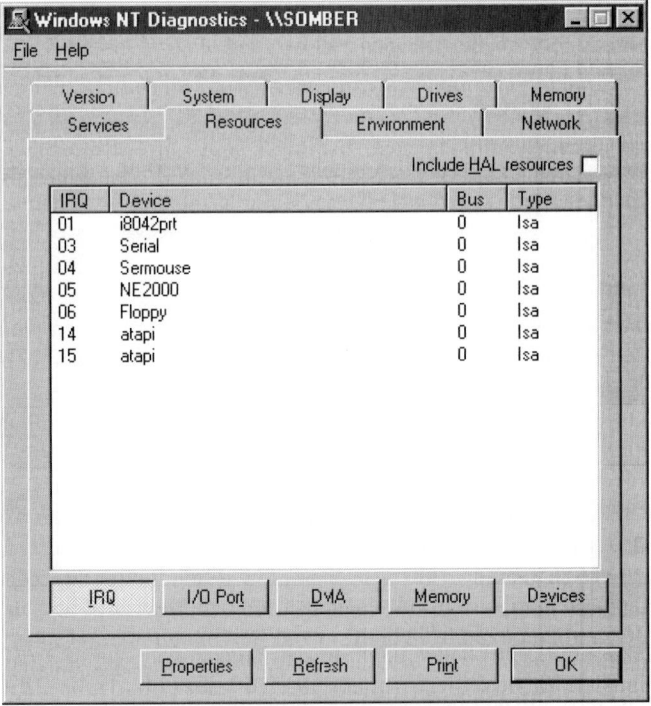

Figure 6-52 Windows NT IRQ and I/O Port Diagnostics

For Windows 3.x:

1. Exit windows.

2. At the DOS prompt, type MSD. Again, look for the IRQ settings.

The box will display all IRQs in your system, and the devices they're assigned to. For Plug and Play devices, Windows will attempt to assign an unused port, and interrupt, to the NIC. That's fine, as long as they are not being used by another device, but if you're getting conflicts, they probably are.

Any unused IRQ will work. However, check your NIC literature for special precautions. If possible, use IRQ 10, and Base I/O address 0300-031F. These interrupt and I/O settings aren't used on most computers, and have become a de facto standard for NICs.

To change the software settings for Win 95, do the following:

1. Click the System icon in the Control Panel.

2. Click the Device Manager tab. The Device Manager window will open. Double click on Network Adapters.

3. Double-Click the installed NIC card and Compatible Properties for the card will open.

NET+ OBJECTIVE
I.2.1

This is shown in Figure 6-53. Notice that under Device Status, Windows tells you if the device is or isn't working properly.

4. Click the Resources tab. This screen shows the IRQ and Base I/O memory address. If the field marked "Use Automatic Settings" is checked, remove the check.

5. Highlight the resource you want to change (IRQ, for example) and press the Change Settings button. An Edit box, depicted in Figure 6-54, will open. Change the IRQ setting and click OK.

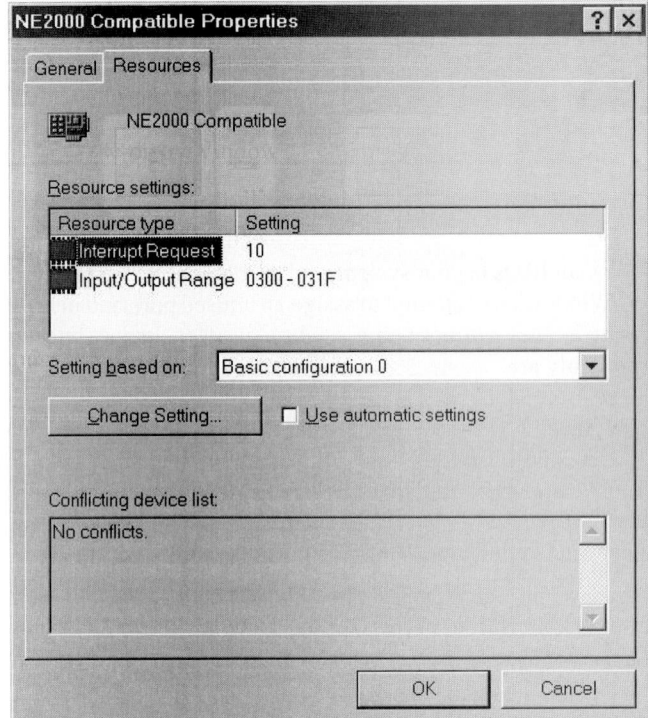

Figure 6-53 Compatible Properties for Win 95 NICs

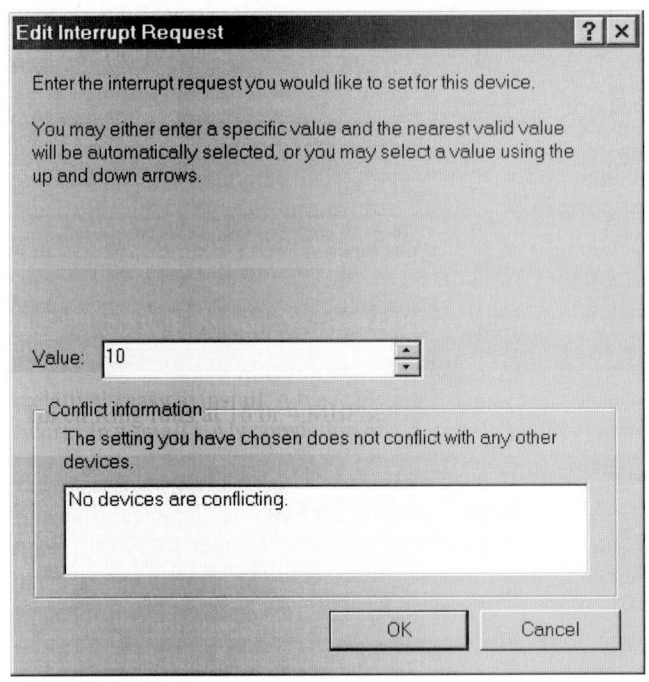

Figure 6-54 IRQ Settings Dialog Box

Note the field near the bottom of the screen labeled Conflicting Device List. If a conflict had been detected, Windows would have told you in this field.

To change the settings for Windows NT, do the following:

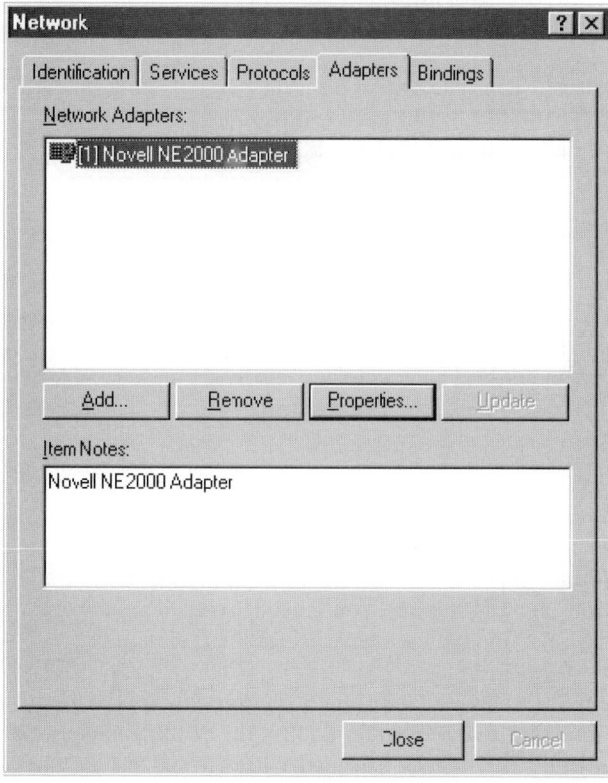

Figure 6-55 NT Network Folder

① From Control Panel, double-click the Network icon. The Network folder (see Figure 6-55) will open.

② Press the Adapter tab to list any installed NIC cards. Select the card to be changed, and press the Properties button.

③ The Network Card Setup dialog box will open, as shown in Figure 6-56. Select the IRQ and I/O, the press the OK button.

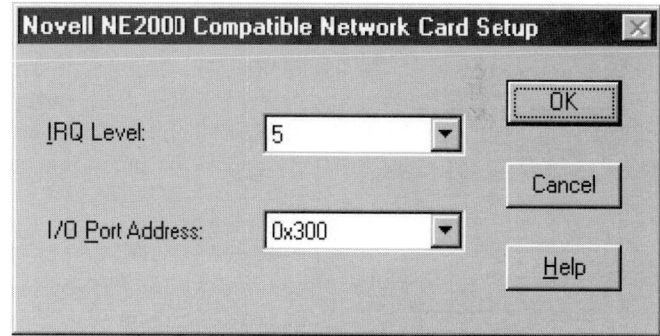

Figure 6-56 NT NIC Setup Dialog Box

NIC Troubleshooting

Let's step back a minute and summarize the steps needed to install and configure a NIC. Once these steps are clear in your mind, you can use them as a guide in troubleshooting problems during the installation, configuration, or operation of the card. The steps are:

① Install the card in an available expansion slot of a client or server.

② If required, configure the IRQ and base I/O address, using DIP switches or jumpers.

③ For Win 95 clients, boot the computer and allow Windows PNP attempt the configuration.

NET+ OBJECTIVE
I.2.1

You should see other servers, printers, computers, etc. that the client is connected to.

(4) If prompted for a driver disk, install the latest drivers.

(5) If available, configure the card for IRQ 10 and I/O 0300-031F. If these are already in use, select an unused IRQ and I/O range.

(6) Check to see if there are any device conflicts.

(7) Once the configuration is complete, restart the computer, and attempt to connect by clicking Entire Network in Network Neighborhood.

Now, where are possible trouble spots likely to occur? The Network + exam identifies three areas: Installation, configuration and general troubleshooting (implying that a trouble wasn't identified in the installation or configuration). You'll need to consider them one at a time. At the end of this chapter, you'll find typical scenarios for these situations.

During the installation, a problem could surface for manually configured cards. If jumpers or switches are involved, these must be set correctly so that the card can access the microprocessor. If not, the processor won't know it's needed. Check to see that the card is seated firmly in an expansion slot of the computer. If it isn't, it doesn't matter how many times you configure it, it's not going to work, or at best, it may work intermittently. A problem during this phase may not involve the card at all. The CAT5 UTP cable may be broken, or the RJ-45 connectors crimped on each end of it may be at fault. This is easily checked with a cable tester.

The NIC configuration allows plenty of opportunities for problems. It's worth noting that a client requires additional setup to be used in a LAN. A considerable amount of work is needed to configure the Network layer settings, but these are done on the assumption that the NIC card is correctly installed, and configured. The most likely source of immediate problems involves resource conflict; interrupts and I/O port addresses. The most common method of checking the card is to see if other devices can be found. Use Network Neighborhood, and check for all devices on the network. Another method is to ping known devices by their IP address. Vendor diagnostics, as well as the diagnostic screens available with Windows (Network Monitor, for example), can also be used to troubleshoot a card that's not communicating with other devices on the network

KEY POINTS REVIEW

This chapter has presented an extensive exploration of local area networks.

- Networks allow communication between various types of computers, sometimes located great distances apart.

- The two main categories of networks are Local Area Networks (LANs) and Wide Area Networks (WANs).

- Local Area Networks are capable of sharing information among users spread around a single room, building, or a metropolitan area. They may be operated as either baseband or broadband networks.

- Baseband networks allow only one user at a time to use the network. Users gain access through the use of Time-Division Multiplexing (TDM).

- Broadband networks allow the network to be used by more than one user at a time, through the use of Frequency-Division Multiplexing (FDM).

- WANs are capable of sharing information between users separated by long distances.

- Packet switching is a technique used by wide area networks to transmit data.

- Wide area networks are capable of connecting different local area networks together through an interface called a gateway.

- Networks are classified according to their types of interface, transmission medium, access protocols, topology, modulation, and data rate (bandwidth).

- An interface is the hardware and signal parameters on the physical level.

- The transmission medium is the type of wire, cable, or fiber used to connect the various network devices.

- Access protocols have to do with the rules and methodology used by the various hardware to allow each user access to the network.

- The most widely used media-access protocols are CSMA/CD (Carrier-Sense Multiple Access/Collision Detection), CSMA/CA (Carrier-Sense Multiple Access/Collision Avoidance), token ring passing, and token bus.

- Network topology is the physical arrangement of the nodes (computers, workstations, or other devices) connected to the network. Examples of network topologies are star, ring, and bus arrangements.

- A star topology consists of a central hub, or switch, connecting the nodes like spokes extending out from it. It is the most widely used topology.

- A ring topology connects the nodes in a continuous loop. Data flows around the ring in one direction.

- Three basic access techniques for ring networks are token passing, fixed slots, and delay insertion.

- A bus topology is a straight-line connection strategy.

- The IEEE 802 standards govern the logical and data link level specs of LANs.

- The lower sublevel of the OSI data link layer is medium-access control, while the upper sublevel is called logical-link control.

- Systems management between the physical OSI layer, the logical-link sublayer, and the medium-access control sublayer is described by IEEE 802.1.

- Logical-Link Control (LLC) is described by IEEE 802.2.

- Medium-access control is described by the IEEE 802.3 (CSMA/CD Ethernet), 802.4 (Token Bus), and 802.5 (Token Ring) standards.

- The two main access methods for LANs are contention and token passing.

- The 802.3 standard (CSMA/CD) was derived from an earlier data-communications effort undertaken jointly by the XEROX, Digital Equipment, and Intel companies, called Ethernet.

- Ethernet networks are designed to detect the collisions that occur when two stations attempt to transmit on the data channel simultaneously.

- Once a collision is detected by a transmitting station, it sends a 32-bit jam signal to give the other transmitting station(s) time to detect the collision.

- After the jam is transmitted, a station will execute a backoff delay of some randomly selected time interval, before trying to transmit again.

- Ethernet networks may operate at 10, 100 or 1,000MBPS data rates, and use UTP, fiber optic, or coaxial cable in the cabling infrastructure.

- A token-passing network passes an access signal, called a token, to each station, based upon a priority table contained in network software. This ensures that each station has time on the network.

- In a token-ring network, the token is transferred to each station sequentially, in a loop architecture.

- FDDI is the Fiber Distributed Data Interface protocol used for sending data at 100 MBPS over fiber-optic cable in LANs. The standard includes a set of protocols corresponding to the first two layers of the OSI model.

- Windows For Workgroups was the first networking software from Microsoft.

- Windows NT replaced WFW, and is specialized for 32-bit applications.

- Due to the complexity of modern networks, support is expected and necessary.

- Network changes require techniques for handling complaints, require the skills of highly organized people, as well as proven strategies for implementing change.

At this point, review the objectives listed at the beginning of the chapter to be certain that you understand and can perform them. Afterward, answer the review questions that follow to verify your knowledge of the information.

LAB MANUAL

Lab Exercises

The lab manual that accompanies this book contains hands-on lab procedures that reinforce and test your knowledge of the theory materials presented in this chapter. Now that you have completed your review of Chapter 6, refer to the lab manual and perform Procedure 7, "NIC Card Installation and Setup."

REVIEW QUESTIONS

The following questions test your knowledge of the material presented in this chapter:

1. Which network operating system used NDS as the directory structure?

2. If an NT server communicates with its clients using the NetBEUI network protocol, why can't the clients be connected to the Internet using this protocol?

3. With which NOS would you expect to utilize a command line interface (CLI) more than the others?

4. A Windows 95 client is to be connected to a NetWare server. What are the requirements for doing so?

5. Fiber optic connector types are specified in the _____ layer.

6. An FDDI symbol group contains _____ data bits and _____ synchronizing bit.

7. What is the signaling rate, and cable type, for 100BaseFX?

8. List two significant differences between Windows For Workgroups and Windows NT.

9. Which two layers of the OSI Reference Model do the IEEE 802.3 protocols include?

10. What type of network is described by the following statement? The nodes are connected by a central hub.

11. Describe the process of contention access in a bus network.

12. Describe the process of detecting collisions on a CSMA/CD network.

13. According to the token recovery procedure for a token bus network, what happens to a station that loses the token?

14. In a token ring network, how does the transmitting station know if its message was received?

15. Consider the following scenario, then develop an appropriate course of action and explain why the action is warranted.

You install a NIC card in a client computer and Windows 95 configures it using PNP software. No problems are identified during the install and you reboot the computer. Once it boots, you check to see if it's operating correctly by going to Network Neighborhood, and choosing the entire network. After a short time, you receive a message indicating that the network can't be accessed. The UTP cable and RJ-45 connectors are checked with a cable tester, and they appear OK. Other clients are able to access the server through a stand-alone hub.

1. Select the statement below that best describes a local area network.
   a. A network connecting computer around the world.
   b. A network connecting computers within a country.
   c. A network connecting computers within a state.
   d. A network connecting computers within a room.

2. In order to be effective, a network should:
   a. Be as large as possible.
   b. Be reliable.
   c. Be connected in a mesh topology.
   d. Not exceed 10MBPS.

3. In a _____ network, nodes attach to the channel in a daisy-chain manner.
   a. Ring
   b. Mesh
   c. Bus
   d. Star

4. In a contention-based LAN, the nodes gain access to the channel by:
   a. Having access to a token.
   b. Competing for the channel.
   c. Receiving permission from a primary station.
   d. Requesting permission from a predecessor.

5. A CSMA/CD frame ensures data is sent to the correct node by:
   a. Including a source and destination address.
   b. Including a frame control field.
   c. Including an Access control field.
   d. Including a frame check sequence field.

6. An installed NIC card is working properly. What will happen if you ping the card using 127.0.0.1?
   a. It will time-out.
   b. The screen will echo the IP of the default gateway.
   c. The screen will show the IP of the machine the card is installed in.
   d. The screen will show the return of four, 32 byte packets.

7. The purpose of the access control field in a token ring frame is:
   a. As a start frame field
   b. To designate source and destination addresses.
   c. To designate the frame as a LLC or MAC protocol.
   d. To carry user data.

8. The maximum data rate of the FDDI standard is:
   a. 100 MBPS.
   b. 20 MBPS.
   c. 10 MBPS.
   d. 2 MBPS.

9. Typically, FDDI is used to:
   a. Provide a wide area connection.
   b. Serve as a port to the Internet.
   c. Recover from network errors.
   d. Interconnect LANs.

10. The purpose of a NIC card is:
   a. To send and receive data frames.
   b. To frame format data.
   c. To check received frames for errors.
   d. To send/ receive frames, to frame format data, to check for errors.

11. In setting up a LAN consisting of eight users, you must be able to provide multiple access to each client but without a server. However, you want the option of adding a server at a later date. Which of the following is the best operating system to install in the clients?
   a.Windows 95/98
   b. Windows NT Workstation
   c. Novell NetWare for Clients
   d. UNIX

12. Which of the following network protocols can be run on a NetWare network?
   a. IPX
   b. NetBEUI
   c. TCP/IP
   d. MS-DOS

13. Which of the following network operating systems is considered to be the most reliable when applications consist of intense graphical or computational tasks?
   a. Novell NetWare
   b. Windows NT
   c. AppleTalk
   d. UNIX

14. Which of the following network operating systems is primarily used in wide area networks?
   a. UNIX
   b. AppleTalk
   c. Novell NetWare
   d. Windows NT

15. Which of the following network operating systems uses the NTFS file structure?
   a. NetWare
   b. UNIX
   c. Windows NT
   d. TCP/IP

Network+ Practice Test

CD-ROM

Additional Net+ Certification testing is available on the CD that accompanies this text. The testing suite on the CD provides Study Card, Flash Card, and Run Practice type testing. The Study Card and Flash Card feature enables you to electronically link to the section of the book in which the question is covered. Choose questions from the test pool related to this chapter.

CHAPTER

7

NETWORK OPERATIONS

LEARNING OBJECTIVES

LEARNING OBJECTIVES

Upon completion of this chapter and its related lab procedures, you should be able to perform the following tasks:

1. Associate IP with its functions.

2. Identify the attributes, purpose, and function of a bridge, router and gateway.

3. Describe the concept of a Data Link layer bridge.

4. Explain routing and Network layer concepts.

5. Identify the use of a repeater.

6. Explain Transport layer concepts.

7. Demonstrate knowledge of TCP/IP fundamentals.

8. Explain the fundamental concepts of TCP/IP addressing.

9. Explain how/when to use the ARP, NBTSTAT, NETSTAT, Ping, Tracert, Ipconfig, and Hostname TCP/IP utilities to test, validate and troubleshoot IP connectivity.

10. Describe a port's purpose in a TCP or UDP setup, and state several basic port values.

11. Describe the purpose of a socket in a TCP setup.

12. State the content and length of a TCP header.

13. State the content and length of a UDP header.

14. State the content and length of an IP header.

15. State the difference between classful and classless IP addresses.

16. Differentiate between internetwork address classes.

17. Given an IP address, determine if it's class A, B or C.

18. Discuss the concept of subnetting IP addresses.

19. Given a network address, subnet address and host address, create a subnet to include network, subnet and host address.

20. Discuss the advantage of CIDR over classful IPs.

21. Discuss the advantages and disadvantages of routers.

22. Describe a typical sequence for MAC/IP frame routing addressing.

23. Given IPs and subnet addresses between two nodes, use the ANDed route determination algorithm to validate a local or remote route.

24. Describe characteristics of the following Address Resolution Protocols: Broadcast ARP, Normal ARP and Proxy ARP.

25. Define a bridge, repeater, router and gateway.

26. Decide if an application is best served by a repeater, bridge, router or gateway.

27. Describe how frames are transferred between networks using bridges.

28. Review the creation process of the Spanning Tree Algorithm for bridges.

29. Differentiate between learning, encapsulation and translation bridging.

CHAPTER 7

Network Operations

INTRODUCTION

The need for data-communication systems, capable of transporting information over great distances at speeds in the hundreds of gigahertz, has resulted in the creation of wide area networks. Recall that back in 1957, AT&T was jubilant at sending 750 bits of data, at a time when a local area network with a hundred computers attached was considered large.

Imagine a million computers on a network, a dozen protocol variations, a mesh of topologies and cable media, data rates as low as 56 kBPS and as high as 600 GBPS. If you can mentally fathom such a smorgasbord of hardware/software, and consider the fact that such networks actually work, you will have a realistic picture of present-day, wide area networks. A startling system in scope and technology, it is inconceivably complex, but monumentally successful.

This chapter discusses the concepts, technologies, standards, and services that comprise the operations that occur on a network—short of extending it to the wide area arena. To join networks, it's not enough to simply access the network media. Data packets must also be routed to the destination node, and also transported with a reasonable degree of reliability in an environment that will detect, and deal with, errors (lost packets, garbled frames, etc.).

In this chapter, we examine the intricacies of the Network and Transport layers. These are realized using what's broadly called internetwork protocols, and specifically the TCP/IP suite of protocols.

The essentials of TCP and IP are discussed first. And since the IP addressing scheme has been over-taxed with the explosion of LANs and the Internet, we'll see how it's been expanded through a system of subnetting. Repeaters, bridges, routers, and gateways—the physical interconnect technologies—are described, along with methods for carrying data between LANs using different access methods. Several transport services, used to increase the performance of networks, are also examined.

NET+ OBJECTIVE
I.1.7

LARGE NETWORKS

A wide area network can span a large geographical area. Generally, a WAN refers to a network that falls outside a city, and one which is used to connect other networks together. Typically, two or more LANs are interconnected to form a wide area network. Of course, these days, interconnected LANs may not necessarily constitute a wide area network. They may be interconnected, and simply be big.

CNST OBJECTIVE
I-A

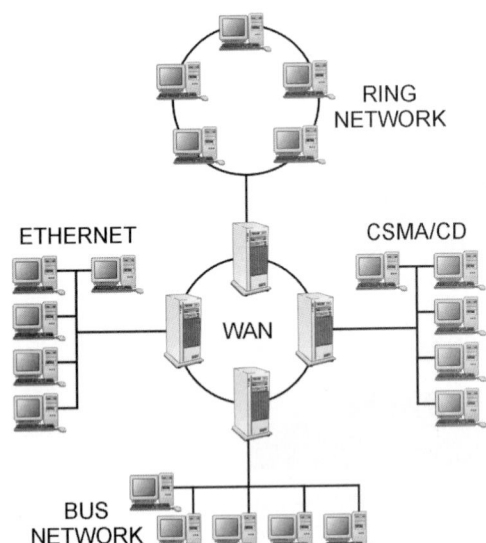

Figure 7-1 LANs Connected in a WAN

PCs, with internetworking software, are connected via the telephone system to a remote host, then to the Internet to become a part of the Internet. Advances in technology during the 1990's have shifted the definition of WANs so that the term has become a bit cloudy. Still, networks grow to become like a sprawling metropolis.

Figure 7-1 illustrates an example of LANs connected to become a WAN. Although the topology and access protocols differ between the LANs, they are able to exchange files in a distributed, wide area network. LANs may be extended, so that they contain hundreds, or thousands, of nodes, with the distance between the LANs crossing the country. To the user on the token-ring network, a file transfer to a station on the distant Ethernet is no more difficult than a walk down the hall.

The reason, of course, is that the complex tasks of the WAN are transparent to the network users. An ideal WAN carries data between stations on a **virtual circuit**. A virtual connection, as shown in Figure 7-2, provides for transparency of the underlying mechanics of data communications—that is, the protocols and technology responsible for transporting the data.

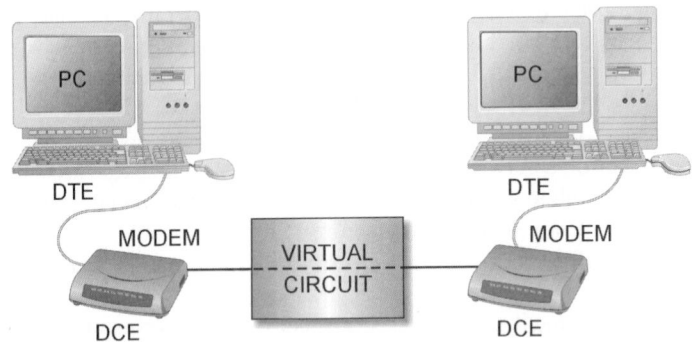

Figure 7-2 WAN Virtual Connection

However, wide-area data communications is a complex system of internet protocols, interacting with devices that make the physical, cross-country hops possible. At the same time, the system is under the control of transport services that are used to operate the network at peak levels of performance.

Much the same can be said about distributed LANs. The biggest difference is that a large LAN doesn't use the protocols that have been specialized for long distance telephone connections such as ISDN (although this is changing as ISDN is now a realistic desktop technology), X.25 Packet Switching, Frame Relay, ATM (also a realistic desktop technology), or SONET and T-Carrier. Instead, the emphasis on a large LAN is the routing of data from node to node, and inventive methods for making the most of the addressing mechanisms at the Network layer.

NETWORK AND TRANSPORT LAYER PROTOCOLS

The Network layer is responsible for routing data frames from a source to a destination node. The Transport layer is responsible for ensuring there's an adequate and reliable connection between the two points. Typically, a frame of data may "hop" from one device to another (usually through routers) on its way to the destination node. The Network layer protocols ensure that a route can be found between the two communicating devices, then sends the packet on its way. At the Transport layer, once a route is selected, the two must maintain an open virtual circuit that is at once capable of detecting errors and providing for a reasonable degree of reliability between the two nodes.

Notice that the intentions of the Network and Transport layers differ. Consequently, there are protocols for both layers with the most common being the TCP/IP suite, the Transmission Control Protocol/ Internet Protocol. Broadly speaking, you can orient TCP and IP to the OSI model as: TCP operates at the Transport layer while IP operates at the Network layer. TCP/IP is an almost universally used protocol because it was designed to be vendor independent, capable of transporting data with no regard to the particular network a computer is attached to. This means that computers on an Ethernet LAN, a wide-area network, or a point-to point connection between a PC and ISP, are viewed as equals by TCP/IP.

Figure 7-3 shows a model for internetworking protocols. This model is a more accurate view of the functions of a suite of protocols that span internets. The word "internet" in this context refers not only to the Internet, but large networks—such as intranets—that may or may not access the Internet.

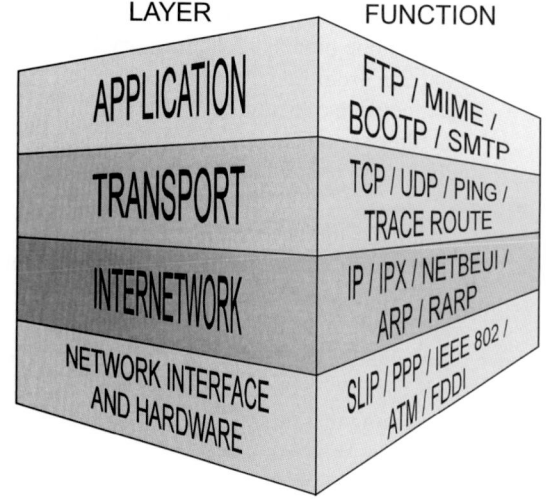

Figure 7-3 Model for Internetworking Protocols

NET+ OBJECTIVE I.6.1

CNST OBJECTIVE IV-B

The model consists of four layers that describe the functionality of events at each. The complete model, as shown, is commonly called the TCP/IP protocol suite. At the Application layer are user functions, such as file transfers and Internet mail. The Transport layer contains protocols dealing with reliable (it's a **connection-oriented** protocol) end-to-end processes. TCP is the most widely used. UDP is the User Defined Protocol, and represents an unreliable (it's **connectionless**) implementation of TCP. Transport layer utilities include Ping, and Trace Route, which are used to troubleshoot the end-to-end connection.

The Internetwork layer includes protocols that frame data so it can be sent from node-to-node. This is a connectionless layer, so it doesn't assume responsibility for any packet sent. (TCP is the reliable half of the suite.) Neither does it provide flow control or error recovery. However, the protocols used at this layer may very well provide error detection, flow control and so on—at least at this layer, but not above it. For example, HDLC provides for flow control and error detection, as do all of the IEEE 802.3 standards. The Internetwork layer does, however, map a route to the destination node so it contains addressing information to that node. The Network Interface and Hardware layer is roughly analogous to the Data Link and Physical layers of the OSI model. As you can see from the wide variety of protocols supported at this layer, the TCP/IP suite can use nearly any Network layer interface.

NET+ OBJECTIVE I.5.1

A Network layer protocol in the OSI model (the Internetwork layer for the Internet model in Figure 7-3) is necessary because protocols for the Data Link and Physical layers don't contain routing mechanisms. Logical-Link Control protocols from the Data Link layer lack the intricate header fields needed to transport data across different types of media and architecture. HDLC, the bit protocol from the LLC sublayer, is not routable. An Internetwork protocol is used to carry the LAN's media-access frame to another location.

What the lower two layers do offer is a physical MAC address. This is the address embedded in a NIC card. It's the address that specifically locates the machine, much like your house number on a street specifically locates you. You also have a Zip code that's used to generally locate you. A Zip code may cover many streets, or small towns, so it's a convenient way for the Post Office to broadly sort mail—separate it into piles according to Zip codes, get each pile to the right Zip code, than let local clerks separate it into actual addresses. The Network layer takes a similar approach in assigning logical addresses that are based on a network address and a machine address. A data packet can be sent to a network address, and it's up to that network to locate the logical machine address.

TCP/IP was a product of the Department of Defense. Bound by law to purchase from the lowest bidder that met the purchasing specifications, it inadvertently created a situation in which one branch of the military bought computers from IBM, another from Wang, and another from DEC. During a war, or other national emergency, the various branches are expected to communicate and support one another. However, it became apparent that they couldn't because the computer vendors were using proprietary internetworking protocols that simply weren't compatible.

**CNST OBJECTIVE
IV-B**

In order to merge vendor incompatibilities, the TCP/IP protocol suite was instituted in 1981, although it had been around, in a different and limited format, since 1969. The military wanted to switch to an alternate communication route if communications were lost at any site due to enemy action, regardless of who supplied the site hardware. TCP/IP was first tested under battlefield conditions in the Gulf War with Iraq. The US and allies did in fact destroy Iraq's known communication centers, but they were still able to communicate by switching to alternate sites, since they were running TCP/IP on their networked computer systems. While this was irritating to the US and allies, it also proved the functionality of TCP/IP—it did exactly as it was designed to do.

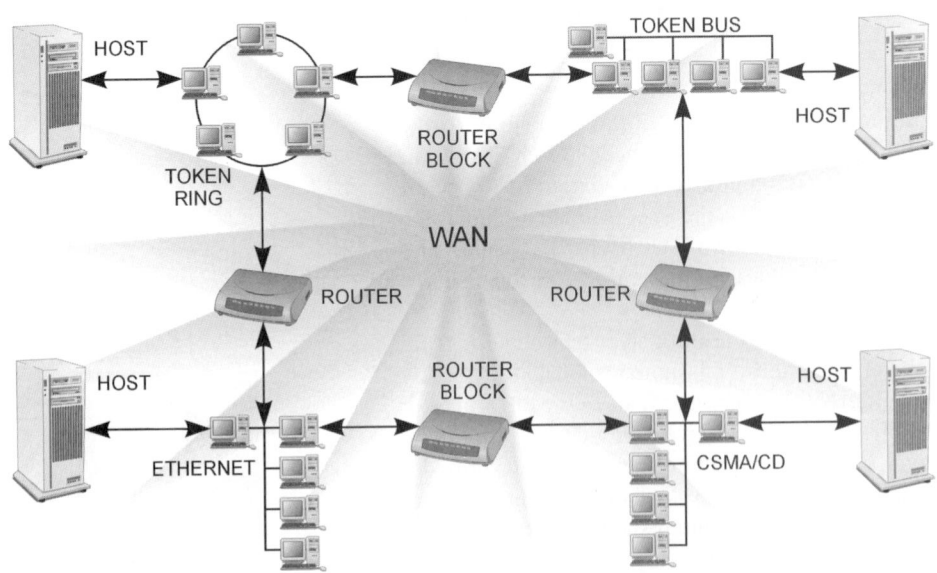

Network layer protocols are abstract devices, existing only in software. As such, they offer a tremendous degree of flexibility because they've designed with little regard to the hardware used to implement them. Figure 7-4 illustrates the universal equality concept of TCP/IP. Several types of networks are connected together to form an Internetwork. The Internet protocol, TCP/IP, transports messages from LAN to LAN. The size of a WAN is unimportant to the protocol; the network shown in Figure 7-4 may be found in an office building, or the four LANs may be distributed in different states, or countries.

Figure 7-4 TCP/IP Treats All Networks Equally

It doesn't matter if PCs are in the LANs, or if they are composed of mainframe computers. As was previously mentioned, TCP/IP is not dependent on the machine type. As a practical point, though, some computers work better with it than do others.

> A router provides an interconnection between networks using the same network layer protocols.

Notice in Figure 7-4 that the four LANs are connected by a **router** block. Routers and gateways are internetworking machines that provide a physical connection for implementing the internet protocol.

NET+ OBJECTIVE
I.6.1

Recall that a bridge doesn't function at the internetworking layer; it focuses on data frames at the data-link layer of the OSI model. It's concerned with the movement of data frames and, as such, is protocol independent. What a bridge does do is to interconnect LANs—those that share the same network portion of the IP address.

A router provides interconnections between networks of similar network protocols, such as TCP/IP, or Zerox's XNS. Routers can send frames with or without the same network portion of an IP address.

Network interconnection machines connect networks, not other machines on a network. When the Ethernet LAN sends a message to the token-bus LAN, the bridge or router transports the message from network to network. When the message arrives at the destination LAN—the token-bus LAN—it's then routed to the correct computer.

How does the message "know" it's at the right machine, or at the right network? The answer to that question lies in the complex addressing scheme used with IP. A 32-bit Address field in the header contains all the information necessary to get the message to the right place. It's the job of the interconnecting machines to interpret the header, and decide on a routing path for the message. All machines connected to a TCP/IP network are assigned unique addresses, and are called hosts, including routers, bridges, gateways, PCs, programmable logic units (PLCs), and, perhaps, printers.

NET+ OBJECTIVE
I.4.1

The LANs in Figure 7-4 show one host on each, but, in fact, there may be hundreds or thousands of hosts.

TCP is based upon reliable, connection-oriented delivery services. The system is reliable because there are end-to-end acknowledgments that the data was received. If it's lost, the sender or receiver will be informed of the loss. There are several mechanisms in TCP for guaranteeing delivery. One is a sliding window mechanism that tracks packets. Typically, data is divided into packets, and the packets are transmitted through the network. They may travel to the destination over different links, and arrive out of sequence. The receiver will acknowledge receipt of sequentially numbered packets. More on this later.

IP, on the other hand, is unreliable, best-effort, connectionless-based delivery. It is a best-effort system, because error control is included for the header, though not for the data field. The error-detection field in the header is a sincere effort to deliver the information. The system is connectionless because there's no acknowledgment that an IP packet arrived.

NET+ OBJECTIVE
I.5.1

TRANSMISSION CONTROL PROTOCOL (TCP)

An interconnected network is a system of interconnected terminals, or local networks, spread over a large area.

TCP is responsible for process-to-process communications between two interconnected devices. A process (identified by a port number) in this context refers to underlying applications such as file transfers, telnet, or e-mail. While, technically, any host running TCP/IP could perform a TCP setup, it's more typically to occur between servers, or routers and servers. TCP provides software services for a common interface between the physical network and user applications. The services run independently of the physical topology, or media access, running at the Physical and Data Link layers. Since the physical parameters of the data that's transferred using TCP are transparent to it, it's able to interconnect networks of different physical attributes, so that the user perceives it to be a single interconnected network—what we call an internet.

TCP/IP is a widely-used, internetworking protocol that is nonproprietary. It is based on a 32-bit addressing scheme, and is the IP used on the Internet.

TCP uses a software abstract called a **socket** to communicate processes. It's used as a programming interface to the communication protocol (TCP, for example). Once set up, a socket includes all addressing information between two communicating devices, the process that's to be called upon, and the transport protocol to be used. It's important to understand that we're backtracking a bit, because a socket is set up before the TCP transmission occurs. It's a requirement for TCP.

Imagine two servers in an internetwork using TCP, and the local server wants to utilize the services of a remote server. Before starting TCP, the servers must set up a connection. The sequence, using sockets, is as follows:

- Initiate: Three parameters are initiated. The **address family** specifies the method of addressing used by the socket, such as Unix. **Type** refers to the type of socket interface to be used. Specifically, type describes a connection-oriented (TCP) or connectionless (UDP) service, as well as direct connections to utilities that are run at a lower level, such as Ping. **Protocol** is the protocol that will be run between the stations such as TCP, IP or UDP.

- Bind: Registers a port address to a socket. In order to do so, two pieces of information are needed: the local address and the local process. Addressing will be IP addresses, while processes refer to the functionality of the service such as file transfers.

- Listen: The local station indicates the number of connection requests it can handle (it can deal with more than one at the same time). It also ensures that the address family, type and protocol are consistent, by listening to the remote server's reply.

- Accept: The remote server accepts the connection by verifying its address, and indicating the process it will be providing.

- Communicate: Exchange between the two servers consists of read/write socket calls.

- Close: Once the socket is closed (which originates from a field of the TCP header) the connection ceases. At this time, no information related to the connection that may be stored in port buffers is retained.

The process that's to be performed in the communication between servers is identified by **port**. A port is a 16-bit number which refers incoming messages to an application that will process them. For example, when you connect to a server on the Internet, and the downloads of text and graphics begin, you're connected to an HTTP application (process) that's specified by a port number (80, in this example). The port is identified as both a source and a destination. The meaning varies with the context. When information is downloaded from the Internet, there may be many source ports that compose the specified Web page. Each of these will be identified by a unique port number. However, all of the information will be sent to destination port number 80, for an HTTP process. To the client requesting the Web page, the destination port will be 80, which is the requested process.

Both UDP and TCP use ports to identify a specific process. Many of the port numbers are standardized, and are referred to as "well-known ports". Similarly, their associated applications are called "well-known services." Table 7-1 lists several well-known port numbers, and their provided services. These ports, from 0 through 1023, are assigned by the Internet Assigned Numbers Authority (IANA). Port numbers from 1024 through 65535 (called **ephemeral** ports) aren't assigned, and are frequently used in user-developed programs.

Table 7-1 Well-Known Ports

SERVICE	WELL-KNOWN PORT NUMBER
FTP	21, 20
Telnet	23
SMTP Mail	25
HTTP (WWW)	80
POP3 (Mail)	110
News	144
IRC	6667

So, a socket is used to setup a connection between two stations, and a port is the service the stations will be using. Once the socket is finished, an association between the two machines will be completed. The association represents a logical connection between the machines that's uniquely identified with the format shown in Figure 7-5.

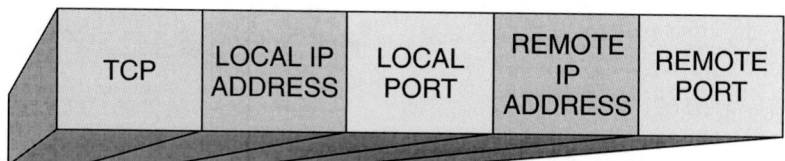

Figure 7-5 Socket Format

TCP is the framework that will ensure data communications between the two machines. To do so, it must fulfill the following services:

- Stream Data Transfer: The application will provide the connection with streams of data bytes, without concern for the number of bytes, or whether the communicating machines can accommodate the total number and rate of delivery. TCP will organize the byte stream into fragments, then pass them on to the IP to be, perhaps, further organized into datagrams. TCP will determine when the fragments are delivered to IP for transmission.

- Reliability: As a connection-oriented and reliable protocol, TCP will expect an acknowledgment from the receiving station for fragments that have been transmitted.

- Flow Control: As byte streams are delivered to TCP from the application, the receiver must tell the sender the number of bytes it can receive before its buffers overflow, this is done during acknowledgments.

- Multiplexing: As mentioned, TCP servers can handle more than one request at a time by assigning port numbers, and multiplexing the requests to well-known ports.

- Logical Connections: A logical connection is set up with sockets (for TCP) and ports (for both TCP and UDP).

- Full-Duplex Operation: Data moves in both directions at the same time during a TCP connection.

These are the fundamental services that TCP is tasked to provide to the applications running on it. In order to do so, it has a prescribed frame format that's used to communicate the level of services to the layers in the protocol suite. The TCP frame is embedded in the Data field of an IP frame. The frame format for TCP is shown in Figure 7-6.

16 BITS	16 BITS	32 BITS	32 BITS	4 BITS	6 BITS	1 BIT EACH	16 BITS	16 BITS	16 BITS	VARIABLE	12 BYTES
SOURCE PORT	DEST. PORT	SEQUENTIAL NUMBER	ACK NUMBER	DATA OFFSET	RESERVED	U R G / A C K / P S H / R S T / S Y N / F I N	WINDOW	CHECK-SUM	URGENT POINTER	OPTIONS	PSEUDO -IP

Figure 7-6 TCP Frame Format

- Source Port (16 bits): The receiver uses its port number when replying.

- Destination Port (16 bits): The destination port.

- Sequence Number (32 bits): This field contains the sequence number of the first data byte in the segment. The next segment will contain the sequence number of the first data byte in its segment. At the receiver, the sequence numbers will be collected, and all must be accounted for to ensure that all data has been received.

- Acknowledgment Number (32 bits): This is the value of the next sequence number that the receiver expects to be sent. This fill is used during acknowledgments—when the ACK bit is set to 1.

- Data Offset (4 bits): This is the size of the header expressed as the number of 32-bit words. It's used to tell the receiver where the header ends and the Data field begins.

- Reserved (6 bits): Not used.

- URG (Urgent Pointer Field) (1 bit): When set, it means that the data contained in the Urgent Pointer field is significant (it may means nothing when the URG bit is 0).

- ACK (Acknowledgment) (1 bit): When set, it means that the Acknowledgment Number field has significant information.

- PSH (Push) (1 bit): When set, any data held in the buffers is sent.

- RST (Reset) (1 bit): Resets the connection.

- SYN (Synchronization) (1 bit): When set, indicates that the Sequence Number field is significant, that the frame received is one of a series of fragments.

- FIN: (Finish) (1 bit): When set, it marks the last fragment to be sent.

- Window (16 bits): The receiver returns this in an ACK to tell the sender the number of bytes it can accept.

- Checksum (16 bits): An error-detection algorithm that looks for bit errors on the TCP header, Data field, and a portion of the IP header (the Source and Destination IP addresses, Protocol, and Length fields).

- Urgent Pointer (16 bits): Specifies the first data octet following the urgent data. This indicates data in a buffer that must be sent immediately.

- Options (variable size): There are three options available in a TCP header. These are the End Of Option List, No operation, and Maximum Fragment Size, which is used to tell the sender the size of the largest fragment it can process.

- Pseudo-IP (typically 12 bytes): Includes the Source and Destination IP address, the protocol being used (UDP), and the length of the UDP datagram. This information is taken from the IP header.

A final field may include padding that's used to fill the header size to a multiple of 32 bits. While a TCP fragment has a variable data field, it's normally constrained by protocols at the lower layers (IP, Ethernet, etc.). As mentioned, once a socket is in place, TCP transmission occurs. The TCP header and data are encapsulated in a lower layer frame, normally IP. IP, in turn, is encapsulated in a lower layer frame such as Ethernet or token Ring.

TCP is an intensive protocol implementation and may not be needed under certain circumstances. IP may be run on a local network, without the benefits of TCP, if the network administrator determines that the network is reliable and efficient. However, if users on the network want to communicate outside of the local environment, a Transport layer protocol is required. Still, TCP may represent overkill for some applications. IPX, the Network layer protocol used with Novell NetWare, offers benefits that IP doesn't, and is frequently run with UDP. Other applications that occur in real-time, such as interactive gaming, can't wait for acknowledgments. Once they arrived, they would be obsolete. For these applications, UDP offers alternative Transport layer access.

User Datagram Protocol (UDP)

UDP is a streamlined implementation of TCP. In fact, in all cases where TCP is run, UDP is also run (though not utilized). UDP is a connectionless (unreliable with no flow control or error recovery) mechanism supplied to the IP. A UDP datagram is encapsulated in the Data field of IP. Essentially, it provides a software interface between the IP and the application to be run. Applications include those run for TCP, such as mail, file transfer (TFTP), or Domain Name Server (DNS).

UDP interfaces applications and the IP via port numbers, such as those shown in Table 7-1. UDP is the protocol specified in the header of an IP packet. Once invoked, it does nothing more than multiplex and demultiplex application processes at the designated ports. The header format for UDP is illustrated in Figure 7-7.

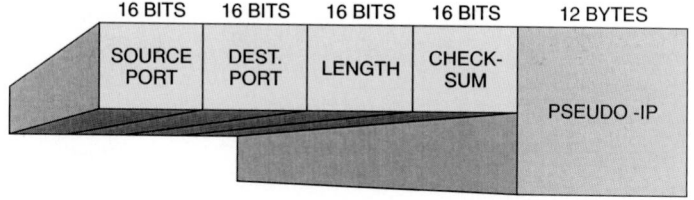

Figure 7-7 UDP Frame Format

The header is 20 bytes in length. Notice that all fields in UDP are a part of a TCP header. This is why UDP is always running when TCP is the specified protocol.

- Source Port (16 bits): The application process port at the sender.

- Destination Port (16 bits): The application process port at the destination.

- Length (16 bits): Total length of the UDP datagram, including the header.

- Checksum (16 bits): Bit error detection algorithm that covers the UDP header, pseudo-IP header, and UDP Data field.

- Pseudo-IP (typically 12 bytes): Includes the Source and Destination IP address, the protocol being used (UDP), and the length of the UDP datagram. This information is taken from the IP header.

As mentioned, UDP is a quick and streamlined Transport layer protocol. It's used in applications where flow control and retransmission of lost packets either can't be done (real-time applications like live broadcasts), or when an upper layer protocol does it. As mentioned, Netware IP uses UDP because it provides for flow control, error detection, etc.

INTERNET PROTOCOL (IP)

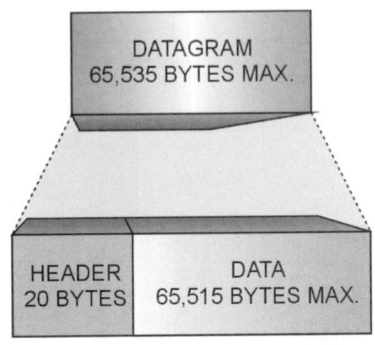

NET+ OBJECTIVE
I.1.3

As mentioned before, IP is a best-effort, unreliable, connectionless protocol. It depends on TCP to provide these attributes. The current version of IP is 4.

IP messages are sent in the form of a **datagram**, shown in Figure 7-8.

A datagram is the unit of measure for an IP transmission. A datagram has a maximum length of 65,535 bytes, including the header, although it could be much smaller. All datagrams contain source and destination addresses (these are the physical MAC-addresses). The datagram is patterned after the addressing methods used with physical networks: it consists of a header field and a data field, as pictured in Figure 7-9. The most-common type of header is 20 bytes long. For a fully-loaded datagram, the maximum Data field length is $65,535 - 20 = 65,515$ bytes. En route to the ultimate destination, datagrams are passed along from device to device, normally through a router or gateway. As it moves up to another layer, such as the Transport layer, TCP (or some other protocol) information is encapsulated within the Data field of the IP frame.

Figure 7-8 Datagram Layout

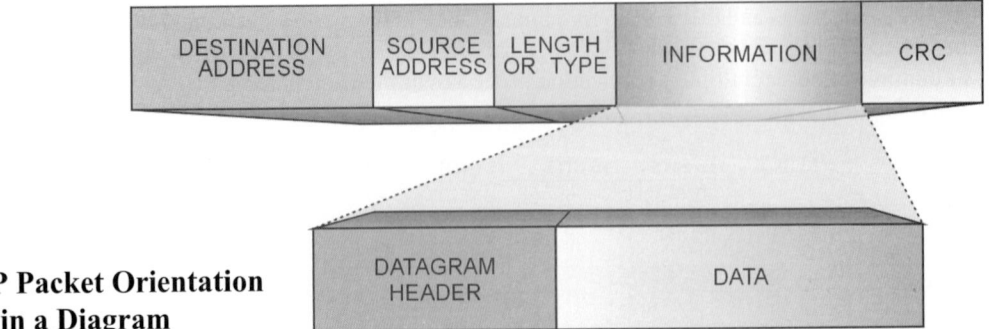

**Figure 7-9 IP Packet Orientation
Within a Diagram**

The IP packet format is depicted in Figure 7-10. The **VR/HL field** contains the software version being used, and the header length. VR and HL both occupy 4 bits of the field. The software version is important because networks, and the machines connecting them, may be running an earlier version. They may not be able to process a datagram encoded in a more recent version, causing the datagram to be rejected. The current version of the IP is 4.

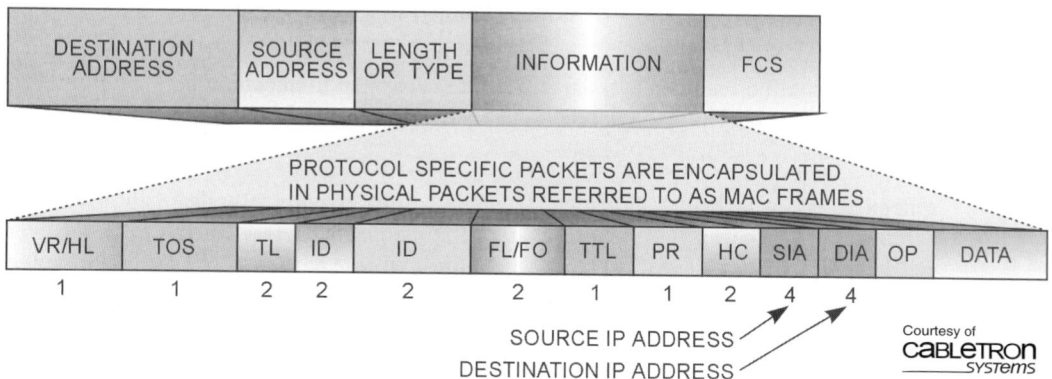

The 4-bit header states the length of the header in 32-bit words. For example, a header consisting of 20 bytes will show 5 in the HL field, which is equal to 20 bytes x 8 / 32 = 5. The IP allows for options in the Header field. Options extend the length of the field, and contain instructions for tracking the datagram across the system.

Figure 7-10 IP Frame Format

The 1-byte **Type Of Service** field, shown in Figure 7-11, describes how the datagram should be treated en route to the destination. Bits 1, 2, and 3 of the field are called **Precedence**. Precedence is an indication of the significance of the datagram to the operation of the network. Datagrams that include control instructions, making the transport quicker or more reliable, are given precedence over datagrams containing word-processing files. The **D, T, and R bits** are indicators of the level of transport service needed for the datagram. D is low delay, T is high throughput, and R is high reliability. These bits provide help to the interconnecting machines as to the route that the datagram is to take. In most cases, a router has several options for routing datagrams passing through it, and will look at the DTR bits before arbitrarily selecting the route. Of course, not all routers or gateways support the type of Service field.

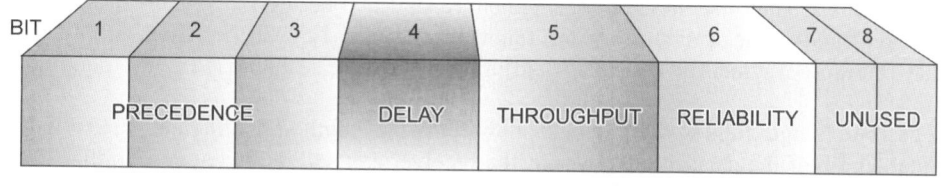

Figure 7-11 Type of Service Field

The 16-bit TL field states the total length of the datagram, measured in bytes. The total length includes the header, and the data. As was previously mentioned, the total length may be a maximum of 65,535 bytes.

The next three fields, ID (Identification), FL (Flag) and FO (Fragmentation Offset), are all related to the fragmentation of a datagram. **Fragmentation** is the process of dividing the datagram, so that the length is smaller. Remember that a wide area network is often a collection of LANs. An Ethernet LAN transmits frames with a maximum length of about 1,500 Bytes. If a datagram is en route to a destination, and has to pass through an Ethernet, the size of the datagram must be compatible with the frame-formatting requirements of the Ethernet, or 1,500 bytes. Because of this, datagrams are fragmented.

> Fragmentation results when datagrams are separated to accommodate the frame lengths of networks through which they pass en route to the destination.

Once a datagram has been fragmented, it remains so until arriving at the destination, where it is reassembled. There is no guarantee that the fragmented packets will arrive at the receiver in the same sequence. The destination, then, must be able to tell which packets belong to which datagrams, which portion of the fragment has arrived, and which fragment is the last. The receiver can reassemble the fragments into the original datagram, by using the information contained in the Fragmentation fields.

The 2-byte **ID field** is a unique number generated for each datagram transmitted over the network. As the datagram is fragmented, the header of the datagram is copied onto each fragment, including the ID field. Then, when the fragments arrive at the receiver, the receiver looks at the ID field and the source address of each packet, to determine the constitution of the original datagram.

The **Flag** is a 3-bit field responsible for controlling fragmentation, and for identifying the last fragment of the datagram. The second bit is the control bit. When the control bit is set, it is an instruction to avoid fragmenting the datagram. A router that sees the bit set will not fragment the datagram, but if it is unable to send the message along without fragmentation, it will disable the datagram and send an error message back to the source station. The first bit, when turned off, identifies the last fragment. This will be the only fragment that has the bit turned off, and the receiver can now determine all fragments of the datagram.

It does so by examining the **Total Length** field of the fragment, and the **Fragment Offset** field. Fragment Offset is a 13-bit field containing a byte count equal to the numerical order of the fragmented datagram. For example, consider a 2,000-byte datagram fragmented into four 500-byte fragments. The first fragment contains an offset of 0, since it begins with the first byte in the field. The second fragment has an offset of 500, because it contains the second 500-byte fragment set. The offset in the third fragment reads 1,000 because it contains bytes 1,000 through 1,499 of the datagram. The last fragment will show 1,500 in the offset, and will also have the more-fragment bit in the Flag field turned off, to indicate that this is the last fragment.

The Total Length field of the fragment shows only the length of the fragment, and not the total length of the datagram. However, the receiver can add the byte-count in the Total Length field to the offset, and determine the size of the datagram. For example, the fourth fragment in the above example will show a total length of 520 bytes (500 bytes in the data field + 20 bytes of header = 520). Subtracting the header bytes gives the size of the data field, 500 bytes. The offset in the fourth fragment reads 1,500. By adding the size of the data field (500 bytes) to the offset (1,500 bytes), the receiver will determine that the original datagram must be 2,000 bytes long (1,500 byte offset + 500 bytes in the data field = 2,000 bytes).

The receiver collects all the fragments with identical IDs, and reassembles them according to the numerical byte-sequence contained in the Offset fields. It will know if any fragments are missing, because the total byte-count must be equal to 2,000.

Time-To-Live is a 1-byte field specifying the time, in seconds, that a datagram may remain on the network. Typically, it is set to 20 seconds. If the datagram, is permitted to move indefinitely, from link to link, it has probably become degraded (the destination address is lost or garbled, etc.), and will never arrive at the receiver. Time-To-Live sets a limit on the time the network is allowed to deliver the datagram.

The 1-byte **Protocol** field describes the protocol governing the datagram. The 16-bit checksum is an algorithm used to check for errors in the header. Note that the header checksum looks only at the header, since the Data field has its own error-detection. The reason for separating the two is that only the headers are examined by interconnecting machines. They process information in the Data field as bit streams. Checking headers for errors saves time when the datagram is moving through the routers or gateways.

The Source and Destination fields contain addresses of the sender and receiver. An Internet address is assigned by the **Network Information Center** (NIC), and is a requirement for connecting to the Internet. However, many corporate WANs also use TCP/IP. These addresses may be of any format the network manager wants to devise, but if the WAN will, at some future date, be connected to the Internet, the proprietary addresses will have to be scrapped and exchanged for addresses assigned by the NIC. It would be wise to make the effort to request addresses from NIC for the possible future connection to the Internet. The following discussion of addresses assumes that the datagram will be formatted for Internet transportation.

IP Addressing

The 32-bit address consists of a network address, and a host address. Only network addresses are assigned by the NIC; the host address is left to the local network manager.

An IP address consists of 32 bits, so, $2^{32} = 4,294,967,296$ unique addresses. While four-billion addresses is a lot, it is finite. A time will come when all four billion addresses have been used. Then what? When IP was first introduced and finalized in the early 80's, no one suspected that the Internet would be such a powerful and consuming force. At that time, 32 bits seemed like enough, especially since the Internet was for scientists, computer nerds, and soldiers. Who could have foreseen that our grandmothers would one day be Web surfing?

In the early days, it seemed that large networks, populated with thousands of machines, would be the future. The potential of client-server systems was untapped, as well as the concept of managing network resources into clusters—or workgroups, as we call them. In the early 80's, 16 kB of RAM was huge, and a 10 MB hard drive was prohibitively expensive. A 32-bit addressing scheme made sense, and has served us well, not withstanding a significant number of critics who attack the system as inefficient and flawed. It's all of that, but only in the context of the huge number of users who require a logical address—a situation that no one could have foreseen.

Of course, things change. The current supply of IP addresses will be depleted in the next 30 years at the current demand rate. Actually, that's less of a problem than having four billion users attached to the Internet—we would have to redefine our definition of slow. But, assuming technology keeps a step ahead of Internet traffic, a time will come when not everyone will be able to use the Internet, because they won't be able to get an IP address (or a MAC address, for that matter).

The current IP is at version 4 (IPv.4), with the experimental version 5 (IPv.5) waiting in the wings. A change to the protocol is proposed for IP version 6 (also known as IP-next generation, IPng), which intends to address (pun intended) the limitations of IPv.4. We'll take a look at a couple of implementations of IPv.4, called **classful** and **classless** IP addressing.

Classful IP

Address classes A, B, and C differentiate in the numbers of networks, and host addresses being utilized by a specific organization. Class A addresses are identified by a logic 0 in their bit-1 position. Class B addresses are identified with logic 10 in the first two bit positions. A class C address contains 110 in the first three bit positions, as shown in Figure 7-12.

BIT	1	2	3	4..	NET ADDRESS	HOST ADDRESS	..32
CLASS A	0	X	X	X X X X X		X X X X X X X X X X X X X X X X X X X X X	
CLASS B	1 X	0 X	X X	X X X X X X X X X X X X X		X X X X X X X X X X X X X X X X	
CLASS C	1	1	0	X X X X X X X X X X X X X X X X X X X X X		X X X X X X X X	
CLASS D	1	1	1	0	MULTICAST		
CLASS E	1	1	1	1	1	RESERVED	

Figure 7-12 IP Address Classes

In terms of calculations, these are the high-order bits in the address. The idea behind address classes is that some large organizations will have a few large networks, and many hosts. Some medium-size organizations will have equal numbers of hosts and networks, while small organizations will have many interconnected networks, with a small number of hosts.

Keep in mind, a **host** is any machine that communicates on the interconnected network. A **network** refers to a physical network—a LAN or WAN. So, the address contains the general location of the receiver (the network address), and the specific location of the destination machine (the host address). Note that these are logical addresses, and not physical addresses. Each host also has a physical address (the MAC address) which locates the machine on its network wire. As you can probably guess, there must be some type of system that will map logical and physical addresses. That system is called a routing protocol, and we'll take a look at it in a later section.

> The Internet address system is separated into five classes that specify the numbers of networks and hosts. The address follows the Decimal Dotted Notation procedure for grouping the address.

NET+ OBJECTIVE
I.6.2

The general structure of the IP classes is also shown in Figure 7-12. Each class separates the 32 bits into a network and a host address. As mentioned above, the sequence of higher-order bits determines the class. Since these are reserved, they aren't available for addressing.

Class A addresses can accommodate $2^{24}-2 = 16,777,214$ hosts, with 24 bits in the host field. The reason 2 is subtracted is that 0.0.0.0 is reserved for the default network, and 127.0.0.10 is reserved for a loopback test. Datagrams can be sent to $2^7-2 = 126$ destination networks. At this time, all class A addresses have been assigned.

The Host field of a class B address has 16 bits; so it can respond to $2^{16}-2 = 65,534$ host machines. With 14 bits in the network field, $2^{14} = 16,384$ networks that may be addressed. The two higher order bits are set to 10, leaving 14 bits for the network address.

In the class C address, the Network field is 21 bits long (the three high-order bits are set to 110, leaving 21 bits for network addresses), for a total of $2^{21} = 2,097,152$ network assignments. The host number contains 8 bits for $2^8-2 = 254$ host machines.

By convention, the address fields of Figure 7-12 are separated into four 8-bit groups. The first byte of a class-A address contains the network number, and the class bit, while the remaining three bytes contain the host address. The first two bytes of a class-B address are the network address, along with the 2-bit class identifier, and the last two bytes are the host number. The network number for a class-C address is in the first three bytes, along with the 3-bit class code, and the host address is in the last byte. This method for expressing TCP/IP addresses is called **Decimal Dotted Notation**.

The binary format for addresses described above is normally converted to base$_{10}$ numbers. For example, consider the class-B address:

bit 32			**bit 1**

Binary (**Base$_2$**)   10000110.10001101.01001010.00010111

Decimal (**Base$_{10)}$**   134 . 141 . 74 . 23

The decimal notation is converted to base$_{10}$ and the dots represent the byte separation. It is the base-ten number that's used when referring to an Internet address, but as you can see, it is a derivative of the binary machine code. In this example, host machine .74.23 is located on network 134.141.

As a matter of numerical interest, the left-most byte, or number, of a class-A network is numbered 1-126. Class-B networks are numbered 128 through 191 and class-C networks are numbered 192 through 223. This provides a quick technique for identifying the classes.

A class-D address signifies a multicast, which is a method for sending data to all hosts or networks. There are two types of broadcasting on networks: directed and limited broadcasts. A **directed broadcast** is used to send data to all of the hosts specified by the network number. Any host portion of the address set to all 1's is a directed broadcast. A **limited broadcast** is used to contact all stations on the local network. A limited address contains thirty-two 1's in the address field.

This type of broadcast is used when a host is first connected to the network, and it sends the limited broadcast to all other hosts on its network, basically asking, "Do any hosts on the network know my address?" All hosts look up the new host's address and respond back with the number. From that point on, the new host knows its address.

IP includes several special addresses that are invalid. All 0s in the host or network fields are interpreted to mean this Host, or this network. It's useful when two machines on the same local network are communicating. When a host does not know the number of the network it's attached to, it may send a message with all 0s in the network field, meaning "this network." Other hosts will respond to the request with the network number, and the host records it for future transmissions. Any network address beginning with 127 is an invalid address. It is used for **loopback testing**. A packet may be looped back to test the integrity of the links, or to measure throughput. When an interconnection machine receives the 127.0.0.1 network address, it sends it back to the source network without transmitting it onto the Internet. In fact, this is a local loopback and never arrives on the network wire.

IP Subnets

In class-B and class-C network addresses, the number of networks is somewhat restricted. Many organizations have the need for adding more of their networks to the Internet, but there are not enough addresses to support the demand. The interim solution has been to create **subnetworks**. Subnets allow a site to divide the host portion of the address into two parts, which define more network address bits, and fewer host address bits. This allows an organization to deploy more networks without requesting additional IPs, and it reduces the number of routes on the Internet, which helps to control congestion.

Figure 7-13 shows a router connected to the Internet. The router services a number of separate networks. The router IP at the Internet interface is a class B 134.141.0.0. All packets with this network address will be received by the router. The router will then determine the correct subnet based on the third octet of the address received from the Internet. Once at the subnet, the packet is sent on to the host identified by the fourth octet of the address.

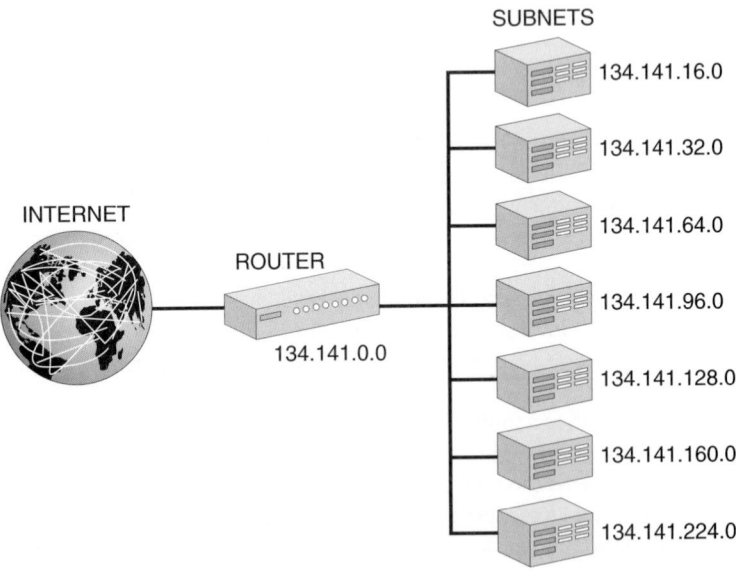

Figure 7-13 Subnetting a Network Address

For example, in the class B address 134.141.16.23, the network address is 134.141. The host address is 16.23. A subnet is created by extending the network address to the third byte so that it becomes 134.141.X, with X = 0 to 254. Host address 23 will be located at one of these subnet addresses. The subnetwork is transparent to machines outside the subnet; they still communicate with host 23 by sending messages to network 134.141. Only at the local network is the subnet created.

Subnetworks are identified by a **default network mask** (or **natural mask**), which is the decimal number 255. A series of 255 masks are used to indicate the boundaries of the mask. Conventionally, in a classful system, the 255 corresponds to the network portion of an IP, so that a class A IP with the first byte reserved for network addresses has a default subnet mask of 255.0.0.0. A class B network has the first two bytes reserved for network addresses, so the default subnet mask would be 255.255.0.0. And a class C network would have a default subnet mask of 255.255.255.0 since the first three bytes are reserved for network addresses. The decimal 255, then, is used to mask the network portion of an IP and only leave open the host portion.

CNST OBJECTIVE
IV-C

The default subnet masks as described are conventional for each class. However, a network manager is free to slice up the mask as needed—within limits, which we'll look at shortly.

Convention beside the point, any address followed by the 255 mask is identified as a host. Keep in mind that the idea of a subnet mask is to artificially create more network addresses. A class B network uses 14 bits of the first two octets, leaving 65,534 host addresses. If you only needed 3,000 host addresses, the remaining 62,534 hosts assignments will be wasted. And if you added a remote network, you would have to request another IP to address hosts on it. The classful system, as you can see, tends to create waste for class A and B IPs.

When a mask is used, a router looks only at the bits constrained by the mask to determine which subnet a packet is addressed to. It follows that router communications must include the mask in the address header of packets it sends and receives. For example, in the class-B address above, the sequence would be:

134 . 141 . 16 . 23, then, 255 . 255 .255 .16.

Now the message will be sent to host .23 on subnet .16 of network 131.141. The **default mask** covers the first two octets since these are the network address octets of a class B IP. The mask in the third octet is used to mark the value of the subnet. The fourth octet, of course, is the value of the host address.

Let's look at another example using the network address 134.141.0.0. This is a class B address, and we want to subnet it to network 96, host 21. This address, using subnetting, would use extended addressing, as shown in Figure 7-14.

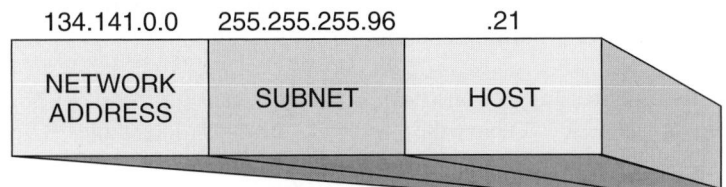

Figure 7-14 Extended Subnet Addressing

This complete address would be carried on the network, and passed between stations and routers or gateways. Outside the network, all packets would arrive addressed to 134.141.X.X. E-mail, for example, sent through the Internet would have no knowledge of the subnetting that occurs at the local level. Once the packet arrives at the class B address, the router will add the subnet string and pass the packet on to the correct subnet address and host.

Notice that this class B address without subnetting accounts for merely a single network address. However, with subnetting, it can create an additional 254 network addresses.

Admittedly, the number of hosts on each network has been drastically reduced (to 254 on each subnet network), but this isn't such a bad thing. Networks are routinely segmented into smaller sizes anyway, for the purposes of better network management (higher throughput, less bandwidth demands, faster speeds, etc.).

Why have more network addresses that host addresses? First, there are more LANs than the addressing scheme can support. Second, a single host address may be used by more than one computer. The host machine may be a communications controller that does the protocol encoding, and has a dozen PCs, or terminals, connected to it. When a PC-user signs onto the Internet, the address of the host—the communication controller—is used. The protocol is not concerned with the arrangement the controller has with the PCs and terminals, since it deals only with packets of data.

Classless IP (CIDR)

By 1992, the Internet Task Force determined that the supply of class B addresses would be exhausted in the mid-nineties. As an interim solution, until IPv.6 solves the problems associated with 32-bit IP addresses, the **Classless Inter-Domain Routing** (CIDR), pronounced "cider", was developed. CIDR is intended to accomplish two primary goals:

- To reduce the current reliance on a classful system.

- To support route aggregation where a single network address can be used to represent the addresses of thousands of hosts. This has the benefit of reducing routing tables that point to network addresses (currently numbering about 30,000+ routes). And reduce the effect of route flapping. First, if a single address can be used to represent 1,000 routes, then the amount of route information that must be maintained in a router is reduced. Flapping refers to changes in route availability. If a router is taken off-line, it's no longer available as a valid route, and a "flap" is then created in the routing tables of all other routers.

Conventional classes are eliminated with CIDR. CIDR routers use a network prefix to determine the line between network address and host address, rather than the first several bits of the address to specify a class. There are still 32 bits in the IP, but all of the bits are used for addressing. And instead of a predetermined dividing line between network and host, the network address may be arbitrarily chosen.

Routers exchange addressing data on a network. If a packet uses a router as a hop to another location, and the router doesn't have the packet address in its router tables, it updates them with it. Whenever a node comes online, it's said to "advertise" its presence and in the process, router tables are updated with the address of the new host. A router that is located at the interface to a group of local networks and the Internet, will advertise all new addresses.

When CIDR is used, the exchanged information between routers contains a mask that specifies the length of the network portion of an IP address. The mask, called a prefix-length, is a bit-count that begins with the left-most bit of the address. For example, an address with 22 bits in the network portion of the address would be advertised with 22 bits in the length-prefix bit-count, and would be called a /22 address. The host address would occupy the last 10 bits of the address.

And classful router won't understand the conventions used with CIDR, so it's common to use network prefixes that are multiples of the class arrangement. Table 7-2 shows commonly used CIDR addressing schemes. By using prefix multiples, host machines will interpret the addresses as if they were classful.

CIDR Prefix Length	Dotted Decimal	Number Individual Addresses
/13	255.248.0.0	512,0000
/14	255.252.0.0	256,000
/15	255.254.0.0	128,000
/16	255.255.0.0	64,000
/17	255.255.128.0	32,000
/18	255.255.192.0	16,000
/19	255.255.224.0	8,000
/20	255.255.240.0	4,000
/21	255.255.248.0	2,000
/22	255.255.252.0	1,000
/23	255.255.254.0	512
/24	255.255.255.0	256
/25	255.255.255.128	128
/26	255.255.255.192	64
/27	255.255.255.224	32

Table 7-2 CIDR Addressing Schemes

Let's look at an example. Assume that an ISP has the class B address 200.25.0.0. With 16 bits in the host, 65,536 addresses can be created. But the ISP wants to assign only 4,096 addresses, beginning at 200.25.16. This requires 12 bits in the host portion of the address, and is the same as 24 class C addresses (4,096/256 = 24). Now, the block of 4,096 addresses can be divided by a power of two. This is typically accomplished by successively dividing the address by two, until the block is composed of a series of consecutively smaller blocks.

Address 200.25.16.0/20 is first divided by two so that now there will be two blocks with 2,048 addresses in each block. One of the blocks is retained and the other is set-aside in order to subdivide. The first part of the process looks like this:

Original block: 200.25.16.0/20 <u>11001000.00011001.0001</u>0000.00000000

First block: 200.25.16.0/21 <u>11001000.00011001.0001</u>0000.00000000

Set-aside: 200.25.24.0/21 <u>11001000.00011001.00011</u>000.00000000

The original block of 4,096 address had been divided into two 2,048-address blocks. The underlined potion of the binary address represent the network portion of the address.

2,048 Set-aside: 200.25.24.0/21 <u>11001000.00011001.00011</u>000.00000000

Second block: 200.25.24.0/22 <u>11001000.00011001.000110</u>00.00000000

1,024 Set-aside: 200.25.28.0/22 <u>11001000.00011001.000111</u>00.00000000

The second block of 2,048 addresses is divided into two blocks of 1,024 addresses.

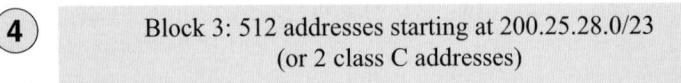

1024 Set-aside: 200.25.28/22 <u>11001000.00011001.000111</u>00.00000000

Third Block: 200.25.28.0/23 <u>11001000.00011001.0001110</u>0.00000000

Fourth block: 200.25.30.0/23 <u>11001000.00011001.0001111</u>0.00000000

By dividing the block of 1,024 address, two blocks of 512 addresses are created. From the single 200.25.0.0/16 address, the ISP has provided four unique blocks of address as in:

1 Block 1: 2,028 addresses starting at 200.25.16.0/21
(or 8 class C addresses)

2 Block 2: 1,024 addresses starting at 200.25.24.0/22
(or 4 class C addresses)

3 Block 4: 512 addresses starting at 200.25.30.0/23
(or 2 class C addresses)

4 Block 3: 512 addresses starting at 200.25.28.0/23
(or 2 class C addresses)

The blocks could have been further subdivided, but it's important to make sure that each block remains a multiple of 2, so that classful routers will interpret the address as classful.

The router-to-Internet interface in this example will advertise an address of 200.25.16.0/16. The /16 will be included in the network prefix. Since the routes to the four networks all occur through a single Internet port of the base router, traffic routes on the Internet have been reduced, or they're said to have been aggregated, since they occur offline from Internet routes. CIDR therefore, represents an interim strategy to aggregate Internet routes, as well as a means to inject flexibility into, and improve the efficiency of the present IPv.4 scheme.

TCP/IP UTILITIES

NET+ OBJECTIVE
I.7.1

TCP/IP comes equipped with a variety of UNIX-like tools to provide a considerable amount of information about your computer, its place in a network, and other devices you're connected to. Not all of the utilities mentioned in this section will be available to you. Which ones you have access to use depends on the utilities that were bundled in your NOS. The most common ones are discussed, along with step-by-step instructions on using them.

Instructions are entered from the DOS shell using a command prompt, assuming the utilities have been installed on your machine. Determine which utilities are installed on a Win 95/98 or NT station by looking in the Program files. Choose Programs from the Start menu, and select the DOS shell. At the C: prompt (or equivalent), enter the command as indicated.

Address Resolution Protocol (ARP) is a convention used to map IP addresses to physical, MAC addresses, and is described in detail in a later section of this chapter. The resolution maps are contained in clients or servers, and include addresses between machines.

At the command prompt, type "arp". Your screen will show the commands available for use with ARP. It's a useful tool for examining the contents of ARP caches on either the client or server station.

At the command prompt, enter "arp -a". You should see the following:

INTERFACE: This is the IP of the machine running the ARP utility.
INTERNET ADDRESS: This is the address of a server that the machine is connected to.
PHYSICAL ADDRESS: This is the Ethernet address of the local machine.
TYPE: This is the connection type from local machine to server, Dynamic or Static.

In addition to querying the ARP cache, entries may be added to it with the -s command, or deleted from it with the -d command.

NET+ OBJECTIVE
I.7.1

The **Hostname** command provides the name of the system on which the command is executed. At the command prompt, enter "hostname". The name displayed on your screen was entered when the NOS (NT, for example) was set up. Note that it refers to a Domain Name System (DNS) name for TCP/IP, rather than the dotted decimal notation number.

Ipconfig is a utility which shows you the addressing information for the system currently connected to. At the command prompt, enter "ipconfig /all". Notice that the information is separated into two categories—server and client (taken from the NIC installed in the client computer) information.

In the network listings, you should see the name of the host (server) that the client machine connects with, along with any pertinent status of the session between client and server.

In the client listings, notice that the MAC address of the NIC installed in the computer is listed in hexadecimal format. Using Ipconfig is an easy way to retrieve MAC addresses without opening the computer case, and reading it from the card. For a quick overview of the configuration, enter "ipconfig". This returns the same information as above, but in abbreviated form.

Note that on Win 95 machines, you must use **winipcfg** to run this tool.

The **nbtstat** (NetBIOS over TCP/IP) tool provides you with information about network names and their corresponding IP address. From the system prompt, type

nbtstat

The screen will fill with commands available with the tool. At the command prompt, type

net view(your server name)

For "your server name", enter the actual name of the server your machine is connected to. As you can see, the list includes all share devices associated with the machine name.

At the command prompt, type "nbtstat -c". This displays the IP address of the machine specified in the step above. The value of this is that it's much more common to refer to network resources by their name, rather than by their IP address. However, it's the address that's used to locate the device when information is sent to it. Consequently, it's the IP which will be needed when troubleshooting.

The **Route** tool is used to list the routing table at the server. You can use it to add or delete routes to a particular address. For example, if you determine a quick route to a remote server, the Route tool is used to add the route to the table (called persistent routing), and each time the specified address is queried, the route will be taken.

Netstat is a tool used to display all current network layer connections. This means you'll see TCP/IP, or UDP, protocols which are active at the time the tool is used. Netstat lists the network connections. At the command prompt, type "netstat". The screen will show all commands used with the Netstat tool. The following will display all connections on the server that your machine is connected to. At the command prompt, type "netstat -r". The display lists all connections, showing which ones are currently active.

Another interesting application of netstat is to view statistics related to the interface of your machine to the network. At the command prompt, type "netstat -e 5". The information listed will show the number of bytes received and transmitted, the type of packets, and of particular interest, the number of errors generated.

If you suspected a client of having a faulty NIC, the exercise above would list any errors which occurred at the client. Adding a number at the end of the above command is optional. As shown, the number "5" is an instruction to update the listing every 5 seconds.

Ping is a widely used tool used to check the status of a connection. An echo packet is sent to a specified address, and returned to your machine, provided the specified address is active. If it's not, you'll receive a message saying that the transaction has timed out. The effect of the Ping tool is similar to measuring continuity with an ohm meter. It checks to see if two network devices are connected. If they are, an echo is returned to the sending station. If they aren't, the ping will time out.

To initiate Ping, enter "ping". The screen will list all commands used with the tool. At the command prompt, type "ping (plus the IP of the server you're connected to)". As you can see from the reply, the connection from your machine to the server is working. Now try pinging to an IP that you're not connected to. At the command prompt, type "ping 123.456.789.123". After a short wait, you should receive the following message: "Request timed out."

What's happened is that the message couldn't find a destination at the specified address, and after a short period, it was discarded. The notation "TTL" stands for Time To Live, and is a field in the IP header. It's an instruction to any devices receiving the packet to discard it if the time specified in the field is exceeded.

Tracert allows you to see the path to an address. When an IP address is specified, Tracert lists the number of hops to the destination, along with the IPs of each router along the way. You can specify the number of hops to the destination in order to determine the most efficient route. It's also a good tool for determining if a problem lies at the remote address, or is within the route to the destination.

For example, assume you ping a remote server, but don't receive a response. The question then becomes: Is the problem at the destination, or at one of the routers along the way? The way to pin-point the problem is to connect to the router at the end of the list, then try to connect to the destination from there. If you can't, the problem most likely lies at that router.

To initiate Tracert, type "tracert". The screen will show all of the Tracert commands. Now type "tracert (plus the IP address of the server your machine is connected to)". This will show the path to your server. Tracert is more appropriate in a wide area environment. You can try using it while connected to the Internet by specifying well known IPs, such as the address to Microsoft or Netscape.

Telnet is a service which allows you to "telephone-net" into another computer. The original idea was that if you were in Atlanta and needed access to information in a computer in Dallas, you could telnet into it. The information was presented on your terminal screen just as if you were sitting in Dallas at a terminal connected directly to the Dallas computer. Telnet remains but its application is specialized and limited.

Originally, you could visit the Library of Congress by telnetting to their site. Now, you go via the Web. Many of the applications invoked using telnet are now handled by servers in a local or wide area network. Still, telnet is a valuable tool, but it use tends to be specialized for companies or educational institutions in which users are working at diskless terminals or stand-alone PCs and need access to resources on a large computer.

A telnet screen can be invoked from the DOS shell by typing telnet. Once you enter it, a telnet terminal emulation screen opens and you must enter the IP address and telephone number of the computer you want to dial into.

FTP (File Transfer Protocol) is a means of downloading files to your computer; or uploading them from your computer to an FTP site. Like e-mail, FTP retains a distinct structure, probably because it too was introduced early in the formation of the Internet. Probably the widest application of FTP is for downloading software, or software enhancements. For example, many vendors have a download section at their Web site. If you've bought a product from them in the past, you can use the site to download the latest revision of the software that's used in the product. Patches, upgrades or fixes to problems are routinely posted at a company's download area.

No Web browsers directly support FTP, but most include FTP software to initiate and control the download. Both Netscape and Explorer allow you to download from a Web site, for example. You can download the most current version of a software upgrade by saving the upgrade to a file, then writing it into non-volatile memory (NVRAM). Network interface cards, modems, and system boards are routinely updated in this way.

To begin an FTP session, enter FTP and the DOS prompt. The prompt will then change to an FTP prompt (FTP). You then enter the address—typically a domain-like name as used on the Internet.

IP ADDRESS RESOLUTION PROTOCOL (ARP)

An Address Resolution Protocol is a router protocol that maps the physical address of a node to the logical address. The three types of ARP protocols are Normal, Proxy, and Reverse-ARP.

An IP is a logical address, used for locating a network. The host portion of the address has little value outside of the local environment other than to specify the logical presence of a node on a LAN. If an address arrives at a router or gateway, the network and host portion will be compared to addresses in its table, and if a match is found, it will accept the packet.

Suppose the router is the base port to the Internet, and connects directly and indirectly to a thousand nodes on distributed LANs. How does it locate the node that matches the host address in the IP? If a node on the LAN wants to send a message to another node on the same LAN, how does the router know the recipient is on the same LAN? Or if the node wants to communicate with a node on a different LAN, how will the router know the difference?

First, a host must resolve the destination node's IP to a MAC address. It does so by using the Address Resolution Protocol (ARP). Let's look at a typical application of router IPs, shown in Figure 7-15. Two routers are being used to interconnect three LANs.

NET+ OBJECTIVE
I.5.1

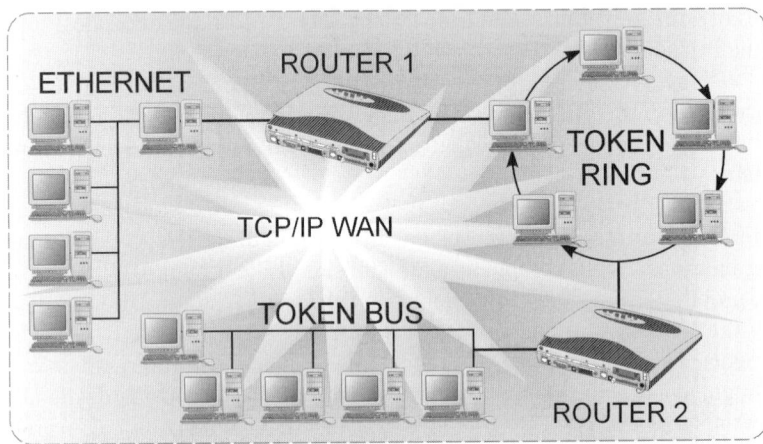

Figure 7-15 Routers Interconnect Many Network Types

NET+ OBJECTIVE
I.1.7

CNST OBJECTIVE
VI-A

A router provides interconnections at the Network layer of the OSI model. As with a bridge, it looks closely at the data frames, and passes only those intended for other network segments, or those intended for entirely different networks. In this respect, the router is capable of conserving greater amounts of bandwidth than a bridge, because the bridge looks only as far as the MAC layer of level two. Bridges are "blind" to internetworking protocols; consequently, they're unable to filter between different networks.

A router is protocol specific. It passes data packets between networks based upon routing information contained in the network layer header.

Typically, the router will decide the best path for the packet to take, which may be the cheapest, or the one requiring the fewest hops between routers. This is a significant departure from a bridge, which maintains alternative paths for data frames. These fallback paths represent unused bandwidth, which must be maintained, and paid for.

The primary disadvantage of a router is that the interconnect protocols must be the same. Examples of Internet protocols are TCP/IP, Novell's **Internet Packet Exchange** (IPX), Digital Equipment Corporation's **DECnet**, or the **Xerox Network Service** (XNS). When used in a wide area network application, each router must be capable of supporting the specific Internet protocol being used, or be able to translate from one to another.

In Figure 7-15, the router interconnects data packets across a network running TCP/IP. The network consists of an Ethernet, Token Ring, and a Token Bus LAN. Notice that the router allows computers on all three LANs to communicate, regardless of the topology and access protocols. The LAN hardware used with the computers may be from diverse vendors, and operate at different bandwidths. The router, because it is basically concerned only with network addresses, is involved in a limited capacity at the Physical layer, and the Data Link layer. This is the reason why the LAN hardware, cabling medium, and access protocols may all be different, but yet the networks can still communicate.

The routing process for the three-LAN wide area network is shown in Figure 7-16. Assume that a PC on the Ethernet LAN sends a message to a PC on the remote, Token Bus LAN. To the right are the MAC addresses of the IP datagram, along with the IP addresses. The first two columns contain destination and source MAC addresses of the router, and the respective LAN nodes. Initially, the MAC source address is the address of the node on the Ethernet LAN, and the destination address is the MAC for router 1. When the frame arrives at the router, the physical addressing fields of the MAC frame are removed, leaving only the IP addresses, data and CRC fields.

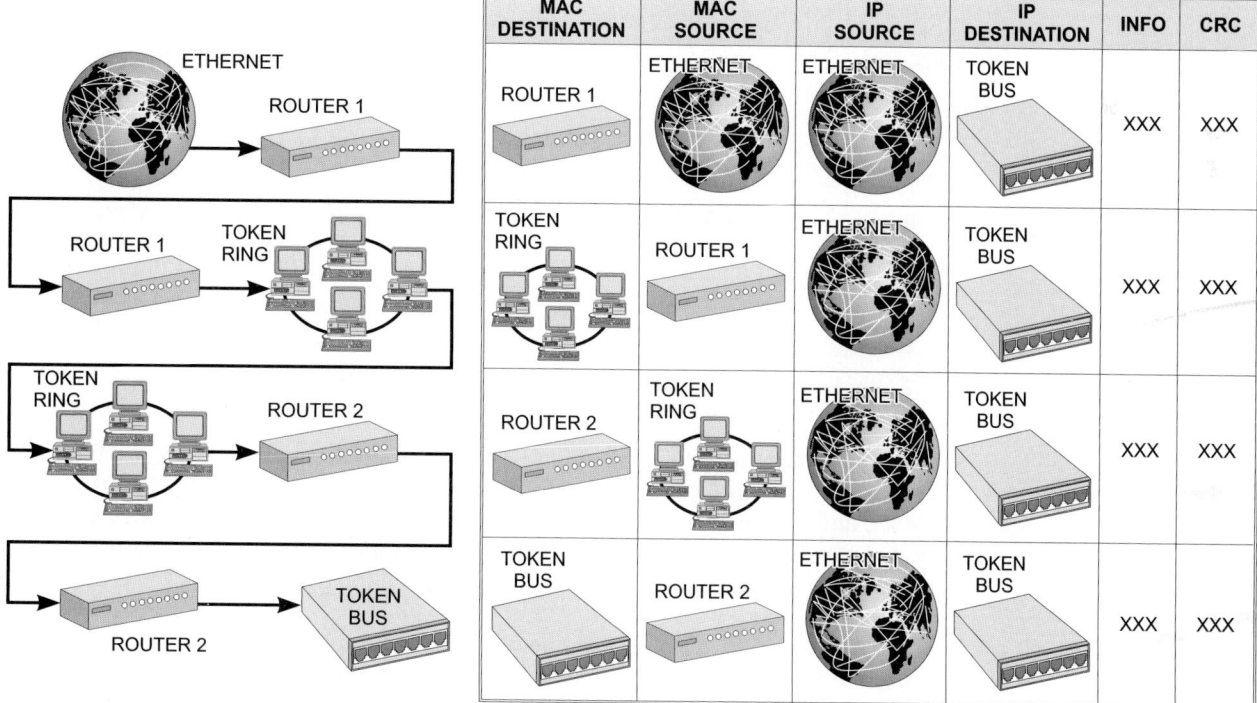

Figure 7-16 MAC and IP Frame Router Addressing

Notice that the IPs never change, because they are the only indication of where the frame is going as it moves from router to router. At each router hop, the router will compare its list of MAC addresses to the destination IP address. If no match exists, it will reframe the MAC addresses and pass the frame on.

Now router 1 reframes the message with new MAC address fields. Keep in mind that router 1 is the source of the message, and the next destination is the Token Ring network. The ultimate destination PC is located on the Token Bus LAN, so the Token Ring LAN doesn't accept the message. Instead, it passes it on to the next router. Once again, the MAC address headers are stripped, and the data, IP address and CRC fields reframed. This time, the source address is the Token Ring LAN, and the destination is router 2. Router 2 strips the MAC headers, and reframes the message with the Token Bus LAN as the destination address, and router 2 as the source address. This is the final destination of the frame, so it doesn't go any further. The message is now delivered to the specific computer on the Token Bus network.

How does the message know where the computer is on the network? Recall from Chapter 5 that the OSI model is a peer-to-peer, hierarchical system. Each function of the upper layers of the model are appended to lower layer functions. This is reviewed in Figure 7-17. Headers from the upper layers of the model are encapsulated within the MAC frame. This is why the source and destination IPs don't change—they aren't affected by physical address changes.

CNST OBJECTIVE
VIII-A

SOURCE   **DESTINATION**

OSI LAYER	HEADER		HEADER	OSI LAYER
APPLICATION	A		A	APPLICATION
PRESENTATION	A P		A P	PRESENTATION
SESSION	A P S		A P S	SESSION
TRANSPORT	A P S T		A P S T	TRANSPORT
NETWORK	A P S T N		A P S T N	NETWORK
DATA LINK	A P S T N D		A P S T N D	DATA LINK
PHYSICAL				PHYSICAL

Figure 7-17 Layers of the OSI Peer-to-Peer Relationship

Included in the information field is the 32-bit source and destination IP address. While the headers surrounding the Information field are stripped and reframed, the field itself remains intact, and is transmitted from network to network until the message arrives at the destination. Recall that it contains a specific network/host address, which is the destination network, as well as the logical address of the destination computer.

The physical and logical addresses now need to be reconciled. That is, a mechanism is needed to allow a node to determine if it can communicate directly to another node, or if it requires the reframing services of a router in order to get a message to it. For example, if the Ethernet node sent a message to another node on its own LAN, it wouldn't have to use the router for stripping and appending the MAC layer addressing. It would simply send the message to the Ethernet destination. Only when the destination node is located on another network does the router have to be involved in determining the physical path.

Route Determination Logic (RDL)

First, a node has to decide if a destination is remote, or local. A local destination is defined as being within the same address space as the source. This includes any subnetted addresses. A remote destination is defined as being outside the network address space, also including any subnetted addresses. This was the example just described. The destination was remote because the Ethernet node was unable to reconcile the Token Ring IP address to its own network IP address. The **Route Determination Logic** (RDL) uses the following algorithm:

(Destination IP AND Source Subnet Mask) = (Source IP AND Source IP Subnet Mask)

The AND in the equation indicates the logical AND operation. If the two operations result in the same value, it's assumed that both nodes reside on the same network, and the messages are sent directly. However, if the two values don't match, the destination is assumed to lie on a remote network, and the source node must utilize the look-up services of a router, or gateway, to determine the MAC address to place in its datagram.

Assume the existence of two networking nodes. Node 1, at IP 150.150. 1. 10, wants to send a message to Node 2, at IP 150.150.2.20, but doesn't know if it can do so directly. To find out, it performs route determination logic by first ANDing the IP of Node 1 with the subnet mask for Node 1, as shown in Table 7-3.

CNST OBJECTIVE
IV-C

Decimal IP		150	150	1	10
Binary IP		10010110	10010110	00000001	00001010
Decimal Mask		255	255	0	0
Binary Mask		11111111	11111111	00000000	00000000
AND	Binary	10010110	10010110	00000000	00000000
Result	Decimal	150	150	0	0

Table 7-3 ANDing Node 1's IP and Subnet Mask

Next, the IP of Node 2 and the subnet mask of Node 1 are ANDed, as shown in Table 7-4.

Decimal IP		150	150	2	20
Binary IP		10010110	10010110	00000010	00010100
Decimal Mask		255	255	0	0
Binary Mask		11111111	11111111	00000000	00000000
AND	Binary	10010110	10010110	00000000	00000000
Result	Decimal	150	150	0	0

Table 7-4 ANDing Node 2's IP and Node 1's Subnet Mask

Since the ANDed results of both operations yields the same address, 150.150.0.0, Node 1 will assume they are on the same network, and send the message directly to Node 2. If they aren't the same, Node 1 will determine that Node 2 is on a remote network. It will first look up Node 2's MAC address in its address cache (located on the local server), and if its found, ARP will cease, Node 1 will add the Node 2 MAC address to its IP datagram, and send the message directly to it. However, if the MAC address isn't in its cache, ARP continues, using one of several protocol implementations.

The ARP finds a specific network within a WAN, and dynamically maps logical addresses with physical addresses. This means that the router will match the Internet address contained in the Information field of the MAC header, to the actual location of the computer. Implied in the protocol is the ability of the router to establish a path, perhaps composed of multiple links, to the destination network. Once the router establishes the map of the logical and physical address of the computer, the computer can't be moved. This is because the router has fixed the physical location of the address of the computer. If the computer is moved, a new address must be assigned, and the router must create a new map to the new destination. Unless...

Actually, a modern router is capable of updating its address list in one of two different ways—dynamically, or statically.

Static routing is accomplished by using preconfigured routing tables that match IPs to MAC addresses. If a router uses static routing, the client can't be moved. The only way to change a static routing table is to manually change it. If the NIC card in a client is changed, the table must be (manually) updated. If the client is moved to another network (its IP changes), the table must also be updated.

Dynamic routers use routing protocols that will automatically update the router cache each time there's a change. Dynamic router protocols are classified as either interior (inside the network domain/subnet) or exterior (outside the network domain/subnet). Examples of exterior routing protocols include Routing Information Protocol (RIP), and Open Shortest Path First (OSPF). An example of an interior routing protocol is Border Gateway Protocol (BGP). Let's look at an overview of ARP implementations.

NET+ OBJECTIVE
I.4.1

CNST OBJECTIVE
VI-A

Broadcast ARPs

Three types of the ARP protocols are depicted in Figure 7-18. Station A wants to send data to B. To do so, A needs to know the local MAC address of B. The local MAC address is the actual address of the computer for station B. Remember, this is placed in the Information field of the Internet MAC frame. Station A sends an ARP, in the form of a MAC broadcast, requesting B's MAC address. Broadcasting on the Internet is a special address; the router must have broadcast capabilities to run ARP. The broadcast ARP is sent to all host networks on the Internet, or wide area network.

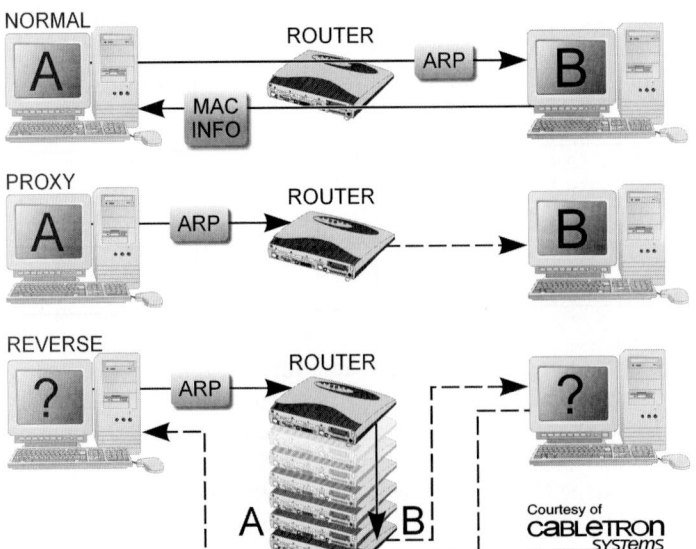

Figure 7-18 ARP Protocolsater

Normal ARPs

When operating in the normal mode, the router will forward the ARP through to station B, as shown in Figure 7-18. In response to the ARP, station B will send a frame back with its MAC information. The router forwards the B response, but with the router's MAC information added. This serves as an acknowledgment to station A that the B station has been located. A normal-type ARP guarantees the system that the destination will be available for message delivery.

Proxy ARPs

In a proxy-type ARP, the router receives the ARP from station A. The router responds to station A's ARP instead of station B responding. In order to do so, the router has already mapped the logical, and physical, location of B. The advantage of a proxy ARP is that network traffic is reduced. The disadvantage is that there is no guarantee that station B will still be at the logical, and physical, location stored in the router map. By this time, it may have been moved, and assigned a new address.

Reverse ARPs

A third type of ARP is the **Reverse Address Resolution Protocol** (RARP). Once again, station A wants to transmit to station B, but the logical addresses of both A and B are unknown. This would mean that the two stations do not know their own Internet addresses. In such a situation, the router bridges the frames, passing them from router to router until the appropriate network accepts the broadcast, and responds with the MAC containing the logical, and physical, address.

There are many academic and vendor proprietary routing protocols, but not all of them will route the common Internet protocols, such as TCP/IP. Due to the significant expense of routers, it is particularly important to evaluate the router against the specific parameters of the interconnected networks into which it will be installed.

A frequent question facing network administrators, when considering plans to expand a network, or to interconnect remote networks, is: Which is better, a bridge or a router?

A network using routers is more expensive, and specific to a given protocol. But a network using routers will utilize all of the communication paths. Since a network built with bridges does not process the network layer protocols, it is cheaper, quicker, and supports multivendor equipment. However, a bridged system also includes stand-by links, organized in a bridge topology, such as the a Spanning Tree Algorithm Topology. While serving to reduce possible collisions, this arrangement also decreases the overall network efficiency.

Therefore, the final decision must be based on price/performance/functionality, versus the actual communication costs.

INTERCONNECT TECHNOLOGY

Interconnect technology refers to devices in the network that transport data messages. These devices may be as simple as an amplifier, or as sophisticated as a statistical multiplexer, with advanced decision-making capabilities. Repeaters, bridges, routers, and gateways are common interconnect machines. Bridges, and routers, have assumed greater and greater roles in internetworking within the last decade. Routers were described in the proceeding section.

Repeaters

> A repeater regenerates network signal bits. Used to link LAN segments, a repeater lacks the ability to route data.

Repeaters regenerate electrical signals. As data travels along a cable run, it is affected by atmospheric noise, copper losses in the cable, as well as the reactive characteristics of the cable. This results in the bit pattern becoming distorted, often to the point that the destination node is unable to tell the difference between a logic 1 and a logic 0.

The basic function of a repeater is shown in Figure 7-19. Data traveling along the cable run has become distorted, due to any of the reasons cited above. The repeater recreates the bit pattern, restoring signal strength and clarity between bit levels. Since repeaters operate at the physical level, they are not concerned with the content of data at the input port. This means they're protocol independent.

Figure 7-19 Regeneration of Data Signal by a Repeater

Because a repeater is a series device in a network, it's concerned with **bandwidth**. The bandwidth of the repeater must be at least equal to the bandwidth of the network it's a part of; and if more than one repeater is used in a network, the path between repeaters cannot be less than the bandwidth of the network. This is illustrated in Figure 7-20.

It makes little sense to utilize repeaters for extending LANs over a wide area. The costs of providing the narrow-band channel would be too excessive. However, they are frequently used to provide remote connections when a node is located more than 50 meters from the Ethernet network, to subdivide large LANs, and to connect LANs that are distributed throughout a city.

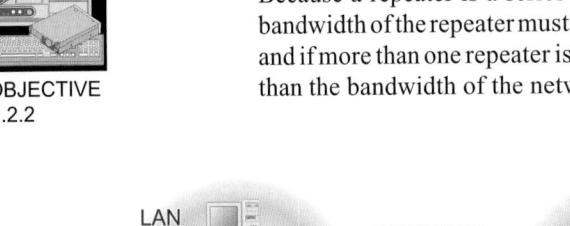
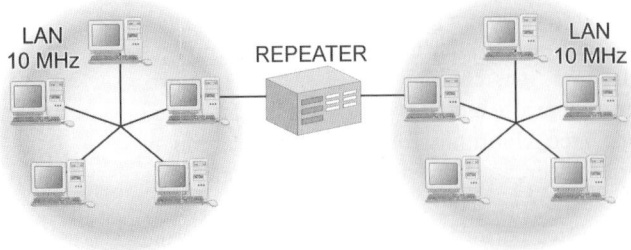

Figure 7-20 Repeater Bandwidth Requirements

Recall that **Ethernet**, or IEEE 802.3 CSMA/CD, restricts bus networks to a length of 2,500 meters. Ethernet segments are limited to 1,500 meters, while 802.3 segments must not exceed 500 meters. The maximum length from the bus to the network station for either type is 50 meters. If a network station is located at a distance exceeding the 50m limit, a repeater is connected at the network interface, as shown in Figure 7-21.

The remote node is located at 100 meters from the network bus, too far to guarantee that the data bits will traverse the cable without being degraded. The repeater is inserted within the 50-meter distance limit, and regenerates the data to the remote node.

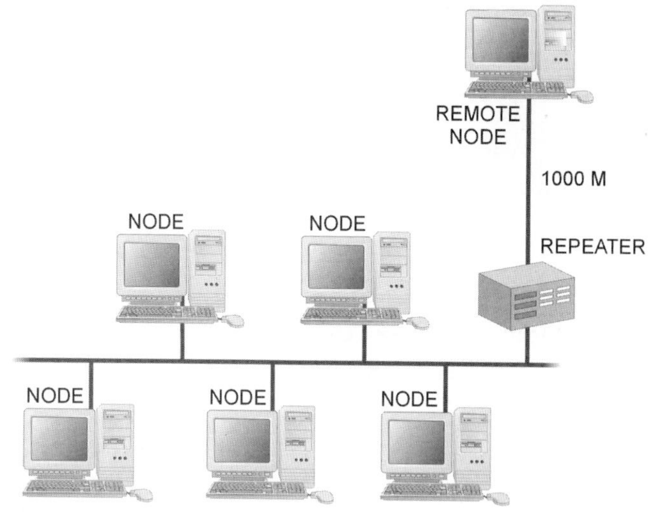

Ethernet LANs are permitted a maximum of 1,024 stations connected to each network. When a network grows beyond the maximum limit, repeaters may be installed to interconnect LANs, as shown in Figure 7-22. Here, the LAN has grown to include 2,000 nodes. The repeater provides a connection between the LAN segments, thus circumventing the station limitation. Note that the distance being served, from the port on each side of the repeater, does not exceed 50 meters.

Figure 7-21 Repeaters Provide Network Access to Remote Nodes

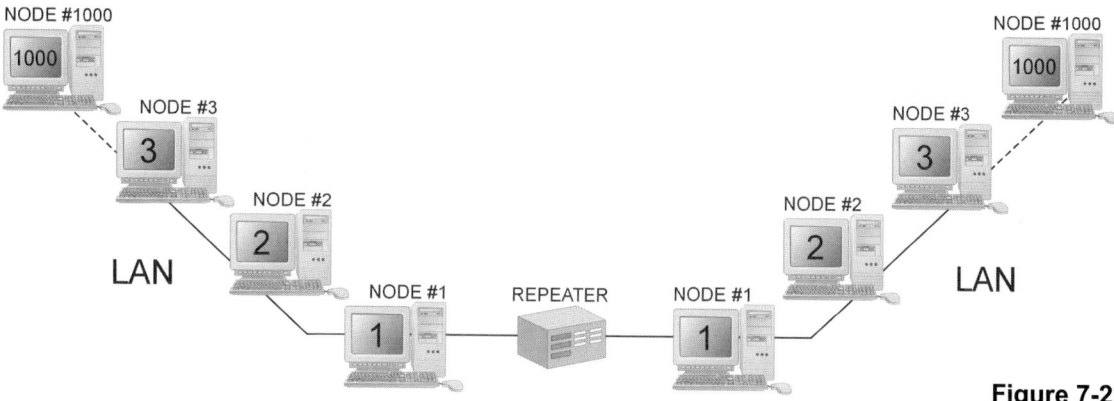

Figure 7-22 Repeaters Interconnect Large LANs

What happens if the distance is greater than 50 meters? This situation often occurs when a network spills over to another building. In such a case, the LANs may be connected by remote repeaters, as illustrated in Figure 7-23. The point-to-point link between the LANs may not be greater than 1,000 meters. Typically, the remote repeater link is a fiber-optic cable, since the external cable faces a greater exposure to noise and distortion.

Repeaters are not only associated with LANs. They may be used to interconnect any of the devices common to internetworking, such as bridges and routers. Increasingly, they are an integral component in situations where a collection of LANs constitute a portion of a wide area network.

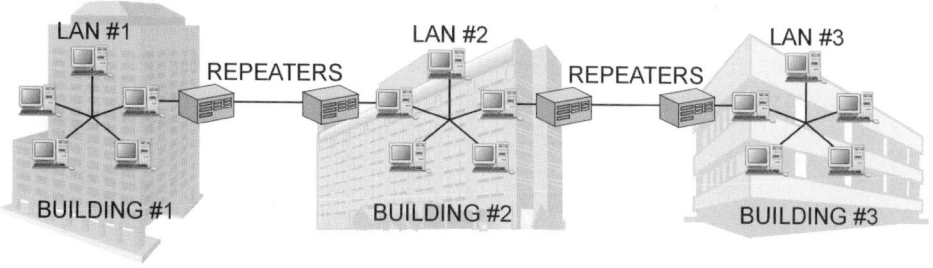

Figure 7-23 Repeaters Connect LANs in Different Buildings

**Figure 7-24 Backbone
Network**

Figure 7-24 shows a WAN consisting of many LANs. Four multiport repeaters (hubs) are shown, each supporting eight segments, and connected to a network **backbone**. A backbone refers to the primary network segment—usually a ring or bus—from which subnetworks are branched off, in a tree configuration. Such is a **Metropolitan Area Network** (MAN).

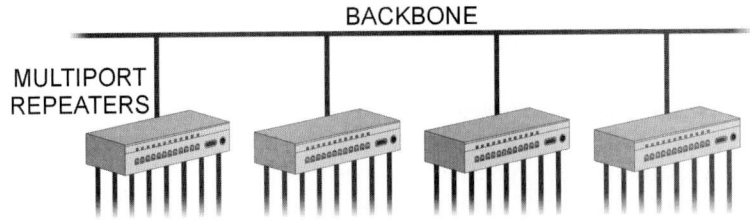

A common practice is to divide large LANs into smaller, more manageable units. As you can see, the distinction between LANs and WANs blurs with the physical size of the network. Keep in mind, though, that repeaters used in data networks are physically connected by the network cabling, which is why it does not make sense to extend their use beyond the area of a city—the cable costs, alone, are too expensive.

Courtesy of
CABLETRON
SYSTEMS

Figure 7-25 Commercial Repeater

Repeaters usually support any of the transmission medium—twisted pair, coaxial cable, and fiber-optic cable, often as a user-selectable option. The IEEE 802.3 standard also specifies several functions that repeaters must take responsibility for. These include the retiming of data frames, the extending of collision fragments, the partitioning of problematic network segments from the others, and reconnecting those segments without further problems. For example, if a repeater finds that a segment has a problem, that segment is disconnected from other segments. Once the problem is resolved, the repeater will reconnect it.

A commercial Ethernet repeater is pictured in Figure 7-25. The repeater is designed to connect two, full-length, thick or thin segments via external transceivers connected to each.

Bridges

A bridge, working at the Data Link level, connects networks. Independent of network protocols, bridges interconnect LANs that may be using dissimilar access methods.

A bridge connects LANs together. The networks may be local, with several LANs scattered throughout a building or office complex, or the LANs may operate at remote locations separated by thousands of miles. Generally, a bridge is used in the local environment, particularly in those situations where several LANs have popped up over a period of years, and it's become necessary to tie them together, and impose order on a network that is about to grow out of control.

Figure 7-26 shows a bridge connecting two Ethernet LANs. A PC on the first LAN, attempting to communicate with a PC on the second LAN, transmits through the bridge. At first glance, this may sound suspiciously like a repeater; after all, the bridge is forwarding packets of data from one LAN segment to another. A repeater operates at the Physical layer of the OSI model, by regurgitating data bits. It's a sophisticated, wideband amplifier.

Bridges operate at the Data Link layer of the OSI model by examining the MAC sublayer address contained in the frame header. This means that they have decision-making capabilities that are not available in a repeater. If, in Figure 7-26, PC A-1 sends a message to PC A-2, the bridge looks into

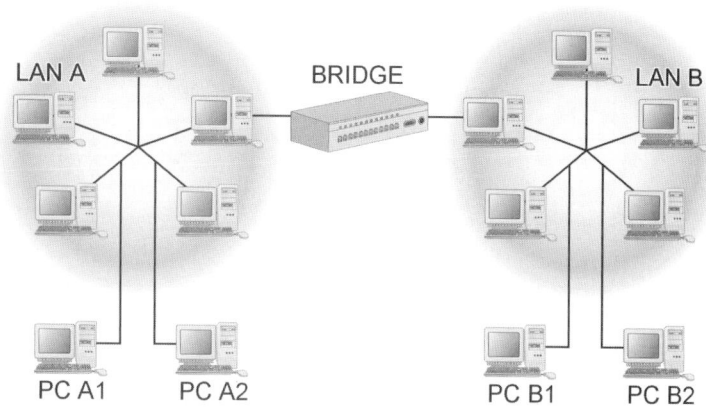

Figure 7-26 Bridge Linking LANs Using Network Protocols

the frame header for the destination address of PC A-1, and decides that bridging is not needed. A repeater, however, is not aware that multiple LANs exist; it simply extends the range of a LAN, and boosts all signals accordingly.

Figure 7-27 illustrates how the bridge handles interlink messages. This time, PC A-1 sends a message to PC B-1 on the second LAN. Recall from Chapter 6 that the MAC sublayer of the Data Link level contains a source and a destination address. When the frame arrives, the bridge decodes the destination address, and forwards it to the next LAN. It also performs the functions of a repeater, such as removing noise and maintaining link management.

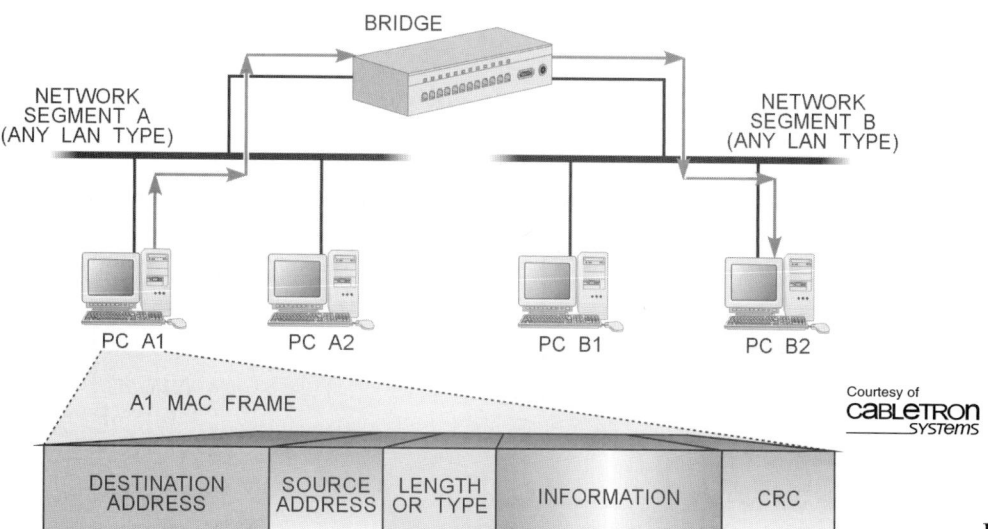

Figure 7-27 Address Resolution Protocols

The advantage of the bridge, in this application, is that much less bandwidth is used to connect the two LANs. From a user's point of view, the two LANs appear as one; but the cost of connecting them is reduced through lower equipment costs, such as using cabling schemes with narrower bandwidths. The two LANs shown in Figure 7-27 may be part of a much larger, wide area network. The bridge is used not only to conserve expensive bandwidth, but also to filter messages on the WAN.

Figure 7-28 shows five LANs connected by bridges. For security reasons, the users of LANs A, B, and C may be denied access to LANs D and E. However, LANs D and E may need access to all other LANs. The bridges are configured to forward all messages with the MAC source addresses of D and E, but to filter access of all messages with the A, B, or C source addresses.

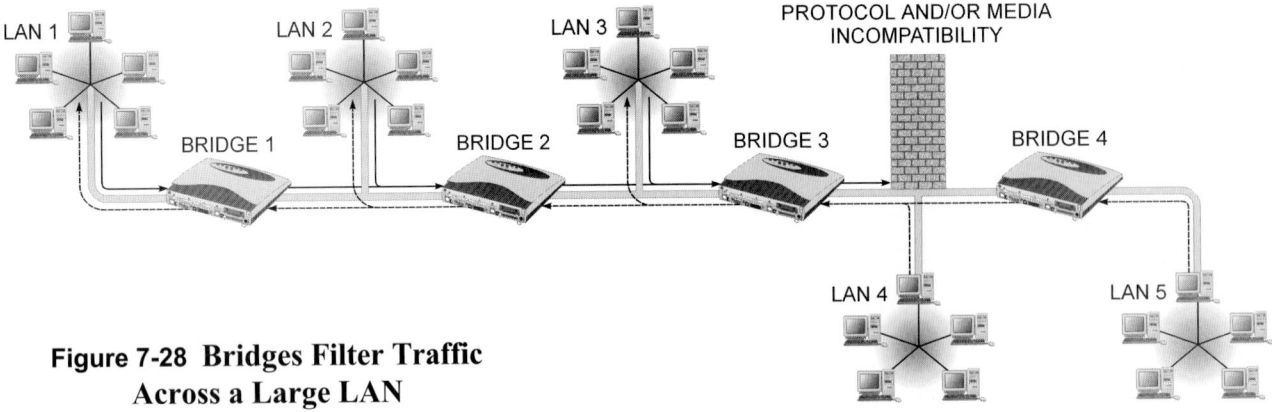

**Figure 7-28 Bridges Filter Traffic
Across a Large LAN**

In addition to extending networks beyond their physical limitations, and to segment users in various workgroups, bridges also provide an interconnection for differing access methods. For example, IEEE 802.3 CSMA/CD (Ethernet) may be connected to an IEEE 802.5 Token Ring network by bridging the two, or these two may be bridged to a fiber-optic FDDI network. To prevent data from circulating around a large bridge network, the **Spanning Tree Algorithm** (described in IEEE 802.1) is employed.

A Spanning Tree Protocol is associated with Ethernet LANs. In Figure 7-29(a), five bridges connect various LANs. When the system is first started, one of the bridges will become the root bridge. From the root bridge, a tree topology will develop based upon a specific path determination process. Figure 7-29(b) shows a typical Spanning Tree Topology.

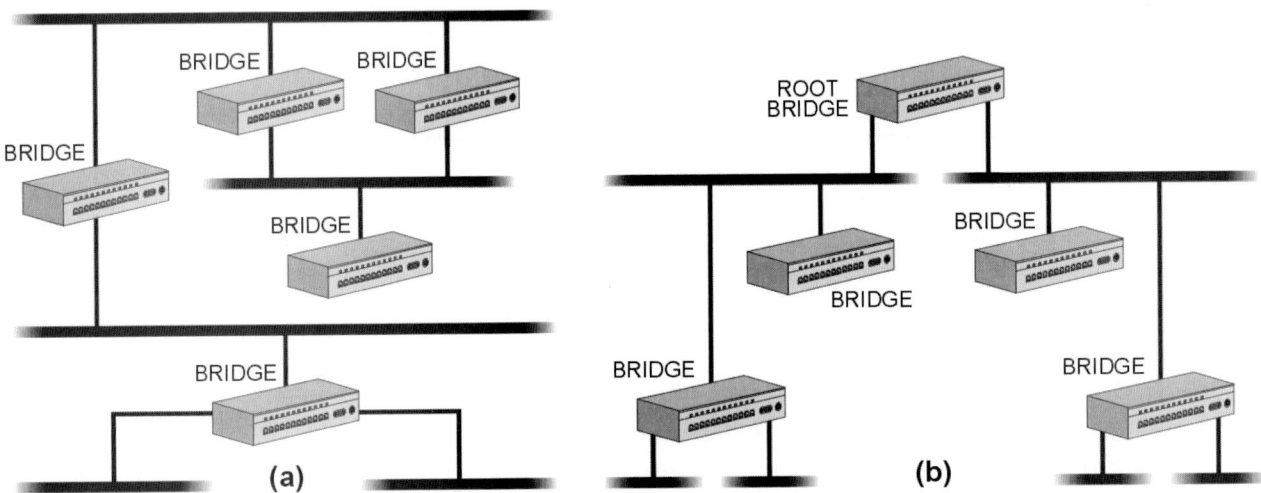

Figure 7-29 Spanning Tree Topology

The root bridge is the bridge with the highest priority, called the **bridge ID**. The bridge ID is composed of two parts, **bridge priority** and the unique **MAC address**. The bridge priority is a two-byte field that's usually set at a default value by the bridge vendor. For example, the default bridge priority for Cabletron is 8000/8001, and for Cisco it's 128.

The MAC address is the address of the bridge, which is considered a node on the network, the same as a PC is a network node. The field is in the extended mode, at six bytes in length.

The bridge that has the lowest numerical value, between the bridge priority and the MAC address, will have the highest priority. The bridge with the highest priority becomes the root bridge, the bridge from which the remainder of the topology is developed.

The logical placement of the remaining bridges is based upon a **Path Determination** process. First, the cost of the path is evaluated. A rule-of-thumb method for estimating the path cost is to divide 1000 by the bandwidth of the network.

$$PC = 1000 / BW$$

For example, the path cost of a 10 MBPS Ethernet network is:

$$PC = 1000/BW$$
$$= 1000/10$$
$$= 100$$

The lowest value is chosen. Keep in mind, there may be many LANs bridged together and operating at several different data rates.

Next, the port priority is calculated. This is based upon the status of the bridge at the time of configuration. The various port states include disabled, blocked, listening, learning, and forwarding. The lowest value has the highest priority.

Finally, the bridge ID is examined. It is the same ID as discussed above. The path topology will be slanted to those bridges connecting networks operating at high data rates, that are not actively learning or forwarding data, and those with the lowest ID. All bridges will accept the configuration parameters of the root bridge, and remain in the active topology until a network failure occurs.

The parameters of the root bridge specify the general characteristics of the bridged system. The root bridge contains a **Hello Timer** that sets the length for how often **Bridge Protocol Data Units** (BPDUs) are generated. BPDUs are encoded signals that specify the configuration of the topology, or serve notice that the topology will change. BPDUs are addressed to the other bridges from the root, and are typically generated every two seconds.

The root bridge also sets a **Max Age Timer** (equivalent to the time-to-live mechanism used with TCP/IP) that specifies the length of time a bridge will wait to receive a BPDU. This is typically set for twenty seconds. Once the timer expires, a topology-change notification BPDU will be sent, and the bridges will reconfigure.

A **Forward Delay Timer**, set by the root bridge, specifies the length of time the bridge will remain in each port state. This is generally set for fifteen seconds. The port states, as previously mentioned, are disabled, blocking, listening, learning, and forwarding. The root-bridge parameters, established by the root bridge, are summarized in Table 7-5.

Table 7-5 Root Bridge and Path Determination

ROOT BRIDGE DETERMINATION	
Bridge ID	Bridge Priority—2 bytes
	Unique MAC Address—6 bytes
Bridge Priority Default	Set by Vendor
Root Bridge	Lowest Numerical Total / Highest Priority
PATH DETERMINATION	
Bridge ID	Bridge Priority—2 bytes
	Unique MAC Address—6 bytes
Path Cost	= 1000 / BW in MBPS
Port Priority	Lowest Numerical Total / Highest Priority

The most serious drawback to the Spanning Tree Topology is that redundant links are maintained in the event of a failure. This is done so that a message will not circle endlessly on a network. If a link should fail, the stand-by link is inserted automatically. While the system reduces errors, it also requires additional bandwidth that may never be used.

Bridging Methods

Once the Spanning Tree Topology is set up, there are several methods available to bridge networks. The most common are Learning, Source Routing, Encapsulation, Translation, and Source Route Translation.

Learning, or transparent, bridging is shown in Figure 7-30.

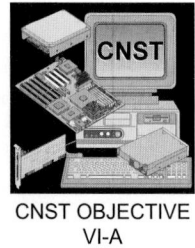

CNST OBJECTIVE
VI-A

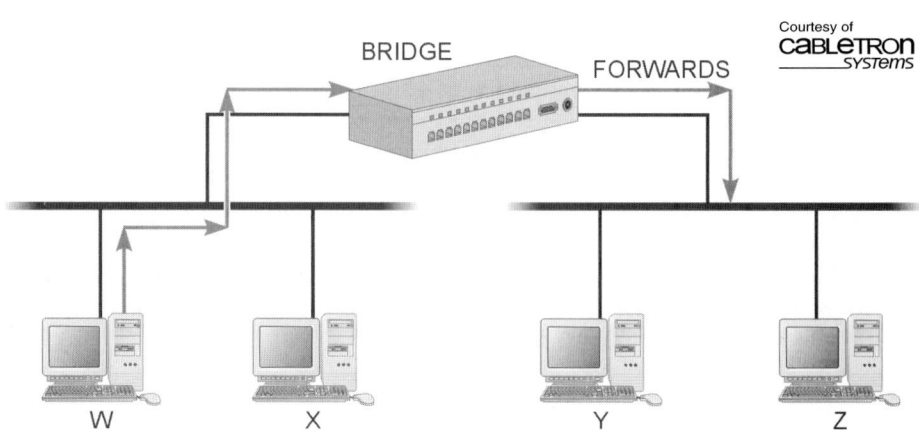

Figure 7-30 Learning, or Transparent, Bridging

A learning, or transparent, bridge is a bridging method that relies on the bridge-compiling maps containing the location of the network nodes.

A learning bridge maintains a **Source Address Table** (SAT) for compiling a map of all addresses on the network. The bridge learns the addresses as the nodes communicate, and stores them in memory. In Figure 7-30, W is sending to X. All transmissions are first routed through the bridge. The bridge then updates the SAT with the learned address of X. The bridge doesn't know what LAN segment X resides in. It forwards the frame to the same segment since X may be located there.

When X responds, the bridge updates the SAT with the address of X. It can do this because all TCP/IP headers contain the destination address. In the future, when W sends to X, or X sends to W, the bridge will filter the frame from any other segments. This is similar to the bridged networks of Figure 7-28. The bandwidth needed to link the two LANs is now available for those that are not on the same segment.

If W sends a message to Z on the other segment, it would first be sent to the bridge. The bridge looks up the address in the SAT and forwards it on to the other segments. If the bridge did not have the Z address in its SAT, it would route it back to the first segment, but since the nodes on that segment would not accept it, the message would return to the bridge. Now, it would be sent to the second segment. Once Z responds, the bridge will add its address to the SAT.

This process continues, with the bridge SAT being updated each time one of the stations communicates with another. In this way, the bridge is learning the addresses of the stations. Transparent bridges learn from the source MAC address. They are used to connect Ethernet, Token Ring, and FDDI networks.

Encapsulation is a bridging method in which the MAC data frame is encapsulated by the network header. The network header is then used as the address identifier for routing the message.

In an **encapsulation bridge**, the MAC frame is encapsulated by the headers of a **transit network frame**. This type of bridge is common where many bridges are used to connect many LANs, or in a situation in which the LANs are connected to a network backbone feeder. A backbone is traditional LAN technology—Ethernet, for example—that feeds sub networks through bridges. Typically, the backbone is constructed of wide-bandwidth media, such as fiber-optic cable. Figure 7-31 illustrates encapsulational bridging.

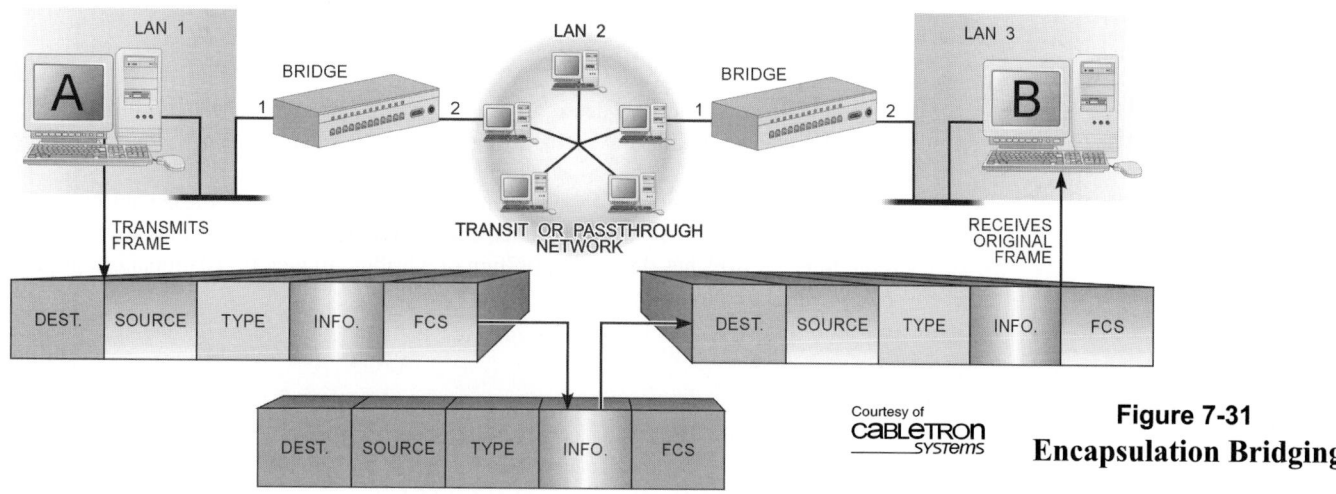

Courtesy of
CABLETRON
SYSTEMS

Figure 7-31
Encapsulation Bridging

Station A, on LAN-1, is sending a message to station B, on LAN-3. To get to the third network, the message passes through the second network, labeled TRANSIT. The MAC frame of station A is encapsulated with headers of the transit network by the bridge. The headers tell the bridges, en route to the destination network, that the frame is to be passed through any network whose header is encapsulating the source frame.

Once the original frame arrives at the destination network, the transit network header is removed and the frame is transmitted on to the destination station.

To use an encapsulation bridge, the MAC types must be the same: CSMA/CD to CSMA/CD, or FDDI to FDDI. They are used primarily with Ethernet and FDDI. Encapsulational schemes are traditionally proprietary, which means they will not support stations connected to other vendors' bridges, through the transit network. This may limit future growth or expansion.

CNST OBJECTIVE
VI-A

> In a **translation bridge**, the source MAC frame is converted to the frame type of the destination network.

For example, in Figure 7-32, a station on the Ethernet network is sending a frame to a station on the Token-Ring network. The source frame, from the Ethernet LAN, is first translated to the frame format of the network connected to the other side of the first bridge, which in this case, is a token bus network.

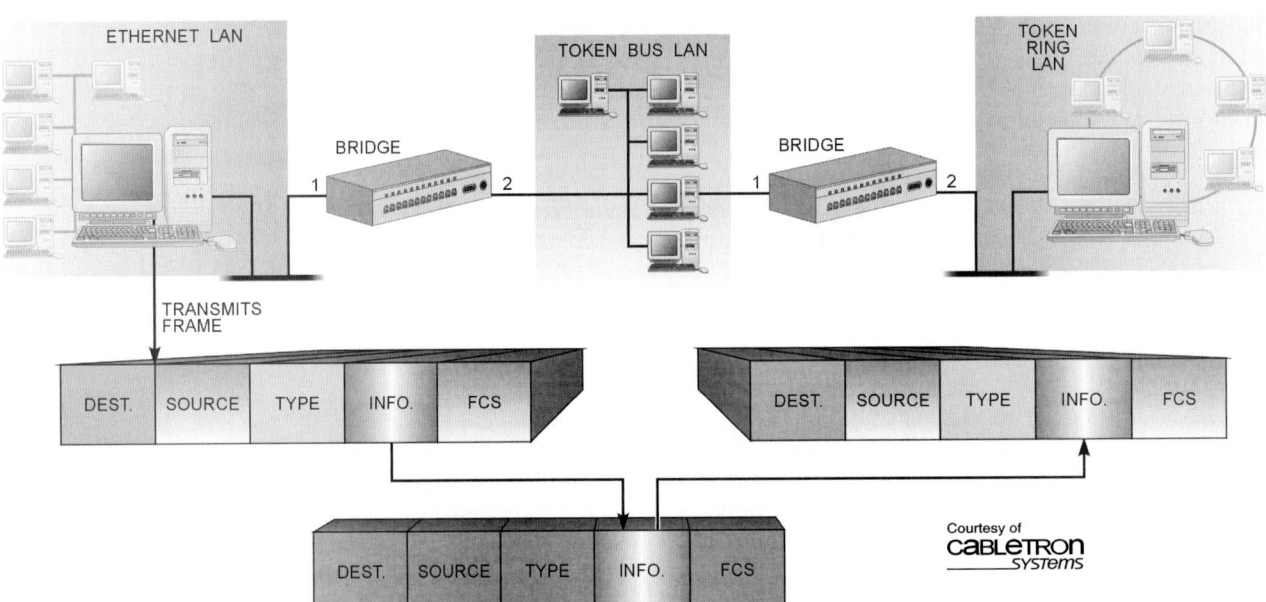

Figure 7-32 Translation Bridging

Since the token bus is not the destination network, the frame is translated to the next networks' frame type. This is the token-ring LAN, and is the destination of the message.

Translational bridges are cited for their interoperability. This refers to the capability of the bridge to work in many LAN environments, and across the product lines of many vendors. Their intelligence stretches the very definition of a bridge. In fact, translational bridges are frequently called **brouters**.

A brouter (bridge/router) is used to interconnect LANs (it's MAC-protocol specific as opposed to a router, which isn't), and also contains routing capabilities that allow packets to be forwarded outside of the subnet domain.

A bridge must work within the local environment, since it doesn't have the ability to route to a network address other than its own. A brouter collects and maintains IP and MAC addresses, and may be called upon to supply these from a transmitting node.

Token-Ring LANs use the IBM bridging method, **Source Routing**. The bridge path is determined by the source station. The bridge examines the Access-Control field of the source frame for the routing information. A variation of the protocol, **Source Route Transparency**, provides either Source Route, Transparent, or Translation bridging when converting from Token Ring to Ethernet.

NET+ OBJECTIVE
I.4.1

Deciding when to use a bridge and when to use a more complex and expensive router can be a daunting decision. Table 7-6 summarizes some of the salient features of both.

Table 7-6 Bridge and Router Differences

ITEM	BRIDGES	ROUTERS
Multiple Active Paths?	Limited due to Spanning Tree Topologies.	Multiple active parallel (meshed) paths available.
Topology Reconfiguration after Network Failure?	Slower, due to network loops.	Reconfiguration is speedy.
Total Number of Stations?	Limited.	Potentially unlimited.
Broadcast Storm Protection?	No.	Filtering uses available bandwidth more effectively.
Packet Size Limits?	Yes.	No.
Congestion Updates?	No.	Yes.
Cost-Effectiveness?	Typically better than routers.	Getting more cost-effective.
Protocol Transparency?	Yes.	No.
Administration and Configuration?	Less required than routers.	More required than bridges.

CNST OBJECTIVE
VI-A

Gateways

A gateway is used to convert from one type of data-communication system to another. For example, it may convert from a system built around the OSI seven-layer architecture to IBM's SNA architecture. It not only physically links the systems, it converts from one protocol to another. Figure 7-33 illustrates a gateway.

NET+ OBJECTIVE
I.4.1

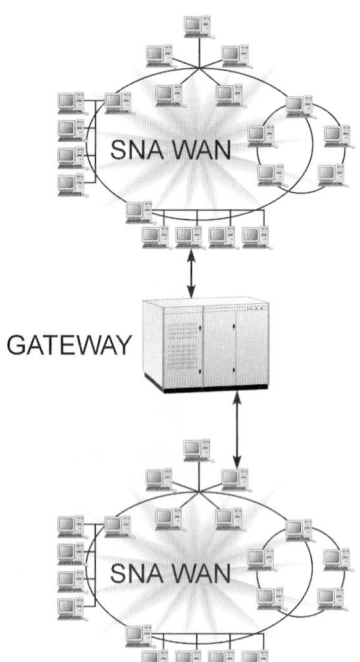

Figure 7-33 Gateways Convert Between Data Communication Systems

The OSI-based system is incompatible with IBM's SNA. However, it's not uncommon for a data-communication network to grow into large entities on the foundation of disparate architectures. At some point, a decision must be made to either scrap them and rebuild, or attempt to merge the systems. The gateway of Figure 7-33 is used to merge the systems.

Gateways must encompass all aspects of a data-communication solution. Figure 7-34 shows the layer of interaction for repeaters, bridges, routers, and gateways. The gateway provides protocol conversion in both directions across the full spectrum of the model; it must do the same for the other architecture it converts to. For this reason, gateways are usually restricted to one type of device conversion. For example, a PC gateway is only for PCs, and will not work with remote terminals.

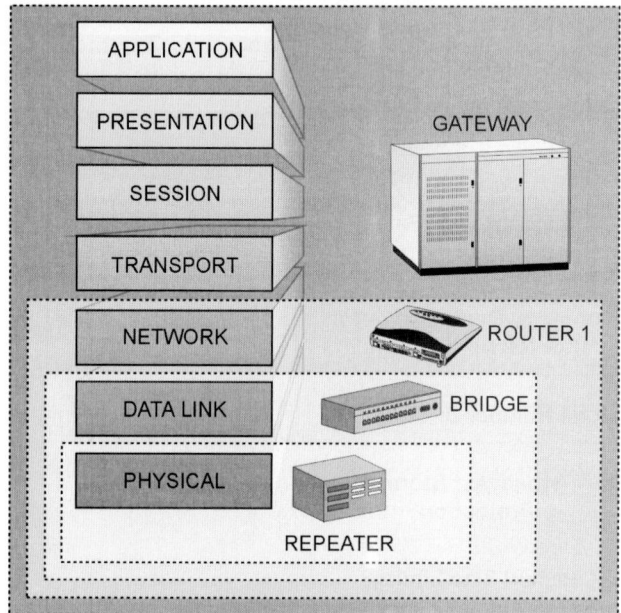

Figure 7-34 Interconnect Technology Interacts with Distinct Layers of the OSI Model

KEY POINTS REVIEW

This chapter has presented an extensive exploration of network operations.

- An interconnected network is a system of interconnected terminals, or local networks, spread over a large area.

- TCP/IP is a widely used, internetworking protocol that is nonproprietary. It is based on a 32-bit addressing scheme, and is the IP used on the Internet.

- Fragmentation results when datagrams are separated to accommodate the frame lengths of networks through which they pass en route to the destination.

- The internet address system is separated into five classes that specify the numbers of networks and hosts. The address follows the Decimal Dotted Notation procedure for grouping addresses.

- A repeater regenerates network signal bits. Used to link LAN segments, a repeater lacks the ability to route data.

- A bridge, working at the Data Link level, connects networks. Bridges are independent of network protocols, and are frequently used to interconnect LANs with different access methods.

- The Spanning Tree Protocol is a logical topology used to organize bridged networks. Fallback links are established to prevent packets from circling endlessly in the network.

- A learning, or transparent, bridge is a bridging method that relies on the bridge-compiling maps containing the location of the network nodes.

- Encapsulation is a bridging method in which the MAC data frame is encapsulated by the network header. The network header is then used as the address identifier for routing the message.

- In a translation bridge, the source MAC frame is converted to the frame type of the destination network.

- Source routing is an IBM bridging method used for token-ring networks. The control field of the source frame contains the routing information.

- A router provides an interconnection between networks using the same network layer protocols.

- Advance Resolution Protocol is a router protocol that maps the physical address of a node to the logical address. Three types of ARP protocols are: normal, proxy, and reverse-ARP.

- A gateway converts data from one communication architecture to another.

At this point, review the objectives listed at the beginning of the chapter to be certain that you understand and can perform them. Afterward, answer the review questions that follow to verify your knowledge of the information.

Lab Exercises

The lab manual that accompanies this book contains hands-on lab procedures that reinforce and test your knowledge of the theory materials presented in this chapter. Now that you have completed your review of Chapter 7, refer to the lab manual and perform Procedures 8, "Client TCP/IP Configuration," 9, "Win 9.X Peer-to-Peer Configuration," 10, "Cisco HP 10Base-T Hub Configuration," 11, "File Shares in Peer-to-Peer LAN," 12, "Planning a Network Installation," 13, "Windows NT 4.0 Server Install, Setup and Configuration," 14, "Client Configuration with Windows 95," 15, "User Account Configuration for Windows NT," 16, "Creating Windows NT Global Groups," 17, "Sharing Windows NT User Directories," 18, "Managing User Accounts on NTFS," 19, "File and Directory Audits," and 20, "Install and Configure Network Printer."

LAB MANUAL

REVIEW QUESTIONS

The following questions test your knowledge of the material presented in this chapter:

1. Examine the Type of Service field shown in Figure 7-11. What layer of the OSI model is represented in the field?

2. Why are TCP/IP datagrams often fragmented into smaller frames?

3. What is the purpose of an internetworking bridge?

4. Describe how a Learning Bridge is used.

5. What are the advantage and disadvantages of a router?

6. Describe the procedure for locating a destination node by using the Broadcast ARP.

7. What is a Normal ARP?

8. What is the purpose of a brouter?

9. At what layer of the OSI reference model do routers operate?

10. What is the function of the port numbers used with TCP/IP?

11. Describe the difference between dynamic and static routing.

12. What is the default subnet mask for a class B IP address?

13. What is the purpose of using a gateway?

14. In a TCP frame format, how many bits are reserved for the destination port?

15. What is the maximum number of stations permitted for an Ethernet LAN?

MULTIPLE CHOICE QUESTIONS

1. The time-to-live field in the TCP/IP header is used to:
   a. Specify the time that a datagram may remain on the network.
   b. Specify the time of data bits.
   c. Specify the time before each network reconfiguration.
   d. Specify the end of a frame.

2. Convert the following Class B, TCP/IP address to a base ten number:
   10000110.10001101.01001010.00010111
   a. 23.74.141.134
   b. 74.134.23.141
   c. 134.141.74.23
   d. 141.23.134.74

3. How is a subnetwork identified using TCP/IP?
   a. By the binary number 10101010.
   b. By the decimal number 255.255.255.
   c. By the decimal number 127.127.
   d. By the binary number 1010.101010.

4. A bridge is used to:
   a. Interconnect only networks of the same access protocol.
   b. Interconnect networks of different access protocols.
   c. Reroute data around LANs.
   d. Replace multiple repeaters.

5. In a learning bridge:
   a. The MAC frame is encapsulated into the network header.
   b. Each bridge translates the address.
   c. The bridge learns the node addresses as they communicate.
   d. The bridge learns the addresses by sending data to each node.

6. When a router uses a normal ARP:
   a. The destination station responds to the ARP.
   b. The router defaults to a bridge.
   c. The router provides the destination address to the requester.
   d. A request for a station's address is sent to all network hosts.

7. When a router uses a reverse ARP:
   a. The address is left unknown.
   b. The frame is sent among routers until the correct network accepts it.
   c. Routing decisions are left to repeaters.
   d. The destination station seeks the sending station.

8. The purpose of a gateway is:
   a. To convert from one type of data communication system to another.
   b. To regenerate data frames.
   c. To provide access to a LAN.
   d. To acknowledge the receipt of routing decisions.

9. An IP address consists of:
   a. A network address only.
   b. 16 bits.
   c. A host address only.
   d. 32 bits.

10. Which of the following is not an ARP?
    a. Normal
    b. Proxy
    c. Forward
    d. Reverse

Network+ Practice Test

Additional Net+ Certification testing is available on the CD that accompanies this text. The testing suite on the CD provides Study Card, Flash Card, and Run Practice type testing. The Study Card and Flash Card feature enables you to electronically link to the section of the book in which the question is covered. Choose questions from the test pool related to this chapter.

CHAPTER 8

WIDE AREA NETWORKS

Upon completion of this chapter and its related lab procedures, you should be able to perform the following tasks:

1. Identify the basic attributes, purpose and function of a gateway, as both a default IP router, and as a method to connect dissimilar systems or protocols.

2. Demonstrate knowledge of TCP/IP fundamentals to include the purpose of DHCP, WINS, DNS, POP3, SMTP, and the purpose of Internet domain name server hierarchies.

3. Explain remote connectivity concepts associated with the distinction between PPP and SLIP, the purpose and function of PPTP and the conditions under which it's used, and the attributes, advantages and disadvantages of ISDN and the telephone (POTS) system.

4. Explain the difference between routable and non-routable protocols.

5. Provide a working definition of a wide area network.

6. Describe how domain names are mapped to IP addresses on the Internet.

7. Describe the ITU model for X.25 packet switching.

8. Draw a block diagram of the X.25 frame format, and state the function of each field.

9. Describe a X.25 exchange using the LAPB protocol.

10. Discuss the reasons that Fast Packet services have emerged.

11. Draw and label a simple sketch of a Frame Relay network.

12. Discuss the advantage of Frame Relay over X.25.

13. Discuss the advantage of ATM over X.25.

14. Describe the relationship of ATM to BISDN.

15. Provide a brief summary of the following routing protocols: RIP, IGRP, OSPF and BGD.

Wide Area Networks

INTRODUCTION

A wide area network covers a large geographical area. How large? Well, larger than a campus setting, or a town. Normally we think of a WAN as interconnecting networks spread around a country or around the world. The Internet is a WAN. A network linking San Francisco, Miami and New York is a WAN. But what about a collection of a dozen LANs in New York City that are interconnected? They cover a relatively small area, so they're LANs. But New York has more people in it than many states, so it's not so small. Then it's a WAN. But they're only LANs. Okay, it's a big LAN. But they're all hooked together. Then it's a WAN. They are a system of interconnected networks, and interconnected networks are generally considered to be a WAN.

Slowly, then, a new definition of a WAN has begun to emerge. A WAN is a network of interconnected networks, and they may cover about any size geographical area. We're beginning to associate the phrase "wide area" to mean a lot of nodes, rather than a big land-mass area. Still, the geographical description remains valid, as well.

In this chapter, think of a WAN most appropriately as the Internet, a true network of networks. We don't know how big the Internet is, since it's autonomous from governments and private industry. One thing is for sure, the Internet is a phenomenon that you have had the great fortune to witness, an incredibly rich window that levels the playing field in terms of knowledge and access to information.

There are numerous ways to access the Internet, and we'll take a look at several of them along with a couple of technologies that have been around for many years, and show no signs of going away. You'll see how the Internet works and review some of the services that are available on it.

And, finally, we'll tour protocols used in routing between networks. Routers represent the glue that holds interconnected networks together by finding paths from one to the other.

NET+ OBJECTIVE
I.1.7

CNST OBJECTIVE
I-A

THE INTERNET

The Internet is a network of networks. It began in the United States in 1969, when four universities—UCLA, UCSB, Stanford Research Institute, and the University of Utah—became four interconnected nodes without a defined exit point. The four sites used different computers to transfers files, and later, e-mail. The interconnection of the four sites originated as a research project funded by the **Defense Advance Research Projects Agency** (DARPA).

DARPA was studying the architecture and protocols of interconnect technology as a defense strategy. The Department of Defense wanted a method of connecting computers, built by different vendors, that allowed them to be able to communicate with each other. That way, if a communication link was lost during battle, an alternative path could be used through another computer system. Developments from 1969 to the present have accelerated the advancement of interconnect technology at a break-neck pace.

> The Internet is a network of networks.

Early protocols, from the beginnings of the Internet, evolved into what would become the present-day TCP/IP suite of interconnect protocols by 1974. These protocols were tested across a wide area network known as **ARPANET**.

ARPANET was a very successful internetworking system, connecting several large research universities, government research centers, as well as a few vendors (notably IBM). As the system grew, the Department of Defense decreed that all users on the Internet employ TCP/IP protocols as an interim strategy, prior to the full development of the ISO OSI Reference Model. At the same time, the ARPANET was split into two groups, due to the size and complexity of the network. The two groups were called the ARPANET, used for additional research in internetworking; and **MILNET**, used for military applications of the technology.

Researchers at the University of California at Berkeley pioneered many aspects of TCP/IP. It became the official wide-area protocol for the Internet in 1982, which, incidentally, was the year the name "Internet" became an official noun.

These scientists used computers with an early version of the UNIX operating system, and in particular, the UNIX utilities that made it simple for users to implement TCP/IP applications. In essence, the quasi standard of internetworking protocols, TCP/IP, had UNIX as a base for its implementation. This is why TCP/IP does not work as well with DOS-based PCs, as with UNIX machines. DOS was intended for stand-alone computers, whereas internetworking was designed into UNIX PCs.

In 1985, the National Science Foundation funded access to its six regional research centers, in the United States, through the ARPANET system. The NSF extended its interest in internetworking by building a long-haul backbone network, operating on a T-1 line at 1.544MBPS, that made access easier. At this point, all of the supercomputers, owned by the NSF, were accessible through ARPANET. In the same year, the NSF partly funded a series of regional networks connecting university research centers to its high-speed backbone, which allowed scientists access to the large computers of the NSF.

The NSF, as the major source of funding and support for the Internet, changed the name of the ARPANET backbone, and regional centers, to **NSFNET**. The NSF was technically the Internet, and access was limited to organizations performing research or educational pursuits—which generally means large universities. But in 1991, the NSF lifted the no-commercial restrictions from the Internet, and in 1995, the NSFNET reverted back to its original status as a research network. The World Wide Web was introduced in 1991, and in 1995, it passed more traffic that any other Internet service. This means that the Web has only been around for less than 10 years! Phenomenal, isn't it?

Originally, you had to pay a hefty fee to directly access the Internet. These days, you pay a nominal fee, and agree (that is, your access service provider agrees) to pass packets intended for other portions of the vast system. Typically, a single-PC subscriber in a residence pays about $20 a month for an Internet connection. All you need is a PC, a modem, the correct protocols (TCP/IP), and a socket to start the transaction.

These software routines are routinely included in off-the-shelf operating system software, such as Windows 95 or 98.

No one owns the Internet—no government, private business, or individual. No one regulates it, either. The closest entity to a regulator is The Internet Society, which is tasked to develop the architecture of the Internet. In recent years, however, many governments around the world have tried to bring it under some type of centralized control (with varying amounts of success), but that control has remained elusive, mostly because the Internet spans national and geographical boundaries. What's legal in this country may be illegal in another country; and if the questionable item originates in this country, how can another country forbid its inclusion on the Internet without first changing the laws of this country?

There's some consensus as to what's illegal—child pornography and credit card fraud, for example. In the United States, it's generally recognized that if "you use it on the Internet in this country, and it's illegal, it doesn't matter where it originates." The ethical and legal debates surrounding the Internet rage daily, with little chance that they'll be sorted out any time soon.

No one knows for sure how many computers are connected to the Internet. Certainly, the number is in the millions. Through subnetting of host computer addresses, the number of computers and users have spiraled beyond the point of reasonable tracking. A list of domain addresses (as in www.microsoft.com, for example) can be assembled, but that doesn't take into account the hundreds or thousands of PCs subnetted to a single, host address.

Virtually all large universities, and private and public research centers, are connected. Most businesses have an Internet presence. Thousands more users have access to portions of the Internet—from its large databases, to e-mail, to the World Wide Web, and to all of the services that are available.

CNST OBJECTIVE
VI-C

What services are available? The World Wide Web (WWW), Gopher, FTP (File Transfer Protocol), Telnet, and e-mail, to name a few. In addition, there are dozens of subsets, including Internet Relay Chat (IRC, also called Chat), mail lists, live video, Voice-over-Internet, etc. The list continues to grow daily.

The WWW is the graphical area of the Internet and is where most of us spend our time—cruising the Web. It requires a graphical interface such as Microsoft Explorer or Netscape Navigator. With the point-and-click capabilities of Web browsers (first popularized by Mosaic), we're free from knowing any of the specialized syntax used with the Internet. For the most part, it resembles Unix commands but with a Web browser, you needn't concern yourself with command prompts that look like dollar signs, forward slashes, or odd looking extensions such as -r.

NET+ OBJECTIVE
I.7.1

The Web, much like the graphical interface pioneered by Apple, brought the Internet to all of us. Rapidly (literally, less that five years), the Web has been extended to include all services on the Internet. At least the browser hides the initiation behind our requests, so that from a Web site, we can start an e-mail program, and it runs transparently under the browser, or files may be downloaded using FTP from another Web site.

> The Web is the graphical area of the Internet. Other services available from the Internet include file transfers, telnet, and e-mail.

However, the other Internet services remain. For example, Gopher, a giant database, originally consisted of a series of menus that compiled information on the Internet.

The most famous gopher was at the University of Minnesota, and you can still go there today to sample the feel of it. Beginning at a top-level menu, you could descend for what seemed like forever, moving from one heading to the next. Search tools were available, and the most widely used one was called Archie. Much of the information originally contained at the gopher sites has now been converted to Web sites.

NET+ OBJECTIVE
I.7.1

Telnet is a service which allows you to "telephone-net" into another computer. The original idea was that if you were in Atlanta, and needed access to information stored on a computer in Dallas, you could telnet into it. The information was presented on your terminal screen, just as if you were sitting in Dallas at a terminal connected directly to the Dallas computer. Telnet remains, but its application is specialized and limited. Originally, you could visit the Library of Congress by telnetting to their site. Now, you go via the Web. Many of the applications invoked using telnet are now handled by servers in a LAN or WAN. Still, telnet is a valuable tool, but its use tends to be specialized for companies, or educational institutions, in which users are working at diskless terminals, or stand-alone PCs, and need access to resources on a large computer.

E-mail still remains intact. It's a separate entity from the Web, and uses a completely different protocol architecture than most of the Internet. Why? The reason is historical. The first e-mail standard was written in 1977 (RFC 733), well before TCP/IP was adopted. File transfers were common in those days, when users, who were primarily academics and researchers, needed a way to discuss their work. E-mail was, and is, a simple method of communicating electronically. It was patterned after the postal system (that is, snail-mail that takes days to get from one address to another), except it's much faster. It calls for simple text messages (in ASCII format—Windows Notepad or Wordpad) that typically are less than 1k bytes in length. With most e-mail software, you can customize your message to include carbon copies, attachments, or links to Web sites.

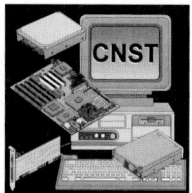

CNST OBJECTIVE
III-A

CNST OBJECTIVE
VI-C

FTP (File Transfer Protocol) is a means of downloading files to your computer, or uploading them from your computer to an FTP site. Like e-mail, FTP retains a distinct structure, probably because it too was introduced early in the formation of the Internet. The widest application of FTP is for downloading software, or software enhancements. For example, many vendors maintain download sections at their Web sites. If you've bought products from them in the past, you can use these sites to download the latest software revisions used in their products. Patches, upgrades or fixes to problems are routinely posted at a company's download area.

No Web browsers directly support FTP, but most include FTP software to initiate and control the download. Both Netscape and Explorer allow you to download from a Web site, for example. As mentioned in the chapter on modems, you can download the most current version of the modem's software by saving the upgrade to a file, them writing it into the memory of the modem. Network interface cards (NICs) can be upgraded in the same way.

For many of us, the Internet is an up-to-date and easily-accessible technical reference library. For business, it's a way to get the message out in a very cost-effective manner, since the Internet—on a cost-per-user basis—is cheap. We visit Web sites to learn about products, as well as to learn about the technology surrounding the product. Many sites include tutorials, written by experts in their fields, that are free from editorial constraints, such as length and complexity, that too often stifle the print media. And, if you're patient, and you follow links to cross-reference facts, you'll forgive writings that aren't clear, are often rambling or occasionally wrong, because these are the creators of the Internet, a vast and sprawling interconnection of diverse networks.

It's an unfortunate occurrence that some sites are protecting specialized information, that not long ago, was freely available in company white papers, but is now only available to verifiable customers.

The Internet, supposedly about free exchange of ideas and practices, exists due to the pursuit, by certain academic pioneers, of an unregulated communication medium that has changed the world in the last decade.

Too often, the papers which are made available on the modern Internet, have a strong marketing slant, so that they tend to read more like an advertisement than an instructional concept paper. It's a trend that we should resist. Those of us who use the Internet as a reference tend to revisit those sites which provide the Internet community with factual, unbiased information. This should also be your approach, while staying away from sites that only want to take from you.

Bulletin Boards are also widely used with the Internet, with more than 2,000 topics currently available. The official name of the Internet bulletin boards is USENET. USENET topics are categorized under seven newsgroups: computers, science, recreational, social, USENET news, miscellaneous, and talk. USENET articles are written by Internet users, covering thousands of subjects. Table 8-1 is a partial listing of topics.

Huge databases, covering topics as diverse as computer networking to recipes for broccoli, are available for viewing, and in some cases, for downloading onto your PC. Access to remote files is typically done with a telnet program, which is an off-the-shelf, software package that allows you to use the public telephone system to log into a remote host from your computer. Once the host is reached, the screen asks for an access code, and login. Both are public login entries, and not protected, as is the case with passwords.

Table 8-2 lists several popular databases.

Internet Chat is similar to e-mail, except it's interactive, and instantaneous. It's the written equivalent to speaking. Terminal conversations are generally topic-oriented, and by using the list command, a user can view descriptions of the current topics, or channels, as they are referred to.

So how does it work? How is it possible to use a local telephone number to access sites all around the world, without paying long-distance charges for the access? Let's take a tour and see how it's done.

Table 8-1 Examples of USENET Topics

Artificial Intelligence
Neural Networks
IBM PCs and Compatible Programs
Cognitive Engineering
Data Communications
Computer Graphics
Employment, Careers
Legalities and Ethics of the Law
Reviews of Star Trek Books, Films, etc.
Antiques
Poems
Food, Cooking, and Recipes
Medicine
Travel

Table 8-2 Example Databases

DATABASE	INFORMATION	ACCESS
History	American history topics.	Telnet: **ukanaix.cc.ukans.edu** Login: **history**
Dartmouth College Library Online System	Info on titles, authors, and publications.	Telnet: **library.dartmouth.edu**
Freenet	News from USA Today, Sports, etc.	Telnet: **freenet-in-{a,b,c}.cwru.edu**
Health Sciences Libraries Consortium	Listings of PC and MAC programs used in health sciences education.	Telnet: **shrwyw.hslc.org** Login: **cbl**
Internet Resource Guide	Internet resources and how to access.	Mail: **info-server@nnsc.nsf.net**
Launchpad	Access to many library systems across the country. Searches and downloads.	Telnet: **launchpad.unc.edu** Login: **launch**
Library of Congress	Records of millions of publications.	Telnet: **locis.loc.gov**
Music Server	Music archives, guitar TAB files, lyrics, MIDI files, and mailing lists.	Anonymous FTP: **ftp.uwp.edu** Path: **/pub/music**
NASA News	Info on current spacecraft and projects.	Finger: **nasanews@space.mit.edu**
PC Magazine	Programs and source code for many PC Magazine utility programs.	Anonymous FTP: **ftp.cco.caltech.edu** Path: **/pub/ibmpc/pcmag**
People on the Internet	Services to search for, and find, someone on the Internet.	Gopher: **yaleinfo.yale.edu** Choose: **People on the Internet**
Searching the Internet	Tools to search the Internet for any specific resource. Uses Archie, Hytelnet, Veronica, Wais, and the WW Web.	Gopher: **yaleinfo.yale.edu** Choose: **Internet Resources | Searching the Internet with...**
Social Security Administration	SSA info, and how to obtain information on others for genealogical purposes.	Anonymous FTP: **oak.oakland.edu** Path: **/pub/misc/ss-info**
Virtual Reality	Articles about single-user virtual reality, with Interactive Fiction archive access.	Anonymous FTP: **ftp.u.washington.edu** Path: **/public/VirtualReality**

CNST OBJECTIVE
VI-C

How the Internet Works

First, let's get some terminology out of the way. Figure 8-1 shows the Microsoft Web site using the Internet Explorer Web browser from Microsoft. We're told we're at this site by looking at the address in the Address field.

http://www.microsoft.com/

So, the Web address for Microsoft is www.microsoft.com. Microsoft also has an IP address. But which is easier to remember—a name, or a number? For most people, the name-version of the address is the least challenging. But machines connected to the Internet only understand numbers—binary numbers, at that. We use naming conventions because they're easier for us to remember and track, but a machine needs to be able to convert from the name that's entered in an address box, to a numerical address.

NET+ OBJECTIVE
I.6.1

Figure 8-1 Microsoft Web Site

A Web address, called a URL, follows the Domain Name System convention. A DNS must be mapped to an IP address, since the two can't be derived from one another.

CNST OBJECTIVE
VI-C

The service that translates names to numbers (IP addresses) is called the Domain Name System, or DNS. Name abbreviations, which correspond to the decimal address, are separated by decimal points into a series of zones. Table 8-3 lists the top-level zone codes, and their meanings. Domain names are unique on the Internet. The organization that assigns them is called InterNIC (www.internic.org/). If you want to set up a Web site using a domain name for your company, you'd request the name from InterNIC, pay a small fee, and within a couple of days, it's done. Your domain name, which is also your Web site address, is then added to the name servers on the Internet.

DNS is a hierarchial system that begins with root name servers, as shown in Figure 8-2. There are about a dozen root servers, and these servers represent the single periods in domain names, as in "." A root server knows where top-level domain name servers are located. For example, if the address you're trying to reach is a .com address, the root server will direct you to a top-level server for .com. There are top-level DNS servers for .org, .net, .edu, and so on. Each top-level DNS server has authority for a domain.

Table 8-3 Top-Level Zone Codes

ZONE	DESCRIPTION
com	Commercial Business
edu	Educational Institution
gov	Government Agency
int	International Organization
mil	Military Site
net	Networking Organization
org	Miscellaneous Non-Profit Organization

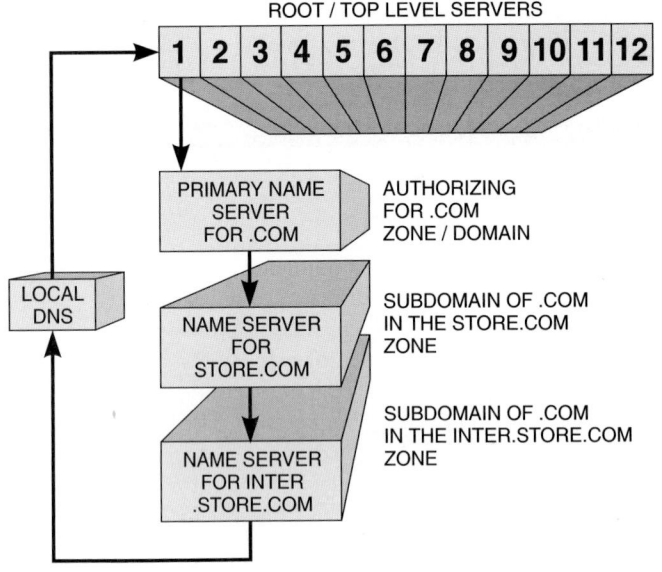

ROOT / TOP LEVEL SERVERS

| 1 | 2 | 3 | 4 | 5 | 6 | 7 | 8 | 9 | 10 | 11 | 12 |

LOCAL DNS

PRIMARY NAME SERVER FOR .COM — AUTHORIZING FOR .COM ZONE / DOMAIN

NAME SERVER FOR STORE.COM — SUBDOMAIN OF .COM IN THE STORE.COM ZONE

SUBDOMAIN OF .COM IN THE INTER.STORE.COM ZONE

NAME SERVER FOR INTER .STORE.COM

Figure 8-2 DNS Server Hierarchy

The authority for a domains is frequently delegated to a subdomain. The DNS server of a subdomain has authority for a zone residing at the subdomain. A subdomain may be further subdivided into more intricate DNS servers that have authority for narrow zones within that subdomain.

Let's look at a fictional example, using the pseudo Internet name of **store.inter.com**. Let's further pretend that the name originates from a retail company called Store, and that it has divisions for Internet products, telecommunications products, and consumer electronics products. The address is read from right to left, and is interpreted as:

1. com—specifies the user as a commercial site.

2. store—represents a subdomain of the .com zone/domain. Some companies use this convention to physically and logically separate their Internet sites. This is often the case with large companies that have a diverse product offering. Note that store.com may also be an equally valid address but will always be associated with inter.store.com.

3. inter—Describes the name of the company of the commercial site, or, in this example, a division within a company; the Internet division of the company called Store. This is usually an abbreviation of the actual company name, university, government agency, etc. When domain names are selected, most companies try to use a name that represents their actual business, without using a name that's too long (it can contain up to 48 characters).

So, for the Internet address, inter.store.com, a subdomain "inter" is in the subdomain "store" which is in the .com domain. Typically, a Web site address is written in lower-case letters because, at one time, the UNIX-based routers and servers on the Internet could only understand lower case. That's not the situation today, but if your request for an address is passed along to an older machine, it may not be able to correctly interpret an address containing capital letters.

Now, let's see what would happen if the above fictional address was entered in the address of a Web browser. The sequence of events are as follows:

- The local DNS server (the DNS server that your computer is assigned to) would first look to see if it has the domain name in its memory cache. We'll assume it doesn't.

- The local DNS server will query a root DNS server for a match to inter.store.com. Functional DNS servers, such as the local DNS to which our example computer is attached, contain a static list of IP addresses for all root DNS servers.

- The root server will refer your DNS to a list of primary .com (domain) servers.

- Your DNS will select one of the .com servers, and ask it for the address of inter.store.com.

- The .com domain DNS server will refer you to a list of store.com subdomain servers (if there are any).

- Your DNS server will query one of the store.com subdomain DNS servers for inter.store.com.

- The store.com subdomain servers may refer you to a list of subdomain DNS servers for inter.store.com. Or, if there are no additional subdomains, it will return the IP address of inter.store.com.

Once the IP of inter.store.com is located by querying through the DNS server hierarchy, your local DNS server will cache all of the information it returns. The next time you enter inter.store.com, your DNS will match the domain name to the correct IP address, because it has it stored in its cache. This reduces the amount of traffic routed through the root and top-level DNS servers (which, in the United States, are the same server).

NET+ OBJECTIVE
I.6.3

Notice in Figure 8-2 that DNS servers may be classified as a **zone** or **domain**. A zone refers to the range of addresses that a DNS server is responsible for. A domain is the name of the address. Depending on the context, they could mean the same thing. The top-level server is responsible for the .com **zone**, and all domain names within the **zone**. This holds true, unless authority for a domain name has been delegated to a subdomain zone. Inter.com is a sub**domain** of the .com **zone**, and this DNS server is responsible for addresses in the inter.com **zone**.

When you set up an Internet connection, you have the option of selecting the IP address of a Primary DNS and a Secondary DNS. These are two physically different servers which should be located on separate networks. When you apply for the authority of domain names, your server IP is added to the list of domain servers. If your DNS crashes and you don't have a secondary DNS, then requests for IPs to domain names on your server will be returned unanswered—it will appear as if the sites maintained in your DNS server don't exist. So, the usual practice is to have a secondary DNS.

A DNS server is responsible for reconciling domain names to IP addresses.

When you access the Internet, you invoke an application on a port at the Internet interface. HTTP is a "well-known" port, at port number 80. HTTP stands for Hyper-Text Transfer Protocol, and is the protocol used to launch an Internet session using HTML, which stands for Hyper-Text Mark-up Language. Then, to get to the Microsoft Web site, you first specify the application port (port 80) using HTTP. The colon, and forward slashes, are Unix conventions used to separate commands, interfaces, or server files and directories.

CNST OBJECTIVE
VI-C

Next, you specify the address (or **Universal Resource Locator**, URL, as it sometimes called) as **www.microsoft.com/**. The DNS will then begin searching for an IP address that matches the domain name **microsoft.com**. The last / character isn't required, but it's a good idea to include it, because some DNS servers search all microsoft.com addresses, eliminating those with /extensions before returning a result. In some Web browsers, the slash is placed by default when you hit the enter key. If yours doesn't, go ahead and include the forward slash because it speeds up the name-to-IP resolution, and gets you to a site faster.

The www tells the HTTP port that this site is a World Wide Web site—and not an FTP site, or a Gopher, or telnet site. What happens if you don't include it? It depends. At worst, the DNS won't find a match, and at best, it'll default to www. HTTP launches HTML which can be run on an FTP or Gopher site, as well as a Web site, so you should specify which service that you want the DNS to search. For example, if you wanted to go to the Microsoft FTP site, you'd enter the address as ftp://ftp.microsoft.com/. Figure 8-3 is a sample of HTML for the Microsoft homepage shown in Figure 8-1.

```
<HTML>
<HEAD>
<META HTTP-EQUIV="Content-Type" CONTENT="text/html; charset=iso8859-1">
<TITLE>Microsoft Corporation Home Page; Welcome to Microsoft</TITLE>
<META http-equiv="PICS-Label" content=(PICS-1.1 "http://www.rsac.org/ratingsv01.html" l gen true comment "RSACi North America Server" by
"inet@microsoft.com" for "http://www.microsoft.com/" on "1997.06.30T14:21-0500" r (n 0 s 0 v 0 l 0)}>
<META NAME="KEYWORDS" CONTENT="products; headlines; downloads; news; Web site; what's new; solutions; services; software; contests;
corporate news;">
<META NAME="DESCRIPTION" CONTENT="The entry page to Microsoft's Web site. Find software, solutions and answers. Support, and Microsoft
news.">
<META NAME="MS.LOCALE" CONTENT="EN-US">
<META NAME="CATEGORY"CONTENT="home page">

<STYLE TYPE="text/css"> <!--.RED  {color:"#FF0000";}
 BODY {font-family:Verdana, Arial, Helvetica, sans-serif;} -->
</STYLE>

</HEAD>
<BODY LEFTMARGIN="0" TOPMARGIN="0" MARGINWIDTH="0" MARGINHEIGHT="0" BGCOLOR="#FFFFFF" TEXT="#000000" ALINK="#003399"
LINK="#003399" VLINK="#003399">

<SCRIPT TYPE="text/javascript">
<!--if ((navigator.userAgent.indexOf("MSIE")!=-1) && navigator.appVersion.substring(0,1) > 3)        {window.location.replace("/ie40.htm"); }//-->
</SCRIPT>

<!--TOOLBAR_START-->
<TABLE WIDTH="100%" CELLPADDING=0 CELLSPACING=0 BORDER=0 BGCOLOR=BLACK>
<TR>
<TD WIDTH=459 ROWSPAN=2 VALIGN="TOP" NOWRAP ><NOBR><FONT FACE="Arial, Helvetica" SIZE=1><A HREF="/">
<IMG SRC="/library/images/gifs/toolbar/home_on.gif" WIDTH=103 HEIGHT=21 ALT="Microsoft Home" BORDER=0></A><A HREF="/products/"
TARGET="_top"><IMG SRC="/library/images/gifs/toolbar/prod.gif" WIDTH=81 HEIGHT=21 ALT="Products" BORDER=0></A><A
HREF="/isapi/gosearch.asp?TARGET=/"><IMG SRC="/library/images/gifs/toolbar/search.gif" WIDTH=68 HEIGHT=21 ALT="Search"
BORDER=0></A><A HREF="/Support/" TARGET="_top"><IMG SRC="/library/images/gifs/toolbar/support.gif" WIDTH=74 HEIGHT=21 ALT="Support"
BORDER=0></A><A HREF="/referral/default.asp" TARGET="_top"><IMG SRC="/library/images/gifs/toolbar/shop.gif" WIDTH=55 HEIGHT=21
ALT="Shop" BORDER=0></A><A HREF="/isapi/goregwiz.asp?target=/regwiz/regwiz.asp"><IMG SRC="/library/images/gifs/toolbar/write.gif" WIDTH=78
HEIGHT=21 ALT="Write Us" BORDER=0></A></FONT></NOBR></TD>

<TD BGCOLOR="#000000" WIDTH="100%" HEIGHT=20><IMG SRC="/library/images/gifs/homepage/1ptrans.gif" WIDTH=1 HEIGHT=1 ALT=""
BORDER=0></TD>
<TD WIDTH=91 ROWSPAN=2 ALIGN="RIGHT" VALIGN="TOP">
<FONT FACE="Arial, Helvetica" SIZE=1><A HREF="/" TARGET="_top"><IMG SRC="/library/images/gifs/toolbar/msft.gif" WIDTH=91 HEIGHT=21
ALT="Microsoft Home" BORDER=0></A></FONT></TD>
</TR>
<TR>
<TD BGCOLOR="#FFFFFF" WIDTH="100%" HEIGHT=1><IMG SRC="/library/images/gifs/homepage/1ptrans.gif" WIDTH=1 HEIGHT=1 ALT=""
BORDER=0></TD>
</TR>
</TABLE>
<!--TOOLBAR_END-->

<BASEFONT FACE="Verdana, Arial, Helvetica" SIZE="3">

<TABLE CELLPADDING=0 CELLSPACING=0 WIDTH=602 BORDER=0>

<TR><!-- spacer row - specify all others with colspan or rowspan-->
<!--1--><TD WIDTH=135><IMG SRC="/library/images/gifs/homepage/1ptrans.gif" WIDTH=135 HEIGHT=1 ALT="" BORDER=0></TD>
<!--2--><TD WIDTH=1><IMG SRC="/library/images/gifs/homepage/1ptrans.gif" WIDTH=1 HEIGHT=1 ALT="" BORDER=0></TD>
<!--3--><TD WIDTH=8><IMG SRC="/library/images/gifs/homepage/1ptrans.gif" WIDTH=8 HEIGHT=1 ALT="" BORDER=0></TD>
<!--4--><TD WIDTH=109><IMG SRC="/library/images/gifs/homepage/1ptrans.gif" WIDTH=109 HEIGHT=1 ALT="" BORDER=0></TD>
<!--5--><TD WIDTH=12><IMG SRC="/library/images/gifs/homepage/1ptrans.gif" WIDTH=12 HEIGHT=1 ALT="" BORDER=0></TD>
<!--6--><TD WIDTH=35><IMG SRC="/library/images/gifs/homepage/1ptrans.gif" WIDTH=35 HEIGHT=1 ALT="" BORDER=0></TD>
<!--7--><TD WIDTH=10><IMG SRC="/library/images/gifs/homepage/1ptrans.gif" WIDTH=10 HEIGHT=1 ALT="" BORDER=0></TD>
<!--8--><TD WIDTH=160><IMG SRC="/library/images/gifs/homepage/1ptrans.gif" WIDTH=160 HEIGHT=1 ALT="" BORDER=0></TD>
<!--9--><TD WIDTH=9><IMG SRC="/library/images/gifs/homepage/1ptrans.gif" WIDTH=9 HEIGHT=1 ALT="" BORDER=0></TD>
<!--10--><TD WIDTH=121><IMG SRC="/library/images/gifs/homepage/1ptrans.gif" WIDTH=121 HEIGHT=1 ALT="" BORDER=0></TD>
</TR>
```

Figure 8-3   HTML Version of Microsoft Site

HTML is used to create the rich text and graphics that you see on Web pages. An HTML document includes links to other files—identified by the HREF tag—and paths for these links are specified when the link is inserted in the document. The link may go to a different server, in another state, or on another continent. All of the files stream in during a download, and are placed on the screen in the location specified in the HTML code.

Dynamic Host Configuration Protocol (DHCP)

Domain Name Servers maintain a database of domain names and their corresponding IP addresses on the Internet. If you have a computer connected to the Internet, you also need an IP for the desired site to match, so that the contents of the site can be returned to appear on your monitor. That is, the remote server you're connecting to has to have an address in order to send files to your computer. There are a couple of ways to do this.

> DHCP is used to dynamically assign IP addresses to domain names.

One method is to permanently assign an IP address to your computer. If you have a stand-alone modem connected to an ISP from your home, you connect to the ISP using a point-to-point (PPP) protocol. Because it's a point-to-point connection, you don't need a physical MAC-layer address, because your location is implied. There's only you at one end of the connection, and the ISP at the other. The ISP may permanently assign you an IP, and you use this number when setting up the connection.

Another method is for the ISP to dynamically assign IPs, which is the more common situation. A dynamic IP assignment means that each time you initiate the connection through your ISP, you'll be given a different IP address. During your Internet session, this will be your IP, and the address to which a remote server downloads files to your computer.

The protocol used for dynamic IP assignments is called **Dynamic Host Configuration Protocol**, or DHCP. When a computer running a DHCP client is booted, it requests an IP from the DHCP server at the ISP. The ISP has been assigned a block of IPs, and enters this range of addresses when the DHCP parameters are first set up. The DHCP server will assign the IP for a "lease period" that's determined by the network administrator. With an ISP, this may be for the duration of an Internet session, or it may be for a specific time, say three hours. At that time, your IP expires and you loose access to the Internet.

Normally, a DHCP server assigns IPs at boot-up of the client computer, and continues the lease until the client logs-off a network—either a LAN connection or an Internet connection. Windows NT 3.5 and up, as well as Windows 95/ 98, have built in support for DHCP. Figure 8-4 indicates that the IPs for the Internet connection shown are assigned (dynamically) by the ISP. When possible, you should use DHCP for assigning user IPs. The advantages of DHCP include:

- It allows the management of IPs to be centralized. While some may argue that this isn't an advantage, you have to remember that IPs are getting less and less available. If you have a user that signs onto the Internet once in the morning to send and receive e-mail, then dedicating an IP to a single, one-hour daily application is very inefficient.

- An IP is a Network layer function and must be mapped to a physical MAC-layer address. With DHCP you can move a client computer without having to reassign the IP, since it will receive a different IP when it reboots.

- DHCP works side-by-side with static IPs—those IPs that are permanently assigned to a network node such as a router or server. This involves a bit of manual intervention, since the block of dynamic IPs (called the DHCP scope) need to be kept separate from the static IPs.

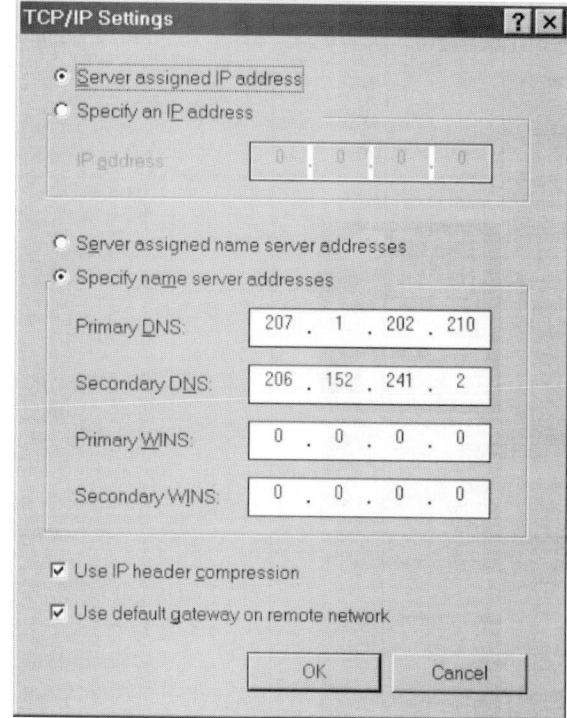

Figure 8-4 Dynamic Assignment of IP Addresses

Windows Internet Naming Service (WINS)

Servers running TCP/IP may also run WINS with Widows NT. WINS contains a look-up table to reconcile computer names to IP addresses. Notice the similarity to the DNS service in which a site is given a name and corresponding IP address. WINS extends to NetBIOS at the Session layer of the OSI model, allowing computer names to be expressed as:

//computername/sharename/path

This is a standard Microsoft convention called Universal Naming Convention (UNC) that's followed with Windows NT. Note that the syntax begins with two forward slashes, followed by the computer name, a single forward slash, then the name of a file, directory, etc. With WINS, you can extend this same convenience to all computers using NT. The advantage is that it relieves you of manually entering NetBIOS and IP addresses for name resolution (This can be done manually in the LMHOST map.) and then manually changing the map tables when there's a change.

> WINS contains a look-up table used to reconcile computer names to IP addresses.

With NetBIOS, a client running NT must broadcast a request for a destination IP. Broadcasts increase traffic on the network, and may in fact be rejected, since not all routers will pass NetBIOS names. If the destination is on a different LAN, this may happen. With WINS, this situation doesn't occur, since a single table lookup is all that's needed to resolve the computer name to an IP address.

Point-to-Point Protocol (PPP)

> The **Point-to-Point Protocol** (PPP) is a communication protocol used to send data across serial communication links.

It's the most widely used wide-area protocol for accessing Internet service providers. Today, it's employed almost universally in stand-alone Internet connections using an ISP, but this wasn't always the case. In the early and late '80s, most of the connections to the Internet were through LANs (with Ethernet being the most common), or public switched networks (X.25). As access to the Internet boomed, the need for resolving IP addresses directly to a desktop computer took on a greater sense of urgency.

Enter PPP. Almost all personal computers support serial, point-to-point communication via EIA/TIA-232 interfaces. Unfortunately, there wasn't a standard that allowed for the encapsulation of IP datagrams to the PC side of the interface. Not only does PPP encapsulate IP frames, it also:

- Assigns and manages IP addresses.

- Communicates in either asynchronous (using start and stop bits) and synchronous (HDLC).

- Can be configured to run more than one Network layer protocol simultaneously. These include IP, IPX, DECnet and Appletalk.

- Includes link configuration, quality testing and error detection.

PPP runs transparently across any Physical layer interface. Typically, these include EIA/TIA-232, V.35, EIA/TIA-422, or EIA/TIA-423. Data rates between the two end points of the link aren't addressed in the protocol. That's left to the physical implementation of the interface. The protocol does require that the link be full-duplex, and use either asynchronous or synchronous operation.

Beyond the physical characteristics of the protocol, PPP specifies three components that comprise the protocol:

- The PPP Link Layer Protocol.

- The PPP Link Control Protocol.

- The PPP Network Control Protocol.

The Link Layer Protocol is based on the structure, frame format and operation of HDLC (High-Level Data Link Control). The frame format of a PPP frame is shown in Figure 8-5. While the format is slightly different than HDLC, its operation is quite similar.

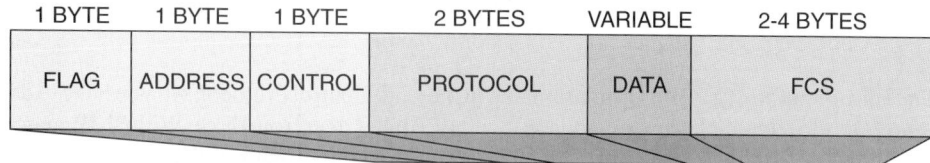

Figure 8-5 PPP Frame Format

Two of the fields in a PPP frame consist of 1-byte **flags** (01111110) that are used to mark the beginning or end of the frame. A 1-byte **address**, containing the bit sequence 11111111, is the standard broadcast address used in HDLC. Since addressing between two points on a link isn't a problem, the actual address is implied by sending frames in the wire between connected nodes. A 1-byte **control** field contains the sequence 00000011. This signifies user data in an unsequenced (LLC, Type 1) frame. The 2-byte **protocol** field identifies the upper-layer protocol encapsulated in the PPP frame. The **data** field contains user data, as well as encapsulated upper-layer frames. By default, the data field is set for a maximum length of 1,500 bytes, but other values are permitted as long as both ends of the connection consent to the larger size. Error detection is handled by the 2-byte **frame check sequence** field. Also, by consent of the communicating stations, this field may be extended to 4-bytes for improved quality of service between the two points.

The Link Control Protocol is responsible for setting up, configuring, maintaining, and terminating the connection. During establishment and configuration, the Maximum Receive Unit (MRU) is specified. The MRU is the maximum length of the data field in the PPP frame. The quality of the link is tested to determine if it's sufficient for communication to occur between the two nodes. Negotiation for Network layer protocols is handled by the Link Control Protocol. Network protocols can be set up and taken down at any time during the communication, and may be run simultaneously. However, both ends of the link have to agree on what protocols will be used.

The Network Control Protocol is concerned with negotiating the dynamic allocation of IP addresses. Depending on the Network layer protocol specified in the protocol field of the PPP frame, this layer will respond differently.

PPP has another advantage in that it can, as an option, employ **authorization protocols**. The purpose of an authorization protocol is to provide a level of security by ensuring that the node requesting a PPP connection is valid.

There are two types of authorization protocols commonly used with PPP:

- Password Authentication Protocol (PAP): This client is authenticated by sending a user name, and password, to the server. The server compares the name and password to its database, and if it's a match, opens the connection.

- Challenge Handshake Authentication Protocol (CHAP): The server generates a random string of bits and sends them, along with its hostname, to the client. The client uses the hostname to look up a cipher key, encrypts the random string, and sends it back to the host. The host uses the same key to decrypt the random string. If it matches the original random string sent to the client, the connection is opened.

CNST OBJECTIVE
IV-B & VI-C

Serial Line Internet Protocol (SLIP) is the forerunner to PPP. It has the same function; to connect nodes in a point-to-point configuration. However, SLIP has some disadvantages when compared to PPP.

SLIP can only transport TCP/IP. PPP cannot only transport multi-Network layer protocols, but it can do them simultaneously. For the user connecting to the Internet from a modem through the telephone system, this doesn't mean much because they will probably be using TCP/IP anyway.

The configuration of a PPP link is automated in the Link Control Protocol. All you have to do is provide the telephone number of the ISP, and PPP takes over from there. With SLIP, many configuration parameters are setup manually. The most important is the IP address. An IP used in a SLIP connection is static; it must be given to you by the ISP and they must give you the IP of the remote server. You enter these when setting up the connections. Other parameters may also need to be setup manually, such as the MRU and Maximum Transmission Unit (MTU), which is the maximum size of a PPP frame.

User authentication can be troublesome in SLIP connections. You have to rely on the ISP for providing a login and password prompt. However, if this differs significantly from the requirements of your computer (operating system, BIOS, etc.), it may not work. To get it to work requires that you make changes to INI login scripts, or create one yourself.

PPP, as mentioned above, verifies clients using either PAP or CHAP. These are standardized for PPP, and routinely included with PPP software.

In summary, SLIP used static assigned IP addresses, while PPP uses dynamically assigned IPs. SLIP lacks the autoconfiguration capabilities of PPP, which means you may have to do some of the configuration manually. SLIP only encapsulates TCP/IP in the data field, which means it won't route Novell (IPX) or Apple (AppleTalk) Network layer protocols.

Point-to-Point Tunneling Protocol (PPTP)

NET+ OBJECTIVE
I.8.1

PPTP is a protocol used to securely transport PPP packets over a TCP/IP network such as the Internet.

PPTP is a protocol used to securely transport PPP packets over a TCP/IP network (the Internet). This makes it an ideal choice for mobile users, or telecommuters, who need access to a remote server, but lack a direct connection for dialing into the server. With PPTP, the user dials into the ISP using a local telephone number, then encapsulates the PPP packet in a TCP/IP frame addressed to the IP of the remote server.

Once the packet arrives at the server the TCP/IP headers are stripped, and the PPP packet, which may be carrying TCP/IP data, or NetBEUI, or IPX packets, is reformatted for the remote server. When responding back to the remote client, the server follows a similar approach. For example, if the remote server is a Windows NT machine, it may encapsulate NetBEUI packets in the PPTP packet, and send them onto the Internet in a TCP/IP packet. At the receiving end, the TCP/IP headers are discarded, and the encapsulated NetBEUI frame is downloaded into the client machine.

PPTP offers two distinct advantages over PPP. It allows non-TCP/IP frames to be sent through the Internet. It requires that data be encrypted (with PPP, encryption is an option) using either PAP or CHAP. The end result is a very secure connection between the client and a remote server that doesn't require the use of expensive dedicated lines between client and server. In effect, a PPTP connection is a virtual private network, since it uses the Internet as the communication medium.

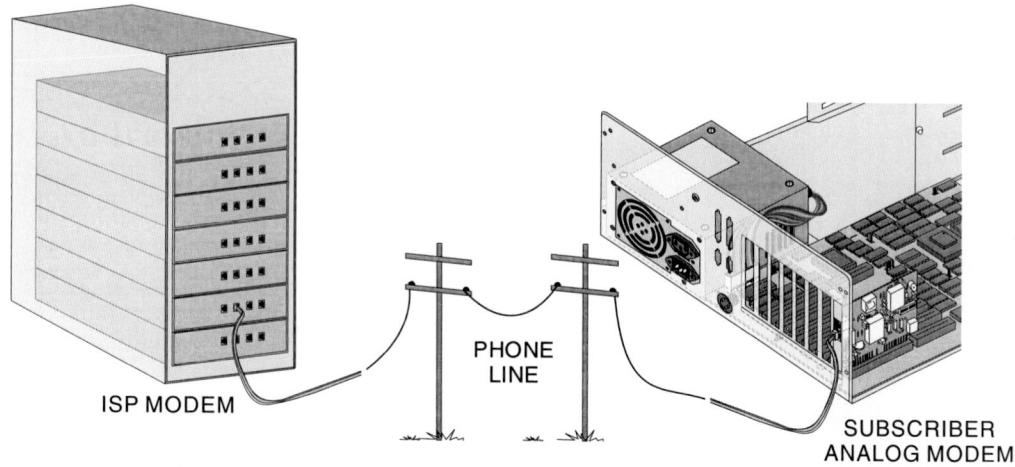

Figure 8-6 PC-to-Internet Connection

Figure 8-6 shows a personal computer connected to the analog telephone system through a modem, and then to the Internet Service Provider.

E-mail

E-mail (electronic-mail) is a system for automatically sending messages from one computer to another, or across the Internet, and generally through a modem over telephone lines. E-mail is a standard offering with Internet access, and is used extensively in businesses as a form of electronic communication.

E-mail is extremely reliable, and can be used to reach a recipient anywhere in the world. There are a couple of reason for this. The first is the almost universal standardized implementation of e-mail, and the second is that it normally communicates through a sort of parallel architecture to the Internet; that is, it tends to have dedicated logical connections and e-mail-specific equipment to handle send and receive functions.

Figure 8-7 shows a typical e-mail screen with headers completed. This is typical of most e-mail software. You're required to insert the recipients e-mail address, specify the sender's e-mail address, and in some packages include a subject. The actual message is entered in the body of the screen, and is in ASCII format.

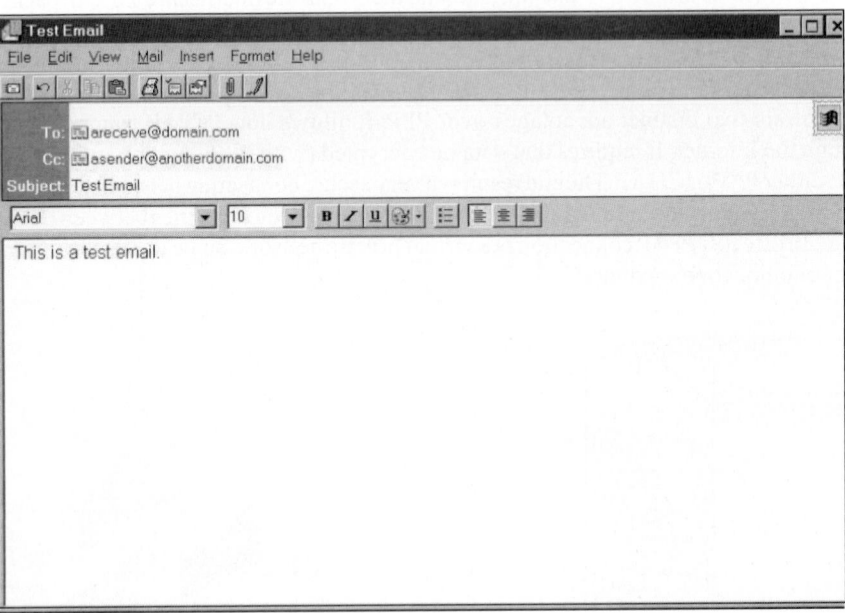

Figure 8-7 E-mail Screen

Notice the format of the sender and receiver names.

> The user name comes before the @ symbol, and usually represents the name of the individual, or business, holding the e-mail account. The domain names of the computer where the e-mail account is maintained are placed after the @ symbol.

You may see that this system is very similar to the DNS used with TCP/IP addressing. When an e-mail is sent, it's first uploaded into an e-mail server (E-mail, as it's organized on most networks, follows a client/server arrangement, with the sender acting as the client and the receiver acting as the server). The local server will query the DNS servers to resolve the receiver's address. Once this is done, the server contacts the remote server that holds the receiver's account and notifies it of a message. The two servers engage in a bit of handshaking that follows the following format:

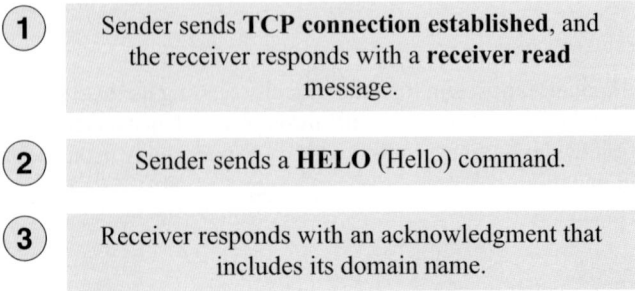

① Sender sends **TCP connection established**, and the receiver responds with a **receiver read** message.

② Sender sends a **HELO** (Hello) command.

③ Receiver responds with an acknowledgment that includes its domain name.

(4) Sender compares the received domain name to the name in the To: field of the message.

(5) Sender sends a **MAIL** command that includes the reverse path back to the sending server. This is done so that any errors will be reported to the correct sending server.

(6) The receiver responds with an **OK**.

(7) There may be more than one recipient of a message, and the sender will now notify the receiver of all recipients one-by-one. The receiver will determine that all receivers are valid, and send back an **OK**.

(8) Sender sends a **DATA** command which is used to tell the receiver that the body of the message will be sent next.

(9) Receiver responds with a **start mail** input.

(10) The sender sends the message line-by-line.

(11) The receiver sends an **OK** for each line received.

(12) Once all lines are sent, the sender sends a **QUIT** command to terminate the session.

(13) The receiver responds with a **service closing** transmission channel command.

The receiver may have messages of its own to send, and if it does, the roles of the two servers will swap, and the forging (beginning with step 5) will be repeated.

SMTP handles all outgoing mail. POP3 is used to receive e-mail.

NET+ OBJECTIVE
I.6.1

As mentioned, e-mail is an end-to-end, logical connection that makes extensive use of acknowledgments and address verification. Most e-mail uses two protocols to send and receive. The first is called **Simple Mail Transfer Protocol** (SMTP). SMTP handles all outgoing mail, and the steps outlined above are examples of a SMTP transaction.

If you had a constant connection to the Internet, SMTP would be all that's needed to send and receive e-mail. But most of us don't, even when the connection is through a network; there are times when we disconnect from the Internet.

If, during one of those times, an e-mail is received, we wouldn't be able to receive it because our end of the SMTP handshaking process would be turned off.

NET+ OBJECTIVE
I.6.1

However, we still want to be able to receive it—usually at our leisure. The protocol used to handle e-mail reception is called **Post Office Protocol v.3**, or **POP3**. There are earlier versions of POP, but they aren't compatible with version 3, and shouldn't be used. POP3 mimics the SMTP end of an e-mail dialogue, and stores the received message until you ask to retrieve it. That way, your e-mail is automatic, and continues to receive when you're not around to handle it yourself, or when you're not connected to the Internet.

The typical implementation for e-mail is to set up an e-mail server that runs SMTP and POP3. In a LAN, the e-mail server handles much of the routine operations, such as the dialogue described in the steps above, without taxing the resources of other Internet servers such as a Web server.

If you connect to the Internet at home, or as a stand-alone, you must set it up separately from your PPP and TCP/IP account. To do so, you need to verify that your ISP is using SMTP for sending, and POP3 for receiving, and the address of the e-mail server. It's typically the same for SMTP and POP3. Figure 8-8 illustrates a setup, using Windows.

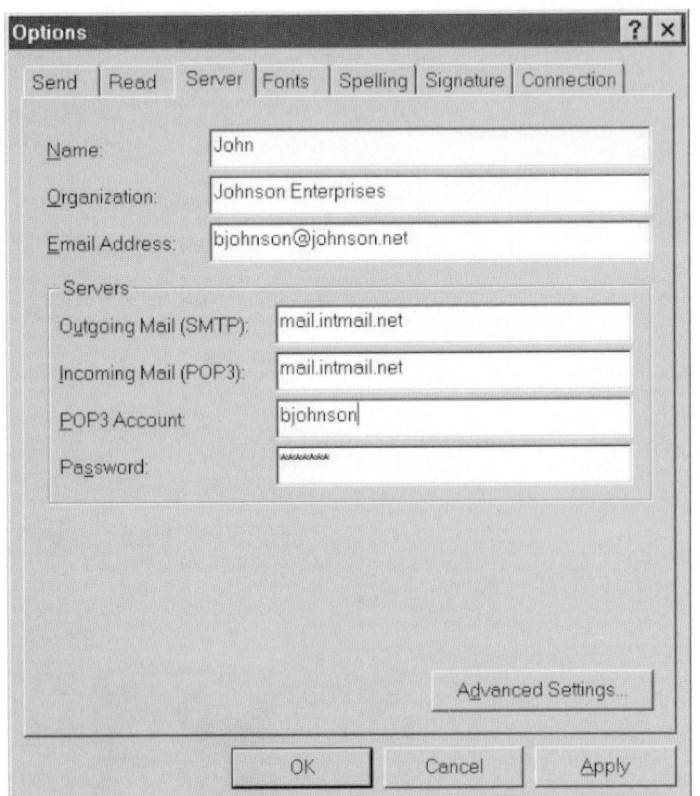

Figure 8-8 E-mail Setup and Configuration

To setup e-mail using Windows:

1 Start Internet Explorer.

2 From the drop-down menu in Explorer, choose Mail and select Read Mail. The e-mail screen will open.

3 In the drop-down menu, click on Mail and choose Options.

4 In the options folder, select the Server tab.

5 Complete the fields as shown in Figure 8-8.

Note that e-mail uses well-known application process ports when it's run. These should be preset in your e-mail software, but if they aren't, or if you try a little experimenting and then discover you can't send or receive e-mail any longer, look for an Advanced Settings button in your e-mail setup. After clicking it, look for outgoing (SMTP) and incoming (POP3) port settings. SMTP is at port 25, and POP3 is at port 110.

Most e-mail software allows you to attach documents to the ASCII text file in the body of an e-mail message. SMTP won't permit this, so another protocol is needed. The **Multipurpose Internet Mail Extension** (MIME) protocol is specifically used for World Wide Web, HTML Internet documents, and can be used to attach music, video, text formats other than ASCII such as Word, or WordPerfect, or graphics. MIME uses a mimecode to translate the attached document into a binary format.

INTERCONNECT TRANSPORT SERVICES

Above the Network layer, data communications is involved in user-to-user circuits, a virtual connection, that makes it seem as if the two communicating nodes are connected by a single wire. A WAN tends to replicate this concept by interconnecting nodes in such a way that they can draw upon various services in order to secure reliable sessions.

An interconnect transport service is a logical concept that describes a network's performance. A transport service is concerned with the performance level, and reliability, of the transmission. Data rate, error control, data packaging methods, and techniques used to establish the connections are all examples of the transport service level provided by a network.

NET+ OBJECTIVE
I.4.1

The following transport service descriptions are protocols, standards, or interfaces. They are most accurately to referred to as interfaces—interfacing to some lower level—since the ultimate implementation of quality occurs at the hardware level. Routers and gateways are the predominate devices used at the WAN level. A gateway is a device that converts from one protocol to another, such as IP to Novell IPX. But it may also be used as a default IP router, as well. A router is used to determine a path from one end-user to another end-user.

Most of the protocols described in this chapter were either proprietary in their origin, or developed by an international standards body such as EIA, ITU (CCITT), ANSI, IEEE, or OSI. Vendors have developed procedures for implementing the protocols that ensure a quality network will result. Protocols continue to evolve and change, and its incumbent on you to remain abreast of developments by visiting the Web sites of standards bodies, and vendors, and buying literature that broadens your understanding of these topics.

It's important to remember that a WAN is services dependent; it should adequately play to Network layer systems as well as respond to issues of quality and reliability at the Transport layer. TCP\IP is one of several internetworking protocols; but it's of little use if it can't be managed to provide end-user connections across a WAN—managed by protocols that are immune to the intricacies of TCP or IP. Most LANs are small enough that acknowledgments, or frame-reject instructions, maintain an adequate service. But if the network grows into the hundreds, or thousands, of connected nodes, then the HDLC responses become too slow and cumbersome to use as a management tool.

NET+ OBJECTIVE
I.1.7

At the WAN level, more efficient means—methods that utilize the minimum amount of precious bandwidth—must be devised. These should be methods that compliment internetworking, and that will reside on the same physical topology as the data. The next several sections examine wide-area protocols that haven't been discussed up to this point—X.25 Packet Switching, Frame Relay, ATM and ISDN.

Packet Switching (X.25)

Packet switching involves transmitting data over a large geographical area, usually in a WAN. This could be from city to city, country to country, or continent to continent. A WAN typically connects **Data Terminal Equipment** (DTE) from one area to a DTE in another area. A DTE is just about any programmable device—a computer, a network of computers, a front-end processor, or controller. The DTE gains access to the WAN through **Data-Communication** (circuit terminating) **Equipment** (DCE). The most common DCE is a modem.

CNST OBJECTIVE
IV-B & VI-B

The ideal WAN limits itself to protocols describing the DTE/DCE relationship as one of simultaneous transmitter and receiver. The communication medium between the transmitting and receiving DTE/DCEs would be a transparent connection. In the terminology of WANs, transparency is referred to as a **virtual connection**, and is depicted in Figure 8-9.

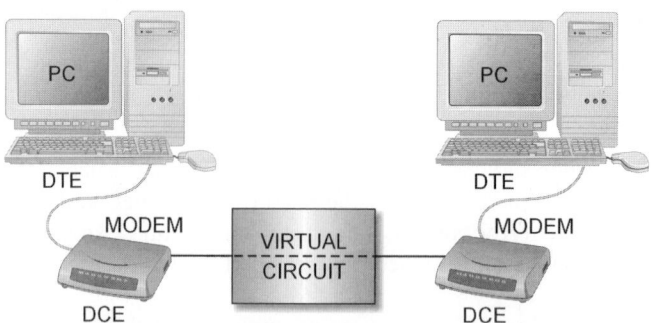

Figure 8-9 WAN Virtual Connection

CNST OBJECTIVE
IV-B & VI-B

The medium appears to the user as a single wire, connecting the transmitter and receiver. The WAN described above is implemented using the packet-switching technique, and data is said to travel over a packet-switching network.

> X.25 packet switching is an older transport protocol used in WANs, and is modeled after the public telephone system. Based on LAPB protocols, it's a reliable, but slow, technology.

The concept of packet switching is embodied in the recommendation of ITU (CCITT) X.25. X.25 is an interface standard that describes the connection of DTEs and DCEs to public switching networks. Essentially, the recommendation is a technology limited to the ports of the DTE, and the ports of the DCE. It is a time-tested technology that's been used successfully since the 1970s. Within the past twenty years, increased data rates, and advances in the physical medium (fiber optics in particular), have caused vendors to question the performance of X.25. Indeed, new techniques will eventually replace conventional packet switching, primarily because X.25 data travels in 64kBPS frames, called packets.

The objective of X.25 is to provide a complete communications system for data transfer. The recommendation is modeled after the public telephone system. The DTE is equivalent to the phone subscriber, and the DCE is equivalent to the central office. Considering the complexities of making a long-distance telephone call, the system is relatively easy to use. X.25 has been designed to provide the same relative ease to users who need to send and receive data.

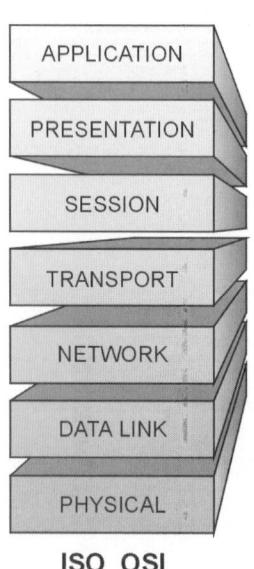

ISO OSI

Figure 8-10 ITU X.25 Recommendation

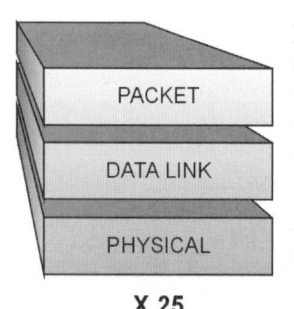

X.25

Messages to be sent through a packet network are broken into pieces (**packets**), and appropriate flags, headers, control, and error-checking fields added. The X.25 protocol adopted a layered approach to data flow that parallels the OSI reference model. As you can see in Figure 8-10, the first three layers of the OSI and the X.25 are the same.

At level 1, the X.25 interface specifications are contained in the X.21 recommendations. X.21 describes physical, electrical, and functional characteristics of level 1. The recommendation specifies a 15-pin synchronous interface that's widely used in Europe, but hasn't gained much of a following in the U.S., due to the prevalence of EIA/TIA-232. The ITU has approved an interface functionally equivalent to EIA/TIA-232 in the X.21 bis recommendation. The word "bis" is a Swiss term for alternate.

The Data Link level (level 2) describes the procedures used by the DTE and DCE for synchronization, control, and error detection. X.25 uses a subset of HDLC, **Link-Access Procedure-Balanced** (LAPB). In Chapter 5, the discussion involving HDLC described the **Normal Response Mode** (NRM): a station was designated as either primary or secondary. A secondary station cannot transmit without receiving permission from the primary. The LAPB protocol is operated in the **Asynchronous Balanced Mode** (ABM). In this mode, a separate primary and secondary aren't recognized. Each station on the network can initiate a transmission, or terminate the connection.

You shouldn't be misled by the "asynchronous" in asynchronous balanced mode. Data flow through an X.25 network is synchronous; "asynchronous" is describing the autonomy of the stations. Each station can transmit a packet of data onto the network whenever it chooses to do so. The Data Link frame format for X.25 is very similar to HDLC, as you'll see shortly.

Level 3, the packet level, describes the format of packets, and includes a Control field header that governs packet exchanges between DTE and DCE.

The user has several services available on a packet-switched network. The network may provide the user with a **virtual circuit**. A virtual circuit is a logical connection through the network. The stations at either end may disconnect the connection at any time. This is quite similar to a subscriber telephone call. The packet network establishes the route of least delay, and maintains it while the transmission takes place. An alternative (and more expensive) service is a **permanent virtual circuit**. Stations at either end of the network are assigned a permanent address, and can communicate at any time without the station dialog inherent in establishing a connection. While more expensive, a permanent virtual connection is quicker because the stations do not have to validate addresses.

A user with a virtual circuit is billed for the time that the connection is in place, and the number of packets that are sent. A permanent virtual circuit user is charged a flat, monthly fee. Packet switching has many other options available to users that are similar to the options offered telephone subscribers. Reverse charges allow a transmitter to bill the receiver for packets sent to it. Local-charge prevention prohibits reverse, or third party, charges. Call redirection, similar to call-forwarding, allows the network to redirect data.

X.25 Packet Frame Format

The frame format for packet networks is shown in Figure 8-11. The actual packet is the network-level header field, and the user data field. The rest of the frame is similar to HDLC. The beginning flag synchronizes the DTE and DCE, and is 8 bits wide, with a value of 01111110. The end flag signals the end of the frame, and also has a bit pattern of 01111110.

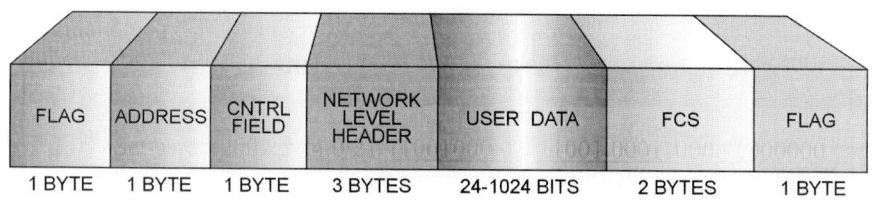

Figure 8-11 X.25 Frame Format

The one-byte address identifies the DTE and DCE. It is a fixed bit pattern, whose assignment to the DTE and DCE depends upon the usage. The address follows the command/response scheme used with unnumbered frames in HDLC. In the case of X.25, the process is simpler since all exchanges are point-to-point between the DCE and DTE.

Since only two devices are involved, the address will only be one of two values: 10000000, or 11000000. When a station (DTE or DCE) sends a command, the address specifies the receiver (DTE or DCE). When a station makes a response, the address specifies the station responding. The specific command or response is contained in the Control field.

The LAPB command address assignments are:

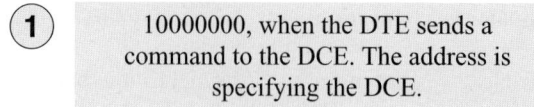

1   10000000, when the DTE sends a command to the DCE. The address is specifying the DCE.

2   1100000, when the DCE sends a command to the DTE. Now, the address specifies the DTE.

The LAPB response address assignments are:

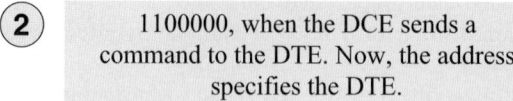

1   11000000, when the DTE responds to a command from the DCE. The address is specifying the DTE.

2   10000000, when the DCE responds to a command from the DTE. The address specifies the DCE.

An example of the command/response is illustrated in Figure 8-12.

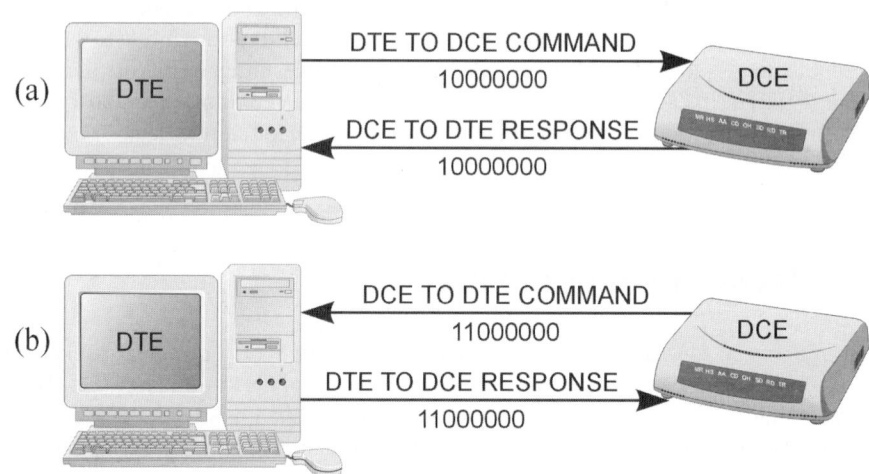

Figure 8-12 Command/Response Assignments of LAPB Protocol

In Figure 8-12(a), the DTE is sending a command to the DCE. The DTE might be sending a **Receive Ready** (RR) in the Control field, asking the DCE if it can receive data.

The DCE makes an appropriate response to the DTE command. In Figure 8-12(b), the roles have reversed. Now the DCE is sending a command to the DTE, and the DTE replies with an appropriate response.

The Control field has basically the same function in LAPB as it did in HDLC. The Control field serves as the data link header. As in HDLC, there are three types of Control fields: **information**, **supervisory**, and **unnumbered**. The Information field controls the transfer of user data. The Supervisory field manages control of the link between DTE and DCE. The Unnumbered field deals with specialized network management functions.

Table 8-4 summarizes the structure of the three types of Control fields. Note that it is very similar to HDLC for Information and Supervisory fields. The Unnumbered field has commands and responses unique to LAPB. **Set Synchronous Response Mode** (SARM) is a request by a station to set up the synch for data transfer. The proper response to a SARM is an **Unnumbered Acknowledgment** (UA). The link initiator then sends a **Set Synchronous Balance Mode** (SABM), which sets the receive and send counters in the stations to zero. These counters track the sequencing of data packets. Again, the appropriate response is UA. A **Command Reject** (CMDR) is sent in response to a frame that was received carrying a prohibited command. For example, if a RR frame is sent before the SARM, the response would be CMDR. A **Frame Reject** (FRMR) would be sent in similar circumstances.

Table 8-4 X.25 Control Fields

FORMAT	COMMANDS	RESPONSES
Information Transfer	I (information)	
Supervisory	RR (receive ready) RNR (receive not ready) REJ (reject)	RR (receive ready) RNR (receive not ready) REJ (reject)
Unnumbered	SARM (set asynchronous response mode)	DM (disconnect mode)
	SABM (set asynchronous balanced mode)	
	DISC (disconnect)	UA (unnumbered acknowledgment)
		CMDR (command reject) FRMR (frame reject)

The **Number Sent** (NS) and **Number Received** (NR) in the Information field are used to ensure proper sequencing between DTE and DCE. Both NS and NR have 3-bit parameters. A station can send 7 packet frames before being sent a response from the receiver. A response is sent using a Supervisory frame which specifies only a NR field. If seven packets are sent to the DCE, it will send a Supervisory frame with RR set, and the NR = 1. Why? The NS from the transmitting station holds the number of frames sent. The NR field in the Information frame is set to the number it expects to receive in the Supervisory frame from the receiver.

Figure 8-13 demonstrates the sequencing.

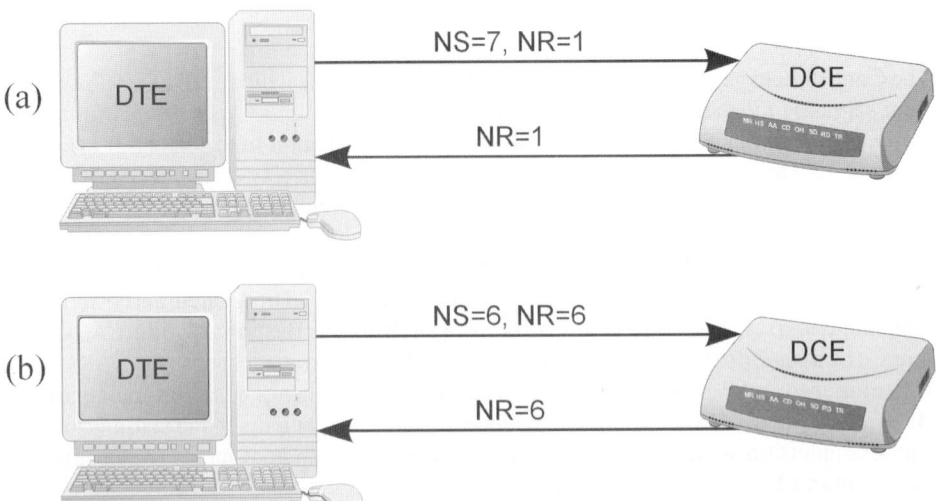

Figure 8-13 Packet Sequencing Procedure

In Figure 8-13(a), the DTE is transmitting the seventh packet (NS = 111). The NR field is incremented by one, to 001. The DCE acknowledges it has received the seventh packet by returning to the DTE the number of the next packet it expects to receive.

A similar situation is shown in Figure 8-13(b). The DTE is sending packet 5. It expects a supervisory return response from the DCE, with NR = 6. The DCE would know a response is expected because the last DTE frame would have the P/F bit set. The DCE received the 5 packets because it sends NR = 6, meaning it expects the next packet from the DTE to be numbered 6. If, in Figure 8-13(b), the DCE had sent NR = 5, the DTE would realize the sixth packet had been lost, because its own NR is set at 6. In this manner, the DTE and DCE check the sequence of packets sent, and received.

The User data field is a minimum of 24 bits long, and a maximum of 1,024. The actual packet is sent in the User data field, along with the network-level header data. The network header is generally 24 bits (3 bytes), and comprises the minimum bit length. Much of the exchange between DTE and DCE consists of commands and responses carried by Supervisory frames. Supervisory frames do not carry user data.

Figure 8-14 illustrates the network-level Header field. The field is responsible for packet format, and for directing an orderly data flow between the DTE and DCE. The header is considered to be part of the packet.

The logical channel group identifies the group of which the channel is a part. The X.25 gateway connecting the DEC to a packet network contains 16 group channels.

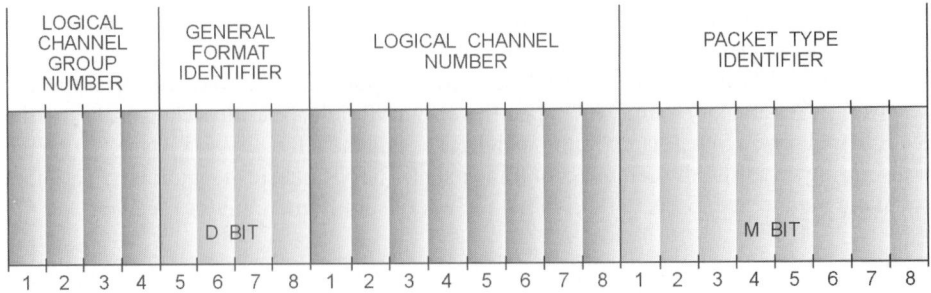

Figure 8-14 Network Level Header Field

Each group channel contains 256 logical channels. As an example, a header may be group channel 7, and logical channel 150. A single gateway supports 40 simultaneous, full-duplex channels.

The **General Format Identifier** (GFI) describes the overall header format. For example, 0001 is the data packet format. Other bit patterns describe diagnostics, flow control (RR RNR, reset indications), and connection setups (call request, call accepted, or incoming call). X.25 networks installed since 1984 have a D-bit option in the general format identifier. D-bit = 1 when the calling station requests delivery confirmation from the called station.

The **Packet Type Identifier** (PTI) describes the function of the packet. The general format identifier may indicates that the packet is a call setup packet. For example, the DCE may send an incoming call to the DTE. The bit pattern for incoming calls is 00001011. Whereas the format identifier is a general indicator of the packet's function, the packet type identifier is a specific indicator of the function. The M-bit contained in the Packet-Type field stands for more data. When the bit is set to 1, additional packets have been transmitted, and should be considered a part of a unit. If the M-bit is turned off, there are no more packets.

The users of packet networks find them to be an advantage for short, bursty traffic. An exchange of small files among field offices several times a day wouldn't cost-justify a dedicated phone line between the users. The packet network would usually be cheaper than public phone lines. Packet networks route the packets dynamically—intelligent nodes in the network select the path offering the least amount of congestion. Efficiency is maximized, while the costs of using the network are thereby kept at a minimum. As mentioned earlier, packet networks also have the advantage of offering a variety of services to data-communication users that are similar to services offered to phone subscribers.

NET+ OBJECTIVE
I.1.5

Fast Packet Services

Fast packet services refer to modified versions of X.25 technology. Frame Relay and ATM are examples of fast packet protocols.

CNST OBJECTIVE
VI-B

Throughout the last two decades, there have been two basic types of network services for wide-area interconnections—X.25-based packet switching, and common-carrier leased lines. X.25 was originally intended as a pay-on-demand system used to move data over analog lines, while the leased lines were available for a fixed, and expensive, rate. Neither is noted for high data rates. Compare the speed of a T1 channel (1.544 MBPS) with a 10MBPS Ethernet LAN, or a 100MBPS FDDI network. Data rates over the wide-area connection are snail-like, compared to the rates of LANs.

The amount of time spent transporting data over the connection to a distant network is a significant cost factor. The challenge for data communications has been to transport the data at faster rates, while providing the quality of service that the X.25 interface and the leased lines are noted for.

The search for greater speed, and wider bandwidth, has resulted in a new form of packet-based technology, called **fast packet**. Fast packet technology is characterized by small packets that avoid much of the overhead associated with traditional X.25 packets. There are two subsets of fast packet switching: **frame relay** and **cell relay**. Frame relay is a fast version of X.25. The cell relay variety is usually referred to as **Asynchronous Transfer Mode** (ATM), after the ITU standard.

Both frame relay and ATM are emerging standards, although there's significant support for them in vendor hardware and marketplace demand. Both are noted for high speeds over WANs, but it appears that ATM will have the ultimate edge, since it is the only internetworking transport service to support voice, data, and video. The following sections provide an overview of frame relay, and a more detailed explanation of ATM.

CNST OBJECTIVE
VI-B

Frame Relay

Frame relay is an interface with a variable-length data field, that was designed for the **Integrated Services Digital Network** (ISDN). It uses a TDM statistical multiplexer for sending messages from many sources over a **Permanent Virtual Circuit** (PVC) to the destination. Note that with a multiplexer, source stations are using the same channel link to the destination. A frame-relay network is illustrated in Figure 8-15.

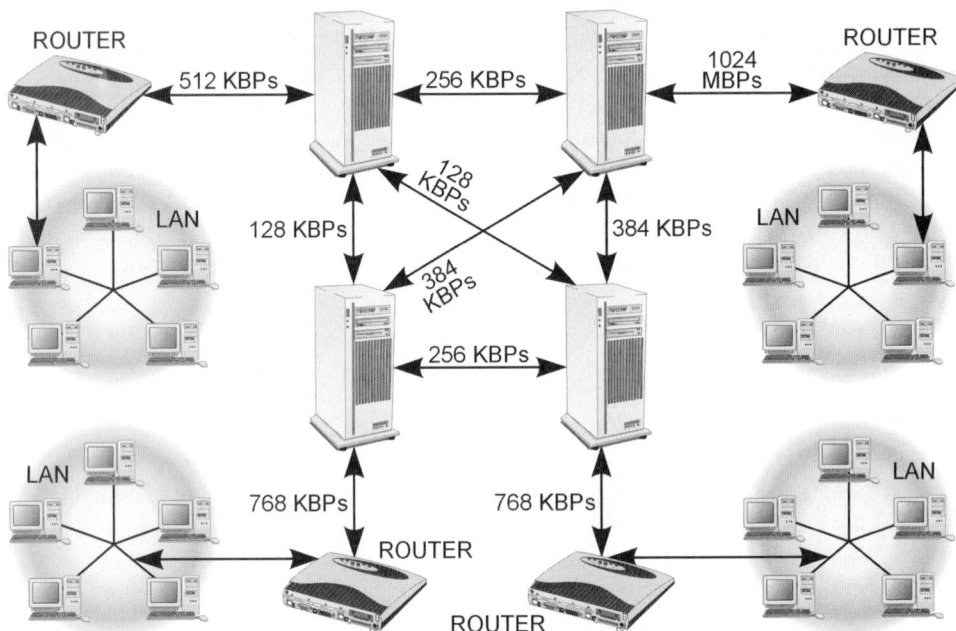

Figure 8-15 Frame-Relay Network

> Frame Relay is a variable-bandwidth, packet-switched technology that utilizes Data Link layer concepts to send data faster than X.25.

In Figure 8-15, four LANs are connected in a WAN using frame-relay switching. The LANs communicate over a permanent virtual circuit. This is set up and maintained by a common carrier, such as AT&T, MCI, etc. The LAN manager specifies which nodes on the LANs will be communicating, and this determines the size and number of PVCs. The frame-relay switch stores the PVC, and will use it when the nodes transmit.

The LANs gain access to the PVC at the carrier **Point Of Presence** (POP). The POP is the physical connection at which the carrier assumes control of the data.

The carriers offer PVCs at varying data rates. The data rate corresponds to channel bandwidth. The LAN user specifies the PVC rates, based upon a best-estimate of node usage. From this estimate, a **Committed Information Rate** (CIR) is derived. The CIR is the sum of the PVC bandwidths for each LAN. The user specifies the CIR bandwidth, and the frame-relay switch multiplexes the LAN nodes onto the assigned PVCs.

The advantage of frame-relay networks is that bandwidth is made variable, and can be matched to the bandwidth needs of the user. This may range from 4 kBPS, to a full T1 1.544MBPS link.

Frame-relay networks work particularly well with mildly bursty data, such as the intermittent keystrokes associated with order entries. They are capable of exceeding the CIR for brief periods, because the switch incorporates a statistical multiplexer. Recall that statistical multiplexers contain buffer pools that allow the data rate to exceed the aggregate rate for short periods.

The reason that frame relay transports data so much faster than X.25 is that it only uses the first two layers of the OSI protocol model, the Physical and Data-Link layers. The significance of this is that the Network-layer functions are not available to frame-relay networks. This translates into higher throughput, which results in higher speeds.

The data-link protocol used by frame relay is the **Link-Access Procedure-D** (LAPD). LAPD was originally designed for ISDN systems, and provides for multiple logical links over the same channels (the permanent virtual circuits shown in Figure 8-15). LAPD is similar to HDLC, but with fewer header fields.

Frame relay transports data at higher rates than X.25, and it is usually implemented at a lower cost than leased lines. Like X.25, users are offered variable amounts of bandwidth. The weakness of frame relay is that it is restricted to data transmissions. In addition, frame relay packets are prone to being lost, when statistical multiplexer buffers approach the overflow point. Due to the flow-control capabilities of multiplexers, data from the LAN nodes is slowed down to avoid losing the packets; this has tended to cast some doubt on the superior data-rate attributes of frame relay.

Asynchronous Transfer Mode

> Asynchronous Transfer Mode is a cell relay standard that uses 53-byte cells for transporting text, voice, video, music or graphic messages.

ATM was developed by AT&T in 1980, as a technique for transmitting voice and data in a packet format. In 1988, the ITU (CCITT) selected ATM as a standard to use with **Broadband ISDN** (BISDN). ATM is the standard which describes cell relay technology.

The strength of ATM, and the reason many believe it will be the transport service of the future for both WANs and LANs, is due to its ability to support large-bandwidth connections, that are scalable to the users needs. **Bandwidth scalability** refers to a channel that is bandwidth-flexible, such as frame relay and X.25. ATM is also noted for providing **bit-level service**. Bit-level service refers to transmissions at the Data Link level; ATM uses only the first two levels of the OSI model.

CNST OBJECTIVE
VI-B

NET+ OBJECTIVE
I.1.5

The ability of a protocol to address individual bits is important to transmitting video. Not only does video require large-bandwidth channels, but the channels must also be of a high quality. This is because the user is much more sensitive to video phase distortion, than noise distortion. That is, our eyes are more sensitive to phase distortion than are our ears.

ATM is the only network service standard capable of carrying voice, data, and video. As Table 8-5 shows, the bandwidth needs of these three classes of data differ considerably. LANs are usually designed for a fixed amount of bandwidth, and the only way to increase the bandwidth is to change to another type of LAN, such as FDDI. However, this may be wasteful if users are only occasionally sending voice or video.

Table 8-5 Bandwidth Requirements for Information Transfer

OBJECT	BASIC	COMPRESSION	COMPRESSED
1-page Business Letter	5 kbits	4:1	1.3 kbits
20-page Document with Graphics	40 Mbits	4:1	10 Mbits
Voice	64 kBPS	8:1	8 kbits
1-page FAX	1 Mbits	14:1	75 kbits
24-bit Computer Image	800 Mbits	100:1	8 Mbits
Full Motion Video (NTSC)	45 MBPS	50:1	1 MBPS
Full Motion Video (HDTV)	150 MBPS	50:1	3 MBPS

Originally, ATM was defined as part of the broadband ISDN model by the ITU, as shown in Table 8-6. Three ATM layers are defined in the BISDN model: the Physical layer, the ATM layer, and the ATM Adaption layer, which replace the first three layers of the OSI model. Note that a network layer is not described. This allows ATM cells to be switched more rapidly than conventional packet switching, since the header will not include routing protocols. This can be accomplished directly with internetworking protocols (TCP/IP).

Table 8-6 BISDN Model

UPPER LAYER SERVICES AND APPLICATIONS	
ATM ADAPTION LAYER	Convergence Sublayer
ATM ADAPTION LAYER	Segmentation and Reassembly
ATM LAYER	Cell Formatting
PHYSICAL LAYER	Transmission Convergence
PHYSICAL LAYER	Physical Medium

The Physical layer describes how the ATM cells are transported, and includes the physical interface, channel media, and data rates. Unlike other technologies, ATM can be operated over many physical layers, and through many physical interfaces. Currently, ATM transports cells through user interfaces (such as a connection to a LAN) at the following data rates:

1	100 MBPS Multimode Fiber Optic.
2	155 MBPS Multimode Fiber Optic.
3	155 MBPS OC3 SONET.
4	45 MBPS DS3 (T3) WAN Interface.

The DS3 interface is targeted to telecommunications carriers which typically use coaxial or fiber cable, and twisted-pair connections to LANs. The 100MBPS fiber connection is targeted to LANs, and specifically to FDDI LANs running twisted-pair cables. The SONET specification reflects the status of current technology, and will no doubt include the higher rates, such as OC-24 (1.2 GBPS) and OC-48 (2.5 GBPS) as the need arises.

The ATM layer of the model describes the **cell format** of ATM. ATM uses small, fixed-size cells, 53 bytes long. The header occupies 5 bytes, while the information field is 48 bytes. The cell format of ATM is pictured in Figure 8-16. The **General Flow Control** (GFC) field provides a method for multiple work stations to use the same interface. ATM cells are statistically multiplexed. The GFC indicates to the multiplexer that more than one station is feeding a single port, and it needs to be aware that the time slot given to the port will contain data from multiple users.

The three, **Virtual Path Identifier** (VPI), and two, **Virtual Channel Identifier** (VCI), fields serve as an addressing mechanism, used by the ATM switches. A virtual channel represents a guaranteed link from source switch to destination switch. Each port on an ATM switch, which is connected to a user station, has a virtual channel to a destination switch. This is illustrated in Figure 8-17.

Users on one LAN site are connected to users on another through a virtual path. A virtual path is a single cable, carrying a number of virtual channels. The VCI, or VPI, indicates the addresses of ATM switches. Once the cell arrives at the destination switch, connection tables are used to send it to the ultimate user destination. Using **virtual switch addresses** allows ATM to be independent of Network-layer routing protocols.

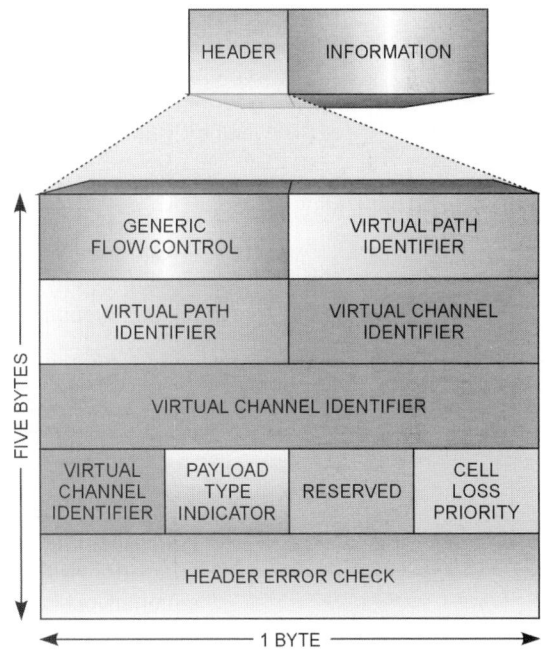

Figure 8-16 ATM Cell Header Format

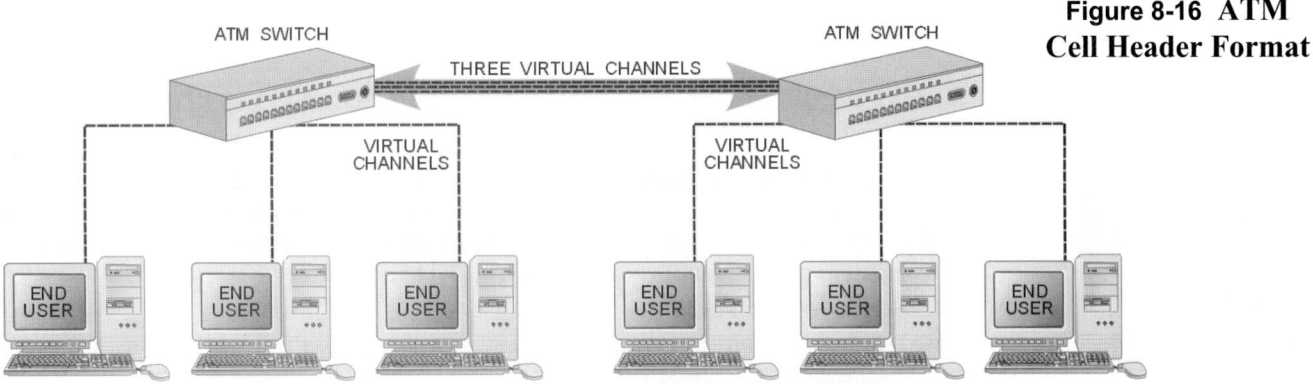

Figure 8-17 ATM Virtual Channels and Virtual Paths

The **Payload Type Indicator** (PTI) identifies the contents of the Information field—user data, management, or control signals. The **Cell Loss Priority** (CLP) contains instruction for dropping cells if the channel becomes congested, and the network is on the verge of crashing. Error detection, and correction, of single-bit errors is accomplished in the **Header Error Check** (HEC) field.

Nearly ten percent of an ATM cell is reserved for the header. This constitutes a considerable amount of relative overhead, and is considered a significant weakness.

The ATM Adaption layer prepares higher-layer data, such as **Switched Multi-Megabit Data** (SMDS), for conversion to cells. SMDS is a cell-based transmission service that provides for a wide variety of access speeds, up to a maximum bandwidth of 45 MBPS, with destination addressing. It is connectionless, meaning it is routed by protocols similar to those discussed in the section on routers. Being cell-based, it has been widely associated with complex ATM networks.

Table 8-7 Classes of the ATM Adaption Layer

Since ATM supports several different types of applications, the CCITT developed classes of ATM adaption layers to respond to the varying characteristics of the applications. The classes are summarized in Table 8-7.

TYPE	SERVICE	APPLICATION	CONTROL
1	Constant Bit-Rate Support		Connection Oriented
2	Variable Bit-Rate Support	Video	Connection Oriented
3	Variable Bit-Rate Support	Frame Relay	Connection Oriented
4	Variable Bit-Rate Support	SMDS	Connectionless Oriented
5	Variable Bit-Rate Support	Simple and Efficient Adaption Layer (SEAL)	Connection or Connectionless Oriented

ATM is being described as the base of network technology for the future. The reason for this is its capability to process multimedia data over any physical network. This means ATM is compatible with all LAN and WAN technologies. Futurists speculate ATM networks will be simultaneously providing users with voice, data, and video services on a workstation, and running on upgraded physical nets, such as Ethernet or token ring.

INTEGRATED SERVICES DIGITAL NETWORK (ISDN)

Integrated Services Digital Network (ISDN) is a set of digital services available for to users over telephone lines. It's an alternative to conventional telephone connections for Internet access or for wide area connections in a multi-user environment. ISDN modems compete with fractional T1, cable modems, and to a lesser degree, Frame Relay.

ISDN takes a layered approach to supplying digital services. The ISDN layers are the Physical, Data Link and Network layers.

ISDN is a complete digital solution from end-user to end-user. The significance of this is that voice, text, graphics, video, music and other material is routinely sent across an ISDN connection at very fast data rates. Because the connection is all digital, data rates can be much higher than an analog telephone connection. With V.90 modems, a user can expect download rates of about 48 kBPS but with ISDN, 128 kBPS are typical. Note that **kilo**, when used with ISDN, is actually 1,000—not the 1,024 that you may associates with powers of 2.

Users are charged a tariff to use ISDN. The equipment needed to interface and use the services is specialized, and limited to ISDN technology. Due to the geographical limits of ISDN, it may not be available in all areas, or if it is, it may not be cost-effective if your facility is located too far from a central office. Currently, you must be within 18,000 feet (3.4 miles) of the CO to receive an ISDN line. The length may be extended if a wide bandwidth repeater is installed, but this cost is passed on to customers, and may very well offset cost advantages of ISDN over a competing technology.

CNST OBJECTIVE
I-A & VI-B

ISDN Terminology

As ISDN frame carries data in a **Bearer channel** (B channel) that has a 64kBPS bandwidth. On older telephone systems, B channels may drop to 56 kBPS. A **Data channel** (D channel) carries supervisor and signaling information at 16 kBPS (and sometimes at 64 kBPS).

There are two types of ISDN connections, a **Basic Rate Interface** (BRI), and a **Primary Rate Interface** (PRI). A BRI connection is composed of two 64kBPS B channels, and one 16kBPS D channel. It's normally referred to as BRI 2B+D. A PRI channel has 23 64kBPS B channels and one 64kBPS D channel. It's normally called PRI 23B+D.

Channel information in an ISDN line is byte-multiplexed, so it's common to aggregate (interleave) the B channels. When this is done, the connection is described by including an H suffix. Typical aggregate rates are:

- H0=6 B channels (384kBPS)

- H10=23 B channels (1,472kBPS)

- H11=24 B channels (1,536kBPS)

- H12=30 B channels (1,929kBPS)

ISDN Interfaces

As mentioned, ISDN comes with its own equipment and interfaces that are needed to establish a physical connection. Refer to Figure 8-18 to place the definitions described below to their place in the physical layout.

ISDN Terminals

- TE1: Terminal Equipment Type 1. A subscriber-side device that is specialized for ISDN. This may include a computer connection or an ISDN telephone. These are both shown, and labeled as TE1.

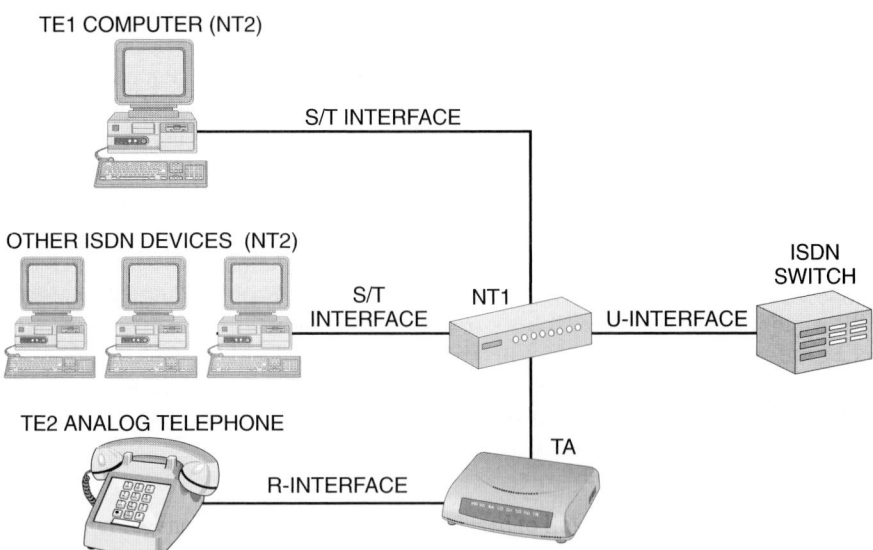

TE1 COMPUTER (NT2)

S/T INTERFACE

OTHER ISDN DEVICES (NT2)

S/T INTERFACE

NT1

U-INTERFACE

ISDN SWITCH

TE2 ANALOG TELEPHONE

TA

R-INTERFACE

Figure 8-18 ISDN Reference Points

- TE2: Terminal Equipment Type 2. Also a subscriber-side device, but one that pre-dates the ISDN standard, such as the analog telephone shown.

Terminal Adapter (TA)

- A terminal adapter is needed only to connect older style equipment to an ISDN line. The analog telephone is shown with a TA because it's not ISDN-ready. TAs are sometimes, incorrectly, called ISDN modems. A TA may be either a stand-alone device, or a printed circuit board inside the TE2 device. If its an external device, it connects to the TE2 via a standard physical interface such as EIA/TIA-232, or V.35.

Network Termination

- (NT1) Network Termination Type 1: An NT1 is a device at the ISDN switch side (in Europe—but at the customer site in North America) of the connection that performs a 2-wire to 4-wire conversion. Four physical wires are used at the subscriber side for full-duplex transmission. Two of the wires are used for transmit, and two for receiving. Many ISDN devices have an NT1 built into them, which makes installations easier and quicker.

- (NT2) Network Termination Type 2: An NT2 handles layer 2 and 3 ISDN protocols. Since these are included in all ISDN devices, they are shown in parenthesis with the TE1 devices.

Reference Interface

ISDN specifies several reference points that define the logical interfaces between terminals and network termination points.

- S Interface: The reference point between subscriber-side ISDN equipment and NT2.

- T Interface: The reference point between NT1 and NT2. Notice that the S and T interfaces are shown on the same line. First, they're electrically identical; second, a S reference is inside the subscriber device.

- R Interface: The reference point between non-ISDN devices and a TA. The analog telephone has an R interface since it's not ISDN equipment.

- U Interface: The reference between the carrier switch and the ISDN device (NT1) at the subscriber site. Keep in mind, ISDN is intended to provide digital connections using the existing 2-wire local loop. The U interface refers to this 2-to-4 wire hybrid.

ISDN Layer Protocol

ISDN provides digital services, at up to 128 kBPS, directly to the desktop for computers, fax or telephones.

The ISDN standard (ITU I and G-series documents) is composed of three protocol layers—the Physical layer, Data Link layer, and the Network layer. They are roughly analogous to the first three layers of the OSI model, and use many of the same conventions and practices.

The Physical layer is responsible frame formatting ISDN data, establishing data rates and signal levels. An ISDN frame consists of 2 bytes of the first B channel (B1), 2 bytes of the second B channel (B2), 4 bits from the D channel (D), 10 bits for link maintenance (L), and 2 bits for synchronization (F), for a total frame length of 48 bits. This is shown in Figure 8-19.

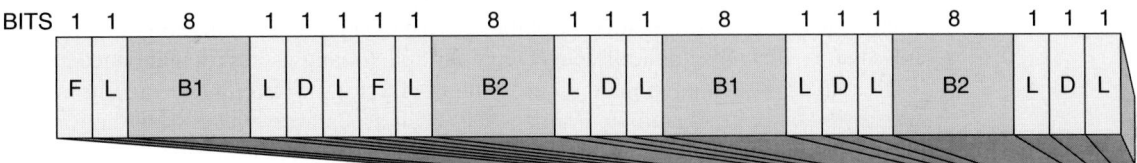

TOTAL FRAME LENGTH = 48 BITS   DATA = 36 BITS   OVERHEAD = 12 BITS
F = SYNCHRONIZATION   L = ADJUST AVERAGE BIT VALUE   B1, B2, D = USER DATA AND SIGNALING

At the U interface, ISDN frames are combined into a single unit that contains five, 48-bit frames. This gives a total length of 240 bits. This is the size of the frame that's sent from the ISDN switch, to the NT1 at the subscriber site. Bit times on an ISDN line are 6.25µS, for a total bandwidth of 160 kBPS. This bandwidth is divided as follows:

Figure 8-19 ISDN Physical Layer Frame

- Overhead: 16 kBPS

- D channel: 16 kBPS

- 2 64BPS B channels: 128 BPS

Data is sent in a superframe consisting of eight, 240-byte frames for a total of 1,920 bits. The Data Link layer uses the LAPD implementation of HDLC. The frame format is shown in Figure 8-20.

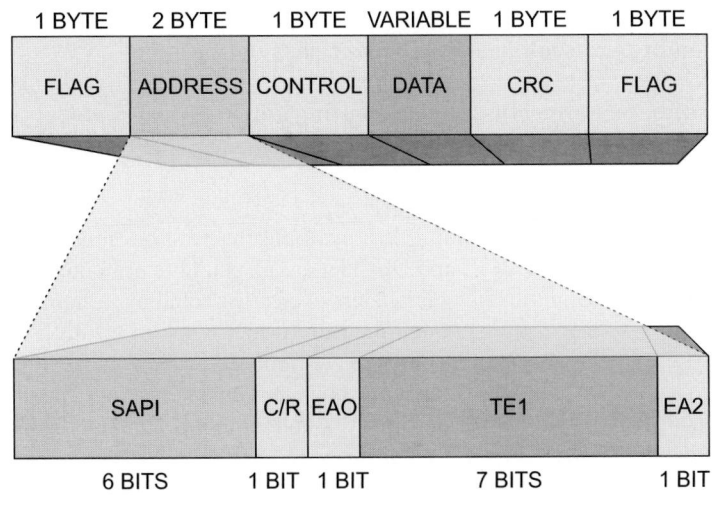

Figure 8-20 LAPD Frame Used with ISDN

The Flag and Control fields are identical to those used in HDLC with Supervisory, Information and Unnumbered frames. The Address field—which may be extended to 2 bytes—differs from HDLC. The C/R field designates the frame as command or response. The EA fields (extended addressing 1 and 2) are used to signify if the address field is 1 or 2 bytes in length. If EA1 is set, the length is 1 byte. The TEI field (**Terminal Endpoint Identifier**) is used to specify a single terminal (0–63_{10}), or multiple terminals (64–126_{10}). A third TEI for broadcast messages is set when the field is configured for 127_{10}. The six-bit SAPI (**Service Access Point Identifier**) identifies the point where layer 2 LAPD provides services to layer 3.

The Network layer is used to specify the type of signaling that will be used on an ISDN line. It may be circuit-switched, Packet-switched, or user-to-user. It addition, the set up, maintenance and termination of the session are handled by the Network layer. The process is very similar to that used with X.25.

An ISDN line is more expensive than an analog telephone line connection (as used by the plain old telephone system, or POTS), but cheaper than a T1 line. It can accommodate multiple users (up to seven devices on the subscriber side), while a POTS line can handle only one. A T1 connection, of course, can multiplex many users. As mentioned earlier, ISDN is much faster than an analog connection, but far slower than either T1 or cable modem access. In some organizations, Frame Relay is an acceptable intermediary between an analog or ISDN connection, and a T1 connection. With Frame Relay, multiple users are supported, data rates are high, but toll charges can easily make it an expensive choice.

ROUTING PROTOCOLS

> A routing protocol is used to route packets from source to destination addresses on a network. Some routing protocols are classified as interior (intra-route), and some as exterior (inter-route).

It's one thing to have a collection of interconnected networks, and another thing to patch them together. Internetworking devices provide a hardware solution for interconnecting networks at the Data Link (bridges), Network (routers) and Transport (gateways) layers. A routing protocol provides a software solution for implementing hardware that allows a network of networks to function.

There are **routing protocols** and **routed protocols**.

Examples of routing protocols include **Routing Information Protocol** (RIP), **Open Shortest Path First** (OSPF), **Exterior Gateway Protocol** (EGP) and **Border Gateway Protocol** (BGP).

NET+ OBJECTIVE
I.4.1

A routed protocol, on the other hand, is a protocol that can be transmitted across an internetwork. IP, TCP, UDP, IPX, and DECNet are all routable protocols. They contain enough addressing information in their headers to ensure a reliable session between users. Some protocols aren't routable because they don't contain enough information (particularly, a logical—IP—address) such as NetBeui, Ethernet, Token Ring or FDDI. In order to send a **non-routable protocol**, it must be combined with a routable protocol, then sent through a network that has the capability to route other protocols; that is, by using a routing protocol.

All routers gather information about other routers by collecting routing information and storing it in tables. A routing table can contain a wide variety of information, but it will, at a minimum, contain addresses of routers that it's aware of, the distance to these routers (expressed in the number of hops to it), and usually some sort of timer that ages the information in the table. This is important, because a router must constantly access the topology around it for changes. If a router within its area goes down, then it's no longer a path through which to send data packets; consequently, it's dropped from the routing tables and they're reconfigured.

In order to keep abreast of topology changes, routers send all, or parts, of the information in their route tables to other routers. These are called **advertisements**, and may be sent every 10 seconds, to an average of every 30 seconds. When an advertisement is received, the router must compare the contents of the advertisement to the information in its table, then make changes as appropriate. Advertisement require time and bandwidth on an internetwork, and the struggle continues to develop protocols that minimize the delay and bandwidth restrictions that result from them. In this section several common routing protocols will be described. Consider the information presented to be introductory, since Internet routing is a vast and complex subject.

Routing Information Protocol (RIP)

A RIP routing table contains the address of the next destination, the next hop on the way to the destination, and some type of metric such as a timer. If the information changes, the router updates its tables, then sends the updated table so that the change will be received by the other routers that it's associated with.

CNST OBJECTIVE
IV-B

A RIP packet contains an Address Family Identifier field that may list up to 25 destinations to be included in the table updates. This means that a RIP router will store the routes to a maximum of 25 other routers in its table. Typically, RIP uses a 30-second timer to send the updates to routers listed in its table. But consider the case when one of its destinations is taken offline. How does it know that a destination router is off the network, and therefore, not accessible as a destination. If a router doesn't receive a RIP packet within a defined time (90 seconds for RIP), it assumes that the router destination is no longer valid, and reports this in the next advertisement. After 270 seconds, the router will assume the invalid destination is not coming back online, and will purge it from its table.

RIP has several notable features that have made it an enduring routing protocol. It sets a hop-count limit of 16. This means that if a destination router is more than 16 hops away, RIP will assume it's unreachable. For distributed networks, this doesn't represent a problem, but for a network the size of the Internet, it limits the effectiveness of RIP. The advantage of a hop limit is that it prevents loops from occurring.

Consider a situation in which a router is down. Since it doesn't transmit update information, it'll be tagged as invalid, and eventually purged from routing tables. But if, before the purge advertisement can be sent, another router sends an update that still lists the invalid router as being available, this message will be added to the tables of other routers. It may possibly be advertised to some routers who have previously received a message that the down-router is no longer available. To them, it will appear as if it's back in the network, when in fact, it's not. To prevent this type of situation, RIP contains a **hold-down**. A hold-down is a timer that prevents routers from advertising changes that may affect routers which were recently removed. The timer is set for the time it takes to update the entire network.

Interior Gateway Routing Protocol (IGRP)

One disadvantage to RIP is its 16-hop routing table destination limit. Consider a network with twenty routers (a medium-sized network) and you can see that RIP will not map all destinations in its tables. The short hop count limits RIP in making routing decisions, as well.

IGRP was developed by Cisco to overcome the weaknesses of RIP. IGRP is a **Distance Vector Interior-Gateway Protocol** (IGP). When a router runs a distance vector protocol, its routing tables are sent to each of its neighbors. They, in turn, send it to their neighbors, who send it on, and so on. In other words, the concepts of hop limits doesn't apply to IGRP. Topology changes propagate to all routers on the network, regardless of their number. Since all routers are sharing information, the distance to any other router can be calculated.

IGRP considers other factors when making routing decisions. Delays, available bandwidth, reliability, and load are metrics which are weighted and included in a routing decision. A network administrator can specify relative weights for any of the metrics, or choose a default value that will decide the optimum path to the destination. As an example, if a router was noted for creating delays (because it's old, slow, over-worked, etc.) the administrator can place a heavier weight on delays for packets that may be sent through this router. This way, a source router will avoid it when calculating the best route to a destination router.

Open Shortest Path First (OSPF)

OSPF is a routing protocol that's **Open** to the public (it's in the public domain). It sends packets based on a calculation that determines the **Shortest Path** to the destination—hence, the rather cryptic sounding name. It's a hierarchial protocol which means that OSPF routers are organized into groups. The groups are called **autonomous systems** (AS), or domains. An AS is a collection of networks under the same administrative control, and using a common routing protocol. As such, OSPF is used as an interior solution for large internetworks, although it can also communicate to exterior networks such as the Internet.

An AS is divided into areas that are composed of connected routers and corresponding hosts. Some of the routers in an area interface to other routers in other areas, usually through a router backbone. These routers are border routers, and they contain all topological information for the area they're assigned to. The topology within an area is invisible to areas outside, and since other areas are unaware of the other's existence, router advertisements are fewer than in RIP or IGRP. A typical OSFP topology is shown in Figure 8-21.

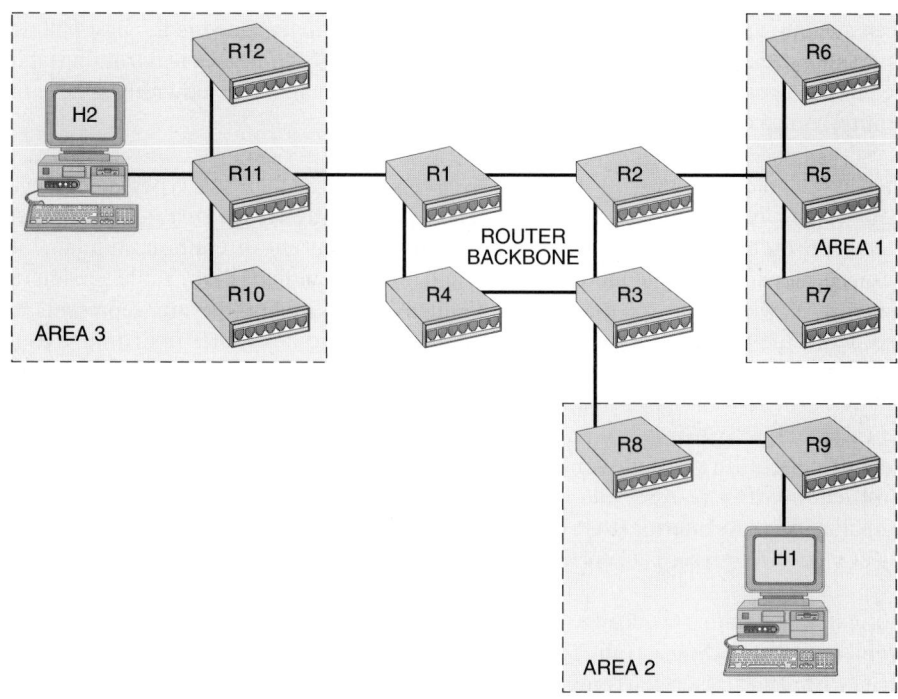

Figure 8-21 OSFP Router Topology

The 12 routers in the network make up an autonomous system. Routers R1, R2, R3 and R4 comprise the network router backbone. Routers R5, R8 and R11 are called border routers, because they border the backbone and their assigned areas.

The backbone routers communicate only with border routers. When the system is first turned on, they send a **hello** protocol to other routers. This identifies other routers in an area, border, or on a backbone. Routers within an area communicate only with other area routers, and their border routers. Periodically, the routers continue to send hello packets, and their receipt validates the router as still being a part of the AS.

OSPF is a **link state protocol** which means it communicates routes based upon the state of a link, various metrics, and then calculates the shortest path to a destination. The calculation is called an SPF (**Shortest Path First**) algorithm, and it considers all reported aspects of a link when making the calculation. Comparatively, RIP and IGRP are distance vector protocols, since they send routing table updates as the primary criteria for mapping routes to destinations.

A **Link State Advertisement** (LAS) is sent to contiguous routers. Backbone routers send LSAs to other backbone routers, and border routers; area routers send LSAs to other routers in their area, and the border routers. Notice that OSPF reduces router advertisements, and as a result, more of the bandwidth is available for data packets.

Border Gateway Protocol (BGP)

The Border Gateway Protocol is used to route between autonomous systems (as is its predecessor, Exterior Gateway Protocol). BGP can also be used to route within an AS. Routing table updates are used with BGP, but the updates also contains a revision that's compared to received updates; if the received revision is the same, then the received update is ignored. If it's not the same, BGP updates cells affected by the new revision.

When sending updates, BGP only advertises what it has determined is the best path to a destination—and not all possible routes (although all routes are retained in its routing table). The metrics upon which BGP makes a decision involve available bandwidth, delays, link stability, and so on.

When communicating with other routers, BGP may send any of four types of messages: Open, Update, Notification or Keepalive. The Open message is the first to be sent after a transport protocol has set up a connection between routers. It contains fundamental information that's needed to reconcile table, and link state, information. Table versions are compared, as well as information about the number of AS that the router represents, the maximum time that can elapse before assuming that another router is offline, and the authentication of valid data.

The Update message provides routing updates. The updates are based on a number of attributes including the current status of a router (unreachable), its AS path, the identification of intra-ASs, and the origin of the update. This can be important if the originating router is interior (RIP, IGRP) or exterior (BGP, EGP), because it will affect the ease of pass-through for packets that are directed toward it.

Notification messages are used to communicate errors between routers. Errors may be of several types, including a **Hold Time Expired**, which means that a router hasn't sent an update within the prescribed time. It should check in shortly beyond the minimum time set in the hold timer, or it will expire. Once it expires, the questionable router will be declared out of the network.

An **Update Message** error means that a field in a received update was invalid. A **Message Header** error indicates an inconsistency in the received header, such as the wrong header length, or an unknown message type. An **Open Message** error is used to report problems with an IP address, or any authentication codes which the receiving router doesn't support. A **Keepalive** message is used to notify the receiving router that the sender is still in the network. Actually, a Keepalive is sent whenever the hold timer is about to expire.

As mentioned, BGP is replacing the Exterior Gateway Protocol (EGP), particularly on the Internet, where by definition, thousands of ASs are connected together.

KEY POINTS REVIEW

- The Internet is a network of networks.

- The Web is the graphical area of the Internet. Other services available from the Internet include file transfers, telnet, and e-mail.

- A WEb address, called a URL, follows the Domain Name system convention. A DNS must be mapped to an IP address, since the two can't be derived from each other.

- A DNS server is responsible for reconciling domain names to IP addresses.

- DHCP is used to dynamically assign IP addresses to domain names.

- WINS contains a look-up table used to reconcile computer names to IP addresses.

- The Point-to-Point Protocol (PPP) is a communication protocol used to send data across serial communication links.

- PPTP is a protocol used to securely transport PPP packets over a TCP/IP network

- With e-mail, the user name comes before the @ symbol, and usually represents the name of the individual, or business, holding the e-mail account. The domain names of the computer where the e-mail account is maintained are placed after the @ symbol. An example of an e-mail address is user@domain.com.

- SMTP handles all outgoing e-mail. POP3 is used to receive e-mail.

- X.25 packet switching is an older transport protocol used in WANs, and modeled after the public telephone system. Based on LAPB protocols, it's reliable, but slow.

- Fast packet services refer to modified versions of X.25 technology. Frame Relay and ATM are examples of fast packet protocols.

- Frame Relay is a variable-bandwidth, packet switched technology that utilizes Data Link layer concepts to send data faster than X.25.

- Asynchronous Transfer Mode is a cell relay standard that uses 53-byte cells for transporting text, voice, video, music or graphic messages.

- ISDN provides digital services, at up to 128 kBPS, directly to the desktop for computers, fax or telephones.

- ISDN takes a layered approach to supplying digital services. The ISDN layers are the Physical, Data Link and Network layers.

- Routing protocols are used to route packets from a source to a destination network address. Routing protocols are classified as interior (intra-route) or exterior (inter-route). Examples of routing protocols include RIP, IGRP, OSPF and BGP.

LAB MANUAL

At this point, review the objectives listed at the beginning of the chapter to be certain that you understand and can perform them. Afterward, answer the review questions that follow to verify your knowledge of the information.

Lab Exercises

The lab manual that accompanies this book contains hands-on lab procedures that reinforce and test your knowledge of the theory materials presented in this chapter. Now that you have completed your review of Chapter 8, refer to the lab manual and perform Procedures 23, "Network Security with Cisco/HP 10Base-T Hub," 24, "TCP/IP Utilities," and 25, "System Commander Partitioning Software."

REVIEW QUESTIONS

The following questions test your knowledge of the material presented in this chapter:

1. Describe the difference between routable and non-routable protocols.

2. What is the purpose of DNS?

3. Define Wide Area Network.

4. What is the cell length of ATM cells?

5. What advantages does Frame Relay offer over X.25?

6. How do PPP and SLIP differ?

7. What is the purpose of DHCP?

8. How does PTPP improve upon PPP?

9. Just exactly what is a WAN?

10. When and where did the Internet actually begin?

11. Why does TCP/IP work better with UNIX, rather than DOS-based PCs?

12. Name at least five Internet services.

13. What is the primary reason for the existence of the File Transfer Protocol?

14. What are the major differences between E-Mail and Internet Chat services?

15. List the zone names for the top-level DNS servers.

MULTIPLE CHOICE QUESTIONS

1. Frame Relay technology provides for:
   a. Data rates less than X.25.
   b. Internetworking addresses within the frame.
   c. Elimination of the common carrier system.
   d. Scalable bandwidth for the user.

2. Fast packet technology using ATM provides:
   a. Fixed frame lengths.
   b. Variable frame lengths.
   c. No header information.
   d. Scalable bandwidth.

3. The layers of the ITU X.25 recommendation are:
   a. Physical, Data Link and Network.
   b. Physical, Data Link and Packet.
   c. Gateway, Router and Bridge.
   d. Application, Presentation and Session.

4. How many computers are connected to the Internet?
   a. Less than a millions.
   b. 65,535.
   c. No one knows.
   d. None—only routers and gateways.

5. Which of the following is not an Internet service?
   a. World Wide Web
   b. File Transfer Protocol
   c. E-Mail
   d. Groundhog

6. A Border Gateway Protocol is used to:
   a. Send packets based on a calculation that determines the shortest path.
   b. Store the routes to a maximum of 25 other routers.
   c. Route between autonomous systems.
   d. Gather information about other servers.

7. A DNS server is responsible for:
   a. Reconciling domain names to IP addresses.
   b. Rerouting data among computers on a LAN.
   c. Downloading network software from ISP vendors.
   d. Checking passwords for users on Department of Defense networks.

8. An Internet address is also known as a/an:
   a. HTML
   b. DHCP
   c. PPP
   d. URL

9. The Point-to-Point Protocol is responsible for all of the following, except:
   a. Encapsulating IP frames.
   b. Assigning IP addresses.
   c. Link configuration.
   d. Data rates.

10. When comparing e-mail with conventional mail service:
    a. E-mail is faster.
    b. E-mail is more expensive.
    c. Conventional mail is less hassle.
    d. Conventional mail is more convenient.

CD-ROM

Net+ Practice Test

Additional Net+ Certification testing is available on the CD that accompanies this text. The testing suite on the CD provides Study Card, Flash Card, and Run Practice type testing. The Study Card and Flash Card feature enables you to electronically link to the section of the book in which the question is covered. Choose questions from the test pool related to this chapter.

CHAPTER
9

NETWORK MANAGEMENT

LEARNING
OBJECTIVES

Upon completion of this chapter and its related lab procedures, you should be able to perform the following tasks:

1. State three areas that comprise the ISO Model for network management.

2. Describe each level of the Organizational model.

3. Describe each level of the Informational model.

4. Describe each layer of the Functional model.

5. Describe modular and tiered configurations.

6. Discuss the need for load balancing in a network.

7. State distributed and centralized network techniques used for load balancing.

8. Contrast simulated, analytical and empirical data collection methods.

9. Calculate network utilization, availability and service time.

10. Discuss the relationship between network utilization and delays.

11. Calculate throughput, response time and queue wait.

12. State a systematic troubleshooting method that will isolate the problem and lead to a resolution.

13. Given an apparent network problem, determine the nature of the action required: Information Transfer, Handholding or Technical service.

14. Given a scenario involving several network problems, prioritize them based on their seriousness.

15. Identify the extent of a given network problem scenario by determining if the problem exists across the network, at a workstation, in a LAN or WAN, and whether the problem is consistent and replicable. Use standard troubleshooting methods to select the appropriate next step, based on this approach.

16. When troubleshooting a given network problem scenario, identify the exact issue, recreate the problem, isolate the cause, and formulate a correction. Then, select the appropriate next step, based on this approach.

17. When determining whether a given problem scenario is attributable to the operator or the system, have a second operator perform the same task on an equivalent workstation, have a second operator perform the same task on the original operator's workstation, and check to see whether the operators are following SOPs. Then, select the appropriate next step based on this approach.

18. For a logical troubleshooting scenario, demonstrate awareness of the need to check for physical, and logical, trouble indicators, including link lights, power lights, error logs and displays, and performance monitors.

19 Identify network troubleshooting resources, including WWW Knowledge bases, telephone technical support, and vendor CDs.

20. Given a symptomatic network problem scenario, determine the most likely cause(s) of the problem, based on the available information. Select the most appropriate course of action after searching for abnormal physical conditions, isolating problems in faulty physical media, checking the status of servers, checking for config problems with DNS, WINS, and a HOST file, checking for viruses, checking the validity of account names and passwords, examining operator logon procedures, and selecting and running appropriate diagnostics.

21. Specify tools that are commonly used to resolve network problems. Identify the purpose and function of common network tools, including, crossover cables hardware loopbacks, tone generators, tone locators.

22. Given a network problem scenario, select the appropriate tools to help resolve the problem. Implement the correction, test the result, document the problem and solution, and give the appropriate feedback.

CHAPTER 9

Network Management

INTRODUCTION

Only within the past several years has network management percolated up from the dizzying array of data-communication issues. As with most events, the evaluation was driven by need. The need to impose umbrella-like order on networks has been overwhelming due to the rapid growth in the industry, the crossover functions of information systems and data communications specialists, and lower component costs.

A few years ago, LANs were somewhat small, with ten to twenty PCs sharing a file server, and a couple of printers. A computer-literate user usually took care of the network. Now, this same LAN may contain 500 computers, spread around fifty different rooms in a city, and interconnected to half a dozen LANs around the country. And what's become of that generous user who used to tinker with that little LAN? He's frantically documenting configuration changes, trying to determine if the latest software release is compatible with the other latest software releases installed yesterday, and the day before. Tariff changes across his WAN have left him trying to decide if he needs to lay off people, hire new people, or just blow up the whole mess.

Network management is a tool for the people who work with networks. It's intended to provide relief for the network administrator described above, and to assist in the maximizing of network resources, providing the highest level of service to users. The most widely used network management is called **Simple Network Management Protocol** (SNMP).

This chapter describes the elements of SNMP, and concentrates on an area of network management used most often by communication technologists—functional network management. Discussed are three functional areas—configuration, performance, and fault management. Troubleshooting methods, and test-equipment descriptions, are also included.

CNST OBJECTIVE
V-B

NET+ OBJECTIVE
I.6.1

MANAGEMENT FUNCTIONS

Network management describes the control and direction of data systems for users, in a climate of integrity and efficient performance. In addition, the term "network management" has come to be associated with a myriad number of data-communications specialties, such as software, hardware, human operators, and local technicians. Each of the preceding specialties fill important support roles in the dynamics of a complete system, with their relative importance being a matter of user needs, rather than an accurate descriptor of managing the complex flow of data in a network.

CNST OBJECTIVE
IX-A

NET+ OBJECTIVE
II.1.1 & II.2.1

NET+ OBJECTIVE
II.5.1 & II.3.2

The ISO takes the broader view of network management, organizing it into five functions.

> The five functions of network management considered to be essential for successful data communications are: **configuration management**, **performance management**, **fault management**, **security management**, and **accounting management**.

Configuration management is the basic mapping of a network. It includes the physical architecture, selection of hardware, protocols, interface and access methods, and the level of service provided to users. The configuration process addresses the need for growth, new technologies, changing personnel, assigning names to all internetworking components, as well as maintaining a complete inventory of the system components.

Performance management is responsible for collecting data, so that the integrity and efficiency of the network can be analyzed. Statistical information of all network components' transactions may be collected into a database for reviewing the need for improvements. How much information should be collected? This varies with the application. Most performance issues establish thresholds that must be exceeded before a transaction or event is reported. For example, a small LAN of five PCs may experience collisions every 15 minutes. The network is operable, and the users learn to live with the problem. But if the collisions began to occur every minute, the users would probably begin to moan and groan. Acceptable performance is relative to the application, and performance thresholds are established with this in mind. In the above example, users may find collisions every five minutes to be the point at which their own efficiency suffers; consequently, this will be the threshold where problems will be reported to the performance database.

As we'll see later in the chapter, performance evaluation contains an after-the-fact premise, as well as a preventive aspect. That is, problems can be corrected after they happen, or they may be predicted, and avoided, before they occur. Performance management includes either of the above, or both.

Fault management is concerned with detecting, diagnosing, and correcting problems. The intent of fault management is that it be automated, not requiring human operator intervention. For example, consider a ring network in which a node becomes disabled, and the ring is broken. The interruption will need to be reported, so that the fault manager can diagnose it as a ring break, and issue a command for rerouting data onto a redundant ring.

As mentioned in the section on performance management, simply detecting and correcting faults may not be sufficient for meeting the performance standards of a network. A fault history database is usually compiled so that trends can be analyzed by the system software for predicting future problems, and for human operators to study the network's history of problems.

Security management includes the issues dealt with in an earlier chapter. User IDs and passwords, browse and data-update access, physical security, file and record access, and access to network components, such as printers, are included in this area.

Accounting management features the cost-effectiveness of network components. The tariff rates of long-distance carriers, delays versus costs of satellite transmissions, the need for investing in new equipment, the cost of a network service to users, as well as the total cost of network services, are areas of concern to accounting management.

The OSI considers configuration, performance, fault, security, and accounting management as part of a functional model of network management. It includes the areas most commonly associated with data communications, and LANs in particular.

The bulk of this chapter focuses on network management functions, particularly configuration, performance, and fault functions. However, it should be noted that network management functions are a subset of network management.

A complete view of network management is shown in Table 9-1.

Table 9-1 ISO Network Management Model

ORGANIZATIONAL MODEL	INFORMATIONAL MODEL	FUNCTIONAL MODEL
Management Domain	Management Information Base	Confirmation Management
Management Subdomain	Entries	Performance Management
Managed System	• Attribute/Value	Fault Management
Managed Object	• Operations	Security Management
	• Messages	Accounting Management

In addition to the functional model, an organizational and informational model are illustrated. The three form a complete model for network management. The **organizational model** attempts to impose systematic order on the network. The **informational model** formally defines network components, and their relationships. The **functional model** is a series of procedures carried out by the network.

The premise of the organizational model is the **object**. An object is a network resource, either physical or abstract. Examples of objects are virtual connections, all layers of the OSI reference model, as well as software commands and messages. Physical objects include network cards, port connections, and so forth. An object is controlled by a **managed system**, comprised of a logical object groupings. Collecting information about how well a LAN is performing may comprise a managed system. A managed system can fall within a management subdomain. Management **domains** group similar subsystems. Performance, and error detection, may be under control of different management systems, but be categorized within the same management subdomain. In turn, a subdomain is organized under a general management domain. For example, a management domain may be responsible for data collection on a LAN. Reports of collisions, throughput, and bottlenecks may be collected in this domain, and the succeeding subdomains, systems and objects, exist to provide the data.

Subdomains, managed systems, and objects often overlap to serve many masters. Information about error detection will also be reported to a domain responsible for correcting errors.

The informational model specifies the characteristics that are maintained in a **Management Information Database** (MIB) in the form of entries. An entry describes the characteristics of an object in three ways: by its attributes and value, by the operations that can be conducted on an object, and by messages that a managed system may report to another managed system. An example of the attribute/value of an object is **priority token allocation** in a ring network. A particular node may need to receive the ring token more often than the other nodes. In this case, the node has an attribute of "priority token", and a value which represents how often the node needs access to the network.

The management information database will also contain a list of operations that can be performed on the object. To continue with the "priority token" example, the list may include a token routing map, and a clock that tracks the time since the priority node last transmitted.

CNST OBJECTIVE
V-B

In order to prioritize the ring token for a particular node, there must be message communication between the token and MIB. These messages will be contained in the database.

The functional model contains management duties as described earlier in this section. It's important to realize that all three areas comprise a network management model. Most features of the organizational and informational model are imbedded in existing networks, and are understood to be performing when "managing" a network. Technically, it is incorrect to consider network management from the perspective of any of the three models. From a practical point of view, it is the functional aspects of a network that concern the user, operators, technicians, and administrators on a day-to-day basis. For this reason, network management functions will be detailed in this chapter.

CONFIGURATION MANAGEMENT

> Configuration management is a physical and logical map of a network.

Configuration management deals with what the network consists of. All devices, or objects, in the network are accounted for by name, as well as by their physical and logical connections. This function of network management also manipulates devices and connections to keep the network running, and delivering the expected level of service.

Issues

Network configuration begins with determining the **needs** of the users who will request services from the network. For stand-alone LANs, these needs may include printer sharing, access levels, file storage and sharing, types of media access, and so forth. For larger, or interconnected LANs, the list of user needs can be quite long—user ID verification, protocol conversion, alternate carrier routes, printer spooling, device initiation, and the use and implementation of communication controllers and multiplexers.

Transparent **connectivity** is achieved with topology tools that determine which devices are connected to the network, thus creating a map for network operators to use. A map is meaningless without device names, and network configuration. Management assigns names to all devices on the network. Any network changes, such as adding, deleting, or creating objects are also included in the topology mapping.

A network is well suited to **modularization** through thoughtful configuration. The configuration may need to be changed to include new equipment, to offer new or expanded services, or to partition a failed section of the network from other users, without interrupting services.

Tiered architectures are also considered an important application of configuration management. In order to initiate, or terminate, network sessions with devices on the network, to track current connections on the network, and to change the configuration of the network, an orderly system of naming devices and imposing order on their organization is needed. The tiered architecture is found in the organizational model in which logical and physical services are called objects. The objects are under the control of managed systems. Network management systems, which are described shortly, address the details of tiered or partitioned architectures.

Configuration management looks at the **on-line monitoring** of networks to determine if modifications should be made. Of particular concern to LANs is **load balancing** and scheduling of network processes. These are vital issues in **distributed environments** (a LAN without a centralized file server). Load balancing is the even distribution of network processes among nodes. For example, if ten computers are connected to a distributed LAN, each PC should share in the responsibility of network management. Now, if these PCs are connected to a WAN containing a dozen LANs, the issue of load balancing can be critical. If one of the twelve LANs has allocated a large share of its resources to network management, the other LANs are getting a free ride at the expense of the users of the overloaded LAN.

There are two approaches to load balancing in configuration management: **detect and fix** overload conditions, or avoid overloads through **scheduling**. In the first approach, the network is continuously monitored, and problems exceeding a defined threshold are compiled until the overload occurs. At this time, the network is reconfigured and the resource load is redistributed.

Scheduling is a management concept that determines what is done, when it's done, and where it's done. In network management, "it" refers to an object, or a network resource. Scheduling presupposes a predestined future, and requires tools for decision making, prioritizing resource functions, and networking, even where there is no predestined future. Even error-correction techniques are based on an understanding of predictable problems. Scheduling in networks is complicated by the varying times required to complete system changes. For example, changes in a computer connected to a network occur much faster than a change transmitted across a network, particularly if network nodes are separated by thousands of miles. If all nodes in a network could be simultaneously advised of a scheduling change intended to normalize the work load of nodes, there would be no need for on-line monitoring. Without continuous monitoring, network modifications that address load balancing will always be "two steps" behind the problem.

The decision making used for scheduling modifications in LANs is founded in **fuzzy logic**. This is logic that presupposes a future event (problem) based upon online monitoring of current network conditions. Fuzzy logic is formulated by a best-effort guess of what is about to happen. This guess is based upon a partial understanding of events and circumstances.

In network management, **artificial intelligence systems** have been effective in assisting network managers with scheduling problems. At the present, artificial intelligence systems are diagnostic tools and generally associated with fault management.

Distributed and Centralized Configurations

Configuration management is concerned with network topology, and network managers must, at some point, decide whether the network resources are to be distributed among nodes, or controlled at a central location. At the LAN level, the discussion revolves around a dedicated **file server**, or the decision to distribute LAN management among network PCs.

The decision to centralize or distribute network management functions will be inadequate or impossible without a basic view of operating systems. The function of all operating systems is to provide a service to a client. In the case of DOS, a PC is the client, and as such, is served by DOS. Without a workable operating system, users are forced to dictate service requests to the PC in machine code.

The idea of associating an operating system with LANs has communication between users as the root. The early LAN operating systems could be fairly simple, since they involved transmitting and receiving messages. The software for controlling these communications could be maintained in each computer's storage area. In short order, users who had been exposed to communications began to ask "what if..." questions about their network. What if I want to add several layers of security? What if one of the computers needs to send more data than the others? What if there was software that could document the volume and type of problems users encountered? The "what if" list went on and on, and was continually addressed through new releases of network software. As users demanded more resources, vendors developed more powerful network software.

Note that a network encompasses a distributed allocation of resources. Since the resources are widespread, why maintain the control in a single machine? Why not provide a network operating system imbedded into the system hardware, rather than built on top of it? This is the present state of network operating systems, and can be found in the products of many IC manufacturers.

Implicit in network software is the need for fairness in sharing the network resources. For small to medium LANs, this isn't too difficult, but as the size of a network grows, so does complexity. It isn't feasible to develop "fair" network hardware for distributed LANs since, as was mentioned earlier, the response time to changes across a network vary.

This brings us to the configuration question: should network management be centralized or distributed? The following sections examine the case for centralized file servers in LANs and distributed network management.

Centralized Systems

A LAN with a centralized network manager is illustrated in Figure 9-1. The network manager is connected into a bus LAN with five other PCs. Typically, the network manager (also called a file server) is dedicated to managing the network. The file server is available for many network resources, such as bus management, collision detection, file write/read storage, compiling statistical lists, and so on.

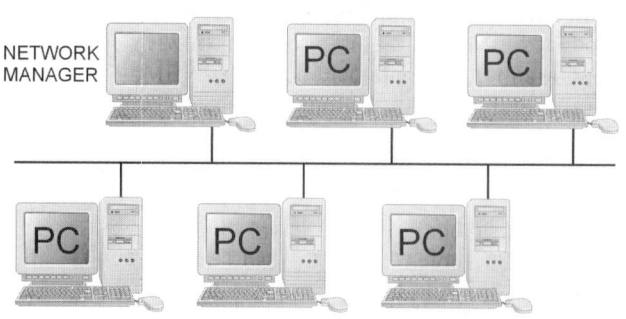

Within the file server resides all aspects of network management. From a maintenance stand, centralized systems make a lot of sense. Skilled personnel need only to be located at a single site, rather than query remote sites and the media between. Troubleshooting the network can take place from a single terminal (the file server in Figure 9-2). Centralized control of LANs makes for simpler implementation of modifications because changes are controlled from a single site. Performance of centralized management is usually superior to distributed systems, although performance is very much dependent on applications. Single servers are more secure than distributed management, simply because it's easier to safeguard one computer than twenty computers.

Figure 9-1 Centralized Network Management

Centralizing networking management does however, have its problems. The worst is that end users suffer under the system due to the lack of control they have. Flexibility for addressing changes of workstations, or an entire LAN, is difficult, particularly if the central host is remote from the point of change. It's also likely that if control is distributed, the network will achieve higher utilization rates and greater efficiencies. But this assumes the distributed sites are staffed by personnel who are qualified at fine-tuning their network.

Distributed Systems

A distributed network management system is shown in Figure 9-2. Each of the PCs contain a network card and the software for managing the network. Management of the network is replicated among the five PCs; that is, there exists a peer consensus of resource utilization. If a change is made, all PCs become aware of the change. This is an improvement over centralized systems, since a user has many sources for data, and doesn't have to que for access at the central server. This is the reason throughput in distributed systems is better than in centralized systems.

Distributed network management of LANs is less memory dependent than centralized systems, because the network shares the memory of all stations, resulting in improved efficiencies.

Typically, distributed systems are slower than centralized systems. Recall that changes propagate much more slowly across the network than within a single computer. When a change or modification is made affecting all workstations on the network, it's not complete until all the stations acknowledge the change. In a centralized system, changes are initiated from the central file server to all the affected stations.

Figure 9-2 Distributed Network Management

A third method of configuring the management of networks includes a little of both distributed and centralized systems. This is illustrated in Figure 9-3. Each host provides remote, centralized network management to groups of LANs. The hosts are distributed, yet connected, to provide high-speed communication exchanges. The hosts are cooperating servers, not unlike the PCs in Figure 9-2. The advantage of this system is that if changes are made, only three servers need assimilate the information. This is a significant time saver, and provides many of the advantages of a central system, such as lower maintenance costs, improved security, and better control over performance.

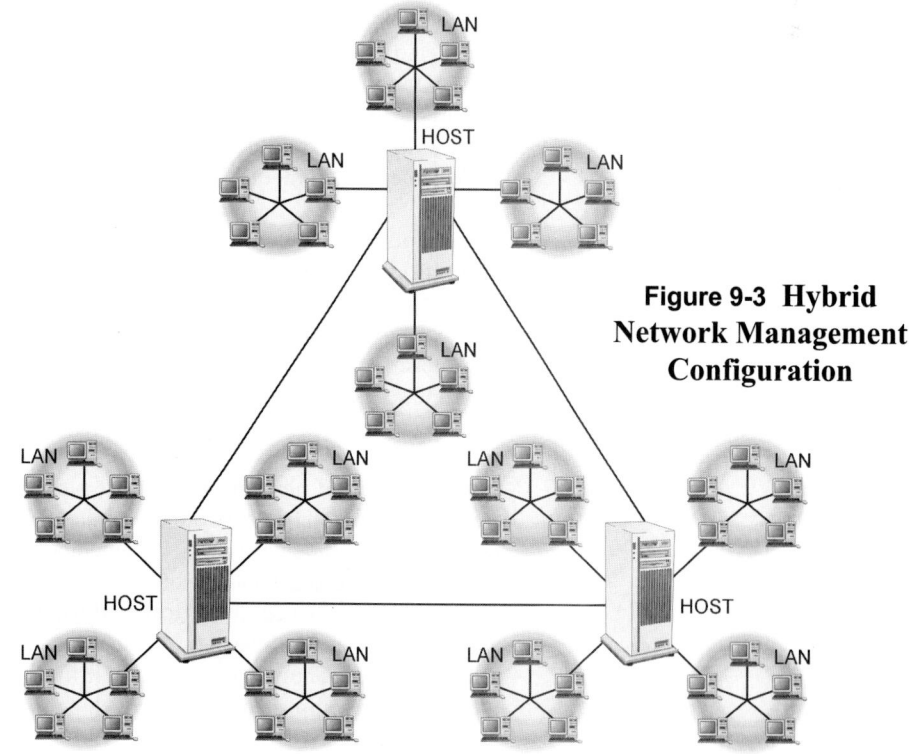

Figure 9-3 Hybrid Network Management Configuration

PERFORMANCE MANAGEMENT

The performance management function is responsible for collecting analytical and empirical data for analyzing the integrity and efficiency of the network.

The purpose of performance management is to analyze the network's operational effectiveness. Generally, this involves evaluating the degree of network utilization, delays that messages encounter en route to the destination, and the **throughput** of the network. Throughput describes the actual amount of data transmitted in a stated period of time.

Measurements are meaningless without agreed-upon evaluation criteria. For example, throughput is measured in bits for LANs, but for WANS, data packets, or frames, are measured. Before analyzing the performance of the network, the evaluation criteria must be developed. Once this is done, there must be agreement on the point, or threshold, that the performance information is considered to be significant. The utilization of a network is measured by considering the ratio of how much time a network is actually used to the time that services are available to users. It's stated as a percentage. One LAN may have a utilization rate of 50%, but another may have a 75% utilization rate. Network managers must determine the **thresholds of performance** parameters, as well as establish the specifics of the evaluation criteria. These are set by default in the software, and are user-selectable.

Once the evaluation thresholds have been set, performance information and statistics are collected in a **database**, which contains current and historical information. Current statistics advise the operators of problems that are occurring, or are about to occur. Once the thresholds are exceeded, the fault-management functions take over in dealing with the problem.

The historical database is maintained so that long-term trends can be analyzed. If, over a period of months, it appears as if the waiting time of transmitted messages is high compared to the total number of messages (system <response time), then network operators can fine-tune the network so that users will spend less time waiting for the services to be completed. The initialization for modifying network components (which is the job of the configuration function) is begun in performance management. The example given earlier of improving the system response rate is a case in point. The performance data has revealed a need to improve the rate, and informs the configuration function. The configuration management implements the needed changes.

The performance management features supported by network management vendors varies a great deal. **Trend analysis** based upon current and historical data is common. User-selectable thresholds, and evaluation parameters, are generally available. Some vendors supply reports of system anomalies. For example, such a report might mention short-term but recurring events, such as an increase in collisions when many users are using the same service. Reports available from the performance database are organized in units of time in most of the software—daily, weekly, monthly, etc.

The realization of performance requirements is a practice in predictability. The common technique for predicting network performance, and then measuring the performance, is based on performance models. A model is a method of analyzing the behavior of a network, and all network management tools make use of it. There are three primary network models used in evaluating performance: **analytical models**, **simulation models**, and **empirical models**. The analytical approach emphasizes average values in a system. Simulation models are developed on desk-top PCs. The network is created in the PC, and analyzed without actually constructing the network. An empirical model is developed by analyzing events as they actually occur.

Simulation models are typically of use in the design stage of a network. The network can be studied to see how it performs under varying loads, topology changes, hardware additions, and so forth. Simulations can also be helpful in evaluating long-term trends.

Analytical models for studying network performance are commonly incorporated into network management software, and maintained in the database as a performance function. They form the base for historical data.

An empirical model is the ultimate in accuracy, since data is extracted from the system as it occurs. In performance management, the techniques of empirical modeling are applied in creating a database of current data.

The majority of data available to network managers is compiled by using the analytical and empirical methods. As mentioned earlier, network performance functions are clustered around network utilization, delays, and throughput. The following sections delineate common types of data available in these three areas. Keep in mind that the information has, at its source, a modeling approach, and as such, is suggesting intelligent and informed guesses.

Network Utilization

Network utilization should be concerned with the degree by which the network is being used. The common-sense reason is to determine if the system is capable of delivering the services expected of it. Or, the network may be endowed with services that are seldom used, and hence, not needed.

Utilization, workload, and response-times are interrelated. If all network components (computers, printers, modems, etc.) are engaged, the utilization will be high. Since the components are being used, the network services are in high demand. When the load on a network increases, **response time** is slower. Response time refers to the time it takes to complete a service.

Response-time from a user's view is quite subjective. However, if there's a consensus that the network is "slow" during times of heavy use, the network manager will be expected to do something about it.

Network utilization is the ratio of the time a network is used to the total time it's available, or:

$$U = TB/T$$

where U = utilization expressed as a percentage, TB = the time that the network is busy, and T = the total time that the network is available.

If a LAN is available for use eight hours a day, and it's used six hours a day, the utilization is found by:

$$U = 6/8 = 75\%$$

Network availability is the amount of time the network services are available to users.

Closely related to utilization is the amount of time the network services are available. **Availability** considers components or services that aren't available and provides the network manager with insight to the time spent on network maintenance. Availability is found by:

$$A = (TB - TD)/T$$

where A = availability expressed as a percentage, TB = time the network is busy, TD = time the network is down, and T = the total time that is available to use the network.

As an example, consider a LAN that's available for 10 hours, but a file server is taken down for maintenance for 1 hour. The time the network is available is found by:

$$A = (10-1)/10 = 90\%$$

This tells the network operator that on this particular day the network was available for 90% of the day. If this data is collected daily, a pattern will eventually emerge in which the manager can develop network reliability reports.

If, in the above example, a single PC were to fail for an hour, in addition to the file server, is the network "down" for the hour it took to fix the PC? The answer is considered to be yes, because without the PC, the network is unable to provide the full range of services it was intended to provide. The availability is now determined as:

$$A = (10-2)/10 = 80\%$$

Network utilization is an indication of the demands for the network's services, and network availability describes the amount of time users can receive access to the network's services. But how does a network manager know if the users are receiving the full benefit of the services? One way is to track the **system service time**.

System service time is the average amount of time a message spends in the system, en route to its destination. It is calculated by:

$$S = B/C$$

where S = system service time, B = busy time, and C = the number of completed messages.

Imagine a LAN in which data is transmitted at 1 kBPS. Ideally, a message could be sent in 1 mS (T = 1/BPS = 1/1000 = 1 mS). In reality, the message contains overhead characters, network devices require time to add and strip the overhead, search files, and so forth. Let's assume that these miscellaneous tasks require 2 mS, so the total amount of time the network is busy is 1 mS + 2 mS = 3 mS. Now, we'll calculate the system service time.

$$S = 3 \text{ mS}/1000$$
$$S = .3 \text{ mS}$$

If the service time is calculated for the ideal LAN, it's:

$$S = 1 \text{ mS}/1000$$
$$S = .1 \text{ mS}$$

Not surprisingly, the amount of time a message spends in the system is higher when machine delays are considered. As more messages are transmitted, so that the network utilization increases, the delays become more pronounced. Rather than increase linearly as the service time formula suggests, there's a nonlinear increase, as shown in Figure 9-4.

The graph shows that as the number of network messages increase, the longer it will take to service each message. A point is reached where the delays increase sharply, and the network is said to contain a **bottleneck**. The performance function tracks the system service time so that when the bottleneck threshold approaches, an alarm is set that initiates fault management to issue interrupts.

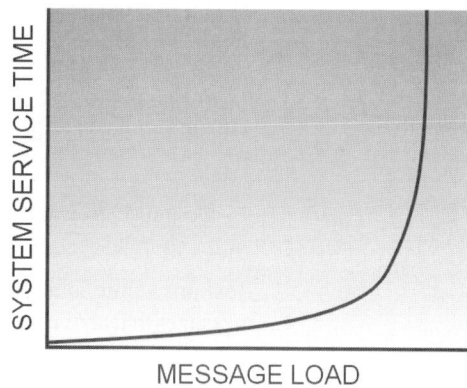

Figure 9-4 System Service Time vs Message Load

Delays

Delays in a network cripple efficiency. The lower the efficiency, the poorer the performance. The network media, software, buffers, memory capacity, and the time needed to read and write files are all examples of network delays. Consider a network in which five users send files to a printer. The printer can print only one file at a time so a line, or queue, is formed. For those files waiting in the printer queue, delays are introduced on the network.

> Throughput describes the number of delivered messages when delays are considered.

The most commonly quoted indication of a network's delay characteristic is **throughput**. Throughput is the actual number of messages sent in a given time. It's calculated by:

$$TP = C/T$$

where TP = throughput, C = the number of messages sent, and T = the total time of the transmission.

The benefits of measuring throughput can be oblique. As in an earlier example, consider a network with a data rate of 1 KBPS. Again, the time to transmit a single bit is 1 mS. But assume we're sending 7-bit ASCII characters with 1 start bit, 1 stop bit, and 1 parity bit. Then, one character contains 10 bits. Our 1 KBPS data stream has 100 characters (1000/10=100). The time needed to transmit one hundred 10-bit characters is 100 x 1 mS = 1 sec. If there were no delays in the network, 100 characters could be transmitted in 1 second.

In fact, there are delays. Assume these delays consume 1.5s. The total time of the transmission is 1 sec. + 1.5 sec. = 2.5 seconds.

$$TP = 100/2.5$$
$$TP = 40$$

The throughput is 40 characters/sec. rather than the transmitted rate of 100 characters/sec.

The throughput rate represents an average of the ideal transmitted time (called **burst rate**) and the **delay time**. It's a very good performance indicator to consider when vendor literature places so much emphasis on network speed. A network may be capable of very high data rates, but if the delays are also high, the throughput will be low. Throughput is a much more meaningful tool for analyzing the system's response time for delivering services to users.

Response time is the time required to deliver a message.

Response time is actually the reciprocal of throughput. As throughput describes the messages that arrive as a function of system delays, response time describes how much time is consumed in delivering a message. Mathematically, it's stated:

$$R = T/C$$

where R = response time, T = total time messages are required to wait in the network, and C = total completed messages.

The performance software will generally determine how much time messages wait in **queues** by averaging the length of all queues in a network. It's determined by:

$$Q = W/T$$

where Q = average queue length, W = total time messages wait in a system, and T = total time of a message run.

The ultimate justification of performance management is to maximize network resources. The LAN manager has analytical and empirical data available in the performance database to draw conclusions about the performance. This is **objective data**.

Equally important is **subjective information**, particularly the complaints of users. It is the network users who are employing the resources of the network. The users' lack of technical understanding of the network results in vague, nonspecific observations of the tools they're working with.

In addition to interpreting performance database information and user concerns, the LAN manager should possess a thorough understanding of all aspects of the network environment. If the network delays are excessive due to heavy loading, should the network be taken apart and reassembled in a different topology? Is the problem in the twisted-pair transmission media, and is it time to upgrade to coax cable? Is the file server inadequate? Strong technical competencies of network managers provide intuitive insight to solutions that should ensure that the network resources are maximized.

FAULT MANAGEMENT

Fault management is concerned with detecting, diagnosing, and correcting problems.

Fault management is intended to detect problems, offer diagnostics, maintain a record of the problems, and in some cases, correct the problems. Companies can experience considerable losses if their networks aren't running smoothly.

The banking industry is heavily dependent on data communications in credit card departments, automated tellers, and for loan processing. Organizations, with far-flung offices that are electronically connected, may simply grind to a standstill if their network goes down.

Looking for problems in a network can be more frustrating than in many industries. The reason is that networks are designed to be transparent to users, and the characteristic that makes them so desirable to laymen is the same characteristic that can hide problems. That is, data communications inherently obscures the technical information needed by technicians. This is the huge advantage of using network analysis software that shows you the underlying activity in a network.

The ideal network is available to users 100% of the time services are requested. In reality, 98% availability is the average. The network manager addresses the 2% of the time that users are idle, because of network problems.

Fault management is usually the first line of defense for managers, because it's preventative. Problem trends may be developing in the network, and the user may not be aware of anything amiss. For example, throughput may gradually decline, and the only symptom noticed by the user is that "the network seems slow today."

Fault management software may accomplish many of the troubleshooting tasks on a network. It's the intent of the software to do this without human intervention, which includes fixing problems in such a way as to keep the network running. For the most part, problems are fixed by **reconfiguring**. If a modem is disabled, data will be routed to another modem, or if a switch is stuck, the data traffic is sent via another switch, and so on. The only true solution to automated fault correction is **redundancy**. This isn't practical in most situations, since, to be fault tolerant, a component will need to be duplicated—computers, printers, cabling, servers, etc.

If the fault management function can't fix a problem, the network manager is usually provided with recommendations of possible causes. But when that doesn't work, it's time to get the hands dirty. The next section describes several troubleshooting strategies

NETWORK TROUBLESHOOTING

In troubleshooting networks, a problem is a deviation from normal conditions.

A network management protocol such as SNMP automates much of the data collection phase that's important to getting a handle on how well a network is performing. Once you determine that some aspect needs attention, then you must determine the most appropriate course of action to take. This may seem oversimplified and obvious, but a network can be complex. Making matters more difficult, it's always supposed to be up and available to the user.

You probably won't be in a position to dawdle while figuring out the problem. You may not be able to take the complete system down, to swap devices in a trial-and-error process, either. Before you begin, then, you need to be able to carefully access the symptoms of a problem, then select the most intelligent course of action.

The logic applied to troubleshooting a network is no different than troubleshooting any equipment or system that doesn't seem to be working properly. The prerequisite first step is to have a complete understanding of how the system functions, when there are no problems.

This means ensuring that you've studied the concepts of networking technology such as architecture, media, protocols, the function of all devices on the network, and how all of the parts fit together. Next, you need to be well versed in conventional practices used to operate and manage the network. This includes configuration of the devices, the effects of changes such as software upgrades, or the introduction of a new device.

Initial Problem Response

Network problems in the field may be communicated via workorders, telephone calls, e-mail, or by an informal approach. Once the problem, or apparent problem, has been handed to you, a decision needs to be made on the next step to take. It's important to recognize that, to one uninitiated in networking, an actual problem is no different than a perceived problem. You must treat perceived problems with the same seriousness that you would an actual problem.

NET+ OBJECTIVE II.4.1

The reason for this is that network users are customers, even if you both work for the same company. To provide value to the service you provide, and to secure a need for your job, your ability to relate well to customers should always guide your actions.

With this in mind, you also need to make a smart decision concerning the level of support that a reported problem warrants. Your time is money; if not specifically to you, then to the company you work for. In all fairness to the organization that pays you, you need to budget your time so that your personal attention to a problem is actually needed. Some problems can be dealt with over the telephone, others by referring the user to printed material, but others require that you conduct an in-person visit.

Table 9-2 lists three initial responses to take when a problem is first reported. The first, **Information Transfer**, is appropriate in a situation where reference material will address the problem just as effectively as if you were going to the client and doing it yourself. Notice that such information may be in many forms. Not all computer users are comfortable, or knowledgeable, with on-line Help screens. Five minutes of quick training on the telephone is a better investment than a couple of hours of in-person help.

Table 9-2 Initial Problem Response

Initial Problem Response	
Response	**Action**
1) Information Transfer	How-to, Standard Operating Procedures, User Manuals, Help Menus
2) Handholding	Telephone support, Step-by-step walk through
3) Technical service	In-person help, machine or network maintenance and diagnostics

Hand-holding means you devote time, usually on the telephone, to working with the user on the problem. Typically, the difficulty level of a problem generating a hand-holding response is greater that a referral for information. Yet, it still doesn't necessitate you dropping whatever you're doing, and going to the customer's workstation.

Many help-desk tasks involve the hand-holding approach, which can save you time, and save your company money. To be successful, though, a hand-holding approach needs some preparation. The following suggestions will be helpful in setting it up:

- Make a list of typical problems that can be resolved over the telephone. Normally, these involve guiding the user through screens leading to configuration settings, and having them read the settings back to you.

- Take the time to list the paths to pertinent information, such as NIC card settings and modem settings. At a server, note the paths to user rights, access, file and directory configuration, domain or workgroup membership, software versions, method of IP assignment, and so forth.

- Consider creating flowcharts as a quick reference.

- Stay with the user until the problem is resolved, or until you escalate it to the next step.

Technical service means you must apply your expertise. This may be in person, or may require your hands-on involvement at a remote terminal. Certainly, if a problem can't be fixed by providing phone support, more drastic action is needed. In the purist sense, technical service involves cutting through red tape, and resolving a problem—perceived or otherwise. Consider the following when offering technical help:

- If the user is located at a distance, determine if the device (computer, router, etc.) can be shipped to you for an exchange.

- Check maintenance agreements and service contracts to determine if the action is specified.

- Check to see if support is available at the site. If so, make the effort to contact them on behalf of the user.

- Go to the location yourself. Some companies charge-back support for computers and networks. If this is the case, you'll need approvals from the site manager, and perhaps, the management at your location. This is where the use of structured workorders is beneficial.

- Stay with the problem until it's resolved.

As an example, suppose you receive a call from a user who needs to know how to get his/her computer to connect to another printer. What is you initial response? Referring them to an SOP, or vendor's user guide, probably won't help. And unless there's an issue of manually changing print rights, you could do this over the telephone.

Step the user through the screens and folders needed to map them to the printer, or print server. At each step, quiz them back on any changes you tell them to make. Once the task is completed, have them print a test page and wait to see if it prints. If so, the job is done, and you can go back to other things.

Or, consider this example. You handle a call from a network operator who tells you that when an NT server was brought-up, it "blue-screened" indefinitely. The server isn't going to boot, and the operator doesn't know what to do next. An information referral won't help much here, either. When this happens with an NT server, it could be one of several problems, all of which involve specialized skills (a hard drive crash, system BIOS problems, lack of RAM, for example).

Consider the skill level of the operator. If you're not sure, go see for yourself. In this scenario, the entire network is down, and this may not be the time for a long-distance learning experience.

Let's assume that a problem has been brought to you, and you've determined that it requires specialized technical assistance—rather than telephone support or a software upgrade. Before going any further in fixing the problem, you then prioritize it according to its overall effect on the operation of the network. Remember, troubleshooting a network often requires a triage approach. You determine what is having the severest effect, and deal with that. It's no doubt very irritating if one user can't print, but it's a bit more important if no users can access application software in a server.

As an example, study the nature of the following problems and prioritize them:

NET+ OBJECTIVE
II.4.2

> a. A server won't boot.
> b. A new user needs a password assigned.
> c. All users on a LAN are unable to print.
> d. The "battery-low" light on a server's backup power supply is blinking.

The first priority is to get the server to boot. This is an immediate problem, and affects all of the network users connected to the server. The second priority is to determine why no LAN users can access their printer. If all other activities appear normal, it should be relatively easy to fix. Third most important item on the list is to replace the battery in the uninterruptable power supply. Finally, the new user should be given a password.

Notice how the network would be affected if the non-booting server took a backseat to the problem of assigning a password to the new user. Clients on the LAN would all be left waiting, while one individual was taken care of. This is seldom in the best interests of a company. But what about the server that has a low-battery light? If it goes down, that's worse than having users who can't print. The fact is, it isn't down, and you can only assume that the server is providing a full range of services. In other words, it's working properly. If, however, the battery were to die, and power dropped out to this server, then another network would be down, and the printer problem would have to wait anyway.

Prioritize problems based upon their overall effect on the operation of the network.

Systematic Approach to Problem Identification

Once a problem percolates up to your immediate attention, you then have to decide the extent of the problem. Does it affect the entire network, a single LAN, or a single user? Is it a problem that, at the moment is localized, but will eventually affect all users (such as a virus). Is the problem associated with specific activities such as logons, printing, or file sharing?

NET+ OBJECTIVE
II.5.1

Table 9-3 lists four steps that CompTIA has specified as a systematic approach to identifying the extent of a problem. These steps assume that you've worked your way through an initial response to a problem, you've decided that technical service is required, and you have prioritized the problems based upon their effect on the network. This would now lead you to deciding the extent of a problem.

First, determine if the entire network is affected by the problem. The best way to do this is to collaborate the problem call with other users. Depending on your resources, you may be able to access problem logs on the affected network, and gather information.

In the second step, localize the problem to a specific function of network machines. If all clients are having a similar problem, shift your analysis to the LAN level. If it doesn't extend to hubs or the server, you've gone too far.

Table 9-3 Steps for Identifying the Extent of a Problem

Steps for Identifying the Extent of a Problem
1) Determine whether a problem exists across a network.
2) Determine whether the problem is workstation, LAN or WAN.
3) Determine whether a problem is consistent and replicable.
4) Use Standard troubleshooting methods.

If, however, network equipment on the LAN is affected, you'll need to look outside of the LAN. Perhaps the LAN is interconnected to another LAN by a router. Check to see if the other LAN is experiencing similar problems. If so, you've now determined that the problem is WAN-wide, so there's no reason to concentrate your efforts on the client computers.

Notice that in the first two steps, you're attempting to establish the boundaries of the problem. A similar technique is used to troubleshoot printed circuit boards for unknown problems. You check sections of the board in gradually increasing areas, until you detect a malfunction. The problem area then lies between the last known good area, and the current boundary.

The third step is not always possible. It depends on the equipment at your disposal. The idea is to determine if you can duplicate a problem by placing a suspect machine in a known good setting. For example, assume a router is the suspect. You would remove it and place it in a mock-setup to see if the problem will surface once all other devices are eliminated. If it does, you've replicated the problem, and can replace the router with a known good one.

The last step is the application of standard troubleshooting techniques. This occurs at any of the above steps, but particularly when you've isolated the problem to a specific network device. There are, of course, many ways to troubleshoot. But in lieu of experience, a basic set of sound techniques may be all you have to begin the process. The following presents two approaches to troubleshooting. Either approach represents a workable method and should be used as a model, to meld with your own personality, style, and technique, with time and experience.

A consistent, methodical approach is necessary when approaching network faults. Figure 9-5 outlines a procedure for identifying the ultimate culprit of a problem.

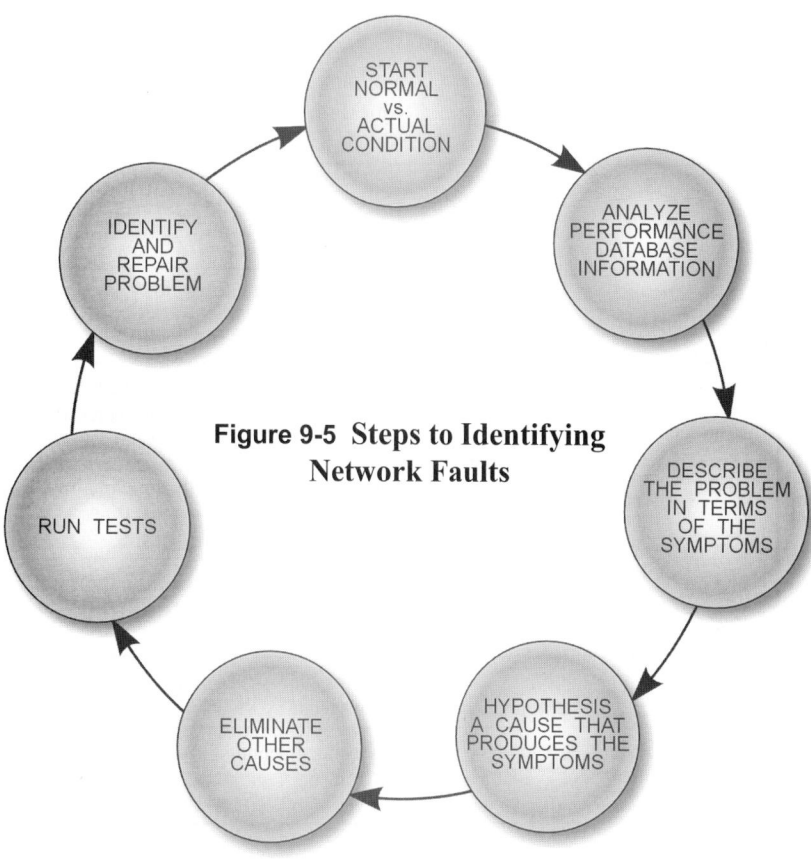

Figure 9-5 Steps to Identifying Network Faults

Before a problem can be classified as such, it must be described in relative terms. Is the network slow? What is normal? A problem is a deviation from the normal condition. If the normal response time is one second, and you notice the time leaps to five seconds, there's a problem. Five seconds is a deviation from the normal one-second response time.

A systematic approach to troubleshooting reduces network downtime.

As the first place to start, **observe the actual vs. Normal conditions**. This is consistent with the accepted troubleshooting techniques of observing the symptoms first. Next, **analyze the performance database** for clues. Are there developing trends similar to the observed conditions? When did the trend begin—yesterday, last week, last month? Keep in mind that many networks appear to be operating, but may actually be riddled with problems. Short of a network crash, or an obviously inoperable network device, a problem may not be obvious. Once the performance data has been analyzed, **describe the problem in terms of the symptoms**. Resist the urge to skip ahead to fix the problem. The lack of thoroughness in analyzing faults can create more problems than any self-induced network malfunction.

When the symptoms can be specifically stated, it's time to **develop a hypothesis** that could create them. The key question to ask is: "Could this problem cause the symptoms I've documented?" If the answer is "no," discard the hypothesis and try again. The pitfall of this technique is that a potential problem may be overlooked, or the total synergism of the network may not fully be understood. A discarded hypothesis may in fact be correct, but this is less likely than precious network time being lost due to rushed and incomplete deductions.

A hypothesis that explains the symptoms is the one to explore. **Eliminate the other causes**, and concentrate on the one. **Tests should be run** using the network software, and appropriate test equipment, in an effort to prove the hypothesis. If this is successful, **fix the problem**. But if the hypothesis doesn't prove to be valid, it's time to go back and re-examine the symptoms. Perhaps a crucial clue was overlooked. The problem could be transient or intermittent. Question the implications of the observed/recorded symptoms, and try again.

Table 9-4 DETECT Troubleshooting Method

Another network troubleshooting approach is shown in Table 9-4. DETECT is a suggested technique from Microsoft, and is an acronym for Discover, Explore, Track, Execute, Check, and Tie-up. DETECT may be helpful to you, because it emphasizes follow-up techniques.

DETECT Troubleshooting Strategy	
Discover	Discover the problem by gathering information related to the problem area. Determine any aspect that's deviating from its normal state or operation.
Explore	Explore the boundaries of the problem. Determine if it's specific to a network, a single client, or a server. Attempt to reproduce the problem in either a mock-network or by isolating nodes that aren't affected.
Track	Track the possible approaches to solving the problem by analyzing past histories of problem logs, talking to peers, contacting vendor support, or referencing vendor documentation.
Execute	Execute a problem solving approach. Ensure you backup the existing parameters, and document each change to the system so it can be returned to its benchmark state.
Check	Check to see if the fix was successful. Make sure the problem is a permanent fix and won't recur.
Tie-up	Tie up the loose ends by documenting the solution and making it available to others. Check back with the client to ensure the problem hasn't resurfaced.

Discover means to discover the problem. Essentially, it's a directive to conduct a root-cause-analysis of the symptoms. A problem may be communicated to you as "I can't get on the network." As a fever is a symptom of an actual illness, this "problem" is symptomatic of an abnormal condition on the network. Again, what's normal? You'll never know unless you establish baseline parameters for all devices you're responsible for.

Document configuration settings, the physical architecture of the network, all permissions and authorities. It's possible that the client was never given assess to the network. Or, it's possible that the client NIC is not communicating. Discover all aspects of the symptom, and the possible causes that may contribute to it.

Explore means to explore the boundaries of the problem. That is, how much of the network is affected by the symptom? Is it a global effect or localized to a LAN, or a single PC? You must think in alternate terms of hardware and software when exploring problems, because they both may have a local or global effect.

For example, consider the problem mentioned previously in which an IP address could be successfully pinged but, a domain name could not. It's unlikely that a hardware problem (such as a router) is causing the problem, because the device works with one of the criteria. But if the server DNS software isn't setup properly for name resolution, the ping will fail on DNS only. And, by extension, the problem should be localized to a single LAN that affects all clients in the LAN.

Track refers to track the possible approaches. This means to figure out the possible solutions to the problem, as identified in the explore strategy. If you're stuck, this is the time to call in any outstanding markers, and do it quickly. And if you're still stuck, get on the telephone and ask for help.

It's extremely important to understand that if the user/customer can't do his/her job because the network is down, it's your fault. Whether it actually is or not is immaterial, because that's the perception, and you must address it quickly and accurately. A problem resolution log can be very helpful in this situation, because if someone else has dealt with similar symptoms, their approach may work in your situation.

Execute means to place a specific troubleshooting approach into action. Decide on a course of action to fix the problem, then do it. A word of caution: Document any changes you make to the network. Then, if your approach doesn't fix the problem, you can return the network to its original state before trying another approach. This may include backing up the contents of a server, or making copies of important files such as the Registry. If the changes may have an undetermined effect on other network devices, consider disconnecting the unit from the network while troubleshooting it.

Check your approach for success. If your fix appears to clear the problem, stick around and make sure it doesn't resurface. Typically, an SOP should be in place that specifies the criteria for checking the success of fixes. This may involve a time period, such as fifteen minutes, or require that a series of tests be run to make sure the changes made are permanent.

Tie up all of the loose ends. Call the user in a day or two, and check to see if the problem has recurred. An anomaly of customers whose experience is perceived as "bad service" is that they don't complain; they simply don't come back, and you may never know why. Document your solution in a log that you share with others. Some of the best problem resolution logs are posted on a company's Web site, and made available to the company's networking personnel, as well as customers.

CompTIA Approach for Troubleshooting

CompTIA cites an approach to troubleshooting network problems for the Network + competencies. The approach is shown in Table 9-5. For the purposes of taking the exam, you should become familiar with the steps in this approach.

Table 9-5 Network Troubleshooting Approach

NET+ OBJECTIVE
II.5.2

Problem Duplication Strategy	
Step 1	Identify the exact problem
Step 2	Recreate the problem on either a mock-network, or on isolated and unaffected nodes.
Step 3	Isolate the cause of the problem.
Step 4	Formulate a correction by working the cause in reverse.

This process calls on many of the techniques previously described, but it's specifically deterministic. This means that once you think you know what the problem is, you should be able to duplicate it. And if you can duplicate it, you can fix the problem by applying a reverse-policy.

A duplication approach is typically easiest to use when a problem is confined to a local environment, either a client, server, or a piece of software running on a LAN. The first step involves identifying the exact problem. To do so, you need to expressly eliminate all other possibilities. How will you know you've done so? There are two ways. The first is by fixing the problem. The second is by duplicating the symptoms of a problem, eliminating them, and then assuming the steps you took to eliminate the problem represent the fix.

Once you recreate the problem, you can trace your steps back, one at a time, until the problem disappears. The point at which it disappears represents the required fix for the problem. At that point, you can apply this knowledge to the actual problem, and it should solve it.

This sounds a bit complicated, and you may wonder why you can't simply approach the problem using a trial-by-error system and achieve the same result. You probably could! However, the network may be partially functional, enough that users are still running applications. In order to troubleshoot the system "live", it'll have to come down, and the users will be idle. Trial-by-error troubleshooting can take a considerable amount of time. The problem duplication approach assumes you have the minimal resources to duplicate the problem in an environment that;s either identical, or very similar, to the one under question.

Once the problem has been recreated in the duplicate network, and a correction to the problem proofed in the duplicate, it stands to reason that it will also fix the actual problem.

Networking companies routinely take this approach for large customers who have purchased support programs. These customers—hospitals, banks, defense agencies, etc.—may not be in a position to take their networks off-line for troubleshooting. They typically pay a hefty fee for problem duplication facilities at the vendor site.

Let's apply the approach to an example scenario. A user complains that she can't access or share files with other members of workgroup. We'll assume that technical service is needed, that the problem has been properly prioritized, and that the extent of the problem has been localized to a workstation. After spending some time at the workstation, you've determined the problem to be a corrupt file in the registry. What's the next step?

According to the approach listed in Table 9-6, you are to recreate the problem. The quickest way to do so would be to move the workstation to another location, and try sharing files. If it still fails, you're diagnosis is correct. Taking this approach a step further, you may swap hard drives with a similar machine. If the problem is replicated in another machine, then you've eliminated all other components in the faulty workstation. In the last step, you must decide on a course of action to fix the problem.

Table 9-6 CompTIA Problem Escalation Protocol

CompTIA Troubleshooting Strategy	
Step 1	Identify the exact problem
Step 2	Recreate the problem on either a mock-network, or on isolated and unaffected nodes.
Step 3	Isolate the cause of the problem.
Step 4	Formulate a correction.

Operator Problems Versus System Problems

At times, a network problem may not be a network problem at all. It may be due to the user operating the system. Recall that the typical user thinks of the network transparently, and that a one-to-one relationship with it is perceived. He/she doesn't usually know what's going on "under the hood." An error message that pops up on the monitor, to he or she, means that there's a network problem.

If you're the one who supports network users, you will first talk with them over the telephone. You may be located in the same building with the user, or your customer may be a thousand miles away. It's silly, then, to jump on an airplane without first eliminating the user as the actual source of the problem. But, keep in mind that tact is essential in these situations, because the user's perception is that the "network is down".

NET+ OBJECTIVE
II.5.3

Table 9-7 lists a simple problem escalation protocol specified by CompTIA that should determine if the user is the problem. First, have another operator perform the same steps as the first operator. The second machine must be functionally the same as the first, and the task must be the same. If the second operator can perform the task, the problem is localized with the first operator.

Next have the second operator, who successfully performed the task on another machine, do the same on the first machine. If the task can now be completed, it's time to do a bit of training with the first operator. If, however, the second operator can't perform the task on the first machine, you can be confident that the problem isn't with the operator. Unless, of course, neither operator is following standard operating procedures for the task they're performing.

Table 9-7 Operator vs System Problem Isolation

Operator Problem Escalation Strategy	
Step 1	Have a second operator perform the same task on an equivalent workstation.
Step 2	Have a second operator perform the same task on the original operator's workstation.
Step 3	Determine if operators are following standard operating procedures.

Ask about their SOP for the task. If the network is properly documented, there will be one available. Have the operator read the procedure while performing it at the workstation. Note each step as it's being read. Have the operator echo the steps that are actually being done. This serves two purposes. The first is so that you can listen for discrepancies in the procedure. The second is so that you can determine if the operator is misinterpreting a good procedure.

Imagine a situation in which you get a call, and the complaint is "I can't save files to my personal directory on the server." You ascertain that all other network functions seem to be working, and suspect that the operator is entering incorrect information. According to the steps outlined in Table 9-7, what is the next step? The next step is the first one. Have a second operator try saving a file to the server directory on an equivalent machine. Let's assume he was successful. What is the next step? Have the second operator try saving the file to the user's directory from the original workstation. We'll assume he was successful. You must now speak with the original operator, and work step-by-step through the process to determine where the problem lies.

If the second operator wasn't able to save a file, then what? Tell he or she, step-by-step, what to do. Hopefully, the steps you cite are from a standard operating procedure. If this works, then make sure that the operators receive a copy of the SOP. If it doesn't work, then the problem lies with the system, and not with the operator.

Networks can be complicated. It's unreasonable to expect those who use them to be as knowledgeable as those who maintain them. Expect operator errors, and plan on a systematic approach for isolating them from actual network problems. When the problem has been resolved, be sure to follow-up in a couple of days to make sure that the customer isn't having more problems—since the problem could be intermittent—and document the resolution in a log. The information can be a valuable source of material for future user training.

Physical and Logical Trouble Indicators

Troubleshooting, in addition to using a systematic approach, requires using as many indicators as you can. Trouble indicators may be as simple as checking a power-on light, and as complex as interpreting software protocol analyzers. A printer, for example, won't print if it's not turned on, no matter how many times its reconfigured.

Table 9-8 lists specific indicators that you should be aware of as a source of troubleshooting information. Sometimes called "dummy lights", these simple indicators can be a ready source of information for quickly resolving a problem. They can also become an uncomfortable reflection of your troubleshooting abilities, if you overlook them.

Nearly all hardware devices have some type of light to indicate basic functions. Check for applied power by looking for a power light. If it's not lit, check to see if power is applied; that is, is the device plugged in? If it's working from an **Uninterruptable Power Supply** (UPS, which is a battery), is the UPS fully charged? Blown fuses can be a source of power failure in boards that are mounted in a chassis. Most of these will also have some type of basic power indicator, usually an LED mounted somewhere on the board. The chassis may be operating, but a crucial board isn't because a fuse is blown. Take the time to make a thorough visual inspection when lack of power appears to be the culprit.

Table 9-8 Physical and Logical Trouble Indicators

Physical and Logical Indicators of Network Trouble
1) Link lights on NIC cards and hubs.
2) Power lights on workstations, printers, servers, hubs, tape back-ups, etc.
3) Error displays such as error messages concerning printers or connections to a server or remote device.
4) Error logs and Displays such as Event Viewer or or graphical displays such as Network Monitor.
5) Performance Monitor for Microsoft operating systems.

Link lights can also provide a basic unit of information as to whether the device is performing it primary function. As with power supply problems, make a thorough visual inspection, particularly when the device is working under a loaded condition. Only then can you determine if the lights are working properly.

Error messages which appear on a monitor may be communicated to you by an operator. The error message may or may not have any significance. Windows products are notorious at generating numbered error messages, and so-called "catastrophic errors". The error that's generated on a screen may only have significance to the native source code of the application software, and to a troubleshooter in the field, may mean nothing. In other cases, it may lead directly to the source of a problem. Collect vendor error codes, document instances when they occur, and record the actions taken to clear the code. Eventually, you'll create a log that's useful in mapping error codes to a problem resolution.

An error log provides historical data about the performance of a network. An error log is setup to "trap" certain events on a network such as collisions, delays, processor usage, interrupt times, etc. You have quite a few options in how you view and analyze the information in an error log. A minimum threshold may be set so that normal conditions are exempted from the log.

For example, an Ethernet LAN is expected to experience collisions. From past history, you may have determined that 100 collisions each day is normal, so the threshold would be set for collisions exceeding 100. You may then further define the log to capture collisions that exceed 100 during a specific time-frame, say from 7:00 AM until 9:00 AM.

Most error logs place the data in a text file, so that it can be readily imported into most off-the-shelf software packages such as Word or Excel.

Closely related to error logs are performance monitors, and protocols analyzers. Windows NT has a Performance Monitor and a Network Monitor. Performance Monitor is used to track attributes on client stations or a server, while Network Monitor tracks attributes across the network. Network Monitor can also display many attributes of an IP packet. In addition, it can be used to chart the network's statistical data such as bandwidth usage, error rates, number of broadcast messages, and so on.

Network Troubleshooting Resources

Knowledge is power, so they say. In the networking business, it represents, at a minimum, relative peace of mind. While none of us can know everything, we can identify sources for information that we either don't use on a routine basis, or simply don't know. Table 9-9 lists three common network troubleshooting resources.

Table 9-9 Network Troubleshooting Resources

Common Network Troubleshooting Resources
1) World Wide Web knowledge bases.
2) Telephone technical support, either inter-company or from the vendor.
3) Vendor CDs and user manuals.

Knowledge in a business that seems to change daily is often hard to come by. The simple 12-port hub of yesterday is now stacked in a group of five similar hubs, and is managed remotely through a circuit card, in a chassis, that's in a wiring closet, in another building. And while standards and adherence to standards are all well and good, you simply can't know everything about the products you're using, unless, of course, you work for the company that manufactures them. Each vendor has their own syntax, so that a NIC card at one manufacturer is a data interface card at another one, and is a network adapter at another.

Acknowledge the widespread use of vendor-specific terminology, acronyms, and syntax, and don't pretend to know it all. Instead, begin building a library of vendor related literature. The library may be only software, or it could also include print-copies of equipment specifications and configuration settings, along with troubleshooting data. Build the reference library, and include cross-reference links to the different types of media in it. There are several categories that your library should include—Telephone support, vendor Web sites, vendor Cds, and printed documentation.

Telephone support for a large manufacturer is most efficiently used when you have a telephone number, and an extension, to an actual person. The normal routing, however, is to call a generic number, leave a message describing your problem, and wait for a call-back. It's worth asking the maximum call-back times from the support department before purchasing equipment from a specific vendor. If they can't quote specific levels of service, think about buying from another company.

Don't overlook expertise within your own organization. Identifying individuals who are strong in areas you're weak in, is smart thinking. Most people, upon hearing a sincere request for help, are more than willing to lend a hand. Take advantage of it, and then extend the same courtesy to others.

Internet Web sites are particularly helpful in identifying technical information sources, ranging from connector pinouts, to flash/NVRAM upgrades, to environmental specifications for a product. Some vendors also publicly post problem resolution logs on their Web sites, and these are helpful if you're having trouble getting a handle on a vendor-specific problem that can't be compared to any established standards. Others provide internal site access for customers, and their own personnel. Examine a vendor, before buying, to see how difficult it's going to be to access troubleshooting information for a product you're interested in.

More often, printed user manuals are disappearing, and in their place is a CD containing all of the information in the original printed documentation, except it's in electronic format. The most common format of the CD is as a postscript **Page Description Format** (PDF) file. PDF files require a PDF "reader", the most widely used being a free download, from Adobe Software, which allows you to view any PDF file. PDF files are convenient because the documents are extensively linked, making it easier to jump across sections of the "manual".

Printed material includes not only vendor documentation, but documentation you create. Problems and associated fixes should be compiled, and maintained, in a library that's available to anyone who needs access to the information. This should be a documented, and approved, SOP which requires network engineers to record the fix. Be sure to date each entry, so that you have some type of revision control for obsoleting information that's been superseded by equipment or software changes.

Organize technical reference material under a master index that notes the location of the different types of resources—actual Web addresses for various products and problem resolution logs, telephone numbers organized by vendor and product, a simple filing system for vendor CDs, that makes it easy to pick the appropriate CD from a shelf, and another equally simple filing system for product printed documentation, and local resolution logs.

Network Problems

Troubleshooting network problems can cover quite a bit of territory. In this section we'll look at several common problem areas. While this isn't meant to exhaust all possible problems you'll encounter while troubleshooting a network, it is an opportunity to apply the troubleshooting methods discussed earlier. Table 9-10 lists the scenarios that may be addressed in the Network+ exam. Refer to it in the following discussion of these areas.

Table 9-10 Typical Network Problem Scenarios

NET+ OBJECTIVE
II.5.6

Network Problem Scenarios
Any of the following issues may be covered:
1) Recognizing abnormal physical conditions.
2) Isolating and correcting problems in cases where there is a fault in the physical media.
3) Checking the status of servers.
4) Checking for configuration problems with DNS, WINS, and HOST file.
5) Checking for viruses.
6) Checking the validity of the account name and password.
7) Rechecking operator logon procedures.
8) Selecting and running appropriate diagnostics.

Physical problems with the network media can be difficult, because the connectors are hidden, and the equipment is normally stored in an out-of-sight location that's—preferably—secured.

But the good aspect of a physical problem (if there is one) is that it will normally show-up during the installation of the network. Assuming the network equipment is working, physical media problems are one of the most common on a network. Anticipate them by preparing as follows:

- Document all physical connection at each entry and exit point in the network.

- Label all connections with a network-wide labeling procedure.

- Collect visuals of connector pinouts, and keep them in an accessible location.

- Maintain a list of each connection on a patch cable.

- Buy, or build, a crossover cable to check the NIC cards.

- Check the fit of all connections where you suspect a problem.

- Check hardware compatibility charts. Windows NT comes with an extensive list of hardware for which the software has been pre-tested for compatibility.

Once a problem has been located in the physical media, it's time to fix it. UTP cabling can be soldered in a splice, if there's a break in it. Chapter 2 lists the pinouts of 8-wire and 50-wire cabling schemes. CAT5 UTP uses eight wires that connect to an RJ-45 connector. The pinout for this connector can also be found in Chapter 2.

Coaxial cable may be thinnet, or thicknet, and each type interfaces to the network media using connection techniques described in Chapter 2.

Fiber optic cabling uses only fiber connectors. Although there is considerable variety in the connectors available, you'll find some standardization in FDDI. The important point about fiber cables is that the connections must be clean, and properly aligned, so there's not a loss of signal at the connection.

A problem that's been determined to be network wide, and isn't in the wiring infrastructure, is likely to be located in the **server**. Run diagnostics on the server, such as Performance Monitor for NT, and then Network Monitor. Analyze the data to see if trends or patterns can be identified for the statistical information.

Name resolution can be a frequent source of problems. Recall from the last chapter that domain names are reconciled to IP addresses using a **Domain Name Server** (DNS). Windows NT uses the **Windows Internet Naming Service** (WINS) to map IPs to computer names when the server is running TCP/IP. HOST refers to the TCP/IP command line tool hostname. When entered, it returns the name of the system on which it's entered. This will be the same name specified in the DNS entry.

A **virus** can cripple a server by consuming hard drive space, creating needless delays, and interfering with server tasks. A virus may run undetected, unlike many Microsoft viruses such as Concept, that provide a visual indication that they're in the operating system. The only prudent approach to viruses is to install virus detection software on the server and clients. Virus software has the disadvantage that it may cause the server and clients to slow down slightly, but this is preferable to having the system crash. Another preventive approach is to forbid user software installations (from floppy disks) until the software has been virus-checked.

A user can't **logon** to a network until a password and logon permission has been set up. This was discussed earlier, but logon problems tend to dominate troubleshooting time for network personnel.

There are two reasons for this, the first being a lack of user training. Understand that in many networks, a user may be required to enter several passwords, one to access the network, another to connect to the Internet, another for e-mail, another for corporate intranets, and so on. It gets confusing. Then, if the user is required to change passwords periodically, the problem is compounded because he/she doesn't understand the process. Commit your logon process to an approved procedure, and use it whenever you are training customers.

The second reason is that permissions aren't well-documented. A customer may have been told that permission for a service has been issued, but the logon still doesn't work. Maybe the problem lies with the operator, and maybe it doesn't. There's a tendency in larger companies to administer some network accounts on a local level, while administering other accounts on a corporate level. The two levels don't always communicate.

One method you can use to get a handle on this type of situation is to canvass users on occasion. Ask them what their logons are, then record the information in a database that can be updated periodically. In addition to the areas listed above, there are numerous other opportunities for problems. Let's take a look at several areas that are noted for being troubleshooting hot-spots. These include:

- The network installation (both hardware and software).

- Boot failures.

- Configuration errors.

- Printing errors.

- Remote access problems.

- Wide-area connectivity.

- Physical and Logical Connectivity.

A **network installation** will go bad if it's not well planned. Refer back to Chapters 1 and 2 for procedures for installing network cabling and hardware. As mentioned above, you must have a thorough understanding of network components, so that you don't try connecting a 10-MBPS Ethernet NIC to a 16-MBPS Token Ring NIC. Installing the NOS is another problematic area during an installation. Windows NT is an easy install, but only if you've done some preliminary planning. The same is true of the later versions of Novell NetWare.

When installing the NOS on a server, make sure that all hardware used on the server is compatible with the operating system. If you're not sure, call the vendor before proceeding, or check the operating system literature. Lack of RAM and hard drive space will also crash an install. Recall from Chapter 1 that a server can't have enough of either.

Assuming a network has been installed properly, **configuration errors** can cause either local or global problems. Make a determination as to the boundaries of the problem—local or global. Decide if the problem occurs on a single client, or on all LAN clients. Discriminate between operations that are working, and those that aren't. For example, all clients may have access to the server applications, but none of them can print. On the other hand, the clients may be able to print but none of them can access server files. Try duplicating the problem on another computer. Try changing logons at the computer that has the problem. The idea is to eliminate as many causes as possible, so that you can describe the problem very specifically.

Configuration settings should be documented to include all IP and MAC addresses, domain names, computer names, and so on. NIC cards and modem settings should be recorded, so that if you suspect a card configuration problem, you can easily check against the actual card settings. In a larger LAN, a chassis-style hub may contain cards for Ethernet, Token Ring or FDDI all in the same hub. It will also have a management card that allows these various access methods to be bridged. A graphical network management software package is invaluable in these situations, since it allows you to see the connections as well as to check IP packet flows.

For clients connected to a server, expect global problems if the server is incorrectly configured. The settings for servers should be meticulously documented, as well. Check them against the documentation before jumping in, and making any changes. If you do make changes, do so one at a time unless you're sure of the outcome. Regardless, document the change, and update the settings documentation, for the machine that you've changed.

A **boot failure** occurs when a machine is turned on, and the operating system won't boot. The boot records are stored on a hard drive, and when a computer is turned on, a dialogue occurs that threads a minimal number of boot records to the system BIOS. Three causes can create bootup problems:

- The operating system is flawed.

- The hard drive has a problem.

- The system board is bad.

The boot files on the hard drive are easier to check by simply booting with a backup disk. Typically, when you install a network operating system, you create a boot backup disk which allows you to bypass the hard drive dialogue, in order to gain access to the remainder of the NOS on the hard drive. If you don't have an emergency boot disk, call the NOS vendor and ask them to send you one. The alternative is to reinstall the NOS, and risk losing all of the information that is stored on the disk.

If you get the system to boot from a backup disk, you can attempt to repair the boot records. If the repairs don't work, change the hard drive. It's more likely to be at fault than the system board. Of course, if replacing the hard disk doesn't fix the problem, you're left with no choice but to remove and replace the system board.

Printing problems can be a headache in nearly any network. Be methodical when you get complaints from users that involve printing. First, check to see if it's localized to a single user, or network-wide. Check all cables and connectors for wear and tear, as well as tight connections at all ports (client PC, hub, print server or printer), then, check the location of the actual equipment against the network floor-plan, to make sure the equipment hasn't been moved or changed. If the problem is local to a single user, log on at another client, and try again. If the other client can now print, you've localized the problem to a single client. Check to see which printer has been selected, to make sure that the client is printing to the correct printer.

Check the amount of hard disk space available. Windows creates two copies of a document when it's printed, and for large print jobs, this can temporarily consume a large section on a hard drive. A client won't be able to print without the correct printer driver installed. Even if it's correct, and you've ruled out everything else, reinstall the driver. It may have become corrupted. Finally, the parallel printer port may not be functioning on the client system board.

Remote Access Service (RAS) allows a user to dial in to a computer from a remote site. The typical complaint is "I can't dial in."

If all else is working properly, assume the problem is localized to the RAS. To be sure, check with other RAS clients. Are they having the same problem, or not? Check to make sure that the client has the necessary permissions for the RAS account. If not, the RAS login will always fail. If all other users are experiencing the same problem, make sure RAS is enabled. With Windows NT, for example, it doesn't start automatically on bootup. You have to manually start RAS.

Authentication, and security callbacks, can be another source of localized RAS problems. If the encryption algorithms aren't compatible, the remote server won't be able to authenticate the client. Most NOSs allow you to disable authentications from the server. Try this (by allowing any type of authentication), and have the client try again.

Callbacks are used as another form of security. When the client dials into the server, it calls back to the number that dialed into it. If the call was sent through a switchboard which used multiple phone lines, the server may not be able to connect back to the client. A similar situation exists when a remote client has been set up to connect to the Internet on a different telephone number if when Netscape or Explorer is started, the dial-out sequence is automatic. Instead of dialing the remote server, the computer may be trying to dial into an ISP.

Physical and logical connectivity refers to the hardware, cabling, connectors and protocols running on a network. After ascertaining if the problem is local or across the network, determine the depth of the problem. A quick visual inspection of cabling may correct the problem. Compare the installed devices against the network floor-plan to ensure equipment hasn't been changed without the proper approvals.

Once the physical connections have been ruled out, the easiest test is to ping. Try pining several clients using 127.0.0.1 which is the local loopback test. Ping the local server as well as other clients on the LAN. Ping routers and default gateways. A ping to the default gateway IP address can eliminate many possible problems because if it works, the client, hub and local server are probably all communicating properly.

Ping is also useful to test by computer domain names. It's possible that an IP ping will work whereas a name ping won't. In the latter case, the physical and logical connections are okay but the DNS isn't configured properly. Chapter 8 lists many TCP/IP utilities that are useful in tracking down connectivity problems.

If a user can't logon, it may mean nothing more than they don't have permission to do so. Check to see if his/her password and logon is valid, then take it a step further to see what permissions have been given. It could be that the resource being accessed has been forbidden.

TEST EQUIPMENT

In addition to network software, a wide range of test equipment is available to network technicians. These range from low-cost **breakout boxes**, to expensive **protocol simulators**. Although this section highlights data-communications-specific test equipment, you shouldn't assume that the familiar multimeters and oscilloscopes aren't equally important.

You should remember about the TCP/IP utilities described in Chapter 8. Ping, as you may recall, is a versatile tool used to perform **loopback tests**. These tests will verify your access to a particular piece of equipment, such as a server or router.

NET+ OBJECTIVE
II.5.7

Breakout Box

The breakout box is one of the most common troubleshooting tools available, used for loopback tests, clock tracing, and signal monitoring. The instrument is connected in-line with cabling, in a serial fashion, in the same way that a ammeter is connected.

> A breakout box is an instrument used for signal monitoring.

Breakout boxes are available for nearly all interface types, and are often used to switch wire connections for test purposes. A commercial breakout box is shown in Figure 9-6.

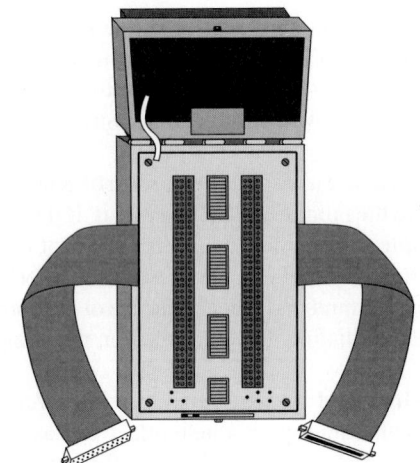

Figure 9-6 Breakout Box

Bit-Error Rate Testers

Bit-Error Rate Testers (BERTs) check for individual bit degradation. A test signal is transmitted through the network, and when it returns, the bits are checked for integrity. BERTs are useful in noisy environments, where electromagnetic radiation is suspected of inducing unwanted voltages into network cabling. They track bit rates, message block errors, and errors that occur on positive or negative transitions. A BERT is pictured in Figure 9-7.

> A bit-error rate tester is used to check for signal degradation in individual bits, messages, and continuous data streams.

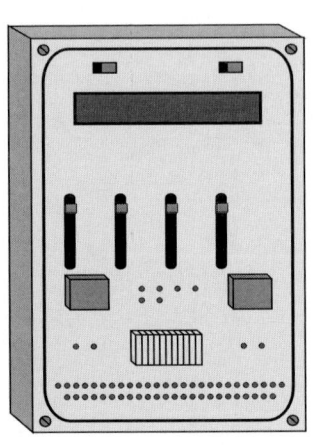

Figure 9-7 BERT

Cable Testers

Cabling problems are nightmares for network managers. If the physical network plant isn't carefully documented, showing each cable and device connection, endless hours can be spent tracing wires around a room, or through a wiring harness. A detailed schematic of the network plant, along with a cable tester, will significantly reduce the amount of time spent troubleshooting cable malfunctions.

> Cable testers are intended for checking continuity, opens, and shorts in network cabling.

Cable testers can be purchased that test twisted pair, or coaxial. They can check each connection on a cable, and determine if the connection is open, continuous, or shorted. Depending on the type of tester, it may also check loop resistance, sheath continuity, insertion loss or line impedance. The status of the cable is displayed by LEDs on most cable testers. Figure 9-8 is a picture of a cable tester.

Some cable testers are called **tone generators** because the indicate wire pairs in an 8-pair UTP by issuing a tone, or with an audible indicating the wire by number. A typical application is a large run of CAT5 cabling, that may include hundreds of wire-pairs. A tone generator can be set so that it will emit a tone when a pair is located. This process is called **tone locating**, or "fox-and-hound."

Another very useful cable tester uses time-domain reflectometry (TDR). A TDR is used to locate cable breaks by working from only one end of a suspect cable. The principle behind the technology is to send a short pulse with a very fast rise-time through one end of the connection. At a cable break, the pulse will reflect due to a mis-match

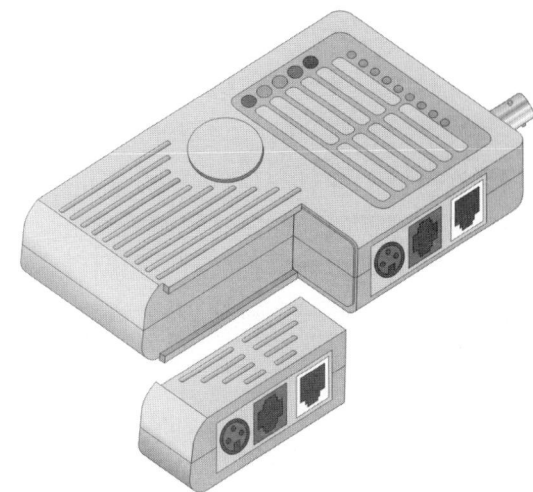

Figure 9-8 Cable Tester

in impedance created by the break. When the reflected pulse is received back by the TDR, it converts the time between sending the pulse and the time to receive the echo, and converts it to inches (or feet, meters, etc.). The accuracy of TDR is very good—within a half inch over several feet of wire to within a thousand feet over 50,000 feet of wire. As you may suspect, accuracy decreases for longer cable runs.

Data Analyzers

> Data and protocol analyzers identify protocol types, transmission speed, and the size of messages.

Data analyzers, and protocol analyzers, are sophisticated diagnostic tools, appropriate for networks in which data may be flowing in a variety of formats. For example, they may be helpful in large networks where a group of LANs are interconnected by a WAN. A data analyzer generally identifies transmission speed, type of protocol, and the number of bits in each character. A protocol analyzer identifies, and decodes, the network protocol. Protocol analyzers are available to identify most common protocols—SDLC, HDLC, X.25, BSC, and Ethernet. The analyzer decodes the protocol into easy-to-understand mnemonics. The mnemonics are displayed on a CRT. Some protocol analyzers allow the operator to display the decoded protocol in ASCII, EBCDIC, or hex. A data analyzer is pictured in Figure 9-9.

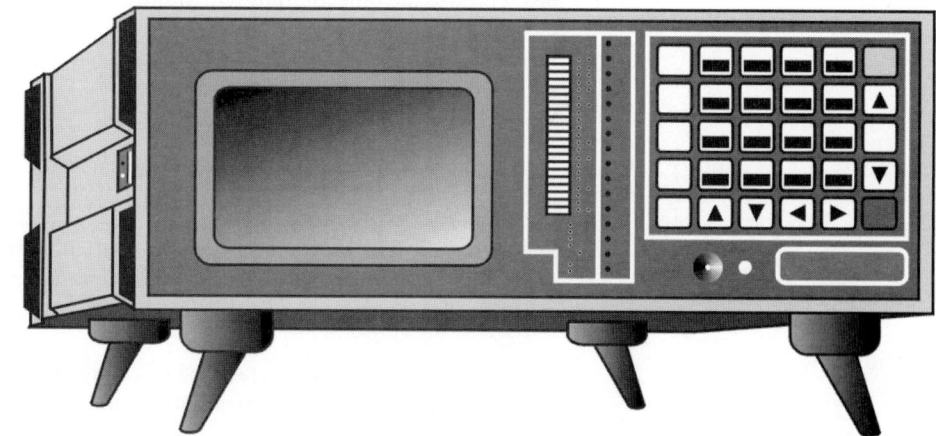

Figure 9-9 Data Analyzer

While protocol analyzers may be a physical piece of test equipment, they're frequently software entities. Network Monitor and Performance Monitor, both used with Widows NT, are examples. They have the advantage of displaying network-related information in both real-time (as it occurs) and in recorded-time (in a log file to be viewed at a later date).

You shouldn't underestimate the value of an old standby troubleshooting tool—the oscilloscope. While a protocol analyzer shows data in binary or hexadecimal, an oscilloscope cab be used to check the integrity of the data against noise. For example, the scope can be used to view spikes on a data stream that couldn't be viewed with many protocol analyzers.

Crossover Cable

A crossover cable is used to directly connect two workstations.

A **crossover cable** may be necessary to troubleshoot NICs or hub ports. A crossover allows you to directly connect two stations, without a hub. Figure 9-10 shows an illustration of a crossover cable. Notice that pairs must remain consistent—RX+ and TX+ as a connection, for example. A crossover is merely a means of connecting the proper transmit pins of one NIC card, to the corresponding receive pins of another NIC card, and vice versa.

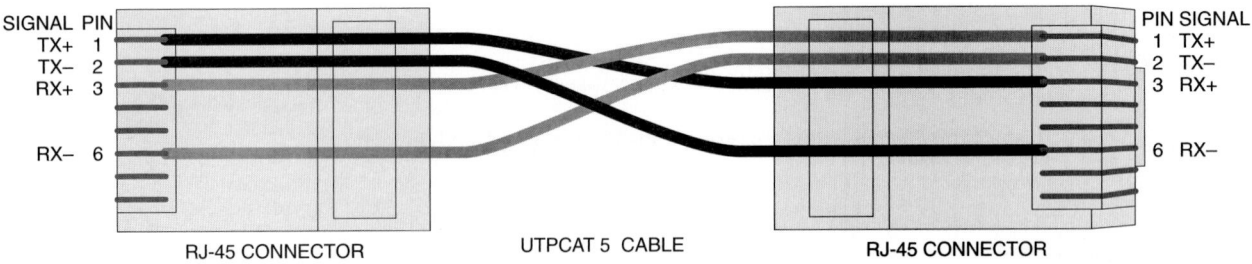

Figure 9-10 Crossover Cable

If two clients are connected together without a crossover, they will invariable collide when they both attempt to transmit at the same time. One may eventually gain access, but it won't last, because the other station will simply try again. Eventually, the link will crash.

A crossover cable is needed to connect two personal computers, or two hubs. A connection from NIC card in a PC to a hub port doesn't need a crossover since the crossover is made internally in the hub. For this connection, use straight-through pinning (pin 1 on one end of the cable connected to pin 1 on the other end of the cable, etc.).

In the absence of markings on a hub port, it's usually safe to assume that the crossover is handled by the hub. **However, check the hub documentation to make sure.** One or more ports are often switchable so you can use the internal crossover, or remove it to connect hubs together. The markings are as follows:

MDI: Media Dependent Interface, when engaged, allows you to use the port for connecting the hub to another hub using straight-through pinning. The hub performs the crossover.

MDI-X: Media Independent Interface-Crossover, when engaged, allows you to use the port for connecting to a NIC card in a PC (or similar device) using straight-through pinning.

KEY POINT REVIEW

- Five functions are associated with network management: configuration, performance, fault, security, and accounting.

- Configuration management is a physical, and logical, map of a network.

- The performance management function is responsible for collecting analytical and empirical data for analyzing the integrity and efficiency of the network.

- Fault management is concerned with detecting, diagnosing, and correcting problems.

- Security management is the safeguarding of all network resources.

- Accounting management focuses on cost-effective issues of the network.

- The ISO model of network management contains three components: a functional model, an organizational model, and an informational model.

- Network utilization is the ratio of network time used, to the total time it's available.

- Network availability is the amount of time the network services are available to users.

- System service time is the average amount of time a message spends en route to its destination.

- Throughput describes the number of delivered messages, considering the delays.

- Response time is the time required to deliver a message.

- In troubleshooting networks, a problem is a deviation from normal conditions.

- A systematic approach to troubleshooting reduces network down-time.

- A breakout box is an instrument used for signal monitoring.

- A bit-error rate tester is used to check for signal degradation in individual bits, messages, and continuous data streams.

- Cable testers are intended for checking continuity, opens, and shorts in network cabling.

- Data analyzers identify protocol types, transmission speed, and the size of messages.

- Protocol analyzers identify and decode network protocols.

- A crossover cable is used to directly connect two workstations.

At this point, review the objectives listed at the beginning of the chapter to be certain that you understand and can perform them. Afterward, answer the review questions that follow to verify your knowledge of the information.

LAB MANUAL

Lab Exercises

The lab manual that accompanies this book contains hands-on lab procedures that reinforce and test your knowledge of the theory materials presented in this chapter. Now that you have completed your review of Chapter 9, refer to the lab manual and perform Procedures 21, "Windows NT Performance Monitor," 22, "Network Monitor," 26, "NetWare Server Setup," 27, "Installing NetWare Client Software," and 28, "Creating a User Account."

REVIEW QUESTIONS

The following questions test your knowledge of the material presented in this chapter:

1. What are the three primary areas covered by the ISO network management model?

2. What does Configuration Management of the Functional model refer to?

3. As described in the text, is a text file created in Notepad an object?

4. What is the advantage of modularizing a network?

5. Describe the "detect and fix" technique for load balancing.

6. Determine the throughput of a 10MBPS network, using 8-bit ASCII, one start bit, one stop bit and no parity. Average delay on the network is 1.5 seconds.

7. Use the calculations from the previous question to determine the response time of the network.

8. A problem occurs when the network parameters _____ from their normal values.

9. How is a problem hypothesis proofed?

10. Which piece of test equipment is used to check for individual bit degradation on a network?

11. To determine if wires are shorted in a CAT 5 cable with RJ-45 connectors, which piece of test equipment is used?

12. You receive a problem call with the following symptoms: A user indicates that upon logon, she's told her password has expired and she must choose a new password. What level of action should you take too resolve the problem?

13. Prioritize the following list of network problems, based on their seriousness.
    a. A client can't access the server from his home.
    b. The server in Building 2 won't boot.
    c. None of the clients on Network A can print.
    d. A client needs a personal directory set up on Server 1.
    e. The vendor has a software upgrade for all NIC cards used on Network B.

14. List four steps used in a systematic approach for identifying the extent of network problems.

15. List four steps used in a systematic approach to troubleshooting network problems.

MULTIPLE CHOICE QUESTIONS

1. Within the Organizational Model are _____ _____, which group similar subsystems.
   a. Performance objectives
   b. Management domains
   c. Attribute values
   d. Fault managers

2. The characteristics of entries in the Informational model are maintained in:
   a. A managed system.
   b. The configuration management area.
   c. The management domain.
   d. The management information database.

3. Which level of the Functional model is responsible for naming all network objects?
   a. Configuration Management.
   b. Fault Management.
   c. Accounting Management.
   d. Performance Management.

4. Which level of the Functional model is responsible for detecting problems?
   a. Accounting Management.
   b. Security Management.
   c. Fault Management.
   d. Performance Management.

5. In a balanced-load network:
   a. The network management functions match the user applications.
   b. The load must match the user applications.
   c. One network or node manages the system.
   d. All networks or nodes share in the management of the network.

6. Determine the utilization of a network that's used 9 out of a possible 12 hours each day.
   a. 75%
   b. 50%
   c. 25%
   d. 0%

7. Determine the availability of a network that's available all day, except between
   the hours of 2:00 AM and 4:00 AM.
   a. 37.8%
   b. 91.7%
   c. 15.6%
   d. 78.4%

8. Determine the system service time of a 2MBPS network, in which the amount of time required to complete the management tasks is 0.5 seconds.
   a. 30 micro seconds
   b. .3 micro seconds
   c. 9.7 micro seconds
   d. 97 micro seconds

9. What is the relationship between message load and system service time?
   a. As the number of messages increases, the longer it takes the system to service the message.
   b. As the number of messages increases, the less amount of time it takes to service messages.
   c. As the number of messages increases, a bottleneck is less likely.
   d. As the number of messages increases, the lower the delays.

10. Determine the throughput of a network in which 500 characters are transmitted in one second, and the total delays are 1.7 seconds.
    a. 105
    b. 149
    c. 173
    d. 294

11. Which of the following steps is not used as a systematic approach to determine whether a problem is attributable to the operator, or the system.
    a. Have a second operator perform the same task on an equivalent workstation.
    b. Have a second operator perform the same task on the original operator's workstation.
    c. Have a second operator perform the same task on a non-networked station.
    d. Check to see if operators are following standard operating procedures.

12. When connecting to an Internet site the "...not enough space in memory" error message is received. A useful troubleshooting tool would not be:
    a. Internet Log.
    b. Performance Monitor.
    c. Network Monitor.
    d. Event Log.

CD-ROM

Net+ Practice Test

Additional Net+ Certification testing is available on the CD that accompanies this text. The testing suite on the CD provides Study Card, Flash Card, and Run Practice type testing. The Study Card and Flash Card feature enables you to electronically link to the section of the book in which the question is covered. Choose questions from the test pool related to this chapter.

CHAPTER

10

ERROR CONTROL AND DATA SECURITY

LEARNING OBJECTIVES

Upon completion of this chapter and its related lab procedures, you should be able to perform the following tasks:

1. Determine if a data word is encoded with even or odd parity.

2. Given a data word, calculate the LRC.

3. Determine the inverted bit in a data word from the LRC.

4. Write a CRC generator polynomial, given the word length.

5. Analyze the CRC generator polynomial to determine the location of feedback taps, and the placement of shift registers.

6. Draw a diagram of CRC hardware, based on creating the polynomial, showing the feedback taps and shift registers.

7. State four potentially weak areas of data security.

8. For a given network installation, explain the problematic environmental or conditional impact caused by room conditions, location of building contents and personal effects, computer equipment, and error messages.

9. Define the following terms as related to fault tolerance, or high availability: mirroring, duplexing, stripping (with/without parity), and tape backup.

10. For a given scenario, select the appropriate workstation backup technique from among tape backup, network drive folder replication, removable media, and multi-generation.

11. Identify the purpose and function of networking elements such as profiles, rights, procedures/policies, administrative utilities, login accounts, groups and passwords.

12. Identify the kinds of test documentation that are usually available regarding a vendor's patches, fixes, upgrades, etc.

13. For a given network maintenance scenario, demonstrate an awareness of standard backup procedures, backup media storage practices, the application of periodic software patches/fixes to the network, the installation of anti-virus software on server/workstations, and the updating of virus signatures.

14. Define encryption.

15. Define decryption.

16. Define plaintext.

17. Define Ciphertext.

18. Define encryption key.

19. Describe the characteristics of unbreakable ciphers, random-key ciphers, and public-key ciphers.

20. Given a block diagram of a single iteration of the Data Encryption Standard, label the blocks, and describe the function of each.

CHAPTER 10

Error Control and Data Security

INTRODUCTION

Error control is the process of minimizing data-bit problems. This chapter examines techniques used for detecting errors at the receiver, as well as correcting errors. For the most part, the errors can be considered to originate between the output port of the transmitter, and the input port of the receiver. The channel between the communicating stations offers the greatest opportunity for causing problems.

Error detection consists of identifying a bad bit, or string of bits.

Error control is a necessary overhead. Since error-detection fields contain no user data, they may be viewed as decreasing the efficiency of a network. The array of error-detection techniques runs the gamut of simple, low-cost implementations, to highly complex systems that will uncover errors, and then correct them. A PC incorporates parity error control when communicating with a printer, but if the PC is wired into a LAN, the error detection that is used is not only more sophisticated, but it's also much more efficient.

The security of the many thousands of computer networks has percolated up the most recent list of things-to-be-worried-about. Networks, while radically altering our lives, have also raised serious questions about privacy, and data integrity. The security section in this chapter focuses on identifying the vulnerabilities in networks, and the practices used to address these weaknesses. For truly sensitive information, data encryption is an option.

The National Bureau of Standards **Data Encryption Standard** (DES) is an effective and proven encryption method that is widely used in government, and the commercial sector. The details of the standard, along with various encryption techniques, are discussed at the end of the chapter.

NET+ OBJECTIVE
I.9.1

Within the client computers and servers in a LAN, the integrity of the data may be compromised due to environmental problems, such as natural disasters, or interference from other equipment. It's important to not only plan for these events, but to recognize the symptoms when they haven't, as yet, been identified.

The most common devices in a network for storing information are the hard drives in the workstations and the servers. As with anything else, these fail from time to time, and the data contained in them can be irrevocably lost. Data backups are an important aspect of planning for fault tolerance and we'll examine the most common practices used to protect the data, while understanding the effect that fault tolerance has on the performance of a networked system.

ERROR DETECTION

The fact that digital data arrives anywhere intact is remarkable, considering the tremendous number of convolutions it's exposed to en route to the receiver. The realities of minute bit times, specificity of protocols, documented standards, and careful equipment selection is that their objective is to not only transport data to a receiver, but to see that the arriving data resembles what was sent.

In this respect, most of data communications is involved in error containment. Predictable problems are identified, and compensated for, and those problems that can't be predicted are anticipated, with the data being treated accordingly.

Error detection is the process of identifying a bad bit, or string of bits. Current error-detection schemes are very effective at catching problem bits, but no system has been problem-adept at detecting all errors. Many detection schemes revolve around a **go-back-to-n** system, which means the transmitter is instructed by the receiver to retransmit bad frames until they're received correctly. Ultimately, a system like this could be argued as perfect, but each retransmission takes time, and costs money.

The following sections begin with a review of **parity**, extend the mechanics of parity to increase its effectiveness, and conclude with **cyclic redundancy checks**.

Parity

Parity was briefly discussed in Chapter 2, and has been referred to in the ensuing chapters. Parity is a simple, and common, method of detecting errors. It doesn't give any indication of where the error can be found, or the number of errors that have occurred, and it doesn't correct errors. Simply put, parity merely detects an error.

Parity checks can be made using either even or odd parity, as shown in Figure 10-1. The parity bit is added after the data, usually 7 or 8 bits. The number of logic 1's in the data is counted, and the parity bit is added to make the total number of data bits, plus the parity bit, equal to an even or odd number.

DATA BITS	(a)	PARITY BIT
1010001		1
1111110		0

DATA BITS	(b)	PARITY BIT
1010001		0
1111110		1

DATA BITS	(c)	PARITY BIT
0000000		0 (even)
0000000		1 (odd)

Figure 10-1 Parity

The first set of data bits in Figure 10-1(a) contains three 1's. A logic 1 parity bit is added to produce a total of four 1's. The second set of data bits contains six 1's (an even number), so the parity bit is 0.

In Figure 10-1(b), odd parity is demonstrated. The same sets of data bits are used, except now the logic 1 parity bit is added whenever the addition makes the total number of 1's equal to an odd number. The first set of data bits contains an odd number of 1's, so the parity bit equals 0. In the second set, there are six 1's, which is an even number. A logic 1 parity bit is used to make a total count equal to seven.

> Even parity consists of adding a logic 1 or 0 to a data word, so that the sum of all logic 1's is an even number. Odd parity consists of adding a logic 1 or 0 to a data word so that the sum of all logic 1's is an odd number.

Even or odd parity has no effect on the performance of a data frame. Neither is better at detecting an error. From the standpoint of analyzing data streams with an oscilloscope, odd parity has the advantage of providing a technician with a bit to look at, when the frame consists of strings of 0's. The set of data bits in Figure 10-1(c) are all 0's. Even parity uses a 0 for the parity bit, while odd parity uses a 1. The odd parity 1 gives the technician an actual bit to see, and serves to break up the bitstream.

The weakness of parity is shown in Figure 10-2. The first set of bits has no errors, and odd parity is being used. In the second set of bits, the first bit (inside the box) is the error. The parity, as calculated by the receiver, is a logic 0. With this one error, the receiver will correctly identify a problem. In the next set of bits, two bits are in error. The receiver will count the number of logic one's in the data, determine a parity bit of 1 should be used, and compare it against the received parity which is also one. It will appear to the receiver that there is no error.

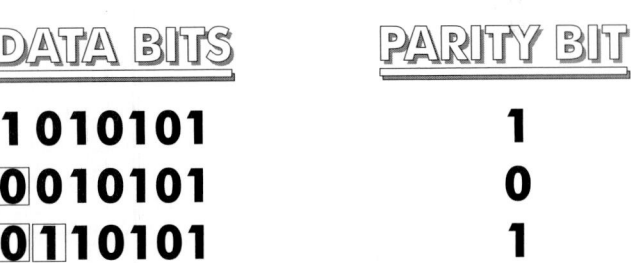

Figure 10-2 Parity Weakness

Parity will only detect an odd number of errors. This is the case no matter if odd or even parity is used. Some parity schemes use two parity bits to check errors across several frames of data. These schemes have the ability to precisely identify which bit is in error. Unfortunately, this drastically increases overhead, while still having the disadvantage of being unable to detect an even number of errors. Statistically, a single parity bit is usually sufficient for identifying errors in about 16 data bits.

Once the transmitter sends the data bits with a parity bit, the receiver counts the number of 1's in the data bits. It generates its own parity bit, and compares it to the parity bit sent by the transmitter. If the two bits are the same, the receiver assumes there's no error. But if they are not the same, the receiver will generally ask the transmitter to retransmit.

Longitudinal Redundancy Checks (LRCs)

Many of the data-frame formats discussed in earlier chapters used a **Block Check Character** (BCC) for detecting errors. The BCC is used for detecting errors in long data streams (up to 256 bits). A BCC uses a parity extension called a **Longitudinal Redundancy Check** (LRC).

Longitudinal redundancy checks, or block character checks, consist of applying odd or even parity to the rows and columns of a block of data words.

When continuous streams of data are sent in a block, each data field in the frame contains an error bit—usually the eighth bit when ASCII is used. The error bits are based upon even or odd parity, as described in the previous section. Immediately following the parity bit is the next data field—or character—and it also has a error bit. The data frame with an **End Of Message** (EOM) indicator, and a BCC, is illustrated in Figure 10-3.

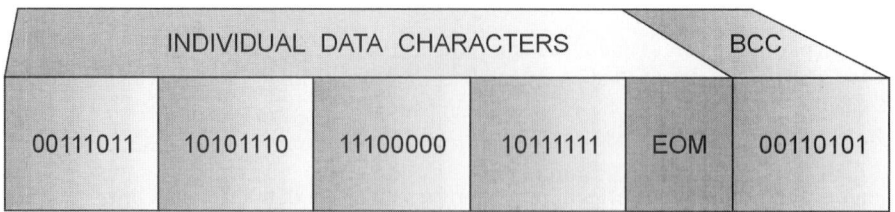

INDIVIDUAL DATA CHARACTERS					BCC
00111011	10101110	11100000	10111111	EOM	00110101

Figure 10-3 Location of BCC in Data Frame

How is the BCC generated? It's convenient to rearrange the format of the data field, as shown in Figure 10-4. The first set of bits in Figure 10-4(a) has seven bits. The eighth bit is an odd parity 1. For each of the four binary characters, an error bit is generated. Next, the four characters are read in a vertical fashion, using odd parity. Reading the left-most bit of the four characters yields 0111, and an odd parity bit, 0, is added. The next column, 0010, also has a 0 parity bit added. The third column 1111 has a 1 parity bit added. Each column is checked, and a parity bit added. The column of parity bits representing the parity of each character is also examined, and an odd parity bit of 1 is added to the columns of **vertical parity bits**. The columned parity of the data bits and parity bits, produces an 8-bit BCC, 00110101. Note that this is the BCC of Figure 10-3.

An LRC is particularly effective in detecting errors. Figure 10-4(b) shows an error in the second bit of the second character. The receiver examines the columns of bits in a similar manner as we have done to produce a BCC. It will produce a BCC in which the second bit is in error. The receiver could examine parity for each character, compare it against the received parity bits, and determine the error has occurred in the second row and second column. If designed to do so, the error could be corrected.

Figure 10-4(c) illustrates two errors along with the BCC determined by the receiver. In the manner described above, the specific errors can be detected and corrected.

The problem with LRCs is a situation when an even number of errors occur in the same column. For example:

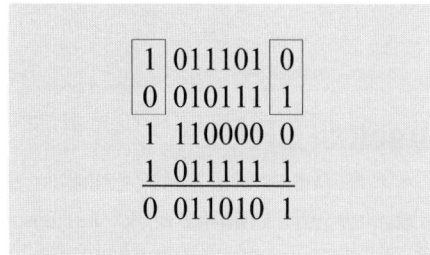

The BCC generated by examining only columns of bits will result in a correct BCC, when in fact there are bit errors. It becomes a question of how often even number column errors occur. LRC represents a significant improvement over simple parity, but, in noisy environments when error probability increases, another technique may be in order.

Cyclic Redundancy Checks (CRCs)

> CRCs operate on blocks of data words by continuously feeding the data back through a series of shift registers and exclusive-OR gates.

Data errors are frequently described as "bursty." This means that data bits in succession—from a few bits to several hundred bits—become garbled. Long-distance telephone lines are particularly prone to **burst noise**, which originates from lightning, microwave interference, crosstalk, or glitches from mechanical switching centers. Burst noise is unpredictable in length and frequency, and because of its unpredictable nature it's sometimes hard to detect as actual noise. For example, a long string of 0's may appear to contain logic 1's when the transmission line has been exposed to burst noise. One technique for detecting errors caused by burst noise is the **Cyclic Redundancy Check** (CRC), also called a **Check-Sum**.

CRC is a widely used error-detecting scheme. It belongs to a broad array of error-detection systems referred to as **convolutional coding**. A convolutional system is noted for its use of continuous feedback in producing an error-detection field. The error-detection field (called CRC, or sometimes used interchangeably with BCC) is sent along with a data frame. A receiver generates its own CRC from the received data, and compares it to the received CRC. If the two match, the receiver assumes no errors. If they don't match, the receiver generally asks for a retransmission.

There are two main aspects of CRC generation. The first is the **feedback**. Data is shifted into a CRC generator serially, and moves through a series of shift registers. When a bit is shifted out of the last register, it's fed back to the first register. This is the origination of the term **cyclic** in Cyclic Redundancy Check. As one bit is shifted out of the registers and fed back, a new data bit is shifted in. This means that in the process of producing the CRC field, all data bits have an historical influence on the CRC.

The second important aspect of CRC generators is the arrangement of the **shift registers** mentioned above. The registers are arranged so that a series of exclusive-OR operations take place. The organization of registers, and the sequence of ex-OR operations, is determined by an algorithm called a **generator polynomial**.

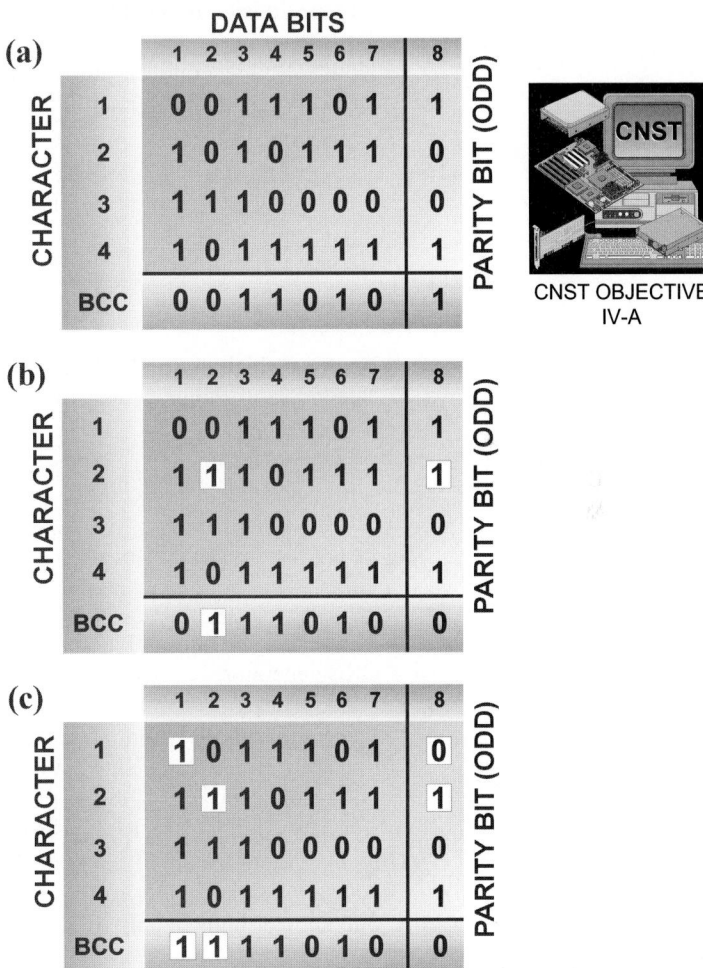

CNST OBJECTIVE IV-A

**Figure 10-4
Generating the BCC**

The generator polynomial is derived by selecting a constant, that, when converted to binary, has the least-significant bit equal to 1, and has a length equal to the CRC field + 1. The organization of shift registers and ex-OR operations will be determined from the constant.

Before working through an example of a CRC generator, it's useful to review some basic arithmetic. If 22 is divided by 7, we have:

$$22 / 7 = 3 \quad R1$$

A **remainder** of one will always result in this division problem as long as the **divisor** is 7 and the **dividend** is 22. If either, or both, divisor and dividend change, it's highly improbable that a remainder of one will result. A CRC generator is based upon the division process. The constant—the generator polynomial—is equivalent to the divisor, the data shifted through the generator is equivalent to the dividend, and the actual CRC is equivalent to the remainder. The **quotient** (the 3 above) is discarded. The unique aspect of CRC generators is that the division is accomplished with exclusive-OR gates.

Now, a CRC generator can be designed. Let's select a CRC word size of three bits. In order to write the generator polynomial, an extra bit is added. So, the constant is 4 bits. We'll use a constant of 1101.

Each bit place in the word is rewritten as a literal with an exponent denoting the bit place:

$$1101 = X^3 + X^2 + X^1 + X^0$$

Next, each bit is multiplied by each literal and like terms are combined. Note that $0 \times X^1 = 0$. This is true of any number multiplied by 0. Also, $1 \times X^0 = 1 \times 1 = 1$. Combining the terms:

$$= (1 \times X^3) + (1 \times X^2) + (0 \times X^1) + (1 \times X^0)$$
$$= X^3 + X^2 + 0 + 1$$
$$= X^3 + X^2 + 1$$

This is the generator polynomial, and it will be used to develop the basic hardware of the CRC generator.

Each term in the polynomial represents a shift register, as shown in Figure 10-5. In drawing the generator, start with 1. Whenever a register number equals an exponent in the polynomial, add an ex-OR sign (an OR symbol in a circle). In the original polynomial, $X^3 + X^2 + 1$, 1 = shift register R^1. Physically connected to it is X^2, or shift register R^2. This register number is equivalent to an exponent in the generator polynomial, so an ex-OR symbol is added. After the ex-OR symbol, the third register, R^3 is added. It is equivalent to X^3 in the polynomial. Immediately following the last register, add another ex-OR gate.

Data from the message frame is fed into the last ex-OR gate. The output from the last ex-OR is fed back to the first ex-OR gate, and the first shift register.

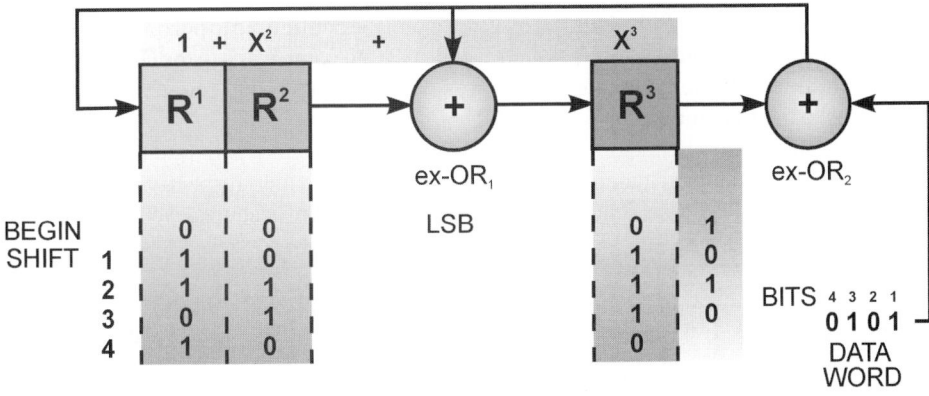

Figure 10-5 CRC Generator Hardware

Figure 10-5 demonstrates the state of our CRC shift registers during each step of a 4-bit word as it shifts through the generator. Although not shown, the registers and ex-OR gates are connected to a system clock. Each bit of the data word is shifted in with the clock pulse. Simultaneously, the contents of the registers shift right one place. Initially, all registers are reset, and contain 0.

Figure 10-5 extends the CRC registers with dotted lines. As each bit of the data word is shifted in, the bit combines with the contents of the registers. Note that the data bits are aligned with the contents of the registers at the time prior to the shift clock.

Step 1

With the first shift, R^1 shifts a 0 to R^2. R^2 shifts a 0 to ex-OR$_1$. R^3 shifts a 0 to ex-OR$_2$. The 1 from the data word shifts into ex-OR$_2$, where a 0 exclusively-ORed with a 1 equals a 1. The 1 from ex-OR$_2$ is fed back and shifted into R^1. It's also fed back to ex-OR$_1$, where it combines with the 0 shifted out of R^2. A 0 exclusively-ORed with a 1 equals a 1. At the end of the first shift clock pulse, the contents of the registers are: $R^1 = 1$; $R^2 = 0$; $R^3 = 1$.

Step 2

At the second shift, R^1 shifts a 1 to R^2. R2 shifts a 0 into ex-OR$_1$. R^3 shifts a 1 into ex-OR$_2$. The 0 from the data word shifts into ex-OR$_2$, producing a 1 at the output. The 1 is fed back and shifted into R^1. The 1 is also fed back to ex-OR$_1$, where it combines with the 0 from R^2 to produce a 1. The 1 output of ex-OR$_1$ is shifted into R^3. Now, the contents of the registers are: $R^1 = 1$; $R^2 = 1$; $R^3 = 1$.

Step 3

With the third shift, R^1 shifts a 1 to R^2. R^2 shifts a 1 to ex-OR$_1$. R^3 shifts a 1 to ex-OR$_2$. The 1 from the data word shifts into ex-OR$_2$ to combine with the 1 from R^3, to produce a 0. The 0 is shifted into R^1. It is also shifted into ex-OR$_1$ where it is exclusively-ORed with the 1 from R^2, producing a 1 at R^3. At the end of the third clock pulse and the input of the third data bit, the contents of the registers are: $R^1 = 0$; $R^2 = 1$; $R^3 = 1$.

Step 4

At the fourth shift, the 0 from R^1 is shifted to R^2. The 1 from R^2 is shifted into ex-OR$_1$. The 1 from R^3 is shifted into ex-OR$_2$. The last bit from the data word—0—is shifted into ex-OR$_2$ to combine with the 1 from R^3, to produce a 1 at the output. The 1 is fed back and shifted into R^3. The 1 is also fed-back to ex-OR$_1$, where it combines with the 1 from R^2 to produce a 0. The 0 is shifted into R^3. The contents of the registers after this last count are: $R^1 = 1$; R2 = 0; R3 = 0.

This last count, 100, equals the CRC. A receiver would be configured to perform an identical operation on the received data. Once it generates a CRC, it compares it to the CRC contained in the data frame. If the two match, there are no errors; if they don't match, the receiver usually asks the transmitter to send again.

Figure 10-6 shows several generator polynomials, along with their respective registers and ex-OR gates. Satisfy yourself that the hardware adheres to the procedure described above.

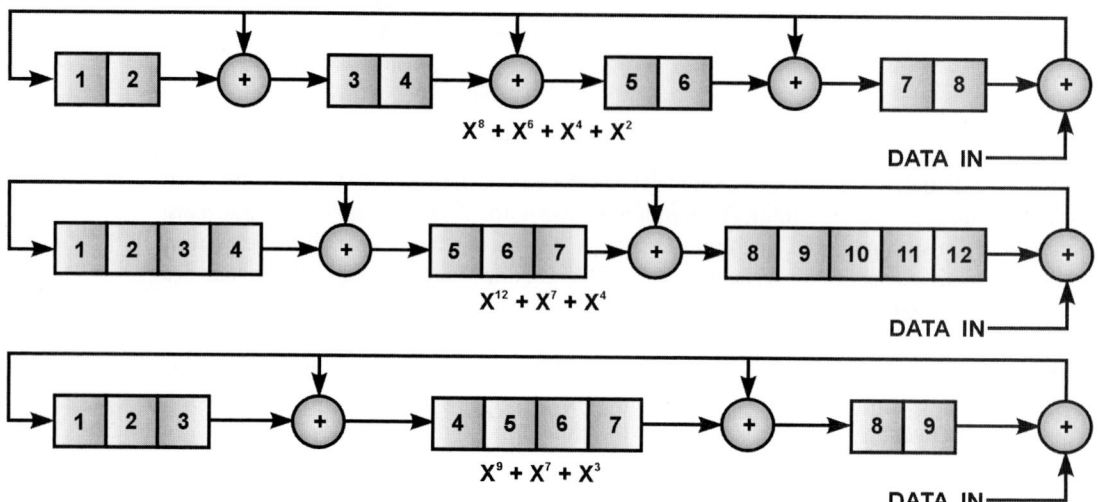

Figure 10-6 CRC Generator Polynomials and Associated Hardware

How accurate is CRC checking? A 16-bit CRC will detect any error burst less than 16 bits. As you'll recall, simple parity won't detect 2-bit errors—or any even-number error. LRC will detect all word errors, unless an even number of errors occur in a column. CRC will detect nearly 99% of errors exceeding 16 bits, when a 16-bit CRC is used.

It's possible that CRC errors could occur in just the right order to generate a correct CRC. But that's highly unlikely, because each bit of the data word shifts slowly through the registers, affecting the final CRC in a cumulative fashion. More likely is that a bit or two of the transmitted CRC could be lost. In that case, the receiver generator CRC wouldn't match the received CRC. The receiver will assume there's an error, and ask for a retransmission.

Most practical frame formats, such as **High-level Data Link Control** (HDLC) and **Synchronous Data Link Control** (SDLC), use a 16-bit CRC. The 16 bits represents overhead, but the characters contained in the information field aren't required to carry an extra parity bit, as LRC does. The bottom line is that a CRC will detect a greater number of errors, with less overhead. For this reason, it's become the favorite of Standards organizations. The most commonly used generator polynomials are:

$$\text{CRC-CITT: } X^{16} + X^{12} + X^5 + 1$$
$$\text{CRC-16: } X^{16} + X^{15} + X^2 + 1$$
$$\text{CRC-12: } X^{12} + X^{11} + X^3 + X^2 + 1$$

Unfortunately, a CRC cannot determine a specific bit error, nor can it be evaluated in reverse to find the problem. Otherwise, sending data would not be required—it could be extracted from a CRC at the receiver.

ERROR CORRECTION

The Huffman code detects and corrects errors by including parity bits with the data bits. The code format for bits is conducted by Hamming rules.

Data may be corrected when it arrives at the receiver. This type of error correction is called **forward error control**, and the most common technique used is the **Huffman Code**. Forward error control is handled by the receiver decoder, and doesn't depend upon a confirmation channel back to the transmitting station. This differs from the **Automatic-Repeat-reQuest** (ARQ) used with the Data-Link protocol, HDLC.

Recall that HDLC transmits up to seven frames, and waits for an acknowledgment from the receiver. If the CRC decoder at the receiver detects an error, a retransmission is requested, beginning with the offending frame.

Modem scrambling, and phase compensation, represent a form of error correction. These techniques are specifically intended to address channel weaknesses, or other predictable problems affecting data from transmitter port to receiver port.

Forward error correction is meant to identify, and correct, bit errors that can't be anticipated. The **Hamming Code** is one of a small, and specific, class of codes known as a **perfect** code. This classification means the code depends upon redundancy to identify a problem. The idea behind redundancy codes is that the data is replicated many times over. With so much duplication, the probability of identifying an error reaches realistic proportions. The mechanism driving Hamming codes, cyclic redundancy, is based upon calculated combinations of parity that identify a bad bit.

Hamming Code

The Hamming code can detect, as well as correct, bit errors. It does this by combining parity bits with the transmitted data bits. The combination is based upon specific Hamming rules, as shown in Figure 10-7(a).

Shown is the format for encoding a 4-bit word. The parity bits (P_X) are located in positions that are powers of two. P_1 is in bit position 1, or 2 to the power of $0 = 1$, P_2 is in bit position 2, or 2 to the 1 power, and P_4 is in bit position 4, or 2 to the 4 power. The data bits (D_X) are placed in the format in ascending order, so that D_3 is the least-significant bit of the 4-bit word, and D_7 is the most-significant bit.

The parity bits are established through even parity of each P-bit, and combination of data bits. The value of the P-bits is determined by the combinations shown in Figure 10-7(b). As an example, let's encode the data bits 0101 ($D_7=0$, $D_6=1$, $D_5=0$, $D_3=1$). Figure 10-7(c) contains the Hamming format for this word, as well as the parity-bit values required to achieve even parity for each combination of parity bit, and data bits.

(a)　　$D_7 \ D_6 \ D_5 \ P_4 \ D_3 \ P_2 \ P_1$

(b)
$$P_1 = P_1, D_3, D_5, D_7$$
$$P_2 = P_2, D_3, D_6, D_7$$
$$P_4 = P_4, D_5, D_6, D_7$$

(c)　　$D_7 \ D_6 \ D_5 \ P_4 \ D_3 \ P_2 \ P_1$
$$0 \quad 1 \quad 0 \quad 1 \quad 1 \quad 0 \quad 1$$

$$P_1 = P_1, D_3, D_5, D_7 = 1$$
$$P_2 = P_2, D_3, D_6, D_7 = 0$$
$$P_4 = P_4, D_5, D_6, D_7 = 1$$

Figure 10-7 Hamming Code Rules

(a)

$D_7 \ D_6 \ D_5 \ P_4 \ D_3 \ P_2 \ P_1$
$1 \ \ 1 \ \ 1 \ \ 1 \ \ 0 \ \ 0 \ \ 0$

$P_4 = P_4, D_5, D_6, D_7 = 1$
$P_2 = P_2, D_3, D_6, D_7 = 0$
$P_1 = P_1, D_3, D_5, D_7 = 0$

(b)

$D_7 \ D_6 \ D_5 \ P_4 \ D_3 \ P_2 \ P_1$
$0 \ \ 1 \ \ 1 \ \ 0 \ \ 0 \ \ 1 \ \ 1$

$P_4 = P_4, D_5, D_6, D_7 = 0$
$P_2 = P_2, D_3, D_6, D_7 = 1$
$P_1 = P_1, D_3, D_5, D_7 = 1$

$D_7 \ D_6 \ D_5 \ P_4 \ D_3 \ P_2 \ P_1$
$1 \ \ 0 \ \ 0 \ \ 1 \ \ 1 \ \ 0 \ \ 0$

$P_4 = P_4, D_5, D_6, D_7 = 1$
$P_2 = P_2, D_3, D_6, D_7 = 0$
$P_1 = P_1, D_3, D_5, D_7 = 0$

$D_7 \ D_6 \ D_5 \ P_4 \ D_3 \ P_2 \ P_1$
$1 \ \ 0 \ \ 1 \ \ 0 \ \ 0 \ \ 1 \ \ 0$

$P_4 = P_4, D_5, D_6, D_7 = 0$
$P_2 = P_2, D_3, D_6, D_7 = 1$
$P_1 = P_1, D_3, D_5, D_7 = 0$

Figure 10-8 7-Bit Hamming Code

Several examples of received codes are shown in Figure 10-9(b), along with the error bit. Verify for yourself that the indicated bit is the error.

The problem with these error-correcting codes is that they occupy a large segment of the data stream. In order to transmit four bits in the Hamming code, three parity bits were added.

The value of $P_1 = 1$, because even parity results when it's summed with the logic 1 of D_3 (D_5 and D_7 are logic 0's). Conversely, $P_2 = 0$, since the sum of the logic 1's of D_3 and D_6 is already an even number. P_4 has to be a logic 1, so that when summed with D_6, even parity results.

Another example is shown in Figure 10-8(a). The 4-bit word, 1110, has been 7-bit, Hamming-encoded to produce 1111000. Several additional examples are shown in Figure 10-8(b). Apply the combination even-parity rules to each 4-bit data word, to ensure you have a firm grasp of the coding technique.

Detection of errors at the receiver decoder is done by even parity checks of the same bit patterns used for encoding. If the parity at the receiver is even for each of the three combinations, there's no error. However, if a bit-error has occurred, the code will identify the offending bit position. Inverting the bad bit corrects the error.

Figure 10-9(a) shows that the encoded word, 1111000, was transmitted. Between the transmitter and receiver, the bit in position 6 was inverted, and the word, 1011000, was received. Now, even parity is applied to each parity bit, and data bits, to produce 110, which correctly identifies the error bit to be in bit position 6. By inverting the error bit, the problem is corrected.

$\quad\quad\quad\quad\quad\quad\quad\quad D_7 \ D_6 \ D_5 \ P_4 \ D_3 \ P_2 \ P_1$
TRANSMITTED $\quad 1 \ \ 1 \ \ 1 \ \ 1 \ \ 0 \ \ 0 \ \ 0$
RECEIVED $\quad\quad\ \ 1 \ \ 0 \ \ 1 \ \ 1 \ \ 0 \ \ 0 \ \ 0$

$P_4 = P_4, D_5, D_6, D_7 = 1, 1, 0, 1 = 1$
$P_2 = P_2, D_3, D_6, D_7 = 0, 0, 0, 1 = 1$
$P_1 = P_1, D_3, D_5, D_7 = 0, 0, 1, 1 = 0$

(a) ERROR BIT POSITION = $110_2 = 6_{10}$

$\quad\quad\quad\quad\quad\quad\quad\quad D_7 \ D_6 \ D_5 \ P_4 \ D_3 \ P_2 \ P_1$
RECEIVED $\quad\quad\ \ 1 \ \ 1 \ \ 1 \ \ 0 \ \ 0 \ \ 1 \ \ 1$
ERROR BIT POSITION = $111_2 = 7_{10}$

$\quad\quad\quad\quad\quad\quad\quad\quad D_7 \ D_6 \ D_5 \ P_4 \ D_3 \ P_2 \ P_1$
RECEIVED $\quad\quad\ \ 1 \ \ 0 \ \ 0 \ \ 1 \ \ 1 \ \ 1 \ \ 0$
ERROR BIT POSITION = $010_2 = 2_{10}$

$\quad\quad\quad\quad\quad\quad\quad\quad D_7 \ D_6 \ D_5 \ P_4 \ D_3 \ P_2 \ P_1$
RECEIVED $\quad\quad\ \ 1 \ \ 0 \ \ 1 \ \ 1 \ \ 0 \ \ 1 \ \ 0$
(b) ERROR BIT POSITION = $100_2 = 4_{10}$

Figure 10-9 Hamming Code Error Correction

In other words, the code eats 43% of the data stream. It's more bit-economical to encode long streams of data. For example, a 15-bit code requires four parity bits (at positions P_8, P_4, P_2, P_1), which represents about 27% of the code length. A 72-bit code contains eight parity bits, representing only 11% of the total length.) Although the efficiency improves with word length, hardware costs at the transmitting and receiving ends increase.

It is the application that drives the need for error correction. The reason that digital music on compact discs sounds so good, is because it's perfect; any errors on the disc are corrected before the music is applied to the audio amplifiers. Routine file transfers, business correspondence, or telephone conversations are seldom expected to be flawless, so it would represent overkill to correct bit errors in these situations.

DATA SECURITY

> Physical, logical, procedural and personnel security must all be analyzed for weakness, and appropriate precautions taken to strengthen any found.

The previous sections dealt with getting information from transmitter to receiver in its original format. It emphasized errors that resulted from unintended events, such as electrical and mechanical failures, channel distortions, atmospheric disturbances, and so forth. In the following sections, data integrity will be analyzed from a different point of view—the protection of data communications from willful interception of data. While extensive networking of computer systems has had tremendous advantages, it's also highlighted the issue of privacy and security of personal data, corporate competitiveness, and governmental considerations. Prior to the widespread use of networks, security was primarily an issue associated with the defense and national security of the government. Within the past decade, telecommunications, and LANs, have facilitated information transfer to the point that ethical questions vie with the benefits of networking. Not only do we, as private individuals, wonder who has access to our personal information, but large corporations have similar concerns.

NET+ OBJECTIVE
I.9.1

In the past, security was limited to the physical aspects of computers and the personnel working with them. Computers were housed in a central location, and access to the room could be controlled with door keys, badges, or sign-in logs. The personnel working with the computers—technicians, programmers, supervisors—were cleared through **background checks**. These practices remain an important part of data security, but the physical environment has been extensively altered.

There are a multitude of stories about computer **hackers**, sitting at home with their PCs and modems, gaining access to sensitive government facilities, financial institutions, or credit bureaus. Who hasn't heard about the hacker who diverts thousands of dollars from electronic fund networks to his own bank account? Security, once the domain of the government, is an issue that's become increasingly important to us due to the accessibility that computer networks have provided.

Figure 10-10 shows the Department of Defense computer network vulnerabilities chart, which profiles potential weaknesses of data-communication systems. These weaknesses may be divided into four categories: **physical**, **logical**, **procedural**, and **personnel**. The following sections provide characteristics and suggestions for addressing the vulnerabilities, as well as planning for faults which are likely to occur. The ultimate security process for computer data is to mask the content of the message through encryption, which will be described in later sections.

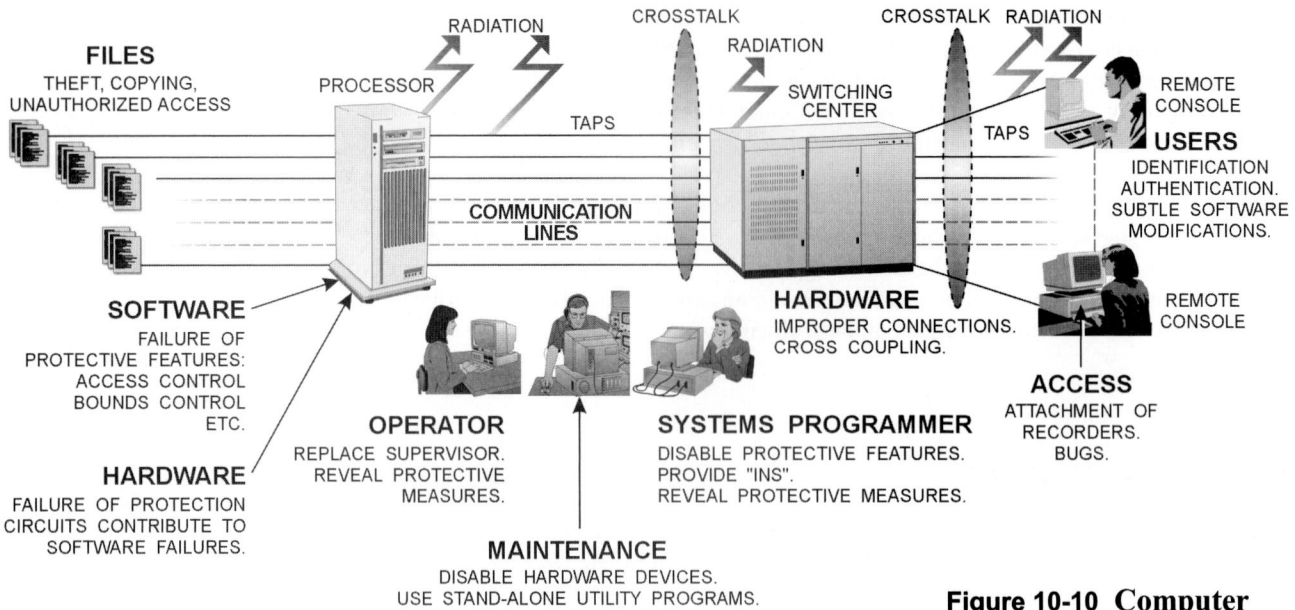

Figure 10-10 Computer Network Vulnerabilities

Physical

The physical element of data security involves **computer hardware**, the facility or office that houses the data, cable runs, and data printouts (hardcopy). Information can be ingeniously encrypted, masked, or hidden in electronic files, but efforts to hide the information will be futile if a technically competent "snoop" encounters little difficulty getting to the data.

NET+ OBJECTIVE
I.9.1

The first place to begin in analyzing physical security is with the obvious: how difficult is it to gain unauthorized access to the hardware? Hardware, in this context, includes remote terminals, communication controllers, multiplexers, servers, client PCs, printers, and cable runs. Many remote terminals, or client workstations, contain a **key lockout** that, when locked, disables the keyboard. Since remote terminals are usually scattered throughout many offices, it's important that users be required to lock the terminal at the end of the day, and take the key with them—rather than tossing it in a desk drawer.

Remote terminals are cabled to a **communications controller**, which serves as an entry/exit port to a modem and the long-distance telephone network. Controllers are sophisticated devices that may be used for verifying user passwords, multiplexing, data compression, error control, or frame formatting. Typically, users in a large network are assigned various levels of access to the network. Each remote terminal is wired to a port on the controller. A savvy user can manipulate access via the ports, if it's known which port carries the data flowing from a user with the desired access. If access to a controller isn't limited, locking out keyboards is like swatting flies with a toothpick.

In a PC-based LAN, the server, typically, is the port to the outside, or WAN, connection. A router connects directly to the server, and while the router is a physical firewall, the server contains software firewall protection. If an intruder manages to get through it, he/she then has access to the system resources.

If cable ports are vulnerable, cable runs beg for hackers. All that's required to tap a twisted-pair cable is to strip away a small amount of insulation from both wires and attach suitable recording equipment. Coax cable is more resistant to **taps**, but generally carries higher frequencies, which produce an increase in radiated energy. In effect, coax cable is a data transmitter, and a very sensitive receiver can capture and store the **radiated data**. The most secure cable medium is fiber-optic cable. Tapping a fiber cable without, interrupting the data flow, is very difficult, and since light doesn't contain the electromagnetic radiation of copper wire, there's no stray energy to capture.

From a security standpoint, it makes sense to install fiber cable, but, economically, it may not be feasible. The best solution for safeguarding wire runs is to control access to them. Locate the **wiring harness** in a locked cabinet, or room, that's separate from the breaker box of the building facilities. Efforts should be made to run cables down walls rather than allowing them to dangle, fully exposed, from ceilings. Avoid placing the cables in the same run as electrical wires, or telephone cable, where anyone with a belt full of tools may have reason to be given access.

At sites in which CPUs, hard drives or tape backups are kept, physical access should be controlled. The memory of a large computer is where the "gold" of the data is kept, and only those with a reason to be in the room should be there. Frequently, personnel records, financial data, medical histories, marketing strategies, or defense data resides in the computer memory. The computer-room traffic can be controlled with **sign-in logs**, **ID badges** issued to authorized employees and guests, or by ensuring that any doors to the room will lock each time they're closed. Entry to the room can be restricted to those with a key.

Physical security planning should also include emergency situations, such as floods, earthquakes, power failures, and fire. Locating a million-dollar computer next to the hundred-year-old boiler is asking for trouble. If it doesn't blow up and incinerate the computer, it may very well float it into the next state when it starts to leak. Small wastebasket fires can quickly escalate into infernos—if there's not a fire extinguisher nearby. The most effective means of dealing with earthquakes is to house a computer in a reinforced facility. And for those small, jarring quakes, anchoring servers will protect much of the computer memory data.

Printouts, modem telephone numbers, written records of passwords and user IDs, or step-by-step instructions of how to utilize the network are all potential problems of physical security. The employment of **properly trained personnel** is the best course of action for preventing information from falling into the wrong hands, and periodic **security audits** will ensure that careless mistakes are kept to a minimum.

Data thieves need not be human beings. Water, for example, may take out your server and destroy all of its data. **Environmental factors** need the same level of attention as other forms of security. Some areas are prone to earthquakes, others tornadoes, some to hurricanes, while other areas get hit with flooding. If your network resides in an area with less-than-reliable electrical service, you chance a server crash each time the electricity drops out.

Consider where you locate critical network components such as servers, routers, hubs and bridges. If they are located too close to large, industrial motors or generators, you'll have problems with **Electro-Magnetic Interference** (EMI). Place them in a basement, and their performance may erode due to excessive moisture. Put these devices in an attic, and the heat will cause them to slow down, and perhaps overheat, and fail.

In a typical installation, critical components are located in a **wiring closet**. Access to the room is controlled, so that physical security is in place. Since the devices which run the network are located in the same room, maintenance and upgrades are easier to perform.

Choose the location of a wiring closet carefully. Make sure there's enough room to make changes on the equipment, that it's well lit, that it's air conditioned in the summer, and heated in the winter. It should be adequately removed from any devices that may cause EMI problems. In addition to motors and generators, put radios, cellular and cordless telephones, and satellite links on the list of items to keep away from. Table 10-1 lists several potential problem areas to consider when placing networking equipment.

Table 10-1 Location of Network Equipment

PHYSICAL DEVICE	ACTION TO TAKE
Servers, Routers, Hubs, Bridges, Gateways	Place in a secured wiring closet
Cabling—UTP, STP, Coaxial	Run at right angles at crossovers, check for taps, coax mat transmit data
Wiring Closet	Ventilate with climate-control, keep well-lit, secure door, floor and walls, dehumidify, and locate away from EMI sources
Storage Devices (disk/tape drives and media)	Secure in locked vault

Consider a case where users complain about the server taking a long time to respond. From a client computer, you log on as the administrator and check for problems, but none are identified on any of the server troubleshooting tools. The server is working, but it's working slow. What environmental factors may be causing the problem?

Depending on the time of year, the first consideration would be heat. If the wiring closet has become too hot, the server will slow. Another factor which could cause this is locating the equipment in a well-ventilated room, but not permitting the ventilation to cool the equipment. At least several inches of free space are needed for fan-cooled hubs and servers. If these units are backed up to a wall, the units will eventually overheat.

What if users complain that at certain times of the day, they loose data, or the server won't respond? After awhile, the problem goes away, and everything appears normal. If heat or humidity were the cause, the problem wouldn't predictably disappear. Due to latency times, if a server became too hot, and then cooled as the air conditioning kicked in, it would require some time to cool. A more likely place to look is for sources of EMI. Radios contain an oscillator that, while capable of delivering low amounts of radiated power, is a source of EMI. It could be that portable generators used to run pumps, or other equipment, are programmed to turn-on at specific times, and these are causing the problem.

Other pieces of network equipment can cause problems. A wireless LAN may interfere with cable-based clients, and the server, if the carrier isn't properly focused. For best results, use wireless systems that have infrared or laser (optical) carriers. Digital transmission facilities such as T-Carriers operate at high data rates, and these rates, if located too close to other equipment or wiring harnesses, could cause EMI interference.

Once you've protected the system against theft, interference and environmental factors, it's time to localize the protection of data. There are two ways of doing so: Provide redundant mass storage devices, and backup the data outside the workstation and server.

Redundant Array of Inexpensive Disks (RAID)

> RAID is a system of fault tolerance that may involve mirroring a disk, or striping multiple disks with data parity.

The standard used for network fault tolerance is the **Redundant Array of Inexpensive Disks**, or RAID. Originally developed at the University of California at Berkeley, RAID was first published as a white paper in 1987. In addition to providing against hardware losses, RAID may increase the performance of a hard drive by distributing read and write operations over multiple disks.

RAID is applied to fixed disks, or hard drives, and references to either of these terms in this chapter shouldn't be applied to other types of mass storage devices such as CD-ROMs, zip drives, floppy drives, optical drives, etc.

There are five levels associated with RAID, but they aren't a measure of how well the data is protected. Rather, they describe how data is distributed among two or more fixed disks, and how data redundancy is achieved. In a PC LAN environment, however, RAID levels 1 and 5 are the most commonly employed.

RAID is implemented through a combination of hardware and software. A Windows NT server, for example, is software-equipped, right out-of-the-box, for RAID 1 and 5. To implement it however, requires additional hardware. Commercial implementations of RAID use the SCSI (see Chapter 1) adapter interface.

We'll take a look at the particulars of each level, as well as define some common RAID terminology along the way.

NET+ OBJECTIVE
II.2.3

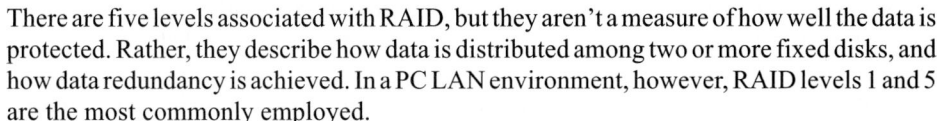
RAID 0

RAID 0 incorporates no redundancy, and therefore, isn't actually a RAID element. What it does do is significantly increase the read/write performance of server hard drives. Figure 10-11 illustrates a RAID 0 implementation.

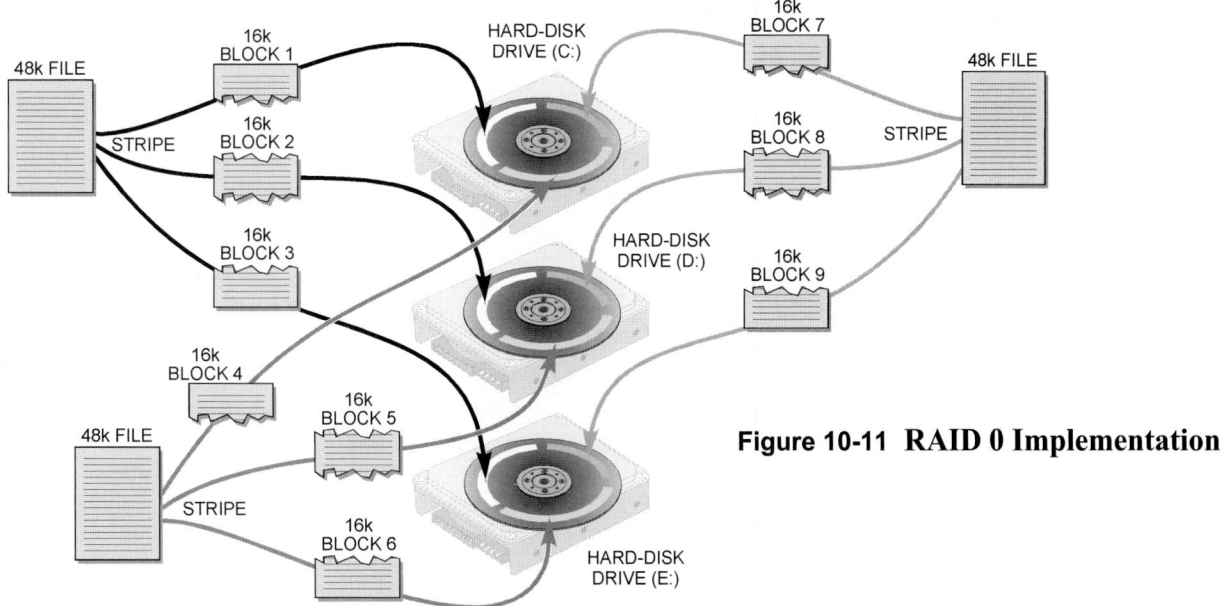

Figure 10-11 RAID 0 Implementation

Shown are three hard drives, with the file data being striped to their fixed disks. Striping means that a block of data is separated, and alternately written to sectors on each of the three disks. For example, assume a 48kB file is written to the disks. RAID 0 will write 16 kB to the first drive, 16 kB to the second drive, and 16 kB to the third drive. In other words, data blocks are striped across the fixed disks.

The date is written serially to each drive, which actually has a negligible effect on the time required to save a file. What does effect the performance of RAID 0 is the size of blocks. If the size is too small, then the commands associated with the write-action, along with additional SCSI commands, may be excessive. This is configurable, and you may need to experiment with it a bit. A good starting point for minimum block sizes is 16 kB.

As mentioned, RAID 0 doesn't provide for redundancy; therefore it has no fault tolerance attributes. RAID 0 provides improved throughput **without parity**. Parity is used with the other levels as a means for regenerating data, if it's lost on any of the fixed disks. If a fixed disk is lost in a RAID 0 system, all data is lost, and there is no means of recovering it; that is, it has no parity for data recovery.

When the block sizes are optimized, RAID 0 provides for improved throughput, particularly for read requests which occur in parallel—even if they are serially read afterwards.

Some RAID systems use a technique called **sector-sparing**, also referred to as **hot-fixing**. With sector-sparing, the disk controller and RAID software will detect a bad sector on a hard drive. When data is written to the bad sector, it will then be moved to a good sector.

RAID 1

RAID 1 copies all of the data on one hard drive, to another hard drive. Figure 10-12 shows an example of RAID 1, in which data on a primary disk is copied to a **mirror** disk. Mirroring is a RAID term meaning simply that all data written to one hard drive is simultaneously written to a backup—or mirror—hard drive.

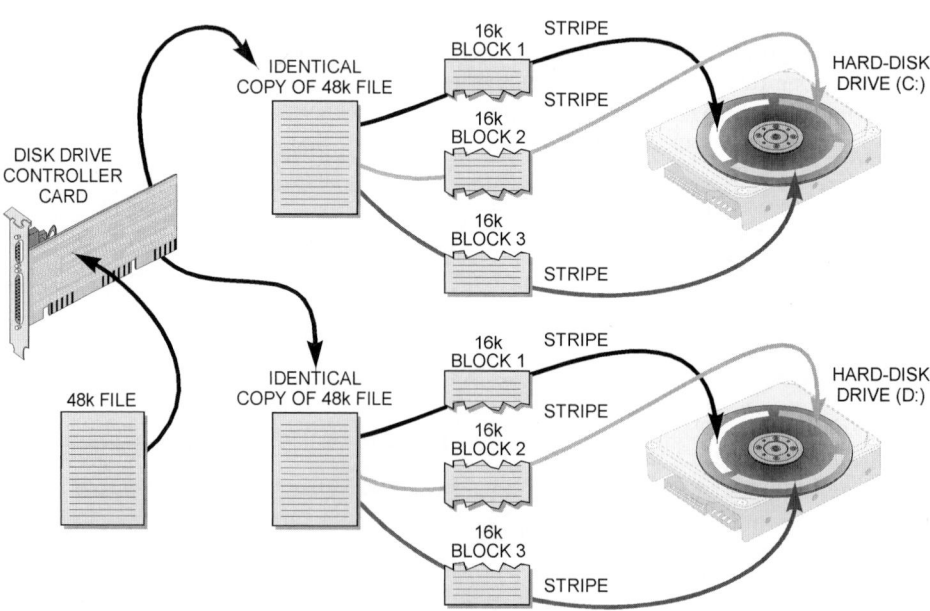

Figure 10-12 RAID 1 Copies Data to a Mirror Disk

The advantage of RAID 1 is that if data on the primary drive is lost, it can still be recovered from the mirror drive. As far as a server is concerned, there's no difference between the two disks. The largest disadvantage of RAID 1 is the cost of duplicate disks. During write operations, the system slows moderately, since data is written to two disks instead of one. However, during read operations, system performance may improve because data can be read from both disks.

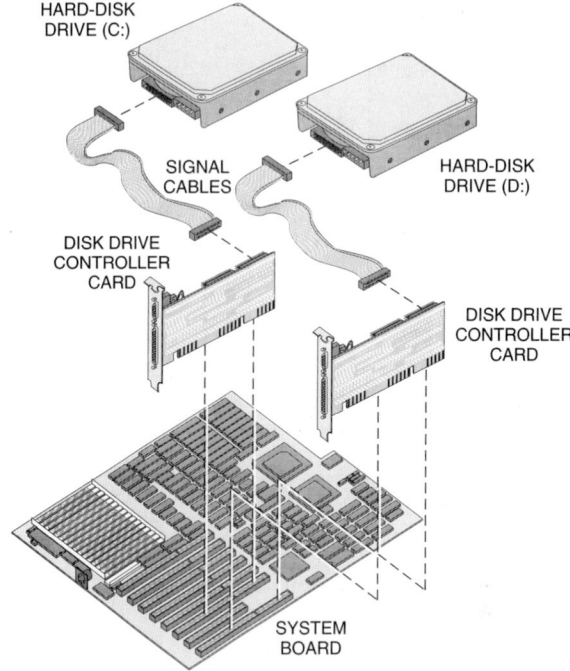

Whether the performance will improve or not depends on how RAID 1 is implemented. One implementation method is called round-robin scheduling. The server alternates between the two drives for read operations. The idea is that as a read operation completes on one drive, it can be immediately started on the next drive. The limiting factor of a hard drive is the mechanical action involved in moving the drive heads from sector to sector on a disk. This is called seek time, and currently averages about 9 mS on most quality hard drives.

In Figure 10-12, if the disk controller is lost, both hard drives are inaccessible. However, you should be able to replace the controller electronics, and be back in business shortly, unless the failing controller takes the drives with it when it goes. A technique for avoiding this possibility is to **duplex** RAID 1, by using separate disk controllers for each fixed disk. Figure 10-13 shows how the hardware is connected. As you can see, duplexing eliminates the disk controller as a single point of failure.

Figure 10-13 Duplexing with RAID 1

RAID 2

RAID 2 uses fault tolerance to distribute data across multiple disk drives, at the bit level. It's a proprietary technique (from Thinking Machines, Inc.) that utilizes disk striping with parity. The parity data is stored on redundant drives, and can be used to regenerate lost data if one of the primary drives fail.

The disadvantage of RAID 2 is the large number of dedicated parity drives which are required. It's typically used in applications where large amounts of data must be written or read from the drives. In a PC LAN, the reads and writes tend to be bursty, and varied in size—with small file sizes being common. The overhead associated with frequent, and small, file transfers means RAID 2 isn't a good choice in this application. Instead, it's typically used for applications such as large audio or video files.

RAID 3

RAID 3 is similar to RAID 2 in that a dedicated parity drive is used to duplicate data. The difference is that data is stripped in bytes, rather than bits, thus reducing the number of redundant drives required. Figure 10-14 shows how data is stored on a mirror disk using parity. Notice that the parity drive will be accessed during each write operation to the disks.

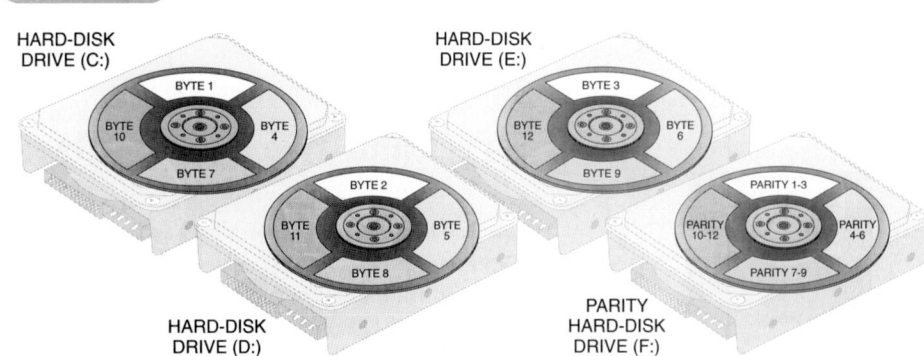

Figure 10-14 RAID 3 with a Parity Disk

This has a tendency to create queues for write operations, and slows down the performance of a server. During a read operation, performance improves, since the disks can be accessed at the same time, and the parity drive isn't needed.

Like RAID 2, RAID 3 is used for large file transfers. It's an improvement because the cost and overhead of the parity disk is reduced.

RAID 4

RAID 4 extends the concept of RAID 2 and 3 by striping disks with blocks of data, rather than bits or bytes. If a block size is set to 18 kB, then a read operation may require accessing a single disk, rather than multiple disks, as in the other two implementations. However, it sill requires a dedicated parity drive, and during a write operation, performance will slow as the data is stored on one or more primary disks, and then written to the parity drive.

RAID 5

RAID 5 stripes both file and parity data across all disk drives. As shown in Figure 10-15, a dedicated parity drive isn't used. For each stripe, a parity stripe is allotted to one of the disks.

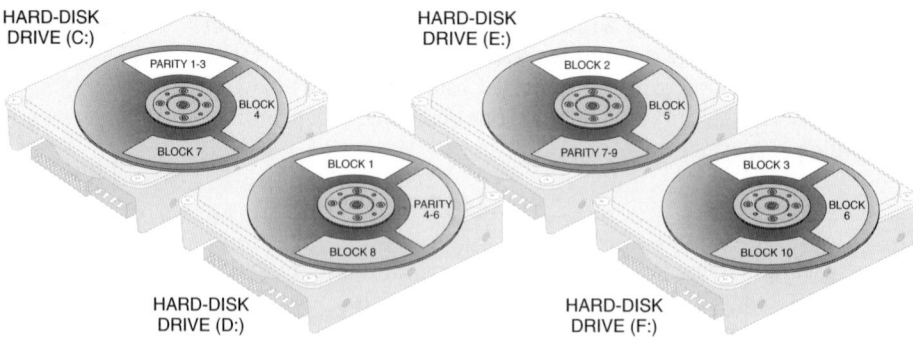

Figure 10-15 RAID 5 File and Parity Striping

RAID 2 through 4 requires one or more dedicated parity drives. For disk reads, this has no effect on server performance, but for write operations, the server slows down, since data is duplicated on the parity drive. RAID 5 overcomes this by striping data to all drives, allowing parallel reads and writes, and speeding up the performance during write operations.

RAID 5 is the most common fault tolerance method used in PC LANs. It makes for a more efficient system than RAID 1, since dedicated mirror disks aren't needed. If a primary disk fails, the server will recreate the lost data from parity stripes on the other disks. If this occurs, read operations will slow considerably, since the server must regenerate data in the parity stripe for the lost drive.

Server and Workstation Backup

NET+ OBJECTIVE
II.2.3

Tape backup, although not a part of the RAID standard, has an equally important fault tolerance role. A tape backup system is used to backup the data stored on fixed disks. This is especially true for data you simply cannot do without! Not only is it used to secure this class of information, it's also used to store data that, while not immediately needed on a server, still needs to be retained.

There are several methods used to tape-back-up server data, and none of them are particularly satisfactory. The most common is a quarter-inch cartridge drive that uses a disk controller in the server. The network operating system routinely contains utility programs that are used to backup data from a hard drive.

What's needed is a strategy for backing up the data. At best, you can expect data transfer rates, from the disk to tape, to average at about 100 MB a minute. If a 10GB hard drive is backed up to tape, the complete transaction will require many hours to complete, and many tapes will need to be changed. Sometimes a full backup is needed—perhaps once a week—but it should be augmented with more efficient planning.

Once the backup hardware is determined, you need to decide on a system for backing up data from the server. Files stored on a server include a bit called the archive bit. This is used to tell the backup software if the file is to be backed up or not. The state of the archive bit—set or not set—determines the backup strategy, unless a strategy is selected that ignores the bit.

Backup practices include the following techniques:

- **Normal Backup**, also called a full backup, means that all data on a hard drive is backed up, regardless of the state of the archive bit.

- **Incremental Backup** occurs only on files that have changed since the last full backup. A change to a file will set the archive bit to one, thus flagging it for the backup.

- A **Differential Backup** occurs for all files that have changed since the last full backup, regardless of whether they changed since the last differential backup. The archive bit is set to 1 when the file is modified and not reset after the backup.

Let's assume you want to back up the server data once a day. That way, at worst, you'll only lose a single day of information, if an earthquake wipes out the server. You could instruct the server to perform a complete backup, or you could back up only those file that have changed since the last backup. There are several variations to an incremental backup as described above, but they revolve around a similar theme. For example, a differential backup is similar to an incremental, except that the selected files are not marked. Similarly, when performing a daily copy, files that have changed on a specific day are backed up, but not marked as such. You should choose a time when server use is light for complete backups, and only back up changed files on a daily basis.

There is no RAID implementation that will allow you to restore fixed-disk data if the hard drives are destroyed by fire, flooding, earthquakes, theft, and so on. Server backups are simply good business practice, as well as common sense. The cost of the tape drive, and the initial system setup, is minimal compared to unrecoverable data.

In addition to tape backup systems, some files and directories are **replicated**. File and directory replication means that specified elements are stored on another computer. The other computer may be another server, or a workstation. Replication is typically used to duplicate logon scripts, system policy files, or large databases. A database is replicated when it's frequently accessed by many users. Once it resides on more than one machine, access times speed-up, because if one server is busy, a user will be off-loaded to the replicated database.

In the usual situation, folders are replicated from one server to another. The machine which copies the folder to another machine is referred to as the **export server**, while the machine that receives the copy is called the **import server**. Folder replication, in addition to copying a file, automatically updates the copy when changes are made to the original. The frequency of the updates are configurable. For example, Windows NT defaults to 5 minutes, but can be set as low as 1 minute between updates.

If a second server isn't available, a workstation may be used for importing folders. The workstation is notified of updates, in the same manner as when replication occurs between servers, but typically, a workstation can only import folder replications. It would not be used to export folders to other machines. The reason is that the workstation software can't support the management functions needed to administer updates.

Since workstations may be used to import folders from servers, and not export folders, they still need a means of backing up their data. How this is done depends on a broad backup strategy designed for each LAN—or, applied to all LANs consistently. The simplest is to assign user directories on a server, and backup the contents as part of the scheduled server tape backup.

Another method used for workstation backups revolves around **removable media**. Removable media refers to floppy disks, tape backups, or recordable CD devices, called a CD-R. Floppy disks, and to a lesser extent, CD backups, aren't a feasible solution for server backups, due to the volume of material on a server versus the volume on a workstation.

Establish standard operating procedures for workstation and server backups. Most organizations defer responsibility for server data away from the client. This means that if you place data on the server, it will be backed up, and you needn't worry about it. Any folders on the workstation are the responsibility of the user. These may be backed up using floppy disk, tape, zip drives, or CD-R, as already mentioned.

Logical

NET+ OBJECTIVE
II.2.10

Logical security techniques involve defending the vulnerabilities of the network software. Almost all network users gain access to a network by entering a **password** and/or **user ID**, at a sign-on screen. User IDs can be of any length, with four to eight characters being the most common. The ID is usually assigned to the user, and consists of alphanumeric characters. The user password may be assigned, or the user may have the option of creating an original password.

User **sign-on screens** provide the first level of logical security. The practice of assigning user IDs (usually by network managers or security officers in information systems departments) ensures that a central authority retains control of the individuals offered network access, as well as a record of all individuals on the network. When users are given the option of changing their password, access security is increased. The most effective sign-on screens won't echo passwords back when the user types them in. But, if the password is compromised, the user may be the first to know, and can correct the problem immediately by changing passwords. The obvious should be avoided when selecting passwords, such as first or last names of users, job titles, birth dates, or the names of the user's children. Network administrators should make a practice of reviewing passwords.

A security policy should include keeping user names and passwords at or below eight characters so as to avoid errors when entering, and to also reduce the likelihood of the user forgetting them. Since most password encryption schemes are case-sensitive, the password should include a mix of upper and lower case letters as well numerals and special characters. Consider the following examples of passwords:

- password
- barney

- aMN8dt$
- aBcDeF

The third password, aMN8dt$, is the most secure since it's not likely that an unauthorized user will attempt it as a random try to crack into the network. The last password, aBcDeF, is next best since it includes upper and lower case letters. However, it doesn't include numbers or special characters. The first two passwords will eventually be discovered. A password called **password** is often the default used during installations. A password called *barney* is the name of the user or one his children.

Passwords and user IDs may be stored in various locations. A LAN without a file server contains both in the system software and each time the software is initiated, sign-on screens for all active PCs will be invoked. If the LAN has a file server, passwords and IDs are maintained at the file server. Figure 10-16 shows a typical example of a user sign-on screen.

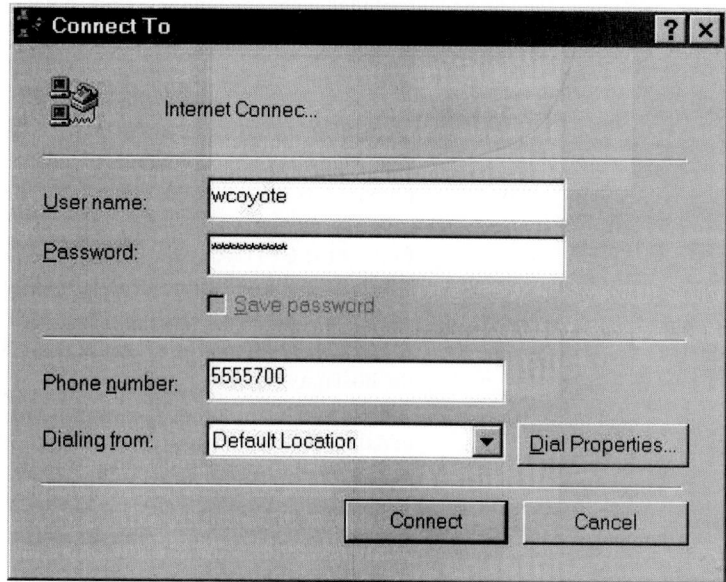

To gain access to network resources, a user will be required to enter the following:

- **Username**: WCOYOTE

- **Password**: roadrunner. Note that passwords are encrypted and, in this example, will echo back as **********

Figure 10-16 Example of User Sign-On Screen

For new users, the password is some default word used by all new users such as *newuser*. At the next logon, the user is prompted to enter a new password, then enter it again to confirm the selection. This is done to provide a measure of security for the user. However, in all network software, this is an option established by the network administrator.

Usernames identify the user on the network and should be unique. The **password** allows the user access to network resources. As previously mentioned, network access is setup and maintained at the server. A **login account** is created for each user that specifies resources they are permitted to access. Note that "resources" in this context refers to any physical and logical objects on a network. These can include access to printers, files and directories, to other servers, as well as access to modify access privileges.

Users should be given the option of changing passwords whenever they want. If this isn't possible, establish a policy that forces them to do so at least once a month. Normally, a notice pops-up when the monthly time limit approaches, say 10 to 15 days before. The user then has two weeks to make the change. If they don't, they'll be prohibited from logging on when the password expires. This is a good system because it incorporates randomness into password changes. If all users change passwords on the same day at the same time, it won't be too difficult for a hacker to be in the right place at that specific time to catch the new password. Randomness makes it far more difficult for this to happen.

Usernames identify the user on the network, and should be unique. The **password** allows the user access to network resources. As previously mentioned, network access is set up and maintained at the server. A **login account** is created for each user that specifies resources they are permitted to access. Note that "resources" in this context refers to any physical and logical objects on a network. These can include access to printers, files, directories, other servers, as well as access to modify the access privileges.

In a typical scenario, **group accounts** are defined by the network administrator. These accounts describe the rights that a user has been given on the system. Examples of rights include System Shutdown or Local Logon.

Once a group account has been set up, a user may be assigned to it. Essentially, groups are a tool that eases the management of user accounts. There will be users who perform similar tasks on a workstation, and utilize similar network services. A group account provides you with the flexibility to create a specific account, and then assign individuals to it.

In wide area networks, sign-on data is usually contained at ports to the WAN, or for diskless workstations, may reside at a communication controller. As was mentioned in the section on physical security, servers are susceptible to invasion by the technically informed. In fact, if a user (**hacker**) can defeat the controller sign-on requirement, a direct connection will result to the host CPU. A server is only moderately more complex than a PC, so defeating the device has a similar level of complexity.

Some distributed networks leave control of network access to a large mainframe **host**. Since the host may be located hundreds, or thousands, of miles from the remote terminal user, user passwords and IDs are quite secure. Unfortunately, this practice also requires that a considerable amount of memory be allotted for logons, when local servers are quite capable of handling the same job.

As mentioned, passwords provide the first level of security to the network. But users are notorious for writing them down, and storing them in an unlocked desk drawer in an unlocked office. How can the network know that the person entering the correct password is the person who actually owns the password?

A technique for authenticating users is the **callback** system. As soon as the sign-on is completed, the remote host disconnects the link, and calls the telephone number of the modem connecting the user's terminal to the network. The user must actually be at that number to receive the call. This prevents an unauthorized user from installing a **terminal emulator** in a home PC, and accessing the remote host through a modem.

The host callback is generally a screen change. The user may be prompted to enter a common code, or, as is frequently the case, told to simply press the ENTER key on the keyboard. Pressing the ENTER key is equivalent to answering the callback.

A PC-based LAN server uses a similar approach. After the system boots, you must CTR-ALT-DEL to force the server to re-boot. Once it does, you enter password information.

Once access is granted to a network, several levels of security should be available. Broadly speaking, the levels are called **browse**, **update**, and **unauthorized access**. A browse function means the user has access to files and may read the information contained in them. The user is generally permitted to print the files as well (although printer access is another security option). While the files may be read (browsed), adding or deleting information isn't allowed at this level. In order to make changes, the user must be given update authority. Now, information can be written to and read from the file. The unauthorized access level forbids the user entry to a file.

When assigning individual user access, there are two terms to understand—**rights** and **profiles**. Rights refer to the authorized permission to perform specific actions on the network. Profiles are the configuration settings made for each user. For example, a profile may be created that places a user in a group. This group has been given certain rights to perform specific actions on the network.

A network administrator may also determine network **policies**. A policy includes system configurations that affect all users. An example of a policy is one built around passwords and logons.

For example, the following lists policies which may be applied to logons with Windows NT:

- Maximum Password Age sets the length of time that a password is used before expiring. At that time, the user must select a new password.

- Minimum Password Age sets the minimum amount of time a password can be used before the user selects another. This is intended to prevent a users from selecting the same password over and over.

- Minimum Password Length is the number of characters that a password must contain.

- Password Uniqueness is used to maintain a history of passwords. The administrator may specify that with each forced password selection, NT will remember previous passwords. This prevents the user from using the same password over and over.

Account Logout/No Account Logout is used to specify what happens when a password is forgotten, or an authorized user attempts to sign on, multiple times, using another's user name. There are two options. First, nothing happens if the administrator checks the No Account Logout box. If the Account Logout box is checked, then a series of dialog boxes opens to set the parameters for the logout.

Policies may be applied to groups as in the above example, or to individuals. An example of this is a policy for making registry changes to remote client computers. Since a registry change contains configuration settings for the client, the complete client system is affected.

Security levels are assigned by network managers or operators. The basis for permitting browse, update, or for denying access to specific files should be the nature of the tasks that the user is required to perform at the terminal. If, in the normal course of his/her job, the user needs access to a file, but lacks the need for changing data contained in the file, the browse access should be permitted, and the update denied.

The logical security safeguards mean little if the physical security of the network is ignored. Writing down modem phone numbers and passwords, or allowing the use, by others, of passwords, defeats the intent of logical security.

User and Share Level Security

At its base level, security can be separated into a **user level** or **share level model**. Or, it may contain elements of both. A good networking practice involves an awareness of both types, then selecting one or both for the system.

User-level security allows an individual or defined groups of users attempting to access network resources to be validated against account information stored at the server. Typically, user-level security, then, is associated with server-based LANs.

NET+ OBJECTIVE
I.9.1

In order to initiate user-level security, the user of a workstation must specify it using the Access Control dialog box in the Network folder. The Access Control dialog is shown in Figure 10-17. In the figure, user-level security has been selected. The user (or group of users) will be validated against at the server domain name **domain**.

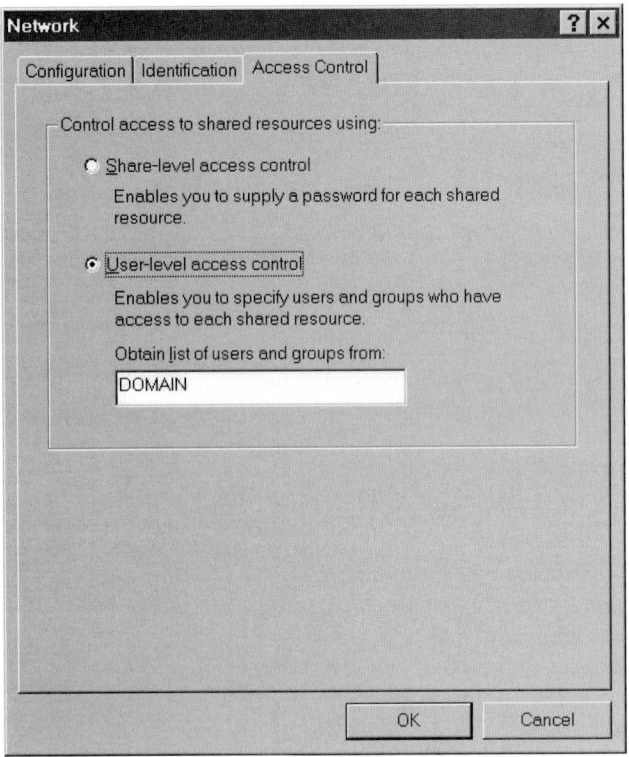

Figure 10-17 The Access Control Dialog Box Located in the Network Folder

User level security involves individually authenticating each user who accesses the network. This is universally done with a user ID and a password. In some networks—the Internet, for example—this may be all that's needed to validate users. In a small LAN, or a departmental network, this may be all that's needed. If, for instance, five users in an engineering department are concurrently working on a product design, they will need access to one another's work. A simple way to do so is to password-protect the network, then permit authenticated users access to all of the information on it.

In a typical scenario, **group accounts** are defined by the network administrator. These accounts describe rights a user has been given on the system. Examples of rights include System Shutdown or Local Logon. Once a group account has been setup, a user may be assigned to it. Essentially, groups are a tool that eases the management of user accounts. From an administrative perspective, they save time over setting security for each user (which is how it must be done with share level access). The option to use group accounts is set at the workstation by specifying user level access.

There will be users who perform similar tasks on a workstation and utilize similar network services. A group account provides you with the flexibility to create one account, then assign individuals to it.

Figure 10-18 shows the top-level screen for user properties. In the figure, a directory (or file, since the process is identical) has been selected to be shared. In Figure 10-19, the share options can be seen in the bottom-right corner of the dialog box and are as follows:

- No Access—this prevents any other users from either reading or modifying the contents of the directory.

- Read Access—Allows other users to read the contents of the directory of file but they may not modify the content.

- Change Access—Allows other users to modify the content of the file.

- Full Access—Allows other users to read as well as modify the file content.

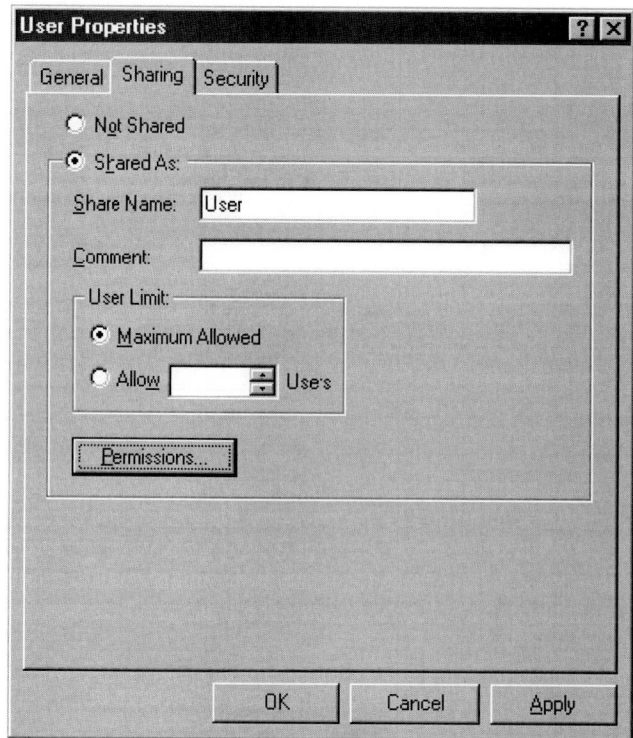

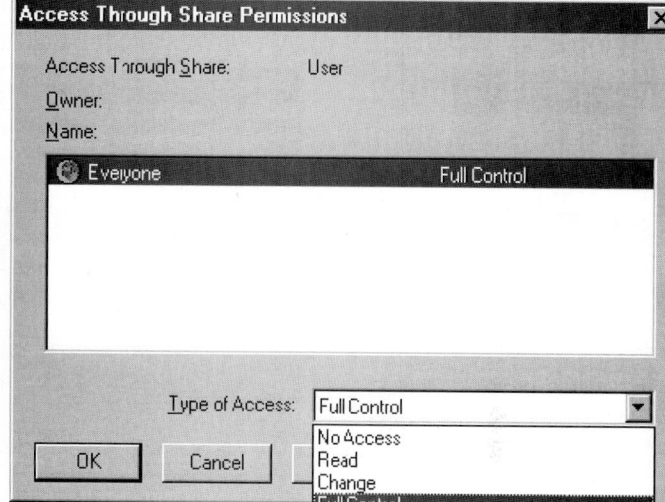

Figure 10-18 Share Tab of User Properties on a Windows NT Server

Figure 10-19 Access Permissions for the User Directory

The screen shot shown in Figure 10-18 is from the group user accounts of Windows NT. Once user-level access is specified on the workstations, group rights are setup at this screen. Then, in order to access a particular resource, the workstation first defaults to the server for password authentication. Once the server authenticates the user password, the workstation checks for additional restriction at the local workstation (share-level access).

In wide area networks, sign-on data is usually contained at ports to the WAN, or for diskless workstations may reside at a communication controller. Servers are susceptible to invasion by the technically informed. In fact, if a user (hacker) can defeat the controller or server sign-on requirement, a direct connection will result to the host resources. A server is only moderately more complex than a PC, so that the skills needed in defeating the device have a similar level of complexity.

Some distributed networks leave control of network access to a large mainframe host or centralized server. Since the host may be located hundreds or thousands of miles from the remote terminal user, user passwords and IDs are quite secure. Unfortunately, this practice also requires that a considerable amount of memory be allotted for logons when local servers are quite capable of handling the same job.

In a variation of this, the user has complete authority for establishing access to his account. This system is employed in a UNIX network but isn't as readily found in NetWare or NT. (Although users have the option, it becomes obscured in rights and policies controlled by the administrator.)

Share-level security involves password protecting each shared resource on a workstation. It's typically associated with workgroup or peer-to-peer LANs, but can also be applied to server-based networks.

Share level access provides a range of security direct to the user that user level doesn't. Unless you have a compelling reason for a specialized user level account, you'll probably grouped with those who have similar needs to your own. The depth of the access is assigned to you; whereas with share level access you determine the depth of security.

Once a user has access to the network, a decision may need to be made that limits their access. For example, should all employees have access to payroll records? While some think this is a good idea, the fact is, it's likely to cause a considerable amount of teeth gnashing and, perhaps, bashing.

Figure 10-20 is an example of a Windows dialog box for setting share-level security on a folder. There are three security options available:

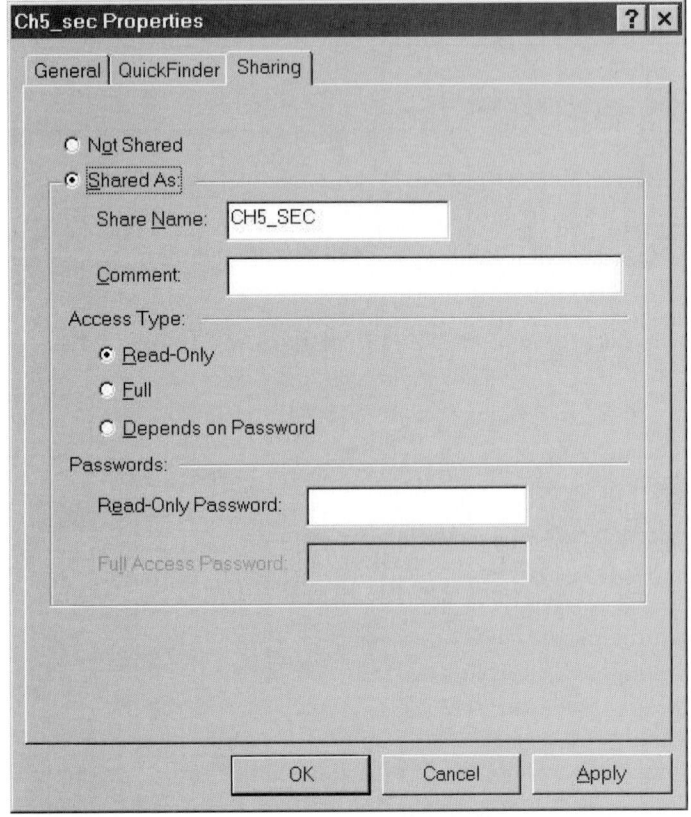

- Read-only allows a user with the read-only password to view the folder contents, but not modify them.

- Full access allows a user with the full-access password to read as well as modify the contents of the folder.

- Depends on password allows you to enter both read-only and full access passwords. Users with one or the other password can access the file.

You may have information in a personal home directory that you simply don't want to share with every employee in the company, and it may not be appropriate to do so. This is the case for share level access and it's not a hard one to make. All network operating systems use some type of shared access.

Passwords provide the first level of security to the network. But users are notorious for writing them down and storing them in an unlocked desk drawer in an unlocked office. How can the network be sure that the person entering the correct password is the person who owns the password?

A technique for authenticating users is the **call-back** system. As soon as the sign-on is completed the remote host disconnects the link and calls the telephone number of the modem connecting the users terminal to the network. The user must actually be at that number to receive the call. This prevents an unauthorized user from installing a terminal emulator in a home PC and accessing the remote host through a modem.

Figure 10-20 Share-level Security Setup on a Folder

The host call-back is generally a screen change. The user may be prompted to enter a common code or, as is frequently the case, told to simply press the enter key on the keyboard. Pressing the enter key is equivalent to answering the call-back.

A PC-based LAN server uses a similar approach. After the system boots, you must CTR-ALT-DEL to force the server to re-boot. Once it does, you enter password information. For remote clients, you have to option of specifying a call-back to the remote user.

Another technique used by many companies whose client computers access the Internet is to install **firewalls** at the Internet ports. A firewall is a filter that operates in a manner that's very similar to a bridge. It's a software object that filters IP addresses containing destination fields which correspond to those on the target network. The firewall contains a pool of authorized source addresses that are permitted access.

If the received packet contains an unknown source address, it's denied access. A firewall works in reverse, as well. It may look at DNS entries and compare those to a list of IP addresses that have been determined to be off-limits to employees.

Procedural

Clearly defined policies and procedures governing data security are essential. Those employees with legitimate needs for accessing the network should have a clear understanding of data safeguards, and written procedures can help to clarify many gray areas. Regulations associated with security should be written clearly, in layman terms, and made readily available to network users. Responsibility for maintaining the procedures should be centralized at local sites so that when a crisis occurs, the procedures followed are current.

NET+ OBJECTIVE
II.3.1

In many cases, a local network manager, or operator, doubles as security manager. It's important that the security responsibilities are handled by an individual with the authority and technical knowledge to adequately oversee data security.

Typical duties of security or network managers should involve issuing **updates** affecting the network to concerned users, eliminating access authorization when employees leave or are transferred, conducting **inspections** to see if the procedures are being followed, and **network training**.

While network managers generally decide the appropriate level of access of users, it's normal procedure to include a one-over-one **signature system** when adding new users or providing update authorities. The signature system helps to avoid situations in which network managers show favoritism or abuse their authority.

NET+ OBJECTIVE
II.3.2

Hardware upgrades and software updates should be proceduralized so they can be installed without adversely affecting other areas on a network. For example, a software patch may be released that addresses a weakness in the original software. The patch may be beneficial to some users but not all and may, in fact, cause some performance losses when installed. For those who need it, the loss in performance is compensated by the benefits of the patch. But for those who don't need it, the patch simply causes problems.

CNST OBJECTIVE
XII-A

The same is true for newer versions of a software package released from the vendor. A procedure should be in place that requires the software to be installed and tested before upgrading all clients and servers. The bugs that the upgrade address may not be appropriate or needed and, consequently, will only disrupt an otherwise functioning system.

Visit the download area of a vendor Web site. You're likely to find fixes, patches or upgrades for hardware or software. These all mean the same thing; an interim solution for bugs which have been discovered either during beta testing or after the product was formally released. The patch will have a file that describes the bug. This is known as test documentation because it typically contains the following information:

- Description of the bug, or known weakness.

- The problem the patch or upgrade is designed to remedy.

- A listing of any known conflict which may arise wen the patch is installed.

- Download and installation directions. These normally are achieved with the download.

- Revision control that follows the dotted decimal revision system of the product. For example, a software package at the time you buy it may be at revision level 1.2. The next scheduled release of the package may be advertised as 1.3. In the meantime, bug fixes, patches and interim upgrades may be at revision 1.2.1 or 1.2.1a, etc.

Before installing an upgrade or patch, read the vendor literature related to it. There are good reasons to do this. The patch may not address your application, it may cause conflicts with other applications in your network, or, the cost of installing the upgrade may not be worth the benefit.

NET+ OBJECTIVE
II.3.2

Similarly, a network operation needs to have documented **computer virus policy** or **procedure**. For example, assume you choose an anti-virus package, and install it on all servers. Should it also be installed on the client machines? Print servers? Hubs and routers?

Consider a network in which you get a call from a user who tells you he/she thinks the workstation was infected with a virus from the server. Impossible, you think, because both client and server have anti-virus software installed. You have a look anyway and, sure enough, it appears the client is infected with a virus. How is this possible since the virus software detects and cleans virus?

The answer is that a new virus has probably been released since you installed the detection software. If you choose McAfee or Norton anti-virus solutions, you also buy periodic updates that are released when a new virus is found. The quickest way to install the updates is to download them from the vendor Web site. You should receive notice when the updates are available, or you can check their Web sites for the latest signatures.

When selecting an anti-virus software package, be aware that there are two basic types available: **Memory-resident,** and **on-demand scanners**. The following describes the differences between the two types:

- Memory- Resident Virus Scanners: Generally only detects a virus but can't correct it; scans only selected files, and will remain active at all times that the computer is turned on.

- On-Demand Virus Scanners: Will detect as well as correct detected viruses; will scan all files on a disk; and must be manually activated.

A commercial anti-virus software package (such as MacAfee Shield or Norton Anti-virus) allow you to configure it for either type, or a combination of both types.

Anti-virus software should be installed on all client computers as well as all servers. At least once a month, the vendor should be queried for the latest version of their anti-virus software. This ensures that the software signature, the coverage of the virus it detects, will remain up to date.

The SOP you put in place needs to address updating installed virus software. Will you do it over the network, via disk at each workstation, or have users do it themselves? No matter which method you choose, document it, enforce it, and stick with it. This is particularly important for workstations since these are likely to be the source of a virus. Many companies forbid employees to install any unauthorized software on computers because of virus problems (as well as piracy issues). This can get tricky for employees who routinely work at home and carry their work back and forth on floppy disks. Consider offering, and requiring, a virus scan to these individuals.

User training and **documentation** is often overlooked. Many technical manuals are written by those long on expertise but short on clarity. One of the most vexing security problems facing non technical users is making the distinction between sensitive and non sensitive data. The problem is compounded when the user must try deciphering excessive amounts of "networkese" terms and, especially, acronyms. If a large network is distributed throughout many locations, the addition of a central assistance desk, manned with a network operator trained to answer the user's questions, will dramatically increase user productivity and decrease time spent on problem solving.

Personnel

A recent study of large network users illustrated the perceived versus actual security threats to a network. The users perceived that hackers and **viruses** were their greatest security threat, but upon examining the realities of security problems, they found that users' curiosity of the network, and **programming errors**, were the culprits in 90% of the security glitches. The people working with, and around, the network caused the majority of the problems.

NET+ OBJECTIVE
II.2.10

Many issues discussed in the previous sections directly involve network personnel. Network managers must restrict access to the network functions and hardware based upon a "job-needed" basis. If an individual doesn't need access to a particular file, access should be denied. In installations where very sensitive information is stored and exchanged, **background checks** are in order. Information affecting national security should only be shared by personnel with the proper **security clearance**.

Unfortunately, it is the personnel who have been cleared, received access to a network, and utilize the network on a regular basis, that are in the best position to misappropriate data, or inflict real damage to the network operation. Due to this, the importance of security should be continually emphasized. Remember, it's been shown that the curiosity of users is mainly responsible for security problems. In many cases, the guilty user is simply trying to "beat the system." While there are no guarantees for ensuring the integrity of network personnel, proper training, clear procedures, common sense physical safeguards, and software obstacles contribute in discouraging the negative aspects of curiosity.

DATA CRYPTOGRAPHY

Cryptography is the process of writing secret messages so that the message intelligence is hidden. In the past, secret communications have been the domain of governments, the military, and intelligence organizations. Today, these agencies still have a considerable need for cryptography, but the applications have broadened in the last decade or so.

It was mentioned earlier in this chapter that curious users represent a greater threat to data security than those with willful intentions of wrongdoing. Ironically, the same curiosity that produced almost instant worldwide communication is also the greatest threat to the product. The majority of the curious seekers will do nothing wrong with the data they find access to, but all users have an ethical and professional responsibility to whatever entity holds the title to that data. Implied in the responsibility is a bias to protect data that may disrupt or damage the lives of individuals, corporations, and government. An invitation to violate privacy has been extended by "all that data out there." Data cryptography is the last line of defense for protecting the sanctity of information.

Electronic fund transfers between financial institutions, banks, savings and loans, brokerage exchanges, and stock exchanges are routinely masked with cryptography. The automatic teller machines also have a need for cryptography usage, with passwords and deposit or withdrawal transactions. The technology for these routine services wasn't installed on a wide base ten years ago, and the applications outside of government for cryptography was limited. The applications of data communications have mushroomed as many corporations have evolved into multinational organizations, and telecommunications has grown to become much more customer oriented.

> Plaintext refers to data which has not been encrypted, while ciphertext is data which has been encrypted.

As individuals, we expect to utilize many of the services available through data communications, but simultaneously expect our utilization to stay out of the daily newspapers. Credit histories, employment records, medical records, or criminal records may all reside in a computer database and may be sent from point to point as needed. There's simply no reason for your neighbor to know that you have a history of delinquent credit, or that you spent a couple of years in prison twenty years ago. But if your neighbor is clever, knowledgeable, and persistent, the information may very well be spewing out of a PC printer.

The basic concept of data cryptography is illustrated in Figure 10-21. The data is encrypted at the transmitter. **Encryption** is the process of transforming data into a secret code. **Decryption** is the process of transforming the secret code back to the original data, and is done at the receiver. The blocks in the figure labelled E and D represent encryption and decryption, respectively.

Figure 10-21 Basic Data Cryptography System

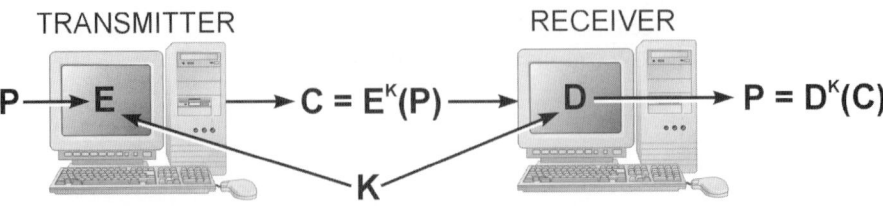

The data to be encrypted is called **plaintext** and is represented as **P**. Once the plaintext has been encrypted, it's referred to as **ciphertext**. Ciphertext is represented with a **C** in Figure 10-16 All encryption techniques require the use of a **key**, shown in the figure as **K**. The key specifies the parameters of the secret code. For example, you may encrypt a message by changing all letters of the message to the next adjacent letter so that the word DATA becomes EBUB. The letter D is followed by E, A by B, T by U, and A by B.

The key used in this example may be written as:

$$K = X + 1$$

where for each plaintext letter (X), the cipher text results by using the next letter in the alphabet.

Encryption keys describe how the plaintext will be operated on to become ciphertext. The process of imposing the key on the plaintext is done with an encryption **algorithm**. The encryption and decryption blocks of Figure 10-11 represent an algorithm that will transform plaintext, through a series of permutations, to ciphertext. The algorithm is implemented in accordance with the encryption, or decryption, key. In our example above of encrypting the word DATA, the algorithm is the necessary hardware and software needed to implement $K = X + 1$.

The encrypted data out of the transmitter of Figure 10-11 is $C = E^K(P)$. This means ciphertext (C) is produced by applying an encryption key (K) and algorithm (E) to the plaintext (P). Decryption takes place at the receiver according to $P = D^K(C)$. This means the plaintext (P) will be recovered by applying the decrypting key (K) and algorithm (D) to the ciphertext (C). These conventions are followed throughout this discussion of data cryptography.

The strength of an encryption scheme is determined by the key and algorithm. As a rule, algorithms are made public and keys are protected. The algorithm should respond to as many key variations as possible and should be designed so as to not reveal the key. In practice, algorithms are available that make it impossible for unauthorized users to derive the key. Thus, encryption systems adhering to widespread standards can be implemented with a very high degree of security.

Since algorithms are in the public domain, the weakness of data encryption is the key. If an unauthorized user has the key, then the plaintext can be recovered. The secrecy of keys is of paramount importance.

Several other components of successful encryption must be considered. The volume of work required to break the encryption code must be impractical. For example, a small army of specialists may be able to break into the files of the local credit bureau; but would it be worth it? Probably not, especially when judgments, bankruptcies, and such, are a matter of public record. Another consideration is that the complexity of the key be excessive to the point that breaking the code is nearly impossible. The current **Data Encryption Standard** (**DES**) offers 65,536 possible keys for use with a single algorithm. The third consideration of successful encryption is related to the time required to break the key. It's possible to try each of the DES keys, one after another, to break a coded message. By the time the correct key is found, the concept of encryption may be obsolete.

In addition, encryption should be successful under several conditions. An unauthorized user shouldn't be able to determine the encryption key, even when large amounts of plaintext, and the corresponding ciphertext, are available. Also, the key should remain hidden when the plaintext, ciphertext, and algorithm can all be compared side by side.

Encryption systems can be divided into three classes: **substitution**, **transposition**, and **product** ciphers. Each of these are shown in Figure 10-22. The substitution class of Figure 10-22(a) is identical to our earlier example of encryption. A substitution cipher substitutes letters of the plaintext with other letters.

Plaintext: **DATA**

Ciphertext: **EBUB** (a)

Key: $K = X + 1$

Plaintext: **DATA**

Ciphertext: **ATAD** (b)

Key: $K = \overline{X}$

Plaintext: **DATA**

Ciphertext: **BUBE** (c)

Key: $K = \overline{X + 1}$

Figure 10-22 Encryption Cipher Classes

Transposition classes of ciphers rearrange the sequence of the plaintext. In the example shown in Figure 10-22(b), the sequence of the letters in the word DATA have been reversed. Other transposition methods may involve route transposition of blocks of data, reversing the order of most- and least-significant bits in data streams, or by arranging messages in columns and transposing the columns.

The product cipher class of Figure 10-22(c) is a combination of substitution and transposition classes. The letters of the word DATA have been substituted by the next adjacent letter and then the order of the letters are transposed by reversing them.

The weakness of substitution encryption is that the code may be broken by analyzing patterns based upon character frequency. For example, the letters E and T are commonly used letters. In our example of enciphering the word DATA, a frequency analysis would quickly reveal that the letter U corresponds to a frequently used letter. After a few trial and error attempts, our simple key would be broken.

Transposition is effective as long as any patterns in the plaintext don't exceed the length of the key. For example, mathematical equations that are long or complex, yet are duplicated many times over in a message, will reveal a pattern to a **cryptanalyst**. If the equations themselves can be derived by examining the redundancy in the ciphertext, the key itself will be revealed. Currently, 100-digit keys can be considered to be fully secure.

By combining substitution and transposition in a product cipher, the revealing nature of **character-frequency analysis** and the statistical properties of the ciphertext can be successfully obscured.

NET+ OBJECTIVE
I.9.1

Encryption Techniques

A number of techniques are available for encrypting data. The more common techniques are discussed below. In practice, encryption techniques incorporate one or more of the encryption classes discussed in the previous section.

Unbreakable Cipher

An unbreakable cipher key is used one time and then discarded. It consists of a randomly generated key of equal length to the plaintext message. An unbreakable code resists analysis due to its complexity and length. A condition must be that there's no duplication in the key (all other keys involve redundancy).

For example, we may encrypt the phrase FAT CAT as:

F = T
A = 12
T = V

C = 14
A = 7
T = R

The code has no redundancy and each character is encoded differently each time it's used.

The problem with unbreakable codes is that they're not practical. Each time a message is to be transmitted through a network, it requires a change of hardware and software to encrypt it. The advantage to unbreakable codes is they are 100% secure.

Random-Key Cipher

A random-key cipher uses logic circuitry to generate a key. Ideally, the same circuitry is used to generate many different keys. In practice, a **random-key generator** is actually a pseudo random-key, because the hardware will eventually duplicate the key.

If the number of possible keys can be counted in the thousands, then the chances of the key being broken, through message analysis, is quite remote. Frequently, random-key ciphers are referred to as **bit-stream ciphers**.

The majority of modern encryption schemes employ random-key generators. The cyclic redundancy circuitry, described earlier in this chapter, resembles random-key hardware. Once data begins shifting through the registers, and combining in the ex-OR gates, it does so according to the initial condition of the registers—that is, the data output is directly influenced by the logic 1's and 0's held in the registers at the time the data is fed through.

The random-key generator used with encryption works the same way. The registers are initially set to the key, and data to be encrypted is then cycled through the generator. Decryption (as in error checking at a receiver) is the inverse of encryption.

Random-key generators are **product ciphers**. They work only on 1's and 0's through substitution and transposition of the bit sequence. They have the added advantage of cyclic redundancy, which produces ciphertext based upon many permutations of the plaintext. Cryptanalysts find it extremely difficult to find patterns in the ciphertext because each generated character is based upon the registers state for many cycles before the character.

The disadvantage to random-key ciphers is that encryption errors will propagate through many characters, before being cycled out of the generator. The advantage of the random-key cipher is that the duplication of keys is unlikely. An 8-bit generator produces 256 keys, a 16-bit generator produces 65,536 keys, while a 24-bit generator provides nearly seventeen million unique keys.

Block Cipher

A block cipher is a substitution cipher. Blocks of plaintext are substituted with ciphertext taken from **block-cipher dictionaries**. Keep in mind, data in this context means 1's and 0's. A block of data is considered to be 64 bits long, and the dictionary has to be capable of storing all block sequences of 1's and 0's.

The disadvantage of block ciphers is that redundant plaintext always results in the same ciphertext. It's a simple and inexpensive method of encrypting data not exceeding one block length. It has limited practical value in larger networks that use the data-link protocols, due to the constant bit-stream duplication in the protocol headers, flags, and frame formats.

An extension of block cipher is **chain-block cipher**. The blocks are chained through exclusive-OR feedback taps, as described for the random-key, bit-stream ciphers. The practice of encrypting bit by bit, or by the block, carries little significance since all data at this level is a series of bits. The data encryption standard utilizes block chaining, but the terminology is more of convenience than of affect.

Public-Key Cipher

One of the problems of receiving a secret message is deciding if the message originated with an authorized user, or was transmitted by someone who had gained access to the key. The assumption of the receiving user is that the message must be valid, or it wouldn't have been sent. The flaw in that kind of logic is that the success of encryption lies in keeping the keys secret, while the object of unauthorized users is to uncover the keys without the knowledge of authorized users. A public-key cipher is intended to authenticate the message sender, as well as perform message encryption and decryption.

Public-key encryption is shown in Figure 10-23(a). If the sender wishes to send a message, the transmitter will request the receiver's public encryption key, E^B. The receiver decrypts the message using its private key. Although related to it, the private key can't be derived from the public key alone.

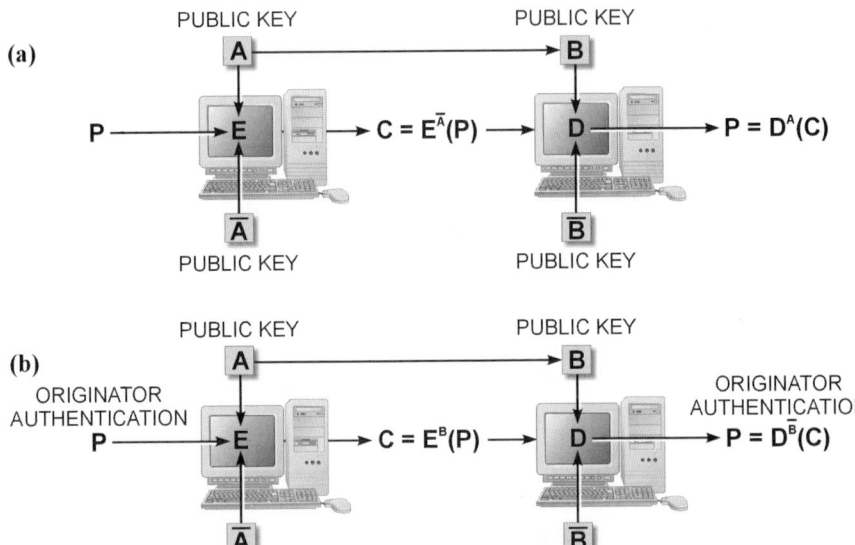

Figure 10-23 Public Key Cipher

Message authentication is shown in Figure 10-23(b). The sender wishes to send a message in which the originator is authenticated. The sender encrypts its address with its private key, and the receiver decrypts the authentication with the sender's public key.

In a practical public-key system, all nodes on the network store the public keys of all other nodes. However, each node has its own, unique, private key. The advantage of public-key ciphers is twofold.

For one thing, the security of private keys is simple, since they are protected at a single location, not at hundreds or thousands of sites. Secondly, erroneous secret messages (such as "launch all of the nuclear weapons") are avoided, since message authentication depends upon possessing a private key.

The challenge in using public-key ciphers is to generate two different keys—one public and one private—in which the encryption/decryption algorithms are related, but where neither key may be derived from the other.

One such public-key cipher is the **Rivest-Shamir-Adleman** (RSA) cipher. Keys are generated by factoring large numbers into **prime numbers**. A prime number is evenly divisible only by itself and 1. The primes are then manipulated mathematically, resulting in message decryption being the inverse of encryption. Message authentication is accomplished by decrypting the authentication with the authenticating station's public key.

The RSA cipher is one of the few ciphers having an inverse encryption/decryption property, based on number primes, which doesn't permit the revelation of either the private or public key with the use of the other.

The success of public-key ciphers lies in the computational difficulty of determining the original number from which the primes are derived. These ciphers assume our limited mathematical knowledge (or lack of computer power) will remain their greatest security. They've not yet seen widespread use, and their effectiveness has yet to be proven.

Data Encryption Standard

> The DES cipher encrypts 64-bit blocks of data through a 56-bit key.

The **National Bureau of Standards** (NBS) adopted the **Data Encryption Standard** (DES) as a mandatory procedure in 1977. It's based upon an IBM cryptographic scheme known as **LUCIFER**. The IBM technique successfully encrypted 64-bit blocks of plaintext, under the control of a 56-bit key. The Bureau of Standards required government organizations to implement the DES, and encouraged commercial vendors to do the same. The DES is the first algorithm offering strength of security over a wide range of applications.

The DES algorithm is shown in Figure 10-24. It is a product cipher that alternately enciphers data through substitution and transposition, under control of the key, and subsets of the key. The plaintext is exposed to sixteen rounds of ciphering, called cipher **iterations**. Within each iteration, the data undergoes transposition by alternating halves of the 64-bit data block between ciphering columns. The columns are labeled L (left) and R (right).

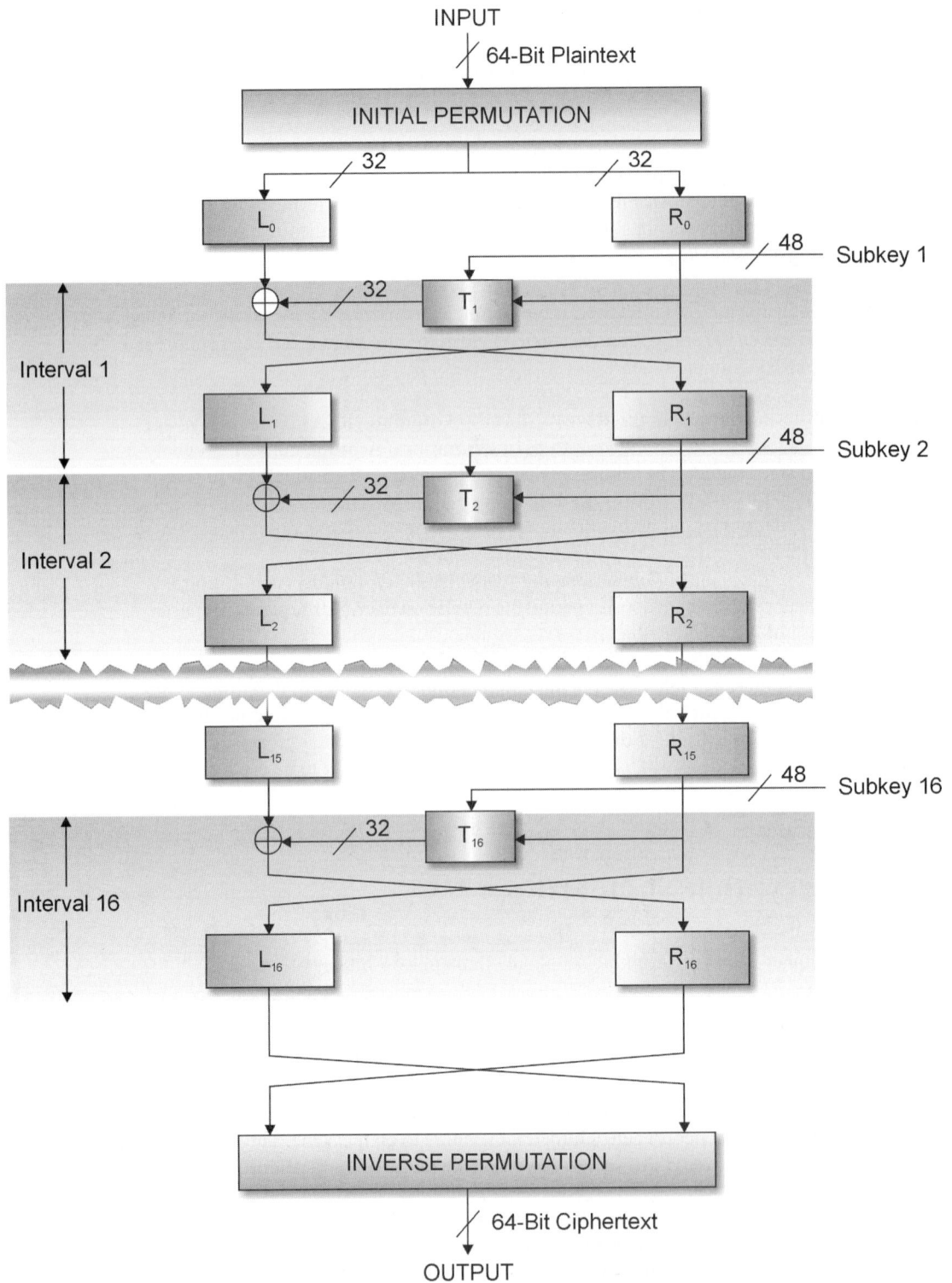

Figure 10-24 The Data Encryption Standard Algorithm

Substitution occurs in the blocks labeled S in Figure 10-25. At each enciphering round, the data is substituted and transposed, according to a 48-bit key that's derived from the original 56-bit key. The subkeys are unique for each iteration.

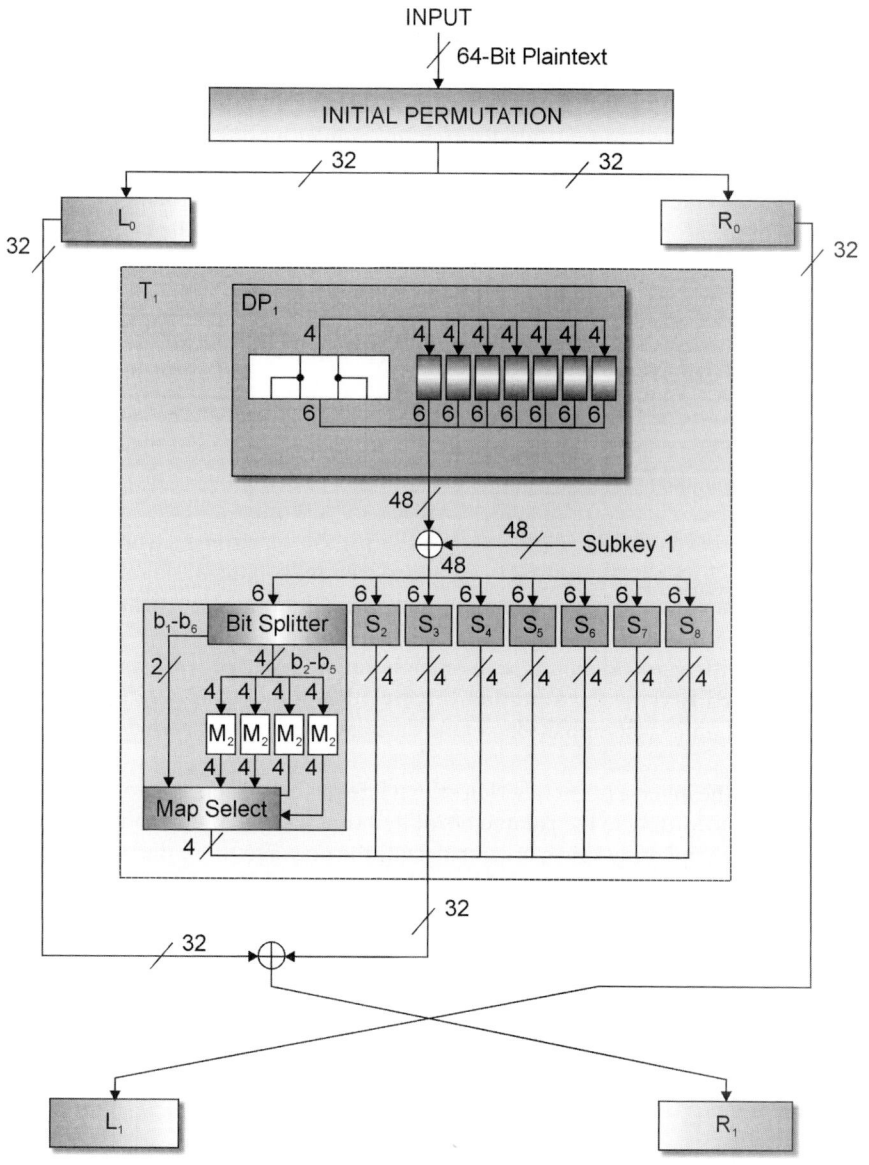

Figure 10-25 Detail of the First DES Iteration

The original DES key is generated at a length of 56 bits. An odd parity bit is then added to each octet to give a total key length of 64 bits. However, the parity bits are stripped away when the subkeys for each of the sixteen iterations are generated. The DES algorithm is capable of generating up to 256 **permutations**, or enciphering results, if it were required that all of the keys be applied to the same plaintext.

A 64-bit block of plaintext is first applied to the block labeled **Initial Permutation**. The plaintext is transposed in this block, and split into two 32-bit segments.

The first round of enciphering begins with L_0 and R_0. At the end of the round, L_0 and R_0 will be transposed. However, before the transposition, substitution takes place in the box labelled T_1 (transformation 1). The substitution process is detailed in Figure 10-25.

The 32 bits of R_0 are first applied to DP_1 (duplicating permutation 1) where the bits are transposed, separated into eight groups of 4 bits, and an additional 16 bits added. The left-most 4-bit group in Figure 10-25 details how the addition of the 2 bits occurs.

Each 4-bit group has 2 bits duplicated in a similar manner, so that DP_1 outputs a total of 48 bits. The 48 bits of DP_1 are ex-ORed to the 48-bit subkey, K_1. Recall that each enciphering round has a unique subkey, derived from the original.

Now the bits are applied to eight **substitution boxes** in groups of six bits. The substitution boxes exchange the binary value of bits 2 through 5, according to a substitution map. Each S-box in the algorithm may select from 16 maps. The maps in each round are unique. The particular substitution map is selected by bits 1 and 6, taken from the bit splitter.

Figure 10-25 shows a detailed blowup of the S_1 substitution box in the lower left-hand corner of T_1. Inputs are duplicated (from bits 2 through 5) into the four individual substitution maps (M_1 through M_4), each of which derives a different 4-bit output.

These four outputs are then sent to the **Map Select Matrix** along with bits 1 and 6. Depending on the values of bits 1 and 6, one of the 4-bit outputs is selected. The same mapping process takes place in all eight substitution boxes.

The 32 bits from the eight S-boxes are ex-ORed with the 32 bits from L_0. The 32-bit output of the exclusive-OR gate is transposed to the right column, and the 32-bit output from R_0 is transposed to the left column. This completes the first iteration (or interval 1).

The following fifteen rounds continue the enciphering. At the end of the sixteenth round, in the block labeled **Inverse Permutation** (Figure 10-24), the inverse transposition of the initial permutation is accomplished, and the data can now be considered ciphertext.

Deciphering is the inverse of enciphering so that after an initial permutation, the ciphertext is transformed according to the parameters of iteration sixteen of the sender. The receiver must know the enciphering key in order to decode the message, since the same subkeys are used at the receiver.

The DES is available in commercial VLSI integrated circuits. The algorithm is permanently stored in the IC, but the 56-bit key is user-selectable. The chip is compatible with the DMA controllers of most PCs, and is primarily used in electronic fund transfers, automatic tellers, and to meet the general security needs of LANs.

Optional DES Modes

The DES algorithm has several options available to users: **electronic codebook**, **cipher feedback**, **cipher blockchaining**, and **output feedback**.

Electronic Codebook

The electronic codebook mode is a simple block cipher, as described earlier. As with all block ciphers, its use should be limited to short messages, since the key may be revealed through character frequency analysis.

Cipher and Output Feedback

The cipher feedback and output feedback modes are both bit-stream ciphers, in which the plaintext never actually enters the cipher algorithm, but is influenced by the key at the start of the process. Cipher feedback encrypts 8-bit blocks, while output feedback encrypts up to 64-bit blocks. During the encryption process, the injection of an error, in either one of the feedback modes, will result in all of the preceding bits being garbled.

Cipher Block Chaining

Cipher block chaining has the most practical characteristics of the DES modes. It specifies that messages be a multiple of 64 bits in length. If an error is injected during enciphering, the 64 bits being enciphered, as well as the next block, will be garbled.

The disadvantage to block chaining is that it doesn't include any method of synchronizing the sender and receiver. If the synchronization—which must be externally applied—is off by as much as a bit, the message will be lost.

KEY POINTS REVIEW

- Error detection consists of identifying a bad bit, or string of bits.

- Even parity consists of adding a logic 1 or 0 to a data word so that the sum of all logic 1s is an even number.

- Odd parity consists of adding a logic 1 or 0 to a data word so that the sum of all logic 1s is an odd number.

- Parity will not detect an even number of errors in a data word.

- A Longitudinal Redundancy Check, or a Block Character Check, consists of applying odd or even parity to the rows and columns of a block of data words.

- A Cyclic Redundancy Check operates on blocks of data words by continuously feeding the data back through a series of shift registers and exclusive-OR gates.

- The arrangement of registers and ex-OR gates in a Cyclic Redundancy Check can be determined by a polynomial generator.

- CRC is primarily used for "bursty" channels, in which long streams of bits are obscured with noise.

- Examples of standard Cyclic Redundancy Check generator polynomials include CRC-CITT, CRC-16, CRC-12, and CRC-32.

- Forward error correction refers to identifying and correcting bad bits at the receiver.

- The Huffman code is an example of a forward error-correction code.

- The Huffman code detects and corrects errors by including parity bits with the data bits. The code format for bits is conducted by Hamming rules.

- The disadvantage to error-correcting codes is that they decrease framing efficiency.

- Data security involves the protection of data and data facilities from unauthorized users.

- Physical, logical, procedural, and personnel security must all be analyzed for security weakness, and appropriate precautions taken to strengthen security.

- Data cryptography is the practice of sending secret messages.

- Plaintext refers to data which has not been encrypted, while ciphertext is data which has been encrypted.

- Data encryption consists of coding data in an encryption algorithm under control of an encryption key.

- Algorithms are usually made available to the public while keys remain secret.

- Data should be encrypted in such a way that it can only be decoded with a key.

- There are three classes of encryption systems: substitution, transposition, and product ciphers.

- Examples of encryption techniques include unbreakable ciphers, random-key ciphers, block ciphers, and public-key ciphers.

- The DES cipher encrypts 64-bit blocks of data through a 56-bit key.

- RAID is a system of fault tolerance that may involve mirroring a disk, or striping multiple disks, with data parity.

At this point, review the objectives listed at the beginning of the chapter to be certain that you understand and can perform them. Afterward, answer the review questions that follow to verify your knowledge of the information.

LAB MANUAL

Lab Exercises

The lab manual that accompanies this book contains hands-on lab procedures that reinforce and test your knowledge of the theory materials presented in this chapter. Now that you have completed your review of Chapter 10, refer to the lab manual and perform Procedures 29, "Cisco 1600 Router," 30, "Configuring Cisco Router Asynchronous Connection," 31, "Routing Across Networks," and 32, "Creating Web Documents."

REVIEW QUESTIONS

The following questions test your knowledge of the material presented in this chapter:

1. Define mirroring, and explain how it's used in fault tolerance.

2. Define Striping, and explain how it relates to fault tolerance.

3. List several environmental factors that may affect a network's performance.

4. What type of information is contained in a vendor's test documentation for patches, fixes and upgrades?

5. What is the purpose of a software patch?

6. Explain how a CRC can be used to identify a single bit error.

7. Write the CRC generator polynomial for a 4-bit word.

8. List the hardware for the CRC generator polynomial for a 4 bit word.

9. Describe the substitution method for an iteration of the DES model.

10. What is the main disadvantage of parity?

11. Which parity is more effective, even or odd?

12. Writing down a password is considered what type of security weakness?

13. Which cable media is the most secure against eavesdroppers?

14. Define an unbreakable cypher.

15. What is the total length of the DES key?

MULTIPLE CHOICE QUESTIONS

1. A server database has proved to be popular, but access times to it have slowed considerably, due to increased use. Choose the most appropriate backup.
   a. Tape.
   b. Folder replication.
   c. Removable media.
   d. CD-R.

2. Which of the following contains configuration settings for individual users?
   a. Profiles.
   b. Rights.
   c. Policies.
   d. Groups.

3. Which of the following refers to system configurations that affect all users?
   a. Profiles.
   b. Rights.
   c. Policies.
   d. Administrative utilities.

4. Encode the data word 1100110 using odd parity.
   a. 11001101
   b. 01001101
   c. 11001100
   d. 10101010

5. What is the major disadvantage of the Hamming code?
   a. It only works with an odd number of bit errors.
   b. It only works with an even number of errors.
   c. It adds high overhead to a frame.
   d. It eliminates overhead bits.

6. In a public-key cipher:
   a. The keys are reproduced by a random number generator.
   b. All nodes have the public keys, but each node also has a private key.
   c. A single key is used to decode all messages.
   d. Encryption isn't necessary.

7. All of the following are optional Data Encryption Standard codes except:
   a. Output feedback.
   b. Electronic codebook.
   c. Input feedback.
   d. Cipher block chaining.

8. Identifying and correcting bad bits at the receiver is called:
   a. Forward error correction.
   b. Reverse error correction.
   c. Standard error correction.
   d. Logical error correction.

9. Data which has not been encrypted is referred to as:
   a. Transtext.
   b. Ciphertext.
   c. Whitetext.
   d. Plaintext.

10. The CRC error-detection method is noted for detecting errors in:
    a. Moist environments.
    b. Hot environments.
    c. Cold environments.
    d. Bursty environments.

11. From the list below, select the word that has been encoded using odd parity.
    a. 01000111
    b. 10110010
    c. 00011100
    d. 11110000

12. Poorly-trained employees are an example of what type of security weakness?
    a. Physical
    b. Personnel
    c. Logical
    d. Procedural

CD-ROM

Net+ Practice Test

Additional Net+ Certification testing is available on the CD that accompanies this text. The testing suite on the CD provides Study Card, Flash Card, and Run Practice type testing. The Study Card and Flash Card feature enables you to electronically link to the section of the book in which the question is covered. Choose questions from the test pool related to this chapter.

CHAPTER 11

SATELLITE COMMUNICATION

LEARNING
OBJECTIVES

LEARNING OBJECTIVES

Upon completion of this chapter and its related lab procedures, you should be able to perform the following tasks:

1. Describe several important events in the history of satellites.

2. Give an example of a satellite used for observation, defense, telephone/data and entertainment.

3. State the components that comprise a satellite system.

4. Describe the difference between an active and passive satellite.

5. Describe what is meant by the terms uplink and downlink.

6. Define a circular orbit.

7. Describe the process of making a footprint using circular orbits.

8. Define an elliptical orbit.

9. Discuss the footprint coverage of elliptical orbits.

10. State the uplink and downlink frequencies for the C, Ka and Ku bands.

11. State the five major sections of a satellite.

12. Describe the purpose of the apogee thruster.

13. Describe the manner in which satellites receive their power.

14. Relate the receive and transmit antennas to the terms uplink and downlink.

15. Describe the process of spot-beaming.

16. Describe the operation of a multi-channel transponder.

17. Explain the function of the command assembly.

18. Describe the sequence of launching a satellite into orbit.

19. Explain how a satellite is placed in its final orbit.

20. Define attitude as it applies to satellites.

21. Explain FDM as used in satellites.

22. Explain FDMA as used in satellites. Give an example of an FDMA system.

23. Explain TDMA as used in satellites. Give an example of an FDMA system.

24. Describe a DAMA system.

25. State the components that comprise an Earth station.

26. Explain the function of the feedhorn, the low noise amplifier, and the actuator.

27. State the requirements for mounting a satellite receive antenna.

Satellite Communication

INTRODUCTION

Satellites were first proposed by Arthur C. Clarke in a 1945 magazine article. He suggested that satellite communication was viable, based upon experiments conducted by Germany with V-2 rockets, during World War II. Unfortunately, the technology for placing a satellite in orbit didn't exist in 1945, but the idea took hold. On October 4, 1957, the Soviets successfully launched Sputnik, the first satellite. The Sputnik weighed 84 pounds, and was a mere beacon. It transmitted an audible signal back to Earth. People were fascinated by the beeping signals coming from the Sputnik. The United States was quick to launch their own satellite, the Explorer I, less than four months later, on January 31, 1958. It weighed 31 pounds, and was packed with scientific instruments that measured radiation in space.

In 1958, the United States launched the first **repeater** satellite. This satellite was capable of receiving a signal transmitted from Earth, and relaying it to another earth station. Satellites in those days were battery powered, so they operated, at most, for a couple of weeks; but this repeater satellite was important because it proved that Arthur C. Clarke's proposal, thirteen years earlier, was indeed practical.

In the early sixties, the Telstar, a satellite for relaying television programs, was launched. For the first time in history, it was possible to witness events as they happened in remote parts of the world, without actually being there. Soon after this, the **International Telecommunications Satellite Consortium** (INTELSAT) was formed, by eleven nations, to research, design and build commercial satellites. Today, INTELSAT has well over one-hundred participating countries, and has launched many satellites.

In 1971, the **Federal Communications Commission** (FCC) permitted corporations to place satellites into orbit for profit. Three for-profit satellites were launched in 1974 by the American Satellite Corporation, RCA, and Western Union, making true worldwide communication possible.

Today, satellites have become a cost-effective alternative to traditional terrestrial communication media, such as the long-distance common carriers. Within the last ten years, the cost of earth stations has decreased considerably, while programming selections from satellites have increased dramatically. There are hundreds of satellites circling the globe. The majority are concentrated 23,280 miles above the Earth, along the equator, in the **geosynchronous orbit** (often called the **Clarke orbit**, in honor of Arthur C. Clarke's 1945 proposal).

As a communication medium, the use of satellites is making a tremendous impact on our lives. Broadly speaking, the cost of leasing a satellite remains high, and the delay, associated with transmitting to and from the satellite, is an obstacle that's not likely to be overcome soon. But, as a vehicle for transporting large volumes of data throughout the world, a satellite is hard to beat.

SATELLITE APPLICATIONS

The fundamental function of a satellite is to serve as a vehicle for long-distance communications. It utilizes a line-of-sight receiver/transmitter, with the unique advantage of being able to relay information to vast areas of the globe. Many predictions, based on the future of satellite technology and applications, hold that the satellite industry is the next "great wave" of opportunity and technological advancement. Since the industry was opened in 1971 to commercialization, several subgroups of satellite users have evolved. With earth, or ground, station systems and antennas becoming cheaper and smaller, the proliferation of satellite usage is predicted to increase. Satellite users can be separated into four, broad subgroups: **observation**, **defense**, **telephone/data**, and **entertainment**. These user subgroups provide a good platform from which satellite applications can be viewed.

Observation

Nearly every evening, TV-news broadcasts contain a weather segment. The weather segment just doesn't seem complete without satellite photos of an approaching hurricane, area maps showing precipitation, or a photo of cloud covering. While meteorologists have come to depend upon satellites for keeping a watchful eye on weather conditions, geologists are satellite advocates as well. Since most of the Earth can be seen from satellites, a geologist can record the minute movement of glaciers, observe the chart-changing river patterns, or monitor any remote volcanoes. Environmentalists may utilize the bird's-eye view of satellites to demonstrate heavily-polluted areas. Since a satellite can be expected to remain operational, and in its orbit, for many years, it is the ideal system for passively observing any changes on the Earth that occur very slowly, over a long time span.

Defense

The military has found several needs for satellites. As an observation system, satellites are difficult to beat. "Spy" satellites may be used to monitor the troop movements of other armies, track their deployment, note the defensive advances of other nations, and so on. A defense satellite also has the capability to serve a dual role as a weapons system, by attaching missiles to the satellite. The **Strategic Defense Initiative** (SDI), commonly called "Star Wars," was envisioned as a very complex system of satellites, intended and able to intercept enemy missiles and destroy them.

Telephone/Data

Trans-global telecommunication was an early beneficiary of satellite technology. Satellites provided a path for connecting callers, separated by thousands of miles, as well as oceans. Many long-distance telephone calls are relayed by satellites. The same satellite carrying voice communication also carries data communication.

Large corporations are finding that satellites are a sound alternative for sending information of all types, including large computer files. Video conferences are beginning to compete with the cost of actually flying business people to a location for important strategy sessions.

Entertainment

Many of us enjoy the benefits of cable television. Cable TV has been possible due to the large coverage of land mass that a satellite transmission is capable of. A single satellite channel can transmit **Home Box Office** (HBO)—the subscriber, 24-hour movie channel—to half of the United States, Canada, the Caribbean, and most of Mexico. Special sporting events can be seen "live," due to satellite transmission. The 24-hour news channel, **Cable News Network** (CNN), relies heavily on relaying news segments from all parts of the world to offices in Washington, D.C. and Atlanta, GA. Personal-use earth stations are becoming ever more popular, as parabolic antenna sizes decrease, along with costs of the earth system.

We're just beginning to tap the endless possibilities of satellite applications. The next decade is sure to bring new uses for satellites—particularly in the areas of medical information (patient histories), police work, and transmitting capabilities for personal earth stations.

BASIC CONCEPTS

A satellite system is best used when the distance between the transmitter and the receiver is great.

Currently, 98% of the Earth is accessible by satellite. The exceptions are the North and South Poles. Within the past 25 years, satellites have come into their own as a reliable, cost-effective, communications medium. They have proved particularly effective as a means of sending large blocks of data, from one location to another. Data rates are much higher than the 19.6kBPS maximum rate of analog long-distance carriers. Much of the modulation and multiplexing is digital, which makes for little noise in the system. The cost of utilizing satellites is generally cheaper than its terrestrial relative—the telephone network. How much cheaper depends upon the number of channels. For example, a leased satellite will cost the user about half the cost of the carriers for 50 full-duplex channels, transmitting at 9.6 kBPS. For a user planning to utilize less than 25 channels, the carriers would be a better bet.

The largest drawback to satellite communications is the time delay. When sending a message and receiving a reply, using transcontinental satellite transmission, the delay encountered ranges from 240 mS to 500 mS. For voice communications, a half-second delay is inconvenient, but tolerable. However, many of the common data-communication protocols send a block of data, and then wait for an acknowledgment before sending another block. The acknowledgment delay could very easily exceed the time required to transmit the data. The effect is to actually decrease the channel capacity.

There are numerous compensators, multiplexers, and emulators that reduce the satellite delays. Essentially, compensators are located at the sending earth station, and provide the sending user with an acknowledgment. What this means is that the compensator doesn't really remove the delay, but serves as a protocol converter by either removing each block data check, or by shortening the time of the check.

The Satellite System

A satellite system consists of the satellite, a transmitting station, and the receiving station.

A satellite is illustrated in Figure 11-1. The transmitting station transmits a signal to the satellite. The satellite receives the signal, converts it to a different frequency, boosts the signal power, and retransmits the signal to the receiving station. The receiving station is tuned to the frequency transmitted from the satellite.

The send and receive stations are referred to as ground, or earth, stations. The most critical components of the station are the final output-power amplifier, usually referred to as the **Low-Noise Amplifier** (LNA), and the antenna. Ground station antennas are of the parabolic type. Parabolic, or dish, antennas are tuned for a particular bank of frequencies. The transmit antenna sends data in the narrow band, from a parabolic reflector that averages in size from several feet, to nearly 60 feet, in diameter. The receive antenna follows the transmit antenna in terms of size. The circuitry that detects data from the carrier is specifically designed so that it can extract very weak signals, even when the signal is nearly lost in noise. Phase-lock loop detectors are the primary component used in detection.

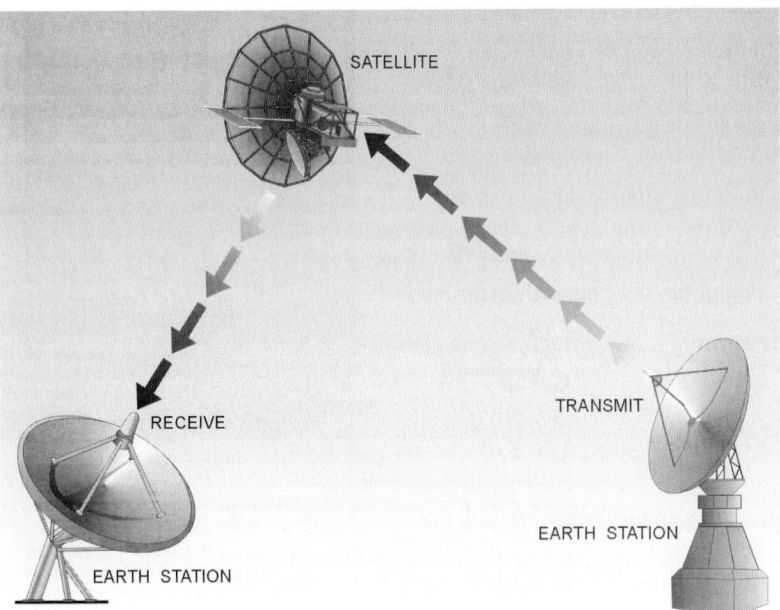

Figure 11-1 Satellite System

Active and Passive Satellites

A passive satellite serves as a signal reflector.

In the early days of satellites, the physical bulk of the satellite was a problem. The maximum payload of a satellite sent into orbit was 2,900 pounds. The problem was being able to include all of the necessary circuitry required in the satellite, and still be able to get it into an orbit. Before the early sixties, it wasn't feasible to do so. Satellites launched in those days were passive satellites. A passive satellite is merely a signal reflector. The transmitting antenna was pointed at the satellite, and the reflector deflected the signal to the receive antenna.

With advancements in the space program, and large-scale integration of semiconductors, it became feasible to launch repeater satellites. These satellites could not only receive the signal from a transmitting ground station, but could also increase the signal's power levels, and then retransmit it to another ground station. These repeater satellites were active satellites!

An active satellite includes circuitry that amplifies a signal. Active satellites are also called repeaters.

Satellite Links

An active satellite receives the modulated carrier at a prescribed frequency, called the **uplink**. The satellite converts the uplink frequency to another frequency, to transmit to the receiver. The other frequency is known as the **downlink**. Today, uplink also refers to the hardware involved in transmitting from the ground station to the satellite. Typically, then, the uplink is the transmitter's carrier frequency/ground equipment, and the satellite's receive antenna. The downlink includes the modulated carrier frequency transmitted from the satellite, the satellite transmit antenna, and the receive equipment at the ground station.

In order for a satellite to remain aloft, it must be placed in orbit at a speed that's fast enough to create a centrifugal force, equal to the gravitational pull of the Earth, but not exceeding the Earth's gravity. The concept is similar to quickly rotating a bucket of water over your head: if you don't rotate the bucket fast enough, you'll get wet; if you rotate it too fast, the bucket will fly out of your hand. In addition, the satellite must be placed in an orbit in which the plane of the orbit slices through the center of the Earth. A satellite positioned at 10 degrees north, would not be able to sustain the orbit. Two of the most common types of orbits will be discussed: **circular** and **elliptical**.

Circular Orbits

Circular orbits—also called geosynchronous orbits—are located 23,280 miles above the Earth. Figure 11-2 shows a satellite in circular orbit. The **major axis** parallels the Earth's equator, while the **minor axis** intersects the equator at a 90-degree angle. A satellite is in a circular orbit when the major axis and minor axis are equal.

A satellite placed in the 23,280-mile orbit will appear, to an earth observer, to be stationary in the sky. This is because the satellite is orbiting the Earth at a speed equal to the rotation of the Earth, and in the same direction of the spin. The 23,280-mile orbit is called the geosynchronous orbit; at this height, the speed of the satellite is the same as the rotational speed of the Earth.

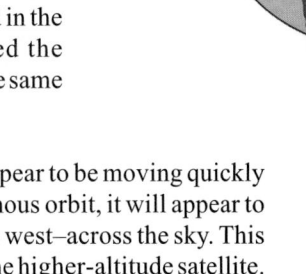
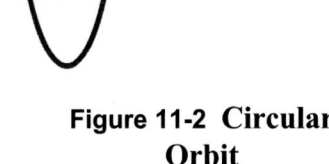

Figure 11-2 Circular Orbit

If a satellite is placed in a lower orbit–say 15,000 miles–it will appear to be moving quickly across the sky. And, if a satellite is placed above the geosynchronous orbit, it will appear to an earth observer to be traveling in the opposite direction–east to west–across the sky. This isn't so, of course, since the Earth is simply spinning faster than the higher-altitude satellite. Figure 11-3 illustrates the relative positions of the orbits.

The geosynchronous orbit (23,280 miles above the Earth) is the most common orbit for telephone, data, and entertainment communication.

The geosynchronous orbit lies directly over the equator. Satellites follow the Earth's west-to-east rotation, at a velocity of about 6,900 mph, and appear to be stationary in the sky. The geosynchronous orbit is a very popular, and crowded, orbit. The reason for its popularity is that satellites, working in unison, can virtually cover the globe. Nearly 20% of the orbit is reserved for satellites launched by the United States.

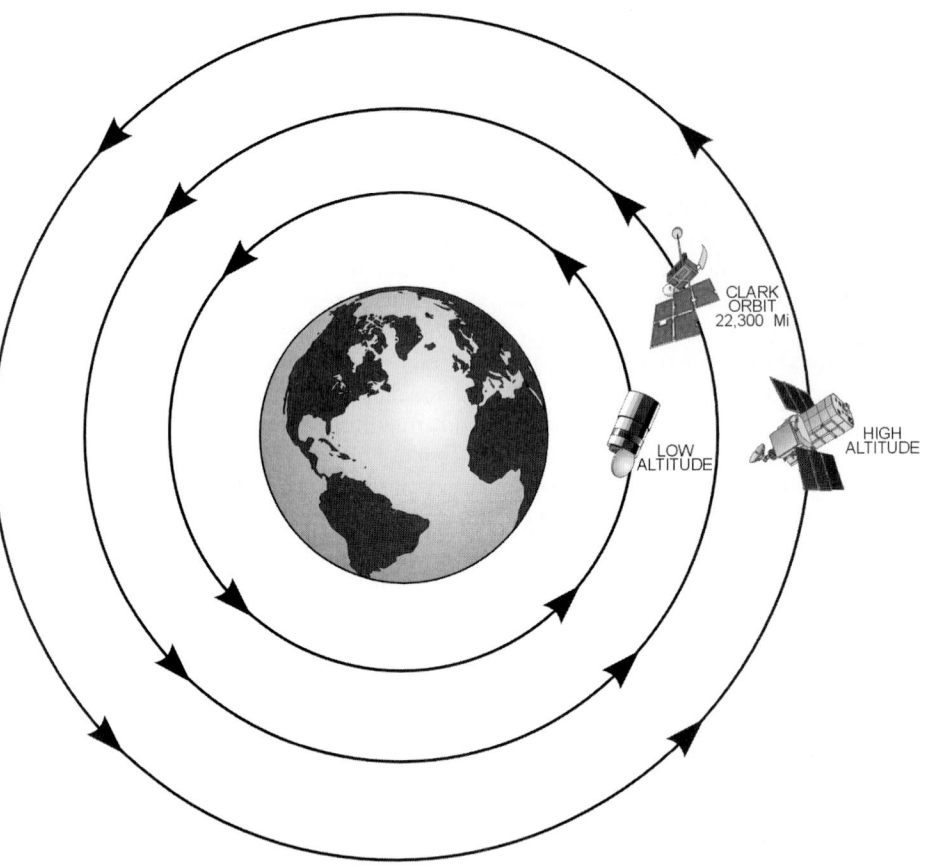

Figure 11-3 Relative Positions of Satellite Orbits

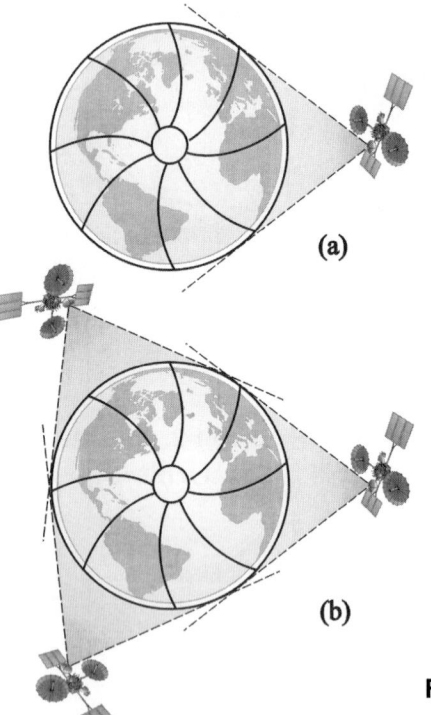

(a)

(b)

Originally, satellites were placed 4 degrees apart (1,833 miles), but recently, the separation has been decreased to 2 degrees (916 miles). Rapid growth in communications markets, and technological advancements, have spurred the change.

To appreciate the value of a satellite in the geosynchronous orbit, refer to Figure 11-4(a). The arc of a satellite in the orbit is 17 degrees, which covers nearly half the Earth's surface. The Earth-coverage of a satellite is referred to as the satellite's **footprint**. Now, in Figure 11-4(b), two more satellites are placed in the orbit, each 120 degrees apart. Within range of these three satellites, 98% of the globe falls within their collective footprint. The remaining 2% is contained in the northern and southern polar regions.

Placing satellites in the geosynchronous orbit means they will remain stationary with the Earth (they'll rotate at the same speed as the Earth), and nearly all of the Earth's surface area is accessible to them. This capability has tremendous implications for defense, telecommunications, data communications, and broadcast radio/television.

Figure 11-4 Earth Coverage of Clarke Orbits

The satellites shown in Figure 11-4(b) communicate with each other by **crosslinks**. Crosslink communication occurs when a satellite transmits directly to another satellite. If Satellite A wished to transmit to an area outside its footprint, it could transmit directly to Satellite B, or C, and one of these satellites would provide the downlink to a ground station.

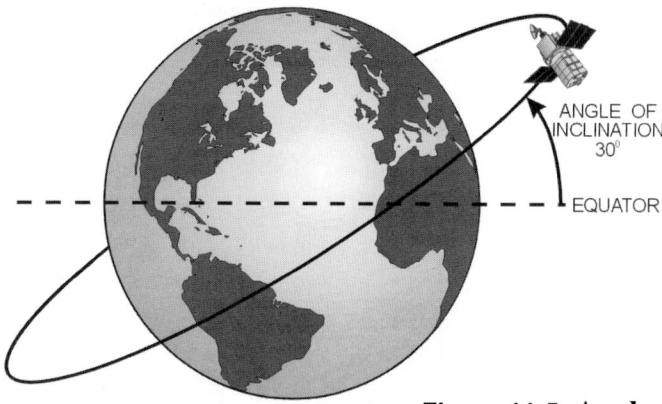

Elliptical Orbits

Satellites, no matter what orbit they're in, must meet the velocity and planer requirements as specified for circular orbits. The elliptical orbit is tilted at an arc between the equator, and 90 degrees. Figure 11-5 illustrates a satellite in an elliptical orbit.

Figure 11-5 Angle of Inclination of an Elliptical Orbit

The satellite is at a 30-degree angle, referenced to the equator. The angle, from the equator to the satellite's orbit, is referred to as the **angle of inclination**.

An elliptical orbit follows a path in which the Earth is off-center in the ellipse.

In Figure 11-6, note that one end of the ellipse is much further away from the Earth than the other. The end furthest from the center of the Earth is the **apogee** of the orbit, while the end nearer the Earth's center is the **perigee**.

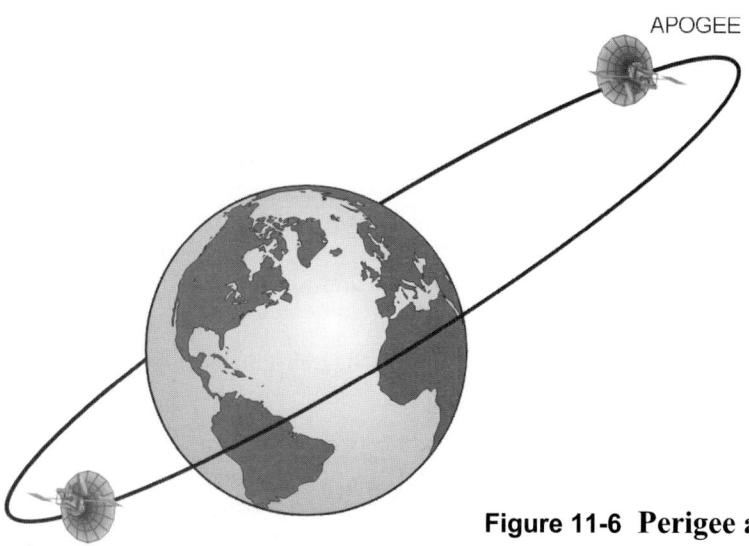

Figure 11-6 Perigee and Apogee of an Elliptical Orbit

How does the satellite stay in orbit? As the satellite approaches the perigee, the gravitational pull of the Earth increases, because the satellite is nearer the Earth. The increased gravitational pull provides the satellite with additional energy, so that it's whipped around the Earth. The increase of energy throws the satellite a distance beyond the Earth. The further the satellite travels, the more this burst of energy decreases, until the satellite is once again pulled back toward the Earth by gravity. At the perigee, the Earth's gravity again whips the satellite toward the apogee, and the cycle repeats itself. Satellites are equipped with **apogee thrusters**, to ensure they remain on course.

The advantage of an elliptical orbit can be seen in Figure 11-7. In Figure 11-7(a), the satellite is orbiting the Earth at a 25-degree angle from the equatorial reference. The shaded area represents the satellite's footprint. In Figure 11-7(b), the incline has been increased to 45 degrees. As you can see, the global coverage increases with the angle of inclination.

SATELLITE FREQUENCIES

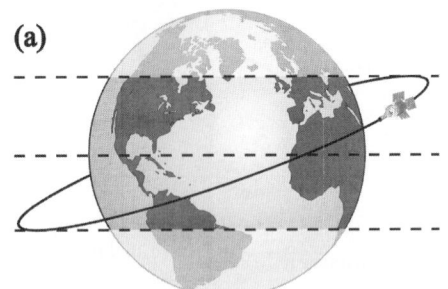

(a)

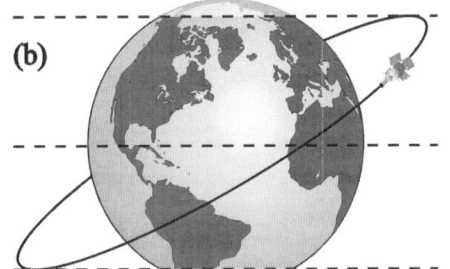

(b)

Figure 11-7 Global Coverage Increases With Orbit Arc

Satellites operate in the gigahertz frequency range, using three bands of frequencies—the C, Ka, and Ku bands (see Table 11-1).

The C band is referred to as the 6/4-GHz band, the Ka band as the 14/12-GHz band, and the Ku band as the 30/20-GHz band. The dual-frequency designations refer to the uplink and downlink frequency ranges.

Table 11-1 Satellite Frequency Bands

BAND	UPLINK	DOWNLINK
C	6 GHz	4 GHz
Ka	14 GHz	12 GHz
Ku	30 GHz	20 GHz

As an example, the **Westar IV** is a Western Union-owned telecommunications satellite. It's located at 99 degrees (over the Pacific Ocean) in the geosynchronous orbit. Channel 8 of the Westar IV uplinks data at 6.245 GHz and downlinks at 4.020 GHz. Another example is the **Gstar I**. The Gstar has subscribed to the 16 frequency ranges in the Ka bank. It uplinks data between 14.030 GHz and 14.470 GHz. It downlinks from 11.730 GHz to 12.171 GHz.

Satellites receive at an uplink frequency, and transmit at a downlink frequency.

The C band is heavily populated. Because of the heavy traffic, and with technological improvements, the separation between satellites was reduced from 4 degrees to 2 degrees, and, in some cases, to 1 degree. Overspill from the C band has gone to the Ka band. As improvements in antennas and satellites continue, the Ka band will soon become filled, and satellite vendors will begin using more and more of the Ku band.

SATELLITE CONSTRUCTION

The majority of satellites are repeaters. They receive a signal (typically from the ground), amplify it, remove noise, and then retransmit the signal (usually to an earth station). The majority of the satellite subassemblies support the satellite's role as a transceiver.

Physically, the satellite must be lightweight, but also very strong, in order to withstand the heavy shock and vibration encountered during the launch. Titanium and beryllium are frequently used in the basic structure of satellites, because they meet these strength and weight requirements, and are less influenced by temperature changes than other metals and alloys. The external shell of the satellite is composed of aluminum, or aluminum alloys.

The high-altitude environment of satellites is a harsh one. Temperature ranges fluctuate widely, gravity is near zero, and the atmosphere is nonexistent. Components within the satellite that may be affected by the environment require special conditioning, from on-board heaters, to shielding that provides protection from X-rays coming from the sun.

Although some satellites are passive, meaning they aren't involved in two-way communication, the majority are active, receiving on one antenna and transmitting on the other. All telecommunication, data, and television satellites are of the active type.

A typical communication satellite is composed of five major sections: the **rocket thruster**, a **power source**, **antennas**, a **transponder**, and a **command assembly**.

Each one of these sections is described next.

Rocket Thruster

The rocket thruster section, as shown in Figure 11-8, is used to control the satellite's apogee. From time to time, satellites drift from their assigned orbits, and need a little nudging to put them back on track. In elliptically orbiting satellites, the apogee is a function of the angle of inclination, which determines the satellite's footprint. Generally speaking, the greater the apogee, the greater the angle. If the apogee falls short, the footprint won't be as wide, and the satellite will be instructed to momentarily fire its apogee thruster. In addition, most satellites have small axial thrusters, mounted on the side of the satellite body, that control the major and minor axis. A small supply of hydrazine propellant is included on the satellite to fuel the thrusters.

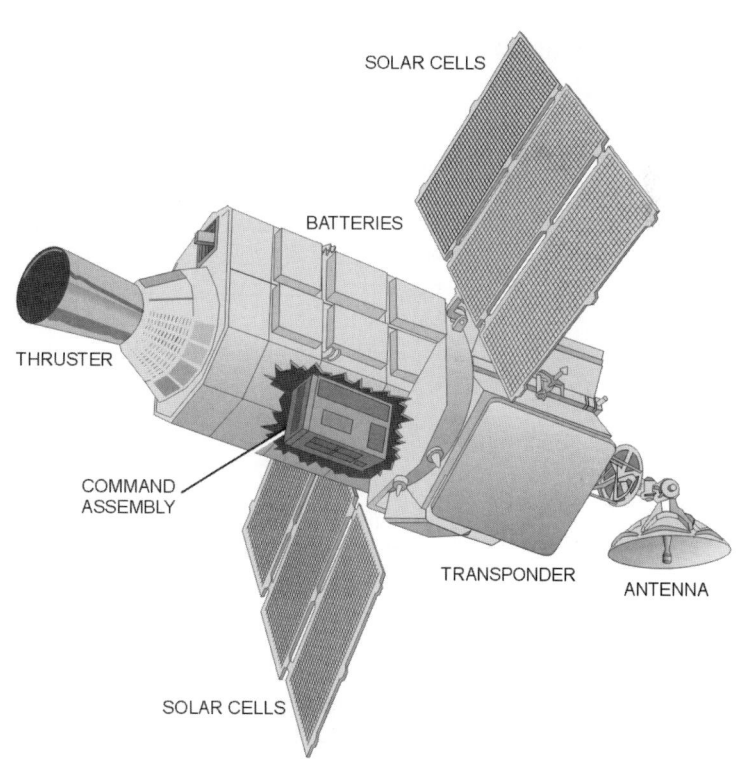

Figure 11-8 Major Sections of a Satellite

Power Source

The source of power for the satellite's electronic circuitry is a combination of batteries and solar cells. In Figure 11-8, the solar cells are mounted around the external body of the satellite. As the satellite rotates, a number of cells are always exposed to the sun.

A body-stabilized satellite is illustrated in Figure 11-9. This type of satellite remains fixed in space. The extruding solar panels are positioned so that they're fully exposed to sunlight at all times. This is an improvement over the rotating satellite. Only about 40% of the rotating satellite's cells are exposed to the sun at any one time.

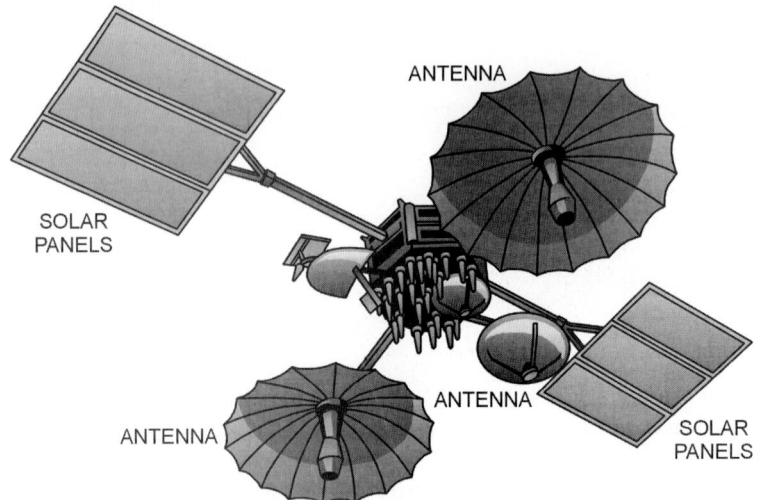

**Figure 11-9
Body-Stabilized
Satellite**

Solar cells are only 10 to 15 percent efficient. A medium-size satellite will contain 30,000 cells that supply a maximum of 250 watts of power. Most satellites contain nickel-cadmium batteries, which are charged by the solar cells. During eclipses, or periods of heightened sun-spot activity, the batteries power the satellite. A light sensor is mounted on the satellite body. If the solar energy is insufficient to power the electronics, the satellite switches to battery power. Larger satellites may garner several kilowatts of power from solar cells.

Antennas

A satellite contains at least three antennas: **receive**, **transmit**, and **telemetry**. The bi-directional telemetry antenna communicates with a ground control station on all aspects of the satellite's operation. The satellite sends the ground station information about its fuel supplies, power sources, ambient temperature, circuitry operation, and orbital position. The telemetry antenna is likely to receive instructions from the ground control station. These instructions may override automated functions for switching from solar to battery power, adjusting the orbit, or adjusting the positioning of solar cell panels.

The receive antenna accepts the uplink modulated carrier from a transmitting ground station, and is tuned to an uplink frequency band. A C-band satellite is equipped with a 6-GHz antenna. The uplink antenna couples the carrier to a wideband amplifier in the transponder.

The downlink antenna is usually a more complex arrangement. The restrictive element in using satellite communications is the size of the ground station downlink antenna. Downlink antennas in the C band are 7 to 18 feet in diameter. It is the physical antenna size that makes their use awkward, especially for mobile ground sites, and residential or office buildings. If the satellite can transmit at higher power levels, the earth station can be made smaller. Or, if the satellite can narrow the **beam width**, the ground antenna size can be reduced.

One method for focusing the satellite transmissions is to polarize the antennas. For example, a satellite may receive a 6GHz signal on a horizontally polarized receive antenna, and transmit at 4 GHz on a horizontally polarized antenna. Simultaneously, it may receive at 6.2 GHz on a vertically polarized antenna, and transmit at 4.2 GHz on a vertically polarized antenna. Essentially, the efficiency of the satellite is increased by greater channel utilization. It is the physical positioning of an antenna that determines the **polarization**. An antenna is vertically polarized when positioned perpendicular to the Earth's surface. An antenna is horizontally polarized when positioned parallel to the surface of the Earth. Broadcast AM radio makes use of vertical polarization, while broadcast FM uses horizontal polarization.

Another method of focusing satellite transmissions is **spot-beaming**. The satellite can use the same antenna for sending an identical carrier to different areas. The antenna is fed by narrow-band **feed horns**, and the reflected wave is then directed to a small area. It is necessary to locate the ground station in the same area as the spot-beam. The ground station can use a smaller antenna because the narrow beam contains a larger amount of power than a corresponding wide-area transmission. Figure 11-10(a) illustrates polarization, and Figure 11-10(b) illustrates spot-beaming.

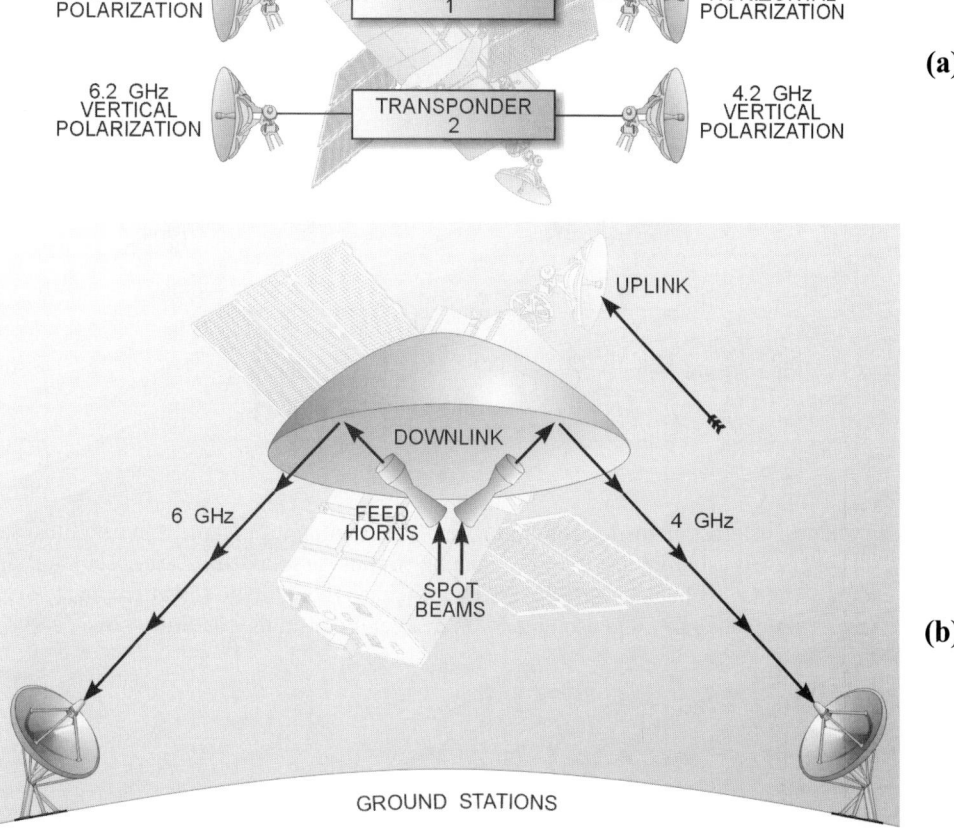

(a)

(b)

Figure 11-10 Antenna Polarization and Spot-Beaming

Figure 11-10 Antenna Polarization and Spot-Beaming

One other method that's increasing in popularity is to use higher frequencies. The higher the frequency, the smaller the ground station antenna. A 30GHz downlink would require the ground antenna to be only about 3 feet in diameter. The higher satellite frequencies cause the system parameters to be more critical, and consequently, increase the cost of the satellite. But, at the same time, the size and complexity of the ground station is decreased. This serves to also reduce the cost of the ground station. In the end, access to satellites will become more available to those of us who may be less affluent.

Transponder

The transponder contains the downlink and uplink electronic circuitry. The operation is very similar to a broadcast-band super heterodyne receiver. The block diagram of Figure 11-11 shows the major components of a 2-channel transponder. Satellite transponders may process from 12 to 24 channels. The modulated C-band carrier is received at the antenna. You can assume that 6.2GHz and 6.4GHz uplinks are received by the antenna, simultaneously. The initial filters are narrow bandpass filters. Channel 1 is resonant at 6.2 GHz, and channel 2 is resonant at 6.4 GHz. The filter outputs are amplified by LNAs, and applied to their respective channel mixers.

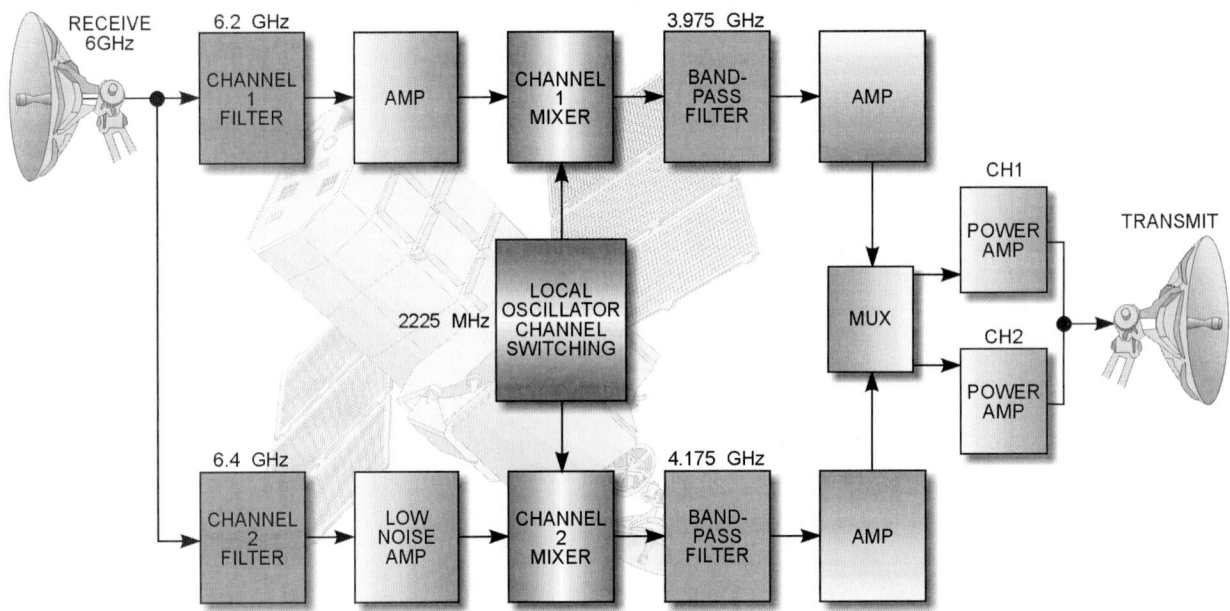

Figure 11-11 Transponder Block Diagram

A single, local oscillator feeds both mixers—a common arrangement in satellites, saving space. There is usually some type of switching circuitry associated with the oscillator, since it can feed up to 24 channels, and be rapidly switched among them. If it attempted to drive 24 mixers simultaneously, the oscillator would severely drain the satellite's power sources.

The received-carrier and local-oscillator signals heterodyne in the mixers. The bandpass filters, following each of the mixers, are tuned to their difference frequencies. In the example shown, these consist of:

Channel 1 = 6.2 GHz – 2.225 GHz = 3.975 GHz
Channel 2 = 6.4 GHz – 2.225 GHz = 4.175 GHz

The difference frequency is the downlink carrier. The downlink is amplified and multiplexed. Each downlink carrier is amplified by a power amplifier at the output of the multiplexer. The transmit antenna relays the carriers to their respective ground stations.

Efficient channel utilization of satellites is achieved through the use of ground station multiplexers. The satellite doesn't multiplex within channels—although, it may multiplex the 12 or 24 channels handled by an individual transponder. This means that each transponder will require only one receive and transmit antenna. Notice that Figure 11-11 shows no modulators or demodulators. The satellite isn't involved in the modulation process.

Command Assembly

The general operation of a satellite is monitored by an on-board command and control subassembly. The command and control system utilizes a microprocessor, with programmed instructions maintained in ROM memory. Ground instructions can be relayed through the telemetry assembly, if directions are needed that aren't included in the ROM. The computer usually contains a small amount of RAM to hold data when calculations are required, or when the satellite is engaged in earth-station dialogue.

The command assembly is also used to monitor vital statistics affecting the satellite, such as orbit drift, battery condition, antenna orientation, and ambient temperatures. Temperatures in the geosynchronous orbit fall between – 40 degrees Fahrenheit and 120 degrees Fahrenheit. On-board heaters activate when the temperature drops, maintaining a more stable environment, since electronic components are adversely affected by temperature changes.

SATELLITE LAUNCH AND ORBIT CONTROL

Satellites are placed into orbit by attaching them to large rockets, and launching them from a facility such as Cape Canaveral, in Florida. A critical launch consideration is the weight of the **payload**, or satellite, and the amount of fuel in the rockets. If the payload is too heavy, the rockets may not be of sufficient size to boost the satellite into its orbit. If the rocket size and amount of fuel is excessive, the launch may exceed 25,000 mph. Then the rocket would escape from Earth's atmosphere, and be lost. Payload/fuel ratios are carefully calculated to ensure that the launch will result in placing the satellite in the proper orbit.

Launch Sequence

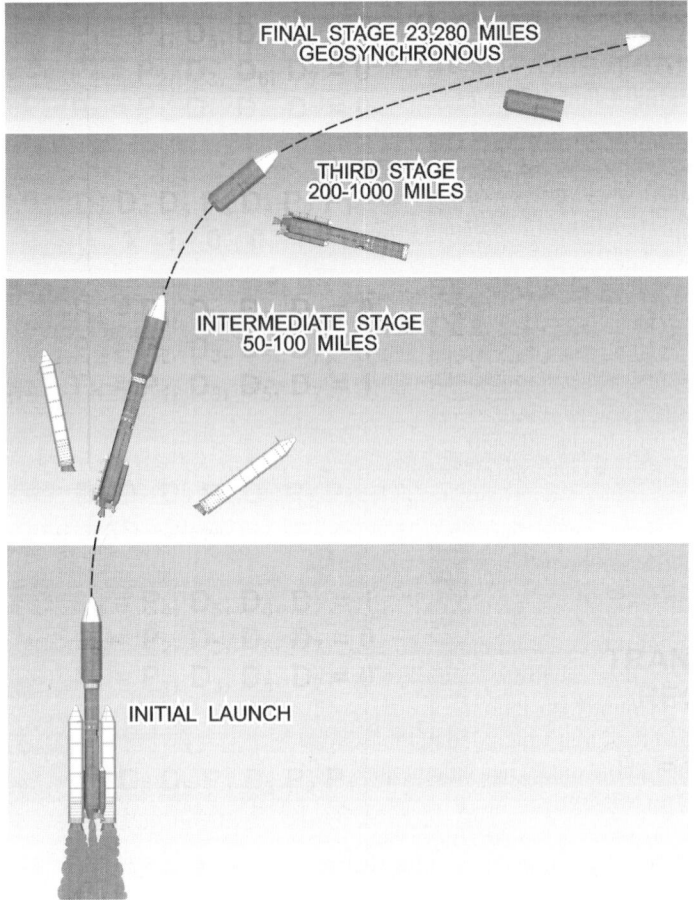

FINAL STAGE 23,280 MILES
GEOSYNCHRONOUS

THIRD STAGE
200-1000 MILES

INTERMEDIATE STAGE
50-100 MILES

INITIAL LAUNCH

Figure 11-12 Rocket Launch Sequence

During the initial launch from the ground, the main booster rockets are ignited, and the rocket rises slowly, overcoming the tremendous resistance of the atmosphere. The launch is monitored on the ground by technicians, receiving information from the telemetry system of the satellite.

At approximately 70 miles above the Earth's surface, the main boosters are deactivated and decoupled from the main rocket assembly, and the booster stage drops into the ocean. With the main boosters gone, an intermediate rocket is ignited. The intermediate stage is smaller than the booster, since the atmospheric resistance is much less at these altitudes. In some satellites, the intermediate-stage rocket is sufficient to place the satellite near the desired orbit. Once the rocket is in the vicinity of the orbit, the intermediate stage is deactivated, and it too—hopefully—drops into the ocean. By this time, the rocket assembly has escaped the larger amounts of atmospheric drag, the resistance of which creates high temperatures on its external elements. The rocket is shielded from the heat by protective **faring**, which is a metal skin placed at its nose. The faring is jettisoned once the intermediate stage is completed.

Occasionally, a third stage may be required to place a satellite near high-altitude orbits. Once all stages have consumed their fuel supply, and decoupled from the main assembly, the satellite will be very near its orbit. The launch sequence is shown in Figure 11-12.

Transfer Orbit

When the stages have been jettisoned, the rocket enters an elliptical transfer orbit, as shown in Figure 11-13. The rocket is likely to make several revolutions in the transfer orbit before entering its final geosynchronous orbit. The purpose of the transfer orbit is to provide fine-positioning commands to the rocket, in preparing to pass it on to the final orbit.

A satellite in the geosynchronous orbit must lie directly over the equator, so on-board thrusters are fired to position it. Since the geosynchronous orbit is quite crowded, timing the transfer to the final orbit must be extremely precise, so as to avoid collisions.

After several revolutions in the transfer orbit, the rocket is given a nudge at the apogee of the transfer orbit. An apogee thruster places the rocket into the final orbit, in the assigned longitude slot. At this point, the rocket may be properly termed a satellite. The satellite will rotate several times as ground technicians analyze the satellite's placement in the orbit, and begin measures to stabilize the orbital path.

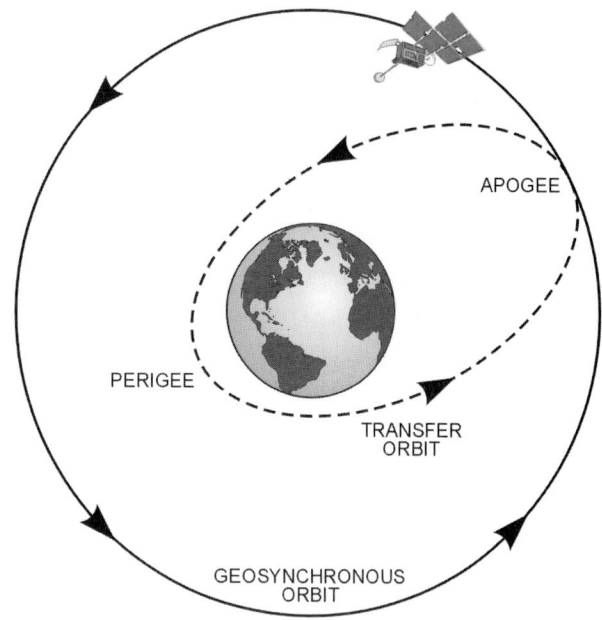

Figure 11-13 Satellite Transfer Orbit

Attitude

Attitude is the final placement of the satellite in the orbit, and the orientation of the satellite to the Earth. The footprint of a satellite is intended to cover a predetermined surface area. For example, a television satellite may be oriented to cover the western half of the United States.

In order to ensure predictable coverage, the satellite must be positioned so that the downlink antenna is focused on the western portion of the country. This process of positioning and orienting is called **attitude stabilization**.

The most common method of controlling the satellite's altitude is called **spin stabilization**. If a satellite is caused to spin at about 100 revolutions per minute, it's less susceptible to pitching and rolling. Figure 11-14 illustrates spin stabilization. Thrusters mounted on the side of the satellite initiate the spinning action. The antennas—which should remain fixed—are connected to the satellite by a **despin axis**. The despin axis is independent of the rotating satellite, so the antennas won't spin. This keeps them pointed at a fixed position on the Earth. Because the position of the antenna needs to be altered periodically, a **despin rotor** permits the antenna assembly to be adjusted, reorienting the antenna to the desired ground location. The geosynchronous orbit isn't exactly circular, because the Earth itself isn't a perfect sphere.

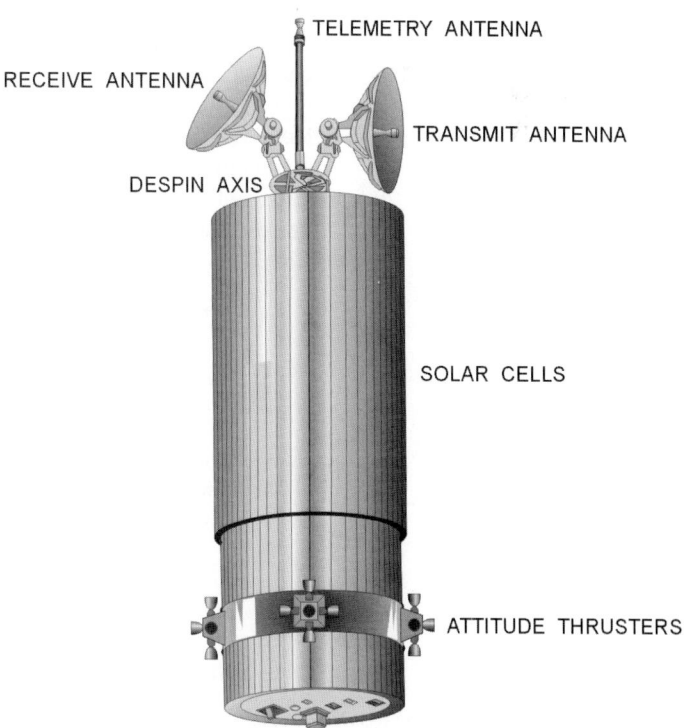

Figure 11-14 Attitude Spin Stabilization

If the satellite has solar cells surrounding the outside shell, the spinning action also provides the maximum amount of exposure to the sunlight. In this way, higher power levels are made available to the satellites electronics. As already mentioned, a satellite that transmits at higher power levels, results in smaller antenna sizes on the ground.

MULTIPLEXING SATELLITE SIGNALS

Channel multiplexing occurs at the receive and transmit sections of satellites, as well as internally in a satellite.

Satellite communication systems' efficiency is increased by multiplexing channels. The quantity of information processed by a satellite is similar to the demands placed on the terrestrial telephone network—the user wants channel space available, as needed.

Satellites use two familiar multiplexing schemes: **Frequency-Division Multiplexing** (FDM) and **Time-Division Multiplexing** (TDM).

These two techniques are modified slightly, so that the satellite is available, on-demand, to many ground-based users. As a result, they are referred to as **multiple-access multiplexing**.

Satellites contain 12 or 24 channels, each having a dedicated transponder with a specified bandwidth—commonly 40 MHz. Multiplexing—either FDM or TDM—can occur within the bandwidth of the individual channels, or the channels themselves may be multiplexed. A user may lease one or more channels of a satellite. For example, **Cinemax**—the 24-hour movie channel—occupies channel 19 of **Galaxy 1**, a geosynchronous satellite located at 134 degrees. The **Disney Channel** is carried on channel 4 of the same satellite. For these channels, multiplexing may occur among the channels, but not within them.

However, the intercontinental **Intelsat 5** provides worldwide telephone/data connections. It contains 27 transponders, with bandwidths varying from 40 MHz to 240 MHz. The total bandwidth is 2,300 MHz, carrying 12,500 voice channels. In order to process this many voice or data channels through 27 transponders, intrachannel multiplexing is a necessity.

Frequency-Division Multiple Access (FDMA)

Satellites utilize **Frequency-Division Multiple Access** by having a range of frequencies allocated within a given bandwidth. For example, a satellite with 12 transponders, and a total bandwidth of 500 MHz, has a channel bandwidth of:

$$BW = 500 \text{ MHz}/12 \text{ channels} = 41.67 \text{ MHz}$$

Each of the 40MHz channels can carry from 300 to 1,200 voice channels, depending on the type of modulation employed. The bandwidth spectrum of the channel is divided to accommodate the needs of the ground-station transmitter. In other words, if a ground station allocated 500 voice channels to the 40MHz transponder channel, each voice channel will occupy 80 kHz of the transponder's bandwidth.

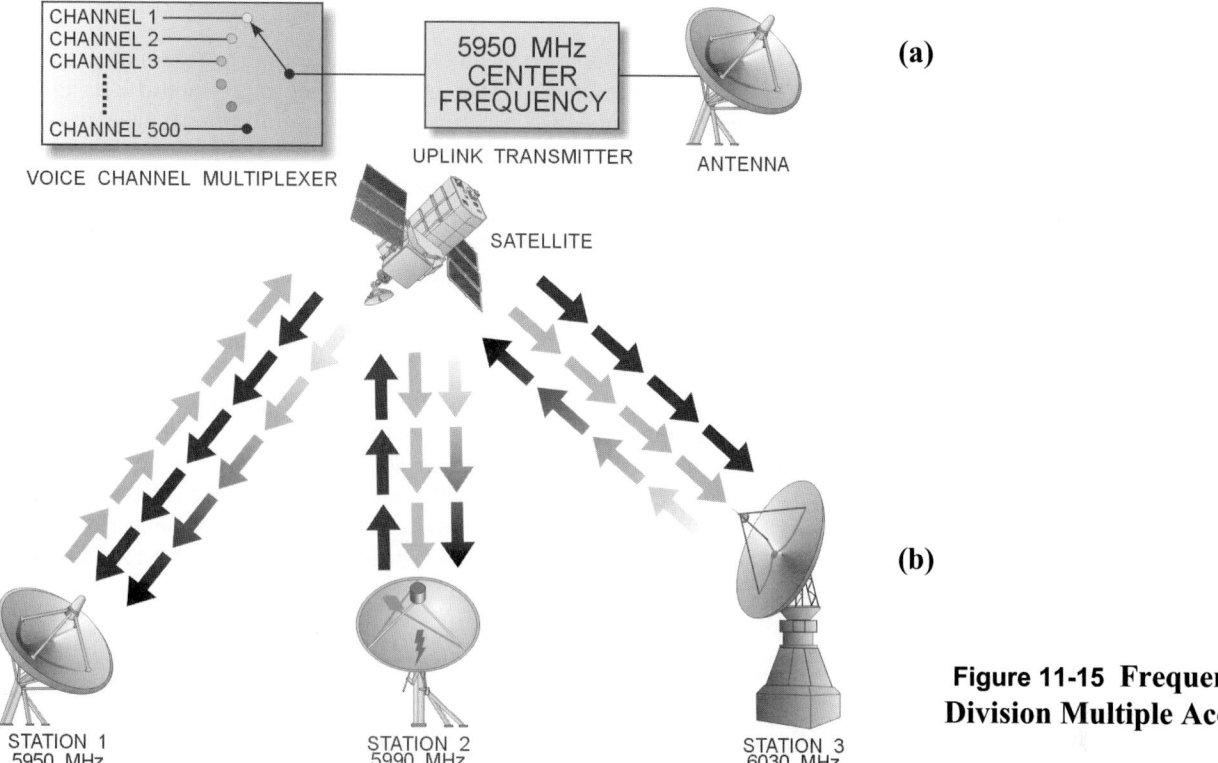

STATION 1 UPLINK 5930 MHz - 5970 MHz

CHANNEL 1
CHANNEL 2
CHANNEL 3
CHANNEL 500

VOICE CHANNEL MULTIPLEXER

5950 MHz CENTER FREQUENCY

UPLINK TRANSMITTER

ANTENNA

(a)

SATELLITE

(b)

STATION 1
5950 MHz

STATION 2
5990 MHz

STATION 3
6030 MHz

Figure 11-15 Frequency Division Multiple Access

If the 500 voice channels originate from a single ground station, they're multiplexed by a terrestrial-based FDM multiplexer, usually into a single, 40MHz transponder voice channel, as shown in Figure 11-15(a). However, discrete division of the transponder bandwidth is relative. If 80 kHz proves to be insufficient for multiplexing the voice channels, the ground-based operator can be creative with the transponder's 40MHz channel bandwidth.

Multiplexing is also done within the satellite, although, at this level, it's more common to multiplex transponder channels. Figure 11-15(b) shows an example of FDM channel multiplexing that provides a multiple-access option. Three earth stations have been assigned a bandwidth of 40 MHz each. Assume each earth station can uplink 500 voice channels to the satellite. Each station has been assigned a transponder channel in the satellite, but any two stations can receive downlink data from the satellite when the third station transmits. This is because the earth stations have multiple access to the downlink transponders, and because of the ability of the satellite to multiplex channels on the downlink.

As mentioned previously, a typical satellite has 12 or 24 transponders, when FDM is used. Each of the channels are tuned to a center frequency in the vicinity of the standard 6GHz uplink frequency. Figure 11-15 shows the three earth stations, tuned to transmit at the uplink frequencies of 5,950 MHz, 5,990 MHz and 6,030 MHz respectively. Each station occupies a 40MHz bandwidth, whose center frequencies correspond to the transponder center frequencies in the satellite. Assume each station is a part of a telephone switching center, responsible for handling 500 voice channels each. The voice channels would be FDM multiplexed, at the earth station, into the 40 MHz of the assigned bandwidth.

Now, Station 1 may contain voice or data calls, a portion of which may need to be sent to the switching facilities of Station 3, and a portion sent to Station 2. Station 1 initializes the transmission by sending a **Request-To-Send** to the satellite. The request usually contains addressing information that tells the satellite which stations are to receive the transmission. In Figure 11-15, Station 1 wants to send information to Station 2 and 3, so the satellite transmits a similar Request-To-Send to each station. When a **Clear-To-Send** is received by the satellite from Stations 2 and 3, it transmits a Clear-To-Send to Station 1.

Station 1 packages the 500 voice channels into a data frame that contains addressing, supervisory, and error-checking information, which is then transmitted to the satellite. Once the satellite receives the data frame, it can choose from several options, such as "picking and choosing" individual voice channels, and directing them to either Station 2 or 3. This complex satellite operation represents a considerable amount of hardware weight (launch expense), as well as increased development costs.

It is more likely that the satellite will broadcast the channel at a downlink frequency, common to Station 2 and 3. Demultiplexers at the earth stations would then be responsible for determining which of the received voice channels were actually intended for the station.

If Station 1 represented a television transmitter that carried 500 TV channels, instead of telephone voice channels, you could more readily see the value of frequency-division multiple access. In Figure 11-15, Station 1 sends 500 channels, and the 500 channels are received by two earth stations. In essence, the satellite has provided 1,000 outputs from the 500 inputs of Station 1. If 10 earth stations (i.e., local cable companies) are designated to receive the 500 transmissions from Station 1, then the satellite has provided 5,000 outputs from the 500 inputs of a single earth station.

Time-Division Multiple Access (TDMA)

Time-Division Multiple Access is used in a similar fashion as FDMA. Many of the earlier satellites favored FDM, but with the rapid expansion of digital communications, such as the T-carrier used with the common carriers, TDM is sure to be the multiplexing scheme used by satellites in the future. A satellite TDM system is shown in Figure 11-16.

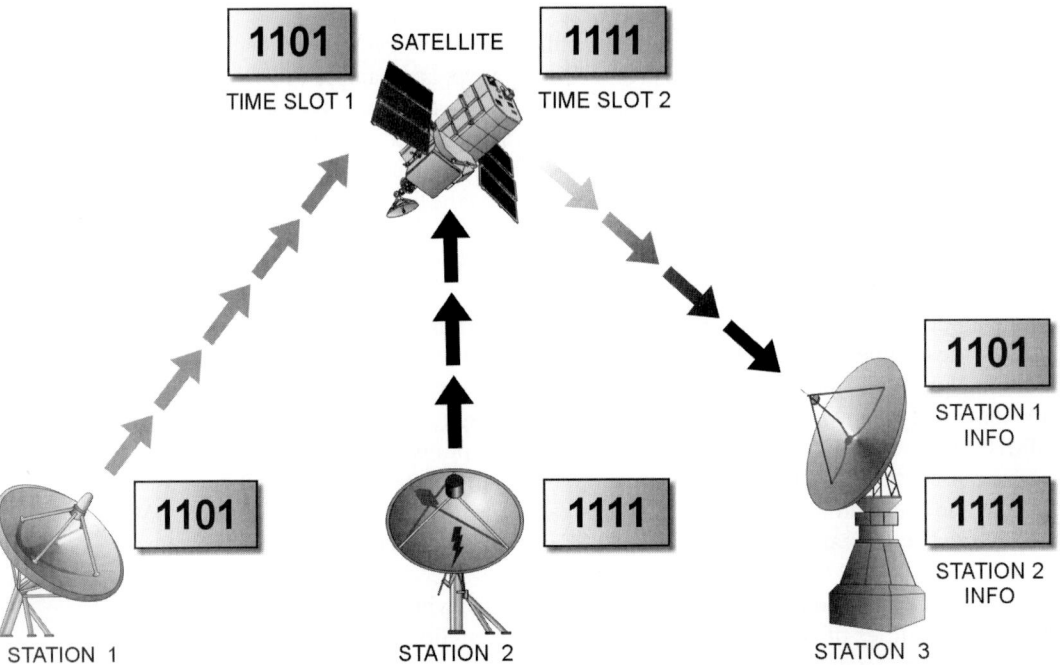

Figure 11-16 Satellite Time Division Multiple Access

Recall from earlier discussions of TDM, that signals are multiplexed by allowing various transmitters access to the full bandwidth of a communication channel for brief time periods, called **time slots**. In a multiple-access system, several earth stations are provided alternating time slots in which they can transmit information to the satellite. Station access to time slots may be conducted on a first-come first-served basis, under control of a routing program. This can be accomplished by competition (as in a contention system), or the slots may be filled strictly by demand.

In Figure 11-16, Stations 1 and 2 are transmitting to Station 3. The transmitting earth stations are assigned the same uplink center frequency. The use of a single frequency is a key advantage of TDM over FDM. Station 1 transmits 1101 to the satellite in the first time slot of the TDM frame. Station 2 has access to the second time slot, and transmits 1111. The satellite receives the time slots at the assigned uplink frequency, amplifies the data signal, removing noise, and transmits the time slots to Station 3. Station 3 demultiplexes the time slots, and routes them to specific addresses.

While Figure 11-16 shows only two uplink stations, dozens, or hundreds, could feed the same satellite. With many stations utilizing the same channel, the satellite becomes a very efficient communication path for transmitting data over long distances, or across oceans, from continent to continent.

Demand Assignment Multiple Access (DAMA)

FDM or TDM are often configured in a **Demand Assignment Multiple Access** (DAMA) scheme. In a DAMA system, none of the channels are dedicated to a subscriber, but are made available to earth stations on an as-needed (demand) basis. This differs from conventional FDMA and TDMA, in which subscribers are assigned to a particular channel, as was the case of Cinemax being assigned to channel 19 of Galaxy 1. DAMA offers earth station users, who send varying amounts of data at indeterminate times, the advantage of only paying for the satellite time actually used.

Supervisory information controlling bandwidth allocation, or time slot information, is generally directed by a central ground-based computer. The computer communicates with the satellite via the telemetry section.

COMMERCIAL AND RESIDENTIAL EARTH STATIONS

In 1984, the commercial satellite industry was deregulated. Among other things, this resulted in the scrambling of many satellite TV programs that, before 1984, weren't scrambled. But as the programs were being scrambled, they were also made available to residential earth-station owners, through subscriptions. A residential owner of a satellite system now pays for many of the same programs carried by cable companies; however, the owner of a satellite "**dish**" pays an average of 25% less than cable subscribers, and can receive up to about 100 free channels, as well as about 100 radio stations transmitted via satellite.

An earth station can be very attractive to a commercial business, with many field offices spread around the country. The field offices may use satellites to transmit daily cash receipts, inventory figures, the results of promotional campaigns, etc., to a central corporate office.

When the field office station isn't sending data, it can receive easy listening background music from channel 8 of **Satcom 2R**, located at 72 degrees in the geosynchronous orbit. The **Satellite Business System** satellite (SBS 4) in the Ku band, has a channel dedicated to automotive sales training. Toyota has a channel on the same satellite, and Ford has a channel on another satellite, in the Ku band. The basic earth station is shown in Figure 11-17.

The satellite signals strike the parabolic antenna, and are reflected to a feed horn. The feed horn is designed to collect the reflected signals, and focus them into a single signal, which is then applied to a **Low-Noise Amplifier** (LNA).

The strength of the signal striking the antenna is very weak, and without some sort of amplification, it wouldn't be of sufficient power to drive the solid-state components of the receiver. The LNA is housed in the same cabinet as the feed horn. The reason for this is that the satellite signal frequencies would be severely attenuated, if they first had to travel through the length of coaxial cable running back to the receiver. The feed horn/LNA module is considered to be a portion of the antenna.

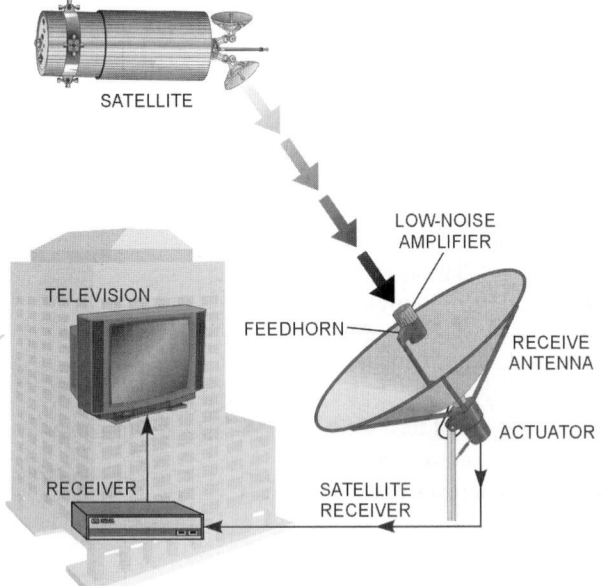

Figure 11-17 Typical Earth Station

In the early eighties, satellite dish owners had to manually move the antenna, if they wished to receive signals from another satellite. These days, antennas are equipped with a remotely controlled actuator. From inside the home or office, the antenna is moved by entering a two-digit code into the satellite receiver. For example, the **Cable News Network** (CNN) is carried on **Satcom 3R**. The user enters a code, such as F3, and the preprogramming in the receiver directs the actuator to move the antenna until it's pointing at the satellite.

Modern earth-station antennas are made of lightweight alloys, so the actuator can be a small motor. Older style antennas were constructed of aluminum, in a screen, or mesh, arrangement. The outside of the antenna was covered with fiberglass, to give the antenna rigidity. However, it also made the assembly susceptible to wind damage. These days, the fiberglass skin is omitted, and the mesh antenna is left exposed. The satellite receiver connects to the LNA by a buried coaxial cable. The receiver is similar to most heterodyne receivers, as can be seen in the block diagram of Figure 11-18.

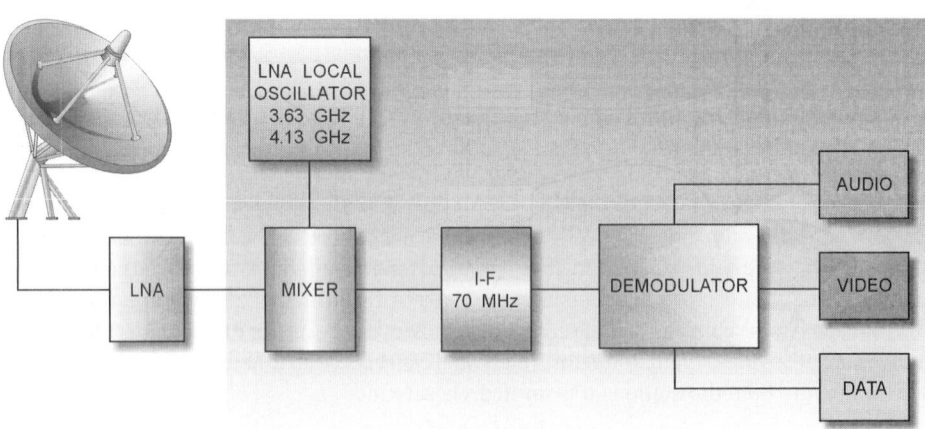

Figure 11-18 Earth Station Receiver

The LNA serves as a preamplifier for the received signal. The downlink signal is fed to the mixer stage, where it's heterodyned with the local-oscillator signal. The local oscillator is tunable over the downlink range of 4.63 GHz to 4.13 GHz. The difference frequency, between the received signal and local-oscillator signal, forms a 70MHz intermediate frequency. The demodulator stage extracts audio, video, or data from the intermediate frequency. The recovered intelligence is then routed to the appropriate load—television, printer, computer, etc.

Earth stations are available with a variety of options, and as you would expect, the more options, the more the system costs. A basic earth station, for a residential customer, costs about $1,800. Figure 11-19 shows the location of satellites in the C and Ku bands in the geosynchronous orbit.

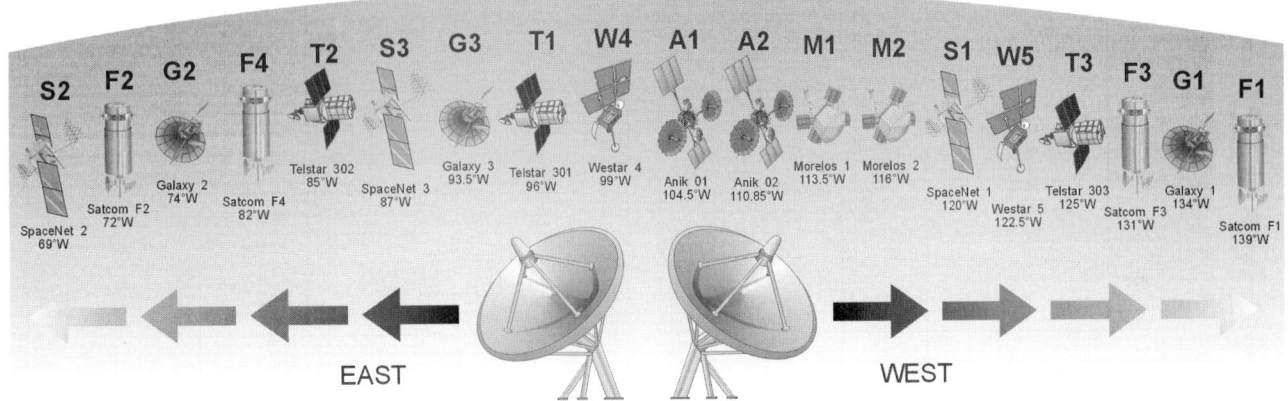

Figure 11-19 Location of Satellites in the Ku and C Bands

On the following page, Table 11-2 lists programming available from each satellite. An asterisk next to a channel means that in order to receive the channel unscrambled, you must subscribe to the channel. Generally, subscriber packages are available for a flat rate, with premium movie channels costing extra.

The earth-station antenna must be solidly anchored, so that it can be trained on the exact position of the satellite. This ensures the reception of the strongest possible signal. For residential applications, the antenna is mounted to a pole that's cemented into the ground. Commercial users often mount antennas on rooftops of buildings. The building then provides a solid foundation for anchoring the antenna.

The technology associated with earth stations has advanced rapidly in the last several years. It takes only a few hours to install, align, and make the station fully operational.

Table 11-2 Programs Available From Satellites

SATELLITE CHANNEL CHOICE

#	SPACENET 2 69°W [S2]	SATCOM 2R 72°W [F2]	GALAXY 2 74°W [G2]	SATCOM 4 82°W [F4]	SPACENET 3 87°W [S3]	TELSTAR 302 85°W [T2]	GALAXY 3 93.5°W [G3]	TELSTAR 301 96°W [T1]	WESTAR 4 99°W [W4]	ANIK D1 104.5°W [AD]	ANIK D2 110.5°W [A2]	MORELOS 1 113.5°W [M1]	SPACENET 1 120°W [S1]	WESTAR 5 122.5°W [W5]	TELSTAR 303 125°W [T3]	SATCOM 3R 131°W [F3]	GALAXY 1 134°W [G1]	SATCOM 1R 139°W [F1]	SATCOM 5 143°W [F5]
1	Zap Movies-PPV (n/a)		sports feeds	Home Shopping Club		news feeds		FOX East (6.2-6.8) ST					sports feeds	Boresight sports	sports, ESPN feed	The Fashion Channel	HBO- (West)		
2		WBBM-CBS-Chicago	StarDust Theater-	Sports Channel-Plus CTNA-(n/a)			sports feeds	CBS programs (West) (6.2-6.8) ST		TSN Sports Network- (n/a U.S.)		XHMT Mexico City (6.2)		University Net Dr. Gene Scott		The Learning Channel	Nashville Network (5.58-5.76) ST	KUSA-ABC-Denver	
3	Zap Movies-PPV (n/a)		First Run PPV-		WBSK-Ind-Boston		sports feeds	recurring & sports feeds		Independant & CBS feeds			sports feeds	sports feeds ATS, Sky Store	ESPN feed	Trinity Broadcasting	WGN Chicago-		
4		WABC-ABC-New York	First Run Promos VA Tech	Guest Cinema 1- (n/a)				ABC feeds		Global TV sports feeds		XHTV Mexico City (6.2)		occasional feeds		Bravo, RAI Vision Interfaith	Disney Channel- (East)	KCNC-NBC-Denver	
5	Channel America			America's Value Network	KTVT-Dallas/ Ft. Worth-			CBS feeds pro sports	NCN Shepherd's Chapel	CBS sports feeds			Christian Television Network	sports feeds		Shop TV Network	Showtime- (East)		
6				MSG Network TelShop				ABC news feeds		MuchMusic (5.41-6.2 wd) ST						Tempo Television	Univision (Spanish)	KMGH-CBS-Denver	
7		ESPN feed		Rainbow PPV-(n/a)	sports feeds		ACTS	CBS programs (East) (6.2-6.8) ST	ESPN news, sports feeds	CBS feeds, sports feeds Newfoundland	CBS, CTV TSN feeds	XHDF Mexico City (6.2)	EENetwork o/v sports feed	CBS (6.2) sports, news feeds	ESPN feeds	ESPN alternate & blackout feeds	CNN-	Prime Ticket Sports FNN	
8			StarDust PPV-sports	PreVue Guide		news feeds	Home Shopping Club	Wold (6.2-6.8) ST	CNN feed	CHCH Hamilton- (n/a U.S.)	sports feeds			college sports, recurring feeds		QVC Network	CNN Headline News-	NBC Network FNN	
9			Tuxedo-StarDust promos	SportsVision Chicago	WPIX-IND-NY-		Cable Value Network	ABC Network (East) (6.2-6.8 wd) ST		WXYZ-ABC- (n/a U.S.)		XHGC Mexico City (6.2)	SelecTV.		ESPN feed	Z Channel- Los Angeles (n/a)	ESPN-	HSE alternate feed	
10	Shipboard Satellite Network		NHK TV feed (Japanese)	SportsChannel-America		ABC Network (West) (6.2-6.8 wd) ST	EWTN	ESPN, ABC sports feeds	ITN	CBC North (Pac.)	Weather Now (7.8 nd) (English & French)					USA- (West)	The Movie Channel- (East)	HSE-Hit Video USA	
11				HV-USA NJT	sports feeds	ABC Network	Mind Extension University	ABC Network (East) (6.2-6.8 wd) ST			CTV (5.76-5.94 nd) ST		Hospital Sat. Network- (n/a)			FNN/SCORE Telshop	CBN- Family Channel	Sunshine Net. sports	
12		WXIA-NBC-Atlanta	sports feeds	SportsChannel-NY-				SNS recurring feeds		news, sports feeds	sports feeds					American Movie Classics-AVN	Arts & Entertainment		
13		NASA feeds	college & pro sports feeds	New England Sports Network		occasional feeds	Weather Channel-	FOX West (6.2-6.8 wd) ST	ESPN feed					ESPN feed college & pro sports		HBO Promos	Country Music TV (5.58-5.76 nd)		
14			college & pro sports feed	Sports Channel-FL Keystone	KTLA Ind-Los Angeles	ATT occasional feeds	C-SPAN II U.S. Senate	CBS news & sports feeds	PBS-A-	TCTV Montreal- (n/a U.S.)	Vision	XEW Mexico City (6.2)	sports feeds			CNN feeds, WA DC, FOX feed NYC	The Movie Channel- (West)	KRMA-PBS-KUBD Denver	
15			sports feeds	Shop at Home	Pro Am Sports Detroit	CBS news feeds (6.2-6.8) ST	Video Hits 1-	ESPN feeds, college sports	CNN feeds	CBC-French	CTV (5.76-5.94 nd) ST					Movietime promos	WWOR-NY- Secaucus, NJ	KWGN-Ind.-Denver	
16			sports feeds			CBS Network (West) (6.2) ST	Home Premiere TV- (n/a)	college & pro sports feeds	Univision news sports	(CBC) House of Commons French	TV5 Quebec (French)		Univision news sports	news, sports feeds	sports feeds	The Travel Channel	Showtime- (West)		
17			sports feeds	CBS programs	sports feeds	CBS programs (East) (6.2-6.8) ST	MTV- (East)	news feeds college & pro sports	PBS-B	Visnews/ London CBC feeds	sports feeds			news, sports feeds		Lifetime- (West)	Inspirational Net (5.58-5.76 nd) ST	3 Angels Broadcasting	
18				Guest Cinema 2- n/a		CBS news, sports feeds (6.2-6.8) ST	MTV- (West)	recurring feeds	HBC-Telemundo news sports feeds	CITV Edmonton- (n/a U.S.)	sports feeds	sports feeds	American Exxxtasy-	recurring feeds		TNT-	TBS-Atlanta		
19			pro sports feeds	Prime Ticket Sports-	college & pro sports feed		Nickelodeon- (East)	recurring, news & sports feeds	college sports	CBC North (Atl)			sports feeds	occasional feeds	Starion-	Request TV 1- (n/a)	Cinemax- (East)		
20			sports feeds	The Nostalgia Channel		CBS news feeds	Lifetime- (East)	sports feeds	London BBC, ESPN, news feeds	CBMT Montreal		occasional feeds	occasional feeds	college & pro sports feeds		BET (6.8-7.38 nd)	Galavision (Spanish)	KDVR-Ind.-Denver	
21		JISO Feed (Japanese)	sports feeds	Home Team Sports-			Viewer's Choice 1-	Wold, ESPN	WTVS-PBS- (n/a U.S.)	CHAN Vancouver- (n/a U.S.)			BTN	ESPN, college & pro sports feeds			USA- (East)		
22		Armed Forces Sat Net (AFRTS)	sports feeds	SC-NE. Silent Net.		CBS news, sports feeds	Nickelodeon- (West)	Fox East ESPN (6.2-6.8 wd)	PBS-C-	WJBK-CBS- (n/a U.S.)	First Choice- (n/a U.S.)			occasional feeds		Home Shopping Club II	VSM Discovery Channel		
23	Zap Movies-PPV (n/a)		sports feeds	Playboy Channel-			Family Net (5.58-5.76 nd)		PBS-D L.D.S. sports				RFD-TV	college & pro sports feeds		Cinemax- (West)	HBO- (East)		
24							C-SPAN I (5.8) U.S. House		ESPN feeds	(CBC) House of Commons English	CTV (5.76-5.94) ST			college & pro sports feeds	SCOLA News	Request TV 2- (n/a)	Disney Channel- (West)	Prime Sports Network	Alaska Satellite TV (5.8)

TRANSPONDERS

NOTES: ST = stereo   wd = wide discrete   nd = narrow discrete   • = encrypted   n/a = not available to U.S. dish owners
Audio on video channels 6.8 unless indicated

KEY POINTS REVIEW

- A satellite system consists of the satellite, the transmitting station, and the receiving station.

- A passive satellite serves as a signal reflector.

- An active satellite includes circuitry that amplifies a signal. Active satellites are also called repeaters.

- A satellite system is best used when the distance between the transmitter and the receiver is great.

- The geosynchronous orbit (23,280 miles above the Earth) is the most common orbit for telephone, data, and entertainment communication.

- An elliptical orbit follows a path in which the Earth is off-center.

- Satellites receive at an uplink frequency, and transmit at a downlink frequency.

- Common satellite frequencies are: C band at 6-GHz uplink and 4-GHz downlink, Ka band at 14-GHz uplink and 12-GHz downlink, and the Ku-band data 30-GHz uplink and 20-GHz downlink.

- A satellite contains five major sub assemblies: rocket thrusters, power source, antennas, transponder, and command assembly.

- Channel multiplexing occurs at the receive and transmit sections of satellites, as well as internally in a satellite.

- Satellites may use frequency-division multiple access (FDMA), or time-division multiple access (TDMA), to multiplex channels.

At this point, review the objectives listed at the beginning of the chapter to be certain that you understand and can perform them. Afterward, answer the review questions that follow to verify your knowledge of the information.

REVIEW QUESTIONS

The following questions test your knowledge of the material presented in this chapter:

1. What was the name given to the first satellite launched by the United States?

2. What year did the commercial use of satellites begin?

3. What type of satellite would be used to track the movements of a glacier?

4. What is the primary component used in detecting the data from a carrier?

5. True or False: Many of the premium movie channels shown on cable TV are sent by satellite.

6. What are the basic components of a satellite system?

7. True or False: A satellite carrying telephone calls is an active satellite.

8. Describe how satellites in the geosynchronous orbit can cover most of the Earth?

9. Why do satellites parked in elliptical orbits have larger footprints that those parked in circular orbits?

10. To an earth-observer, how will a satellite in an orbit 10,000 miles above the Earth appear?

11. How is the downlink signal produced from the uplink signal in the satellite transponder?

12. What is one method used to focus satellite transmissions, so as to utilize a smaller earth station receive antenna?

13. Satellites are powered from a combination of _____ and _____?

14. What is the function of the satellite apogee thruster.

15. Which satellite section is responsible for monitoring the onboard systems?

MULTIPLE CHOICE QUESTIONS

1. The temporary orbit first assumed by a satellite, and used for making fine adjustments, before entering the final orbit is called the:
   a. Geosynchronous orbit.
   b. Transfer orbit.
   c. Circular orbit.
   d. Elliptical orbit.

2. The attitude of a satellite refers to the:
   a. Orientation of the satellite to the surface of the moon.
   b. Orientation of the satellite to the North pole.
   c. Orientation of the satellite to the Equator.
   d. Orientation of the satellite to the surface of the Earth.

3. The total bandwidth of a channel may be either frequency-division multiplexed or time-division multiplexed using:
   a. FDMA.
   b. TDMA.
   c. DAMA.
   d. None of the above.

4. A satellite multiplexing system usually associated with digital data is:
   a. FDMA.
   b. TDMA.
   c. DAMA.
   d. None of the above.

5. Channel bandwidth is made available on an as-needed basis in which satellite multiplexing system?
   a. FDMA.
   b. TDMA.
   c. DAMA.
   d. None of the above.

6. A 100MHz transponder is using FDMA with 24 channels. What is the bandwidth of each channel?
   a. 2.085 MHz.
   b. 4.17 MHz.
   c. 8.34 MHz.
   d. None of the above.

7. The signal that's transmitted from an Earth station to a satellite receiver is called the:
   a. Ellipse.
   b. Orbit.
   c. Downlink.
   d. Uplink.

8. To cover most of the globe, using satellites in a circular orbit, they must be placed _____ degrees apart.
   a. 15.
   b. 30.
   c. 60.
   d. 120.

9. A complete satellite system is composed of the transmit Earth station, receive Earth station, and the:
   a. Satellite.
   b. LNA.
   c. Solar cells.
   d. Apogee thruster.

10. A satellite using FDMA has a bandwidth of 250 MHz, and is using 25 transponders. What is the bandwidth of each channel?
    a. 20 MHz.
    b. 15 MHz.
    c. 10 MHz.
    d. 5 MHz.

11. Why is a low noise amplifier located near the antenna?
    a. Because it also serves as the antenna.
    b. Because it's too large to fit in the receiver.
    c. Because the carrier frequency of the downlink is less than 100 kHz.
    d. Because the downlink signal is very weak.

12. The component of an Earth station that focuses the received signal on the antenna is the:
    a. Feedhorn.
    b. Low noise amplifier.
    c. Actuator.
    d. Receiver.

CD-ROM

Net+ Practice Test

Additional Net+ Certification testing is available on the CD that accompanies this text. The testing suite on the CD provides Study Card, Flash Card, and Run Practice type testing. The Study Card and Flash Card feature enables you to electronically link to the section of the book in which the question is covered. Choose questions from the test pool related to this chapter.

APPENDIX

A

GLOSSARY

Glossary

A

Access Protocols: The class of protocols in the LLC and MAC sublayers of the data-link layer of the OSI reference model. Media-access protocols include CSMA/CD, CSMA/CA, token bus, and token ring.

Accounting Network Management: One of five ISO functions of network management; the cost-effectiveness of the network, tariff rates, and new equipment-needs analysis, are among the areas included.

Active Satellite: A repeater satellite that includes amplifiers for increasing the signal strength before retransmitting it back to an earth station.

Adaptive Equalization: The dynamic sampling and evaluation of data transmitted through the telephone network. An adaptive equalizer compensates for intersymbol interference as it occurs.

Address Resolution Protocol (ARP): A wide-area network routing protocol used to map the MAC addresses of nodes to logical network addresses.

Administrative Utilities: Tools for network managers to setup or change user accounts.

Algorithm: The steps used to solve a problem. Error-detection fields, such as cyclic redundancy checks, are organized under a specific algorithm.

Alternate Mark Inversion (AMI): A digital encoding technique used with long-distance telephone systems. Logic 0's are represented with 0V, and logis 1's by alternating the channel voltage between +V and –V.

Amplitude Modulation (AM): A method of superimposing data on a carrier in which the carrier amplitude is directly proportional to the data amplitude, and the rate of carrier amplitude changes is directly proportional to the data frequency.

Analog Loopback Test: A test carrier generated by modems to simulate reception and detection of analog carriers.

Angle of Incidence: The angle at which light enters a fiber-optic cable.

Angle of Inclination The angle of a satellite's orbit, as referenced to the equator.

Answer Modem The modem receiving data from a transmitting modem. The answer modem responds on a specified answer channel.

Antenna Antennas are used in the transmission and receiving of microwaves and other radio waves. A satellite contains separate transmit and receive antennas, as well as a telemetry antenna for communicating with the ground control station.

Anti-Tinkle and Speech Muting: The section of a telephone responsible for preventing high-voltage spikes from entering the speech circuitry.

Anti-virus software: Software used to detect and/ or clean known computer viruses.

Apogee: The end of an ellipse orbit of a satellite furthest from the center of the Earth.

Apogee Thrusters: A small thruster mounted on the body of satellites that ensures the satellite cab be moved and remain in its orbit.

Application Layer: Layer seven of the OSI reference model. The only layer in which users have direct contact with the model, it's the user interface for initiating application software programs such as FTP or HTTP.

Approvals: The individual who authorizes certain activities. It normally refers to access and passwords on a network, as well as approval of standard operating procedures.

ASCII: A 7-bit terminal code capable of producing 128 unique characters.

Asynchronous: A transmission method that uses start and stop bits to separate frames. It is typically used with personal computers.

Asynchronous Balanced Mode (ABM): An alternative form of the asynchronous response mode for configuring HDLC exchanges. In the balanced mode, network stations are peers and may initiate as well as terminate exchanges.

Asynchronous Response Mode (ARM): One of two modes for configuring HDLC exchanges. In the ARM mode, stations retain the primary/secondary designation, but the secondaries may transmit without first receiving permission from the primary.

Asynchronous Transfer mode (ATM): A fast packet service capable of carrying voice, data, and video.

Atmospheric Noise: Noise that is the result of lightning and sunspot activity. Atmospheric noise tends to distort large segments of data.

Attenuation: The undesirable weakening of a signal.

Attitude Stabilization: The process of properly positioning and orienting a satellite.

Automatic Gain Control: A modem circuit that provides a flat response of the received data.

B

Backbone: A primary network segment from which subnetworks branch off in a tree configuration.

Backoff Delay: The condition a transmitter enters following a collision on a CSMA/CD network. Backoff delays are variable, and may occur up to sixteen times before an error is generated.

Balancing Network: A telephone circuit connected across the hybrid that samples the caller's voice, and applies it to the receive circuit. This provides the voice feedback necessary for the caller to adjust the volume of his voice.

Bandwidth: A range of frequencies in which nodes transmit and receive data. Since channel capacity is directly proportional to bandwidth, large bandwidth channels carry more information than narrow bandwidth channels.

Baseband: Refers to networks that communicate without carriers. Generally, baseband networks transmit at data rates of less than 10 Mhz.

Baseline: Statistical data that shows the normal operation of a network.

Baud Rate: The number of data symbols transmitted per second. Baud=BPS/N, where BPS is bits per second, and N is the number of bits per symbol.

Baudot: An older terminal code, commonly representing up to 32 characters with a 5-bit code.

Beamwidth: The physical size of a satellite's footprint on the Earth.

Best Effort Service: Refers to protocols—particularly internetworking protocols—in which errors are checked in the header, but not in the data field of the message.

Binary Synchronous Communication (BSC): A character-oriented protocol developed by IBM. The size of the data field varies, by multiples of eight, with 128 bytes common.

Bit-Error Rates (BER): A measure of the bit errors per transmitted symbol.

Bit-Error Rate Tester: Network test equipment used to check for individual bit degradation.

Bit Interleaving: The system used with time-division multiplexing in transmitting channel data in alternating bits.

Bit-Level Protocol: A class of protocols in which syncronization between stations is achieved at the bit level. HDLC and SDLC are common bit protocols.

Bit Rate: The frequency of the data; also referred to as bits per second (BPS).

Bit Stuffing: A method of achieving text transparency with HDLC, also called zero insertion. For any data stream in the information field containing six consecutive logic 1's, a 0 bit is inserted after the fifth bit. The inserted bit is removed at the receiver.

Block Character Check (BCC): A one- or two-byte error-detection field, associated with the BSC protocol frame, and based on longitudinal redundancy checks.

Block Cipher: A class of substitution ciphers in which blocks of plaintext are replaced with ciphertext taken from block-cipher dictionaries.

Bootp: The Bootstrap Protocol defines how to determine the IP of a diskless system when bootstrapped. It's used when an IP is assigned to a remote node from a server.

BORSCHT Functions: An acronym that describes the control, management, and use of the telephone system. BORSCHT stands for Battery, Overvoltage Protection, Ring trip, Supervision, Coding, Hybrid, and Testing.

Bottleneck: The critical point in which network message delays have increased, until data flow is at a standstill.

Breakout box: Network test equipment used for loopback tests, clock, and signal monitoring. Breakout boxes are connected in parallel with the cable under test.

Bridge: An internetworking machine that connects networks (LANs) of different access methods. Operating at the Data Link layer, it is independent of Network-layer protocols such as TCP/IP.

Bridge Protocol Data Units (BPDU): Encoded signals used with Spanning Tree Protocol that specify the configuration of the topology or serve notice that the topology will change.

Broadband: A method of transmitting in which the data modulates a carrier frequency. Typically, broadband networks operate in excess of 10 Mhz.

Brouter: A bridge/router is used to interconnect LANs at the local level, as well as route packets to different network addresses.

Browse: Refers to read-only access to files.

Buffer Overflow: A condition in which the temporary storage of a receiver, i.e., multiplexer, receives more data than space exists to store it.

Buffer Pools: A method of organizing multiplexer memory. All terminals compete for storage space.

Bus Topology: The most common method of arranging network nodes, a network bus is characterized by the use of a network interface for connecting each station to the bus.

Busy Signal: A telephone signal indicating the called number is occupied. A busy signal consists of a dual tone of 480+620 Hz, 2 seconds on, and .5 of a second off.

C

Cable Labeling Conventions: A scheme used to label the entry and exit points of network cable, that can be reconciled to the attached device.

Cable Tester: Network test equipment used to check cables for opens, shorts, and continuity.

Callback: A data security measure in which a host computer calls the modem of a station user who has initiated a network sign-on. If the dialed modem responds as expected, the station is assumed to be in a valid location.

Carrier Recover: The section of a modem that aids in calculating the amount of phase distortion in a received signal.

Carrier-Sense Multiple Access/Collision Detect (CSMA/CD): The IEEE 802.3 standard for bus networks, based upon the original Ethernet, and functionally the same.

Carson's Rule: A method of calculating bandwidth of an FM signal. BW = 2(DFc + Fm), where Fc is the deviation produced by the modulating signal, and Fm is the modulating signal frequency.

Central Office: The central point where all telephones within an exchange are connected. Each office can serve up to 10,000 subscribers.

Centralized Network: A network in which control and management of the network lies in a central computer. The attached work stations are forbidden to make changes to the network. LANs with a file server are centralized networks.

Channel Bank: The equipment needed to combine the channels of T-carrier facilities, referred to as digital banks.

CHAP: Challenge Handshake Authentication Protocol, used with PPP. The server generates a random string of bits and sends them, along with its hostname, to the client.

Character-Level Protocol: A class of protocols in which synchronization between stations is achieved with data characters. BSC is an example.

Character Stuffing: The method used with BSC for achieving text transparency. Within the frame, all control characters are preceded by DLE. In the data field, any character similar to a control character is prefaced with two DLE characters. The additional characters are removed at the receiver.

Characteristic Impedance: The value of pure resistance that a cable is to be terminated with in order to transfer the maximum amount of signal strength to a load. It is dependent upon the effective capacitance and inductance of the cable, and is calculated by: Zo = the square root of the inductance, divided by the capacitance of the cable.

Cheapernet: A term describing 10base2-type LANs, using RG-58 coaxial cable.

Ciphertext: Encrypted plaintext.

Circular Orbit: Geosynchronous orbit, located 23,280 miles above the Earth.

Cladding: The potion of a fiber-optic cable encircling the core material.

Class A IP Address: The first three digits of Class-A networks are numbered 1-126.

Class B IP Address: The first three digits of Class-B networks are numbered 128 through 191.

Class C IP Address: The first three digits of Class-C networks are numbered 192 through 223.

Clear-to-Send (CTS): An RS-232C signaling pin, initiated upon completion of the modem training time.

Client Configuration Documentation: Set of data that describes configuration parameters of a workstations. It includes IP, COM port assignments, IRQ assignments, amount of RAM, type of CPU, as well as other information pertinent to the operation and interface of the client.

Coaxial: A transmission cable consisting of two conductors insulated from one another, and enclosed in a polyethylene jacket.

Code Violation: Indicates that the bit transitions on a CSMA/CD network are too long or too short. This occurs when there's a collision between stations.

Collision Window: The first 464 bits of data transmitted on a CSMA/CD network. If there is to be a collision, it will occur within this window.

Command Assembly: The section of a satellite responsible for monitoring factors that may affect the satellite's operation, as well as providing management of the other sections.

Command State: The condition noted by a modem detecting a dial tone on the telephone circuit.

Compander: A compressor/expander used in the PCM encoding process that ensures both small- and large-amplitude signals will produce an identical coding change.

Concentrator: A network device that serves as an interface between stations, particularly in situations in which networks may be interconnected by a backbone.

Conditioned Lines: Fee-based telephone data channels that contain specific phase-delay and signal-attenuation characteristics.

Configuration Network Management: One of five ISO functions for network management; includes the physical architecture, selection of hardware, protocols, interface and access methods, and the level of service provided to users.

Congestion Signal: A telephone signal indicating a busy network. The congestion signal is a dual, 480+620-Hz tone that's on for .2 second, and off for .3 second.

Connection-oriented Transport: A protocol that assigns sequence numbers to frames passed into the LLC, and tracks them at the receiving node. At the Data Link layer, it's the same as Type II LLC.

Connectionless Transport: A protocol that doesn't track the sequence of frames or packets of frames. A connectionless service, at the Data Link layer, is Type I LLC. See Connection-oriented Transport.

Consultative Committee for International Telephony (CCITT): An international standards organization responsible for developing the telecommunications standards.

Contention-based Systems: A general term describing CSMA/CD-type networks, in which stations vie for access to the network. Ethernet is a contention-based protocol.

Conversion Time: The time required for an analog-to-digital converter to reach full-scale resolution.

Convolutional Coding: Refers to error-detection schemes noted for the use of continuous feedback in producing the error-detection field of data frames. An example is cyclic redundancy checks.

Core: The center part of a fiber-optic cable that carries data in the form of light, and constructed of glass or plastic.

Critical Angle: The angle at which light propagates along the core of a fiber-optic cable.

Crosslink: A satellite-to-satellite communication path for transmission in the Geosynchronous orbit.

Crossover Cable: A cable used to directly connect two computers, or hubs, in which the receive and transmit wires of a twisted pair, or other cable, have been reversed.

Crosstalk: Electromagnetic distortion resulting from two conductors, lying in close proximity, in a parallel plane. Crosstalk is generally associated with twisted-pair cables.

Cryptography: The process of writing secret messages, so the intelligence of the message is hidden.

Cyclic Redundancy Check (CRC): A widely used error-detection technique, based upon convolutional coding of the data stream.

D

Data Analyzer: Network test equipment used to identify data rates, protocol types, and number of bits in each character.

Data-Communication Equipment (DCE): Any device directly involved in transmitting and receiving data. Examples are modems and multiplexers.

Data Compression: The process of encoding data, so that the data is transmitted with fewer bits. Examples of data-compression techniques are the Huffman and Dictionary methods.

Data-Encryption Standard Cipher (DES): The official encryption technique of the National Bureau of Standards. The DES is based on a 56-bit key from which sixteen 48-bit keys are derived to encrypt 64-bit blocks of plaintext.

Data-Link Layer: Layer two of the OSI reference model. The data-link layer provides for point-to-point exchanges between network nodes. Frame formatting, error control, and access to the network are functions of the data-link layer.

Data Rate: The frequency at which information is transmitted across a communication channel.

Data Set Ready (DSR): An RS-232C pin that, when initiated, tells the host DTE that the connection between two modems is active.

Data-Signal Rate Selector (DSRS): Designated as pin 23 on the RS-232C interface, it is used in modems that have the ability to automatically shift to varying data rates.

Data Terminal Equipment (DTE): Any device in which its primary purpose is the manipulation of data. Examples are computers and terminals.

Data Terminal Ready (DTR): An RS-232C interface pin initiated by the answer DTE, to indicate it will accept an incoming call.

Database: A large collection of similar data, usually stored in a host computer.

Datagram: The unit of measure of a TCP/IP transmission; it consists of a maximum of 65,535 bytes.

DC Shift: The gradual build-up of voltage, caused by the capacitive and inductive reactance of transmission cables.

Decibel: The standard criteria for evaluating the distortion performance of signal quality. The common method for evaluating power losses, and gains, is with the formula: db = 10log (Po/Pi).

Decimal Dotted Notation: The process of dividing the 32-bit TCP/IP addresses into four 8-bit groups. The groups are separated by a decimal point, and expressed in base ten.

Decryption: The process of recovering the intelligence from encrypted data.

Default gateway: The term is taken literally to mean a "gateway to other networks", and not as a device that performs protocol conversions. In this context, it's the same as a router. See gateway.

Delay: Refers to frequency, or phase, delays in data transmission that are undesirable.

Delta Modulation: A variation of pulse-code modulation. The DM output consists of positive and negative pulses that correspond to the quantized amplitude variations.

Demand Assignment Multiple Access (DAMA): A method of configuring TDM or FDM for satellites, in which channels are made available on an as-needed, or demand, basis.

Descrambler: A section of a modem responsible for removing the scrambling algorithm initiated at the transmitting modem.

Despin Axis: A device connected to the antennas of a satellite, that keeps the antennas pointed at a fixed position on the Earth.

Despin Rotor: A device that permits satellite antennas to be adjusted, so as to point to a desired ground location.

Detect and Fix: A technique for balancing the workload among network stations; it's characterized by an historical orientation, in that the problem is corrected after it's been identified.

Dial Tone: The telephone dial tone that originates from a 350/440-Hz oscillator, at the local office.

Dictionary Concentrator: A data-compression technique that establishes unique bit patterns, based upon the content of the data to be transmitted.

Differential Phase-Shift Keying (DPSK): A modulation method used in modems, in which the symbol phase encoding is based upon the phase position of the previous symbol. Up to 16 bits-per-symbol have been used with DPSK.

Digital Loopback Test: A modem check that is used for testing the transmit and receive sides of both modems, as well as the connection between the two.

Distortion: The degradation of signal quality, usually measured in decibels, and referenced to a standard value.

Distributed Network: A network in which control and management of software is shared by the work stations.

Domain: An element of the Organizational Model of the ISO network management function; refers to a group of similar subsystems consisting of objects.

Domain Name System (DNS): A database system used to map host names, IP addresses and e-mail routing.

Downlink: The modulated carrier transmitted from a satellite, the satellite transmit antenna, and the receive equipment at the ground station.

Down-Side: In a token-ring network, down-side is the side of the receiver the data enters; the up-side is the side of the receiver the data exits.

Drive Mapping: The process of creating a drive letter to connect to another network resource.

Dual-Tone Multifrequency (DTMF): A method of tone dialing using a twelve-button keypad, and dual tones representing each of the twelve buttons.

Duplexing: Used in RAID implementations to provide a dedicated hard drive controller for each hard drive.

Dynamic Host Configuration Protocol (DHCP): A protocol used to dynamically assign IP addresses to clients and nodes. It's gradually replacing the Bootp protocol.

Dynamic routing: Routers that advertise updates and collect updated routing addresses are called dynamic routers.

E

Earth Station: The source of satellite transmissions, also called the ground station.

EBCDIC: An 8-bit terminal code capable of producing 256 unique characters.

Electronic Industry Association (EIA): A professional trade organization that develops many standards.

Elliptical Orbit: A satellite orbit tilted at an arc in reference to the equator, and in which the Earth is off-center in the ellipse.

Encapsulation Bridge: A bridging method in which the MAC frames of the transmitting stations are placed in the information field of a transmitted network frame. The access methods of all nodes must be the same to use this method.

Encryption: The process of transforming data into a secret code.

Energy Detector: A section of a modem that samples the output of the automatic gain control, to determine if the data signal meets the minimum requirements for successful data exchanges.

Environmental factors: A reference to the physical surroundings of network equipment such as temperature, humidity, electrical interference, and security measures.

Equalization: The process of compensating for phase-jitters and frequency attenuation. Data may be equalized at the transmitter (pre-equalization), or dynamically (adaptive equalization).

Ethernet: The forerunner of the IEEE 802.3 standard for bus networks. Ethernet was developed jointly by XEROX, Digital Equipment, and Intel. It is functionally identical to CSMA/CD, and often used interchangeably in literature.

F

Fairing: Metal skin placed over the nose of a rocket, protecting it from the heat during launch.

Fast Packet Services: A version of X.25 packet switching that transports messages at much higher data rates. Includes frame relay and ATM.

Fault Analysis: Refers to established procedures for locating and correcting malfunctions.

Fault Network Management: One of the five ISO functions of network management; concerned with detecting, diagnosing, and correcting problems.

FDM Hierarchy: An organizational structure used by the long-distance carriers, primarily for analog systems. The system is based on a group of 12 channels, each occupying a 4kHz bandwidth. Five groups comprise a super group; ten super groups are included in a master group; a jumbo group contains 5 master groups; and a multiplexed group consists of 3 jumbo groups.

Fiber Distributed Data Interface (FDDI): The ANSI standard for transmitting 100 MBPS data over fiber-optic cable in local-area networks.

Fiber Optics: Transmission cable in which data is transported as light. Fiber-optic cable is noted for high data rates and wide bandwidths.

File Server: A network station dedicated to managing a local-area network. A LAN with a file server is a centralized network, and all exchanges between nodes are under control of the file server.

File Transfer Protocol (FTP): The protocol used to transfer files by copying the file from one system (computer) to another.

Fix: An interim solution for bugs which have been discovered either during beta testing or after the product was formally released. See patch.

Folder Replication: Method used to backup data. Typically associated with copying a database from server to client to that more than one copy of the database exists.

Footprint: The geographical coverage of a satellite transmission.

Forward Delay Timer: Set by the root bridge of the Spanning Tree Protocol, it specifies the length of time the bridge will remain in each of the port states (disabled, learning, blocking, listening, or forwarding).

Forward Error Control: Error correction that occurs at the receiver, such as the Huffman Code.

Fractional T1: A portion of the 24-channel T1 facility for lease to small- or medium-size companies.

Fragmentation: The process of dividing TCP/IP datagrams so that the length is smaller. This may be necessary to pass the datagram over LANs that have smaller frame requirements than TCP/IP.

Frame: The collection of fields containing link control and management, as well as user information.

Frame-Check Sequence (FCS): The error-detection field of HDLC frames, one or two bytes long.

Frame Relay: A fast packet service that is similar to the X.25 interface. It provides variable data rates.

Frequency-Division Multiple Access (FDMA): A modified version of FDM for satellites, that allocates the total bandwidth to a number of transponders.

Frequency-Division Multiplexing (FDM): In an FDM system, a wide bandwidth is divided among many dedicated channels.

Frequency Modulation (FM): A modulation method in which the carrier frequency changes in direct proportion to the data amplitude, and the rate of carrier frequency change is directly proportional to the data frequency.

Frequency Noise: Noise that is of a constant period, but of varying amplitude. A common source of frequency noise is the 60 Hz radiated from wiring.

Frequency-Shift Keying (FSK): A modulation technique used with modems, in which the phase of the carrier is shifted higher, or lower, to represent a logic 1 or 0.

Full Duplex: A system that permits simultaneous data flow between nodes.

G

Gateway: A wide-area network interconnection machine, that converts from one type of data communication system to another.

Generator Polynominal: In error-detection techniques, it is the organization of shift registers and exclusive-OR operations, under the control of a specific algorithm.

Geosynchronous Orbit: A circular satellite orbit located 23,280 miles above the Earth's surface, also called the Clarke orbit.

Groups: The practice of organizing individuals into related groups, all of whom have a general need to a class of information.

H

H88 Loading: The practice of installing 88-mH coils every 6,000 feet along the telephone network. H88 loading attenuates the signal, providing a flatter frequency response.

Half Duplex: A system that permits data flow between nodes, in only one direction at a time.

Hamming Code: A technique for detecting and correcting errors, requiring a significant amount of overhead.

Handholding: An initial response to a problem in which you devote time, usually on the telephone, to working with the user on the problem.

Handshaking: The dialog exchanged between communicating stations that sets up the link.

Hardware Loopback: The ping utility, and its many variations.

Header: All fields of data frames that do not include user information. While the header is necessary to establish and maintain the link, it also reduces the efficiency of the exchange.

High-level Data-Link Control (HDLC): The official data-link protocol of the International Standards Organization. HDLC is a bit-oriented protocol suitable for most network environments and topologies.

Hub-1: A high-speed switch at the center of a star network.

Huffman Code: A forward error-correction technique.

Huffman Concentrator: A data-compression method in which the data is sampled, and those bit sequences with higher occurrence rates are given abbreviated bit patterns.

Host: Any machine that communicates on the network. It normally refers to a device that has a dedicated or assigned IP address.

Hybrid: A transformer interface that provides for full-duplex operation of the telephone system. A telephone includes a 2- to 4-wire hybrid, and the central office maintains a 2- to 4-wire hybrid.

HyperText Transfer Protocol (HTTP): The protocol used to link files on the Internet.

I

Ideal Signal Point: A predetermined position in the signal-point constellation of a modem modulator. The ideal signal point is separated from the position of the received signal by an amount equal to an error signal.

Idle Token: The state of a token-ring network when the token is in transition between stations.

IEEE 802 Standards: A series of standards approved by the IEEE to address the implementation of recommendations of the ISO at the physical and data link layers of the OSI reference model. The standards are not all completed, but encompass:

802.1 High-Level Interface
802.2 Logical-Link Interface
802.3 CSMA/CD
802.4 Token Bus
802.5 Token Ring
802.6 Metropolitan Area Networks
802.7 Broadband LANs
802.8 Fiber Optics
802.9 Integrated Voice Data

Information transfer: An initial response to take when a problem is first reported. Information Transfer, is appropriate in a situation where reference material will address the problem as effectively as you going to the client, and doing it yourself.

Impulse Noise: Sporadic noise resulting from relays, motors, generators, and switches. It is usually of short duration, and in close proximity to the affected equipment.

Information Frame: An HDLC frame type used to carry user information. Information frames are represented with a logic 0 in the frame-identifier field of the control field.

Information Service: A large database. Usually, access to an information service is made available for a fee.

Interconnect Transport Service: Software overlaid on the protocols, that addresses the performance of a network.

Interface: Describes the physical connection between dissimilar devices. A common example is the RS-232C interface connection between PCs and printers.

International Direct-Distance Dialing (IDDD): A worldwide telephone numbering system that allows the direct dialing of any number in the world, without the assistance of an operator.

International Standards Organization (ISO): A large, professional, trade organization responsible for many standards.

Internet: A WAN used for education and research, that uses TCP/IP protocols. The Internet is the largest of wide-area networks with controlled access.

Internetworking Protocol (IP): A Network layer protocol used in conjunction with TCP, to route between logical addresses.

Intersymbol Interference: The blurring together of data symbols caused by distributed channel reactance.

Iteration: The sixteen rounds of ciphering in the Data-Encryption Standard.

J

Jam: The state of a CSMA/CD network following the detection of a collision, in which the transmitters continue to send data for 32 bits.

Jam Pattern: A series of logic 1s generated after a collision is detected on a CSMA/CD network.

Jitter: The unavoidable delay in arrival times of symbols. It's created by harmonic distortion of the logic levels carried by the symbols.

K

Key: Specifies the parameters of a secret code, and is used to encrypt and decrypt the data.

L

Learning Bridge: Also called Transparent Bridge. It is a bridging method that utilizes source-address tables for compiling a map of all addresses on the network.

Line Interface: The RJ-11 telephone jack that couples data onto the telephone network.

Line of Sight: Communication method associated with microwaves. The transmit and receive antennas must be arranged in a straight path.

Link Access Protocol-Balanced (LAPB): A subset of HDLC used with X.25 packet switched networks. All stations on a LAPD network are peers.

Load Balancing: The even distribution of network processes among the nodes of a peer-to-peer LAN.

Local-Area Network (LAN): A LAN is characterized by a collection of nodes connected together in a limited geographical area, and operating under a single protocol.

Local Exchange Loop: The two-wire circuit from the telephone to the central office, and the wires connecting the two.

Logical Indicators: Network management software used to identify problems. Examples include TCP/IP utilities, Network Monitor, or Performance Monitor.

Logical-Link Control (LLC): A sublayer of the data-link layer of the OSI reference model. The LLC is responsible for frame formatting and the conventions necessary to establish a reliable link.

Login Account: A script that specifies the privileges of an individual or group access to the network resources.

Longitudinal Redundancy Check (LRC): A parity-based error-detection method in which the bits in blocks of data are arranged in columns and rows, and a block error field is generated.

Loop Length Compensation: A circuit in a telephone that regulates the speech levels of callers, regardless of the distance separating them.

Loopback Test: Modem tests that check the operation of local and remote modems, as well as the connection between the two.

Low-Noise Amplifier (LNA): The output power amplifier of a satellite Earth station.

M

MAC Address: All nodes, or stations, on the network have a unique address. A 6-byte length is permitted, as the original version of Ethernet specified a 6-byte address. IEEE 802.3 permits a 2-byte alternative, but this is seldom used.

Major Axis: A satellite orbit that parallels the equator.

Managed System: A component of the Organizational Model of ISO network management; managed systems are a logical grouping of objects.

Manchester: A common encoding method in which logic 1s are represented by the high-to-low mid-bit transition, and logic 0's are represented by the low-to-high mid-bit transition.

Mark: The steady state condition of a channel represented by a logic 1.

Max Age Timer: A parameter set by the root bridge of the Spanning Tree Protocol that specifies the length of time a bridge will wait to receive a BPDU.

Maximum Port Speed: A setting that allows you to specify the port speed for a modem.

Media: The type of physical connection used between network nodes. Examples are twisted-pair wires, coaxial cables, fiber optics, and microwaves.

Media Access Unit (MAU): A hardware device associated with coaxial cable. An MAU contains circuitry that allows a workstation to access the network media.

Medium-Access Control (MAC): A sublayer of the data link layer of the OSI reference model. The MAC is responsible for ensuring that network stations gain access to the network.

Mesh: In a pure mesh network, each node has a physical link (coax, twisted pair, microwave, fiber optic) connection to all other nodes.

Microwave: A type of transmission media. Data is modulated onto a carrier, and transmitted through the atmosphere.

Minor Axis: A line intersecting the equator at a 90-degree angle.

Mirroring: A RAID method of backing up hard drive data. In a mirrored configuration, the data on one disk is duplicated to another disk.

Modal Dispersion: Distortion found in fiber-optic cables that results from the light arriving at the receiver at different times.

Modem: An acronym for modulator/demodulator. Modems are required to transmit data between stations separated by 50 feet, or more.

Modulation: The process of superimposing data onto a carrier. Examples are AM, FM, and PM.

Multiplexer: A device capable of transmitting more than one signal over the same channel.

N

Name Resolution: System for reconciling Internet names, IP addresses and physical addresses so they point to the exact location of the destination node, no matter where it's located.

Network: A group of computers and peripherals connected together, so that data may be exchanged between them.

Network Availability: The amount of time that network services are available: $A = (TB\text{-}TD)/T$: where A = availability; TB = time the network is busy; TD = time the network is down; T = total time the network is available.

Network Drawing: A sketch of a network. A network drawing is used to identify network components as well as the cable labels.

Network Interface Card (NIC): A network interface card contains a transceiver for sending and receiving data frames on and off a network, as well as the Data Link layer hardware needed to format the sending bits and to decipher received frames.

Network Layer: Layer three of the OSI reference model. The network layer implements the virtual connection of the upper layers, by mapping a data route among the point-to-point links.

Network Management Model: The ISO description of network management; includes an organizational model, an informational model, and a functional model.

Network Utilization: The ratio of the time a network is used, to the total time the network is available. $U = TB/T$: where U=utilization; TB = time the network is busy; T = total time the network is available.

NIC diagnostics: Tools used to assist in troubleshooting connectivity problems.

Node: A generic term describing any device that is connected to a network.

Noise: Undesirable interference of data signals that distorts the data.

Noise Factor: The ratio of noise at the input of a communication system to noise at the output. It is calculated by: $NF = 10 \log ((Si/Ni)/(So/No))$

Nonreturn To Zero (NRZ): An encoding technique in which logic 1's are represented by $+V$ and logic 0's by $-V$.

Non-routable Protocols: Protocols that aren't routable because they don't contain enough addressing information in their headers. MAC layer protocols such as Ethernet, Token Ring or FDDI are examples of nonroutable protocols.

Normal Response Mode (NRM): One of two modes for the configuring of HDLC protocols. All stations are designated as primary or secondary. Secondaries are forbidden to transmit without first receiving permission from the primary.

Nyquist Rate: The Nyquist Channel Information Theory states that if the data is sampled at a rate of at least twice the highest transmitted frequency, then the original data will be accurately recovered at the receiver.

O

Object: Refers to any network resource, such as software commands or network interface cards.

Off-hook: A term describing the handset lifted from the cradle of a telephone.

On-hook: A term describing the handset resting in the cradle of a telephone.

On-line State: The condition a modem enters when it has access to the telephone network.

Open-System Interconnection (OSI) Model: The standard model, developed by the International Standards Organization, which describes a complete data communication system. The model includes a hierarchial relationship between seven distinct levels: layer 1, the Physical layer; layer 2, the Data-Link layer; layer 3, the Network layer; layer 4, the Transport layer; layer 5, the Session layer; layer 6, the Presentation layer; and layer 7, the Application layer.

Operator Versus System model: A model used for determining if a problem lies with the client or network operator, or the network.

Originate Modem: The modem that initiates a call. The originate modem communicates with the answer modem, by transmitting over the originate channel.

Overhead: The portion of a data frame that does not contain user data. Overhead reduces the efficiency of communication exchanges.

P

Packet Assembly/Disassembly (PAD): The process of organizing data frames into packets of frames, sometimes used to refer to the synchronizing flags preceding BSC frames.

Packet Switching: The process of dividing data into packets for transmission over a WAN. X.25 is the conventional method of packet switching, in which data travels at 64 kBPS in MAC-like packets.

Parity: An error-detection system based on an odd, or even, count of logic one's in a data word.

Passive Satellite: Also called a reflector satellite, it is characterized by the absence of a repeater.

Password: An encrypted and secret word entered at the sign-on screen of a work station; usually used in conjunction with user IDs. If the password and ID match the password for the user, maintained in the computer files, access is granted to the network.

Password Authentication Protocol (PAP): Protocol used with PPP. The client is authenticated by sending a user name and password to the server.

Patch: A software enhancement that addresses a weakness in the original release of hardware or software. See upgrade and fix.

Payload: The weight of a satellite, including the satellite subassemblies and instrumentation.

Peer-to-peer networks: Control of the network is distributed among the nodes, meaning there is no server connected to the network. All nodes are servers as well as clients.

Performance Network Management: One of five functions of the ISO network management; responsible for collecting data, so that the integrity and efficiency of the network can be analyzed.

Perigee: The end of an elliptical orbit nearest the Earth's center.

Period: The time of a data bit. Period = 1/F: where F is the frequency.

Permanent Virtual Circuit: A leased channel in which stations at each end are assigned permanent addresses, so that they may communicate at any time without the normal exchange of dialogue.

Permutation: The complete encryption process. In the DES system, up to 256 permutations may be imposed on the same plaintext.

Phase Modulation (PM): A modulation method in which the amount of phase distortion is proportional to the data amplitude, and the rate at which phase shifts occur is proportional to the data frequency.

Phase-Shift Keying (PSK): A modulation technique used with modems in which the phase of the carrier is shifted for each change of logic levels.

Physical Indicators: Lights, LEDs, error messages, etc. that provide messages related to network problems.

Physical Layer: Layer one of the OSI reference model. The physical layer includes hardware interfaces and the connection medium. It is the only layer at which data bits are actually transferred.

Plaintext: The data to be coded into a secret message.

Point-to-Point: A network topology in which data is exchanged between only two stations.

Point-to-Point Protocol (PPP): A communication protocol used to send data across serial communication links. It's the most widely used wide area protocol for accessing Internet service providers.

Point-to-Point Tunneling Protocol (PPTP): A protocol used to securely transport PPP packets over a TCP/IP network (i.e., the Internet).

Polarization: Refers to the orientation of an antenna in reference to the Earth. Antennas positioned perpendicular to the ground are vertically polarized, while antennas positioned parallel to the ground are horizontally polarized.

Policies: System configurations that affect all users.

Post Office Protocol-Version 3 (POP3): An e-mail protocol used with SMTP.

Precedence: Part of the Type of Service field of a TCP/IP datagram; it provides an indication to the network routers and bridges as to the significance of the datagram.

Predecessor: A method of referring to stations on a token-ring network. The station sending the token is the predecessor to the station receiving the token.

Pre-equalization: The process of compensating for known distortion at the receiver.

Presentation Layer: Layer six of the OSI reference model. The presentation layer is responsible for determining the syntax used between communicating stations. This includes screen formats, terminal codes such as ASCII and EBCDIC, and provisions for language conversions.

Printer Port Capture: The process used to connect to a printer on a network.

Print Server: A computer used to queue requests to a printer. It's used in a network in which several users utilize the same printer.

Problem Extent Model: A systematic approach to identifying the boundaries of a problem.

Product Cipher: A class of encryption systems that combines substitution and transposition techniques.

Profiles: The configuration settings made for each user.

Protocol: A set of rules describing the exchange of data on a network. Examples include BSC, HDLC and TCP/IP.

Protocol Analyzer: Network test equipment that identifies and decodes the common protocols, such as HDLC, Ethernet, and TCP/IP.

Public Key Cipher: An encryption technique intended to authenticate the message sender, as well as to perform encryption and decryption. In this type of cipher, a public key and a private key are used, but neither may be derived from the other.

Pulse-Amplitude Modulation (PAM): A variation of analog pulse modulation. A PAM signal consists of a series of pulses whose amplitude corresponds to the amplitude of an analog signal.

Pulse-Code Modulation (PCM): A form of digital pulse modulation. PCM is produced by quantizing an analog waveform to a series of pulses; then, converting the pulses to a binary-encoded signal.

Pulse-Duration Modulation (PDM): A form of analog pulse modulation. A PDM signal is achieved by varying the width of sampled pulses, in direct proportion to the amplitude of the modulating analog waveform.

Pulse Modulation: The most common technique of modulating signals within the telephone system. Pulse modulation includes Pulse-Amplitude Modulation, Pulse-Duration Modulation, Pulse-Code Modulation, and Delta Modulation.

Q

Quadrature-Amplitude Modulation (QAM): A modulation method used with modems. The data is represented with amplitude and phase shifts in the carrier.

Quantization Error: The amount of error produced in the analog-to-digital conversion process. It's typically expressed in 1 or 1/2 bit.

Queue Length: The time a network spends waiting in a queue: $Q = W/T$; where Q = average queue length, W = total time messages wait in the system, T = total time of a message run.

R

Random-Key Cipher: A cipher that uses logic circuits to generate a large number of keys. The number of possible keys discourages potential code breakers.

Received Line-Signal Detect (RLSD): An RS-232C command that modems exchange following the training period.

Receiver: The data-terminal equipment that accepts data from a sender.

Redundant Array of Inexpensive Disks (RAID): Consists of five levels of fault tolerance practices that are used with servers for protecting data, or improving the read/ write performance of the server.

Refraction: The bending of a light wave when it is passed through materials of different densities.

Remote Loopback Test: A modem test in which a local modem instructs the remote modem to perform a digital loopback test, and provide the local modem with the results.

Repeater: An interchannel amplifier that not only increases the signal amplitude, but also removes noise and distortion.

Request-to-Send (RTS): The RS-232C pin that initiates an exchange between modems.

Response Time: The amount of time consumed in delivering a message in the network, $R = T/C$: where R = response time; T = total time messages are required to wait in the system; C = total completed messages.

Rights: Refers to the right to perform specific actions on the network.

Ring: One of two wires connecting the telephone to the central office. The ring wire is typically the red wire.

Ringback: A telephone signal sent back to inform a caller that the called number is ringing. It consists of a 440/480-Hz tone that's on for 2 seconds, and off for 4 seconds.

Ringer: The circuit in a telephone that signals an incoming call with a 90-V, 20-Hz signal that's on for 2 seconds, and off for 4 seconds.

Ring Indicator (RI): An RS-232C command sent to the DTE from the modem, indicating a call has arrived.

Ring Topology: A network topology arranged with the nodes connected end-to-end, in a daisy-chain manner, that resembles a circle.

Ring Wrap: The process of by-passing a failed station or link segment on an FDDI network.

Rocket Thruster: The section of a satellite that lifts it into its orbit.

Rotator: A device found in modems that generates an error signal equal to the phase delay of a received signal.

Routable Protocols: A protocol that can be transmitted across an internetwork. IP, TCP, UDP, IPX, and DECNet are all routable protocols.

Router: An internetworking machine that operates at the network layer of the OSI model. It is protocol-specific to internetworking protocols.

RS-232C: An EIA interface commonly used to connect personal computers to peripherals. It supports one receiver and one transmitter at data rates up to 20 kBPS. A logic 1 is specified at –3V to –25V, and a logic 0 at +3V to +25V.

RS-449: An EIA interface that offers balanced and unbalanced modes of operation. The unbalanced mode is described in RS-422 and specifies up to 10 receivers and one transmitter at data rates up to 100 kBPS. The balanced mode is described in RS-423 and supports 10 receivers and one transmitter at data rates up to 10 MBPS. The logic 1 for both modes ranges from –3.6V to –6V, and a logic 0 falls between +3.6V and +6V.

RS-485: An EIA interface designed for a multiuser environment. Up to 32 transmitters and receivers are supported at data rates up to 10 MBPS. A logic 1 is represented by –1.5V to –6V, and a logic 0 by +1.5V to +6V.

S

Satellite: An orbiting communication system characterized by wide bandwidth capabilities and global coverage.

Scheduling: A network management technique used to balance the workload between nodes; it is a future-oriented system that attempts to anticipate problems and correct them before they occur.

Scrambler: The section of a modem that encodes the data to be transmitted in order to avoid distortion, such as intersymbol interference.

Server: A powerful computer on a network which contains a network operating system (NOS) and manages the flow of data on the network.

Security Network Management: One of the five functions of ISO network management; includes factors affecting physical security, file and record access, and the use of passwords and user Ids.

Serial Line Internet Protocol (SLIP): The forerunner to PPP. It has the same function; to connect nodes in a point-to-point configuration. SLIP only transports TCP/IP.

Serial Network Interface (SNI): An SNI is found in the network controller cards used with CSMA/CD LANs. It serves as an interface between the interface controller and the transceiver, by Manchester II-encoding the data.

Serial Protocol: Point-to-point, physical communication protocol. Examples are PPP and SLIP.

Session Layer: Layer five of the OSI reference model. The Session layer is responsible for managing the end-to-end dialog of the network stations. This may include half- or full-duplex operation, and the inclusion of synchronization headers attached to data frames.

Signal Noise To Quantization Ratio (SQR): A general indication of the quality of a quantizer.

Signal-to-Noise Ratio (SNR): The measure of desired signal power to the amount of noise contained in the signal. It is found by: SNR = Ps/Pn.

Simple Mail Transfer Protocol (SMTP): Used to route outgoing e-mail, and in some applications, incoming e-mail.

Simple Network Management Protocol (SNMP): This protocol defines packet exchanges.

Simplex: A system of one-way communication.

Socket: A software abstract used to communicate processes. It's used as a programming interface to the communication protocol (TCP, for example).

Source Routing: An IBM bridging method used with token-ring networks.

Space: The condition of a channel represented by a logic 0.

Space-Division Multiplexing (SDM): A multiplexing technique common with the telephone system. In an SDM system, a single channel is dedicated to a single receiver and transmitter.

Spanning Tree Protocol: Used with bridged networks to determine network paths for data messages. It prevents the messages from circling through the network endlessly, by establishing fall-back routes.

Speech Channel: The portion of the telephone channel used for speech. The speech channel has a frequency range from 300Hz to 3,300Hz.

Spin Stabilization: A method of controlling the attitude of a satellite. The spinning action is initiated by thrusters mounted on the side of the satellite.

Spot-Beaming: A method of focusing satellite transmissions that sends a narrow beam to small, ground-based antennas.

Standard Operating Procedure (SOP): A document used to maintaining control and consistency on a network. It's an approved document that is designed to convey knowledge, as opposed to data, to the reader.

Star Topology: A topology for arranging network nodes, characterized by a central hub that serves as a switch for connecting the stations.

Start Bit: The first bit in an asynchronous data frame that signifies the beginning of the frame.

Static Routing: A static router has its routing tables updated manually.

Statistical Time-Division Multiplexing (STDM): A modified version of TDM. An STDM multiplexer collects and stores data at the aggregate rate of the terminals feeding the multiplexer, enabling the data to be processed at very high rates for short periods.

Stop Bit: The final bit in an asynchronous data frame, that signifies the end of the frame.

Stripe parity: Used with disk striping by adding redundant data in the form of parity blocks. The parity may be a dedicated drive, or the parity blocks may be spread across multiple hard drives.

Striping: The process of spreading data on hard drives across more than one drive.

Subnet mask number: The decimal 255, then, is used to mask the network portion of an IP and only leave open the host portion. The subnets for each class are: Class A: 255.0.0.0, Class B: 255.255.0.0, and Class C: 255.255.255.0

Subnetwork: Identified by a default network mask (or natural mask), which is the decimal number 255. Subnetworks use the subnet mask in order to extend the use of a single IP address. There are class A, B and C subnetwork masks.

Subscriber Line-Interface Card (SLIC): An interface circuit between the analog local loop, and the digital switching centers of the telephone system.

Subscriber Loop: Another term for the local loop that contains the telephone, central office, and the two wires connecting the two.

Substitution Cipher: A ciphering technique in which substitute alphanumeric characters replace the alphanumeric characters of the plaintext.

Successor: A method for identifying stations on a token-ring network. The station receiving the token from the transmitter is the successor.

Supervisory Frame: A control-field frame type of HDLC, represented by the dibit 01 in the frame identifier field. Supervisory frames are used to inform a station of various conditions existing on the network.

Switch Hook: The telephone switch that connects the telephone to the central office, when the handset is lifted.

Switching Hub: Includes a switching backplane that allows any port to be connected to any other port on an as-needed basis. In other words, a switching hub assigns ports dynamically and under control of the hub.

Synchronous: A method of transmitting data frames in which each bit, or frame, is tracked in unison by the receiver and transmitter. Typically, synchronous transmission is used at higher data rates.

Synchronous Data-Link Control (SDLC): An IBM data-link protocol. SDLC is the forerunner of the OSI protocol HDLC. The two are functionally the same.

Synchronous Optical Network (SONET): Fiber-optic system used to interconnect wide-area network at speeds from 54.84 MBPS to 2.5 GBPS.

Synchronous-to-Asynchronous Converter: The section of a modem that converts received data into the format suitable for personal computers or peripherals.

System Service Time: The average amount of time that a message spends in the system, S = B/C: where S = system service time; B = busy time; and C = the number of completed messages.

T

Tape Backup: Method used to backup hard drive data on a server or client.

Target Token Rotation Time Value: An FDDI number generated for the purpose of assigning a single station to initiate the transmission token.

T-Carrier: The TDM digital hierarchy of the long-distance telephone carriers.

TCP/IP utilities: UNIX-based tools which can be used to provide a considerable amount of information about your computer, its place in a network, and other devices you're connected to. Typically used in troubleshooting. Examples include ping and ipconfig.

TDM Hierarchy: The digital multiplexing scheme used by the long-distance carriers, often called the T-Carrier. The T1 system contains up to 24, 64-kHz channels at a rate of 1.544 MBPS; the T2 consists of 96 channels transmitting at 6.312 MBPS; the T3 includes 672 channels transmitting at 44.736 MBPS; and the T4 includes 4032 channels transmitting at 274.176 MBPS.

Technical service: An initial response to a problem in which you must apply your expertise. This may be in person, or may require your hands-on involvement at a remote terminal.

Telemetry: Refers to the telemetry antenna on a satellite. Control signals passing to the satellite from a ground station, and data signals passing from the satellite to the ground station, are transmitted via the telemetry antenna.

Terminal Code: Binary numbers representing alphanumeric characters and special control functions. Examples are ASCII, EBCDIC, and Baudot.

Text Transparency: The practice of ensuring that user data remains separate and distinct from frame header data. Two common techniques for achieving text transparency are character stuffing and bit stiffing.

Throughput: A general term describing the ratio of frame header to user data contained in the frame. High throughput indicates a network is operating with high efficiency, and is calculated by TP = C/T: where TP = throughput; C = the number of messages sent; and T = the total time of the transmission.

Time-Division Multiple Access (TDMA): A satellite multiplexing scheme, in which ground stations are provided alternating time slots for sending data to the satellite.

Time-Division Multiplexing (TDM): A multiplexing technique in which a single carrier frequency contains the data from many channels. Each terminal is assigned a time slot in which it has access to the full bandwidth of the channel.

Timing Recovery Element: A device in modems that measures the synchronization between the receiver and transmitter.

Tip: One of the two wires connecting the telephone to the central office. The tip wire is typically the green wire.

Token: A network signaling element used by stations to gain access to a token ring, or token bus, network.

Token Bus: The IEEE 802.4 local area network. Stations connect to the network through interface adapters, and gain access to the network when they possess the token.

Token-based System: A ring, or bus, network that uses a signaling token for station access.

Token Recovery: Describes the process used in token-based networks for recovering the access token, when a station node fails.

Toll Exchange: A series of centers used by the long-distance carriers to route long-distance calls. The toll exchanges consist of a class-4 toll center, a class-3 primary center, a class-2 sectional center, and a class-1 regional center.

Tone Generator: Test equipment used to generate an audible for locating wire pairs in UTP cable.

Tone Locator: Test equipment used to identify wire pairs in UTP cable.

Topology: Refers to the physical architecture of a network. Examples are ring, star, and point-to-point networks.

Training Detector: The section of a modem responsible for establishing compatibility between the modems during handshaking.

Training Period: The process of exchanging data streams between modems that establishes a common dialog.

Transceiver: A network component that simply receives and transmits signals. It lacks the sophistication to manage or massage the signal.

Transceiver Interface: A circuit associated with 802.3 CSMA/CD protocols that provides isolation between the network cabling, and the network interface. Collision detection is monitored by the transceiver interface.

Translation bridge: A bridging method in which the MAC frames of the transmitting station are converted to the frame type of the destination station.

Transmission Control Protocol (TCP): Used to establish a reliable connection between client and server, or other network devices.

Transmission Control Protocol/Internet Protocol (TCP/IP): A widely used internetworking protocol, that's independent of vendor hardware, and is characterized by a 32-bit addressing scheme.

Transmitter: The network device that sends data to a receiver.

Transparency: A general term describing the degree to which user data remains separate from header data.

Transponder: Contains the receiver and transmitter of a satellite.

Transport Layer: Layer four of the OSI reference model. The transport layer ensures a virtual communication path by assigning node addresses. In addition, five classes of network service are specified that describe the robust nature of the network.

Transposition Cipher: An encryption technique in which the sequence of the plaintext is rearranged.

Troubleshooting model: A process of systematically identifying and correcting a network problem.

Trunk Line: A common pathway between telephone company central offices. Trunk lines are reserved, and not available for direct subscriber connections.

Twisted Pair: A communication medium consisting of two conductors insulated from one another, and twisted together. Twisted pairs comprise the majority of installed telephone cables.

U

Unauthorized Access: A phrase referring to security measures in which a user is denied access to a file or directory.

Unbreakable Cipher: An encryption technique in which the key is used only once.

Universal Asynchronous Receiver/Transmitter (UART): An integrated circuit that formats data characters to be transmitted, as well as received. UARTs are found in personal computers.

Universal Name Convention (UNC): Microsoft method of naming computers. It follows the convention \\computername\filename.

Unnumbered Frame: An HDLC control-field frame type. Unnumbered frames are responsible for initiating and terminating station links, and are represented by the dibit 11 in the frame identifier field.

Unreliable Service: Refers to protocols, particularly TCP/IP, in which there is no end-to-end acknowledgement of received messages.

Update: Refers to a type of security access in which the user is authorized to write to files; the changing of such files.

Upgrade: An interim solution for bugs which have been discovered either during beta testing or after the product was formally released. See patch.

Upgrade Maintenance: The process of comparing software or hardware version of an installed component to the latest version available from the component vendor.

Uplink: A satellite transmitter carrier frequency, the transmitter ground equipment, and the satellite transmit antenna.

Up Side: Refers to the side of a station, on a ring network, that data exits.

User Datagram Protocol (UDP): A simpler implementation of TCP, but without the reliability of TCP.

User-Defined Buffer Allocation: A technique for organizing multiplexer buffer-pool memory. With this method, all terminals are assigned dedicated buffer space based upon their estimated need.

User ID: A security measure consisting of a word, or combination of letters and numbers, entered at the sign-on screen by the user. Usually used in conjunction with a password.

V

Variable-Gain Amplifier: A modem amplifier used to increase the level of weak signals.

Virtual Connection: A logical connection that appears to the user to be independent of data frames, encoding, protocols, and all of the underlying mechanisms of data exchange.

Virus signature: The known-viruses that anti-virus software detects. It's usually referenced by the release version of virus detection software.

Voice Channel: A telephone channel that extends from 0 Hz to 4000 Hz. Included in the voice channel is the 3kHz speech channel, called the in-band signaling range; and the ranges from 0 Hz to 300 Hz and 3300 Hz to 4000 Hz, called the out-of-band signaling range.

W

Well-known port number: A 16-bit number which refers incoming messages to an application that will process them. An example of a well-known port number is 80, used for HTTP.

Wide-Area Network (WAN): A network encompassing a large geographical area. Usually, WANs are considered to cover distances beyond a metropolitan area.

Windows Internet Naming Service (WINS): Contains a look-up table used to reconcile computer names to IP addresses; associated with Windows NT and 9x clients.

Word Interleaving: A process used to transmit time-division multiplexed channels in the T-carrier system. Each channel is separated into 8-bit words, and the channel words are transmitted one after the other.

Workstation: A stand-alone computer, or a computer that has application programs stored on it, and that can be launched from it. In many cases, a client and a workstation are the same.

Workstation Backup: Method used to backup user and operating system information of a client computer.

X

XMODEM: A simplified modem protocol used with many personal computers for accessing large databases.

Z

Zero-Dispersion: Refers to commercial grades of fiber-optic cable in which the light is transmitted at 1.3 microns and 1.5 microns, with very low losses.

INDEX

M

N

RC Jet-Cobra Race Car SE-1030

Leave the competition in the dust....build this 1/18 scale, 2 wheel drive Baja racer from Marcraft. Select one of two forward speeds, punch the turbo power and go for it. The Jet-Cobra features a 5-function pistol grip controller that incorporates a turbo-boost circuit. Independent front and rear suspension provide excellent handling on sharp, high-speed corners. You'll find state-of-the-art IC technology coupled with fundamental transistor circuitry to demonstrate important electronics components such as: RF signal transmission and reception, digital information encoding and decoding, and motor control theory. A 72-page manual provides a thorough understanding of the electronics principles. As low as $36.95.

MARCRAFT Electronics Kits

PC Technician's Tool Kit IC-345

This professional technician's kit contains 29 of the most popular PC service tools to cover most PC service applications. Zipper case is constructed out of durable vinyl with room for an optional DMM and optional CD-ROM service disks. Includes: case (with zipper) has external slash pocket for extra storage (13½" L x 9¾" H x 2 3/8" W), slotted 3/16" screwdriver, IC Inserter, slotted 1/8" screwdriver, 3-prong parts Retriever, Phillips # 1 screwdriver, self-locking tweezers, Phillips # 0 screwdriver, tweezers, precision 4 pc (2 slotted / 2 Phillips) screwdriver set, inspection mirror, driver handle, penlight, # 2 Phillips / slotted ¼" screwdriver bits, 6" adjustable wrench, # T-10 Torx / T-15 Torx screwdriver bits, 4 ½" mini-diagonal, ¼" nut driver, 5" mini-long nose, 3/16" nut driver, anti-static wrist strap, 5" hemostat, part storage tube, IC Extractor. (Note: Meter not included) As low as $36.95

Sonic Rover SE-1029

The Rover is an exciting hands-on electronics project, providing an easy way to learn basic transistor, amplifier and switching circuitry. It teaches the fundamentals of sound detection and amplification, as well as switching circuits, DC motors and gear ratios. The front-mounted microphone sensor can be activated by a touch or noise. When the sensor encounters an object, or hears a loud voice command, it will automatically stop, back up, turn to the left 90 degrees, and then resume its forward motion. A dual-colored LED switches between Green and Red to indicate forward and reverse motion. The 48-page manual details breadboarding explorations and circuit construction for this 9-transistor project. As low as $13.95.

ower Supply SE-1014

project that teaches half-wave, full-wave, and full-wave, and l-wave bridge rectification. When finished, it's a usable power pply featuring four d.c. output voltage selections. An isolation nsformer is included and is enclosed in a durable case for fety. The manual has 32 pages of information. As low as $9.95

Analog Multimeter SE-1028

The Analog Multimeter teaches the importance of electronic "basics". This project functions as an AC/DC meter and is designed to cover all aspects of meter theory including diode rectification and protection...and how resistors are used to limit current and drop voltage. This kit is first breadboarded and tested in a series of informative circuits and explorations, which are detailed in the 48-page instruction manual. As low as $26.95.

ORDERING INFORMATION

School Purchase orders: Terms are net 30 days.
Direct Student orders: Must be accompanied by check, money order, credit card or shipped C.O.D. Shipping Charge: $5.00 per kit to cover shipping and handling charges, for C.O.D. orders add $5.50.

QUANTITY DISCOUNT PRICE LIST

odel	Description	1-4	5-9	10-99	100+
E-1014	Power Supply	12.95	11.95	10.95	9.95
E-1028	Analog Multimeter	32.95	30.95	28.95	26.95
E-1029	Sonic Rover	17.95	16.95	14.95	13.95
E-1030	R/C Race3 Car	42.95	40.95	37.95	36.95
-345	Deluxe Tech Tool Kit	39.95	38.95	37.95	36.95

Order Toll Free
1-800-441-6006

MARCRAFT

Marcraft International Corporation
100 N. Morain - 302, Kennewick, WA 99336

MARCRAFT
Your IT Training Provider
(800) 441-6006

A+ Certification

This book provides you with training necessary for the A+ Certification testing program that certifies the competency of entry-level (6 months experience) computer service technicians. The A+ test contains situational, traditional, and identification types of questions. All of the questions are multiple choice with only one correct answer for each question. The test covers a broad range of hardware and software technologies, but is not bound to any vendor-specific products.

The program is backed by major computer hardware and software vendors, distributors, and resellers. A+ certification signifies that the certified individual possesses the knowledge and skills essential for a successful entry-level (6 months experience) computer service technician, as defined by experts from companies across the industry.

Network+ Certification

Network+ is a CompTIA vendor-neutral certification that measures the technical knowledge of networking professionals with 18-24 months of experience in the IT industry. The test is administered by NCS/VUE and Prometric™. Discount exam vouchers can be purchased from Marcraft.

Earning the Network+ certification indicates that the candidate possesses the knowledge needed to configure and install the TCP/IP client. This exam covers a wide range of vendor and product neutral networking technologies that can also serve as a prerequisite for vendor-specific IT certifications. Network+ has been accepted by the **leading networking vendors** and included in many of their training curricula. The skills and knowledge measured by the certification examination are derived from industry-wide job task analyses and validated through an industry wide survey. The objectives for the certification examination are divided in two distinct groups, Knowledge of Networking Technology and Knowledge of Networking Practices.

i-Net+ Certification

The i-Net+ certification program is designed specifically for any individual interested in demonstrating baseline technical knowledge that would allow him or her to pursue a variety of Internet-related careers. i-Net+ is a vendor-neutral, entry-level Internet certification program that tests baseline technical knowledge of Internet, Intranet and Extranet technologies, independent of specific Internet-related career roles. Learning objectives and domains examined include Internet basics, Internet clients, development, networking, security and business concepts.

Certification not only helps individuals enter the Internet industry, but also helps managers determine a prospective employee's knowledge and skill level.

Linux+ Certification

The Linux+ certification measures vendor-neutral Linux knowledge and skills for an individual with at least 6 months practical experience. Linux+ Potential Job Roles: Entry Level Helpdesk, Technical Sales/Marketing, Entry Level Service Technician, Technical Writers, Resellers, Application Developers, Application Customer Service Reps.

Linux+ Exam Objectives Outline: User administration, Connecting to the network, Package Management, Security Concept, Shell Scripting, Networking, Apache web server application, Drivers (installation, updating, removing), Kernel (what it does, why to rebuild), Basic printing, Basic troubleshooting.

Server+ Certification

Server+ certification deals with advanced hardware issues such as RAID, SCSI, multiple CPUs, SANs and more. This is vendor-neutral with a broad range of support, including core support by 3Com, Adaptec, Compaq, Hewlett-Packard, IBM, Intel, EDS Innovations Canada, Innovative Productivity, and Marcraft.

This book focuses on complex activities and solving complex problems to ensure servers are functional and applications are available. It provides an in-depth understanding of the planning, installing, configuring, and maintaining servers, including knowledge of server-level hardware implementations, data storage subsystems, data recovery, and I/O subsystems.

Data Cabling Installer Certification

The Data Cabling Installer Certification provides the IT industry with an introductory, vendor-neutral certification for skilled personnel that install Category 5 copper data cabling.

The Marcraft *Enhanced Data Cabling Installer Certification Training Guide* provides students with the knowledge and skills required to pass the Data Cabling Installer Certification exam and become a certified cable installer. The DCIC is recognized nationwide and is the hiring criterion used by major communication companies. Therefore, becoming a certified data cable installer will enhance your job opportunities and career advancement potential.

Fiber Optic Cabling Certification

There is a growing demand for qualified cable installers who understand and can implement fiber optic technologies. These technologies cover terminology, techniques, tools and other products in the fiber optic industry. This text/lab book covers basics of fiber optic design discipline, installations, pulling and prepping cables, terminations, testing and safety considerations. Labs will cover ST-compatible and SC connector types, both multimedia and single mode cables and connectors. Learn about insertion loss, optical time domain reflectometry, and reflectance. Cover mechanical and fusion splices and troubleshooting cable systems. This Text/Lab covers the theory and hands-on skills needed to prepare you for fiber optic entry-level certification.